CliffsAP®

Statistics

CliffsAP®

Statistics

by

David A. Kay

WILEY

Wiley Publishing, Inc.

About the Author

David A. Kay has taught mathematics for 35 years and has been teaching at Moorpark College since 1981. He is currently the chairman of Moorpark's Mathematics Department and has taught Statistics and Honors Statistics for more than 10 years. He is the author or contributing author of several books on test preparation.

I would like to thank my son, Bryan Kay, for his contributions with the preparation of the manuscript. His guidance during the editing process was invaluable.

I would like to thank Phil Abramoff for reviewing the manuscript for technical accuracy and for his assistance in preparing the practice exams.

I would like to thank my wife, Ellen, for her patience, understanding, encouragement, and for keeping me on task.

I would like to thank Jerry Bobrow for his guidance and suggestions.

Publisher's Acknowledgments

Editorial

Project Editor: Kelly D. Henthorne

Acquisitions Editor: Greg Tubach

Technical Editor: Philip Abramoff

Production

Proofreader: Henry Lazarek

Wiley Publishing, Inc. Composition Services

CliffsAP® Statistics

Published by:
Wiley Publishing, Inc.
111 River Street
Hoboken, NJ 07030-5774
www.wiley.com

Copyright © 2005 Bobrow Test Preparation Services

Published by Wiley Publishing, Inc., Hoboken, NJ
Published simultaneously in Canada

Kay, David A.
  CliffsAP statistics / by David A. Kay.--1st ed.
      p. cm. -- (CliffsAP)
  Includes bibliographical references and index.
  ISBN 0-7645-7313-6 (pbk. : alk. paper)
  1. Mathematical statistics--Examinations, questions, etc. 2. College
entrance achievement tests--Study guides. I. Title. II. Series.
    QA276.2.K39 2004
    519.5'076--dc22
2004022069

Printed in the United States of America

10 9 8 7 6 5 4 3 2 1

1B/RT/RS/QU/IN

WILEY

Table of Contents

PART I: INTRODUCTION

PART II: SUBJECT AREA REVIEWS WITH SAMPLE QUESTIONS AND ANSWERS

PART III: AP STATISTICS PRACTICE TESTS

INTRODUCTION

Introduction

AP Statistics Exam Content

The topics covered on the AP Statistics Exam are divided into four main areas:

- **Exploring Data:** Describing patterns and departures from patterns (20%–30%)

  Analysis of data using graphical and numerical techniques; interpreting information from graphical and numerical displays and summaries.
  - Constructing and interpreting graphical displays of distributions of univariate data
  - Summarizing distributions of univariate data
  - Comparing distributions of univariate data
  - Exploring bivariate data
  - Exploring categorical data
- **Sampling and Experimentation:** Planning and conducting a study (10%–15%)

  Collecting data using a well-developed plan, including clarifying the question and determining which method of data collection and analysis should be used.
  - Overview of data collection methods
  - Planning and conducting surveys
  - Planning and conducting experiments
  - Generalizing results from observational studies, experiments, and surveys
- **Anticipating Patterns:** Exploring random phenomena using probability and simulation (20%–30%)

  Using probability to anticipate what a distribution should look like under given conditions.
  - Probability
  - Combining independent random variables
  - The normal distribution
  - Sampling distributions
- **Statistical Inference:** Estimating population parameters and testing hypotheses (30%–40%)

  Using statistical inference to select appropriate statistical models.
  - Estimation using point estimates and confidence intervals
  - Tests of significance

AP Statistics Exam Format

The AP Statistics Exam is divided into two equally weighted sections. Each section of the exam is distinct.

- Section I
  - Number of multiple choice questions—40
  - Time allowed for Section I—90 minutes
- Section II
  - Part A
    - Number of free response questions—5
    - Recommended time spent—65 minutes

- Part B
  - Number of investigative tasks—1
  - Recommended time spent—25 minutes
- Time allowed for Section II—90 minutes

You are allowed to work on Section I for 90 minutes. You may do the multiple-choice questions in any order. Work easy ones first and difficult ones as time permits. If you skip questions, be careful to mark the correct answer on the answer sheet. You may work on only Section I questions during this 90-minute portion of the exam. You cannot return to this section after the 90-minute time limit has elapsed. Do not take uneducated guesses; only guess when you can eliminate one or more answer choices. One-fourth the number of incorrect answers is subtracted from the number of correct answers.

You are allowed to work on Section II for 90 minutes. You may do the free-response questions in any order. Be careful to budget your time properly. Most students spend 65 minutes on the first 5 free-response questions and about 25 minutes on problem 6 (the investigative task). If you are spending more than 13 to 15 minutes on any free-response question, consider moving on to another question; return if you have time. Do not leave any free-response question unanswered; a partial response may earn some points.

Calculator Policy

Students are expected to bring to the exam a graphing calculator with the following statistical capabilities: standard statistical univariate and bivariate summaries; linear regression; and univariate and bivariate displays (scatterplots, histograms, and boxplots).

Students can bring two calculators to the exam. You may not store notes in your calculator. Programs that add statistical functionality to older calculators are permitted. During the exam, you cannot use minicomputers, pocket organizers, electronic writing pads, or calculators with QWERTY keyboards.

The most commonly used calculator on the exam is the TI-83/4 series of graphing calculator. This text refers to the TI-83/4 calculator in many examples and explanations.

Calculators should be used for computation and as an aid in evaluating patterns. When answering free-response questions, be sure to include your reasoning, not just calculator results. Correct reasoning is worth more than numerical accuracy.

Free-Response Questions

When answering free-response questions, make sure that your answers are well organized and clearly stated. Do not skip steps. Write formulas, make substitutions, and solve. Make it easy for the person reading your exam to follow your reasoning. Emphasize key steps in the solution. Write answers in complete sentences.

Read questions carefully. Responses should be given in the context of the question. Do not just give numeric answers. Conclusions of hypothesis tests and interpretations of confidence intervals should always be included and written in the context of the problem.

State and check assumptions you use when performing hypothesis tests and when finding confidence intervals.

Define all symbols. Use proper symbols when referring to populations and samples. Be consistent in the use of symbols. The correct use of vocabulary is very important.

Learn to read and interpret computer output as well as statistical graphs and charts.

Be accurate. Round only final answers, not intermediate steps.

Read the entire question and then answer all of the parts. Partial answers are better than no answer at all.

Advanced Placement Exam Grades

The multiple-choice section of the exam is computer scored. The free-response section is scored by readers. The two scores are combined and converted to a 5-point scale.

AP Grade	Qualification
5	Extremely well-qualified
4	Well-qualified
3	Qualified
2	Possibly qualified
1	No recommendation

A grade of 3 or better is usually considered a passing grade. Some schools require a grade of 4 or better for credit. Contact the schools to which you plan to apply; admissions can tell you what score you need for college credit.

How AP Grades Are Determined

Section I. On the AP Statistics Test, one-fourth the number of wrong answers is subtracted from the number of correct answers. (This discourages random guessing.)

$$(\text{correct} - (1/4) * \text{wrong}) * 1.2500 = \text{Section I score}$$

Section I score will be greater than or equal to zero (a negative score is recorded as zero).

Section II. Questions 1–5 each count for 7.5% of the composite score. Question 6 counts for 12.5%. Each question is scored on a scale of 1–4 and then multiplied by the appropriate weight. The maximum weighted score for this section is 50 (50% of the composite score).

$$(\text{Question 1 score} * 1.8750) + (\text{Question 2 score} * 1.8750) +$$
$$(\text{Question 3 score} * 1.8750) + (\text{Question 4 score} * 1.8750) +$$
$$(\text{Question 5 score} * 1.8750) + (\text{Question 6 score} * 3.1250)$$
$$= \text{Section II score}$$

Composite Score

$$\text{Composite score} = (\text{Section I score}) + (\text{Section II score})$$

AP Statistics Composite-to-AP Grade Conversion

Composite score*	AP Grade
68–100	5
53–67	4
40–52	3
29–39	2
0–28	1

Scoring Free-Response Questions

Score Descriptors	Statistical Knowledge	Communication
	Important components of problem; demonstration of statistical concepts and techniques that lead to a correct solution	Explanation of what and why; drawn conclusions stated
4 Complete	■ Demonstrates complete understanding of problem's statistical components ■ Shows a correct relationship among the components (creativity or novelty is good) ■ Uses appropriate statistical techniques; uses them correctly ■ May have minor arithmetic errors, but answers are still reasonable	■ Clearly, completely explains what to do and why, using correct terminology and appropriate organization ■ States appropriate assumptions and caveats ■ Uses diagrams or plots when appropriate; visuals help describe the solution ■ States an appropriate, complete solution
3 Substantial	■ Demonstrates substantial understanding of problem's statistical components ■ Shows a relationship among the components (may have minor gaps) ■ Uses appropriate statistical techniques ■ May have arithmetic errors, but answers are still reasonable	■ Clearly explains what to do and why using correct terminology; not perfectly organized; may be slightly incomplete ■ May omit necessary assumptions or caveats ■ Uses diagrams or plots when appropriate; visuals help describe the solution ■ States a conclusion that follows the analysis but may be somewhat incomplete
2 Developing	■ Demonstrates some understanding of problem's statistical components ■ Shows little of any relationships among the components ■ Uses some appropriate statistical techniques; omits or misuses others ■ May have arithmetic errors that make answers unreasonable	■ Some explanation of what to do, but explanation may be vague, difficult to interpret; some terminology may be inappropriate ■ Uses diagrams incompletely or ineffectively; or might be missing needed diagrams ■ Incomplete conclusion
1 Minimal	■ Demonstrates limited understanding of problem's statistical components (fails to identify important ones) ■ Shows little ability to organize a solution; may use irrelevant information ■ Misuses or omits appropriate statistical techniques ■ Has arithmetic errors that make answers unreasonable	■ Minimal or unclear explanation of what to do or why; explanation may not match solution ■ Fails to use diagrams or plots; or uses them incorrectly ■ Incorrect solution; or fails to state a conclusion
0	■ Shows little to no understanding of statistical components	■ No explanation of legitimate strategy

PART II

SUBJECT AREA REVIEWS WITH SAMPLE QUESTIONS AND ANSWERS

Exploring Data: Interpreting Graphical Displays of Distributions of Univariate Data

A **frequency distribution** is a listing that pairs each value of a variable with its frequency. Frequency distributions in table form are useful but do not give the viewer a feel of what patterns might exist. Graphical representations of the data provide a better picture of the distribution. No one best choice exists when it comes to a graphical display. The most common types of graphical displays include dotplots and bar charts, stemplots, histograms, and cumulative frequency plots.

Dotplots and Bar Charts

A **dotplot** represents each piece of data as a dot positioned along a scale or axis. The scale can be either horizontal or vertical. The horizontal position is more common. The frequency is represented by the other axis.

EXAMPLE:
The following represent the ages of 21 club members. Describe the distribution in general terms.

22	24	19	17	20	27	24	23	26	17	19
22	25	21	21	22	22	21	21	20	22	

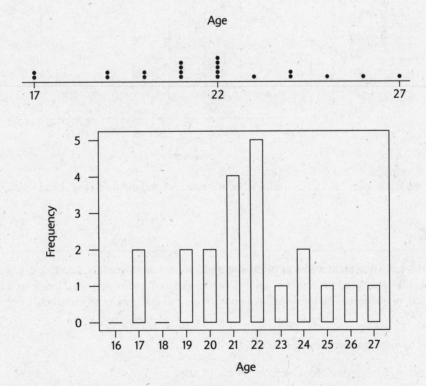

The data is mound-shaped and fairly symmetric. Both the dotplot and the **bar chart** convey the same information. The relative frequency of the data is shown by the height of the dots or the height of the bar.

Dotplots and bar charts are useful in depicting categorical or qualitative data. Each column (row) of dots in a dotplot or each column in a bar chart is used to represent a category of data.

EXAMPLE:

Bryan found 16 pens in his desk: 7 black, 4 blue, 3 red, and 2 green. The following dotplot displays this data.

Pen Color Distribution

EXAMPLE:

Lawnmower sales vary depending on the season. A garden supply store sold 90 lawnmowers during the spring, 85 during the summer, 30 during the fall, and 10 during the winter. Display this information in a bar chart.

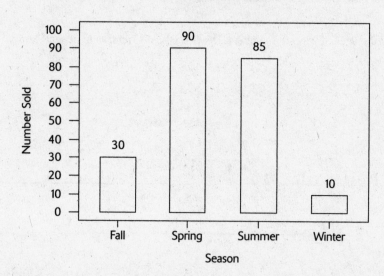

Listing the value at the top of each bar can be useful when the scale is spread out and the actual value is difficult to judge.

Stemplots

Stemplots, sometimes known as **stem and leaf plots**, use digits to represent the data. Leading digits are used to form the stem, and trailing digits are used to form the leaves. What to use as the stem and what to use as the leaf should be determined by the data in question. The following example shows two different configurations.

EXAMPLE:

Construct a stemplot to display the following quiz scores:

58	62	62	63	65	65	65	68
69	72	72	75	76	78	79	81
84	84	85	92	94	95	98	

Grouping by 10:

Quiz Scores

```
5 | 8
6 | 22355589
7 | 225689
8 | 1445
9 | 2458
```

Grouping by 5:

Quiz Scores

```
5 |
5 | 8
6 | 223
6 | 55589
7 | 22
7 | 5689
8 | 144
8 | 5
9 | 24
9 | 58
```

Both of the plots are useful in showing the distributions of the data.

Placing two stemplots back-to-back can be useful in comparing two distributions.

EXAMPLE:
Compare the following two sets of test scores using back-to-back stemplots:

Rudy's scores on 20 tests were 39, 40, 43, 44, 47, 49, 53, 55, 55, 56, 58, 59, 62, 62, 63, 65, 75, 78, 87, and 88.

Sonya's scores on the same 20 tests were 46, 47, 47, 48, 54, 55, 56, 58, 62, 62, 63, 65, 65, 68, 68, 69, 75, 75, 76, and 87.

```
    Rudy      Sonya

        9 | 3 |
    97430 | 4 | 6778
   986553 | 5 | 4568
     5322 | 6 | 22355889
       85 | 7 | 556
       87 | 8 | 7
```

Histograms

Bar charts represent categorical or qualitative data. Histograms are bar charts that represent a frequency distribution of a variable that is quantitative. The horizontal scale represents values of the variable and is labeled with class boundaries or class midpoints. The vertical scale represents the frequency (quantity) or relative frequency (percentage) of the values in each class. Bars in a histogram touch each other. Although histograms can be constructed from given data, the exam does not stress this technique. Questions on the exam use histograms to display data and ask test takers to interpret the histograms.

Important items concerning histograms:

- Bar charts are used for categorical, qualitative data. Histograms are used for quantitative data.
- Classes, or bars, are of equal width and touch each other.
- The number of classes depends on the quantity of data and what you are trying to display.
- If a data element falls on a class boundary, it belongs to the class on the right. If the boundaries of a class are 20 and 30, and x is a data element, then $20 \leq x < 30$.
- All data elements must fit into a specific class. Do not extend the histogram far beyond data values.

EXAMPLE:

The following is a summary of results from a survey concerning the ages of 800 students at a private university: 320 were between 18 and 20 years old ($18 \leq x < 20$); 240 were between 20 and 22 years old ($20 \leq x < 22$); 80 were between 22 and 24 years old ($22 \leq x < 24$); and 160 were between 24 and 26 years old ($24 \leq x < 26$). The following frequency histograms represent this data, one using class boundaries (or cut points) and the other using class midpoints.

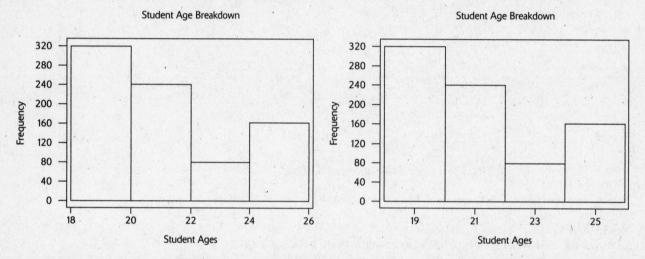

The data could also be represented by a relative frequency histogram. First calculate the relative frequency for each class: $320/800 = .4$, $240/800 = .3$, $80/800 = .1$, $160/800 = .2$. Notice that the shapes of the two histograms are the same. The only difference is in the vertical scale.

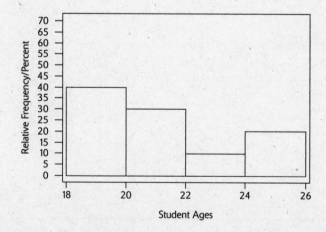

The TI-83/4 can display histograms. In the Window settings, Xscl refers to the class width. Xmin and Xmax are set to the left and right side boundaries of the histogram. Set Ymin and Ymax so that the entire graph is visible. The following screen shots of a TI-83/4 show the steps required to plot a histogram of the following data values: 7, 7, 7, 8, 8, 8, 8, 8, 9, 9, 10, 10, 10, 10, 10,10, 11, 11, 11, 11, 12, 12, and 13.

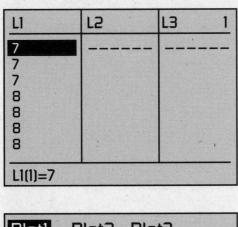

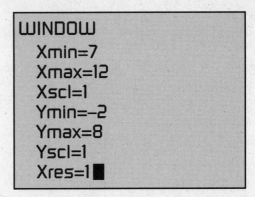

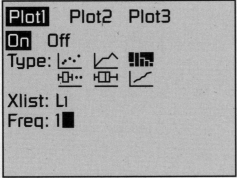

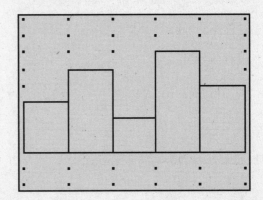

The TI-83/4 can also display a histogram given a frequency distribution table, such as the data from the preceding example. In this case, enter the midpoints of the classes into L1 and the frequency for each class into L2. In the Window settings, set Xmin to 18, Xmax to 26, Xscl to 2. Set Ymin and Ymax to show the entire graph. Some room can be left at the bottom and top to display TRACE information. Enter STATPLOT and set Xlist to L1 and Freq to L2. The following screenshots demonstrate this procedure.

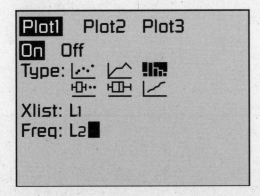

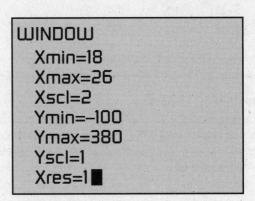

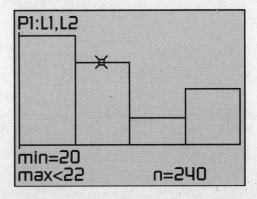

EXAMPLE:

Based on the following histogram, what could be said about the weights of the 200 fish caught during the contest?

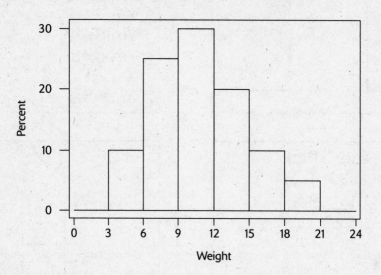

The histogram shows the following:

0–3	0	0%
3–6	20	10%
6–9	50	25%
9–12	60	30%
12–15	40	20%
15–18	20	10%
18–21	10	5%
21–24	0	0%

Observations could include the following: fish weights were between 3 and 21 pounds; 60% of the fish weighed between 9 and 18 pounds; 35% of the fish weighed more than 12 pounds; 110 fish weighed between 6 and 12 pounds.

EXAMPLE:

Since the heights of the columns of a histogram represent the frequency of each class, you can determine the relative frequency of classes even if the frequency is not known. Divide each column (class) into approximately equal sized rectangles. Count the total number of rectangles. The relative frequency can be approximated by dividing each column total by the grand total.

The following histograms show the number of miles driven annually by the employees of a small company:

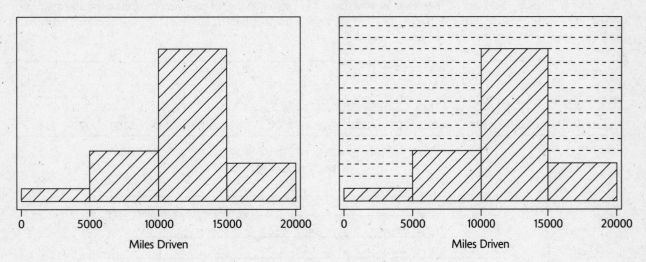

To determine the relative frequency, divide as follows: 1/20 = 5%, 4/20 = 20%, 12/20 = 60% and 3/20 = 15%. Therefore, 75% of the employees drive more than 10000 miles annually, and 20% drive between 5000 and 10000 miles annually.

Cumulative Frequency Charts

A **cumulative frequency chart**, often known as an *ogive*, can represent either total frequency or total relative frequency.

EXAMPLE:
The following chart shows the relative frequencies of ages of freshman at a private university. The cumulative frequency chart can be drawn using this data.

Age Range	Percentage of Enrollment	Cumulative Percentage
18–20	40	40
20–22	30	70
22–24	10	80
24–26	20	100

Cumulative Percentage of Enrollment

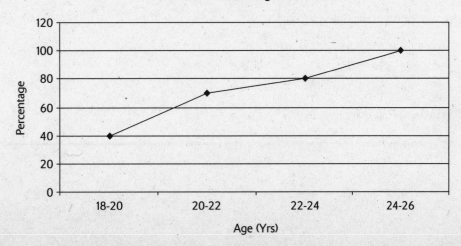

EXAMPLE:
Cumulative frequency charts can be used to show how fast values are changing over one interval compared to another interval. For example, this cumulative frequency chart shows that this elephant's most rapid growth occurred between year 3 and 4, and most growth occurred before year 7.

Age (Yrs)	1	2	3	4	5	6	7	8	9	10	11	12
Weight Gain (kg)	1000	300	700	2000	1200	1100	700	100	60	40	20	10
Cumulative Weight (kg)	1000	1300	2000	4000	5200	6300	7000	7100	7160	7200	7220	7230

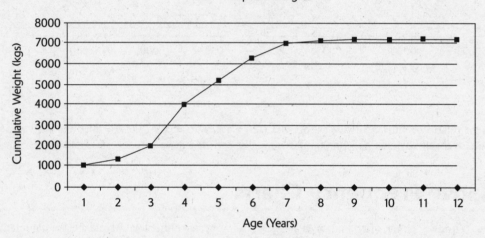

Cumulative line graphs can be difficult to read. The shape of a cumulative line graph can show whether the distribution is shifted to the left, shifted to the right, or is symmetric. See the discussion that follows on "Shape" and the example within that section for a comparison of shifted distributions and how they affect a cumulative line graph.

Center and Spread

The center and spread of a distribution can be defined as follows:

> *Center*—The point in the distribution where approximately half of the values (area) lie to the left and approximately half of the values (area) lie to the right.

> *Spread*—Sometimes known as the range, the spread extends from the minimum value to the maximum value in a distribution.

EXAMPLE:
What is the center and spread of the following data?

58 62 62 63 65 65 65 68
69 72 72 75 76 78 79 81
84 84 85 92 94 95 98

The center is 75, and the spread is from 58 to 98.

Clusters and Gaps

Some distributions are concentrated about several values with space between these concentrations. These concentrations are called *clusters,* and the spaces between them are called *gaps.* Note that the gaps contain no members of the distribution.

EXAMPLE:
These two distributions contain clusters and gaps:

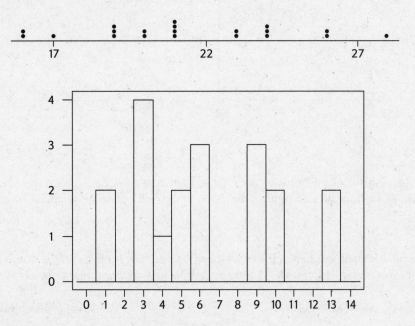

Outliers and Other Unusual Features

An **outlier** is a data entry that is far removed from the other data entries. Outliers can have an adverse effect on some statistical measures and, therefore, must be treated with care. The decision to include or exclude an outlier should be considered carefully. (A more formal definition will be discussed in the next chapter.)

EXAMPLE:
The following histograms contain outliers. Note that outliers may be on one side of the distribution or on both sides of the distribution.

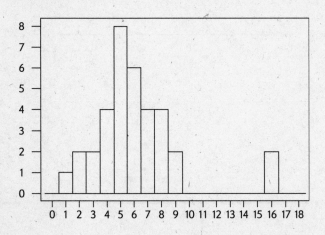 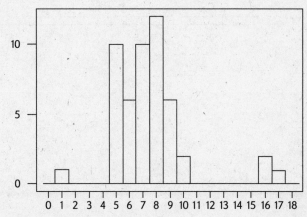

EXAMPLE:
The following continuous distributions contain outliers:

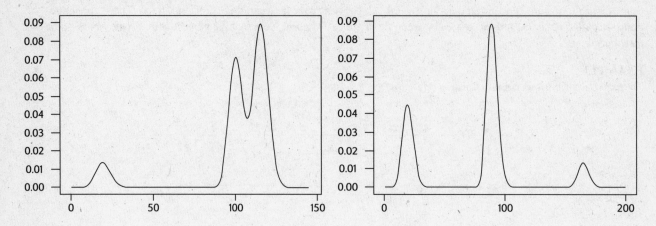

Shape

One very important characteristic of a distribution is its shape. Distributions made up of a single mound can be classified as **symmetric, skewed left,** or **skewed right.** If the values of the distribution are evenly distributed, it is called a uniform distribution.

EXAMPLE:
Each of these distributions is made up of a single mound. Note that the *skew* is the *tail* of the distribution. The uniform distributions are uniform or nearly uniform. The symmetric distributions are symmetric or nearly symmetric.

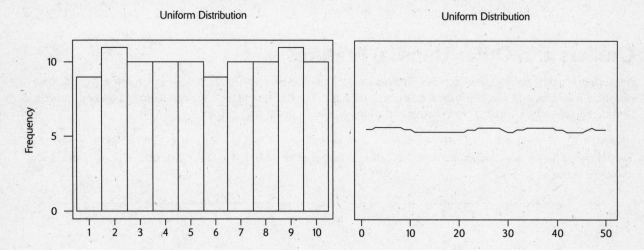

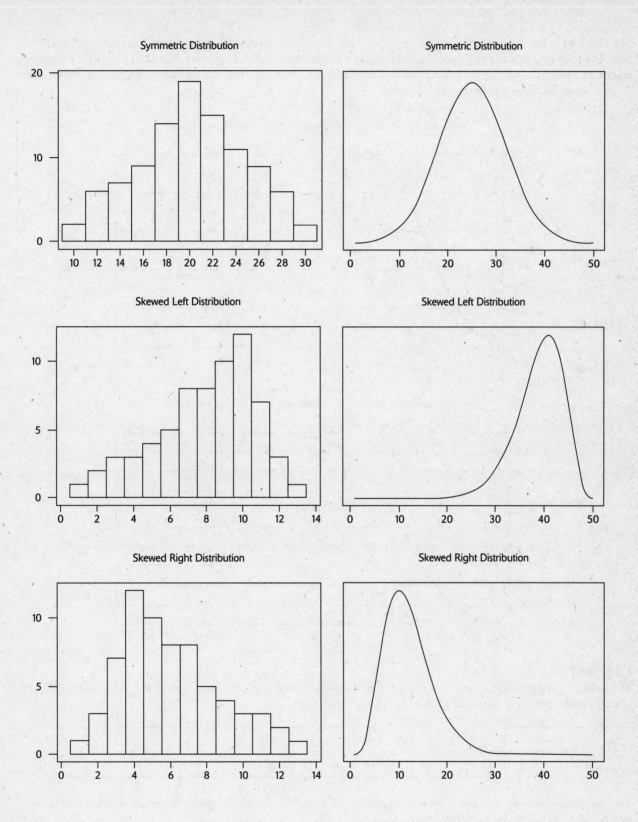

The relationship between a relative frequency graph and its cumulative relative frequency graph is an important one to note. The following two sets of graphs demonstrate this relationship. The first diagram is a set of three relative frequency graphs (skewed right, symmetric, and skewed left) and the second diagram shows the corresponding cumulative frequency graphs. Notice the shape of the cumulative graphs.

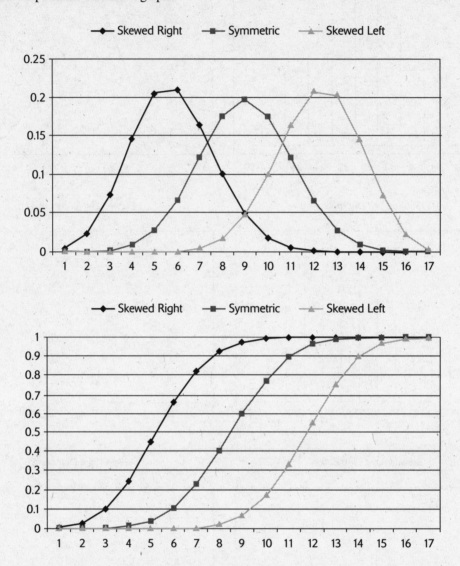

EXAMPLE:

The following represents the amount of product sold each day for ten days for a salesman. Graph the frequency distribution and the cumulative frequency distribution on the same graph.

Day	1	2	3	4	5	6	7	8	9	10
Amount Sold	1	10	15	14	12	8	5	3	2	1

This frequency distribution shows a skew to the right. Notice that the cumulative graph rises more quickly during the first few days as compared to the last few days.

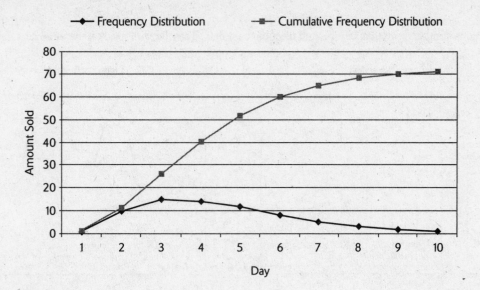

If the amounts sold were reversed, the distribution would be skewed left and the cumulative graph rises more rapidly during the last few days.

Day	1	2	3	4	5	6	7	8	9	10
Amount Sold	1	2	3	5	8	12	14	15	10	1

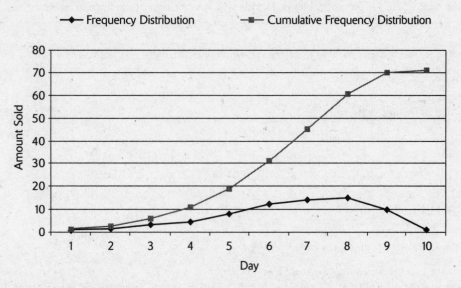

Distributions made up of a single mound of data are said to have one **mode**. A mode is a high point in the distribution. Each of the distributions in the previous example (demonstrating shape) have a single mode. Some distributions have more than one mode. If the distribution had two main mounds, then it is bimodal. Distributions with more than two mounds are considered multimodal.

EXAMPLE:

These distributions contain more than one mound of connected data. They have more than one mode.

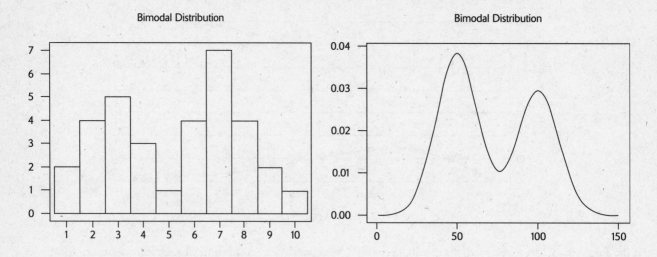

Review Questions and Answers

Multiple Choice Questions

Directions: Solve each of the following problems. Decide which is the best of the choices given.

1. Which of the following is/are suitable to determine whether a distribution is skewed?

   I.   Stemplot

   II. Histogram

   III. Cumulative frequency charts

   A. III only

   B. I and II

   C. I and III

   D. II and III

   E. I, II, and III

2. Which of the following statements is false?

   A. Continuous distributions may have gaps or outliers.

   B. A skewed right distribution and a skewed left distribution cannot be compared using a back-to-back stemplot.

   C. Histograms are never continuous.

   D. In histograms, the area of the bars may be used to compute relative frequency.

   E. A frequency histogram can be constructed from a cumulative frequency chart.

3. Which statement is best represented by this histogram?

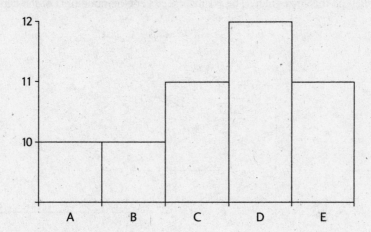

A. The histogram is skewed right.
B. Division D sold more than A and B combined.
C. Division D made 1/3 of all sales.
D. Division C sold more than division B.
E. Division C sold twice as much as division B.

4. If a relative frequency distribution is symmetric, the sum of the relative frequencies is:

A. 0.5
B. 0.68
C. 1.00
D. 100
E. Cannot be determined from the information given

5. Which of the following are true statements about histograms?

I. Midpoints are just as useful in determining class width as boundaries.
II. They are useful in displaying cumulative frequencies.
III. They are used to display categorical data.

A. I only
B. II only
C. I and II
D. I and III
E. II and III

6. This histogram represents the weights of 16 fish caught in Lake Thomas on April 1. Which of the following statements is true based on this histogram? The *x*-values represent the midpoints of the class.

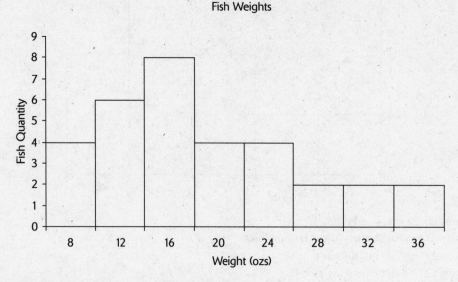

Fish Weights

A. More than half of the fish caught weighed less than 16 ounces.
B. Half the fish caught weighed between 16 and 24 ounces.
C. The relative frequency for fish weighing between 22 and 30 ounces is 0.1875.
D. The distribution is skewed left.
E. More than half of the fish caught weighed at least 16 ounces.

7. In a histogram, integer data is grouped into five classes. The classes contain the following age ranges:

Class	I	II	III	IV	V
Age Range	12–17	18–23	24–29	30–35	36–41

What is the numeric width of each class?

A. 5.5
B. 6.0
C. 6.5
D. 7.0
E. 7.5

8. A 4-class histogram is used to display information about the height (to the closest inch) of 30 club members. The minimum height is 57 inches, and the maximum is 80 inches. If the right boundary of the fourth class is 82 and the width of each class is an integer value, what would be the largest possible value of the boundary between the first and second classes?

A. 60 inches
B. 61 inches
C. 62 inches
D. 63 inches
E. 64 inches

9. Which of the following is not true about histograms?

    A. The bars must touch each other.

    B. The width of each class must be the same.

    C. A histogram for a given set of data may be symmetric or skewed depending on the selection of class width and boundaries.

    D. Histograms may have gaps and clusters.

    E. Histograms may represent categorical data.

10. Which of the following is true?

    A. Histograms convey more information than stemplots.

    B. Dotplots are not used for categorical data.

    C. Relative frequency histograms convey less information than frequency histograms.

    D. The largest value of a set of data can be determined by observing a histogram of the data.

    E. If a stemplot for a set of data shows a gap, then a histogram for the same data will also show a gap.

11. This dotplot represents the number of people applying for jobs at a company during March.

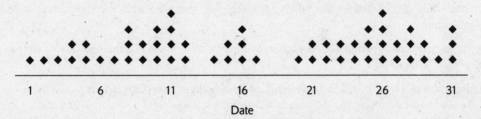

If the first is a Monday, what is the approximate relative frequency of people applying for a job on a weekend (Saturday and Sunday)?

    A. 0.17

    B. 0.19

    C. 0.21

    D. 0.23

    E. 0.25

12. Which of the following is true about this back-to-back stemplot?

Team A		Team B
994	16	68
8776442110	17	47889
99888863	18	346679
94431	19	113367799
986554	20	01136688
97755	21	144566

    I. The team with the highest score was the team with the lowest score.

    II. The distribution for Team A is skewed right, and the distribution for Team B is skewed left.

    III. Team A had a higher average score than Team B.

    A. I only

    B. I and II

    C. I and III

    D. II and III

    E. I, II, and III

13. Which of the following statements is false?

    A. A symmetric distribution can have outliers.

    B. A skewed left distribution cannot have outliers on the right.

    C. A skewed right distribution may have outliers on the right.

    D. A symmetric distribution may have more outliers than a skewed distribution.

    E. Stemplots are suitable for showing outliers.

Multiple Choice Answers

  1. E. Stemplots and histograms directly show whether a distribution is skewed. Using a cumulative frequency chart, the frequency chart can be constructed, and a determination can be made if the distribution is skewed. Also, left and right skewed distributions have distinctive cumulative frequency charts.

  2. B. Back-to-back stemplots are very appropriate to use to compare the shapes of two distributions. Response **C** is true because histograms are used for discrete data—not continuous data. Response **D** is true if the scales of the histogram are accurate. Response **E** is true because frequency histograms and cumulative frequency histograms can be determined from each other. Relative frequency can be determined from frequency, but frequency cannot be determined from relative frequency.

  3. D. The histogram is skewed left. Because the scale on the left does not start at zero, the actual areas that the bars show are misleading.

  4. C. The symmetry of a distribution does not have anything to do with the fact that the sum of all the relative frequencies must be equal to 1.

  5. C. The class width of a histogram can be determined by calculating the difference between the midpoints of adjacent classes or by calculating the difference between the left and right boundaries of a class. Histograms can represent either frequency or cumulative frequency. Histograms are not used for categorical data.

  6. C. Choices **A**, **B**, and **E** are each false because 16 is a midpoint, and the distribution of fish weights within the class is unknown. Choice **D** is false because the distribution is skewed right. The relative frequency for the fish in the classes between 22 and 30 can be determined by adding to find the total frequency for the classes. That total is 32. Then find the total frequency for the classes between 22 and 30. This total is 6. Six divided by 32 is 0.1875.

  7. B. The width of a class is determined by finding the difference between midpoints of adjacent classes or by subtracting the left and right boundary values of a class. The second class, for example, has left and right boundaries of 17.5 and 23.5, respectively. Therefore, the class width is 6.

  8. C. The statement of the problem implies that the values of the boundaries are integers. A chart demonstrates that the largest possible value for the required boundary of 61 occurs when the class width is 7. If the class width is 6, then the left boundary of the histogram is 58. This is not possible because the smallest data value is 57.

       `<----Class 1---><----Class 2---><---Class 3---><---Class 4--->`

58	64	70	76	82
54	61	68	75	82

  9. E. This is an important distinction between histograms and bar charts. Histograms are not used for categorical data.

  10. C. A relative frequency distribution can be constructed from a frequency distribution. A frequency distribution cannot be constructed from a relative frequency distribution. Therefore, a frequency distribution conveys more information than does a relative frequency distribution.

  11. B. If the first is on a Monday, then the weekends fall on days 6, 7, 13, 14, 20, 21, 27, and 28. The total number of dots above weekends is 11. The total number of dots is 57. Dividing, you get approximately 0.19.

12. B. Choice III is not accurate. Team A had a lower average score than Team B. Choices I and II are accurate.

13. B. Outliers usually lie in the direction of the skew, but not always. Distributions can be drawn easily with an outlier on the opposite side from the skew. The other choices are accurate.

Free-Response Questions

Directions: Show all work. Indicate clearly the methods you use. You will be graded on method as well as accuracy.

1. The following are test scores from 40 students in a tenth-grade math class. Construct a histogram with 6 classes and use it to describe the shape of the distribution.

97	95	88	74	69	86	70	79
99	90	89	97	59	67	78	96
88	66	76	92	98	77	62	84
76	85	48	69	63	98	49	91
80	58	99	85	63	60	97	96

2. Compare and contrast these two distributions using a back-to-back stemplot.

Distribution A:

105	65	27	33	94	79	48	45
53	85	66	108	59	70	22	71
54	47	23	39	93	89	73	56
101	77	73	66	96	22	82	34
99	76	77	34	86	68	54	108
109	88	64	47	98	67	96	84
35	88	59	68	97	28		

Distribution B:

43	59	102	86	48	27	74	66
31	99	112	95	61	20	57	50
22	63	21	31	79	57	26	56
33	66	32	45	104	89	43	82
63	77	44	57	83	47	21	34
37	96	33	36	96	76	83	65
106	37	104	84	48	79		

Free-Response Answers

1. The minimum value in the distribution is 48, and the maximum value is 99. Because both of these numbers plus all those in between must be contained in the distribution, you can subtract to find the range of values of the data. The difference between 99 and 48 is 51. If you keep the class width as an integer, you could make the class width 9. The six classes then would be 54 units wide. The actual choice for the beginning and end points of the histogram will determine its shape. You must start lower than the minimum data value of 48 and extend higher than the maximum data value of 99. Enter the 40 numbers into a list, such as L1, in the TI-83/4.

If the left edge of the histogram begins at 47 and there's a class width of 9, then the class boundaries would be 47, 56, 65, 74, 83, 92, and 101. The following screenshots display the output of the TI-83/84:

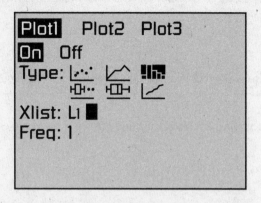

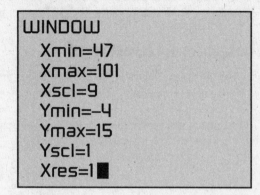

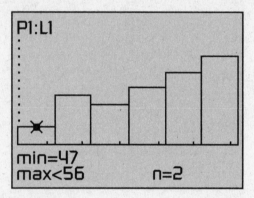

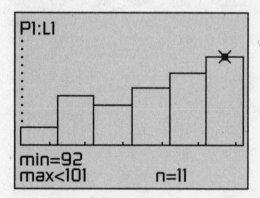

If the left edge of the histogram begins at 46 and there's a class width of 9, then the class boundaries would be 46, 55, 64, 73, 82, 91, and 100. The following screenshots display the output of the TI-83/84:

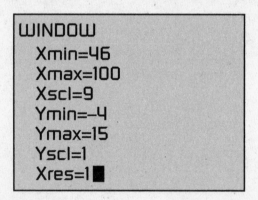

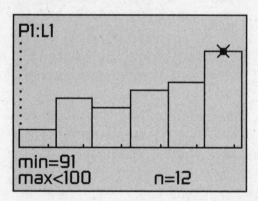

Although the frequency of the last two classes changes by one each as the boundaries are shifted, the shape of the distribution remains approximately the same. This distribution is definitely skewed left. One half of the entire distribution is located in the last two classes.

2. Create a back-to-back stemplot.

Distribution A		Distribution B
87322	2	011267
95443	3	112334677
8775	4	3345788
996443	5	067779
8876654	6	133566
97763310	7	46799
9886542	8	233469
9876643	9	5669
98851	10	2446
	11	2

Distribution A is skewed to the left (the low numbers) and distribution B is skewed to the right (the high numbers). Distribution B has the smallest value (20) of both distributions; it also has the largest value (112). The average value of distribution A appears to be greater than that of distribution B. Neither distribution has any outliers, and neither distribution has gaps or clusters. Both distributions contain the same number of data values (54).

Exploring Data: Summarizing Distributions of Univariate Data

When presented with a set of collected data, patterns and other characteristics are usually not obvious. Graphs and charts can help organize the data but still lack precision. The branch of statistics that analyzes data and describes features of the data is known as **Descriptive Statistics.** Essential elements of descriptive statistics include finding averages, measures of spread or deviation, as well as other measures that allow for comparisons between data sets.

Measuring Center: Median, Mean

Two main measures of central tendency are *median* and *mean*. Although both the median and the mean are measures of the center of a set of numbers, the common usage of the word "average" refers to the mean.

The **median** is the middle number in a series of ordered numbers. The order of the numbers can be either ascending or descending. If the data set contains an odd number of values, then there is one exact median. If the data set contains an even number of values, then the median is the average of the two middle numbers.

The **mean** is the sum of all the members of the data set divided by the number of numbers in the data set. If an entire **population** is under consideration, the Greek letter μ is used to specify the mean. If a portion of a population, known as a **sample,** is used, then the symbol $\bar{x}$ is used. If x is a variable that represents the sample values in the data set, then the mean is denoted by $\bar{x} = \dfrac{\sum x_i}{n}$.

EXAMPLE:
Find the median and mean of the following set of numbers: 12, 12, 15, 16, 16, 17, 19, 21, 21, 21, and 22.

To find the median manually, the numbers, if out of order, must be ordered. (Technology tools, such as the TI-83/4 calculator, can find the median of a set of numbers without ordering them.) In this example, the middle number in the ordered list is 17. An odd number of values exists in this data set so there is one number in the middle. The mean is found using the formula $\bar{x} = \dfrac{\sum x_i}{n} = \dfrac{192}{11} = 17.455$.

In this example, if the number 22 is changed to 30, the median would remain the same, but the mean would increase in value because the sum of the numbers increased. Therefore, the median is said to be more **resistant** than the mean to extreme values, called **outliers,** in data sets.

EXAMPLE:
Find the median and mean of the following set of numbers: 17.2, 18.1, 20.5, 22.2, 23.6, and 23.8.

This set of numbers is already ordered. Because the list has an even number of values, the median is the average of the two middle values. Add 20.5 and 22.2. Then divide by 2. This gives a median of 21.35. The mean is found using the formula $\bar{x} = \dfrac{\sum x_i}{n} = \dfrac{125.4}{6} = 20.9$. If the smallest value decreased by 50%, there would be no change in the median, but the mean would decrease from 20.9 to 19.467.

EXAMPLE:

Consider the following stem and leaf plot:

Quiz Scores

5	5578
6	223455589
7	225689
8	1445
9	58

Which would you expect to be larger, the mean or the median, and why?

This distribution is skewed right, toward the higher numbers. (Mentally rotate the graph so that the smaller numbers are on the left and the larger numbers are on the right.) The higher numbers, 95 and 98, are considered extreme values in this distribution because they are in the tail. They have more of an effect on the mean since the median is more resistant to extreme values. You would expect the mean to be higher. In this case, the median is 69, and the mean is 71.48.

Measuring Spread: Range, Interquartile Range, Standard Deviation

Two sets of numbers can have the same mean and the same median, but be very different. For example, the following two sets of numbers each have a mean of 80 and a median of 80.

Set A: 100, 90, 80, 70, and 60

Set B: 82, 81, 80, 79, and 78

Although Set A and Set B have the same mean and median, Set A is more spread out than Set B. Several statistical measures are used to describe the spread of a distribution.

The **range** of a distribution is nothing more than the difference between the largest data value and smallest data value (range = maximum – minimum).

The **interquartile range** of a distribution is the range of the middle 50% of the data. That is, the range of the data we have left after discarding the upper and lower 25% of the numbers in a data set. If Q1 represents the median of the bottom half and Q3 represents the median of the upper half of an ordered distribution, then the interquartile range is defined as IQR = Q3 – Q1.

EXAMPLE:

Find the range and interquartile range of the following set of 21 numbers: 3, 5, 5, 6, 6, 8, 9, 9, 12, 13, 15, 15, 16, 17, 20, 22, 22, 23, 23, 26, 27. Repeat without the largest value (27). Repeat again without the largest two values (26 and 27).

The following table shows the three lists along with five specific values. These values are the minimum, the maximum, the median, Q1 and Q3. The range and interquartile range are calculated as follows:

$$range = maximum - minimum$$
$$interquartile\ range = Q3 - Q1$$

	Set X		Set Y		Set Z
Minimum = 3	3	Minimum = 3	3	Minimum = 3	3
	5		5		5
	5		5		5
	6		6		6
	6		6	Q1 = 6	6
Q1 = 7	8	Q1 = 7	8		8
	9		9		9
	9		9		9
	12		12		12
	13		13	Median = 13	13
Median = 15	15	Median = 14	15		15
	15		15		15
	16		16		16
	17		17		17
	20		20		20
	22	Q3 = 21	22	Q3 = 20	22
Q3 = 22	22		22		22
	23		23		23
	23		23	Maximum = 23	23
	26		26		
Maximum = 27	27	Maximum = 26			

Set X contains 21 numbers. One number, 15, is in the middle; therefore the median is 15. When determining the values of Q1 and Q3, the median is excluded. Q1 is the median of the lower 10 numbers and Q3 is the median of the upper 10 numbers.

$$\text{range of Set X} = \text{maximum} - \text{minimum} = 27 - 3 = 24$$

$$\text{interquartile range of Set X} = Q3 - Q1 = 22 - 7 = 15$$

Set Y contains 20 numbers. Two numbers are in the middle, so the median is their average, or 14. When determining the values of Q1 and Q3, the median is not excluded since an even number of values exists. Thus, Q1 is the median of the lower 10 numbers and Q3 is the median of the upper 10 numbers.

$$\text{range of Set Y} = \text{maximum} - \text{minimum} = 26 - 3 = 23$$

$$\text{interquartile range of Set Y} = Q3 - Q1 = 21 - 7 = 14$$

Set Z contains 19 numbers. One number, 13, is in the middle; therefore the median is 13. When determining the values of Q1 and Q3, the median is excluded. Q1 is the median of the lower 9 numbers and Q3 is the median of the upper 9 numbers.

$$\text{range of Set Z} = \text{maximum} - \text{minimum} = 23 - 3 = 20$$

$$\text{interquartile range of Set Z} = Q3 - Q1 = 20 - 6 = 14$$

These five numbers (minimum, Q1, median, Q3, and the maximum) are called the **5-number summary.** These five values may be found using a technology tool such as the TI-83/4. Using the STAT menu and the EDIT submenu, enter the list of numbers in one of the available lists. Use the STAT menu and the CALC submenu and choose 1-variable statistics. Enter the appropriate list. Scroll down and find the 5-number summary.

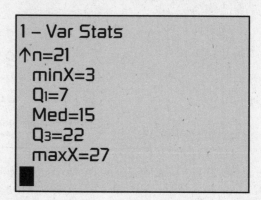

The **variance** of a distribution is the average of the sum of the squared differences between the mean and each value in the data set. The variance of a population uses Greek letters and is represented by the following formula:

$$\sigma^2 = \frac{\sum(x_i - \mu)^2}{n}$$

The variance of a sample uses English letters and is represented by a slightly different formula:

$$s^2 = \frac{\sum(x_i - \overline{x})^2}{n - 1}$$

Notice that for variances of samples, the divisor is $n - 1$, not n.

The **standard deviation** is the square root of the variance.

$$\sigma = \sqrt{\frac{\sum(x_i - \mu)^2}{n}} \text{ or } s = \sqrt{\frac{\sum(x_i - \overline{x})^2}{n - 1}}$$

The representation of the standard deviation formula on the AP Statistics Exam is as follows:

$$s_x = \sqrt{\frac{1}{n - 1}\sum(x_i - \overline{x})^2}$$

It is important to distinguish between these two forms of standard deviation. The population standard deviation is used when you describe the spread of an entire population. The sample standard deviation is used when you are working with samples. The following example will use the sample standard deviation.

Technology tools such as the TI-83/4 can find the standard deviation directly from a list of numbers. Calculation formulas also can be used as shown in the following example.

EXAMPLE:

Find the variance and standard deviation of the following sample set of numbers: 12, 14, 15, 15, 17, and 18.

The following table summarizes the process of finding the mean and then the sample standard deviation. First, calculate the mean. Then, subtract the mean from each of the numbers in the data set. Square these results. Add the squares and then divide by one less than the sample size. This gives the variance. The square root of the sample variance is the sample standard deviation.

x	$x - \overline{x}$	$(x - \overline{x})^2$
12	−3	9
14	−1	1
15	0	0
15	0	0
17	2	4
17	2	4
$\Sigma x = 90$		$s^2 = \dfrac{\sum(x - \overline{x})^2}{n-1} = \dfrac{18}{5} = 3.6$
$\overline{x} = \dfrac{\sum x}{n} = \dfrac{90}{6} = 15$		$s = \sqrt{3.6} = 1.897$

To use the TI-83/4 to find the mean and standard deviation, enter the numbers into one of the lists under STAT and EDIT. Then enter STAT, CALC, and choose "1-Var Stats."

Enter the list number for the calculations:

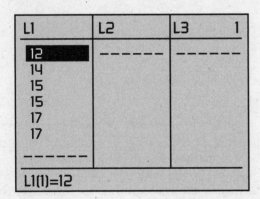
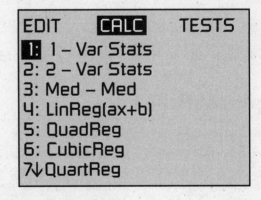

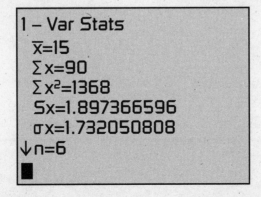

Measuring Position: Quartiles, Percentiles, Standardized Scores (z-Scores)

The position of an entry in an ordered data set can be looked at in several different ways:

Ordinal placement: The absolute rank of a number within an ordered data set states how many numbers are larger or smaller than the given number including the number itself. For example, this list may represent the ages of the children in a school play: 6, 6, 7, 8, 9, 9, 10, 12, 13, 13, 14, 16, 18, and 19. The child who is 10 years old is the 7th youngest, or the 8th oldest child.

Percentile: Percentile indicates the percentage of values smaller than the given value. For example, if a number is the 5th largest in a set of 84 numbers, then it is larger than 78 of the 84 numbers. Therefore, its percentile would be $\frac{78}{84} = 0.929$, or the 93rd percentile.

Quartile: The first quartile, Q1, is the same as the 25th percentile. The third quartile, Q3, is the same as the 75th percentile. The second quartile is the 50th percentile, which corresponds to the median.

z-score: The z-score indicates how many standard deviations above or below the mean the given value lies. If the value is larger than the mean, then the z-score is positive. If the value is smaller than the mean, then the z-score is negative. For example, if a distribution of numbers has a mean of 32.5 and a standard deviation of 4.7, then the z-score of the number 38 can be calculated by using the following formula: $z = \frac{x - \mu}{\sigma} = \frac{38 - 32.5}{4.7} = 1.17$. Notice that the z-score is positive since 38 is larger than the mean. This formula relates four important values. You can rewrite the formula so that it is solved for the raw data value instead of the z-score. This form is useful when you want to determine a value that has a given z-score. The transformed formula is $x = z\sigma + \mu$. For example, if a distribution has a mean of 32.5 and a standard deviation of 4.7, then the raw data value corresponding to a z-score of $z = -2.3$ can be calculated as follows: $z\sigma + \mu = (-2.3)(4.7) + 32.5 = 21.69$.

EXAMPLE:

The mean price of a home in a small city is $322,000 with a standard deviation of $26,000. Find the z-score of a home selling for $310,000. Find the value of a home that has a z-score of 1.3.

To find the z-score: $z = \frac{x - \mu}{\sigma} = \frac{310000 - 322000}{26000} = -0.46$.

To find the value: $z\sigma + \mu = (1.3)(26000) + 322000 = 355800$.

Empirical Rule

The empirical rule is also known as the 68–95–99.7 rule. The empirical rule states that in a bell-shaped, symmetric distribution, such as the normal distribution, approximately 68% of all the data lies within one standard deviation from the mean. Also, approximately 95% lies within two standard deviations from the mean, and approximately 99.7% lies within three standard deviations from the mean. In the figure that follows, the numbers on the horizontal axis represent the z-scores with vertical bars one standard deviation apart.

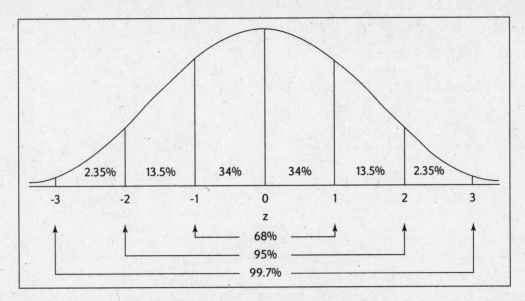

From this graph, it is clear that almost all data in a bell-shaped symmetric distribution, like the normal distribution, lies within three standard deviations from the mean. If there are no outliers or other extreme values in the data set, then the standard deviation should be approximately one-sixth of the range of the data. This is a very rough approximation and should be used as a "first guess" at the standard deviation for this type of distribution.

EXAMPLE:

In a bell-shaped, fairly symmetric distribution, the mean is 150, and the standard deviation is 20. Approximately what percent of the distribution lies between 130 and 190? between 90 and 110? What should be the approximate range of the data in this distribution?

Since 130 lies one standard below the mean and 190 lies two standard deviations above the mean, the approximate percentage of this distribution that lies between 130 and 190 is 34% + 34% + 13.5% = 81.5%. Since 90 lies three standard deviations below the mean and 110 lies two standard deviations below the mean, the approximate percentage of this distribution that lies between 90 and 110 is 13.5%. Since the standard deviation of this bell-shaped, symmetric distribution is 20, the range should be approximately 6 times 20 or about 120. This is a very rough approximation.

Comparing Measures of Central Tendency

When a distribution is symmetric, the mean, median, and mode are equal. If the distribution is skewed right, the mean is more than the median, and the median is usually more than the mode. If the distribution is skewed left, the mean is less than the median, and the median is usually less than the mode. The mean is affected more by extreme values so that the mean will be closer to the tail of a skewed distribution than the median. The figures that follow are examples of distributions that commonly occur:

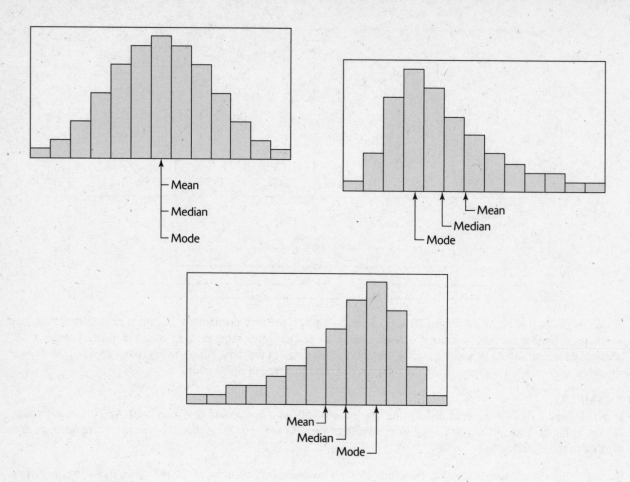

Using Boxplots

A **boxplot** (box and whisker plot) is a graph that shows the 5-number summary. That is, the 5-number summary is the minimum value, the first quartile (Q1), the median, the third quartile (Q3), and the maximum value of a distribution.

An **outlier** is a member of a distribution that lies more than 1.5 times the interquartile range (IQR) above Q3 or below Q1. Outliers are extreme values. The TI-83/4 can display boxplots either with or without outliers. Boxplots are useful in describing distributions that are highly skewed.

EXAMPLE:
Given the following set of numbers, determine whether there are any outliers and plot the distribution using a boxplot (box and whisker plot): 2, 3, 5, 5, 6, 7, 7, 7, 8, 9, 9, 9, 10, 10, 10, 10, 10, 11, 11, 12, 14, 14, 14, 15, 16, 18, 18, 18, 18, 19, 19, 20, 20, 22, 22, 24, 24, 24, 25, 26, 26, 27, 28, 28, 28, 33, 45, 50, 55, and 66.

Since this distribution contains 50 ordered numbers, the median is the average of the 25th and 26th values, Q1 is the 13th value, and Q3 is the 38th value. Therefore, Q1 is 10, and Q3 is 24. The IQR (interquartile range) is Q3 – Q1 = 24 – 10 = 14. Next, multiply the IQR by 1.5, giving 21. Thus, any value more than 21 greater than Q3 or lower than 21 less than Q1 would be outliers. The value of 45 is exactly 21 greater than Q3 and, therefore, does not qualify as an outlier. The values of 50, 55, and 66 do qualify as outliers.

If these 50 values are entered into a list in the TI-83/4, Q1 and Q3 can be determined by choosing STAT, CALC, and "1-Var Stats." Using STATPLOT, a boxplot can be drawn showing the outliers. Use the TRACE key to easily determine which values are outliers.

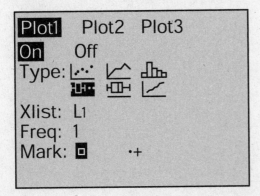

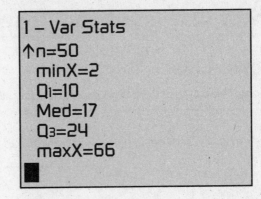

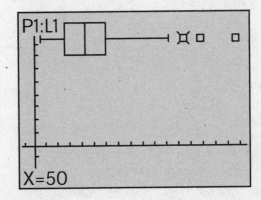

The Effect of Changing Units on Summary Measures

Changing units, such as degrees to radians, feet to meters, and hours to days, do have an effect on summary measures. When units are changed, usually one of two changes takes place. Either a constant is added to each data value, or each data value is multiplied by a constant factor (or possibly both).

If a constant is added to (subtracted from) each data value, the measures of central tendency will increase (decrease) by that constant value, but the measures of spread will not change. If each data value is multiplied by a constant factor, the measures of central tendency, as well as measures of spread will increase (or decrease) by that factor. The following table summarizes these changes.

	Central Tendency (Mean and Median)	Spread (Range, IQR, and Standard Deviation)
Adding a constant	Add constant	Remains the same
Multiplying by a constant	Multiply by constant	Multiply by constant

EXAMPLE:

If a distribution has a mean of 44 and a standard deviation of 12, what will be the new mean and standard deviation if 22 is added to each value in the distribution?

The measure of central tendency, the mean, will increase by that constant. Thus, the new mean will be 66. The measure of spread, the standard deviation, will not change from its value of 12.

EXAMPLE:

If a distribution has a mean of 44 and a standard deviation of 12, what will be the new mean and standard deviation if each data value in the distribution is multiplied by 1.75?

The measure of central tendency, the mean, will increase by a factor of 1.75. Thus, the new mean will be 77. The measure of spread, the standard deviation, will also increase by a factor of 1.75. Thus, the new standard deviation will be 21.

Review Questions and Answers

Multiple Choice Questions

Directions: Solve each of the following problems. Decide which is the best of the choices given.

1. Life span data is shown in this histogram. Which of the following is/are false?

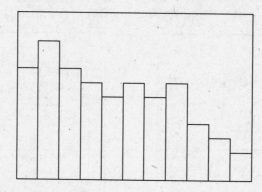

   I.   The median is greater than the mean.
   II. The histogram is skewed right.
   III. The IQR is one half of the range.

   A. I only
   B. II only
   C. III only
   D. I and III
   E. I, II, and III

2. The mean score on a standardized test is 125 with a standard deviation of 25. Use the empirical rule to determine the appropriate percentile rank of someone who scored 152.

   A. 68
   B. 75
   C. 79
   D. 85
   E. 92

3. The following is the 5-number summary of a set of animal weights: a, 12, b, 16, and c. If a boxplot is drawn to show outliers, what is maximum length of either boxplot whisker?

   A. the larger of $(12 - a)$ and $(c - 16)$
   B. the larger of $(b - a)$ and $(c - b)$
   C. 6
   D. 8
   E. cannot be determined from the given data

4. The mean of a bell-shaped, symmetric distribution is 0, and the standard deviation of the distribution is 5. If 5 is added to each value in the distribution and then the resulting values are each divided by 5, what would be the new mean and standard deviation?

    A. mean = 0, standard deviation = 1
    B. mean = 1, standard deviation = 1
    C. mean = 0, standard deviation = 2
    D. mean = 1, standard deviation = 2
    E. mean = 5, standard deviation = 1

5. How many outliers are there in this data set?

1, 2, 4, 8, 16, 32, 64, 128, 256, 512, 1024

    A. 0
    B. 1
    C. 2
    D. 3
    E. 4

6. Use this back-to-back stemplot to determine which team's scores had a larger IQR and how much larger?

Team A		Team B
	3	23678
87765	4	5668
98643	5	0277
3220	6	36679
99875	7	

    A. Team A, 2
    B. Team A, 4
    C. Team A, 6
    D. Team B, 2
    E. Team B, 4

7. Which of the following is/are resistant to outliers and other extreme values?

    I. mean
    II. median
    III. standard deviation

    A. I only
    B. II only
    C. III only
    D. I and III
    E. II and III

8. Logan scored 76 on his math test and 82 on his English test. The mean class score on the math test was 72 with a standard deviation of 3. The mean class score on the English test was 78 with a standard deviation of 5. What is the difference in z-scores between Logan's English and math test scores?

    A. 2.13
    B. 0.53
    C. 0
    D. −0.53
    E. −2.13

9. Which of the following would be greatly affected by outliers?

    I.   IQR

   II. range

  III. median

   A. I only

   B. II only

   C. I and II

   D. I and III

   E. II and III

10. Given a bell-shaped, symmetric distribution with a mean of 50 and a standard deviation of 10, which of the following would be an accurate statement about the z-score of Q1?

   A. $-2 \leq z \leq -1$

   B. $-1 \leq z \leq 0$

   C. $0 \leq z \leq 1$

   D. $1 \leq z \leq 2$

   E. $z < -2$ or $z > 2$

11. The mean of a mound-shaped distribution is 60. The median of the same distribution is 55. How many of the following statements are true?

    I.   The standard deviation can be determined by knowing the IQR.

   II. The standard deviation is less than 6.

  III. The z-score of the median is positive.

  IV. The distribution is skewed right.

   V. IQR > 5

   A. 0

   B. 1

   C. 2

   D. 3

   E. 4

12. Aaron is checking the values of all of the cards in his card collection. If 26 of the cards had a value of $11 each, 16 had a value of $15 each, 17 had a value of $18 each, 22 had a value of $20 each, and 9 had a value of $30 each, what is the average value of his card collection?

   A. $16.47

   B. $16.88

   C. $17.13

   D. $18.00

   E. $18.80

13. Use this cumulative frequency graph to determine the IQR and the median value of the distribution.

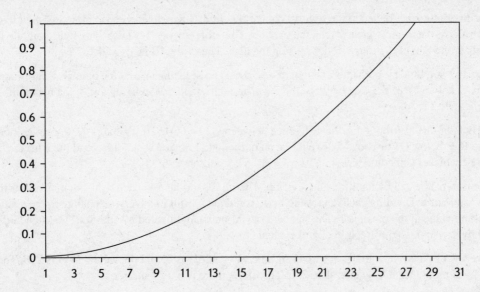

    A. 9, 19.5
    B. 10, 19.5
    C. 9, 20
    D. 10, 20
    E. 11, 20

14. The salary schedule of a school district has six columns. The number of employees in each column is shown in the chart that follows. The salary increases as you move from column 1 to column 2 to column 3, and so on.

Column	1	2	3	4	5	6
# of Employees	32	58	110	230	650	90

Which of the following statements is accurate?

    A. The distribution is skewed right with a mean salary that is greater than the median salary.
    B. The distribution is skewed right with a median salary that is greater than the mean salary.
    C. The distribution is skewed left with a mean salary that is greater than the median salary.
    D. The distribution is skewed left with a median salary that is greater than the mean salary.
    E. Without knowing the salary for each column, the relationship between mean and median salaries cannot be determined.

15. According to the empirical rule, a value in a distribution that is two standard deviations above the mean would lie at approximately what percentile?

    A. 34th percentile
    B. 68th percentile
    C. 84th percentile
    D. 95th percentile
    E. 97th percentile

Multiple Choice Answers

1. D. This distribution is skewed to the right so choice II is true. Since the median is more resistant to outliers and extreme values, the mean is greater than the median. Therefore, choice I is false. The IQR could be less than or greater than one half of the range. It depends on the data. Therefore, III is also false.

2. D. Since 152 is a little more than one standard deviation above the mean and the empirical rule states that there is approximately 34% of the data between the mean and one standard deviation above the mean, the approximate percentile of 152 is 85.

3. C. The IQR of this distribution is the difference between Q3 and Q1. This value is 4. Any value more than 1.5 times the IQR below Q1 or above Q3 would be an outlier and graphed as a dot beyond the whisker. Therefore, the longest whisker you could have in a boxplot showing outliers is 6.

4. B. The mean is affected by addition and division. Therefore, adding 5 to each data value increases the mean by 5 to a new value of 5. Dividing each data value by 5 would also result in a likewise change in the mean. Therefore, the resulting value of the mean is 1. The standard deviation is not affected by addition. The standard deviation is affected by division. Therefore, it, too, will evaluate to 1.

5. B. There are 11 data values in this distribution. The value of Q1 is 4, and the value of Q3 is 256. The IQR is 252. Only 1024 is more than 378 greater than 256. Therefore, there is only 1 outlier.

6. A. For team A, Q1 is 48 and Q3 is 75. The IQR for team A is 27. For team B, Q1 is 38 and Q3 is 63. The IQR for team B is 25. Therefore, the IQR for team A is 2 greater than the IQR of team B.

7. B. Since the standard deviation is calculated using the mean, and the mean is not resistant to outliers, only choice II is correct.

8. D. Calculate the z-score for each test. For the math test, $z = \frac{x - \mu}{\sigma} = \frac{76 - 72}{3} = 1.33$. For the English test, $z = \frac{x - \mu}{\sigma} = \frac{82 - 78}{5} = 0.80$. The difference between English and math is $0.80 - 1.33 = -0.53$.

9. B. The range would be affected by an outlier. The IQR and median are resistant to outliers.

10. B. The value of Q1 is at the 25th percentile. One standard deviation below the mean is at the 16th percentile. Therefore, Q1 is within one standard deviation below the mean.

11. B. Choice I is false since the IQR has no relationship to the standard deviation. Choice II is false. Consider the following distribution values: 55, 55, 55, 75. This distribution has the required mean and median and has a standard deviation that is greater than 5. Consider the following distribution values: 55, 55, 55, 55, 55, 66, 66, 66, 67. This distribution has the required mean and median and has a standard deviation less than 6. Choice III is false. The median is less than the mean, so its z-score would be negative. Choice IV is true. The distribution is skewed right since the mean is greater than the median. Choice V is false. Consider the following distribution values: 55, 55, 55, 55, 55, 55, 85. This has the required mean and median and has an IQR of zero.

12. C. This is a weighted distribution. The easiest way to calculate the result is to use two lists in the TI-83/4 calculator. Enter the values into L1 and enter the quantities into L2. Then press STAT, CALC, 1-var Stats, and enter L1, L2. Then press ENTER again.

13. B. Carefully draw gridlines at 0.25, 0.50, and 0.75. Follow the curve down to the values on the x-axis. The x-value at the 25th percentile (Q1) is 14. The x-value at the 75th percentile (Q₃) is 24. Therefore, the IQR is 10. The x-value at the 50th percentile (median) is 19.5.

14. D. This distribution is skewed left. Since it is skewed left, the median will be greater than the mean. Therefore, choice D is correct.

15. E. The empirical rule states that 34% of the distribution lies between the mean and one standard deviation above the mean. Also, 13.5% lies between one and two standard deviations above the mean. Therefore, two standard deviations above is between the 97th and 98th percentile.

Free-Response Questions

1. The following represents the street price of a random sample of point-and-shoot digital cameras (rounded to the nearest dollar):

217	590	178	420	320	995	160
362	192	385	1210	165	460	177
724	221	210	263	250		

Use a boxplot and a histogram to discuss the shape and characteristics of this distribution including outliers, symmetry, median, and mean.

2. A bell-shaped, symmetric distribution, suitable for use with the empirical rule as well as z-score computations, has a mean of 200 and a standard deviation of 50. Q1 has a z-score of –0.8, and Q2 has a z-score of 0.75. What values in this distribution would be considered outliers?

Free-Response Answers

1. First, enter the data into a list in the TI-83/4 calculator. Sorting the numbers is not necessary but allowed. Set up two plots, one boxplot and the other a histogram plot. Set window parameters so both graphs are visible at the same time. Also calculate the mean, standard deviation, and 5-number summary.

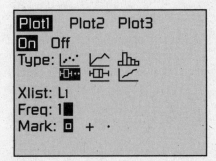

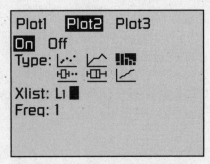

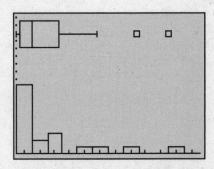

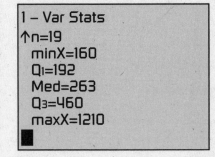

The boxplot shows two outliers, 995 and 1210. The histogram, as well as the boxplot, shows a skewed right distribution. Depending on the choice of class width, the histogram shows gaps and clusters. In a skewed right distribution, the mean will be larger than the median. The mean is 395, and the median is 263. The interquartile range (IQR) is Q3 – Q1 = 460 – 192 = 268. Outliers are more than 1.5 times the IQR above Q3 (or below Q1). Therefore, outliers are values greater than 460 + (1.5)(268) = 862. Two of the values in this distribution are greater than 862.

2. First calculate the value of Q1 and Q3.

$$Q1 = z\sigma + \mu = (-0.8)(50) + 200 = 160$$
$$Q3 = z\sigma + \mu = (0.75)(50) + 200 = 237.5$$

Next, calculate the interquartile range (IQR).

$$IQR = Q3 - Q1 = 237.5 - 160 = 77.5$$

To calculate the lower boundary, subtract 1.5 times the IQR from Q1. To calculate the upper boundary, add 1.5 times the IQR to Q3.

Lower boundary = Q1 − (1.5)(IQR) = 160 − (1.5)(77.5) = 43.75

Upper boundary = Q3 + (1.5)(IQR) = 237.5 + (1.5)(77.5) = 353.75

Therefore, outliers would be values less than 43.75 or greater than 353.75.

Exploring Data: Comparing Distributions of Univariate Data

Several distributions can be compared at the same time using **multiple dotplots, back-to-back stemplots, parallel boxplots,** and **cumulative frequency charts.** Special features of multiple distributions can be compared including center and spread, clusters and gaps, outliers, and distribution shapes.

Multiple Dotplots

More than one dotplot can be graphed using the same axis. The positions of the graphs are usually one above the other. This way, several features of the distribution can be observed at the same time.

EXAMPLE:
The following data represents the sales figures of two employees for 21 days:

Employee A: 1, 3, 4, 4, 5, 6, 6, 6, 7, 7, 7, 7, 8, 8, 8, 8, 8, 9, 9, 10, 10

Employee B: 1, 1, 2, 2, 3, 4, 4, 4, 5, 5, 5, 5, 6, 6, 6, 6, 7, 7, 7, 8, 9

Construct a multiple dotplot to compare these two distributions.

```
                                    *
                            *       *
                        *   *       *
                *       *   *   *   *   *
        *       *   *   *   *   *   *   *
    0   1   2   3   4   5   6   7   8   9   10

                        *   *
                    *   *   *   *
            *   *       *   *   *   *
            *   *   *   *   *   *   *   *
    0   1   2   3   4   5   6   7   8   9   10
```

From this multiple dotplot, several characteristics can be compared easily. The data for employee A is more skewed than is the data for employee B. Its range is also greater. The data for employee A shows a gap at 2 with an extreme value at 1, possibly an outlier. The mean and median appear to be greater for employee A. The data for employee B is more symmetric, although not quite mound shaped.

Back-to-Back Stemplots

Placing two stemplots back-to-back with the same stem allows for distribution comparisons.

EXAMPLE:
Compare the following two distributions using a back-to-back stemplot.

Set X: 48, 56, 56, 57, 57, 57, 57, 58, 58, 58, 62, 64, 64, 64, 68, 69, 69, 73, 73, 74, 74, 76, 82, 83, 89, 93, 99

Set Y: 56, 56, 57, 58, 64, 64, 66, 68, 71, 72, 73, 75, 75, 78, 78, 79, 85, 85, 86, 89, 96

Set X		Set Y
8	4	
888777766	5	6678
9984442	6	4468
64433	7	12355889
932	8	5569
93	9	6

From the preceding stemplot, Set X has the larger range and the higher maximum. Set Y has the larger mean and median. Both sets are somewhat mound-shaped with set X being more skewed. These distributions do not have any clusters or gaps and do not have any extreme values.

Parallel Boxplots

Although back-to-back stemplots are limited to two plots, parallel boxplots can compare several distributions at the same time.

EXAMPLE:

Use the data in the preceding example and compare using parallel boxplots.

Set X: 48, 56, 56, 57, 57, 57, 57, 58, 58, 58, 62, 64, 64, 64, 68, 69, 69, 73, 73, 74, 74, 76, 82, 83, 89, 93, 99

Set Y: 56, 56, 57, 58, 64, 64, 66, 68, 71, 72, 73, 75, 75, 78, 78, 79, 85, 85, 86, 89, 96

Using the TI-83/4 calculator, enter Set X in list 1 and Set Y in list 2. Set up two boxplots and graph together.

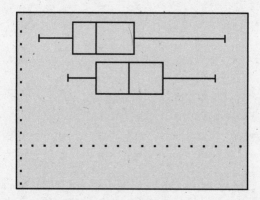

The top graph, that of Set X, shows a pronounced skew to the right. The bottom graph, that of Set Y, shows a fairly symmetric distribution. The mean and median are clearly larger in the bottom graph as are Q1 and Q3. The range is larger for Set X.

EXAMPLE:

The parallel boxplots shown represent the weights of samples of fish taken from a lake stocked with trout. What can be said of the weight of these trout over the seven years shown?

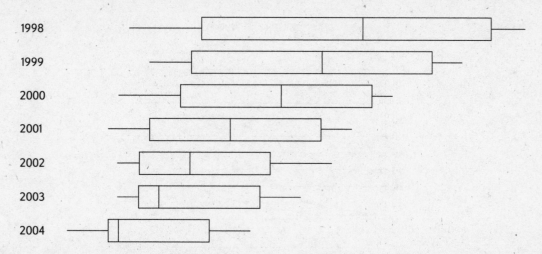

Each year the median fish weight has decreased. Although from 1998 to 2000 the distributions were approximately symmetric, starting in 2002, the distributions have become more and more skewed to the right. The range and IQR have also decreased over time. The maximum weights of fish in the lake have decreased faster than the minimum weights. No outliers are found in the samples.

Cumulative Frequency Plots

One of the most difficult graphs for students to read is the cumulative frequency plot. Distributions that are symmetric, skewed left, and skewed right have distinctive cumulative frequency plots. Compare the following three graphs. Notice how the cumulative frequency plot changes depending on whether the frequency plot is symmetric, skewed right, or skewed left.

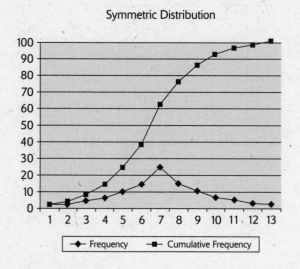

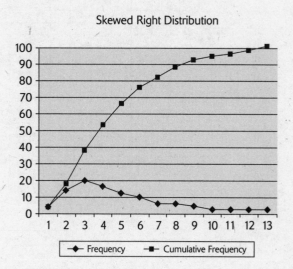

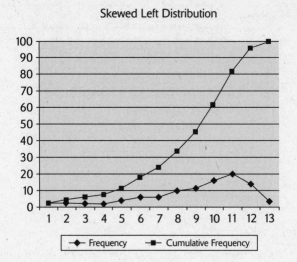

Skewed Left Distribution

EXAMPLE:

This chart shows two cumulative frequency charts, one for Department A and one for Department B. Use the chart to describe the sales patterns of the two departments.

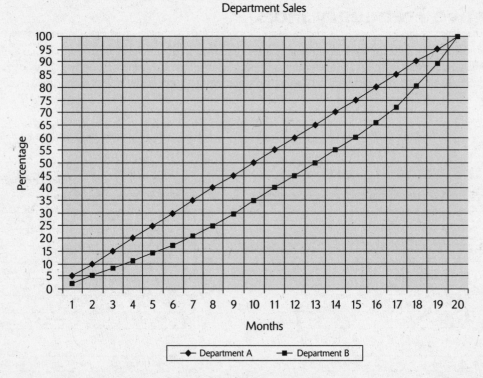

Department Sales

Department A had consistent sales month after month. Department B increased its rate of sales as time went on. This chart does not indicate that both departments sold the same amount but does compare their percent of sales month by month for the 20-month period. Department A sold half of the total by month 10, but Department B did not reach half of its sales until month 13. The interquartile range (months to sell 75% minus months to sell 25%) for the Department A plot is 10, and the interquartile range for the Department B plot is 9.5.

Review Questions and Answers

Multiple Choice Questions

Directions: Solve each of the following problems. Decide which is the best of the choices given.

1. Scores on a math test from two different classes are compared using the following back-to-back stemplot.

Class X		Class Y
98776	5	03467
9952	6	3589
7640	7	27889
52	8	38899
43	9	

   Which of the following statements are true?

   I. The range of distribution X is greater than the range of distribution Y.
   II. The median of distribution X is greater than the median of distribution Y.
   III. The mean of distribution X is greater than the mean of distribution Y.
   IV. The standard deviation of distribution X is greater than the standard deviation of distribution Y.

   A. All four statements are true.
   B. Three of the statements are true.
   C. Two of the statements are true.
   D. One of the statements is true.
   E. None of the statements is true.

2. If two distributions are symmetric and have the same range and the same mean, then which of the following statements are true?

   I. They have the same standard deviation.
   II. They have the same median.
   III. They have the same IQR.

   A. I only
   B. II only
   C. III only
   D. II and III
   E. I, II, and III

3. The following histograms show the results of a sample of the scores from two competing teams.

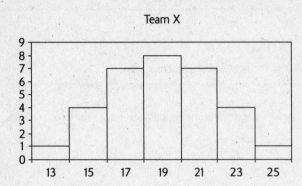

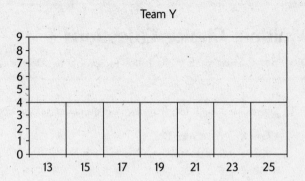

Estimate the standard deviations for the distributions of Team X and Team Y.

A. 2.5, 5
B. 2.5, 4
C. 3, 3
D. 3, 4
E. 3.5, 5

For problems 4 and 5, use the following parallel boxplots:

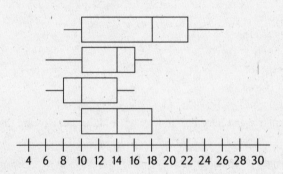

4. Which of the following are true statements?

I. The IQR of the first is equal to the range of the second.
II. The range is different for all four boxplots.
III. The sum of the medians for the first and third is equal to the sum of the medians for the second and fourth.

A. II only
B. I and II
C. I and III
D. II and III
E. I, II, and III

5. Using symmetry as a guide, which two boxplots should have means that are the closest to each other in value?

A. first and second
B. first and fourth
C. second and third
D. second and fourth
E. third and fourth

6. Two distributions have identical boxplots. How many of the following must be true about the two distributions?

    I.   They have the same range.
    II. They have the same IQR.
    III. They have the same mean.
    IV. They have the same median.
    V. The distributions have the same dotplots.

    A. 1
    B. 2
    C. 3
    D. 4
    E. 5

7. Two distributions have identical boxplots. How many of the following may be true about the two distributions?

    I.   They have the same range.
    II. They have the same IQR.
    III. They have the same mean.
    IV. They have the same median.
    V. The distributions have the same dotplots.

    A. 1
    B. 2
    C. 3
    D. 4
    E. 5

Multiple Choice Answers

1. E. All four statements are false. Statement I is false since the range of Class X is 38 and the range of Class Y is 39. Statement II is false since the median of Class X is 69 and the median of Class Y is 72. Statement III is false since the mean of Class X is 70.8 and the mean of Class Y is 71.4. Statement IV is false since the standard deviation of Class X is 12.4 and the standard deviation of Class Y is 13.2. The mean and standard deviation of each distribution is most easily found by entering the data values into a list and performing 1-variable Stats.

2. B. If two distributions are symmetric and have the same median, they will have the same mean. The IQR and the standard deviation depend on the concentration of data about the mean/median. Consider the following two symmetric distributions. They have the same range, the same mean, and the same median, but have different IQRs and different standard deviations.

Distribution 1:

       1   5   6   7   8   9   13

Distribution 2:

       1   2   3   7   11   12   13

3. D. The distribution for Team X appears to be a bell-shaped, symmetric distribution. The empirical rule can be applied to give an approximation for its standard deviation. According to the empirical rule, 68% of the data (area) lies within one standard deviation from the mean. Using the vertical scale as a guide, the sum of the areas of the three middle classes is 44. The total area is 64. Dividing gives 44/64 = .6875. Since with width of the three columns is 6, an approximation for the standard deviation of Team X is 3. It is clear that the standard deviation of Team Y must be greater than that of Team X.

4. E. All four statements are true. Statement I is true since the IQR of the first distribution is 12, and the range of the second distribution is also 12. Statement II is true since the ranges of the four distributions are 18, 12, 10, and 16, respectively. Statement III is true since the sum of the medians for the first and third distribution is 28 and the sum of the medians for the second and fourth distributions is also 28.

5. B. In a skewed distribution, the mean is closer to the tail of the distribution than the median. The mean of the first distribution should be less than 18, and the mean of the fourth distribution should be more than 14. Therefore, their difference of means should be less than 4. The mean of the second distribution should be less than 14, and the mean of the third distribution should be more than 10. This difference is also less than 4. Since the ranges of the first and fourth distributions are greater than the ranges of the second and third distributions, it is more likely that there will be more "movement" of their means away from their medians. This will result in a smaller difference for the first and fourth distributions.

6. C. The range, IQR, and median are all components of a boxplot. Therefore, they would be the same. Mean and dotplots would depend on the concentration of the data within the distribution and, therefore, might not be the same.

7. E. All five statements *may* be true. I, II, and IV, *must* be true. III and V *may* be true.

Free-Response Questions

Directions: Show all work. Indicate clearly the methods you use. You will be graded on method as well as accuracy.

1. This parallel boxplot shows the relationship between three distributions. Discuss these relationships including comments concerning the lengths of the *whiskers* and their meaning.

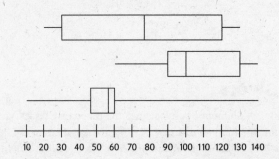

2. Construct a back-to-back stemplot for two distributions. Each distribution should have the same median. One distribution should be skewed right with one outlier. The other distribution should be symmetric and bell-shaped.

Free-Response Answers

1. The whiskers in boxplots are useful in showing concentrations within the distribution. Since Q1 and Q3 are the edges of the box in the boxplot and they represent the 25th percentile and the 75th percentile, it means that each whisker of a boxplot contains 25% of the data. Short whiskers represent concentrations of data. Long whiskers show spread-out data. The same holds true about the size of the box and the placement of the median. Each half of the box represents 25% of the data. A short box indicates concentrations of data, and a long box shows data that is spread out. The top boxplot in the figure has very short whiskers compared to the length of the box. This shows a high concentration of data between 20 and 30 and between 120 and 130. The top boxplot is symmetric. The bottom boxplot shows a very high concentration of data between 57.5 and 60. There is also a high concentration of data between 47.5 and 57.5. The bottom boxplot also shows a skewed right distribution. The middle boxplot shows a skewed left distribution. Concentrations are between 90 and 100 and between 130 and 140. The bottom boxplot has the largest range. It is clear that the upper two boxplots do not have outliers. Since the IQR is so small in the bottom boxplot, at least one outlier exists in each whisker.

2. When constructing the stemplot, it is probably easier to start with the symmetric distribution. After it is in place, insert the other distribution's median and work out from there. Make a note of the IQR so that an appropriate outlier can be determined. The following is a sample back-to-back stemplot that meets the requirements of the problem. Notice that the symmetric distribution will have a symmetric dotplot as well as boxplot.

5	2	22334578
345	3	134566779
55555	4	334569
345	5	23459
5	6	2345
	7	4567
	8	489
	9	
	10	
	11	
	12	
	13	9

The previous two chapters dealt with univariate data, data relationships of one variable. This chapter discusses *bivariate data*, data relationships of two variables. Paired data is usually represented in scatterplots, points plotted on a plane using two axes. Linear patterns or relationships are of particular interest, and finding linear functional relationships helps statisticians make predictions.

Analyzing Patterns in Scatterplots

Scatterplots are used to show relationships of bivariate data. Pairs of points are graphed on a plane. The first value is called the **explanatory variable** or independent variable and is usually graphed along the horizontal axis. The second value is called the **response variable** or dependent variable and is usually graphed along the vertical axis. Scatterplots are used to determine whether any patterns exist in the data. An existing pattern, such as a linear relationship, does not mean that there is a causal relationship, simply that there is a relationship. Scatterplots can show whether any unusual patterns exist, such as outliers or influential points.

EXAMPLE:
Graph the following data as a scatterplot. The data represents grams of protein and grams of carbohydrates in a sample of energy bars.

PROTEIN	CARBOHYDRATES
2	45
2	48
3	32
3	44
5	38
6	32
8	33
8	30
8	33
9	32
10	25
11	24
13	22
16	26
20	20
22	12
26	18
26	16
28	10

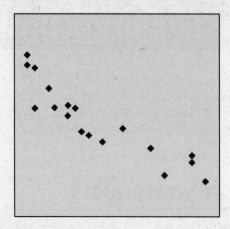

Notice that the graphed points appear to trend in a downward direction. The pattern appears to be somewhat linear. There appears to be an inverse relationship between the number of grams of protein and the number of grams of carbohydrate. There does not appear to be any extreme influential points or any outliers.

EXAMPLE:
Use the TI-83/4 to graph the data in the previous example in a scatterplot.

To use the TI-83/4 calculator to graph a scatterplot, enter the data into two lists, such as L1 and L2. Press STAT, EDIT, and enter the data. Then choose STATPLOT and select one of the plots, such as Plot 1. Choose the scatterplot icon. Make sure that the two lists match the lists where the data was placed. Choose the mark you want plotted for each point. Leave the frequency set to 1. Deselect or clear all equations so that they will not be plotted over the points. Select ZOOM and then ZoomStat to set the correct window limits. You can also set the window limits manually by selecting WINDOW and setting the appropriate values. Select GRAPH. The following screenshot shows the points graphed and the point representing 16 grams of protein and 26 grams of carbohydrate highlighted.

```
P1:L1,L2
     ▫
   ▫▫
      ▫
   ▫  ▫ ▫▫
         ▫
       ▫▫   ⋈
       ▫        ▫
                  ▫
              ▫     ▫
X=16........Y=26........
```

Correlation and Linearity

Scatterplots are used to look for patterns of data that are linear, or approximately linear. Linear relationships can be positive or negative in the same way that the slope of a line can be positive or negative. A relationship is positive if one variable increases in value as the other variable increases in value. A relationship is negative if one variable decreases in value as the other variable increases in value. These relationships can be strong, mild, or weak. Strong linear relationships exist when the plotted points are close to being on a straight line. Mild and weak linear relationships exist as the points spread farther away from being on a straight line.

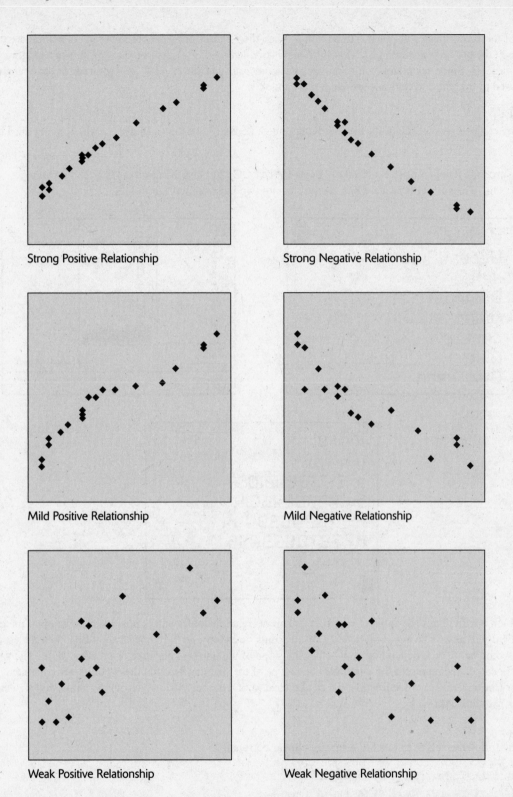

Strong Positive Relationship

Strong Negative Relationship

Mild Positive Relationship

Mild Negative Relationship

Weak Positive Relationship

Weak Negative Relationship

The strength of a linear relationship can be measured mathematically by finding the **correlation coefficient** of the plotted points. The formula used on the AP Statistics Exam to find the correlation coefficient is $r = \frac{1}{n-1}\sum\left(\frac{x_i - \overline{x}}{s_x}\right)\left(\frac{y_i - \overline{y}}{s_y}\right)$.

Thus, the correlation coefficient is simply the sum of the products of the z-scores of the coordinates of each point. The correlation coefficient can by found using this formula, which will also require finding the standard deviation of the x-coordinates using $s_x = \sqrt{\frac{1}{n-1}\sum(x_i - \overline{x})^2}$ and a similar formula to find the standard deviation of the y-coordinates.

The mean of the x-coordinates also needs to be found. Then the z-scores of each coordinate of each point are then multiplied, and all the products are summed. This sum then is divided by $(n - 1)$. As you can see, this is a lengthy, time-consuming process. Since calculators with Statistics Packages, such as the TI-83/4, are required for the exam, they should be used to find the correlation coefficient more quickly.

EXAMPLE:
Calculate the correlation coefficient for the following points: (2, 5), (3, 4), (5, 7), (6, 6), and (8, 7) using the TI-83/4 calculator.

First make sure that "Diagnostics" is turned on. Press CATALOG (2nd and the number 0). Scroll down to "DiagnosticsOn." Press ENTER twice. Enter the points into two lists, such as L1 and L2.

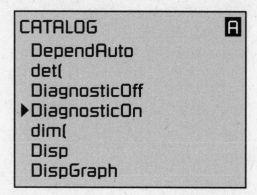

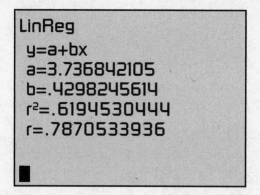

The correlation coefficient is the value of r, or 0.787. This correlation coefficient is positive. The value of the correlation coefficient will always be between −1 and 1. If all points lie exactly on the same straight line, then the correlation coefficient would be −1 or 1, depending on whether the slope of the line was negative or positive. *Note:* The values of a and b that are calculated represent the y-intercept and slope of the line that best fits these points. (See the next section.) *Note:* Either LinReg($ax + b$) or LinReg($a + bx$) can be used to find the regression coefficient, slope, and y-intercept. Statisticians use LinReg($a + bx$).

EXAMPLE:
Which of the following sets of points has a stronger linear correlation?

  Set A: (1, 1), (2, 4), (3, 5), (4, 7), (5, 9), (6, 12)
  Set B: (1, 2), (2, 3), (3, 6), (4, 8), (5, 11), (6, 11)

Enter the points into lists in the calculator. The scatterplot with both sets plotted on the same axes is shown below. Set A is plotted with the squares, and Set B is plotted with the pluses. The correlation coefficient of each set of points is calculated.

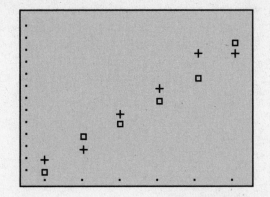

```
LinReg
 y=a+bx
 a=-.8666666667
 b=2.057142857
 r²=.9830594185
 r=.9914935292
■
```

```
LinReg
 y=a+bx
 a=-.2666666667
 b=2.028571429
 r²=.962328985
 r=.9809836824
■
```

The correlation coefficient of Set X is 0.991. The correlation coefficient of Set Y is 0.981. Set X has a stronger correlation. That is, closer to 1 if positive or closer to –1 if negative. Both of these values represent very strong positive correlation.

The terms "strong," "mild," and "weak" are relative. Care should be taken when giving labels to correlation. This table gives some rough guidelines:

Description	Value of Correlation Coefficient
Strong Positive Correlation	$0.85 \le r \le 1$
Mild Positive Correlation	$0.5 \le r < 0.85$
Weak Positive Correlation	$0.1 \le r < 0.5$
Strong Negative Correlation	$-1 \le r \le -0.85$
Mild Negative Correlation	$-0.85 < r \le -0.5$
Weak Negative Correlation	$-0.5 < r \le -0.1$

When correlation is very close to zero, labels should not be applied.

If a strong correlation exists between two variables, it does not imply that an increase in one variable will cause an increase in the other variable. If each of two stocks rise in price one dollar per week over a 10-week period, the correlation coefficient of their prices as taken as ordered pairs would be $r = 1$. Even with strong positive correlation, you cannot say that the increase in one stock price caused the other stock to rise in price.

Influential points or outliers can have a dramatic effect on the value of the correlation coefficient. The correlation coefficient is *not* resistant to influential points.

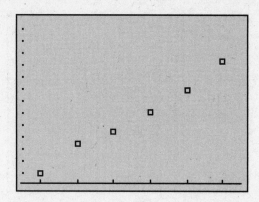 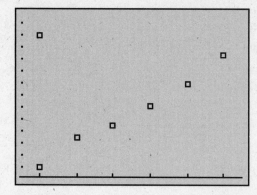

The graph on the left has a correlation coefficient of $r = 0.991$, a strong positive correlation. The graph on the right has a correlation coefficient of $r = 0.492$, a weak positive correlation. Worse yet, if the points that do appear to be quite linear are closer together, you get the following results:

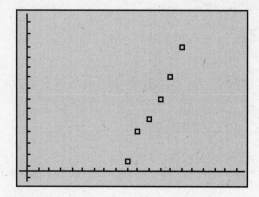 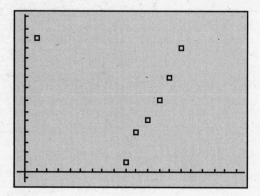

The graph on the left has a correlation coefficient of $r = 0.991$, a strong *positive* correlation. The graph on the right has a correlation coefficient of $r = -0.114$, a weak *negative* correlation. Not only does the influential point reduce the positive correlation coefficient, it actually makes it negative.

Some points to remember:

- The correlation coefficient is not resistant to influential points.
- A *linear* correlation coefficient is a measure of linear correlation. Therefore, a linear correlation coefficient near zero does not indicate that there is no correlation, just no linear correlation.
- The correlation coefficient does not indicate slope, only how close to a straight line the points are and the direction of the line, either falling or rising.
- A strong linear correlation does not indicate cause and effect.
- Linear correlation coefficients are always between 1 and –1, inclusive.
- If $r = 1$, there is a perfect positive correlation between the two variables.
- If $r = -1$, there is a perfect negative correlation between the two variables.
- The closer the value of the correlation coefficient is to either 1 or –1, the stronger the linear relationship is between the two variables.
- The linear correlation coefficient is a unitless measure.

The formula for the linear correlation coefficient can be written several different ways, each yielding the same results.

The form of the formula used on the AP Statistics Test is

$$r = \frac{1}{n-1}\sum\left(\frac{x_i - \bar{x}}{s_x}\right)\left(\frac{y_i - \bar{y}}{s_y}\right) \text{ where } s_x = \sqrt{\frac{1}{n-1}\sum(x_i - \bar{x})^2} \text{ and } s_y = \sqrt{\frac{1}{n-1}\sum(y_i - \bar{y})^2}$$

A version of the formula that is easier to use in calculations is

$$r = \frac{\sum x_i y_i - \frac{\sum x_i \sum y_i}{n}}{\sqrt{\sum x_i^2 - \frac{(\sum x_i)^2}{n}}\sqrt{\sum y_i^2 - \frac{(\sum y_i)^2}{n}}} = \frac{s_{xy}}{\sqrt{s_{xx}}\sqrt{s_{xy}}}$$

This calculation formula can be simplified by multiplying both the numerator and denominator by n:

$$r = \frac{n\sum x_i y_i - \sum x_i \sum y_i}{\sqrt{\left(n\sum x_i^2 - (\sum x_i)^2\right)\left(n\sum y_i^2 - (\sum y_i)^2\right)}}$$

The values in this formula $(n, \sum x_i, \sum y_i, \sum(x_i^2), \sum(y_i^2), \sum x_i y_i)$, can be easily found using the TI-83/4. Enter the values of the x and y coordinates of the points into two lists, such as L1 and L2. Press STAT, CALC, and choose "2-Variable Stats." Enter list numbers if necessary. Scroll down to find all required values.

EXAMPLE:

Find the correlation coefficient using the calculation formula and compare with the correlation coefficient found using the TI-83/4 directly.

Hours Studied for a Quiz	Grade on the Quiz
1	68
2	75
2	64
3	68
5	76
6	74
6	76

Although the needed values can be found by hand, using the calculator is more efficient. First, enter the values into L1 and L2 on the TI-83/4. Press STAT, CALC, and choose "2-Variable Stats." Scroll down to obtain needed values.

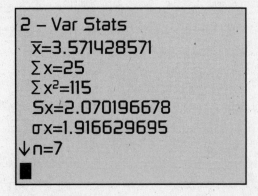

```
2 - Var Stats
↑ȳ=71.57142857
  Σy=501
  Σy²=35997
  Sy=4.825527358
  σy=4.46757022
↓Σxy=1830
■
```

```
LinReg
 y=ax+b
 a=1.583333333
 b=65.91666667
 r²=.461400818
 r=.67926491
■
```

Use the calculation formula to find the correlation coefficient.

$$r = \frac{n\sum x_i y_i - \sum x_i \sum y_i}{\sqrt{\left(n\sum x_i^2 - \left(\sum x_i\right)^2\right)}\sqrt{\left(n\sum y_i^2 - \left(\sum y_i\right)^2\right)}}$$

$$r = \frac{7(1830) - (25)(501)}{\sqrt{\left(7(115) - (25)^2\right)}\sqrt{\left(7(35997) - (501)^2\right)}}$$

$$r = 0.67926491$$

This value matches the value of the correlation coefficient found using the calculator's STAT package.

The value of r^2 is called the **coefficient of determination.** It measures the percentage of the variation in the dependent variable (usually y) that is explained by the variation in the independent variable (usually x). This variation in the independent variable results in the calculation of the least-squares regression line.

Least-Squares Regression Line

If the scatterplot and the correlation coefficient indicate that a linear correlation exists between two variables, then a line best describes this linear relationship. This line is known as the **least-squares regression line.**

EXAMPLE:
Find a linear equation that fits the data from the previous example. Graph the line on the same graph as a scatterplot of the data. Use this line to predict the quiz grade for someone who studies 4 hours.

First, use the data to construct a scatterplot.

Hours Studied for a Quiz	Grade on the Quiz
1	68
2	75
2	64
3	68
5	76
6	74
6	76

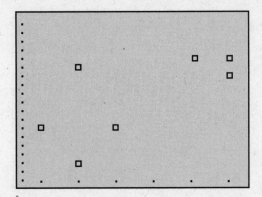

Choose two points on the scatterplot through which a line can be drawn that approximates the linearity of the points. In this case, choose (1, 68) and (6, 76). Find the slope of the line through these two points and calculate the equation of the line.

$$m = \frac{y_2 - y_1}{x_2 - x_1} = \frac{76 - 68}{6 - 1} = 1.6$$
$$y - y_1 = m(x - x_1)$$
$$y - 68 = (1.6)(x - 1)$$
$$y - 68 = 1.6x - 1.6$$
$$y = 66.4 + 1.6x$$

Enter the equation into the calculator and plot on the same graph as the scatterplot. The line should pass through the two points selected previously.

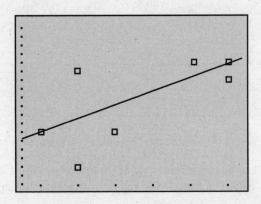

To use this line to predict a value, simply substitute that value in the preceding equation.

$$y = 66.4 + 1.6x$$
$$y = 66.4 + (1.6)(4)$$
$$y = 66.4 + 6.4$$
$$y = 72.8$$

The predicted value can also be found using the TRACE function on the calculator.

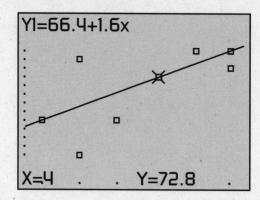

Therefore, if someone studies 4 hours, a quiz score of approximately 73 might be expected.

This line appears to fit the points quite well, but is there a better choice for this line? The answer is yes.

First, calculate the **residual** for each point. This is the difference between the observed value and the value predicted by the equation of the line for the dependent variable. Using the line and data from the previous example, the residuals can be computed.

Hours Studied for a Quiz (x)	Grade on the Quiz (y)	Predicted Value y = 66.4 + 1.6x	Residual	Residual²
1	68	68	0	0
2	75	69.6	5.4	29.16
2	64	69.6	−5.6	31.36
3	68	71.2	−3.2	10.24
5	76	74.4	1.6	2.56
6	74	76	−2	4
6	76	76	0	0

The total of the squares of the residuals is 77.32, and the sum of the residuals is −3.8.

The best fit line also known at the least-squares line is the line that minimizes this total of the squares of the residuals. This technique allows for the best compromise and for an equilibrium between the errors.

The formula used on the AP Statistics Exam for the least-squares line is

$$\hat{y} = b_0 + b_1 x$$

where

$$b_1 = r \frac{s_y}{s_x} \text{ and } b_0 = \bar{y} - b_1 \bar{x}$$

A calculation formula for the slope, b_1 is

$$b_1 = \frac{n \sum x_i y_i - \sum x_i \sum y_i}{n \sum x_i^2 - \left(\sum x_1\right)^2}$$

In these formulas, $b_1 = r \frac{s_y}{s_x}$ represents the slope of the line, and $b_0 = \bar{y} - b_1 \bar{x}$ represents the y-intercept. In reality, these values are found directly using the statistical package in the calculator.

EXAMPLE:

Find a linear equation that *best* fits the following data. Find the linear correlation coefficient as well as the coefficient of determination. Graph the line on the same graph as a scatterplot of the data. Use this line to predict the quiz grade for someone who studies 4 hours. Compare the results to those of the previous example.

Hours Studied for a Quiz	Grade on the Quiz
1	68
2	75
2	64
3	68
5	76
6	74
6	76

Enter the data into two lists such as L1 and L2. Press STAT, CALC, and choose LinReg(a+bx). *Note:* There are two linear regression equations on the TI-83/4. This is the second one. Press ENTER. Enter list numbers if necessary. Press ENTER again.

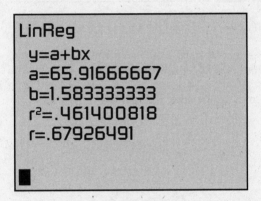

```
LinReg
 y=a+bx
 a=65.91666667
 b=1.583333333
 r²=.461400818
 r=.67926491
```

The linear correlation coefficient is $r = 0.679$, which is mild positive correlation. The coefficient of determination is $r^2 = 0.461$. Therefore, 46% of the variation in quiz score is explained by the variation in study hours. The rest is due to the randomness of the sample.

Since this form of the equation of a line uses b as the slope and a as the y-intercept, the equation of the least-squares regression line is

$$\hat{y} = b_0 + b_1 x$$
$$\hat{y} = 65.9167 + 1.5833x$$

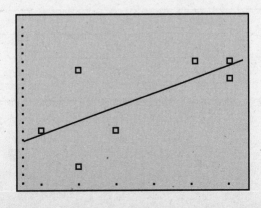

Therefore, the predicted quiz score for 4 hours of studying is

$$\hat{y} = 65.9167 + 1.5833x$$
$$\hat{y} = 65.9167 + 1.5833(4)$$
$$\hat{y} = 72.25$$

To show that this is a more accurate result than that obtained in the previous example, calculate the new residuals.

Hours Studied for a Quiz (x)	Grade on the Quiz (y)	Predicted Value $\hat{y} = 65.9167 + 1.5833x$	Residual	Residual²
1	68	67.50	0.50	0.25
2	75	69.08	5.92	35.05
2	64	69.08	−5.08	25.81
3	68	70.67	−2.67	7.13
5	76	73.83	2.17	4.71
6	74	75.42	−1.42	2.02
6	76	75.42	0.58	0.34

The total of the squares of the residuals is 75.31, and the sum of the residuals is 0.

This is a smaller sum of squares than that obtained with your estimate in the previous example. Since this calculated line is the least-squares or best fit line, it has the lowest sum of squared residuals. Also, the sum of the residuals is 0.

The estimated equation and result from the previous example was as follows:

$$\hat{y} = 66.4 + 1.6x$$
$$\hat{y} = 66.4 + (1.6)(4)$$
$$\hat{y} = 66.4 + 6.4$$
$$\hat{y} = 72.8$$

There is a slight difference. The estimate was quite good.

A chart that is generated by a statistical program such as MiniTab usually appears on the test. Learn to read it. Following is a chart for the data in this example. The coefficients of the least-squares regression line are listed under Coef in the table. The constant is the y-intercept, and the Hour, in this case, is the slope of the line. The value of R-Sq is the coefficient of determination, which is the square of the linear correlation coefficient.

The regression equation is

Grade = 65.9 + 1.58 Hours

Predictor	Coef	StDev	T	P
Constant	65.917	3.101	21.26	0.000
Hours	1.5833	0.7650	2.07	0.093

S = 3.879   R-Sq = 46.1%   R-Sq(adj) = 35.4%

EXAMPLE:

Use the following data to determine the linear correlation coefficient and predict the value of y when x is 0.7.

x	−6	−3	1	4	3	2	−4	1	−3	−1	5
y	−11	−7	1	8	5	5	−6	2	−5	0	9

First, enter the coordinates of the points into two lists in your calculator and press STAT, CALC, and choose LinReg (a + bx). The resulting output shows the linear correlation coefficient as well as the coefficients for the regression line.

```
LinReg
 y=a+bx
 a=.2564469914
 b=1.820916905
 r²=.9765339185
 r=.9881973075
■
```

A chart from a statistical package such as MiniTab shows the coefficient of the least-squares regression line. They are listed under Coef in the following chart.

The regression equation is

Y = 0.256 + 1.82 X

Predictor	Coef	StDev	T	P
Constant	0.2564	0.3197	0.80	0.443
X	1.82092	0.09409	19.35	2.23E + 11

S = 1.060   R-Sq = 97.7%   R-Sq(adj) = 97.4%

The correlation coefficient r is very close to 1, showing strong positive linear correlation. From the data in this display, the equation for the least-squares line (regression line) is

$$\hat{y} = 0.256 + 1.821x$$

Using this equation for the least-squares line, a prediction can be made for what y would be when x is 0.7:

$$\hat{y} = 0.256 + 1.821x$$
$$\hat{y} = 0.256 + (1.821)(0.7)$$
$$\hat{y} = 0.256 + 1.275$$
$$\hat{y} = 1.531$$

Residual Plots, Outliers, and Influential Points

The residual is the difference between the observed value of y and the predicted value, $\hat{y}$. The vertical lines in the plot that follows represent this difference, known as a residual. As shown in the previous example, residuals are minimized in the determination of the least-squares line. The term "least-squares" refers to the line that has the smallest sum of the squares of the residuals of all the points in the plot—that is, the smallest total area of the squares.

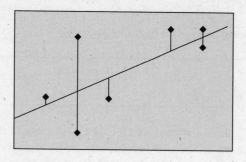
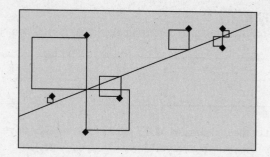

There are two common uses for residuals:

- To determine whether a linear model is the correct choice to represent the relationship between the variables
- To determine whether there are any outliers in the plot

To determine whether a linear model is the correct choice for a particular set of points, plot the residuals against the independent variable. If the residual plot shows a noticeable pattern that is not linear, then the independent variable and dependent variable may not be related linearly. The graph on the left, in the following sets of images, shows no pattern, so a linear model is acceptable. The graph on the right shows a nonlinear pattern, so a linear model is not acceptable.

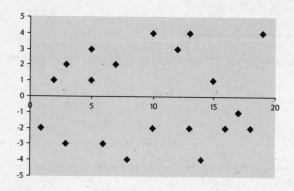
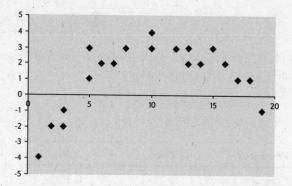

EXAMPLE:

Determine whether a linear model is appropriate for the following table of values showing the number of hours studied for a final exam and the exam score for 19 students.

Student No.	Hours Studied	Score on Final
1	2	9
2	2	22
3	3	14
4	4	9
5	5	18
6	6	10
7	8	33
8	8	24
9	9	20
10	9	32

Student No.	Hours Studied	Score on Final
11	10	22
12	11	16
13	12	32
14	14	39
15	19	30
16	22	26
17	24	46
18	26	35
19	28	38

First, plot the points in a scatterplot. Look for an obvious linear pattern.

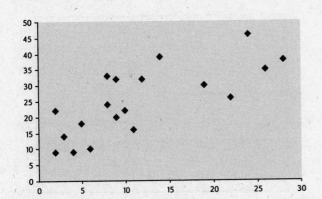
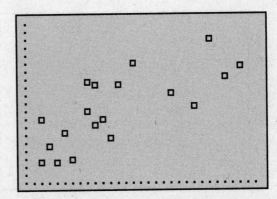

There does appear to be a linear pattern to the plotted points. Next, calculate the equation for the least-squares line. Then determine the residuals for each plotted point. Graph these residuals against the independent variable. Residuals can be found on the TI-83/4 calculator.

Enter the values for the pairs of points into two lists, for example, L1 and L2. Calculate the least-squares regression line. Press STAT, CALC, and choose LinReg(a + bx). Enter list numbers if necessary. Press ENTER. The resulting equation for the least-squares line for these points is $\hat{y} = 13.525 + 0.982x$.

The regression equation is

Score = 13.5 + 0.982 Hours

Predictor	Coef	StDev	T	P
Constant	13.525	3.002	4.50	0.000
Hours	0.9821	0.2116	4.64	4.30E+15

S = 7.427   R-Sq = 55.9%   R-Sq(adj) = 53.3%

The residuals can be stored in L3 as follows: Press 2nd LIST; choose 7:RESID; press STO, L3, ENTER. This stores the residuals into L3. Press STATPLOT; choose a plot; and set the data lists to L1 and L3. Press ZOOM, ZoomStat, and then ENTER. The resulting graph will be that of the residuals.

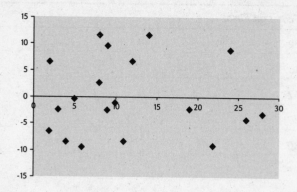
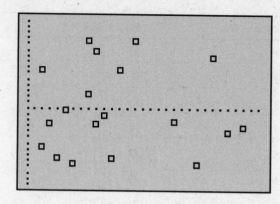

From these residual plots, there is not a noticeable pattern. Therefore, a linear model is appropriate for this relationship.

Outliers are points that fall outside the overall pattern of points. Outliers may be easily found by using residual plots because they will fall far from the other points in the plot. Boxplots can also be used to find outliers. The plots that follow show a scatterplot of the sample data. Next is a residual plot of the sample data. Finally is a boxplot of the residuals. The outlier is most easily seen on the residual plot and the boxplot.

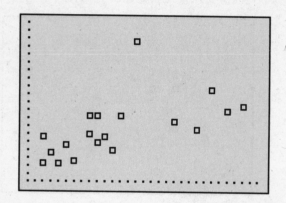
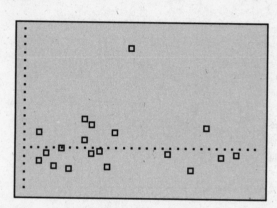

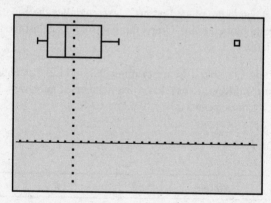

Influential points dramatically affect the slope and/or y-intercept of the least-squares line. The following graph shows a scatterplot with three labeled points:

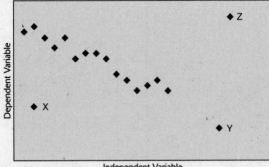

Point X may be an outlier because its y-value is small compared to the other points with similar x-coordinates. Because there are several other points with approximately the same x-value, its affect on the least-square line is minimal, and so it is not an influential point. Point Y is far separated from the other points, so it might be an outlier. Point Y might or might not be an influential point. It lies on the overall pattern of the other points and is very close to the least-squares line, so it is probably not an influential point—depending on how close it is to the least-squares line. Point Z is far removed from the overall pattern of the points; it is an outlier with respect to x. It does not have other points with approximately the same x-value to help balance it. It is an influential point. Influential points are usually outliers relative to the x-values of the sample points.

The following four scatterplots show the sample data points from the preceding graph along with the least-squares line. The first graph excludes points X, Y, and Z. The second graph includes point X. Although the least-squares line did change slightly, it was not a significant change. The correlation coefficient did indicate a drop in correlation. The third graph includes point Y. Because point Y was very close to the original least-squares line, there was almost no change in the least-squares line or the correlation coefficient when point Y is included. The fourth graph includes point Z. The least-squares line is dramatically changed by the inclusion of point Z. The correlation coefficient is significantly lower as well. Point Z is definitely an influential point.

$$y = 25.7 - 0.875x$$
$$r = -0.954$$

$$y = 22.9 - 0.625x$$
$$r = -0.630$$

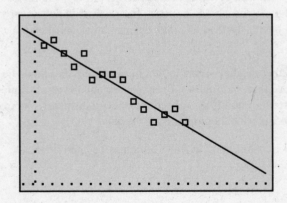

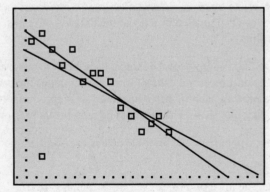

$$y = 26.0 - 0.934x$$
$$r = -0.969$$

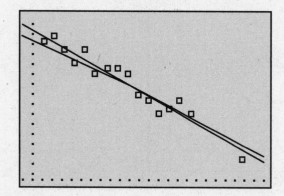

$$y = 22.1 - 0.327x$$
$$r = -0.395$$

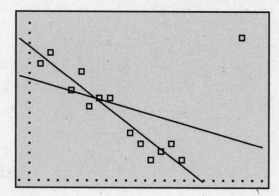

To graph a residual plot on the TI-83/4, use the following method:

- Enter the sample data points into L1 and L2.
- Enter STAT, CALC, LinReg(a + bx).
- Enter L1, L2, Y1 (*Note:* Y1 is located under VARS, Y-VARS, Function).
- This calculates the least-squares regression line and places it in Y1.
- Either calculate the residuals and store them in L3 by entering L2 – Y1(L1) STO L3 or Enter LIST, RESID STO L3.
- Enter STATPLOT, choose a plot, choose scatterplot, and enter L1 and L3 as the lists.
- Enter ZOOM and choose ZoomStat.

Transformations to Achieve Linearity: Logarithmic and Power Transformations

The previous two sections are concerned with linear models—that is, relationships that can be modeled using a straight line. A linear relationship exists in many, but certainly not all, bivariate relationships. If the pattern of the data is non-linear, a different model is more appropriate. Exponential growth and decay, quadratic curves, powers, and roots, are all appropriate for bivariate relationships. An important fact to note is the AP Statistics Test deals with only bivariate data that can be modeled by a linear relationship or that can be transformed into data that can be modeled by a linear relationship.

Examine the scatterplot of the sample data. Look to see whether the data seems to fit a linear pattern. Examine the residual plot. Look for a pattern. If the scatterplot of the data appears to follow a linear pattern and the residual plot shows a random pattern, then a linear model is appropriate for the data. If the scatterplot shows a distinctive curve or the residual plot shows a nonrandom pattern, then a linear model is not appropriate for the data.

If the basic pattern on the bivariate data is exponential, then a logarithmic transformation may be appropriate.

EXAMPLE:
Consider the price of a stock over an 18-month period.

Month	1	2	3	4	5	6	7	8	9
Price ($)	23	25	28	31	34	38	42	46	51
Month	10	11	12	13	14	15	16	17	18
Price ($)	57	63	69	77	85	94	104	114	127

The scatterplot shows a pattern that is not linear. The pattern appears to be exponential. Note that the correlation coefficient for the least-squares line for these points is quite high, with a value of 0.97. The residual plot shows a definite pattern, therefore indicating that a linear model would not be appropriate, even though the correlation coefficient is high.

Scatterplot

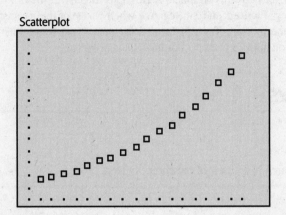

Residual plot

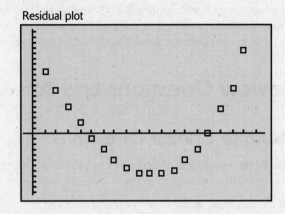

To graph the scatterplot of the original points using the TI-83/4, enter the *x*-coordinates of the points in L1 and the *y*-coordinates in L2. Set up a scatterplot using these two lists and use ZoomStat to create the graph. For the residual plot, calculate the least-squares regression line using STAT, CALC, LinReg(a + bx). Then store the residuals in L3 using LIST, RESID STO L3. Change the STATPLOT to use L1 and L3. Use ZoomStat to create the graph.

Because a linear model is not appropriate, and the data does appear to be exponential, try a **logarithmic transformation.** Take the log of each *y*-coordinate and store in L4. In this example, the natural log (ln) is used. Using the common log (log(y)) would produce similar results. Change the STATPLOT to use L1 and L4. Use ZoomStat to create the graph. Create a residual plot of the transformed data.

Scatterplot of transformed data (1n(y))

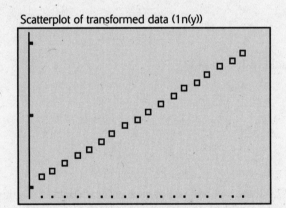

Residual plot of transformed data

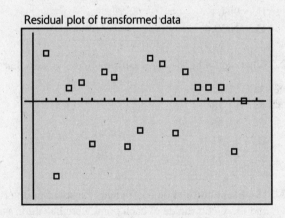

The scatterplot of the transformed data is indeed linear, and the residual plot of the transformed data shows a random pattern. Therefore, a linear model would be appropriate for the transformed data. The correlation coefficient of the least-squares line for this transformed data is a very high 0.999. *Note:* If you want to project the stock price for month 24, you can use the least-squares line for the transformed data.

$$\hat{y} = 3.03 + 0.10x$$
$$\hat{y} = 3.03 + 0.10(24)$$
$$\hat{y} = 5.43$$

Since this value was calculated using the ln(y) transformation, it must be converted back using the exponential e^x.

$$y = e^x$$
$$y = e^{5.43}$$
$$y = 228$$

Therefore, if the trend continues, the price of the stock should be approximately 228 at month 24.

When performing transformations to achieve linearity, it can be difficult to determine whether a transformation is appropriate and then which transformation to use. The TI-83/4 calculator performs nonlinear regressions directly. If the raw data is not linear, try QuadReg, CubicReg, QuartReg, LnReg, ExpReg, PwrReg, and SinReg. See whether one of these transformations produces linearity. If not, try the reciprocal (1/x) and other powers. Try transformations on both the x-coordinate as well as the y-coordinate. Sometimes, a different transformation applied to each coordinate is appropriate.

Review Questions and Answers

Multiple Choice Questions

Directions: Solve each of the following problems. Decide which is the best of the choices given.

Use the following information for problems 1 and 2:

After evaluating several dozen randomly chosen lightbulbs of the same type from different manufacturers, a statistician determined that there was a linear correlation coefficient of 0.80 when plotting cost (in dollars) versus bulb life (in hours). The least-squares regression line had a slope of 1084 and a y-intercept of –35.4.

1. What would be the approximate life expectancy of a bulb that costs $0.95?

   A. 796.5
   B. 840.3
   C. 867.2
   D. 994.4
   E. 1050.4

2. What would be the approximate price of a bulb that would last 1600 hours?

   A. $1.21
   B. $1.28
   C. $1.46
   D. $1.51
   E. $1.53

3. The linear correlation coefficient of a set of points is –0.75. If the x-coordinate of each point is doubled in value and the y-coordinate of each point were halved in value, which of the following statements most accurately describes what will happen to the correlation coefficient?

   A. It will increase by an unknown amount.
   B. It will decrease by an unknown amount.
   C. It will stay the same.
   D. It will change by a fixed amount.
   E. The answer cannot be determined from the information given.

4. The correlation of a set of 25 points is positive. If two points are chosen at random and a line is drawn through these two points, which of the following could be true about the slope of that line?

  I.   The slope is positive.
  II. The slope is negative.
  III. The slope is zero.
  IV. The slope is undefined.

  A.   None of the above
  B.   One of the above
  C.   Two of the above
  D.   Three of the above
  E.   All four of the above

5. Which of the following statements is true about the correlation coefficient r?

  A.   Removing an extreme value from the data will increase r.
  B.   Removing an extreme value from the data will decrease r.
  C.   Removing an extreme value from the data will not change r.
  D.   If r decreases, so will the coefficient of determination.
  E.   The coefficient of determination is positive if r is positive.

6. Which of the following statements are true?

  I.   A residual plot with no pattern indicates that a linear model is appropriate.
  II. A residual plot with no pattern indicates that the correlation between the variables is 0 or close to 0.
  III. Nonlinear variable relationships result in nonlinear residual plots.

  A.   I and II
  B.   I and III
  C.   II and III
  D.   I, II, and III
  E.   None of the above are true.

7. Which of the following are true about a point that is an outlier with respect to the response variable but is not an outlier with respect to the explanatory variable?

  I.   Significantly affects the slope of the regression line.
  II. Significantly affects the correlation.
  III. Significantly affects the y-intercept of the regression line.

  A.   I only
  B.   II only
  C.   I and II
  D.   II and III
  E.   I, II, and III

Use the following information for problems 9 and 10:

The following table shows the salaries of 10 employees (in $1000's) along with the purchase price of the cars they drive (in $1000's).

Salary	27	62	42	18	35	20	55	25	27	26
Car Price	21	39	28	11	24	13	36	18	20	16

8. Using the information in the table, what would be the expected value of a car driven by an employee with a salary of $30,000?

    A. $20,300
    B. $20,500
    C. $20,700
    D. $20,900
    E. $21,100

9. Using the information in the table, what would be the expected value of the salary for an employee who drives a car valued at $30,000?

    A. $43,550
    B. $44,400
    C. $45,650
    D. $47,800
    E. $49,850

10. Which of the following are true about the data represented by this scatterplot?

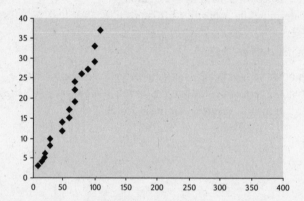

    I.   The points show a strong positive correlation.
    II. The value of the slope of the regression line is greater than the value of the correlation.
    III. The correlation of the points is greater than the correlation of the points in the residual plot.

    A. I only
    B. I and II
    C. I and III
    D. II and III
    E. I, II, and III

11. Which of the following will have an effect on the correlation between two variables?

    I.   Adding −4 to each value of the x-variable
    II. Multiplying each value of the y-variable by 3
    III. Exchanging the values of the x-variables and the y-variables

    A. I and II
    B. I and III
    C. II and III
    D. I, II, and III
    E. None of them will have an effect on correlation.

12. A data set with 5 points has a correlation of 0.8 and a linear regression line with a slope of 0.8. Which of the following statements are true?

   I. A sixth point can be added so that the resulting slope is 1.

   II. A sixth point can be added so that the resulting correlation is 1.

   III. A sixth point can be added so that the resulting slope is –1.

   IV. A sixth point can be added so that the resulting correlation is –1.

   A. I and III

   B. II and IV

   C. I and II

   D. III and IV

   E. I, II, III, and IV

13. The relationship between A and $\sqrt{B}$ shows a strong negative linear correlation. Which of the following is true?

   A. The residual plot of the variables A and B will show a random pattern, and the scatterplot of the variables A and B will show a linear pattern.

   B. The residual plot of the variables A and B will show a nonrandom pattern, and the scatterplot of the variables A and B will show a linear pattern.

   C. The residual plot of the variables A and B will show a random pattern, and the scatterplot of the variables A and B will show a nonlinear pattern.

   D. The residual plot of the variables A and B will show a nonrandom pattern, and the scatterplot of the variables A and B will show a nonlinear pattern.

   E. Residual plots cannot be used with quadratic relationships.

14. Which of the following are true?

   I. A linear correlation of 0.9 shows a stronger linear relationship than a linear correlation of –0.9.

   II. A linear correlation of 0.9 shows more of a cause-and-effect relationship than a linear correlation of –0.9.

   III. A linear correlation close to 0 indicates a nonlinear relationship.

   A. I only

   B. II only

   C. III only

   D. Two of the statements are true.

   E. None of the statements is true.

15. The correlation coefficient of a set of points is $r = 0.8$. The standard deviation of the x-coordinates of the points is 2.1, and the standard deviation of the y-coordinates of the points is 1.2. Find the slope of the least-squares line.

   A. 0.46

   B. 0.96

   C. 1.40

   D. 1.68

   E. 2.02

16. One of the points in a set of points is (4, 8). What is the residual for this point if the equation of the regression line for these points is $\hat{y} = 3.6 + 1.8x$?

   A. –1.8

   B. –2.4

   C. –2.8

   D. –3.2

   E. –3.6

17. An exponential relationship exists between the explanatory variable and the response variable in a set of data. The common log of each value of the response variable is taken, and the least-squares line has an equation of $\log(y) = 7.3 - 1.5x$. What would be the value of the response variable if $x = 4.8$?

   A. 0.1
   B. 1.1
   C. 1.3
   D. −1.0
   E. −2.3

18. Pre-test scores versus post-test scores for a class of 120 college freshman English students were graphed. The residual plot for the least-squares regression line showed no pattern. The least-squares regression line was $\hat{y} = 0.9x + 0.2$ with a linear correlation of $r = 0.76$. What percent of the variation in post-test scores can be explained by the variation in the pre-test scores?

   A. 52.0%
   B. 57.8%
   C. 76.0%
   D. 90.0%
   E. Cannot be determined from the information given

Multiple Choice Answers

1. D. The correlation coefficient is not used in the determination of the answer. Substitute the cost of $0.95 into the regression equation to determine the approximate life expectancy of the bulb.

$$\hat{y} = 1084x - 35.4$$
$$\hat{y} = (1084)(0.95) - 35.4$$
$$\hat{y} = 994.4$$

2. D. The correlation coefficient is not used in the determination of the answer. Substitute the life expectancy into the regression equation to determine the approximate cost of the lightbulb.

$$\hat{y} = 1084x - 35.4$$
$$1600 = 1084x - 35.4$$
$$1635.4 = 1084x$$
$$1.51 = x$$

3. C. Adding a constant to each value of the x- or y-coordinates or multiplying the x- or y-coordinates by a constant does not alter the correlation coefficient. Therefore, it remains the same.

4. E. The fact that the overall correlation of 25 points is positive does not indicate the relationship of two randomly chosen points. The two chosen points could lie on the same horizontal line, resulting in a slope of 0. The two chosen points could lie on the same vertical line, resulting in an undefined slope. Positive and negative slopes are also possible. Therefore, all four could be true.

5. E. Removing an extreme value usually will improve the correlation. Since the sign of the correlation coefficient is not known, it might be positive or negative. If it is positive, then removing the extreme value will increase r. If it is negative, then removing the extreme value will decrease it. Therefore, answer choices A, B, and C are not correct. If r is negative, then a decrease in r will result in an increase in r^2. Therefore, answer choice D is not correct. Choice E is correct since the coefficient of determination is never negative. It is the square of the correlation coefficient.

6. B. A residual plot with no obvious pattern indicates that a linear model is appropriate for the relationship. Although the correlation could be close to 0 and have a residual plot with no pattern, there is no indication that the implication is not true. Therefore, answer choice I is true and II is false. Nonlinear relationships do result in nonlinear residual plots, so answer choice III is true.

7. B. Consider the following two scatterplots. The first has no outlier. The second adds an outlier with respect to the response variable (*y*-coordinate). The addition of the outlier significantly affects the correlation but does not significantly affect the regression line. Therefore, only choice II is true.

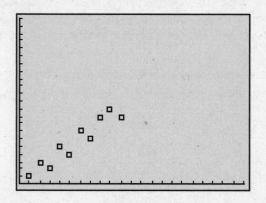
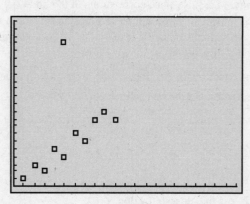

Slope = 0.982

y-intercept = 0.8

correlation = 0.95

Slope = 0.900

y-intercept = 2.1

correlation = 0.49

8. A. Calculate the equation of the least-squares regression line. Enter the values in the chart into two lists in the TI-83/4 calculator and perform a linear regression. The correlation is strong with $r = 0.988$. The equation for the regression line is $\hat{y} = 1.73 + 0.62x$. Substitute the value of the salary and solve for the car price.

$$\hat{y} = 1.73 + 0.62x$$
$$\hat{y} = 1.73 + (0.62)(30)$$
$$\hat{y} = 20.33$$

Thus, answer choice A is the closest to the correct answer.

9. C. Calculate the equation of the least-squares regression line. Enter the values in the chart into two lists in the TI-83/4 calculator and perform a linear regression. The correlation is strong with $r = 0.988$. The equation for the regression line is $\hat{y} = 1.73 + 0.62x$. Substitute the value of the car price and solve for the salary.

$$\hat{y} = 1.73 + 0.62x$$
$$30 = 1.73 + 0.62x$$
$$28.27 = 0.62x$$
$$45.597 = x$$

Thus, answer choice C is the closest to the correct answer.

10. C. The scatterplot shows a strong linear pattern that has a positive slope. The correlation is therefore positive. Thus, choice I is true. Strong linear relationships have residual plots that show random patterns with very low correlation. Thus, choice III is true. Since the scales on the plot are different, you cannot say that the slope of the regression line is greater than 1. (The correlation would be close to 1.) Thus, choice II is false. Therefore, answer C is correct.

11. E. Adding a constant to each value of one of the coordinates will not change the correlation. Neither will multiplying by a positive constant. (Multiplying by a negative constant will change the sign on the correlation.) Exchanging variables also does not change the correlation. It will probably change the slope of the regression line, but not its sign.

12. A. If five points have a correlation of 0.8, it means that they do not lie on the same straight line; otherwise they would have a correlation on 1 or −1. Adding another point does not change the fact that they do not lie on the same straight line. Thus, choices II and IV are false. The slope of the regression line can be changed considerably by influential points. Thus, choices I and III are true.

13. D. If there is a strong linear relationship between A and $\sqrt{B}$, then there will be a nonlinear relationship between A and B. A nonlinear relationship yields a residual with a nonlinear pattern.

14. E. Choice I is false since correlations of 0.9 and –0.9 show the same strength of correlation, only one regression line has a positive slope and one regression line has a negative slope. Choice II is false since correlation does not imply causation. Choice III is false since a correlation close to 0 does not imply any specific type of pattern, but it is probably random.

15. A. The equation for the slope of the regression line can be written in terms of the standard deviations of the x- and y-coordinates and the regression coefficient: $m = r \dfrac{s_y}{s_x}$. Substituting the appropriate values and solving gives

$$m = r \frac{s_y}{s_x}$$
$$m = (0.8)\left(\frac{1.2}{2.1}\right).$$
$$m = 0.457$$

Choice A is the closest in value.

16. C. Substitute the x-coordinate into the regression equation to obtain $\hat{y}$. Then calculate the residual, $y - \hat{y}$.

$$\hat{y} = 3.6 + 1.8x$$
$$\hat{y} = 3.6 + (1.8)(4)$$
$$\hat{y} = 10.8$$

Subtracting gives $8 - 10.8 = -2.8$

17. C. The least-squares line of the transformed y-variable can be used to approximate y-values for given x-values. First, evaluate log y using the equation:

$$\log(y) = 7.3 - 1.5x$$
$$\log(y) = 7.3 - (1.5)(4.8)$$
$$\log(y) = 0.1$$

Since the equation of the least-squares line was for the transformed y-values, the answer must be transformed back using $y = 10^{\log y}$.

$$y = 10^{\log y}$$
$$y = 10^{0.1}$$
$$y = 1.259$$

The best answer choice is C. Choice A is not correct since it is the value of log y. Choice B is not correct since that is the answer you get if you used e^x instead of 10^x.

18. B. The coefficient of determination is the square of the correlation. The equation of the least-squares regression line is not used in the calculation.

$$r^2 = (0.76)^2$$
$$r^2 = 0.5776$$

Free-Response Questions

Directions: Show all work. Indicate clearly the methods you use. You will be graded on method as well as accuracy.

---

1. Data from an experiment is standardized. That is, the values of the bivariate data, x and y, both have standard deviations of 1. The coefficient of determination of the data is 0.25. Describe the pattern of the scatterplot of the data and the slope of the least-squares regression line.

2. The following represents the scores received by 10 students on the first two exams in a history class:

Test A	38	53	90	44	74	51	97	88	53	67
Test B	54	63	88	46	80	48	96	86	52	60

    A. Draw a scatterplot of the data.
    B. Calculate the correlation r of the data as well as the equation of the least-squares line.
    C. Should the regression line be used to make predictions? If so, what is the predicted score on Test B if a student got a 70 on Test A?

3. Give an example of four data points that have a very strong positive correlation but have a regression line that should not be used for predictions. Include a discussion of the effect of outliers or influential points.

4. The following residual plot shows a nonlinear pattern:

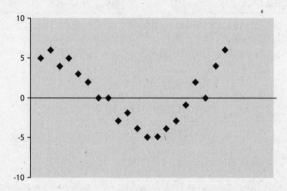

If the linear regression least-squares line for the original data is $\hat{y} = 3x + 7$, discuss why the predicted value of $\hat{y} = 52$ when $x = 15$ is inaccurate. What might be done to give a better prediction?

5. The following data shows an exponential relationship:

x	2	4	6	8	10	12
y	2	4	7	14	28	55

    A. Use a transformation that would create a linear relationship.
    B. Use the least-squares line of this transformed relationship to predict the value of y when x is 16.

6. A bivariate relationship between x and y has a correlation of r. The least-squares regression line for the data has a slope of m. Discuss the relationship between r and m. If 3 is added to each value of x, how does this relationship change? If each value of x was multiplied by 3, how does this relationship change?

7. The equation of the least-squares line for a set of points is $\hat{y} = -8 + 4.6x$. If 75% of the variation in y is explained by the variation in x, what is the ratio of the standard deviations of the x and y-values?

Free-Response Answers

1. The official AP Statistics form of a regression line is given by $\hat{y} = b_0 + b_1 x$, where the slope is represent by b_1. The correlation, r, the standard deviations of the x and y variables, s_x and s_y, and the slope, b_1, are related by the following equation: $b_1 = r \frac{s_y}{s_x}$. If the x and y variables are standardized with standard deviations of 1, then this equation simplifies to $b_1 = r$. The coefficient of determination is given as $r^2 = 0.25$. Therefore, the correlation is either $r = 0.5$ or $r = -0.5$. Since the standard deviations are equal to 1, the slope of the regression line is either

$b_1 = 0.5$ or $b_1 = -0.5$. With a correlation of only ±0.5, the regression line would not be a very accurate predictor. The scatterplot would show points that have a weak linear correlation. If the scales on both axes were the same, the trend would be rising or falling with a slope of ±0.5.

2. The scatterplot produces a pattern that appears to have a strong positive correlation:

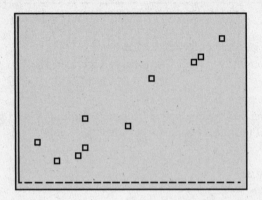   

The correlation is strong with a value of 0.94. The regression equation can be used to make predictions. To calculate a prediction of the score on Test B if the student got a 70 on Test A, solve for the response variable:

$$\hat{y} = 0.84x + -12.46$$
$$\hat{y} = (0.84)(70) + 12.46$$
$$\hat{y} = 71.26$$

With a grade on Test A of 70, a student can expect a grade of 71 on Test B.

3. Consider the four points (1,3), (2,2), (3,1), and (20, 20). The scatterplot and calculations of the regression line and correlation are shown here:

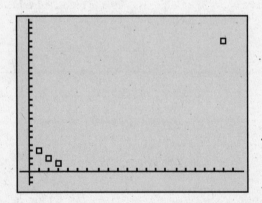   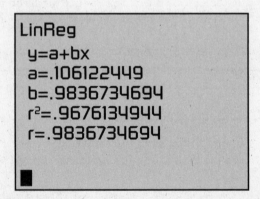

It is clear from the calculations that these points have a very strong positive correlation, and your first thought might be to use the regression line to make predictions. But consider the boxplots of the variables:

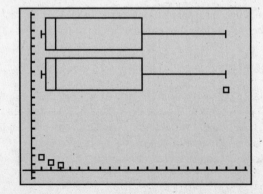

Although there are no official outliers with respect to either variable, the point (20, 20) is truly an influential point. Without it, the regression line and correlation coefficient would change significantly. Because this one influential point changes the outcome so dramatically, the data should be viewed with caution.

4. A residual plot that is nonlinear indicates that a linear model is not appropriate for the original data. It is difficult to tell whether the value of 52 is lower or higher than what it should be since the horizontal scale is missing from the residual plot. If the x-value of 15 is on the left or the right side of the graph, then the value is lower than what it should be. If the x-value of 15 is in the middle of the graph, then the value is higher than what it should be. Possibly a transformation of one or both variables might provide a more linear model.

5. A scatterplot of the original data definitely shows a nonlinear pattern.

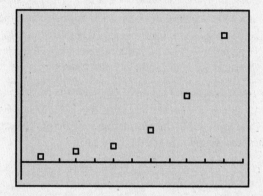

Since the plot appears to be exponential, a log transformation might help produce a more linear model. Take the natural log of the response variable. Store the results in L3 and graph L3 as the response variable instead of L2.

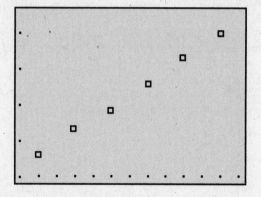

L1	L2	L3	3
2	2	------	
4	4		
6	7		
8	14		
10	28		
12	55		
------	------		

L3 = 1n(L2)■

This scatterplot produces a linear relationship. Calculate the correlation and regression of this transformed relationship.

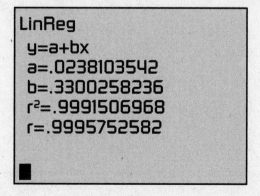

```
LinReg
 y=a+bx
 a=.0238103542
 b=.3300258236
 r²=.9991506968
 r=.9995752582


 ■
```

To use this least-squares line to make the prediction, solve for y using the value of 16 for x. Then transform back using e^x:

$$\hat{y} = 0.33x + .02 \qquad\qquad \hat{y} = e^x$$
$$\hat{y} = (0.33)(16) + .02 \qquad\qquad \hat{y} = e^{5.3}$$
$$\hat{y} = 5.3 \qquad\qquad\qquad \hat{y} = 200.33$$

Therefore, the predicted value for y when x is 16 is approximately 200.

6. The official AP Statistics form of a regression line is given by $\hat{y} = b_0 + b_1 x$, where the slope is represented by b_1. The correlation, r, the standard deviations of the x and y variables, s_x and s_y, and the slope, b_1, are related by the following equation: $b_1 = r\frac{s_y}{s_x}$. Since the standard deviations are both positive, the sign of the slope and the sign of the correlation must be the same. Adding 3 to each value of a variable or multiplying each value of a variable by 3 will change the value of the slope but not the correlation. Even though the slope's value will change, the sign of the slope will remain the same because the correlation did not change.

7. The equation that relates slope, correlation, and standard deviations is $b_1 = r\frac{s_y}{s_x}$. From the given equation, the slope of the regression line is 4.6. Since 75% of the variation in y is explained by the variation in x, the coefficient of determination is $r^2 = 0.75$. This implies that the correlation $r = \pm 0.866$. Substituting the values for the slope and correlation in the preceding formula and solving for the ratio gives:

$$b_1 = r\frac{s_y}{s_x}$$

$$4.6 = (0.886)\frac{s_y}{s_x}$$

$$5.31 = \frac{s_y}{s_x}$$

$$0.188 = \frac{s_x}{s_y}$$

Therefore, the ratio of the standard deviations of the x- and y-variables is 0.188.

Exploring Data: Exploring Categorical Data—Frequency Tables

Descriptive statistics, including bivariate analysis, uses charts and tables to find relationships in sets of data. These relationships involve data that, for the most part, is quantitative. This chapter concentrates on data that is qualitative—**categorical data.** Examples of categorical data include religion, political party affiliation, gender, place of birth, citizenship status, and blood type. Quantitative data can be classified as categorical if ranges of values are grouped. For example, age is quantitative, but if ages are grouped, such as "Under 25" or "25 and Older," then the data becomes categorical.

Marginal and Joint Frequencies for Two-Way Tables

Relationships between categorical variables are best shown using **contingency tables.** The relationships usually revolve around the dependence or independence of the variables.

EXAMPLE:
The gender breakdown for student enrollment at four colleges in a California community college district are as follows:

College A	Female = 3832	Male = 4228
College B	Female = 6765	Male = 5590
College C	Female = 2889	Male = 3388
College D	Female = 5580	Male = 5612

Organize this data into a two-way contingency table.

This table relates the two categorical variables, college and gender.

	Female	Male
College A	3832	4228
College B	6765	5590
College C	2889	3388
College D	5580	5612

The names of the colleges are called the row variable, and the gender is called the column variable.

Totals can be added to both the rows and columns. These totals are added in the margins so they are called marginal frequencies.

EXAMPLE:
Use the data from the previous example to create a two-way contingency table with marginal frequencies. Write the marginal frequencies as proportions and percentages of the totals:

	Female	Male	TOTAL
College A	3832	4228	8060
College B	6765	5590	12355
College C	2889	3388	6277
College D	5580	5612	11192
TOTAL	19066	18818	37884

The marginal frequencies for the colleges are as follows:

$$\text{College A} = \frac{8060}{37884} = 21.3\%$$

$$\text{College B} = \frac{12355}{37884} = 32.6\%$$

$$\text{College C} = \frac{6277}{37884} = 16.6\%$$

$$\text{College D} = \frac{11192}{37884} = 29.5\%$$

The marginal frequencies for gender are as follows:

$$\text{Female} = \frac{19066}{37884} = 50.3\%$$

$$\text{Male} = \frac{18818}{37884} = 49.7\%$$

EXAMPLE:
Display the data in the previous example in bar graphs.

Bar graphs are used to display categorical data. Each graph displays the totals of one of the categories:

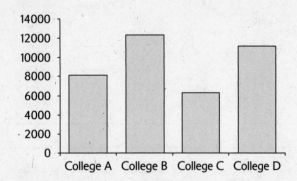
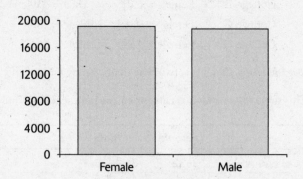

Conditional Relative Frequencies and Association

The table of data in the previous examples provides more information than marginal frequencies. The data inside the table provides information about the relationship, or association of the two categorical variables. These are called conditional relative frequencies.

EXAMPLE:
Use the data from the previous examples to calculate the percentages of females at each of the four colleges and the percentages of males at each of the four colleges. Use the data to calculate the gender percentages of students at each college.

	Female	*Male*	**TOTAL**
College A	3832	4228	8060
College B	6765	5590	12355
College C	2889	3388	6277
College D	5580	5612	11192
TOTAL	19066	18818	37884

To calculate these conditional relative frequencies, computation will take place in only one column or row from the table. To calculate the percentage of all the female students that attend College A, divide the number of female students at College A by the total number of female students. Remember, these quantities are relative to an individual row or column total, not the grand total.

For the females:

$$\text{Relative frequency of female students attending College A} = \frac{3832}{19066} = 20.1\%.$$

$$\text{Relative frequency of female students attending College B} = \frac{6765}{19066} = 35.5\%.$$

$$\text{Relative frequency of female students attending College C} = \frac{2889}{19066} = 15.2\%.$$

$$\text{Relative frequency of female students attending College D} = \frac{5580}{19066} = 29.3\%.$$

For the males:

$$\text{Relative frequency of male students attending College A} = \frac{4228}{18818} = 22.5\%.$$

$$\text{Relative frequency of male students attending College B} = \frac{5590}{18818} = 29.7\%.$$

$$\text{Relative frequency of male students attending College C} = \frac{3388}{18818} = 18.0\%.$$

$$\text{Relative frequency of male students attending College D} = \frac{5612}{18818} = 29.8\%.$$

To calculate the percentage of students at College B who are female, divide the number of female students at College B by the total number of students at College B.

For students at College A:

$$\text{Relative frequency of College A students who are female} = \frac{3832}{8060} = 47.5\%.$$

$$\text{Relative frequency of College A students who are male} = \frac{4228}{8060} = 52.5\%.$$

For students at College B:

$$\text{Relative frequency of College B students who are female} = \frac{6765}{12355} = 54.8\%.$$

$$\text{Relative frequency of College B students who are male} = \frac{5590}{12355} = 45.2\%.$$

For students at College C:

$$\text{Relative frequency of College C students who are female} = \frac{2889}{6277} = 46.0\%.$$

$$\text{Relative frequency of College C students who are male} = \frac{3388}{6277} = 54.0\%.$$

For students at College D:

$$\text{Relative frequency of College D students who are female} = \frac{5580}{11192} = 49.9\%.$$

$$\text{Relative frequency of College D students who are male} = \frac{5612}{11192} = 50.1\%.$$

Different types of bar charts can illustrate these percentages. Stacked bar charts and clustered bar charts show these conditional relative frequencies.

EXAMPLE:

Use the results from the previous example and construct stacked bar charts and clustered bar charts by college and gender.

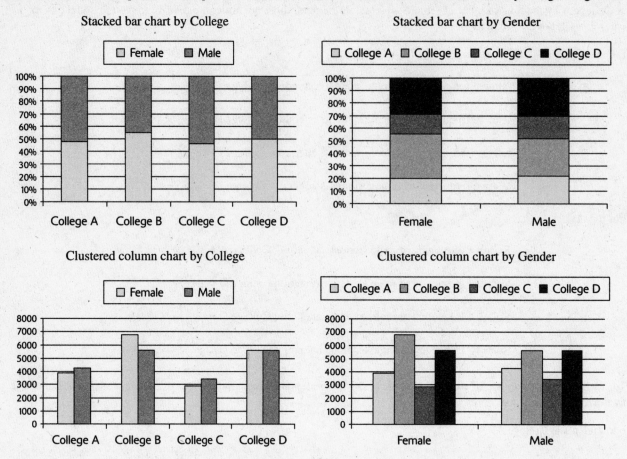

Although two-way contingency tables are useful, be careful of hidden variables that can change, or even reverse categorical percentages. This phenomenon is known as **Simpson's Paradox** and is illustrated in the next example.

EXAMPLE:

You are trying to decide which of two vegetables to serve at a banquet. A random sample of 600 people is divided into two groups. Three hundred fourteen people were asked whether they like broccoli and 286 people were asked whether they like spinach. Use the table of responses here to determine which vegetable is more popular.

	Yes	*No*
Broccoli	148	166
Spinach	153	133

Calculate the percentage of those who said they like spinach and calculate the percentage of those who said they like broccoli. Should you serve the one that received the higher percentage?

Calculate the percentage of those who like broccoli and spinach by dividing the number of "yes" responses by the total.

$$\text{Percentage who like broccoli} = \frac{148}{148 + 166} = \frac{148}{314} = 0.471 = 47.1\%.$$

$$\text{Percentage who like spinach} = \frac{153}{153 + 133} = \frac{153}{286} = 0.535 = 53.5\%.$$

From these results, you might conclude that because a substantially higher percentage of people like spinach, you should serve spinach at your banquet.

You would be making a mistake if you don't consider any *hidden variables* that could change, or reverse your conclusion. If the original sample of 600 people was made up of children and adults and separate data was collected for each, evaluating each subset of data could be useful in helping make the correct decision.

The following table of responses is broken down into two subsets: Children and Adults. Note that corresponding data adds up to the original total.

Children	Yes	No
Broccoli	110	155
Spinach	43	88

Adults	Yes	No
Broccoli	38	11
Spinach	110	45

Now, separately for children and adults, calculate the percentage of those who like broccoli and spinach by dividing the number of "yes" responses by the total.

$$\text{Percentage of CHILDREN who like broccoli} = \frac{110}{110 + 155} = \frac{110}{265} = 0.415 = 41.5\%.$$

$$\text{Percentage of CHILDREN who like spinach} = \frac{43}{43 + 88} = \frac{43}{131} = 0.328 = 32.8\%.$$

$$\text{Percentage of ADULTS who like broccoli} = \frac{38}{38 + 11} = \frac{38}{49} = 0.776 = 77.6\%.$$

$$\text{Percentage of ADULTS who like spinach} = \frac{110}{110 + 45} = \frac{110}{155} = 0.710 = 71.0\%.$$

The results are interesting. When you consider the adults and children separately, each group favored broccoli by about 8%. But, if you consider both subgroups together as one group, spinach is favored by about 6%. This is **Simpson's Paradox** and results from the unbalanced nature of the subgroup responses. Overall, the yes/no ratio was about the same. But when the data is separated, adults have a much higher approval rating of both vegetables and children have a much lower approval rating of both vegetables. Combining all the information into one chart *hid* the effect of age on vegetable preference.

Statistical results, such as these, can be used to mislead consumers by not showing enough detail.

Review Questions and Answers

Multiple Choice Questions

Directions: Solve each of the following problems. Decide which is the best of the choices given.

Use the following information for problems 1–6:

A waiter kept track of all the dinner guests at his tables during a weekend job assignment. He recorded whether each guest ordered an appetizer and whether they ordered dessert. This table summarizes the results. For example, 44 people ordered dessert but did not order an appetizer. Use the information in the table to answer the following questions.

	Ordered an appetizer	Did not order an appetizer
Ordered a dessert	30	44
Did not order a dessert	12	24

1. What percentage of the people served by the waiter ordered dessert?

   A. 38%
   B. 42%
   C. 49%
   D. 67%
   E. 74%

2. What percentage of the people served by the waiter ordered an appetizer?

   A. 38%
   B. 42%
   C. 49%
   D. 67%
   E. 74%

3. What percentage of the people served by the waiter ordered either a dessert or an appetizer, but not both?

   A. 44%
   B. 49%
   C. 51%
   D. 56%
   E. 64%

4. Which of the following is the second most likely to occur?

   A. Order dessert, but no appetizer
   B. Order an appetizer, but no dessert
   C. Order both an appetizer and dessert
   D. Order an appetizer
   E. Does not order dessert

5. What percentage of people served by the waiter who ordered dessert also ordered an appetizer?

   A. 27%
   B. 38%
   C. 41%
   D. 68%
   E. 78%

6. What percentage of people served by the waiter who didn't order an appetizer ordered dessert?

   A. 40%
   B. 55%
   C. 60%
   D. 65%
   E. 92%

Use the following information for problems 7–9.

The following table represents the election results of a ballot proposal:

	Freshman	Sophomore	Junior	Senior
Yes	210	180	110	130
No	165	210	245	140

7. Which of the following orders represents approval percentages from highest to lowest?

   A.   Freshman, Sophomore, Junior, Senior
   B.   Freshman, Senior, Sophomore, Junior
   C.   Senior, Freshman, Junior, Sophomore
   D.   Senior, Sophomore, Freshman, Junior
   E.   Sophomore, Senior, Junior, Freshman

8. What percent of the "yes" votes were sophomores?

   A.   13%
   B.   21%
   C.   29%
   D.   47%
   E.   86%

9. Which class had an approval percentage closest to the overall school approval percentage?

   A.   Freshman
   B.   Sophomore
   C.   Junior
   D.   Senior
   E.   Not enough information in the table to determine the answer.

Use the following information for problems 10–12.

Four departments in a company, A, B, C, and D, are responsible for sales of the four different products, W, X, Y, and Z, that the company sells. The following stacked bar chart shows the sales records of units sold by each of the four departments. During the reporting period represented by the chart, the company sold the same number of units of each of the four products.

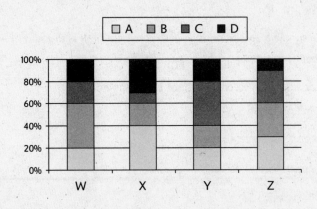

10. What percentage of male students favor the petition?

    A. 28%

    B. 37%

    C. 43%

    D. 58%

    E. 67%

11. What percentage of female evening students favor the petition?

    A. 34%

    B. 37%

    C. 40%

    D. 58%

    E. 63%

12. What percentage of students are daytime students?

    A. 32%

    B. 40%

    C. 46%

    D. 54%

    E. 68%

Multiple Choice Answers

1. D. Totals can be added to the chart to help determine the answer.

	Ordered an appetizer	Did not order an appetizer	TOTAL
Ordered a dessert	30	44	74
Did not order a dessert	12	24	36
TOTAL	42	68	110

To find the percentage of people who ordered dessert, divide the number of people who ordered dessert by the total number of people: $\frac{74}{110} = 0.672 = 67\%$.

2. A. Using the table in answer 1, divide the number of people who ordered an appetizer by the total number of people: $\frac{42}{110} = 0.382 = 38\%$.

3. C. The number of people served a dessert or an appetizer but not both is the sum of 44 and 12. This sum is then divided by the total number of people: $\frac{44 + 12}{110} = \frac{56}{110} = 0.509 = 51\%$.

4. D. To answer this question, the five percentages must be computed.

Choice A: Order dessert, but no appetizer: $\frac{44}{110}$

Choice B: Order an appetizer, but no dessert: $\frac{12}{110}$

Choice C: Order both an appetizer and dessert: $\frac{30}{110}$

Choice D: Order an appetizer: $\frac{42}{110}$

Choice E: Does not order a dessert: $\frac{36}{110}$

Since all the denominators are the same, the second largest is the one with the second largest numerator, or choice D.

5. C. This is a conditional relationship. Here you work in only one row or one column of the table. In this case, you are given that the person ordered dessert. Therefore, divide by the total on the "ordered dessert" row:
$\frac{30}{74} = 0.4054 = 41\%$.

6. D. This is another conditional relationship. In this case, use the "did not order an appetizer" column:
$\frac{44}{68} = 0.647 = 65\%$.

7. B. To answer this question, add totals to the chart.

	Freshman	Sophomore	Junior	Senior	Total
Yes	210	180	110	130	630
No	165	210	245	140	760
Total	375	390	355	270	1390

Calculate the "yes" percentage for each class.

Freshman: $\frac{210}{375} = 0.560$

Sophomore: $\frac{180}{390} = 0.462$

Junior: $\frac{110}{355} = 0.310$

Senior: $\frac{130}{270} = 0.481$

Ordered from highest to lowest is Freshmen, Seniors, Sophomores, and Juniors, which is answer choice B.

8. C. There were 630 yes votes, and 180 were cast by sophomores. Therefore, divide 180 by 630: $\frac{180}{630} = 0.2857 = 29\%$.

9. B. The overall approval percentage is $\frac{630}{1390} = 0.453 = 45\%$. Using the results from problem 7, the approval percentage of Sophomores is the closest.

10. C. Totals can be added to each of the charts (see the preceding). Divide the yes votes by the total:
$\frac{242}{567} = 0.427 = 43\%$.

11. E. Divide the yes votes by the total: $\frac{24}{38} = 0.631 = 63\%$.

12. E. Divide the total number of daytime students by the total number of students: $\frac{290 + 395}{567 + 433} = \frac{685}{1000} = 0.685 = 68\%$.

Note: The data in problems 13–15 is an example of Simpson's Paradox. Using the data from the charts, the student approval percentage by gender shows a higher percentage of males favoring the petition. However, if the daytime and evening subgroups are calculated separately, each shows that females have a higher approval percentage.

Overall:

Male: $\frac{242}{567} = 0.427 = 42.7\%$

Female: $\frac{159}{433} = 0.367 = 36.7\%$

Daytime:

Male: $\frac{80}{290} = 0.276 = 27.6\%$

Female: $\frac{135}{395} = 0.342 = 34.2\%$

Evening:

Male: $\quad \frac{162}{277} = 0.585 = 58.5\%$

Female: $\quad \frac{24}{38} = 0.632 = 63.2\%$

It is clear that although in each subgroup the female voters voted a higher yes percentage than the male voters, the reverse was true of the total. This paradox seems odd at first. Consider the fact that the two subgroups were unbalanced. The daytime voters did not favor the petition, but the evening students did. The daytime students cast more votes than the evening students. In the daytime, more female voters cast their vote. In the evening, many more males cast their vote. The unbalanced nature of the voting leads to this paradox. By simply looking at the overall statistics, important trends go unnoticed.

Free-Response Questions

Directions: Show all work. Indicate clearly the methods you use. You will be graded on method as well as accuracy.

1. Information was collected at a restaurant whose dinners include soup or salad. Although some diners ask for both soup and salad, and some diners have neither, these cases were excluded from the data. The number of people requesting soup or salad along with their gender was tabulated and is presented in the following two-way table:

	Male	*Female*
Soup	120	60
Salad	220	160

Examine the marginal as well as conditional distributions. Compare and contrast the results.

2. Student evaluations are conducted in classes at the end of the school year. Many teachers believe that the evaluations are influenced by the grade the students receive in the class, with better teacher evaluations coming from those students with higher grades. Here are the results of the number of high and low evaluations given to two teachers from students with both high and low grades in the classes.

	Teacher A	*Teacher B*
High evaluations from students with high grades	110	40
Low evaluations from students with high grades	40	10
High evaluations from students with low grades	10	40
Low evaluations from students with low grades	40	120

Which teacher had a higher percentage of high evaluations? Look at the data in more than one way.

3. A comparison was made of the pass/fail rates for the three teachers in a small math department. Separate information was collected from male and female students. A reporter noted that females had a higher pass rate for the department as a whole but when each teacher's pass/fail rate was examined individually, the opposite was true. Was the reporter correct? The following chart lists the number of students in each category. Evaluate the data and discuss why this might be true.

	Male Students		Female Students	
	Pass	*Fail*	*Pass*	*Fail*
Teacher A	82	20	82	22
Teacher B	240	103	76	36
Teacher C	58	6	128	20

Free-Response Answers

1. First, add totals to each row and column so that the marginal distributions and conditional distributions can be calculated.

	Male	*Female*	*Total*
Soup	120	60	180
Salad	220	160	380
Total	340	220	560

These are the marginal distributions:

Percent of male diners: $\frac{340}{560} = 0.607 = 60.7\%$

Percent of female diners: $\frac{220}{560} = 0.393 = 39.3\%$

Percent of diners ordering soup: $\frac{180}{560} = 0.321 = 32.1\%$

Percent of diners ordering salad: $\frac{380}{560} = 0.679 = 67.9\%$

These are the conditional distributions:

Percent of male diners ordering soup: $\frac{120}{340} = 0.353 = 35.3\%$

Percent of male diners ordering salad: $\frac{220}{340} = 0.647 = 64.7\%$

Percent of female diners ordering soup: $\frac{60}{220} = 0.273 = 27.3\%$

Percent of female diners ordering salad: $\frac{160}{220} = 0.727 = 72.7\%$

Percent of soup eaters who are male: $\frac{120}{180} = 0.667 = 66.7\%$

Percent of soup eaters who are female: $\frac{60}{180} = 0.333 = 33.3\%$

Percent of salad eaters who are male: $\frac{220}{380} = 0.579 = 57.9\%$

Percent of salad eaters who are female: $\frac{160}{380} = 0.421 = 42.1\%$

It is clear that each pair adds up to 100%. Salads are heavily preferred over soup by both men and women. The preference for salads is greater in women than men.

2. First, add totals for each column so that the conditional distributions can be calculated.

	Teacher A	Teacher B
High evaluations from students with high grades	110	40
Low evaluations from students with high grades	40	10
High evaluations from students with low grades	10	40
Low evaluations from students with low grades	40	120
Total	200	210

Using the data in the preceding chart, another chart can be constructed that combines the results for students with high and low grades.

	Teacher A	Teacher B
High evaluations	120	80
Low evaluations	80	130
Total	200	210

Conditional distributions are calculated for each teacher.

Teacher A:

Percentage of high evaluations: $\frac{120}{200} = 0.600 = 60.0\%$

Percentage of low evaluations: $\frac{80}{200} = 0.400 = 40.0\%$

Teacher B:

Percentage of high evaluations: $\frac{80}{210} = 0.381 = 38.1\%$

Percentage of low evaluations: $\frac{130}{210} = 0.619 = 61.9\%$

It is clear that overall, Teacher A (60.0% high evaluations) received a higher percentage of high evaluations than did Teacher B (38.1% high evaluations). But consider the hidden variable of student grades. Conditional distributions are calculated separately for students with high grades and students with low grades.

Students with high grades:

	Teacher A	Teacher B
High evaluations	110	40
Low evaluations	40	10
Total	150	50

Teacher A:

Percentage of high evaluations: $\frac{110}{150} = 0.733 = 73.3\%$

Percentage of low evaluations: $\frac{40}{150} = 0.267 = 26.7\%$

Teacher B:

Percentage of high evaluations: $\frac{40}{50} = 0.800 = 80.0\%$

Percentage of low evaluations: $\frac{10}{50} = 0.200 = 20.0\%$

Students with low grades:

	Teacher A	Teacher B
High evaluations	10	40
Low evaluations	40	120
Total	50	160

Teacher A:

Percentage of high evaluations: $\frac{10}{50} = 0.200 = 20.0\%$

Percentage of low evaluations: $\frac{40}{50} = 0.800 = 80.0\%$

Teacher B:

Percentage of high evaluations: $\frac{40}{160} = 0.250 = 25.0\%$

Percentage of low evaluations: $\frac{120}{160} = 0.750 = 75.0\%$

For students with high grades, Teacher B (80.0% high evaluations) received a higher percentage of high evaluations than did Teacher A (73.3%). Likewise, for students with low grades, Teacher B (25.0% high evaluations) received a higher percentage of high evaluations than did Teacher A (20.0%).

So, overall, Teacher A receives a higher percentage of high evaluations, but if you consider each subgroup separately, Teacher B receives a higher percentage of high evaluations. This inconsistency is known as Simpson's Paradox. Why does this occur? In this case, Teacher A taught most of the better students who received better grades. Teacher B, teaching less capable students, appears to get better ratings from both groups. So who got higher ratings? Depends on the way you look at the data.

4. This table presents the data as it was presented in the problem.

	Male Students		Female Students	
	Pass	Fail	Pass	Fail
Teacher A	82	20	82	22
Teacher B	240	103	76	36
Teacher C	58	6	128	20

In order to compare the overall results to the male and female subgroups, two additional tables are useful. Totals are added to each table.

	Male Students		
	Pass	Fail	Total
Teacher A	82	20	102
Teacher B	240	103	343
Teacher C	58	6	64
Total	380	129	509

	Female Students		
	Pass	Fail	Total
Teacher A	82	22	104
Teacher B	76	36	112
Teacher C	128	20	148
Total	286	78	364

The overall department pass rate for male students: $\dfrac{380}{509} = 0.747 = 74.7\%$

The overall department pass rate for female students: $\dfrac{286}{364} = 0.786 = 78.6\%$

Therefore, overall for the department, females did have a higher pass rate. But if each teacher is considered separately, the opposite is true.

Teacher A pass rate for male students: $\dfrac{82}{102} = 0.804 = 80.4\%$

Teacher A pass rate for female students: $\dfrac{82}{104} = 0.788 = 78.8\%$

Teacher B pass rate for male students: $\dfrac{240}{343} = 0.700 = 70.0\%$

Teacher B pass rate for female students: $\dfrac{76}{112} = 0.679 = 67.9\%$

Teacher C pass rate for male students: $\dfrac{58}{64} = 0.906 = 90.6\%$

Teacher C pass rate for female students: $\dfrac{128}{148} = 0.865 = 86.5\%$

This is an example of Simpson's Paradox. In this case, the teacher who taught the most males (Teacher B) had the lowest pass rates for both males and females. The teacher who taught the most females (Teacher C) had the highest pass rates for both males and females. The unbalanced nature of the data leads to the conclusion that overall, a higher percentage of female students passed, but each individual teacher passed a higher percentage of male students.

Sampling and Experimentation: Overview of Methods of Data Collection

Everyday, statements appear in newspapers, magazines, and on television that involve the use of data. Statements such as "The average home price is now $456,000," "Sixty-three percent of college students eat in restaurants at least four times a week," and "The average cost of a college education has increased 47% in the past two years" involve collecting and analyzing data. Everything a statistician does relies on data. Accurate data and valid data collection methods are essential to ensure valid results. Incorrect data or data collected with poorly designed methods can lead to incorrect conclusions.

Data consists of information derived from measurements, observations, counts, or responses. **Statistics** is a science. It is the science of collecting, organizing, summarizing, analyzing, and interpreting data. There are two main types of sets of data: populations and samples. A **population** is a collection of all of the measurements, observations, counts, or responses that you are interested in analyzing. A **sample** is a subset or part of a population. Statisticians usually deal with samples because working with an entire population is usually difficult, costly, or even impossible.

Characteristics of a population are called **parameters.** The mean of a population is a population parameter. The standard deviation of a population is a population parameter. Measures that identify characteristics of a sample are called **statistics.** (The word "statistics" should not be capitalized. The capitalized version is the name of the science.) The mean of a sample is a sample statistic. The standard deviation of a sample is a sample statistic.

EXAMPLE:
Classify each of the following as either a sample or a population:

  The height of each employee in a company.

  The speed of every other car passing a point on a highway during a given hour.

  A questionnaire from 350 students in a school of 2000 students.

  The area of each state in the United States.

  The number of pages contained in each of the encyclopedia in a library.

The height of each employee in a company is data from a population. Data is obtained from every member in the set of company employees. The speed of every other car is data from a sample since only some of the cars are used. Questionnaires from 350 of 2000 students is also a sample. Only a portion of the entire set of students is sampled. The area of each state would be a population since all the states are included. Since each encyclopedia is included in the data set, this is also an example of a population.

The populations listed in the previous example, although fitting the definition of *population*, are quite small. Populations can be very large. A study of tuna fish includes the population of all tuna. This is an extremely large population. Most of the tuna that exist are not even accessible for study. It would be impossible to work with the entire population. Studies using samples of tuna would be more appropriate. A study of all 18-year-old males in the United States would be a population of more than 2,000,000 people. It would be very difficult and very costly to conduct a study using this entire population. Using a sample of 18-year-old males would be much more efficient.

Census

When measurements are taken for every member of a population it is called a **census.** Most people equate the word census with the tabulation of U.S. population data conducted every 10 years. The last U.S. Census was conducted in 2000. It is the intent of our government to collect data on every member of the U.S. population, which is an impossible task. Many of the people living in the United States are missed and do not appear in the census figures. The U.S. census is, of course, not the only census. Anytime a study is made of an entire population, a census is the result. It is possible to conduct a census of all students taking a specific class in a specific community college. It is also possible, but more difficult, to conduct a census of all students attending a specific community college. It would not be practical to try to conduct a census of all students in all community colleges.

Sample Survey

It is the intent of a **sample survey** to collect data from a representative portion of a population and to record the results. The way the sample is determined may vary, but the goal is that inferences about the entire population can be drawn from data taken in the sample survey. Political polls are examples of sample surveys. Statements about the entire population of voters are made based on the results of the poll. Surveys may be conducted in person, through the mail, with questionnaires, or on the telephone. No matter how the data is collected, it is important that it be representative of the population. The researcher makes no attempt to alter or change the population. A well-executed sample survey can obtain valid data without the time and expense of conducting a census.

Experiment

In designed, researcher-controlled studies, called **experiments,** the researcher maintains some control over the subjects of the study. By controlling certain aspects of the experiment, the researcher can determine the effect, if any, changes in the explanatory variable has on the outcome, or response variable. Subjects are usually divided into two groups, the *treatment group* and the *control group*. Medical studies are often experiments. Test groups are divided in two, with one half given certain medication and the other half given some placebo. If both the subjects and the researchers are unaware of which group received the placebo and which group received the medicine, the experiment is called a double-blind study. Testing the effectiveness of artificial sweeteners by asking opinions after giving half the test subjects a beverage sweetened by sweetener A and half of the test subjects the same beverage sweetened by sweetener B and then comparing the results would also be an experiment. In a properly designed experiment, more information is obtainable than from an uncontrolled study.

Observational Study

Observational studies are similar to experiments except that the researcher has no control over which subjects are placed in the control group and which in the treatment group. If a researcher is studying to see whether increased sleep time prior to the test results in better scores on IQ tests, the researcher cannot artificially control the sleep time of the control and treatment groups. Data is obtained from all subjects, and the results are examined for possible relationships. A researcher may observe a group of young children and note which children speak loudly and which speak softly. The researcher then looks for factors that might be related, such as height or weight. Unlike controlled experiments, a researcher conducting an observational study makes no attempt to control any part of the study.

EXAMPLE:

As a researcher, you are interested to see whether aerobic exercise is more effective in weight loss than strength training. Which of the following two studies would be considered an observational study and which one would be an experiment?

A. Data was collected by observing people at a gym, noting the kind of exercise they were doing and the resulting amount of weight loss.

B. Data was collected by observing two groups of people. One group was asked to concentrate on strength training and the other group on aerobic exercise. Both groups were given the same diet to follow.

The first is an example of an observational study. The researcher is not controlling any aspect of the study. The observed data then is analyzed, and conclusions may be drawn from the results.

The second is an example of an experiment. The researcher is controlling the study. The researcher divides the test subjects into two groups, and different treatments are applied to each group.

Both experiments and observational studies are examples of valid statistical studies, but experiments are more useful in establishing cause-and-effect relationships than observational studies.

Review Questions and Answers

Multiple Choice Questions

1. Which of the following are true of a double-blind experimental design?

   I.   Subjects react differently if they know they are in the treatment group.
   II.   Researchers react differently if they know who is in the treatment group.
   III.   Results are more reliable from a double-blind study.

   A.   I only
   B.   II only
   C.   I and III
   D.   II and III
   E.   I, II, and III

2. Which of the following statements is true?

   A.   In an observational study, interaction is required between test subject and researcher.
   B.   In an experiment, test subjects know whether they are in the control group of the treatment group.
   C.   Observational studies are more useful in establishing cause-and-effect relationships than experiments.
   D.   In an experiment, researchers must know which group is the control group.
   E.   Sample surveys are examples of observational studies.

3. Which of the following would be considered observational studies?

   I.   A researcher wants to determine whether taking vitamin E supplements can lower blood pressure. The blood pressure of each of 150 randomly selected subjects is measured. A vitamin E supplement is given to each subject. Six months later, the blood pressure of each subject is measured again and compared with the first measurement.
   II.   A researcher wants to determine whether taking vitamin E supplements can lower blood pressure. The blood pressure of each of 150 randomly selected subjects is measured. Three groups of 50 subjects each are formed. One group is given a certain daily dose of vitamin E. The second group is given twice the daily dosage of the first group. The third is given a pill that contains no vitamin E. Six months later, the blood pressure of each subject is measured again and compared with the first measurement.
   III.   A researcher wants to determine whether taking vitamin E supplements can lower blood pressure. The blood pressure of each of 150 randomly selected subjects is measured. Each subject is asked whether they take a daily dose of vitamin E supplements. The subjects are placed into two groups depending on whether or not they took vitamin E supplements. Results are tabulated.

   A.   I only
   B.   II only
   C.   III only
   D.   I and II
   E.   I, II, and III

4. Which of the following are true statements about cause and effect?

   I. Cause-and-effect relationships should not be drawn from experiments because researchers have an influence over test subjects.
   II. Cause-and-effect relationships are difficult, but not impossible, to draw from observational studies.
   III. Cause-and-effect relationships are better indicated from well-designed experiments than from well-conducted observational studies.

   A. I only
   B. II only
   C. III only
   D. II and III
   E. I, II, and III

5. A researcher wants to determine whether drinking red wine is better at reducing blood pressure than drinking white wine. Two studies are designed. In the first study, 200 people who have not had wine for 6 months are randomly selected. The blood pressures of the 200 subjects are taken. Half of the subjects are asked to drink 1 glass of red wine daily for 6 months, and the other half of the subjects were asked to drink 1 glass of white wine daily for 6 months. The blood pressures of the 200 subjects were taken again after the 6-month study. In a second study, 100 subjects who only drink red wine and 100 subjects who only drink white wine are selected. The blood pressures of the 200 subjects are taken. Results are tabulated. Which of the following is true about these two studies?

   A. The first study is an experiment, and the second study is an observational study.
   B. The first study is an observational study, and the second study in an experiment.
   C. Both studies are experiments.
   D. Both studies are observational studies.
   E. The second study in more likely to show a cause-and-effect relationship than the first study.

6. A researcher wants to determine the average height of students who attend a large college. Which of the following would be the most appropriate technique to use?

   A. An experiment
   B. An observational study
   C. A census
   D. A sample survey
   E. All would be appropriate for determining the answer.

7. Which of the following statements is false?

   A. Existing situations are used in observational studies.
   B. In an experiment, researchers divide subjects into groups, apply a treatment to one of the groups, and observe differences.
   C. Cause-and-effect relationships are more likely to come from experiments than observational studies.
   D. In observational studies, researchers control group composition.
   E. Observational studies are less likely than experiments to cause disruption in a subject's routine.

8. Which of the following statements are true about the process of dividing groups in an experiment?

   I. A researcher divides the subjects into two groups so that the subjects do not know which group they are in.
   II. A researcher divides the subjects into two groups so that the subjects do know which group they are in.
   III. The subjects request which group they want to be in, but the researcher's decision is final.

   A. I only
   B. II only
   C. III only
   D. I and III
   E. II and III

9. As a researcher, you are interested in the effectiveness of traffic school for those people who get tickets for running red lights. You are interested to see whether traffic school is more effective for females than males. You divide traffic school attendees into two groups, males and females, and observe their driving records for the next 3 years. This situation can best be described as which of the following?

   A. A census
   B. An experiment
   C. An observational study
   D. A sample survey
   E. A double-blind study

10. As a researcher, you are interested to see whether stretching exercises coupled with diet is a more effective weight loss program than diet alone. You randomly select a group of 100 women and 100 men. You give the men the diet without the stretching routines. You give the women the diet with the stretching routines. You monitor their progress for 2 months. Which of the following would best describe this study.

   A. Flawed observational study
   B. Flawed experiment
   C. Controlled observational study
   D. Controlled experiment
   E. Blind study

11. A teacher is interested to see whether grading homework has an effect on test results. She randomly divides each of her classes into two groups. She grades the homework from one of the groups and simply checks off the homework for the other group. The test scores from each of the two groups were similar. Which of the following study designs was used?

   A. An experiment
   B. An observational study
   C. A random study
   D. A survey since the results were similar
   E. A placebo

12. You want to assess the ice cream flavor preferences of students at your school. You decide to randomly select 100 female juniors and administer a questionnaire. Which of the following statements are true?

   I. By choosing only female juniors, you will have a limited experiment.
   II. By choosing only female juniors, your sample is flawed, and the results of the study are suspect.
   III. By choosing only female juniors, you have created a limited observational study.

   A. I only
   B. III only
   C. I and II
   D. II and III
   E. None of the preceding is a true statement.

Multiple Choice Answers

1. **E.** The purpose of a double-blind experiment is not to influence the subjects of the experiment. If subjects know which group they are in, their expectation of success or failure will cause poor results. Researchers can also react differently if they know which group is which. More reliable studies result when a double-blind style is used.

2. **E.** In observational studies, no interaction occurs between subject and researcher. In experiments, test subjects should not know which group they are in because of expectation of results. Experiments are more useful in determining cause-and-effect relationships. Researchers might not know which group is the control group, as in double-blind studies. The correct choice is E; sample surveys are examples of observational studies.

3. **C.** The first two choices are examples of experiments since the researcher is applying a treatment. Only the third choice is an observational study since no treatment was applied; only observations were made.

4. **D.** Cause-and-effect relationships may be drawn from well-designed experiments, thus choice I is false and III is true. Choice II is also true. Although cause-and-effect relationships come more often from experiments, under certain rare occasions, cause-and-effect relationships can be drawn from observational studies.

5. **A.** A treatment was applied to the two groups in the first study, making it an experiment. No treatment was applied in the second study. Cause and effect is more likely to come from the first study, an experiment.

6. **D.** No treatment is necessary. It is not realistic to measure every student who attends the college; thus, a census would not be appropriate. Therefore, a random sample should be used. Thus, a sample survey is most appropriate in this case.

7. **D.** Observational studies obtain data from existing situations. Researchers do not form control groups in observational studies. All other choices are true statements.

8. **A.** In experimental design, subjects do not have input as to the group they want to be in. Usually they do not even know there are groups. Indicating preference could have an effect on expectations for success, or failure, and alter results.

9. **C.** As a researcher, you are not applying any special treatment to either group. Group membership is not random. As a researcher, you are simply observing whether male or female attendees have better driving records.

10. **B.** Since a separate treatment is used for each of the two groups, this is an experiment. Since men were not given the stretching exercises, no comparison can be make. The flaw in the experiment results from not dividing each group, men and women, into two subgroups. Give half the men and half the women the exercises along with diet and the other half of the men and half of the women the diet alone. This would be a better experimental design.

11. **A.** This is an experiment. She randomly divided the classes and applied a different treatment to each group. Subjects in each group were treated differently, although the results were similar. This does not indicate a flawed design, just no differences were observed.

12. **D.** No special treatment is applied and, therefore, this is not an experiment. Since juniors may have different preferences than the student body at large, choice II is true. What the study does produce are the preferences of female juniors. This observational study is limited to female juniors.

Sampling and Experimentation: Planning and Conducting Surveys

What is the goal of a statistical study? The object is usually to make generalized statements about a population using data from a sample drawn from the population. Although controlled experiments are used to obtain information about a given population, data usually is gathered through simple observation. The choice of the sample is critical in order to obtain a representative set of data from the population. For example, if the goal of the study is to find the average price of products sold in a supermarket, it would not be a good idea to use a sample of meat products for our study. This would yield a higher than average price. If the goal of the study is to find the average cost of a camera, it would not be appropriate to only use models found in a drug store. These models would have average prices well below those found in camera stores. Obtaining samples that truly represent the population in question is essential.

The first several chapters of this book discussed **descriptive statistics**—that is, techniques to describe and document data. Subsequent chapters will discuss **inferential statistics.** Inferences made about a population using data samples drawn from the population are meaningless if the data samples do not accurately reflect the population. This chapter discusses techniques of collecting sample data that increase the probability that the sample data accurately represents the population.

Characteristics of a Well-Designed and Well-Conducted Survey

Data selection techniques involve probability and chance. Random selection does not guarantee that the sample data will be representative of the population.

EXAMPLE:
A political poll needs to be conducted. People are selected at random as they exit a movie theater, and they are questioned about an upcoming bond issue. Would this sampling technique produce a representative sample of the population that will vote on the bond issue?

No. Different segments of the population may have different views of a bond issue. Older citizens might not be represented in the sample if the movie was of interest to young adults. Therefore, older citizens' views about the bond issue would not be represented in the sample. Although valid sampling techniques may be used, the entire population was not available for selection. Also, some people might not be willing to stop and answer questions. Some people might not know about the bond issue and might not have formed opinions at the time of the survey.

Populations, Samples, and Random Selection

The best way to determine information about a population is to conduct a **census.** This would provide accurate results since all members of the population are considered. In most cases, populations are very large, and it is not practical or possible to conduct a census. A sample from the population must be used to find estimates of population parameters. Samples do not have to be large in order to accurately represent a population. A sample of less than 100 could be used to estimate the mean weight of a population of fish in a lake. A sample of 1200 could be used to estimate the likelihood that a state ballot proposition would pass in an upcoming election. These samples must accurately represent their populations. The objective of sampling techniques is to produce samples that are free of bias that every possible sample has the same probability of being selected.

Different samples can, and do, produce different estimates of population parameters. After all, they are estimates. These differences are called sampling errors. Sampling errors are expected and are stated in terms of a probability of being within a given amount of the actual population parameter. Errors can be reduced by increasing the sample size.

EXAMPLE:

A large shipment of apples is received at a warehouse. Five different samples are selected to determine the average weight of an apple in the shipment. The average weight of the apples in each sample is determined. Although the sample averages are close in value, they are not the same. Does this mean that the sampling techniques were in error? Does each sample produce a good estimate of the actual average weight of all the apples in the shipment?

The average weight of all the apples in the shipment is not known. Each sample produces an estimate of the average weight. Each sample estimate could be valid, even though they are different. If good sampling techniques were used to make each selection, each sample is valid, and some variation in the results is expected. It is critical that each sample be representative of the entire population of apples.

Sources of Bias in Surveys

Bias occurs in surveys when one outcome is favored over another. Bias can be intentional or unintentional. Most bias occurs because the sampling process did not produce representative samples.

Undercoverage Bias

This type of bias occurs when part of the population is excluded from the sampling process.

EXAMPLE:
A survey of college students to determine their feelings about a building expansion is taken at lunchtime in the cafeteria. This survey shows undercoverage bias since it excludes evening students. A survey is taken of motorists at a gas station asking them whether they favor rent control. This survey shows undercoverage bias since it does not include people who do not have cars and use public transportation. These excluded people might be mostly renters and have a very different opinion than home owners.

Voluntary Response Bias

This type of bias occurs when the sample is self-selected. People with strong opinions are more likely to want to participate. When people offer to be included in a survey, their opinions are not usually representative of the population.

EXAMPLE:
The city council wants to determine the opinion of residents about installing speed bumps on a particular street. A questionnaire is sent out to all residents in the neighborhood. Only a small percentage of the questionnaires are returned, and most of those do not want the speed bumps. This is an example of voluntary response bias. The small response probably included those people most interested in the speed bumps, either because they use the street where the bumps are to be installed, or they live on the street. Their strong opinions will produce biased results.

Nonresponse Bias

This type of bias occurs when people chosen for a survey refuse to respond or are unable to respond.

EXAMPLE:
A several page questionnaire is sent out by a car dealership seeking information about your satisfaction with the new car you recently purchased. Although you like the car, you don't want to take the time to fill out the lengthy questionnaire. This represents a nonresponse bias. Someone who is dissatisfied with their new car might be more likely to fill out the long questionnaire. This could also lead to voluntary response bias.

Wording Bias

The way a question is worded can influence the results. If the question is stated in a way to emphasize the positive aspects of the situation, it is more likely to result in a favorable response. If the question is stated with a negative emphasis, an unfavorable response might be more likely.

EXAMPLE:
Opinions about a local tax to help schools build new gymnasiums is the subject of a survey. A positive response is more likely if the question focuses on "helping young people stay in school by encouraging participation in after school athletics" than if the question focuses on "the tax will cost property owners $320 in additional taxes each year."

EXAMPLE:
A prescription drug manufacturer is more likely to get a favorable response from a survey if it emphasizes the benefits of taking a new medication for diabetes than if it emphasizes the side effects. (Notice that in commercials on television about prescription drugs, most of the time is spent talking about the positive aspects, and the last few seconds relate the negative side effects.) The wording of a question can produce an intentional or unintentional wording bias.

Response Bias

Response bias occurs in several situations. If an oral interview is conducted or if the questionnaire is not anonymous, the respondent may want to please the interviewer rather than give their true opinion. If questions are of a personal nature, respondents might not tell the truth. If a question is phrased in a way that makes it difficult to understand, the respondent might be embarrassed that they do not understand and give a false answer.

EXAMPLE:
A teacher wants to determine whether he presented the material in a chapter in a way that students enjoyed. He asks the students in his class to choose a number from 1 (bad) to 5 (good) that represent their opinions of his teaching style. He asks them to write the number at the top of their chapter test. Would this technique produce biased results?

Students usually want to please their teacher, especially while he is grading their test. Students are more likely to give favorable replies if their responses are not anonymous.

Selection Bias

If a sample is chosen simply because it is easy to obtain, it is known as a **convenience sample.** If you want to choose five students in your class and you choose the five that sit closest to you, you have obtained a convenience sample. Convenience samples might or might not produce biased results. If the convenience aspects of the sample are related in any way to the survey, then bias has occurred.

If a survey about child care is taken on a popular website, several types of bias can occur. First, only people who visit the website, and, therefore have or use computers, are included in the survey. Not all visitors to the website might choose to participate. Only those with a particular interest in the question being surveyed would have a tendency to answer. The type of website could have a lot to do with the responses. The survey on a financial website would probably produce different results than the survey on a marriage and counseling website.

Unintentional Bias

It is difficult for a person to choose survey subjects randomly. If you ask someone to choose five random digits chosen from the digits 0 through 9, they are very likely to choose five different digits. Although they think they are choosing randomly, they are not. After choosing the first random digit, they mentally eliminate that digit when choosing subsequent digits. If the random choice is left to the interviewer, this unintentional bias can occur. If you have ever taken a multiple choice test and for a particular problem you have no clue as to which answer is correct, you can make a random selection. If you think back to see how many of your previous choices were "a" and how many were "b," then you are introducing unintentional bias in your random selection of an answer. The best way to avoid unintentional bias is to use acceptable selection techniques as illustrated in the following sections.

Simple Random Sampling

In a convenience sample, the interviewer is able to choose the respondents. In a voluntary sample, respondents choose to be included in the sample. In either of these two situations, human choice enters into the selection process and, therefore, might produce bias. In order to eliminate this human choice aspect of sample selection, random selection is used to determine sample membership. This technique helps eliminate many of the forms of bias that can invalidate results of a survey. Most of us are familiar with the "draw the names from a hat" technique. An object representing each member of the population is placed in a "hat," and a sample is then "randomly" drawn from the hat.

In a **random sample,** each member of the population is equally likely to be selected for inclusion in the sample. In a **simple random sample,** a sample of a given size is chosen from the population in such a way that every sample of that size has an equal chance of being selected. A distinction exists between the individual member of a population and a sample drawn from the population. In a simple random sample, every possible sample as well as each individual has an equal chance of being selected.

Computer software, as well as calculators with statistical functions, can choose simple random samples from a population.

A simple random sample can be produced easily on the TI-83/4. If you want to produce a simple random sample of 7 integers chosen from the integers from 1 through 10, use the randInt(1, 10, 7) function located under the MATH and PRB menus. (Note that duplicates might appear. If duplicates appear, additional integers can be selected until a simple random sample has been created.)

Random digit tables are also used to produce simple random samples. A table of random digits is a string of the digits 0, 1, 2, 3, 4, 5, 6, 7, 8, and 9 chosen so that each entry in the table is equally likely to be any one of the digits. Each pair of digits in the table is equally likely to be a two-digit number from 00 to 99. Each trio of digits in the table is equally likely to be a three-digit number from 000 to 999. These random digit tables are long strings of digits arranged in rows and columns to make them easier for people to read. The fact that all combinations of digits are equally likely to occur enables us to use these tables to produce simple random samples.

EXAMPLE:

Suppose that you are a car dealer and have 150 cars on your used car lot. You want to choose three of these cars to put on sale and advertise to the public. You want to choose a simple random sample of three cars using a random digit table.

Number the cars from 1 to 150. Randomly choose a starting location in the table of random digits. The lines in the table you have chosen contain the following digits:

| 36146 | 15570 | 28593 | 42089 | 99282 | 59640 | 15323 | 97054 | 09916 | 05321 |
| 21549 | 18432 | 13720 | 02218 | 02789 | 81003 | 49092 | 79044 | 50912 | 08388 |

Since your car numbers range from 1 through 150, choose 3-digit numbers starting at the beginning of the first row. Use only those numbers in the range from 1 through 150. The first 3-digit number is 361. This is out of the range, so it is skipped. The next 3-digit number is 461. This, too, is out of the range and is not used. So is 557. The next 3-digit number, 028, is in the proper range, so the first car to be put on sale is car number 28. The next usable number is 053, near the end of the first row. The third car number would be 137. Therefore, car #28, car #53, and car #137 would be put on sale.

Stratified Random Sampling

Dividing the population into groups and then randomly selecting members from all groups is a technique that helps to produce an unbiased sample. A **systematic random sample** results when members of a population are put in some order and then every 10th, 100th, 1000th, or other interval is chosen. For example, if 20 people need to be selected from 200 seated in a theater, divide the population into 20 groups of 10 each. Choose a random individual from the first 10, for example, person number 4. Then choose every 10th person—that is, number 14, number 24, number 34, and so on. Although systematic random sampling helps reduce bias, it does not produce a simple random sample since each possible sample of size 20 does not have an equal chance of being selected. For example, using the preceding illustration, it is not possible to choose person number 4 and person number 8 in the same sample.

To produce a stratified random sample, divide the population into groups of similar individuals, called strata. For each stratum, choose a simple random sample and then combine these into one large sample. For example, if 20 students are to be chosen from a school's population consisting of 25% freshmen, 30% sophomores, 20% juniors, and 25% seniors, divide the school population into these four strata. Since 25% of 20 is 5, choose a simple random sample of size 5 from the freshman. Choose a simple random sample of size 6 from the sophomores. Choose a simple random sample of size 4 from the juniors. Choose a simple random sample of size 5 from the seniors. Combine these 20 students to make your overall random sample.

Multistage sampling is another technique to obtain samples that truly are representative of the population. This technique involved dividing the population into groups. Each group then is divided into subgroups. A random selection is made of these subgroups. Then simple random samples are taken from each chosen subgroup. Multistage sampling is very common in national surveys.

EXAMPLE:
Your school's student population is made up of 55% democrats, 35% republicans, and 10% other. You want to select 100 students who will be asked questions about political concerns. How would you construct a stratified random sample for this purpose?

Divide the sample of 100 in the same proportion as the entire student population. Out of the 100 in the sample, 55% should be democrats, 35% should be republicans, and 10% should be other. Thus, use simple random samples to select 55 of the democrats, 35 of the republicans, and 10 of the other. Combine to give your sample of 100 students.

EXAMPLE:
Given the information from the preceding example, how would you refine the selection process if you knew that approximately 60% of each political affiliation were female and 40% were male?

Subdivide each political affiliation group into two subgroups, female and male, resulting in six subgroups: female democrats (33%), male democrats (22%), female republicans (21%), male republicans (14%), female other (6%), and male other (4%). Use simple random samples to choose 33 of the female democrats, 22 of the male democrats, 21 of the female republicans, 14 of the male republicans, 6 of the female other, and 4 of the male other. Combine to create your sample of 100 students.

Review Questions and Answers

Multiple Choice Questions

Directions: Solve each of the following problems. Decide which is the best of the choices given.

1. A researcher wants to interview 10 of the more than 150 people waiting in a long line to buy tickets to a concert. He walks up to the first person in line who is wearing a hat and interviews the next 10 people in line. Which of the following are true statements?

   I.   This is a simple random sample.
   II. This design may result in selection bias.
   III. This design suffers from response bias.

   A. I only
   B. II only
   C. I and III
   D. II and III
   E. I, II, and III

2. When a student newspaper at a local high school took a poll of students at the school, they found that 86% said they drank alcoholic beverages in the past month. When the students were polled by the PTA, only 36% said they drank alcoholic beverages in the past month. What type of bias caused the large difference in results?

    I.   Wording bias
   II. Sampling bias
  III. Response bias

    A. II only
    B. III only
    C. I and II
    D. II and III
    E. I, II, and III

3. A statistics class is made up of 20 female and 16 male students. A committee of 8 students needs to be selected. Each student is given a number from 1 to 36. A random number table is used to repeatedly select two-digit numbers until eight different numbers in the range of 1 to 36 are generated, thus forming a committee of 8 students. After the committee was formed, it was discovered that all 8 of the students were male. One of the female students in the class complained that this could not be random since only male students were selected. Which of the following statements is true?

    A. A sample of size eight is not large enough to produce random results.
    B. The method used did produce a random sample, even though only males were selected.
    C. It is so unlikely to have all eight students be male that it is not a random sample.
    D. Since the results do not reflect the composition of the class, it is not representative; therefore, it is not random.
    E. A random number table cannot be used in this type of selection.

4. A political questionnaire is sent out to all 220,000 residents in a congressional district. Only 15,500 are returned. Of those 15,500 returned questionnaires, only 165 said that the congressman was doing a poor job in representing them. What kind of sample does this represent?

    A. A cluster sample
    B. A systematic sample
    C. A representative sample
    D. A stratified random sample
    E. A self-selected sample

5. Why would one use a stratified random sample instead of a simple random sample?

    A. Because a stratified sample usually produces a more representative sample
    B. Because a smaller sample can be used
    C. Because stratified samples are easier to collect
    D. Because there is less bias in a stratified sample
    E. Because systematic random samples are more random than simple random samples

6. Tom wants to survey customers of a local bank. He stands at the door of the bank and talks to every 50th customer leaving the bank. Which of the following are true?

I.   This is a simple random sample.
II. This is a systematic random sample.
III. This is a stratified random sample.

   A. I only
   B. II only
   C. III only
   D. I and II
   E. I and III

7. Each of the following three designs suffers from a form of bias. Identify the bias for each design.

I.   A school vice principal questions a random selection of students about cheating on tests and techniques they might have used recently.
II. A local radio talk show invites listeners to phone in their opinions on abortion.
III. Readers of a medical journal are taking surveys about issues concerning welfare.

   A. I–response bias, II–voluntary response bias, III–selection bias
   B. I–voluntary response bias, II–undercoverage bias, III–response bias
   C. I–selection bias, II–response bias, III–undercoverage bias
   D. I–response bias, II–voluntary response bias, III–undercoverage bias
   E. I–voluntary response bias, II–response bias, III–undercoverage bias

8. A random number table is to be used to generate five random integers from 1 to 25. Use the following table. Start with the first row and read left to right, then top to bottom. What is the 5th random integer?

32111	74541	74511	25273	19336
42192	40935	52042	95282	87083
28109	10508	97961	95677	98904

   A. 5
   B. 10
   C. 19
   D. 20
   E. 21

9. A survey is taken of students who finished Professor Toohard's math class. They were asked whether they would take the same professor again for a different class. Of the 85 students who responded, 67 said they would not take the professor for another class. Which of the following statements is true?

   A. The size of the survey is not large enough to produce meaningful results.
   B. Choosing a random sample of these 85 responses would improve the reliability of the survey.
   C. Response bias is evident in this survey.
   D. The survey suffers from undercoverage bias since some of the students did not reply.
   E. This is a valid survey, and the results are meaningful.

10. A telephone book is used as a source of addresses. A questionnaire about local housing issues is mailed to 1000 randomly selected households, of which 625 returned the questionnaire. What kind of bias exists in this study?

   I.   Undercoverage bias
  II.   Response bias
 III.   Unintentional bias

  A.   I only
  B.   II only
  C.   I and II
  D.   I and III
  E.   II and III

11. Which of the following samples does not suffer from undercoverage bias?

  A.   A sample of college students drawn from calculus classes
  B.   A survey of 300 respondents to bulk email
  C.   A sample of homeowners drawn from county property tax records
  D.   A sample of doctors taken from membership rosters of the American Medical Association (AMA)
  E.   A survey of motorists at a local traffic school

12. A survey of expectant mothers was taken at the office of an OB-GYN. The survey question was, "Since smoking while pregnant has been shown to increase the risk of birth defects, do you feel that an OB-GYN should advise his patients not to smoke while pregnant?" This survey suffers from which of the following types of bias?

   I.   Wording bias
  II.   Sampling bias
 III.   Response bias

  A.   II only
  B.   III only
  C.   I and II
  D.   II and III
  E.   I, II, and III

13. Jack and Jill have been asked to conduct a survey of the membership of a club in which they are members. Using a systematic sample, they want to survey 5% of the membership. They obtain an alphabetized roster of the club membership. Jill wants to make sure that she is included in the survey. Her name is the 17th one on the list, so they start there and choose every 20th name after that. Which of the following statements are true about this survey?

   I.   An alphabetized roster should not be used.
  II.   This is not a systematic random sample.
 III.   Response bias is guaranteed by including Jill in the survey.

  A.   I only
  B.   III only
  C.   I and II
  D.   II and III
  E.   I, II, and III

14. You have decided to use an online retailer to buy a specific book on organic gardening. On the website are 24 reader reviews for the book you were thinking of buying, and most of the reviewers were not happy with their purchase. Based on these reviews, you decide to choose another book. Which of the following statements are true about these reviews?

    I.   They suffer from undercoverage bias.
   II. They suffer from response bias.
  III. They suffer from selection bias.

    A.   I and II
    B.   I and III
    C.   II and III
    D.   I, II, and III
    E.   There is no bias since the reviews were voluntary.

Multiple Choice Answers

1. **D.** This is not a simple random sample because each possible sample of size 10 does not have an equal chance of being selected. The researcher has used a convenience sample. This might result in selection bias since people standing next to each other might be friends and, therefore, think alike and share the same opinions. This design also suffers from response bias because people might not be truthful in their responses if their friends are listening.

2. **B.** The wording of the question and the way the students were selected are not at issue in this problem. As students are influenced by peer pressure, they would overstate their response because that is the cool thing to say. Students are more likely to understate their response to adults, especially parents and their friends. Thus, a response bias contributed to the different results.

3. **B.** The fact that a result is rare does not mean the procedure was not random. Sample size has nothing to do with the way the sample was selected. Small sample sizes might not be representative of the population, but the selection procedure is not at fault. A more representative sample should be obtained with a larger sample size.

4. **E.** Random selection was not used in the distribution of the questionnaires since everyone in the district received one. Only some returned the questionnaire; their doing so makes it a voluntary self-selected sample. This type of survey also suffers from nonresponse bias since only those with strong feelings will respond.

5. **A.** If a sample is small, the chance of producing one that is nonrepresentative is higher with a simple random sample than with a stratified random sample. The ease of collection is about the same for these two types of samples. Convenience samples may be easier to collect but are not simple random samples or stratified samples. Systematic random samples are not more random than simple random samples since only the selection in the first stratum is random. The desire for a smaller sample size is not a good reason to choose a stratified random sample.

6. **B.** This represents a systematic random sample. The selection is random, and subsequent selections are at fixed intervals, essentially dividing the population into strata. In stratified random samples and simple random samples, the interval between selections is not fixed.

7. **D.** The first design suffers from response bias. Students are not likely to tell the truth when being asked questions by the vice principal of the school. They don't want to get into trouble. They might be embarrassed or scared to tell the truth. The second design suffers from voluntary response bias. Listeners who call in to talk shows have strong opinions about certain topics, especially abortion, welfare, taxes, and religion, and do not necessarily share the views of the general population. The third design suffers from undercoverage bias. Readers of medical journals are usually highly educated and might not share the views of the entire population when it comes to welfare.

8. **E.** Select two-digit numbers starting with the first two digits on the first row. Skip those that are out of the appropriate range. Continue across the first row and then on to the second row. Continue until the required sample size is obtained. In this case, the first acceptable number is 11, the second is 17, the third is 12, the fourth is 19, and the fifth is 21.

9. **C.** Response bias is evident in this survey. Students with strong opinions are more likely to respond. Randomizing selection of the respondents will not help since the responses are biased. All students were included in the survey, so undercoverage bias is not an issue. Small sample sizes can produce meaningful results in a well-designed and well-conducted survey.

10. **C.** Undercoverage bias exists since many people have unlisted numbers and do not appear in the telephone book. These people might have opinions that differ from the population as a whole since they are more concerned with privacy. Response bias exists since respondents determine whether they are included in the study. No unintentional bias exists since the sample was randomly selected.

11. **C.** Since all homeowners are on the property tax rolls, this choice does not suffer from undercoverage. All other choices are restrictive and do not include the entire population during sample selection.

12. **E.** This survey suffers from all three of these forms of bias. First, wording bias is evident; the wording of the question almost forces a positive response. Second, sampling bias exists; only expectant mothers are included in the survey. Third, response bias exists; what expectant mother would tell her doctor she does not want to be told how to reduce the risk of birth defects.

13. **D.** When using a systematic sample, an alphabetized list is not necessary. Although this is a systematic sample, it is not a systematic *random* sample. The intentional inclusion of Jill not only removes the random start point in the first strata, it also introduces response bias.

14. **A.** Not all of the readers visit the website and read the reviews; thus, undercoverage bias exists. Readers with strong feelings are more likely to respond and write a review; thus, response bias exists. Since all readers who visit the website have an opportunity to write a review, no selection bias exists.

Free-Response Questions

Directions: Show all work. Indicate clearly the methods you use. You will be graded on method as well as accuracy.

1. To determine the opinions of teenagers about abortion, a survey is to be taken. Write questions that involve wording bias. Phrase one question to favor abortion and the other to oppose it. Both questions should ask for an opinion about abortion.

2. Explain why systematic random samples are, or are not, simple random samples.

3. You want to use a random number table to simulate the rolling of a fair die. You want to roll the die 10 times. Construct two different procedures to carry out this process and use the following random number table to demonstrate them.

32111	74541	74511	25273	19336
42192	40935	52042	95282	87083
28109	10508	97961	95677	98904
32949	63434	28963	10330	54554

4. A club membership consists of 40 women and 50 men. You want to select 4 women and 5 men to serve on a committee. Construct a procedure to obtain a systematic random sample and a procedure to obtain a stratified random sample.

5. Explain why a convenience sample of people at a party would, or would not, be an appropriate sample for a survey about alcohol abuse.

6. You randomly select 2000 names from the subscription list of a magazine designed for hunters. You mail a questionnaire about gun control to these readers and receive 800 responses. You randomly select 300 of the 800 responses for inclusion in your study. What forms of bias are evident in this design?

Free-Response Answers

1. Wording bias can easily change the outcome of a survey. Care should be taken to avoid wording that influences the way people respond.

   Here is a question written to favor abortion:

   A woman should not be forced to continue a pregnancy if it can be determined that the baby suffers from birth defects. Do you favor a woman's right to have an abortion?

   Here is a question written to oppose abortion:

   A woman should not be allowed to kill an unborn child because all life is sacred and pregnancies should be continued until birth. Do you favor a woman's right to have an abortion?

2. Systematic random samples are not simple random samples. In a simple random sample, all possible samples of size n must have the same chance of being selected. Systematic random sample members are drawn from strata. This process eliminates many possible n-sized samples from being selected. Although systematic random samples might be more representative of the population, they are not simple random samples.

3. One sampling design to yield 10 integers in the range of 1 to 6 is to create a systematic sample. Consider each group of 5 to be a stratum. Begin at a random location in the first stratum—for example, the second digit, which is the number 2. Move to the second stratum and select the second digit, which is the number 4. Continue until 10 numbers are selected. If the number is larger than 6 or less than 1, skip it. The 10 numbers obtained using this technique are 2, 4, 4, 5, 2, 2, 5, 5, 2, and 3.

32111	74541	74511	25273	19336
42192	40935	52042	95282	87083
28109	10508	97961	95677	98904
32949	63434	28963	10330	54554

   A second sampling design to yield 10 integers in the range of 1 to 6 is to use a convenience sample. Find a random starting location. One technique might be to use the first 2 digits in the table to determine how many digits to skip before beginning the convenience sample. In this case, it is the number 32. If you skip 32 digits, reading left to right, top to bottom, you would start with the 9 in the second row, second group. Using that as a starting point, record the first 10 digits that are in the range of 1 to 6. The digits would be 3, 5, 5, 2, 4, 2, 5, 2, 2, and 3.

4. The first sampling design is to use a systematic sample. Consider the 40 women. Create a list of their names. Divide the list into 4 groups of 10 names each. Choose a random starting location in the first group—for example, the third name. Select that name. Select the third name in each of the other three groups. These are the names of the four women who will serve on the committee. Now consider the 50 men. Create a list of their names. Divide the list into 5 groups of 10 names each. Choose a random starting location in the first group—for example, the third name. Select that name. Select the third name in each of the other four groups. These are the names of the five men who will serve on the committee.

   The second sampling design is to use a stratified random sample. Consider the 40 women. Create a list of their names. Divide the list into 4 groups of 10 names each. Choose a random name in the first group. Select that name. Choose a random name in the second group. Select that name. Continue the process for each of the remaining two groups. The four selected names are the names of the women who will serve on the committee. Consider the 50 men. Create a list of their names. Divide the list into 5 groups of 10 names each. Choose a random name in the first group. Select that name. Choose a random name in the second group. Select that name. Continue the process for each of the remaining three groups. The five selected names are the names of the men who will serve on the committee.

5. Convenience samples might lead to several kinds of bias. Asking people at a party where alcohol is being consumed about alcohol abuse would probably create a biased sample in and of itself. A convenience sample probably would compound the bias. Friends who might be standing near each other might share the same views about many issues, including alcohol abuse. Using a convenience sample in this situation would not be a good idea and probably would result in a biased sample.

6. Several forms of bias exist in this design including undercoverage bias, response bias, and nonresponse bias. Readers of a hunting magazine would probably share positive views about gun ownership. This group of readers is not a representative sample of the general public when it comes to gun control. Therefore, undercoverage bias is suggested. Since this group of readers probably have strong views about gun control, they might answer more often than the general public, therefore, exhibiting nonresponse bias. There is also an expectation among hunters that gun control is not a good idea. This expectation might lead to a response bias not found in the general population. In order to try to avoid this form of bias, a magazine covering a topic unrelated to guns might be more appropriate for a subscription list.

You can collect meaningful data in many ways. Statisticians use vocabulary that might sound similar but might have very different meanings. The meaning of common terminology is often confused. Use statistical vocabulary with care.

The two general types of statistical studies are **observational studies,** as discussed in the previous chapter, and **experiments.** When using an observational study, a researcher makes observation of the participants or subjects in the study. The researcher does not ask the subjects to change their behavior or try to control them in any way. The researcher simply observes and records those observations. The researcher then uses the data obtained from observing the sample to say something about the population from which the sample was drawn. In experiments, researchers have control over something, and they then try to measure the effect of what they are trying to control. A study actually becomes an experiment if the researchers do something to or for the subjects and observe the response.

Characteristics of a Well-Designed and Well-Conducted Experiment

When conducting observational studies, you must take care to limit bias. When conducting experiments, you must make sure that the response being measured is really caused by what the researcher is controlling. A well-designed experiment isolates that which is being studied through proper randomization techniques. Depending on the circumstances, researchers might choose between observational studies and experiments to collect their data. Many times, one method is preferred over the other. Sometimes, experiments are not possible.

EXAMPLE:
Consider the task a researcher might have to compare the effectiveness of two different diets. The researcher could survey a sample of people using diet number one and another sample of people using diet number two. The researchers could collect data from each sample concerning participants' starting weight, ending weight, and length of time on the respective diet. Comparisons then could be made and conclusions drawn from the data.

The drawback to this study is that there might be some unmeasured factors that will affect one set of dieters more than the other. Possibly one of the diets tries to control sugar intake more than the other diet. Therefore, more subjects who are diabetic might use the sugar restrictive diet than the other diet. Diabetics might have an easier, or harder, time losing weight on any diet, thus invalidating the results.

Proper experimental design could help eliminate this problem. Subjects who want to go on a diet could be randomly assigned to one of the two diets. By appropriate randomization techniques, the fact that some dieters are diabetic would not affect one diet more than the other; thus, this variable could be controlled.

EXAMPLE:
Suppose that a researcher is asked to determine whether more traffic accidents are caused by people who drink beer or people who drink wine. It would be difficult, if not illegal, to construct an experiment in which you ask some of your subjects to drink wine and some subjects to drink beer and then send them out driving so that you could tabulate the number of accidents they cause. In this case, as observational study would be more appropriate. Data about the type of alcohol consumed by drivers who caused accidents while driving under the influence of alcohol could be collected and analyzed.

Treatments, Control Groups, and Experimental Units

Researchers use different terms to describe the subjects of an experiment. The most common term is **experimental unit,** which represents a single entity. It can be a person, an animal, or a thing. When experimental units are people, the term subject or participant is usually used. The specific experimental condition that is being applied to these experimental units is called the treatment. Experimental units are divided into groups. Groups that receive the treatment are called **treatment groups.** Researchers create **control groups,** which are treated identically to all other groups with the exception that they do not receive the actual treatment.

EXAMPLE:
A researcher wants to determine whether listing the calorie content of desserts on the menu would influence a diner's dessert selection. Half of the parties (the treatment group) dining at an upscale restaurant are given menus with the dessert calorie content listed. Half of the parties (the control group) are given traditional menus. Appropriate random selection is used to determine which parties (experimental units) go into each group. By using good experimental design, other variables, such as the type of dinner ordered, can be controlled so that they do not affect one group more than the other group.

Random Assignments and Replication

Good experimental designs control variables that might have an influence on the outcome of the experiment. Good control is essential to be sure that any differences between the control group and the treatment group are caused only by the treatment variable and not any other variable. **Explanatory variables** explain or cause differences in the **response variable.** Two techniques to help control explanatory variables that are not treatment variables are random assignment and **replication.** Randomization is used to help balance groups so that the effect of these lurking variables is minimized. Random selection is used to determine which group, treatment, or control an experimental unit is placed in. Some individual experimental units are affected more by these lurking variables than others. By using random selection techniques, the overall groups can be balanced with respect to all variables except the treatment variable. Even with randomized selection, variation can occur. By using replication and repeating the experiment with as many experimental units as possible, these variations can be minimized.

EXAMPLE:
A teacher wants to determine whether a particular teaching approach will help improve student learning. The amount of previous knowledge a student has about a topic would be considered a lurking variable when using testing as a method to determine effectiveness. Replication could be used to balance these differences.

Researchers randomize with respect to *treatment type* and with respect to *treatment order*. If one treatment is being tested, then the experimental units need to be placed in either the treatment group or the control group.

The experimenter cannot be allowed to personally choose in which group to place each experimental unit. Some experimenters feel that if they equally divide experimental units with respect to as many lurking variables as possible and place half in the treatment group and half in the control group that they have done a good job of balancing. Good experimental design requires that random techniques, not experimenter choice, be used to determine the assignment of groups. The use of random number tables or statistical calculators with random number generators are the preferred way of choosing which experimental units get assigned to each group. If all subjects of an experiment are to receive all treatments, then the order of the treatments should be determined by randomization. If each subject in an experiment is to determine their preference for five different flavors of herbal tea, the order of tasting of the teas must be randomized.

Sources of Bias and Confounding, Including Placebo Effect and Blinding

When the response in an experiment is due to variables in addition to the treatment variable and the effect of these variables cannot be separated from the effect of the treatment variable, then these variables are referred to as **confounding variables.** That is, a confounding variable is a variable that has an effect on the response variable and is also related in some way to the explanatory (treatment) variable. The main problem with confounding variables is that they might have more of an effect that the treatment variable. A **lurking variable** looks like a confounding variable—that is, it could have an effect on the results of the experiment, but is not measured or used in the experiment. Proper randomization of experimental units should minimize or eliminate the effect of lurking variables. Proper experimental design helps control the effects of confounding variables. It is harder to control these variables in observational studies.

EXAMPLE:

A company that specializes in helping students prepare for the ACT advertises that, "If you took the ACT once and you did not like your score, take our course, and your score will improve." If you want to conduct an experiment to test this claim, you must be careful of a confounding variable. Suppose a student takes the ACT, does poorly, takes the preparation course this company is offering, repeats the test, and the score improves. Remove the confounding variable. Is the increase in score due to the preparation course or just the fact that these people have taken the test before? An increased comfort level with taking the test might contribute to an increased score. The experiment could be structured to control for this confounding variable.

Many statistical studies involve testing the effectiveness of drugs. A **placebo** looks identical to the actual drug but contains no active ingredient and so has no real physical effect. Humans want to be helped by the medication that is administered to them. If they think they are receiving a drug to help their condition, they tend to improve even if it turns out that the drug is a placebo. This is called the **placebo effect.** Since patients tend to respond to any treatment administered by their doctors, even a placebo, researchers must design experiments to control the placebo effect. Researchers randomly divide the patients into two groups. One of the groups receives the real medication and is referred to as the treatment group. The other group receives the placebo and is referred to as the control group. The patients are not told into which group they have been placed so they will not be influenced by their group association.

The two main sets of participants in experiments are the subjects, or experimental units, and the researchers. Well-designed experiments are **double-blind.** In a double-blind experiment, neither the subjects nor the researchers know to which group, treatment, or control, subjects have been assigned. If a researcher knows that a subject is in the control group, they do not expect a treatment effect, and their measurement of a response might be understated. If a researcher knows that a subject is in the treatment group, they might overstate a response simply because they expect it. An experiment might also be single-blind. In this case, only one of the participants, either the subjects or the researchers, knows to which group the subjects have been assigned.

Completely Randomized Design

If all the experimental units (subjects of the experiment) are randomly assigned to either the control group or to the treatment group, then the experiment has a **completely randomized design.** The following diagram illustrates a completely randomized design with one treatment group and one control group.

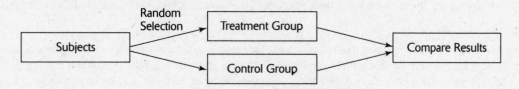

If the experiment involves more than one treatment group—for example, three treatment groups—the diagram may be modified as follows:

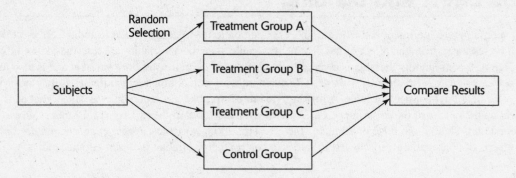

It is important to remember that the control group, receiving no treatment or a placebo that looks like a treatment, is actually a treatment group.

EXAMPLE:

A study is being conducted to compare the effectiveness of three medications to reduce cholesterol levels in adults. Five hundred subjects have volunteered to participate in this study. Design a double-blind, completely randomized experiment for testing the effectiveness of these three medications.

First, you must decide whether to include a control group in which volunteers will be given a placebo instead of one of the three medications being tested. If only one medication was being tested, a placebo-based control group would be necessary in order to be able to make a comparison. In this case, you could compare the effectiveness of the three medications to each other without a control group. We will choose to include a placebo-based control group. Medical personnel will be in contact with the subjects to run blood tests to monitor their progress. To be a double-blind experiment, both the subjects and the medical personnel must not know into which group the subjects have been placed.

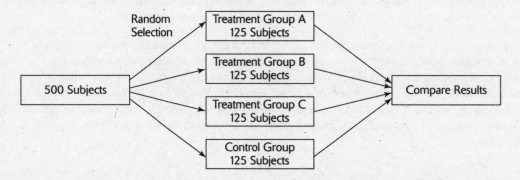

Randomized Block Design, Including Matched Pairs Design

Completely randomized designs work well when variability among experimental units is unknown or minimal. If known variability exists among the subjects of the experiment and the effect of these variables cannot be separated from the treatment variables, then these variables are known as confounding variables. **Blocks** should be used to isolate these sources of variability among the subjects when these confounding characteristics can be identified for each subject.

EXAMPLE:

The experimental design in the preceding example does not take into account any known variability among the subjects. If, for example, it is known that the medications are more effective in men, then gender becomes a confounding variable and can be controlled for with the use of **blocking** since the gender of each subject can be determined. Men and women subjects are separated into two blocks, and a completely randomized design is used for each block. If the 500 subjects consisted of 300 men and 200 women, the following block design might be appropriate:

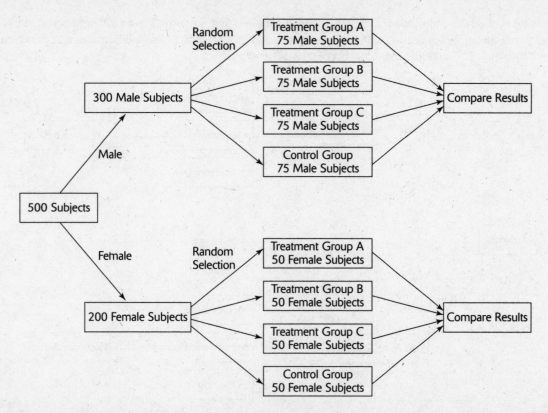

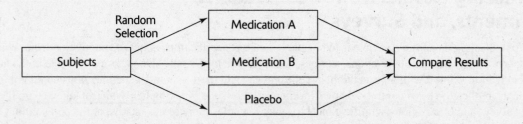

If an experimental design uses closely matched pairs of subjects, uses the same subject for each of two treatments, or uses each subject in a before-and-after experiment, it is called a **matched pairs** design. When the design applies two treatments to each subject, the *order* of the treatments must be randomized. In this type of matched pairs design, it is extremely important that a double-blind randomized assignment be used.

EXAMPLE:

A golf club manufacturer has designed a new style of golf club that it claims will help golfers hit the ball farther. Fifty golfers are randomly selected, and the hitting distance is determined for each with several types of clubs. Then the golfers are each given a set of the new clubs, and they are asked to practice with them for six months. After the practice period, their hitting distances are again determined. A comparison is made for each golfer between their hitting distance before receiving the new clubs and after practicing with them for six months. This design is a match pairs design since before and after distances are paired for each golfer.

EXAMPLE:

Two different pain medications are to be tested to determine their effectiveness. Each medication uses a different mechanism for blocking pain, and the two medications do not affect each other's effectiveness. Compare three different experimental designs for testing these medications.

For the first method use a completely randomized design. In this design, no control exists for known differences in the subjects. Randomization is used to control unknown differences.

For the second method use a block design. In this design, blocks are used to control known differences that can be separated from the treatment. When dealing with human subjects, gender and age are classic differences that can be controlled with blocking. This example uses blocking to control for gender.

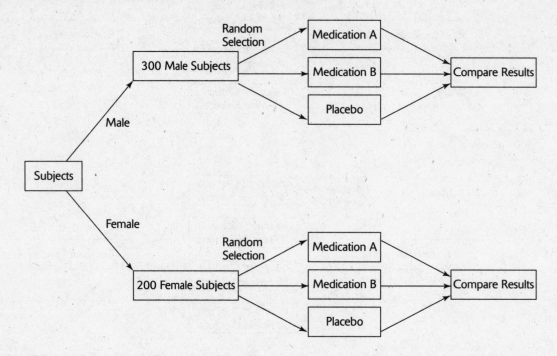

For the third method use a matched pairs design. Matched pairs is a type of block design. In this case, each subject will be given each medication separated by a period of time so as not to confuse effectiveness. The order that the two medications are administered for each subject is randomly selected. This design also uses blocking to control for gender, and each subject receives both treatments in a random order.

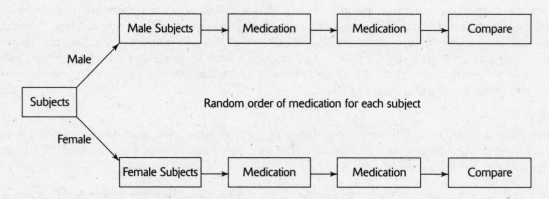

Generalizing Results from Observations, Experiments, and Surveys

The intent of collecting data from a sample is to be able to make generalizations about the population from which the sample is taken. This is true for observations, surveys, and experiments. Sample size plays a direct role in the accuracy of the generalization. Almost without exception, larger samples yield more accurate generalizations about populations. In experiments, replication helps control unknown lurking variables, and blocking helps control known variables in the sample. In surveys and observations, stratification helps make samples more representative of the population. Clearly specialized samples should be avoided no matter what method of data collection is used.

Review Questions and Answers

Multiple Choice Questions

Directions: Solve each of the following problems. Decide which is the best of the choices given.

1. You are designing an experiment to test the effectiveness of two new medications. You randomly assign 240 subjects to one of three groups. One of the groups is given a placebo, and the other two groups each receive one of the two new medications. Neither the subjects nor the researchers know into which group each subject is placed. This represents what kind of experimental design?

   A. A double-blind three block design
   B. A double-blind matched pairs with control group design
   C. A block design with randomization
   D. A completely randomized design
   E. A control block design

2. You are designing an experiment to test the effectiveness of two new medications. You know that males and females respond differently to the medications. You randomly assign the 120 male subjects to one of three groups. One group is given a placebo, and the other two groups each receive one of the two medications. You randomly assign the 120 female subjects to one of three groups. One group is given a placebo, and the other two groups each receive one of the two medications. Neither the subjects nor the researchers know into which group each subject is placed. This represents what kind of experimental design?

   A. A double-blind three block design
   B. A double-blind matched pairs with control group design
   C. A block design with randomization
   D. A completely randomized design
   E. A control block design

3. The manufacturer of a new toothpaste claims that the new product helps whiten teeth. Sixty subjects were randomly selected and had the whiteness of their teeth measured during an examination. Each subject used the new toothpaste for four months. The whiteness of their teeth was again measured, and the results of the two measurements were compared. Which of the following is true?

   A. This is not an experiment since no control group was used.
   B. This is not an experiment since the study was not blind.
   C. This is an experiment using a matched pair design with each subject acting as their own control.
   D. This is an experiment using a completely randomized design.
   E. This is an observational study using a completely randomized design.

4. Which of the following is the best description of replication?

   A. Asking subjects the same question in different ways
   B. A technique of increasing the number of treatments used in an experiment
   C. A technique of increasing the number of subjects in an experiment to help decrease variation caused by chance
   D. A tendency for subjects to be influenced by knowing what group they are in
   E. A technique of distributing subjects into random groups

5. You are designing an experiment with one treatment and one control group. You are blocking for two different variables, gender (M, F) and blood type (A, B, AB, O). If you want each group to contain 20 subjects, what is the total number of subjects needed for the experiment?

    A. 120
    B. 160
    C. 240
    D. 320
    E. None of the above

6. In the design of experiments, _____ is used to control known variables, and _____ is used to control unknown variables.

    A. Blinding, randomization
    B. Pairing, blocking
    C. Randomization, blocking
    D. Blocking, randomization
    E. Randomization, pairing

7. Before and after experiments, those that use the same subjects for pre-testing and post-testing a treatment, use what type of design?

    A. Double-blind design
    B. Blocking with control design
    C. Completely randomized design
    D. Blocking without control design
    E. Matched pair design

8. Which of the following are true statements?

    I. All blocking techniques involve matched pair design.
    II. When using matched pair design, subjects may be their own control.
    III. In a matched pair design, all subjects may receive the same two treatments but in a random order.

    A. II only
    B. I and II
    C. I and III
    D. II and III
    E. I, II, and III

9. Which of the following represents a tendency for subjects to respond well to any treatment?

    A. Placebo effect
    B. Blocking
    C. Blinding
    D. Matched-pairs
    E. Replication

10. In experimental design, which of the following should be used to deal with unknown variables?

    I. Randomization
   II. Replication
  III. Control

    A. III only
    B. I and II
    C. I and III
    D. II and III
    E. I, II, and III

11. You are designing a study to test the effectiveness of a new medication. Blood type is known to have been a confounding variable in the past, so you divide the subjects by blood type. For each blood type, you randomly assign subjects to either a treatment group or a control group. The subjects do not know to which group they have been assigned. Which of the following describes this experimental design?

    A. Complete randomization, blinding, blocking
    B. Stratification, randomization, blinding
    C. Blocking for control, blinding, randomization
    D. Matched pair, blinding, randomization
    E. Systematic selection, blinding, control for blood type

12. Twelve subjects are given a pre-test. They are then provided with materials to help improve their test scores. Subjects then are given a post-test, and the scores of each subject are compared. Which experimental design does this represent?

    A. Blocking
    B. Double-blind
    C. Matched pairs
    D. Replication
    E. Randomization

13. There are 80 used cars on a lot at a local dealership. Which of the following procedures will yield a simple random sample of 20 of these cars?

    A. Select the 20 cars parked closest to the office.
    B. Write down the license numbers of all 80 cars in a list. Randomly select one of the first four cars on the list. Select every fourth car thereafter from the list.
    C. Write down the license numbers of all 80 cars in a list. Divide the list into 20 groups of four each. Randomly select one car from each group.
    D. Write down the license number of all 80 cars on 3×5 cards, one per card. Shuffle the deck of cards several times. Select the fourth card in the deck. Shuffle the cards again. Select the fourth card in the deck. Repeat until 20 cars have been chosen.
    E. Write down the license numbers of all 80 cars in a list. Divide the list into two groups of 40 each. Randomly select 10 cars from each group.

14. An experiment is being designed to determine the effectiveness of three different cat food supplements. Since data existed for diets without supplements, no control was used in the experiment. The researcher has decided to block for three different species of cat and also for gender. How many groups of cats will be needed for the experiment?

    A. 8
    B. 10
    C. 12
    D. 18
    E. 24

Multiple Choice Answers

1. **D.** No blocking was used in this design. All subjects were randomly assigned to one of the three groups. Matched pairs were not used. This is a completely randomized design.

2. **C.** This design used blocking to group males and females separately. Each block is a completely randomized design. Two blocks are used. Matched pairs are not used in this design.

3. **C.** This is a before-and-after experiment. It is a matched pair design. Confounding variables were not considered in the design of this experiment. It is possible that subjects brushed longer and actually increased the whitening effect of the toothpaste.

4. **C.** In general, increasing the sample size will better control variation caused by chance. Replication is a technique for increasing the sample size through repetition. Increasing the number of treatments does not necessarily increase the number of subjects. Answer choice D refers to the placebo effect, and answer choice E refers to randomization.

5. **D.** Blocking for gender (M, F) and for blood type (A, B, AB, O) results in 8 blocks: M-A, M-B, M-AB, M-O, F-A, F-B, F-AB, and F-O. Each of these 8 blocks uses two groups, a treatment group and a control group. This gives a total of 16 groups. If 20 subjects are to be placed in each of the 16 groups, then a total of 320 subjects are needed.

6. **D.** Blocking is used to control known variables (confounding variables), and randomization is used to control for unknown variables.

7. **E.** Before and after experiments use a matched pair design. Matched pair designs are a form of blocking.

8. **D.** Statement I is false since *some* blocking techniques are matched pair designs. Statement II is true. In before-and-after designs, subjects usually act as their own control. Statement III is true. If all subjects receive the same treatment but in a different random order, a matched pair design was used.

9. **A.** The placebo effect represents the tendency for some subjects to respond to any treatment, even a placebo. Many subjects want to be helped by a treatment, and that influences their response. Randomization and replication are used to minimize the placebo effect.

10. **B.** Control is used to minimize the effects of confounding variables—known to have an effect that interferes with the response of the treatment variable. Blocking is a control design. Replication and randomization minimize variation due to unknown variables.

11. **C.** Blocking is used to control the effects of blood type. Blinding was used since subjects did not know to which group they were assigned. Randomization occurs within each block.

12. **C.** A before-and-after experiment uses a matched pairs design. Although matched pairs is a form of blocking, answer choice C is better than answer choice A. The selection process of the 12 students was not stated.

13. **D.** Placing the license numbers on 3 × 5 cards and shuffling provided a random selection for the cars. Since all remaining cars are available for each selection, the design is that of a simple random sample. The fact that the fourth card is selected does not matter. The first card could also have been chosen. Answer choice A is not correct since that is a convenience sample. Convenience samples are not random. Answer choice B represents a systematic random sample. Answer choices C and E are stratified random samples.

14. **D.** Blocking for three species of cat divides the subjects into three blocks. Blocking also for gender divides each of the three blocks into two blocks, yielding six blocks altogether. Each of these blocks is randomized into three treatment groups, giving a total of 18 treatment groups.

Free-Response Questions

Directions: Show all work. Indicate clearly the methods you use. You will be graded on method as well as accuracy.

1. A researcher randomly selected a group of 200 students who had taken both an algebra class and a statistics class in college. Each of these students was asked which class they liked better. Of the 200 students, 99 said they liked statistics better and 101 students said they liked algebra better. Based on these results, the researcher concluded

that neither class stood out as a favorite. Was this an experiment or an observation study? Was there a possible confounding variable? If so, what might it be?

2. A bar owner offers his customers free nuts, which are in bowls on all of the tables. He has two different types of nuts. The two varieties look and taste the same, but one variety has a much higher potassium content than the other. The bar owner would like to determine whether serving the variety with added potassium, which costs more than the other variety, will get the customers to order more drinks. Design an experiment to test the two nut varieties.

3. Many years ago, some physicians dispensed medication directly to their patients. One dishonest doctor gave out sugar pills instead of real medication to some of his patients to save money. Many of the patients who received these sugar pills actually had their symptoms vanish, and they felt better even without getting the real medication. Explain how this can happen.

4. Twenty-four containers, arranged in four rows of six containers each, are on a counter near a window. The rows are parallel to the window. Twenty-four plants, 8 each of 3 varieties, will be grown to test a new fertilizer. You want to feed half of the plants the new fertilizer (treatment group) and half the old fertilizer (control group). You are concerned that proximity to the window might be a confounding variable. Design a procedure for determining how to select which plants should be placed in each container and which ones receive each treatment.

5. Use a completely randomized design to construct an experiment that studies whether taking a garlic supplement in tablet form can reduce the occurrence of colds during the winter.

6. An experiment to test the effectiveness of four different medications is being designed. Four hundred subjects have volunteered to participate. Construct a procedure to randomly select subjects so that each subject will be assigned to one of the four treatment groups. It is more important that each subject has the same chance of being assigned to each treatment group than it is to have equal-sized treatment groups.

7. As a restaurant owner, you are interested in determining whether people who order a drink before dinner spend more on their meal (excluding the drinks) than people who do not order a drink. Over a period of two weeks, you record data on 320 customers who ordered drinks before their meals and 460 customers who did not order a drink before their meals. After tabulating the results, you find that the drinkers spent considerably more than the non-drinkers. Is this an experiment or an observational study? Explain.

8. Subjects in an experiment have been selected to receive one of two different treatments or a placebo. Two different measurements are periodically taken with respect to each subject, one of which is objective and one is subjective. Discuss why this experiment should be double-blind.

9. A researcher wants to determine whether performance in statistics classes can be influenced by the expectation of success. A statistics teacher will be teaching 15 sections of statistics over a two-year period. He wants to tell the students in some sections that "females perform better in statistics than males." In some other sections he wants to say "males perform better in statistics than females." Design an experiment that uses treatment groups and control groups and blocks for the difference between day and evening sections.

Free-Response Answers

1. This is an observational study since the researcher had no control, and there was no treatment. As for the question of favoring either statistics or algebra, there might be a confounding variable masking some interesting facts. Gender might be a confounding variable. For example, females might favor statistics over algebra by a wide margin, and males might favor algebra over statistics by a wide margin. Blocking for gender and studying each gender separately might yield very different results.

2. The experiment should be run over a several week period to control chance variations in drinking habits on different days of the week or month. Use a random number table, or other technology tool such as the TI-83/4, to choose either even or odd numbers each morning. If the number is even, serve the potassium-fortified nuts that day. If the number is odd, serve the regular nuts that day. Keep track of sales. Compare sales figures after a

several week period. This is a double-blind experiment. The customers who order the drinks do not know they are subjects in an experiment. The staff in the bar does not know that an experiment is in progress and, therefore, will not influence the customers. Blocking was not used. Randomization and replication were used to minimize variation caused by chance.

3. Some patients react favorably from taking a sugar pill or placebo. This is known as the placebo effect. When people think they are receiving a real treatment, some react as though the treatment was real, even though it is a placebo. It is difficult to know whether the real medication would have worked better with proper experimental design. Control groups and treatment groups should be randomly created, not left to the discretion or opinion of a physician.

4. Since proximity to the window is a confounding variable, block for nearness to the window by assigning each of the four rows to a different block. There may be some left-right variation within each row, so stratifying may help by assigning the treatment fertilizer to the odd-numbered containers and the control fertilizer to the even-numbered containers. For each row, randomly select one of each type of plant and randomly assign it to the odd-numbered containers. For each row, randomly select one of each type of plant and randomly assign it to the even-numbered containers. Repeat the process for each row. Blocking helps control the effects of sun and heat near the window. Randomization controls variation in containers caused by chance.

WINDOW					
1	2	3	4	5	6
7	8	9	10	11	12
13	14	15	16	17	18
19	20	21	22	23	24

5. Recruit volunteers for the experiment. Randomly divide the volunteers into two equal groups. Use a random number table or technology tool to randomly select half of the volunteers and place them in the treatment group. Place the other half of the volunteers in the control group. The treatment group will receive the garlic supplement. The control group will receive a placebo that looks and tastes like the garlic supplement but does not contain garlic. This experiment should be double-blind: neither the researchers who will be providing the supplements nor the subjects themselves should be informed which group each subject has been assigned.

6. In order to assign each subject to one of the four treatment groups, a random number table, a calculator like the TI-83/4, or some other technology tool should be used. One method to repeatedly select a random number from 1 to 4 using a random number table would be to start at a random location. If the digit is a 1, 2, 3, or 4, use it. If not, then skip that digit and continue. To repeatedly select a random number from 1 to 4 using the TI-83/4, use the function randInt(1,4). Continue to select random numbers from 1 to 4 and assign the next subject to that treatment group. Repeat until all subjects have been assigned to a treatment group. Each treatment group should end up with approximately one-fourth of the subjects. Since treatment group selection was random for each subject, balanced group assignment is unlikely.

7. This is an observational study. The researcher (restaurant owner) did not control anything. No treatment was imposed on any subject. Each customer made his own decision as to which group to be in, drinker or nondrinker. Although drinkers spent considerably more money than nondrinkers, it might or might not be significant; random variation might have caused the differences. Repeating the experiment in other restaurants, locations, and months of the year would reinforce the results.

8. In a double-blind experiment, neither the subjects nor the researchers know to which group subjects have been assigned. Blind design for the subjects is important to control the placebo effect. In this experiment, blind design should also be used with respect to the researchers. For objective measurement, such as lab work on blood samples, blinding is not as important since researchers are simply recording factual data. For subjective measurements, such as how subjects are feeling, how they look, or how fast they respond to questions, blinding is very important. If a researcher knows what treatment a subject is receiving, their expectation of success or failure could interfere with their interpretation of subjective information.

9. Divide the 15 sections into the 9 daytime sections and the 6 evening sections. Use a random number table, or some other technology tool, to randomly select 3 of the 9 daytime sections to receive treatment A (females do better than males). Randomly select 3 to receive treatment B (males do better than females), and select the remaining 3 to be the control and not be told anything about gender performance differences. Randomly select 2 of the 6 evening sections to receive treatment A (females do better than males). Randomly select 2 to receive treatment B (males do better than females), and select the remaining 2 to be the control and not be told anything about gender performance differences. This is a single-blind design. Do not tell the students about the experiment. By dividing the sections into day and evening sections, you are blocking by time. You are randomizing within each block. Two treatments and a control are used. Compare the results.

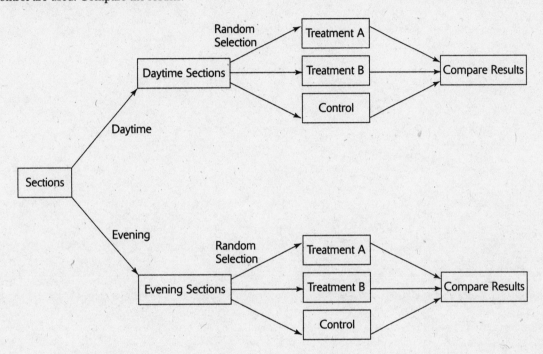

Anticipating Patterns: Probability as Relative Frequency

Much of Statistics is based on the study of probability. Probability measures the likelihood that a chance event will occur. A **probability experiment** represents some action through which results are collected. These results can be measurements, responses, or counts. A probability experiment consists of a sequence of attempts called trials. An **outcome** is the result of a single trial. All possible outcomes form the **sample space** for the experiment. An **event** is one or more outcomes and forms a subset of the sample space. An event that consists of a single outcome is called a **simple event.** If an event cannot occur, then that event's probability of occurring is zero. If an event must occur, then it is a sure thing, and that event's probability of occurring is 1. Thus, the probability that an event will occur is $0 \leq P(E) \leq 1$.

Probability is defined in three different ways: theoretical, empirical, and subjective.

Theoretical probability (also referred to as the **probability of an event**) is used when each possible outcome in the sample space is equally likely to occur. This is what mathematically *should* happen. If the probability that event E will occur is written as $P(E)$, then theoretical probability is defined as

$$P(E) = \frac{\text{the number of outcomes in E}}{\text{the total number of outcomes in the sample space}}$$

You can think of this formula as

$$P(E) = \frac{\text{total favorable outcomes}}{\text{total outcomes}}$$

EXAMPLE:
A standard six-sided die is rolled. Find the probability for each of the following events:

- **A.** rolling an 8
- **B.** rolling a 5
- **C.** rolling a 2
- **D.** rolling an even number

First determine the sample space. A standard die has six sides. With a fair die, each side has an equal chance of being rolled. The outcomes in the sample space are $\{1, 2, 3, 4, 5, 6\}$.

A. The number 8 is not in the sample space. Therefore, there are no favorable outcomes.

$$P(E) = \frac{0}{6} = 0$$

B. One of the outcomes in the sample space is favorable.

$$P(E) = \frac{1}{6} = 0.167$$

C. One of the outcomes in the sample space is favorable.

$$P(E) = \frac{1}{6} = 0.167$$

D. Three outcomes in the sample space are even: 2, 4, and 6.

Thus, three of the outcomes in the sample space are favorable.

$$P(E) = \frac{3}{6} = 0.500$$

EXAMPLE:

A deck of cards (standard) is shuffled and a card is randomly drawn. What is the probability of the following events?

    A.   drawing a diamond

    B.   drawing a king

    C.   drawing a red card

First determine the sample space. A standard deck of cards consists of 52 cards. Each suit (spades, hearts, diamonds, and clubs) consists of 13 cards (A, 2, 3, 4, 5, 6, 7, 8, 9, 10, Jack, Queen, and King). The spades and clubs are black in color; the hearts and diamonds are red in color.

  A. Thirteen of the 52 cards in the deck are favorable.

$$P(E) = \frac{13}{52} = 0.250$$

  B. Four of the 52 cards in the deck are kings.

$$P(E) = \frac{4}{52} = 0.077$$

  C. Twenty-six of the 52 cards in the deck are red.

$$P(E) = \frac{26}{52} = 0.500$$

EXAMPLE:

If two standard dice are rolled, what is the probability that the sum of the uppermost sides adds up to 8? At least 8?

A table helps summarize the results of rolling two dice. The values in the left column represent the possible outcomes of die number one. The values in the first row represent the possible outcomes of die number two.

	1	*2*	*3*	*4*	*5*	*6*
1	2	3	4	5	6	7
2	3	4	5	6	7	8
3	4	5	6	7	8	9
4	5	6	7	8	9	10
5	6	7	8	9	10	11
6	7	8	9	10	11	12

The table shows 36 possible outcomes. Five of the outcomes are the sum of 8. Therefore,

$$P\left(\text{rolling an } 8\right) = \frac{\text{number of outcomes} = 8}{\text{total number of outcomes}} = \frac{5}{36} = 0.139.$$

There are 15 outcomes that are at least 8 in value. Therefore,

$$P\left(\text{rolling at least an } 8\right) = \frac{\text{number of outcomes} = 8}{\text{total number of outcomes}} = \frac{15}{36} = 0.417.$$

Empirical probability uses the results of a probability experiment. The relative frequency of an event E is the empirical probability of that event.

$$P(E) = \frac{\text{the frequency of event E}}{\text{the total frequency}} = \frac{f}{n}$$

EXAMPLE:

A large container is filled with thousands of small candies, all the same size and shape, differing only by color. The candies are thoroughly mixed. Eighty-five of the candies are randomly selected from the container. The following is the color breakdown of the 85 candies.

Candy Color	Number Selected (f)
Red	12
Green	36
Blue	27
Brown	10
Total (Σf)	85

Based on this experiment, if another candy is randomly selected from the container, what is the probability that it will be green?

The relative frequency of selecting the color green, as determined by this experiment, is $\frac{36}{85}$. Therefore, the empirical probability of selecting a green candy is $P(E) = \frac{f}{n} = \frac{36}{85} = 0.424$.

EXAMPLE:

Tamara is collecting data for a project in her Statistics class. She is standing at the exit of a school parking lot and is observing cars as they leave. Of the 245 cars that have left the parking lot, 96 were domestic and 149 were foreign. What is the probability that the next car to leave the parking lot will be foreign?

Since 149 our of a total of 245 cars were foreign, the empirical probability (the probability determined by an experiment) would be $P(E) = \frac{f}{n} = \frac{149}{245} = 0.608$.

Subjective probability, sometimes referred to as personal probability, is based on personal experience, not experimental data. For example, you might know from past experience that you usually can find a parking spot in a particular lot at school. When asked by a friend what is the probability of finding a parking spot in the lot, you might respond, "Your probability of finding a parking spot in the lot is 0.85."

Law of Large Numbers

As the number of times you perform a probability experiment increases, the resulting empirical probability (what did happen) will approach the theoretical probability (what should happen). This is known as the **law of large numbers.**

EXAMPLE:

The gambling game of roulette consists of spinning a wheel with 38 numbers (1–36, 0, and 00), 18 of which are even. A bouncing ball randomly selected one of the numbers. The theoretical probability of the selected number being even is

$$P(E) = \frac{\text{favorable outcomes}}{\text{total number of outcomes}} = \frac{18}{38} = 0.474$$

Since the theoretical probability of picking an even number is less than one-half, does that mean you will always get less than one-half even numbers in any number of spins?

Certainly not. Anything can happen over the short term. Ten spins could result in 10 even numbers. As the number of spins increases, the cumulative relative frequency of even numbers will approach the theoretical probability. The following chart shows the results of 500 spins of the roulette wheel and the cumulative empirical probability of the spin being even. For the first 100 spins, the empirical probability was fluctuating. At first, quite rapidly. As the number of spins increased, the cumulative empirical probability started to approach the theoretical probability of 0.474.

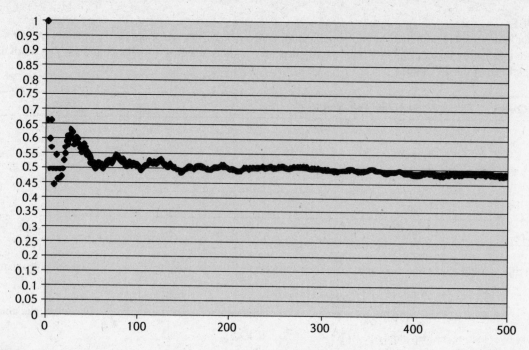

EXAMPLE:

A standard die has six sides, each with the same chance of ending face up when the die is rolled. The probability of rolling a 3 is

$$P(E) = \frac{\text{favorable outcomes}}{\text{total number of outcomes}} = \frac{1}{6} = 0.167$$

Although the theoretical probability of rolling a 3 is 0.167, the results of an experiment can, and will, vary widely. As the number of rolls increases, the cumulative relative frequency of rolling a 3 will approach the theoretical probability. The following chart shows the results of 500 rolls of the die and the cumulative empirical probability (cumulative relative frequency) of the roll being a 3. For the first 100 rolls, the empirical probability was fluctuating. As the number of rolls increases, the cumulative empirical probability started to approach the theoretical probability of 0.167.

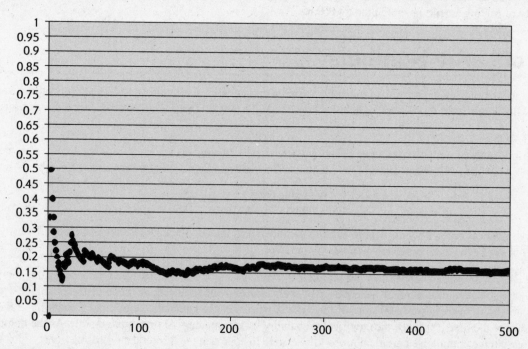

Addition Rule, Multiplication Rule, Conditional Probability, and Independence

If the probability that something will happen is 0.65, then the probability that it will not happen is 0.35. These are said to be **complementary events.** If E represents an event, then E' represents the complement of the event. The probability of the complement of a event is one minus the probability of the event. If E represents an event, then

$$P(E') = 1 - P(E)$$

It is sometimes easier to find the probability of the complement of an event that it is to find the probability of the event directly. Finding probability using this indirect method is very useful.

EXAMPLE:
If the probability that an event E will occur is 0.12, what is the probability of E''?

$$P(E') = 1 - P(E)$$
$$P(E') = 1 - 0.12$$
$$P(E') = 0.88$$

If two events cannot occur at the same time, they are said to be mutually exclusive.

EXAMPLE:
Randomly draw a card from a standard deck. If event E represents drawing a heart and event F represents drawing a spade, then these two events, E and F, are mutually exclusive since a card cannot be both a heart and a spade at the same time.

If the occurrence of one event is not influenced or affected by the occurrence of another event, then the events are said to be **independent events.**

EXAMPLE:
In a probability experiment, you are flipping a coin once and rolling a die once. The occurrence of a tail when you flip the coin does not influence in any way the probability of rolling a 4 with the die. These two events are independent events.

EXAMPLE:
In the game of craps, two dice are repeatedly rolled, and the sum of the two dice is calculated for each roll. The fact that you have rolled a 7 on one roll of the dice does not influence or change the probability of rolling a 7 on the next roll. The two successive rolls of the dice are independent events.

If event X and event Y are *independent*, then the probability that they will occur in sequence is the product of their individual probabilities. This is the **multiplication rule for independent events.**

$$P(X \text{ and } Y) = P(X \cap Y) = P(X) \cdot P(Y)$$

This rule can be extended for any number of independent events.

EXAMPLE:
If a die is rolled three times, what is the probability that the first roll will be an even number, the second roll will be an odd number, and the third roll will be a 4?

Since these three events are all independent, the probability they will occur in sequence is the product of their individual probabilities. If event X is rolling an even number, event Y is rolling an odd number, and event Z is rolling a 4, then

$$P(X \text{ and } Y \text{ and } Z) = P(X) \cdot P(Y) \cdot P(Z) = \left(\frac{3}{6}\right)\left(\frac{3}{6}\right)\left(\frac{1}{6}\right) = \frac{1}{24} = 0.042$$

A **conditional probability** is the probability of some event occurring, given that some other event has already occurred. The conditional probability of event X occurring, given that some other event Y has already occurred, is written as $P(X|Y)$. For example, $P(M|N)$ would be the probability of the occurrence of event M given that event N has already occurred. It would be read as "the probability of M, given N."

As stated earlier, two events are considered independent if the occurrence of one of the events does not change the probability of the other event from what it would have been had the first event not occurred. Thus, two events, X and Y, are independent if

$$P(X|Y) = P(X) \quad \text{or} \quad P(Y|X) = P(Y)$$

Actually, these two conditional relationships are related. If one is true, the other must be true. If one is false, the other must be false.

If $P(X|Y) = P(X)$, then $P(Y|X) = P(Y)$, and the events are independent.

If $P(X|Y) \neq P(X)$, then $P(Y|X) \neq P(Y)$, and the events are dependent.

EXAMPLE:

Are events X (drawing a heart from a shuffled deck of cards) and Y (rolling a 5 on a single die) dependent or independent?

There are 13 hearts in a deck of 52 cards. Therefore, the probability of event X is

$$P(X) = \frac{\text{favorable outcomes}}{\text{total number of outcomes}} = \frac{\text{number of hearts}}{\text{total number of cards}} = \frac{13}{52} = 0.250$$

If we consider the conditional probability of event X given that event Y has occurred, the result of rolling a die does not change the probability of selecting a heart from a deck of cards. Therefore,

$$P(X|Y) = P(X)$$

Thus, the events, X and Y, are independent.

Alternately, there are six sides on a die. Therefore, the probability of event Y is

$$P(Y) = \frac{\text{favorable outcomes}}{\text{total number of outcomes}} = \frac{\text{number of 5's}}{\text{total number of sides}} = \frac{1}{6} = 0.167$$

If we consider the conditional probability of event X given that event Y has occurred, the result of drawing a card from a deck does not change the probability rolling a 5 on a single die. Therefore,

$$P(Y|X) = P(Y)$$

Thus, the events, X and Y, are independent. If either $P(X|Y) = P(X)$ or $P(Y|X) = P(Y)$, the events are independent.

EXAMPLE:

This table summarizes the number of diners in a restaurant who ordered an appetizer and the number of diners who ordered dessert.

	Appetizer (A)	No Appetizer (A')	TOTAL
Dessert (D)	16	22	38
No Dessert (D')	10	12	22
TOTAL	26	34	60

A diner is selected at random. What is the probability that the diner

    A.   orders dessert
    B.   orders an appetizer
    C.   orders dessert, given that they ordered an appetizer
    D.   orders an appetizer, given that they ordered desert

The first two parts represent the probability of an event. The second two represent conditional probabilities.

    A. $P(D) = \dfrac{\text{favorable outcomes}}{\text{total outcomes}} = \dfrac{38}{60} = 0.633$

    B. $P(A) = \dfrac{\text{favorable outcomes}}{\text{total outcomes}} = \dfrac{26}{60} = 0.433$

    C. $P(D|A) = \dfrac{\text{favorable outcomes}}{\text{total outcomes}} = \dfrac{16}{26} = 0.615$

    D. $P(A|D) = \dfrac{\text{favorable outcomes}}{\text{total outcomes}} = \dfrac{16}{38} = 0.421$

The symbol for "and" is "$\cap$". Using this symbol, the **multiplication rule** involving conditional probabilities is

$$P(A \cap B) = P(A) \cdot P(B|A).$$

Reversing the roles of A and B gives

$$P(A \cap B) = P(B) \cdot P(A|B).$$

The form of this rule that is used on the AP Statistics Test solves for the conditional probability.

$$P(A|B) = \frac{P(A \cap B)}{P(B)} \quad \text{or} \quad P(B|A) = \frac{P(A \cap B)}{P(A)}$$

EXAMPLE:
Given:

    $P(A) = 0.4$
    $P(B) = 0.7$
    $P(A|B) = 0.55$

Find:

  A. $P(A \cap B)$
  B. $P(B|A)$

Part A is solved using the product rule for conditional probabilities.

  A. $P(A \cap B) = P(B) \cdot P(A|B)$

          $= (0.7)(0.55)$

          $= 0.385$

Part B is solved using the quotient form of the product rule for conditional probabilities.

  B. $P(B|A) = \dfrac{P(A \cap B)}{P(A)}$

          $= \dfrac{0.385}{0.4}$

          $= 0.9625$

EXAMPLE:

Twenty percent of men show early signs of losing their hair. Two percent of men carry a gene that is related to hair loss. Eighty percent of men who carry the gene experience early hair loss.

A. What is the probability that a man carries the gene and experiences early hair loss?

B. What is the probability that a man carries the gene, given that he experiences early hair loss?

If event G represents men who carry the gene and event H represents men who experience early hair loss, then $P(H) = 0.2$, $P(G) = 0.02$, and $P(H|G) = 0.8$.

Part A:

$$P(G \cap H) = P(G) \cdot P(H|G)$$

$$= (0.02)(0.8)$$

$$= 0.016$$

Part B:

$$P(G|H) = \frac{P(G \cap H)}{P(H)}$$

$$= \frac{0.016}{0.2}$$

$$= 0.08$$

The **addition rule** results in an *or* relationship for probabilities. If *or* is represented by "$\cup$", the formula is

$$P(A \cup B) = P(A) + P(B) - P(A \cap B)$$

This represents the *inclusive or*. The occurrence of both events is included in the *inclusive or*.

EXAMPLE:

A card is randomly selected from a shuffled deck. What is the probability that the card is a *heart* or a *king*?

This represents a situation in which an overlap exists in the two events. The *king of hearts* is a member of both events. Therefore, these events are NOT mutually exclusive.

$$P(A \cup B) = P(A) + P(B) - P(A \cap B)$$
$$P(\text{heart or king}) = P(\text{heart}) + P(\text{king}) - P(\text{heart and king})$$
$$= \frac{13}{52} + \frac{4}{52} - \frac{1}{52}$$
$$= \frac{16}{52}$$
$$= 0.308$$

EXAMPLE:

Sixty percent of the students in a class are juniors. If 25% of the students are math majors and 40% of the math majors are juniors, then if a student is selected at random from the class, what is the probability that the student is a junior or a math major?

Writing the given relationships symbolically, $P(J) = 0.6$, $P(M) = 0.25$, and $P(J|M) = 0.4$, the first task is to find $P(J \cap M)$.

$$P(J \cap M) = P(M) \cdot P(J|M)$$
$$= (0.25)(0.4)$$
$$= 0.1$$

Using $P(J \cap M)$, the next step is to find $P(J \cup M)$.

$$P(J \cup M) = P(J) + P(M) - P(J \cap M)$$
$$= (0.6) + (0.25) - (0.1)$$
$$= 0.75$$

EXAMPLE:
In a large lecture class at a local college, 60% of the students are female and 40% are male. Records show that 15% of the female students and 20% of the male students are seniors.

A. If a student is chosen at random from the class, what is the probability that the student is a senior?

B. If a randomly chosen student is a senior, what is the probability the student is male?

The solution may be found using the probability formulas directly, or a chart may be drawn to help organize the data. First, the conditional probability formulas may be used.

A. $P(S \cap M) = P(M) \cdot P(S|M) = (0.4)(0.2) = 0.08$

$P(S \cap F) = P(F) \cdot P(S|F) = (0.6)(0.15) = 0.09$

$P(S) = P(S \cap M) + P(S \cap F) = 0.08 + 0.09 = 0.17$

B. $P(M|S) = \dfrac{P(S \cap M)}{P(S)} = \dfrac{0.08}{0.17} = 0.471$

Second, a chart may be used to organize the data.

	Senior (S)	Not a Senior (S')	Total
Male (M)	0.080		0.400
Female (F)	0.090		0.600
Total	0.170		1.000

Note: Although the rest of the table could be filled in, it is not necessary.

A tree diagram is a useful tool to visually display some types of conditional relationships.

EXAMPLE:
A company uses four machines to produce widgets. Machine A produces 30% of the widgets of which 3% are defective. Machine B produces 25% of the widgets of which 5% are defective. Machine C produces 10% of the widgets of which 4% are defective. Machine D produces 35% of the widgets of which 2% are defective. All produced widgets are placed in a storage area. If one widget is selected at random from the storage area, what is the probability that it is defective?

The following tree diagram shows the relationships between good and defective widgets for the four machines.

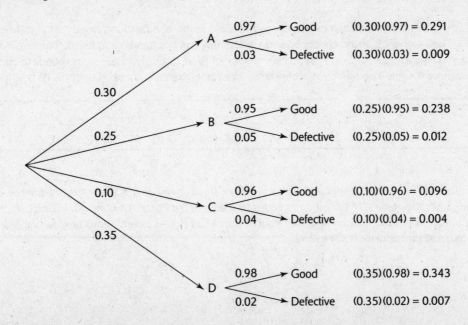

The probability that a defective widget is chosen is the sum of the probabilities of the four defective results.

Probability of defective widget = 0.009 + 0.012 + 0.004 + 0.007 = 0.032 = 3.2%

The following table summarizes the relationships and formulas for probability.

Description of Probability	Formula
Theoretical Probability	$P(E) = \dfrac{\text{the number of outcomes in E}}{\text{the total number of outcomes in the sample space}}$
Empirical Probability	$P(E) = \dfrac{\text{the frequency of event E}}{\text{the total frequency}} = \dfrac{f}{n}$
Complementary Events	$P(E) + P(E') = 1$, $P(E') = 1 - P(E)$
Multiplication Rule	$P(A \cap B) = P(A) \cdot P(B\|A)$
Multiplication for Independent Events	$P(A \cap B) = P(A) \cdot P(B)$
Quotient Rule (restated multiplication rule)	$P(A\|B) = \dfrac{P(A \cap B)}{P(B)}$
Addition Rule	$P(A \cup B) = P(A) + P(B) - P(A \cap B)$
Addition Rule for Mutually Exclusive Events	$P(A \cup B) = P(A) + P(B)$

Discrete Random Variables and Their Probability Distributions, Including Binomial

Some outcomes of probability experiments are counts or measurements. Whenever this occurs, the outcome is called a **random variable.** A random variable represents a numerical value that is assigned to an outcome of a probability experiment. There are two types of random variables.

A random variable is **continuous** if it has an infinite number of possible outcomes and can be represented by an interval on a number line.

A random variable is **discrete** if it has a countable or finite number of possible outcomes that can be listed.

EXAMPLE:
The number of customers that place orders at the drive-through window at a fast food restaurant each hour is a discrete random variable. The number of customers per hour is finite. They can be counted and listed. The possible values of the discrete random variable, x, are 0, 1, 2, 3, 4, 5, and so on. One of these possible values corresponds to each hour the drive-through window is open. The following table shows an example of customer counts for a 10-hour period.

Hour	1	2	3	4	5	6	7	8	9	10
Customers per hour (x)	8	4	9	12	7	16	4	7	9	12

EXAMPLE:
The amount of time it takes to serve each customer at the drive-through window at a fast food restaurant is a continuous random variable. Since the amount of time it takes could be a decimal, it cannot be counted. Instead, the results form intervals on the number line. The amount of coffee poured into a cup is also a continuous random variable. The amount cannot be counted, and the measure is not exact.

A **discrete probability distribution** lists each possible value the random variable can assume, along with the probability for that value. A discrete probability distribution must meet the following conditions:

1. The probability for each value of the discrete random variable must be between 0 and 1, inclusive: $0 \leq P(x) \leq 1$.
2. The sum of all the probabilities is 1: $\Sigma P(x) = 1$.

Use these steps to construct a discrete probability distribution:

1. Make a frequency distribution for each possible outcome.
2. Find the sum of the frequencies in the distribution.
3. Find the probability (relative frequency) for each possible outcome by dividing its frequency by the sum of the frequencies.
4. Make sure that the probability for each outcome is between 0 and 1, inclusive, and that the total of the probabilities is 1.

EXAMPLE:

In a class of students, 3 students have no siblings, 5 have 1 sibling, 6 have 2 siblings, 5 have 3 siblings, 4 have 4 siblings, and 1 has 5 siblings. Construct a discrete probability distribution for this data.

First, find the total frequency for the distribution. Add the frequencies for each possible number of siblings: $3 + 5 + 6 + 5 + 4 + 1 = 24$. Next, calculate the probability (relative frequency) for each number of siblings:

$$P(0) = \frac{3}{24} = 0.125 \qquad P(1) = \frac{5}{24} = 0.208 \qquad P(2) = \frac{6}{24} = 0.250$$

$$P(3) = \frac{5}{24} = 0.208 \qquad P(4) = \frac{4}{24} = 0.167 \qquad P(5) = \frac{1}{24} = 0.042$$

Check to make sure that each probability is between 0 and 1, inclusive. Check to make sure that the total of the probabilities is 1. *Note:* If you have rounded several probabilities, it is possible, due to round off error, that the total is not exactly 1.

This discrete probability distribution is shown in the following table, where x represents the number of siblings:

x	0	1	2	3	4	5
$P(x)$	0.125	0.208	0.250	0.208	0.167	0.042

EXAMPLE:
Suppose that a fair coin is tossed three times. If x represents the total number of *heads*, create a discrete probability distribution for x.

There are four possible values for x. They are 0, 1, 2, and 3. The probability of each may be determined by listing the possibilities. The probability of getting a *head* or a *tail* when you toss a coin is 0.5. There are eight possible outcomes when you toss a coin three times:

$$HHH = (0.5)(0.5)(0.5) = 0.125$$
$$HHT = (0.5)(0.5)(0.5) = 0.125$$
$$HTH = (0.5)(0.5)(0.5) = 0.125$$
$$HTT = (0.5)(0.5)(0.5) = 0.125$$
$$THH = (0.5)(0.5)(0.5) = 0.125$$
$$THT = (0.5)(0.5)(0.5) = 0.125$$
$$TTH = (0.5)(0.5)(0.5) = 0.125$$
$$TTT = (0.5)(0.5)(0.5) = 0.125$$

One results in 3 heads, three result in 2 heads, three result in 1 head, and one results in 0 heads. If x represents the number of heads resulting from tossing a coin three times, then this table shows the discrete probability distribution.

x	0	1	2	3
$P(x)$	0.125	0.375	0.375	0.125

Many probability experiments have only two possible outcomes. These outcomes are called *success* and *failure*. A coin has two sides, so if you want to toss a coin and get *heads*, you have success if you toss a *head* and failure if you toss a *tail*. The result of a game is either a win or a loss. The win could be considered the success, and the loss could be considered the failure.

A **binomial experiment** is a probability experiment that satisfies the following four conditions:

1. The experiment is repeated a fixed number of times, or trials, and each trial is independent of the other trials.
2. There are only two possible outcomes for each trial. These possible outcomes are success (S) and failure (F).
3. The probability of success, $P(S)$, is the same for each trial.
4. The random variable, x, is a count of the number of trials that result in success.

The preceding example, involving tossing a coin three times and determining the probability of tossing a certain number of heads, is a binomial experiment. It is repeated a fixed number of times (three). It only results in two possible outcomes—success (heads) and failure (tails). The probability of success (heads) is the same for each toss (0.5).

The probabilities associated with binomial experiments are **binomial probabilities.**

Common notation used in reference to binomial distributions are

n	number of trials (number of times the experiment is repeated)
p	probability of success in a single trial
q	probability of failure in a single trial ($q = 1 - p$)
k	number of successes in n trials
$\binom{n}{k}$	combinations of n things taken k at a time

Also written as $_nC_k = \dfrac{n!}{k!(n-k)!}$

The **binomial formula** for determining the probability of k successes in n trials in a binomial experiment is

$$P(X = k) = \binom{n}{k} p^k (1-p)^{n-k}$$

EXAMPLE:

A die is rolled 20 times. What is the probability of rolling a 6 exactly 4 times?

This is a binomial experiment. The die is rolled a finite number of times. There are only two possible outcomes, success (rolling a 6) and failure (not rolling a 6). The probability of rolling a 6 does not change from trial to trial. Apply the binomial formula.

$$P(X = k) = \binom{n}{k} p^k (1-p)^{n-k}$$

$$P(4) = \binom{20}{4}\left(\frac{1}{6}\right)^4 \left(\frac{5}{6}\right)^{16}$$

$$P(4) = 0.202$$

The TI-83/4 calculator contains a set of distribution functions. One of the functions is the binomial distribution. To solve this example using this function, select DISTR and then choose binompdf(20,1/6,4). Three values are entered into the function: n, p, and k. The format is binompdf(n, p,k). For added accuracy, enter the probability of success as a fraction when necessary.

EXAMPLE:

Thirty-five percent of all employees in a large corporation are women. If 12 employees are randomly selected, what is the probability that at least 4 of them are women?

First, is this a binomial experiment? It is; since it is repeated a fixed number of times (12), there are only two possible outcomes—success (woman) and failure (not a woman)—and the probability remains constant for each trial (0.35).

What does "at least 4" mean? Out of 12 trials, this means selecting 4, 5, 6, 7, 8, 9, 10, 11, or 12 women. The probabilities for each of these could be calculated using the binomial formula and then added up. But there is an easier way. *It is sometimes easier to determine the probability of the complement on an event than to determine the probability of the event itself.* This is true in this case. It is easier to determine the sum of the probabilities of selecting 0, 1, 2, and 3 women and then to subtract that sum from 1.

$$P(0) = \binom{12}{0}(0.35)^0(1 - 0.35)^{12-0} = 0.006$$

$$P(1)\binom{12}{1}(0.35)^1(1 - 0.35)^{12-1} = 0.037$$

$$P(2) = \binom{12}{2}(0.35)^2(1 - 0.35)^{12-2} = 0.109$$

$$P(3) = \binom{12}{3}(0.35)^3(1 - 0.35)^{12-3} = 0.195$$

Therefore, the probability of selecting at least 4 women is

$$P(k \geq 4) = 1 - (0.006 + 0.037 + 0.109 + 0.195) = 0.653$$

The TI-83/4 calculator contains two different binomial distribution functions. One is the probability distribution function (binompdf()), and the other is the cumulative distribution function (binomcdf()). The cumulative distribution function adds all the probabilities of the random variable from 0 to the value of k. (The calculator uses the pdf function repeatedly and adds the results.) To solve this example using this function, select DISTR, choose binomcdf(12,0.35,3), and subtract this result from 1. Three values are entered into the function: n, p, and k. The format is binomcdf(n,p,k). Using the data from this example, here are some probabilities calculated with the TI-83/4 calculator:

$$P(4) = \text{binompdf}(12,0.35,4) = 0.237$$
$$P(k \leq 4) = \text{binomcdf}(12,0.35,4) = 0.583$$
$$P(k \geq 6) = 1 - \text{binomcdf}(12,0.35,5) = 0.213$$

Note: One of the conditions for the use of the binomial distribution is that the probability of success does not change from trial to trial. This condition is relaxed somewhat in certain situations. If the population from which items are selected is very large, but finite, removing one success from the population will alter the proportion of remaining successes slightly. If the population is large enough, this minor change will not alter results significantly, and the binomial distribution may be used.

EXAMPLE:

A basketball player makes 74% of his free throw attempts. In one game, the player attempts 5 free throws. What is the probability he will make at least one of his attempts?

The complement of making at least one free throw is not making any of the free throws. It is easier to calculate the value of the complement and subtract from 1 to get the desired result.

$$P(0) = \binom{5}{0}(0.74)^0 (1 - 0.74)^{5-0} = 0.001$$

$$P(k \geq 1) = 1 - P(0) = 1 - .001 = .999$$

EXAMPLE:

A player wins a game of chance 45% of the time. If the player plays the game 200 times, what is the probability the player will win *exactly* 45% of the games?

First, calculate the number of games to win. Forty-five percent of 200 is 90. This is a binomial probability. The probability of winning exactly 90 of the 200 games played is

$$P(k = 90) = \binom{200}{90}(0.45)^{90} (1 - 0.45)^{200-90} = 0.057$$

$$P(k = 90) = \text{binompdf}(200, 0.45, 90)$$

EXAMPLE:

A player wins a game of chance 45% of the time. If the player plays the game 200 times, what is the probability the player will win *at least* 45% of the games?

First, calculate the number of games to win. Forty-five percent of 200 is 90. This is a binomial probability. It would be too time-consuming to calculate all 111 probabilities using the binomial formula. Even finding the complement and subtracting from 1 using the formulas would require 91 computations. This problem is best solved using a technology tool such as the TI-83/4. The probability of winning at least 90 of the 200 games played is

$$P(k \geq 90) = 1 - \text{binomcdf}(200, 0.45, 89) = 1 - 0.473 = 0.527$$

EXAMPLE:

The probability that a visitor to a record store will actually buy something is 0.4. If 10 people visit the store, calculate the probability that none of them buy something. What is the probability that exactly 1 will buy something? Also, calculate the probability that exactly 2, 3, 4, 5, 6, 7, 8, 9, and all 10, will buy something. List all 11 probabilities in a table.

Using the binomial formula:

$$P(k = 0) = \binom{10}{0}(0.4)^0 (1 - 0.45)^{10-0} = 0.006$$

$$P(k = 1) = \binom{10}{1}(0.4)^1 (1 - 0.45)^{10-1} = 0.040$$

$$P(k = 2) = \binom{10}{2}(0.4)^2 (1 - 0.45)^{10-2} = 0.121$$

$$P(k = 3) = \binom{10}{3}(0.4)^3 (1 - 0.45)^{10-3} = 0.215$$

$$P(k = 4) = \binom{10}{4}(0.4)^4 (1 - 0.45)^{10-4} = 0.251$$

$$P(k = 5) = \binom{10}{5}(0.4)^5 (1 - 0.45)^{10-5} = 0.201$$

$$P(k = 6) = \binom{10}{6}(0.4)^6 (1 - 0.45)^{10-6} = 0.111$$

$$P(k=7) = \binom{10}{7}(0.4)^7(1-0.45)^{10-7} = 0.042$$

$$P(k=8) = \binom{10}{8}(0.4)^8(1-0.45)^{10-8} = 0.011$$

$$P(k=9) = \binom{10}{9}(0.4)^9(1-0.45)^{10-9} = 0.002$$

$$P(k=10) = \binom{10}{10}(0.4)^{10}(1-0.45)^{10-10} = 0.000$$

(*Note:* The value in the last formula rounds to zero, but is a small positive number.)

Using the binomial distribution function in the TI-83/4 calculator, eleven separate functions can be entered:

binompdf(10,0.4,0) = 0.006
binompdf(10,0.4,1) = 0.040
binompdf(10,0.4,2) = 0.121
binompdf(10,0.4,3) = 0.215
binompdf(10,0.4,4) = 0.251
binompdf(10,0.4,5) = 0.201
binompdf(10,0.4,6) = 0.111
binompdf(10,0.4,7) = 0.042
binompdf(10,0.4,8) = 0.011
binompdf(10,0.4,9) = 0.002
binompdf(10,0.4,10) = 0.000

All 11 results may be obtained at one time by leaving off the value of k and entering

binompdf(10,0.4) = {0.006, 0.040, 0.121, 0.215, 0.251, 0.201, 0.111, 0.042, 0.011, 0.002, 0.000}

These results can be stored in a list by selecting STO L1. Since these 11 probabilities are all the probabilities of all possible values of the random variable, their sum is 1.

List all 11 probabilities along with the value of the discrete random variable. This is the discrete probability distribution.

x	0	1	2	3	4	5	6	7	8	9	10
$P(x)$	0.006	0.040	0.121	0.215	0.251	0.201	0.111	0.042	0.011	0.002	0.000

The combinations formula, $\binom{n}{k} = {}_nC_k = \dfrac{n!}{k!(n-k)!}$, may be used to help count the number of ways a few objects may be chosen from a larger group of objects.

EXAMPLE:
There are 20 male students and 24 female students in a class. A committee of 8 students is to be chosen consisting of 5 female students and 3 male students. How many such committees can be formed? If 8 students are randomly chosen from the class, what is the probability 5 female students and 3 male students will be chosen?

The 5 female students must be chosen from the 24 female students and the 3 male students must be chosen from the 20 male students.

$$\text{\# of committees} = ({}_{24}C_5)({}_{20}C_3) = 48,454,560$$

To find the probability that the 8 randomly students will consist of 5 female and 3 male students, simply divide the number of favorable committees by the total number of committees of 8 students.

$$P\left(5 \text{ female, } 3 \text{ male}\right) = \frac{\left(_{24}C_5\right)\left(_{20}C_3\right)}{\left(_{44}C_8\right)} = \frac{48,454,560}{177,232,627} = 0.273$$

Simulation of Probability Distributions, Including Binomial and Geometric

A simulation is a mathematical process to approximate a real-life situation. Many probabilities are hard to calculate because they are time-consuming, costly, or difficult to obtain. In these cases, it is easier to use a computer, calculator, or some other technology tool to simulate the real-life situation. If you simulate an occurrence n times and the favorable outcome occurs x times, then the simulated (estimated) probability of this occurrence is the quotient of x and n. This estimate of the real-life situation will improve as n is increased.

On the AP Statistics Test, the use of a random number table is the preferred method for generating random numbers. This way, there is some consistency in the results that makes the test easier to grade. Simulations usually occur in the free-response questions on the exam.

This random number table will be used for the examples in this section.

36146	15570	28593	42089	99282	59640	15323	97054	39916	05321
21549	18432	73720	52218	02789	81003	49092	79044	50912	08388
87334	50174	30962	23607	88691	29294	87179	45443	51370	69555
92043	59814	60673	56569	22035	43311	56013	62846	69030	47559
47681	72704	49759	76359	12525	32143	15882	36916	08097	90578

If you want to simulate a probability of 70% (0.7), consider the digits 0, 1, 2, 3, 4, 5, and 6 as success and the digits 7, 8, and 9 as failure. That way, you will simulate success 7 times out of 10. If you want to simulate a probability of 35% (0.35), select two digits at a time with the two-digit numbers from 00 to 34 representing success and the two-digit numbers from 35 to 99 representing failure.

EXAMPLE:
A basketball player makes 70% of his free throw attempts. Use simulation to estimate the probability that he will make at least 8 of his next 10 free throw attempts.

To estimate the probability, simulate repeated series of 10 free throws each. Determine how many of those series result in making at least 8 of 10 free throws. This is a simulation of the binomial distribution.

Starting with the first row, let the first 10 digits represent the 10 free throws, with the digits 0, 1, 2, 3, 4, 5, and 6 representing a success, and the digits 7, 8, and 9 representing a failure. Determine whether at least 8 of the 10 digits are in the success range. Record either a Y for yes or an N for no. Repeat the process with the second 10 digits. Continue across the first row for the 5 groups of 10 digits each. Repeat for rows 2 through 5 in the table. The table is shown here arranged in groups of 10 digits each. The groups with at least 8 digits in the success range (0–6) are underlined.

<u>3614615570</u>	2859342089	9928259640	<u>1532397054</u>	<u>3991605321</u>
<u>2154918432</u>	7372052218	0278981003	4909279044	5091208388
8733450174	<u>3096223607</u>	8869129294	8717945443	<u>5137069555</u>
9204359814	<u>6067356569</u>	<u>2203543311</u>	<u>5601362846</u>	6903047559
4768172704	4975976359	<u>1252532143</u>	1588236916	0809790578

Out of the 25 groups of 10 digits each, 10 of the groups represent a success with at least 8 digits in the range from 0 through 6. Therefore, according to this simulation, the probability of making at least 8 of the next 10 free throws is

$$\frac{\text{number of success}}{\text{number of trials}} = \frac{10}{25} = 0.400$$

Compare this answer to the one obtained using the binomial formula:

$$P(8) = \binom{10}{8}(0.7)^8(0.3)^2 = 0.233$$

$$P(9) = \binom{10}{9}(0.7)^9(0.3)^1 = 0.121$$

$$P(10) = \binom{10}{10}(0.7)^{10}(0.3)^0 = 0.028$$

Therefore, using the binomial formula, the answer is actually the sum of these three probabilities: 0.233 + 0.121 + 0.028 = 0.382. The TI-83/4 provides this calculated result by using (1 – binomcdf(10,.7,7). This result is very close to the simulated result of 0.400. The simulated result used only 25 trials. A better approximation using simulation would be possible with an increased number of trials.

EXAMPLE:

Jason is at a carnival. He wants to win a stuffed animal at the coin toss game. He has been told that there is only a 6% chance that a quarter tossed toward the plates will actually remain on a plate. Only one toss resulting in the quarter remaining on a plate will win the stuffed animal. Jason has brought 10 quarters with him to play the game. Use simulation to determine the approximate probability that he will win the stuffed animal before he runs out of quarters.

This is a simulation of the **geometric distribution**. The geometric distribution represents the probability of the first occurrence of an event occurring on a particular trial. In this simulation, Jason will win the stuffed animal with a success anywhere within the first 10 trials. Group the random digits from the random number table in groups of 20.

36146155702859342089	99282596401532397054	3991605321
2154918432	73720522180278981003	49092790445091208388
87334501743096223607	88691292948717945443	5137069555
9204359814	60673565692203543311	56013628466903047559
47681727044975976359	12525321431588236916	0809790578

(The first two groups of 20 digits are on the first row. The third group of 20 is split between the first and second row. The pattern continues.)

Each group of 20 digits represents 10 two-digit trials, with a success being a two-digit number in the range from 00 to 05. In each of the 12 series of 20 digits each (the last 10 digits are not used), the underlined digit pairs represent a success. In each group of 20 digits, if more than one digit pair is in the success range, (0 to 5), only the first pair is underlined, since Jason stops tossing after a success. In the 12 series of tosses (10 tosses each), a success occurred in 6 of the series. Therefore, according to this simulation, the probability of winning the stuffed animal before the 10 quarters run out is

$$\frac{\text{number of success}}{\text{number of trials}} = \frac{6}{12} = 0.500$$

Compare this answer to the one obtained by using the formula for the geometric distribution. In the geometric distribution, each series of trials begins with failures and ends with the first success. In this example, the probability of success is 0.06. To determine the probability of a success within the first 10 attempts, use the formula for the geometric distribution.

If p is the probability of success on any attempt, then the probability that the first success will occur on trial number x is

$$P(x) = p(1 - p)^{x-1}$$

In this simulation, $p = 0.06$. We calculate the probability of success on any of the first 10 attempts.

$$P(1) = 0.06(1 - 0.06)^{1-1} = 0.060$$
$$P(2) = 0.06(1 - 0.06)^{2-1} = 0.056$$
$$P(3) = 0.06(1 - 0.06)^{3-1} = 0.053$$
$$P(4) = 0.06(1 - 0.06)^{4-1} = 0.050$$
$$P(5) = 0.06(1 - 0.06)^{5-1} = 0.047$$
$$P(6) = 0.06(1 - 0.06)^{6-1} = 0.044$$
$$P(7) = 0.06(1 - 0.06)^{7-1} = 0.041$$
$$P(8) = 0.06(1 - 0.06)^{8-1} = 0.039$$
$$P(9) = 0.06(1 - 0.06)^{9-1} = 0.037$$
$$P(10) = 0.06(1 - 0.06)^{10-1} = 0.034$$

Since Jason is looking for a success in the first 10 attempts, add these 10 probabilities. The probability of winning the stuffed animal is

$$0.060 + 0.056 + 0.053 + 0.050 + 0.047 + 0.044 + 0.041 + 0.039 + 0.037 + 0.034 = 0.461$$

Our simulation gave a probability of winning at 0.500. Very close to the actual value of 0.461 considering only 12 series were used. Increasing the number of series would improve the already good approximation.

The TI-83/4 calculator may be used to find these probabilities using the calculator's built-in functions. For example, the probability that the first success will occur on the 8th attempt can be found using: geometpdf(.06,8) = 0.039. The "-----pdf()" functions find individual probabilities. Cumulative functions (from zero) are also available. The TI-83/4 calculator finds the cumulative result (probabilities from 0 to 10) using only one cumulative function: geometcdf(0.06,10) = 0.461.

EXAMPLE:

Five green, two blue, and three yellow marbles are placed in a container. Five marbles are selected at random from the container. Use simulation to determine the approximate probability that the selection consisted of three green, one blue, and one yellow marble.

To use simulation to solve this problem, digits can be assigned to each marble color in the same proportion and quantity as the marbles themselves. Let the digits 0, 1, 2, 3, and 4 represent the five green marbles. Let the digits 5 and 6 represent the two blue marbles. Let the digits 7, 8, and 9 represent the three yellow marbles. Select groups of five digits each from a random number table. Skip any that have repeated digits. Determine the colors represented by the digits. Determine whether the group of five digits represents five marbles of the appropriate colors. If so, underline the group. Repeat 50 times. Determine the proportion of groups that satisfy the color selection.

The following shows skipped groups in strike-through type. Groups that represent the desired color combination are underlined.

~~36146~~	~~15570~~	28593	42089	~~99282~~	59640	~~15323~~	97054	~~39916~~	05321
<u>21549</u>	18432	~~73720~~	~~52218~~	02789	~~81003~~	~~49092~~	<u>79044</u>	<u>50912</u>	~~08388~~
~~87334~~	<u>50174</u>	<u>30962</u>	<u>23607</u>	~~88691~~	~~29294~~	~~87179~~	45443	<u>51370</u>	~~69555~~
92043	59814	~~60673~~	~~56569~~	~~22035~~	~~43311~~	56013	~~62846~~	~~69030~~	~~47559~~
47681	~~72704~~	~~49759~~	76359	~~12525~~	~~32143~~	~~15882~~	~~36916~~	~~08097~~	90578

Thirty-one groups were skipped because they contained duplicates. Of the remaining 19 groups, 6 met the proper color representations and 13 did not. Therefore, using this simulation, the probability of selecting three green, one blue, and one yellow marble is

$$\frac{\text{number of success}}{\text{number of trials}} = \frac{6}{19} = 0.316$$

The actual probability may be computed using a counting technique involving combinations.

$$P(3 \text{ green}, 1 \text{ blue}, 1 \text{ yellow}) = \left(\frac{(_5C_3)(_2C_1)(_3C_1)}{_{10}C_5} \right) = 0.239$$

The difference between the simulation and the actual value is quite small considering the small number of repetitions.

Mean (Expected Value) and Standard Deviation of a Random Variable

A **random variable** takes on numerical values determined by the outcome of a random event. The probability distribution of a random variable, x, tells us what the possible values of x are and what probabilities are assigned to each of the values. The **expected value** (E) is the mean of the distribution. The AP Statistics Test uses the following formula for expected value:

$$E(x) = \mu x = \Sigma x_i p_i$$

This is nothing more than the sum of the products of each possible value of the random variable multiplied by the probability of the occurrence of that value.

EXAMPLE:

In a large class at a local high school, 15% of the students have no siblings, 27% have one sibling, 34% have two siblings, 18% have three siblings, 6% have four siblings, and 2% have five siblings. What is the expected value for the number of siblings for a student in this class? In other words, what is the average number of siblings for students in this class?

First construct a probability distribution showing the possible values of the random variable along with their probabilities. Find the products of each value of the random variable and its probability of occurrence. Add these products. This total is the expected value of the random variable. It is also called the mean of the distribution.

x_i	$P(x_i)$	$x_i P(x_i)$
0	0.130	0.000
1	0.270	0.270
2	0.340	0.680
3	0.180	0.540
4	0.060	0.240
5	0.020	0.100
		$E(x) = \mu_x = \sum x_i P(x_i) = 1.830$

The AP Statistics Test uses the following formula for the *variance* for a probability distribution.

$$Var(x) = \sigma_x^2 = \sum (x_i - \mu_x)^2 p_i$$

The **standard deviation** for a probability distribution is the square root of the variance.

$$\sigma_x = \sqrt{\text{variance}} = \sqrt{\sigma_x^2}$$

EXAMPLE:

Use the information in the preceding example and compute the standard deviation of the distribution.

Three additional columns need to be added to the chart in the example.

x_i	$P(x_i)$	$x_i P(x_i)$	$x_i - \mu_x$	$(x_i - \mu_x)^2$	$(x_i - \mu_x)^2 p(x_i)$
0	0.130	0.000	−1.830	3.349	0.435
1	0.270	0.270	−0.830	0.689	0.186
2	0.340	0.680	0.170	0.029	0.010
3	0.180	0.540	1.170	1.369	0.246
4	0.060	0.240	2.170	4.709	0.282
5	0.020	0.100	3.170	10.049	0.201
		$\mu_x = \sum x_i p(x_i) = 1.830$			$\sigma_x^2 = \sum (x_i - \mu_x)^2 p(x_i) = 1.360$

The standard deviation is the square root of the variance.

$$\sigma_x = \sqrt{\text{variance}} = \sqrt{\sigma_x^2} = \sqrt{1.360} = 1.166$$

EXAMPLE:

A company sells three types of backpacks. They make a $12 profit on type A, an $8 profit on type B, and a $6 profit on type C. Twenty percent of the backpacks they sell are type A; 50% of the backpacks they sell are type B; and 30% of the backpacks they sell are type C. What is the expected profit (mean) from selling a backpack? What is the standard deviation of this distribution?

$$\mu_x = \sum x_i p(x_i) = (12)(0.20) + (8)(0.50) + (6)(0.30) = \$8.20$$

$$\sigma_x = \sqrt{\sum (x_i - \mu_x)^2 p_i} = \sqrt{(12 - 8.2)^2 (0.2) + (8 - 8.2)^2 (0.5) + (6 - 8.2)^2 (0.3)} = 2.088$$

This problem can be easily done on the TI-83/4 calculator. Enter the numbers 12, 8, and 6 in L1. Enter the probabilities (0.2, 0.5, 0.3) in L2. Select 1-Var Stats and enter L1, L2. The mean and standard deviations are given.

The **mean of a binomial distribution** is simply the product of n and p. The variance is the product of n, p, and 1-p. The standard deviation is the square root of the variance.

EXAMPLE:

The probability that a spin of a roulette wheel will result in the color red is 0.474. The wheel spins 8 times. What is the mean and standard deviation of this binomial distribution?

$$\mu_x = np = (8)(0.474) = 3.792$$

$$\sigma_x = \sqrt{np(1-p)} = \sqrt{(8)(0.474)(0.526)} = 1.412$$

EXAMPLE:

A multiple choice quiz has five questions. Each question has four answer choices. A student guesses randomly for each question on the test. The student could get 0 questions correct, 1 question correct, 2 correct, 3 correct, 4 correct, or all 5 correct. What is the expected number of questions this student will get correct and what is the standard deviation?

For this problem, $n = 5$ and $p = 0.25$.

$$\mu_x = np = (5)(0.25) = 1.25$$

$$\sigma_x = \sqrt{np(1-p)} = \sqrt{(5)(0.25)(0.75)} = 0.968$$

The following is a summary of the formulas for mean, variance, and standard deviation for probability distributions in general, and, more specifically, the binomial distribution.

Formulas for a random variable (generalized)

Expected value (mean) $\quad E(x) = \mu_x = \sum x_i p(x_i)$

Variance $\qquad\qquad\quad \sigma_x^2 = \sum (x_i - \mu_x)^2 p(x_i)$

Standard deviation $\qquad \sigma_x = \sqrt{\sum (x_i - \mu_x)^2 p(x_i)}$

Formulas for a binomial distribution with n trials, a probability of success of p, and number of success of x.

Expected value (mean) $\quad \mu_x = np$

Variance $\qquad\qquad\quad \sigma_x^2 = np(1-p) = npq$

Standard Deviation $\qquad \sigma_x = \sqrt{np(1-p)} = \sqrt{npq}$

Linear Transformation of a Random Variable

Data can be transformed to make it more manageable, but how does this transformation alter the mean and variance of the data? One transformation might involve adding a constant to every member of the set of data. Another transformation might involve multiplying each member of the set of data by a constant. A transformation might include both the addition of a constant and the multiplication by a constant. Any of these transformations are referred to as linear transformations. You also can expand a data set by multiplying each data element by 10, or shift the set of data by adding 20 to each data value. How do these transformations change the mean or variance of the data?

If each data value is multiplied by k or if c is added to each data value, or some combination of the two, a transformation has occurred. The equations that follow show what happens to the mean and variance under these transformations.

If each member of the set of data is multiplied by a constant k, then the mean and standard deviation increase by factor of that amount:

$$\mu_{kx} = k\mu_x$$
$$\sigma_{kx} = k\sigma_x$$

If a constant is added to each member of the set of data, then the mean increases by that amount but the standard deviation remains the same:

$$\mu_{c+x} = c + \mu_x$$
$$\sigma_{c+x} = \sigma_x$$

EXAMPLE:
A set of data is made up of temperature readings in degrees C. You want to change the data so that the readings are listed in degrees F. This is a linear transformation that includes multiplying each temperature reading in degrees C by 9/5 and then adding 32 to the answer. The mean and standard deviation of the data before the transformation were 42 and 4.2, respectively. What will be the new mean and standard deviation?

$$\mu_{32+\left(\frac{9}{5}\right)x} = 32 + \left(\frac{9}{5}\right)\mu_x = 32 + \left(\frac{9}{5}\right)(42) = 107.6$$

$$\sigma_{32+\left(\frac{9}{5}\right)x} = \left(\frac{9}{5}\right)\sigma_x = \left(\frac{9}{5}\right)(4.2) = 7.56$$

153

How do you deal with the means and variances of two variables if you want to combine them?

The mean of a sum of two random variables equals the sum of the means. If two random variables are added, the new mean is simply the sum of the two original means.

$$\mu_{A+B} = \mu_A + \mu_B$$

If two variables are *independent,* then the variance of the sum is the sum of the variances.

$$\sigma^2_{A+B} = \sigma^2_A + \sigma^2_B$$

Note that this applies to the variances, not the standard deviations. For the standard deviations, if two variables are *independent,* then the standard deviation of the sum is the square root of the sum of the variances.

$$\sigma_{A+B} = \sqrt{\sigma^2_A + \sigma^2_B}$$

These formulas for the combining of two random variables can be extended to three or more random variables.

EXAMPLE:

Two machines produce ball bearings. The first machine produces an average of 89 ball bearings per second with a standard deviation of 3. The second machine produces an average of 84 ball bearings per second with a standard deviation of 2. What is the mean and standard deviation of the combined production of the two machines?

The combined mean is the sum of the means of the two machines.

$$\mu_{A+B} = \mu_A + \mu_B = 89 + 84 = 173$$

To combine the standard deviations, first determine variances.

$$\sigma_{A+B}\sqrt{\sigma^2_A + \sigma^2_B} = \sqrt{3^2 + 2^2} = \sqrt{9 + 4} = \sqrt{13} = 3.606$$

Review Questions and Answers

Multiple Choice Questions

Directions: Solve each of the following problems. Decide which is the best of the choices given.

1. Use the information in the following table to determine $P(W \cap F)$ and $P(M|A)$.

	B	W	A	Total
M	7	12	4	23
F	9	7	5	21
Total	16	19	9	44

    A. 7/19, 4/44
    B. 7/21, 4/9
    C. 7/44, 4/9
    D. 7/44, 4/23
    E. 7/21, 4/44

2. Use this tree diagram to determine $P(Y|N)$.

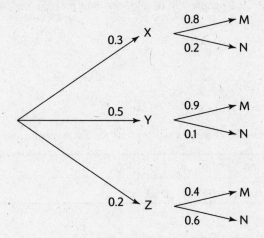

    A.   1/18

    B.   1/9

    C.   1/5

    D.   5/23

    E.   5/9

3. Two workers work independently on a project. Roy processes 32 applications per hour with a standard deviation of 2.6 applications per hour. Ted processes 40 applications per hour with a standard deviation of 6.4 applications per hour. What is the mean and standard deviation of their combined work?

    A.   36, 6.9

    B.   36, 9.0

    C.   72, 6.9

    D.   72, 9.0

    E.   72, 4.5

4. Of all the candles produced by Brite-Lite Candle Corporation, 0.01% do not have wicks. If a retailer buys 10,000 candles from Brite-Lite, what is the probability that all the candles have wicks? What is the probability that at least one candle will not have a wick?

    A.   0.368, 0.632

    B.   0.9999, 0.0001

    C.   0.99, 0.01

    D.   0.01, 0.99

    E.   Cannot be determined from the information given

5. Only one person in 12 will take the time to return a questionnaire mailed to them from their city council. If 40 questionnaires are mailed, what is the probability that exactly 4 will be returned?

    A.   0.112

    B.   0.192

    C.   0.570

    D.   0.762

    E.   0.888

6. Approximately 3 in 10,000 people will develop a certain skin problem each year. In a group of 1000 people, what is the probability that at least 2 people will develop the skin problem next year?

    A. 0.033

    B. 0.037

    C. 0.259

    D. 0.741

    E. 0.963

7. In a company-sponsored contest, the chance of wining various amounts of money is given here:

Prize ($)	500	100	50	1	0
Win Probability	0.01	0.03	0.11	0.50	0.35

What is the expected value and standard deviation of the prize?

    A. 130.2, 14

    B. 14, 53.66

    C. 53.66, 130.2

    D. 14, 42.42

    E. 53.66, 14

8. In a survey of students that was conducted at a junior high school, 30% of the students said they like broccoli and 15% of the students said they like spinach. If every one of the students who said they like spinach also said they like broccoli, what proportion of the students responding to the survey said they liked at least one of the two vegetables?

    A. 3/20

    B. 3/10

    C. 9/20

    D. 11/20

    E. 7/10

9. During a given month, the probability that event A occurs is 0.75, the probability that event B occurs is 0.60, and the probability they both occur is 0.50. Are these two events independent? Are they mutually exclusive?

    A. Yes, yes

    B. Yes, no

    C. No, yes

    D. No, no

    E. No, cannot be determined from the information given

10. Let $x = P(A)$, $y = P(B)$, and $z = P(A \cap B)$. Which of the following facts would indicate that events A and B are dependent events?

    I. $xy < z$

    II. $z > 0$

    III. $xy > 0$

    A. I only

    B. I and III

    C. II and III

    D. I, II, and III

    E. None of the facts would indicate dependence.

11. In which of the following games would you have the best chance of winning?

    A. Toss a coin 20 times. You win if you get more than 11 heads.

    B. Toss a coin 10 times. You win if you don't get 4, 5, or 6 heads.

    C. Toss a coin 7 times. You win if you get at least 5 heads.

    D. Toss a coin 4 times. You win if you get at least 3 heads.

    E. Toss a coin 5 times. You win if you get exactly 3 heads.

12. If A and B are two events such that $P(A) \cdot P(B) > 0$, which of the following is a true statement?

    A. Two mutually exclusive events are independent.

    B. Two mutually exclusive events may be independent.

    C. Two mutually exclusive events are not independent.

    D. Two independent events are mutually exclusive.

    E. No relationship exists between mutually exclusive and independent events.

13. Which of the following events are true?

    I. The standard deviation of a random variable is always positive.

    II. The variance of a random variable is always greater than the standard deviation.

    III. The law of large numbers implies that as a probability experiment is repeated, the variance will approach zero.

    A. I only

    B. II only

    C. I and II

    D. II and III

    E. None of the above statements is true.

14. As a payment for helping at home, you have been given a choice of either a flat payment of $5, or a chance of randomly drawing a bill from a box. The box contains one $100 bill, two $20 bills, seven $10 bills, ten $5 bills, and thirty $1 bills. Which choice gives you the greatest expected payment?

    A. Flat payment because the expected value of selecting a bill from the box is less than $5.

    B. Flat payment because the expected value of selecting a bill from the box is equal to $5, and it is better to have a sure thing.

    C. Draw from the box because the expected value of selecting a bill from the box is greater than $5.

    D. Draw from the box because the expected value of selecting a bill from the box is equal to $5, so you have nothing to lose.

    E. Flat payment because the expected value of selecting from the box cannot be determined.

15. A die is rolled three times. What is the probability that all three rolls resulted in different numbers?

    A. 0.500

    B. 0.556

    C. 0.578

    D. 0.596

    E. 0.606

16. A standard deck of cards consisting of 52 cards, 13 in each of 4 different suits, is shuffled, and 4 cards are drawn without replacement. What is the probability that all four cards are of a different suit?

    A. 0.004

    B. 0.010

    C. 0.105

    D. 0.121

    E. 0.223

For problems 17–19, use the information in the following table. The information came from 272 employment applications. Some were handwritten, and some were typed. Some contained mistakes, and some did not.

	Mistakes	No Mistakes	Total
Typed	38	66	104
Handwritten	122	46	168
Total	160	112	272

17. What is the probability that an application was typed and had no mistakes?

   A.   0.243
   B.   0.449
   C.   0.551
   D.   0.589
   E.   0.635

18. What is the probability that an application was typed, given that mistakes were made?

   A.   0.140
   B.   0.238
   C.   0.365
   D.   0.589
   E.   0.831

19. What is the probability that an application was handwritten or had mistakes?

   A.   0.243
   B.   0.449
   C.   0.726
   D.   0.757
   E.   0.762

20. On a recent administration of a state bar exam, 22% of the test takers passed the test, 78% of those who passed were first-time test takers, and 60% of those who failed were first-time test takers. What percent of first-time test takers passed the test?

   A.   17%
   B.   27%
   C.   47%
   D.   64%
   E.   73%

21. Which of the following investments gives you the best opportunity to make money (highest expected value)?

   Investment A: You have a 20% chance of making $50,000 and an 80% chance of losing your $8000 investment.
   Investment B: You have a 10% chance of making $100,000 and a 90% chance of losing your $8000 investment.
   Investment C: You have a 40% chance of making $30,000 and a 60% chance of losing your $14,000 investment.

   A.   Either A or B, but not C
   B.   Either A or C, but not B
   C.   Either B or C, but not A
   D.   All three investments have a negative expected value.
   E.   The expected value is different for each investment.

22. The probability function, $g(x) = 0.02x$ is defined for $x = 8, 9, 10, 11,$ and 12. What is the mean of this probability distribution?

    A. 10

    B. 10.2

    C. 20

    D. 50

    E. This is not a probability distribution.

23. The formula, $P(x = 7) = \binom{12}{7}(0.4)^7(0.6)^5$, was used to compute a probability from a probability distribution. What is the standard deviation for this probability distribution?

    A. 1.697

    B. 2.191

    C. 2.88

    D. 4.8

    E. Not enough information is given to compute the standard deviation.

24. A large corporation offers its employees one of three pension plans, A, B, or C. Records show that 70% choose plan A, 20% choose plan B, and 10% choose plan C. Also, 60% of those who choose plan A are married, 20% of those who choose plan B are married, and 60% of those who choose plan C are married. If a married employee is selected at random, what is the probability the employee is in plan A?

    A. 0.42

    B. 0.43

    C. 0.70

    D. 0.81

    E. 0.86

25. Given two independent events, X and Y, such that $P(Y) = 0.2$ and $P(X \cup Y) = 0.4$, what is the value of $P(X)$?

    A. 0.05

    B. 0.20

    C. 0.25

    D. 0.30

    E. Cannot be determined from the information given

26. A doctor's office sends half of its lab work to Lab X, one-fourth of its lab work to Lab Y, and the remainder to Lab Z. From Lab X, 1 report in 10 is late, from Lab Y, 1 in 8 is late, and from Lab Z, 1 in 12 is late. What is the probability that a late lab report came from Lab Y?

    A. 0.021

    B. 0.031

    C. 0.050

    D. 0.304

    E. 0.333

27. Which of the following are true?

    I.   If $P(A \cap B) = P(A) \cdot P(B)$, the events A and B are independent.

   II. If $P(A \cup B) = P(A) + P(B)$, the events A and B are mutually exclusive.

  III. If $P(A \cap B) = 0$, the events A and B are mutually exclusive.

  IV. If $P(A) = P(A|B)$, the events A and B are independent.

    A. III only

    B. IV only

    C. I and II

    D. I, II, III, and IV

    E. Three of the above statements are true.

Multiple Choice Answers

1. C. The intersection of row F and column W contains the number 7. This represents the intersection of the two events. Divide by the total, 44, to get the probability. The conditional probability restricts you to a single row or column. In this case, that is the A column. The new total is not 9. The part of 9 that is in the M row is 4. Divide to get the probability.

2. D. First calculate the products for all paths that end in N. Their sum becomes the denominator, and the path beginning at Y becomes the numerator.

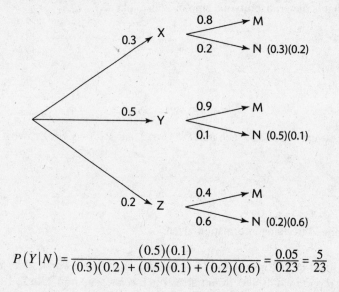

$$P(Y|N) = \frac{(0.5)(0.1)}{(0.3)(0.2) + (0.5)(0.1) + (0.2)(0.6)} = \frac{0.05}{0.23} = \frac{5}{23}$$

3. C. The mean of the sum is the sum of the means. The standard deviation of the sum is the square root of the sum of the variances.

$$\mu_{R+T} = \mu_R + \mu_T = 32 + 40 = 72$$

$$\sigma_{R+T} = \sqrt{\sigma_R^2 + \sigma_T^2} = \sqrt{2.6^2 + 6.4^2} = 6.9$$

4. A. This problem is best solved by finding the complement of the event. If you want to find the probability of *at least one*, it is easier to find the probability of *none* and subtract from 1.

$$P(x = 0) = (0.9999)^{10000} = 0.368$$

$$P(x \geq 0) = 1 - P(0) = 1 - 0.368 = 0.632$$

5. B. This is a binomial distribution. Solve by either using the formula for the binomial distribution or using the built-in function in the TI-83/4.

$$\text{binompdf}(40, 1/12, 4) = 0.192$$

$$P(4) = \binom{40}{4}\left(\frac{1}{12}\right)^4\left(\frac{11}{12}\right)^{36} = 0.192$$

6. B. This is a binomial distribution. It makes no sense to try to calculate all 999 probabilities and add them together. It is far easier to calculate the probability of 0 and 1, add them, and then subtract the total from 1. It is also easier to use the built-in "cdf" function that will sum binomial probabilities from 0: $1 - \text{binomcdf}(1000, 0.0003, 1) = 0.037$.

7. B. To get the mean of this distribution, multiply each value of the random variable by its probability and then add:

$$\mu = (500)(0.01) + (100)(0.03) + (50)(0.11) + (1)(0.5) + (0)(0.35) = 14$$

The variance of the distribution is the sum of the products of the squares of the differences between the value of the random variable and the mean, and the probability of the random variable. The standard deviation is the square root of the variance.

$$\sigma^2 = (500 - 14)^2(0.01) + (100 - 14)^2(0.03) + (50 - 14)^2(0.11) +$$
$$(1 - 14)^2(0.50) + (0 - 14)^2(0.35) = 2879.5$$
$$\sigma = \sqrt{2879.5} = 53.66$$

Both of these values can be calculated quickly and easily in the TI-83/4 by entering the values of the random variable in L1 and the probabilities in L2. Then use STAT CALC 1-Var Stats L1,L2 to get your answer directly.

8. B. Since spinach is a subset of broccoli, $P(S \cup B) = P(B) = 0.30 = \frac{3}{10}$.

9. D. If the events were independent, then

$$P(A \text{ and } B) = P(A) \cdot P(B) = (0.6)(0.75) = 0.45$$

Since you are given that $P(A \text{ and } B) = 0.50$, the events are not independent. If the events were mutually exclusive, there would be nothing in the intersection. Since the intersection is not zero, the events are not mutually exclusive.

10. A. Choice I indicates dependence since independence implies that $z = xy$. Choice II only tells us that the intersection is not empty, so the events are not mutually exlusive. All choice III tells us is that both events can happen, but nothing about their relationship.

11. B. Calculate the probability of each. They are all binomial distributions.

Choice A: $1 - \text{binomcdf}(20, 0.5, 11) = 0.252$

Choice B: $\text{binomcdf}(10, 0.5, 3) = 0.172$

                $1 - \text{binomcdf}(10, 0.5, 6) = 0.172$

                Add the two sides to get 0.344.

Choice C: $1 - \text{binomcdf}(7, 0.5, 4) = 0.227$

Choice D: $\text{binompdf}(5, 0.5, 3) = 0.3125$

Choice E: $1 - \text{binomcdf}(4, 0.5, 2) = 0.3125$

The best probability of winning is choice B.

12. C. Two mutually exclusive events cannot be independent if both events have a positive probability of occurring. Mutually exclusive implies that the intersection is empty. Independent implies that the intersection is the product of the two event probabilities.

13. E. Choice I is false since it is possible to have a standard deviation of 0 if the random variable can take on only one possible value. Choice II is false since the square of a number that is less than one is smaller than the original number. Choice III is false since the law of large numbers simply states that the empirical probability will approach the theoretical probability as an experiment is repeated over and over.

14. **C.** The box's expected value is greater than 5.

Multiply each value of the random variable by the probability. Add them to get the expected value. There are 50 total bills. Divide each quantity of bills by 50 to get the probability. Or enter the values of the bills in L1 and the probabilities in L2. Select STAT CALC 1-Var Stats L1,L2 and get the expected value (mean) of $5.80.

15. **B.** A die has six sides. If it is rolled three times, there are (6)(6)(6) = 216 possible outcomes. Some of these result in all three rolls being different, and some rolls include duplicates. The probability of rolling all different numbers is a quotient between the favorable outcomes over the total number of outcomes. The first roll can be any of the 6 sides since it will not match anything. The second roll is limited to 5 choices, since one has already been selected by the previous roll. The third roll is limited to 4 choices, since the first two rolls have selected two of the choices.

$$P(\text{all different}) = \frac{(6)(5)(4)}{(6)(6)(6)} = 0.556$$

16. **C.** The first card selected will not match anything since it is the first card drawn. The second card drawn must avoid the remaining cards from the first suit drawn. The third card drawn must avoid both of the first two suits drawn, and the fourth card drawn must avoid all three suits of the cards already drawn.

$$P(\text{4 different suits}) = (1)\left(\frac{39}{51}\right)\left(\frac{26}{50}\right)\left(\frac{13}{49}\right) = 0.105$$

17. **A.** This intersection is read directly from the table.

$$P(T \cap N) = \frac{f}{n} = \frac{66}{272} = 0.243$$

18. **B.** This is a conditional probability. You want to know the probability given that mistakes were made. This isolates the "mistakes" column.

$$P(T|M) = \frac{38}{160} = 0.238$$

19. **D.** This is the union of a row and column in the table. Add any values in either the "handwritten" row or the "mistakes" column.

$$P(H \cup M) = \frac{38 + 122 + 46}{272} = 0.757$$

20. **B.** This problem may be solved with the help of either a table or a tree diagram.

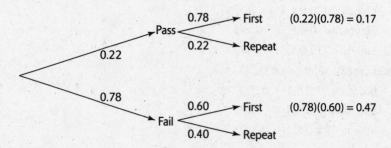

Note that you do not have to write down the probabilities or names on paths you do not use. In this case, the "repeat" values are not used.

$$P(P|F) = \frac{0.17}{0.17 + 0.47} = \frac{0.17}{0.64} = 0.27$$

Using a table gives the same information.

	Pass	*Fail*	*Total*
First Time	(0.78)(0.22) = 0.17	(0.60)(0.78) = 0.47	0.64
Repeat			
	0.22	0.78	1.00

Again, it is not necessary to fill in what you do not need.

21. **B.** Calculate the expected values for each investment.

Investment A: $(0.2)(50000) - (0.8)(8000) = 3600$

Investment B: $(0.1)(100000) - (0.9)(8000) = 2800$

Investment C: $(0.4)(30000) - (0.6)(14000) = 3600$

Investments A and C have the same expected value and both are higher than investment B.

22. **B.** One method is to create a probability distribution table for the data.

x	8	9	10	11	12
P(g(x))	0.16	0.18	0.20	0.22	0.24

Next, calculate the mean.

$$\mu = (8)(0.16) + (9)(0.18) + (10)(0.20) + (11)(0.22) + (12)(0.24) = 10.2$$

You can also use the TI-83/4 calculator. Put the numbers 8, 9, 10, 11, and 12 in L1. Move the cursor to the heading (name) in L2. Enter L1*0.02. This will fill L2 with the correct values based on the function. Then select STAT CALC 1-Var Stats to obtain the mean, as well as the standard deviation.

23. **A.** This is the binomial formula. From it you can tell that $n = 12$, $p = 0.4$, and therefore, $q = 1 - 0.4 = 0.6$. Use the formula for the standard deviation of a binomial formula: $\sigma = \sqrt{npq} = \sqrt{(12)(0.4)(0.6)} = 1.697$

24. **D.** This problem may be solved with a tree diagram.

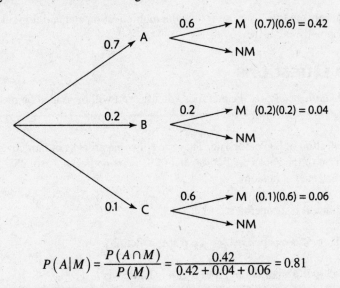

$$P(A|M) = \frac{P(A \cap M)}{P(M)} = \frac{0.42}{0.42 + 0.04 + 0.06} = 0.81$$

25. C. You are given that these are independent events. This implies that the intersection of the events is the product of their respective probabilities.

$$P(Y|X) = P(Y) \text{ since they are independent}$$
$$P(X \cap Y) = P(X) \cdot P(Y)$$
$$P(X \cup Y) = P(X) + P(Y) - P(X \cap Y)$$
$$P(X \cup Y) = P(X) + P(Y) - P(X) \cdot P(Y)$$
$$0.4 = P(X) + 0.2 - P(X) \cdot (0.2)$$
$$0.2 = (0.8)P(X)$$
$$P(X) = \frac{0.2}{0.8}$$
$$P(X) = 0.25$$

26. D. This problem may be solved using a tree diagram.

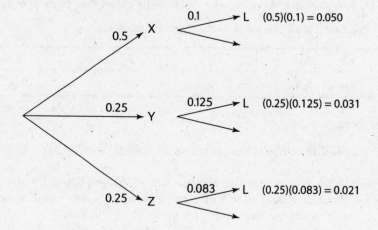

Note that only those necessary paths were filled in.

$$P(Y|L) = \frac{0.031}{0.050 + 0.031 + 0.021} = \frac{0.031}{0.102} = 0.304$$

27. D. All of these statements are true. They all follow the multiplication and addition rules as well as the definitions of independent and mutually exclusive.

Free-Response Questions

Directions: Show all work. Indicate clearly the methods you use. You will be graded on method as well as accuracy.

1. A bookstore has a collection of books for sale. They are either paperbacks or hardcovers and either fiction or nonfiction. Forty percent of the books are fiction, and 65% are paperbacks. Also, 25% of the fiction books are hardcover. A book is selected at random.

   a. What is the probability it is a paperback?

   b. What is the probability it is a paperback, given that it is fiction?

   c. What is the probability it is nonfiction, given that it is hardcover?

   d. What is the probability it is either nonfiction or paperback?

2. A manufacturer states that only 10% of the boxes of cereal they produce are underweight. You randomly select 15 boxes of cereal produced by this manufacturer and find that 5 are underweight.

   a. What is the probability of selecting 5 or more underweight boxes of cereal in a sample of 15 if the percentage of underweight boxes is what the manufacturer claims?

   b. What is the probability of selecting 5 or more underweight boxes of cereal in a sample of 15 if the underweight percentage was 40%?

   c. Comment on the manufacturer's claim.

3. Given two events, A and B, state why each of the following is not possible. Use formulas or equations to illustrate your answer.

   a. $P(A) = -0.46$

   b. $P(A) = 0.26$ and $P(A') = 0.62$

   c. $P(A \cap B) = 0.92$ and $P(A \cup B) = 0.42$

   d. $P(B) = 0.24$ and $P(B|A) = 0.32$

   e. $P(A \cap B) = P(A) \cdot P(B)$ and $P(B) > P(B|A)$

4. A basketball player is successful on 70% of his free throw attempts. A reporter stated that this basketball player averages 6 successful free throws per game. Use simulation to determine the average number of free throw attempts per game needed to average 6 successful free throws per game. Run 10 trials.

5. Forty percent of all cars do not stop at a particular stop sign. How many cars, on average, would you have to observe to see 8 cars actually stop at the stop sign? Use simulation to determine your answer. Conduct 10 trials.

6. A random variable M has a mean of 12 and a standard deviation of 3. If each value of M is multiplied by 4 and then 6 is added to the result, what will be the new mean and standard deviation?

7. At a local school, 90% of the students take the SAT, and 15% of the students take both the SAT and the ACT. Based on the information provided, which of the following calculations are not possible, and why? What can you say based on the data?

   a. P(ACT|SAT)

   b. P(SAT|ACT)

   c. $P(SAT \cup ACT)$

   If you know that everyone who took the ACT also took the SAT, how would that change your answer?

Free-Response Answers

1. First translate the information in the problem into statistical notation.

$$P(F) = 0.40$$
$$P(P) = 0.65$$
$$P(H|F) = 0.25$$

You immediately see that there are three variables showing up, so a direct use of the formulas would be difficult. A better approach would be a tree diagram or a table.

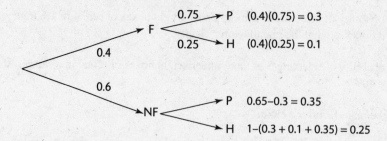

Since 40% of the books are fiction, fill in the 0.4 and the 0.6. Since 25% of the fiction are hardcover, fill in the 0.25. Multiply to get the 0.1. Next, subtract 0.25 from 1 to get the 0.75. Multiply to get the 0.3. Since 65% of the books are paperback, subtract to get the 0.35. Finally, add the three probabilities and subtract to get 0.25. After the tree diagram is filled in, answering the question is direct.

a. $P(P) = 0.65$

b. $P(P|F) = 0.75$

c. $P(N|H) = \dfrac{0.25}{0.1 + 0.25} = 0.714$

d. $P(N \cup P) = 0.25 + 0.35 + 0.3 = 0.9$

	P	H	Total
F	0.3	0.1	0.4
NF	0.35	0.25	0.6
Total	0.65	0.35	1.00

2. This is a binomial distribution. To do this problem directly using the formula would require finding the probabilities for 0, 1, 2, 3, and 4 underweight boxes, adding them, and subtracting from 1.

$$P(x = 0) = \binom{15}{0}(0.1)^0(0.9)^{15} = 0.206$$

$$P(x = 1) = \binom{15}{1}(0.1)^1(0.9)^{14} = 0.343$$

$$P(x = 2) = \binom{15}{2}(0.5)^2(0.5)^{13} = 0.267$$

$$P(x = 3) = \binom{15}{3}(0.5)^3(0.5)^{12} = 0.129$$

$$P(x = 4) = \binom{15}{4}(0.5)^4(0.5)^{11} = 0.043$$

The probability of 5 or more underweight is

$$1 - (0.206 + 0.343 + 0.267 + 0.129 + 0.043) = 0.012.$$

Using the TI-83/4

$$1 - \text{binomcdf}(15,0.1,4) = 0.013 \text{ (difference due to round-off error)}$$

This result is unlikely, but possible. The claim by a manufacturer should be right at least 90% of the time, not 1.2% as the manufacturer implies.

Using the probability of 40% gives a more realistic answer.

$$1 - \text{binomcdf}(15, 0.4, 4) = 0.783 \text{ or } 78.3\%.$$

The claim of only 1% underweight boxes is grossly understated. It should be more in the order of at least 40%.

3. a. It is not possible to have a negative probability. The correct formula is

$$P(E) \geq 0$$

b. The complement of two events must add to 1. These do not. The correct formula is

$$P(E) + P(E') = 1$$

c. The intersection of two sets is always a subset of each set. It is not possible for an intersection to have a greater probability than a union. The correct formula is

$$P(A \cup B) \geq P(A \cap B)$$

d. Adding a condition to the probability of an event cannot increase it, only decrease it. The correct formula is

$$P(A) \geq P(A|B)$$

e. Two events cannot be both independent and dependent at the same time. The first relationship shows that events A and B are independent since their intersection is the product of the probabilities. The second relationship shows that the events are dependent since the probability changed when a condition was added.

4. Using the given random number chart, develop a plan to simulate the basketball player shooting free throws.

36146	15570	28593	42089	99282	59640	15323	97054	39916	05321
21549	18432	73720	52218	02789	81003	49092	79044	50912	08388
87334	50174	30962	23607	88691	29294	87179	45443	51370	69555
92043	59814	60673	56569	22035	43311	56013	62846	69030	47559
47681	72704	49759	76359	12525	32143	15882	36916	08097	90578

Let the digits 0, 1, 2, 3, 4, 5, and 6 represent a successful free throw, and 7, 8, and 9 represent a miss. Start in the first row and count until you have six successes. Record this number. Continue counting again until you have six successes. Record this number. Repeat 10 times. Successes are underlined in the table. The sixth success in each sequence is in **bold.**

In the first sequence, the sixth success occurred on the sixth try. In the second sequence, the sixth success occurred on the ninth try. In the third sequence, the sixth success occurred on the eleventh try, and so on. The first 10 sequences have the following lengths: 6, 9, 11, 7, 8, 8, 7, 9, 7, and 11. Find the mean of these 10 numbers.

$$\mu = \frac{6 + 9 + 11 + 7 + 8 + 8 + 7 + 9 + 7 + 11}{10} = \frac{83}{10} = 8.3$$

So, based on this simulation, the player shoots an average of 8.3 free throws per game. This is very close to the calculated number found by dividing 6 by 0.7.

5. This simulation is similar to the previous problem.

36146	15570	28593	42089	99282	59640	15323	97054	39916	05321
21549	18432	73720	52218	02789	81003	49092	79044	50912	08388
87334	50174	30962	23607	88691	29294	87179	45443	51370	69555
92043	59814	60673	56569	22035	43311	56013	62846	69030	47559
47681	72704	49759	76359	12525	32143	15882	36916	08097	90578

Forty percent of all cars do not stop. Therefore, 60% do stop at the stop sign. Let the digits 0, 1, 2, 3, 4, and 5 represent those cars that stop at the stop sign. The digits 6, 7, 8, and 9 represent those cars that do not stop. Start in the first row and count until you have eight successes. Record this number. Continue counting again until you have eight successes. Record this number. Repeat 10 times. Successes are underlined in the table. The eighth success in each sequence is in **bold**. In the first sequence, the eighth stop occurred on the eleventh digit. In the second sequence, the eighth stop occurred on the fifteenth digit. The first 10 sequences have the following lengths: 11, 15, 12, 11, 10, 10, 14, 12, 13, and 17. Find the mean of these 10 numbers.

$$\mu = \frac{11 + 15 + 12 + 11 + 10 + 10 + 14 + 12 + 13 + 17}{10} = \frac{125}{10} = 12.5$$

So, based on this simulation, you would have to observe an average of 12.5 cars in order to see 8 cars that stop at the stop sign. This is close to the calculated answer found by dividing 8 by 0.6.

6. Both multiplication and addition change the mean. Only multiplication changes the variance and standard deviation.

$$\mu_{6+4x} = 6 + (4)\mu = 6 + (4)(12) = 54$$
$$\sigma_{6+}4x = (4)\sigma = (4)(3) = 12$$

7. The information provided does not tell you how these two events overlap or whether the ACT is a subset of the SAT. You do know that there is an overlap since 90% + 15% is more than 100%. Without knowing this relationship, none of the probabilities can be calculated. The best you can do is to give a range of values for each. Let S = SAT and A = ACT.

   a. The least amount of overlap (the smallest intersection) possible is 5% and the most is 15%, which occurs when A is a subset of S. Thus, $0.05 \leq P(A \cap S) \leq 0.15$. If the intersection is 5%, then $P(ACT|SAT) = \frac{0.05}{0.90} = 0.056$. If the intersection is 15%, then

   $$P(ACT|SAT) = \frac{0.15}{0.90} = 0.167.$$

   Therefore, $0.056 \leq P(ACT|SAT) \leq 0.167$

   b. Similarly, if the intersection is at the minimum of 5%, then $P(SAT|ACT) = \frac{0.05}{0.15} = 0.333$. If the intersection is at the maximum (when A is a subset of S) of 15%, then $P(SAT|ACT) = 1$.

   Therefore, $0.333 \leq P(SAT|ACT) \leq 1$.

   c. Finally, if the intersection is at the minimum of 5%, then $P(SAT \cup ACT) = 1$. If the intersection is at the maximum (when A is a subset of S) of 15%, then $P(SAT \cup ACT) = 0.900$.

   Therefore, $0.900 \leq P(SAT \cup ACT) \leq 1$.

   If everyone who took the ACT also took the SAT, then A is a subset of S. In this case, as illustrated previously,

   a. $P(ACT|SAT) = \frac{0.15}{0.90} = 0.167$

   b. $P(SAT|ACT) = 1$

   c. $P(SAT \cup ACT) = 0.900$

Anticipating Patterns: Combining Independent Random Variables

Probability distributions of random variables may be studied alone or in combination with one another. The interaction between random variables, or the lack of it, is complex. If the occurrence of an event changes the probability that another event will occur, the events are related in some way, and they are said to be dependent. The interaction of dependent events was studied in the previous chapter through the use of conditional probabilities. Combining dependent events is very complex and beyond the scope of AP Statistics. On the other hand, independent events may be combined quite easily.

Notion of Independence versus Dependence

The definition of **independent events:**

Two events, X and Y, are said to be independent if and only if the occurrence of one of the events does not affect the probability of the occurrence of the other event.

In many situations, it is very easy to determine whether two events are independent. If two events are clearly unrelated, they are independent.

EXAMPLE:
Are the events *tossing a coin* and *rolling a die* independent?

Clearly, the answer is yes. Say, you flip a coin and then roll a die. The fact that the coin flip resulted in a tail does not change the probability of getting a 4 when you roll the die. The fact that the roll of the die resulted in a 4 does not change the probability of getting a tail when you flip the coin. These two events are independent.

A common notation when dealing with multiple events at the same time is to indicate the value of each event in the probability formula. If the probability of event X is 0.45 when the value of the random variable X is 7, then you write $P(X = 7) = 0.45$. If the probability of event X and event Y is 0.25 when the value of the random variable X is 2 and the value of the random variable Y is 3, then you write $P(X = 2, Y = 3) = 0.25$.

Many calculations require that events be independent.

EXAMPLE:
When two dice are rolled, what is the probability that the total on the two dice will be 5?

First consider the different ways two dice sum to 5. They are 1+4, 2+3, 3+2, and 4+1. The calculation of the probability that the first die is a 1 and the second die is a 4 is simply the product of their individual probabilities. Similarly, with the other possible combinations. The results are then added.

If the first die is represented by event X and the second die is represented by event Y, $P(X = 1) = \frac{1}{6}$ and $P(Y = 4) = \frac{1}{6}$.

The four probabilities are

$$P(X = 1, Y = 4) = P(X = 1) \cdot P(Y = 4) = \left(\frac{1}{6}\right)\left(\frac{1}{6}\right) = \frac{1}{36}.$$

$$P(X = 2, Y = 3) = P(X = 2) \cdot P(Y = 3) = \left(\frac{1}{6}\right)\left(\frac{1}{6}\right) = \frac{1}{36}$$

$$P(X = 3, Y = 2) = P(X = 3) \cdot P(Y = 2) = \left(\frac{1}{6}\right)\left(\frac{1}{6}\right) = \frac{1}{36}$$

$$P(X = 4, Y = 1) = P(X = 4) \cdot P(Y = 1) = \left(\frac{1}{6}\right)\left(\frac{1}{6}\right) = \frac{1}{36}$$

Therefore, the probability the dice sum to 5 is

$$P(X + Y = 5) = \left(\frac{1}{36}\right) + \left(\frac{1}{36}\right) + \left(\frac{1}{36}\right) + \left(\frac{1}{36}\right) = \frac{4}{36} = \frac{1}{9} = 0.111$$

This answer required that the two events, X and Y, be independent. The result on one die did not change, in any way, the probability of a result on the other die. The probability of rolling a 4 on the second die is the same as the probability of rolling a 4 on the second die given that you rolled a 3 on the first die. That is, $P(Y = 4) = P(Y = 4|X = 3)$. This notation gives more information than using $P(Y) = P(Y|X)$.

A **two-way table,** also known as a **contingency table,** is a table of observed frequencies in which the rows correspond to one of the variables and the columns correspond to another variable. These tables are useful in determining whether two variables are independent or dependent.

EXAMPLE:

The following two-way table provides information about the probabilities of buying paint and paintbrushes by customers at a home improvement store.

	Bought paintbrushes	*Did not buy paintbrushes*
Bought paint	0.08	0.06
Did not buy paint	0.04	0.82

This table shows that most customers bought neither paint nor paintbrushes. How do you tell whether the purchase of one of the two items influences the purchase of the other item? Adding totals to the table will help.

	Bought paintbrushes	*Did not buy paintbrushes*	*Total*
Bought paint	0.08	0.06	0.14
Did not buy paint	0.04	0.82	0.86
Total	0.12	0.88	1.00

By adding column and row totals, you determine the probability that a customer buys paint and the probability that a customer buys paint brushes.

$$P(\text{buying paint}) = 0.08 + 0.06 = 0.14$$
$$P(\text{buying paintbrushes}) = 0.08 + 0.04 = 0.12$$

You also determine some conditional probabilities. These are found by dividing the cell location corresponding to one variable by the total, in the row or column, corresponding to the other variable.

$$P(\text{buying paint}|\text{buying paintbrushes}) = \frac{0.08}{0.12} = 0.667$$

$$P(\text{buying paintbrushes}|\text{buying paint}) = \frac{0.08}{0.14} = 0.571$$

Now look at the probability of buying paint, with no condition. Compare that with the probability of buying paint, given the added condition that the customer bought paintbrushes. They are not the same. So,

$$P(\text{buying paint}) \neq P(\text{buying paint}|\text{buying paintbrushes})$$

Similarly,

$$P(\text{buying paintbrushes}) \neq P(\text{buying paintbrushes}|\text{buying paint})$$

You can conclude that the buying of paint does influence the purchase of paintbrushes, and the purchase of paintbrushes does influence the purchase of paint. Since the probability of an event changed when it became conditional on the occurrence of another event, the two events are dependent.

EXAMPLE:

The following table, which includes totals for the row and column variables, shows the probabilities of tossing a coin and getting heads and rolling a die and getting a 4.

	Die—4	Die—not 4	Total
Coin—heads	$\frac{1}{12}$	$\frac{5}{12}$	$\frac{1}{2}$
Coin—not heads	$\frac{1}{12}$	$\frac{5}{12}$	$\frac{1}{2}$
Total	$\frac{1}{6}$	$\frac{5}{6}$	

$$P(\text{heads}) = \frac{1}{2} \qquad P(\text{heads}|4 \text{ on die}) = \frac{\frac{1}{12}}{\frac{1}{6}} = \frac{1}{2}$$

and

$$P(4 \text{ on die}) = \frac{1}{6} \qquad P(4 \text{ on die}|\text{heads}) = \frac{\frac{1}{12}}{\frac{1}{2}} = \frac{1}{6}$$

Thus,

$$P(\text{heads}) = P(\text{heads}|4 \text{ on die})$$
$$P(4 \text{ on die}) = P(4 \text{ on die}|\text{heads})$$

The probability of getting heads did not change when the condition of rolling a 4 was added. Also, the probability of rolling a 4 did not change when the condition of tossing heads was added. Therefore, these two events are independent.

In general: Two events, X and Y, are independent if and only if

$$P(X) = P(X|Y) \text{ or } P(Y) = P(Y|X)$$

In this example, you use *or* because if one condition exists, the other must exist. Either both of the previous conditions exist, or neither exists.

If event X and event Y are independent, then the conditional probability formulas simplify:

$$P(X \cap Y) = P(X) \cdot P(Y|X) = P(Y) \cdot P(X|Y) \text{ becomes } P(X \cap Y) = P(X) \cdot P(Y)$$

If two events are independent, then conditional row and column ratios are the same as total row and column ratios.

If $P(X) = a$, $P(X') = b$, $P(Y) = c$, and $P(Y') = d$, with $a + b = 1$ and $c + d = 1$, then

Events	Y	Y'	Total
X	ac	ad	a
X'	bc	bd	b
Total	c	d	1

$$P(X) = \frac{a}{1} \text{ and } P(X|Y) = \frac{ac}{c} = \frac{a}{1}$$
$$P(Y) = \frac{c}{1} \text{ and } P(X|Y) = \frac{ac}{a} = \frac{c}{1}$$

EXAMPLE:

Event A has two possible values, 5 and 25. Event B has three possible values, 6, 8, and 10. The following probabilities are known:

$$P(A = 5) = 0.25$$
$$P(B = 8) = 0.24$$
$$P(A = 25 \cap B = 6) = 0.33$$
$$P(A = 5 \cap B = 10) = 0.08$$
$$P(B = 8|A = 5) = 0.24$$

Are events A and B independent or dependent?

Draw a two-way table filling in the information you have.

	A = 5	A = 25	Total
B = 6		0.33	
B = 8	0.06		0.24
B = 10	0.08		
Total	0.25		1.00

The values of 0.25 and 0.24 are column and row totals. The values of 0.33 and 0.08 are written directly into the intersections in the table. The conditional probability is different. From the conditional probability formula:

$$P(A = 5 \cap B = 8) = P(A = 5) \cdot P(B = 8|A = 5) = (0.25)(0.24) = 0.06$$

You now have enough information to fill in the rest of the table in the following order:

$$P(A = 5 \cap B = 6) = 0.11$$
$$P(A = 25 \cap B = 8) = 0.18$$
$$P(B = 6) = 0.44$$
$$P(B = 10) = 0.32$$
$$P(A = 25) = 0.75$$
$$P(A = 25 \cap B = 10) = 0.24$$

	A = 5	A = 25	Total
B = 6	0.11	0.33	0.44
B = 8	0.06	0.18	0.24
B = 10	0.08	0.24	0.32
Total	0.25	0.75	1.00

For events A and B to be independent, each conditional probability (the intersections of the rows and columns) must be equal to the product of their row and column totals. They are. Also, for each value of $x = \{5,25\}$ and $y = \{6,8,10\}$

$$P(A = x) = P(A = x|B = y) \text{ and } P(B = y) = P(B = y|A = x)$$

This is true, for example:

$$P(A = 25) = 0.75$$

$$P\left(A = 25 \mid B = 6\right) = \frac{0.33}{0.44} = 0.75$$

$$P\left(A = 25 \mid B = 8\right) = \frac{0.18}{0.24} = 0.75$$

$$P\left(A = 25 \mid B = 10\right) = \frac{0.24}{0.32} = 0.75$$

These are all the same, also. Therefore, events A and B are independent.

Mean and Standard Deviation of Sums and Differences

Does a relationship exist between the means of several sets of numbers and the mean of a set made up of the sums or differences of the elements of those sets? How about a similar relationship for variances? How about extending the relationship to random variables? To answer these questions, consider the following several examples of the means and variances of sums and differences of

- two or more sets of numbers
- two or more dependent random variables
- two or more independent random variables

EXAMPLE:
Consider two sets of numbers: A = {3,5,7} and B = {4,12}. Form two additional sets of numbers, one made up of the sums of all the combinations of numbers, one from each set, and the other made up of the differences. Then calculate the mean and the variance of each of the four sets. Is there a relationship between the means or variances of these sets?

$$A = \{3,5,7\}$$
$$B = \{4,12\}$$
$$C = \{(3 + 4),(3 +12),(5 + 4),(5 + 12),(7, + 4),(7 + 12)\} = \{7,15,9,17,11,19\}$$
$$D = \{(3 - 4),(3 -12),(5 - 4),(5 - 12),(7, - 4),(7 - 12)\} = \{-1,-9,1,-7,3,-5\}$$

$$\mu_A = \frac{3 + 5 + 7}{3} = 5$$

$$\sigma_A^2 = \frac{(3 - 5)^2 + (5 - 5)^2 + (7 - 5)^2}{3} = \frac{8}{3}$$

$$\mu_B = \frac{4 + 12}{2} = 8$$

$$\sigma_B^2 = \frac{(4 - 8)^2 + (12 - 8)^2}{2} = 16$$

$$\mu_C = \frac{7 + 15 + 9 + 17 + 11 + 19}{6} = 13$$

$$\sigma_C^2 = \frac{(7 - 13)^2 + (15 - 13)^2 + (9 - 13)^2 + (17 - 13)^2 + (11 - 13)^2 + (19 - 13)^2}{6} = \frac{112}{6} = \frac{56}{3}$$

$$\mu_D = \frac{(-1) + (-9) + (1) + (-7) + (3) + (-5)}{6} = -3$$

$$\sigma_D^2 = \frac{\left((-1) - (-3)\right)^2 + \left((-9) - (-3)\right)^2 + \left((1) - (-3)\right)^2 + \left((-7) - (-3)\right)^2 + \left((3) - (-3)\right)^2 + \left((-5) - (-3)\right)^2}{6} = \frac{112}{6} = \frac{5!}{3}$$

The mean of the sum is equal to the sum of the means.

$$\mu_{A+B} = \mu_C = \mu_A + \mu_B$$
$$13 = 5 + 8$$

The variance of the sum is equal to the sum of the variances.

$$\sigma^2_{A+B} = \sigma^2_C = \sigma^2_A + \sigma^2_B$$
$$\frac{53}{3} = \frac{8}{3} + 18$$

The mean of the difference is equal to the difference of the means.

$$\mu_{A-B} = \mu_D = \mu_A + \mu_B$$
$$-3 = 5 - 8$$

The variance of the difference is equal to the SUM of the variances. (*Note:* SUM)

$$\sigma^2_{A-B} = \sigma^2_D = \sigma^2_A + \sigma^2_B$$
$$\frac{53}{3} = \frac{8}{3} + 18$$

These relationships may be generalized to any number of sets.

The mean of a sum of sets equals the sum of the means of the sets.

The mean of a difference of two sets equals the difference of the means of the two sets.

The variance of a sum of sets equals the sum of the variances of the sets.

The variance of a difference of two sets equals the sum of the variances of the two sets.

EXAMPLE:

This example illustrates *dependent random variables.*

You are given two random variables, A and B. There are four possible values for variable A (2, 5, 9, and 10) with probabilities of 0.35, 0.20, 0.25, and 0.20, respectively. There are three possible values for variable B (3, 4, and 8) with probabilities of 0.40, 0.35, and 0.25, respectively. The following distribution table shows their joint probabilities. The totals have been added for convenience. They are not part of the distribution table.

		2	**5**	**9**	**10**	**Total**
				A		
	3	0.20	0.05	0.10	0.05	0.40
B	**4**	0.10	0.05	0.10	0.10	0.35
	8	0.05	0.10	0.05	0.05	0.25
	Total	0.35	0.20	0.25	0.20	1.00

Do the expected values (means) for each of the random variables add to give the mean of the sum? Use the formula $E(X) = \mu_X = \Sigma x_i p_i$.

$$E(A) = \mu_A = \Sigma a_i p_i$$
$$= (2)(0.35) + (5)(0.20) + (9)(0.25) + (10)(0.20)$$
$$= 5.95$$
$$E(B) = \mu_B = \Sigma b_i p_i$$
$$= (3)(0.40) + (4)(0.35) + (8)(0.25)$$
$$= 4.60$$

When combining the variables, work with individual joint probabilities instead of the totals.

$$E(A + B) = (2 + 3)(0.20) + (5 + 3)(0.05) + (9 + 3)(0.10) + (10 + 3)(0.05) +$$
$$(2 + 4)(0.10) + (5 + 4)(0.05) + (9 + 4)(0.10) + (10 + 4)(0.10) +$$
$$(2 + 8)(0.05) + (5 + 8)(0.10) + (9 + 8)(0.05) + (10 + 8)(0.05)$$
$$= 10.55$$
$$E(A) + E(B) = E(A + B)$$

This example demonstrates the general rule about random variables and expected values. Also, this holds true for the difference as well as the sum. The general formula becomes

$$E(A) \pm E(B) = E(A \pm B)$$

You now compute the variances and see whether this same relationship holds. Use the formula
$Var(X) = \sigma_x^2 = \sum (x_i - \mu_x)^2 p_i$.

$$Var(A) = \sigma_A^2 = \sum (a_i - \mu_A)^2 p_i$$
$$= (2 - 5.95)^2(0.35) + (5 - 5.95)^2(0.20) +$$
$$(9 - 5.95)^2(0.25) + (10 - 5.95)^2(0.20)$$
$$= 11.2475$$
$$Var(B) = \sigma_B^2 = \sum (b_i - \mu_B)^2 p_i$$
$$= (3 - 4.6)^2(0.40) + (4 - 4.6)^2(0.35) + (8 - 4.6)^2(0.25)$$
$$= 4.04$$
$$Var(A + B) = (2 + 3 - 10.55)^2(0.20) + (5 + 3 - 10.55)^2(0.05) + (9 + 3 - 10.55)^2(0.10) +$$
$$(10 + 3 - 10.55)^2(0.05) + (2 + 4 - 10.55)^2(0.10) + (5 + 4 - 10.55)^2(0.05) +$$
$$(9 + 4 - 10.55)^2(0.10) + (10 + 4 - 10.55)^2(0.10) + (2 + 8 - 10.55)^2(0.05) +$$
$$(5 + 8 - 10.55)^2(0.10) + (9 + 8 - 10.55)^2(0.05) + (10 + 8 - 10.55)^2(0.05)$$
$$= 16.4475$$

The variances DO NOT add up. In general, the rule does not hold for variances of random variables. The reason the variances did not add up was because the random variables, A and B, were *dependent*. The joint probabilities were not those that would be expected if the variables were independent.

What about *independent* random variables? Can you construct a two-way joint probability distribution table that guarantees independence of the variables?

EXAMPLE:

This example illustrates *independent random variables*.

You can construct a table to guarantee independence. Do you remember the multiplication rule for independent variables? It is simply the product of the event probabilities. This is the procedure you will use to generate the values that go in the interior of the table. You will start with the data from the previous example except

		A				
		2	**5**	**9**	**10**	**Total**
	3	0.14	0.08	0.10	0.08	0.40
B	**4**	0.1225	0.07	0.0875	0.07	0.35
	8	0.0875	0.05	0.0625	0.05	0.25
	Total	0.35	0.20	0.25	0.20	1.00

Each intersection is the product of the row total and the column total. For example,

$$P(A = 2, B = 3) = P(A = 2) \cdot P(B = 3) = (0.35)(0.40) = 0.14$$

Complete the rest of the table in a similar manner.

$$E(A) = \mu_A = \Sigma a_i p_i$$
$$= (2)(0.35) + (5)(0.20) + (9)(0.25) + (10)(0.20)$$
$$= 5.95$$
$$E(B) = \mu_B = \Sigma b_i p_i$$
$$= (3)(0.40) + (4)(0.35) + (8)(0.25)$$
$$= 4.60$$
$$E(A + B) = (2 + 3)(0.14) + (5 + 3)(0.08) + (9 + 3)(0.10) + (10 + 3)(0.08) +$$
$$(2 + 4)(0.1225) + (5 + 4)(0.07) + (9 + 4)(0.0875) + (10 + 4)(0.07) +$$
$$(2 + 8)(0.0875) + (5 + 8)(0.05) + (9 + 8)(0.0625) + (10 + 8)(0.05)$$
$$= 10.55$$

Note that even though the joint probabilities on the interior of the table changed, the expected value of the sum did not. Now consider the variances.

$$Var(A) = \sigma_A^2 = \sum (a_i - \mu_A)^2 p_i$$
$$= (2 - 5.95)^2(0.35) + (5 - 5.95)^2(0.20) +$$
$$(9 - 5.95)^2(0.25) + (10 - 5.95)^2(0.20)$$
$$= 11.2475$$
$$Var(B) = \sigma_B^2 = \sum (b_i - \mu_B)^2 p_i$$
$$= (3 - 4.6)^2(0.40) + (4 - 4.6)^2(0.35) + (8 - 4.6)^2(0.25)$$
$$= 4.04$$
$$Var(A + B) = (2 + 3 - 10.55)^2(0.14) + (5 + 3 - 10.55)^2(0.08) + (9 + 3 - 10.55)^2(0.10) +$$
$$(10 + 3 - 10.55)^2(0.08) + (2 + 4 - 10.55)^2(0.1225) + (5 + 4 - 10.55)^2(0.07) +$$
$$(9 + 4 - 10.55)^2(0.0875) + (10 + 4 - 10.55)^2(0.07) + (2 + 8 - 10.55)^2(0.0875) +$$
$$(5 + 8 - 10.55)^2(0.05) + (9 + 8 - 10.55)^2(0.0625) + (10 + 8 - 10.55)^2(0.05)$$
$$= 15.2875$$

The variances now add up since the variables are independent.

So, to summarize:

For dependent or independent random variables, A and B:

$E(A \pm B) = E(A) \pm E(B)$

$\mu_{A \pm B} = \mu_A \pm \mu_B$

$\mathrm{Var}(A + B) = \mathrm{Var}(A) + \mathrm{Var}(B)$

For independent random variables, A and B only:

$\sigma^2_{A \pm B} = \sigma^2_A + \sigma^2_B$

Review Questions and Answers

Multiple Choice Questions

Directions: Solve each of the following problems. Decide which is the best of the choices given.

For problems 1–4: Each of the following is a joint probability distribution table for the random variables M and N.

Table I	N = 1	N = 2	Table II	N = 1	N = 2
M = 1	0.06	0.54	M = 1	0.56	0.06
M = 2	0.04	0.36	M = 2	0.14	0.24

1. Which of the tables provides information that will lead you to the conclusion that the variables M and N are independent random variables?

   A. I only
   B. II only
   C. I and II
   D. Neither chart provides the information needed.
   E. No conclusions can be drawn from the charts.

2. Using Table I, what is the expected value of M?

   A. 1.3
   B. 1.4
   C. 1.5
   D. 1.6
   E. 1.7

3. Using Table II, what is the expected value of N?

   A. 1.3
   B. 1.4
   C. 1.5
   D. 1.6
   E. 1.7

4. Using Table I, what is $E(M + N)$?

   A. 2.7
   B. 2.9
   C. 3.1
   D. 3.3
   E. 3.5

For problems 5–9: The following is a joint probability distribution table for two random variables, A and B.

		A		
		1	**2**	**3**
	1	0.05	0.05	0.15
B	**2**	0.30	0.10	0.05
	3	0.05	0.05	0.20

5. What is the probability distribution for the variable B?

   A. $P(B = 1) = 0.05, P(B = 2) = 0.05, P(B = 3) = 0.15$
   B. $P(B = 1) = 0.40, P(B = 2) = 0.20, P(B = 3) = 0.40$
   C. $P(B = 1) = 0.25, P(B = 2) = 0.45, P(B = 3) = 0.30$
   D. $P(B = 1) = 0.05, P(B = 2) = 0.30, P(B = 3) = 0.05$
   E. Cannot be determined since the variables are dependent

6. What is the probability distribution for the variable A?

   A. $P(A = 1) = 0.05, P(A = 2) = 0.05, P(A = 3) = 0.15$
   B. $P(A = 1) = 0.40, P(A = 2) = 0.20, P(A = 3) = 0.40$
   C. $P(A = 1) = 0.25, P(A = 2) = 0.45, P(A = 3) = 0.30$
   D. $P(A = 1) = 0.05, P(A = 2) = 0.30, P(A = 3) = 0.05$
   E. Cannot be determined since the variables are dependent

7. Find $P(A = 2, B = 1) - P(A = 1, B = 2)$.

   A. 0.05
   B. −0.05
   C. 0.25
   D. −0.25
   E. 0

8. Find $P(A = 1 | B = 3)$.

   A. 0.05
   B. 0.15
   C. 0.167
   D. 0.35
   E. 0.70

9. Find $P(A = 3 \cup B = 2)$.

  A. 0.15
  B. 0.30
  C. 0.45
  D. 0.80
  E. 0.85

10. The following is information from the probability distributions of two independent random variables, A and B. The possible values for A are 1, 2, and 3. The possible values for B are 1, 2, 3, and 4.

$$P(A = 1) = 0.1$$
$$P(A = 2) = 0.3$$
$$P(B = 1) = 0.2$$
$$P(B = 1) = 0.3$$

The joint probability $P(A = 2, B = 2) = 0.09$. Find $P(A = 2, B = 4)$.

  A. 0.03
  B. 0.04
  C. 0.05
  D. 0.06
  E. 0.07

11. The following is information from the probability distributions of two independent random variables, A and B. The possible values for A are 1, 2, and 3. The possible values for B are 1, 2, and 3.

$$P(A = 1) = 0.4$$
$$P(B = 3) = 0.4$$

The joint probabilities $P(A = 2, B = 1) = 0.2$ and $P(A = 3, B = 3) = 0.08$. Find $P(A = 2, B = 2)$.

  A. 0.04
  B. 0.06
  C. 0.10
  D. 0.14
  E. 0.30

12. The following is information from the probability distributions of two independent random variables, A and B. The possible values for A are 1, 2, and 3. The possible values for B are 1, 2, and 3. The joint probabilities $P(A = 2, B = 1) = 0.2$ and $P(A = 3, B = 1) = 0.4$. Which of the following may be determined from the information given?

  I. $P(A = 1)$
  II. $P(A = 1, B = 1)$
  III. $P(A = 2, B = 2)$

  A. I only
  B. II only
  C. III only
  D. I and II
  E. II and III

13. If A and B are independent random variables, $E(A) = 80$, $Var(A) = 10$, $E(B) = 60$, and $Var(B) = 4$, then what is $E(A - B)$ and $Var(A - B)$?

A. $E(A - B) = 20$ and $Var(A - B) = 6$

B. $E(A - B) = 20$ and $Var(A - B) = 14$

C. $E(A - B) = 140$ and $Var(A - B) = 6$

D. $E(A - B) = 140$ and $Var(A - B) = 14$

E. Cannot be determined from the information given.

14. If A and B are random variables, $E(A) = 200$, $Var(A) = 20$, $E(B) = 100$, and $Var(B) = 10$, then which of the following is not possible to determine?

I. $\mu_{A + B}$

II. $Var(A + B)$

III. $\sigma_{A + B}$

A. I only

B. I and II

C. I and III

D. II and III

E. I, II, and III

15. A dice game consists of rolling one regular die (6 sides numbered 1–6) and one die in the shape of a regular octagon (8 sides numbered 1–8). Each die is fair. You roll the two dice. What is the mean and standard deviation of the differences of all possible rolls of the dice?

A. $\mu = 1$ and $\sigma = 0.6$

B. $\mu = 1$ and $\sigma = 2.9$

C. $\mu = 1$ and $\sigma = 4.0$

D. $\mu = 5$ and $\sigma = 2.9$

E. $\mu = 5$ and $\sigma = 4.0$

Multiple Choice Answers

1. A. First, add totals to the rows and column for each table.

Table I	N = 1	N = 2	Total	Table II	N = 1	N = 2	Total
M = 1	0.06	0.54	0.60	**M = 1**	0.56	0.06	0.62
M = 2	0.04	0.36	0.40	**M = 2**	0.14	0.24	0.38
Total	0.10	0.90		**Total**	0.70	0.30	

In Table I, all the joint probabilities are products of the row and column totals. This is not true for Table II. Therefore, Table I leads to the conclusion that the variables are independent.

2. B. The expected value of a variable is the sum of its possible values multiplied by their respective probabilities. Using Table I,

$$E(M) = (1)(0.6) + (2)(0.4) = 1.4$$

3. A. The expected value of a variable is the sum of its possible values multiplied by their respective probabilities. Using Table II,

$$E(N) = (1)(0.7) + (2)(0.3) = 1.3$$

4. D. Method 1: Find the expected values of M and N separately, then add.

$$E(M) = (1)(0.6) + (2)(0.4) = 1.4$$
$$E(N) = (1)(0.1) + (2)(0.9) = 1.9$$

Adding gives 3.3.

Method 2: Use the joint probabilities.

$$E(M + N) = (1 + 1)(0.06) + (1 + 2)(0.54) +$$
$$(2 + 1)(0.04) + (2 + 2)(0.36)$$
$$= 3.3$$

5. C. Add totals to the table.

		A			
		1	**2**	**3**	**Total**
	1	0.05	0.05	0.15	0.25
B	**2**	0.30	0.10	0.05	0.45
	3	0.05	0.05	0.20	0.30
	Total	0.40	0.20	0.40	

The probability distribution for B is the row totals.

6. B. Using the table given in answer number 5, the probability distribution for A is the column totals.

7. D. This is the difference of the two joint probabilities.

$$0.05 - 0.30 = -0.25$$

8. C. This is a conditional probability: $P\left(A = 1 \middle| B = 3\right) = \frac{0.05}{0.30} = 0.167$.

9. D. This is the union of a row and a column.

Method 1: Use the addition rule: $P(A = 3 \cup B = 2) = P(A = 3) + P(B = 2) - P(A = 3 \cap B = 2)$.

$$0.40 + 0.45 - 0.05$$
$$= 0.80$$

Method 2: Add up the individual joint probabilities from the table.

$$P(A = 3 \cup B = 2) = 0.15 + 0.05 + 0.20 + 0.30 + 0.10 = 0.80$$

10. D. Create a table and fill in the values for the probabilities that are given. Using the fact that the variables are independent, the product of row and column totals is the joint probabilities. Complete rows and columns when possible. The joint probabilities in column $A = 2$ must add to 0.30.

		A			
		1	**2**	**3**	**Total**
	1	0.02	0.06	0.12	0.20
	2		0.09		
B	**3**	0.03	0.09	0.18	0.30
	4		0.06		
	Total	0.10	0.30	0.60	

11. A. Create a table and fill in the values for the probabilities that are given. Using the fact that the variables are independent, the product of row and column totals is the joint probabilities. Complete rows and columns when possible.

		A			
		1	**2**	**3**	**Total**
	1	0.20	0.20	0.10	0.50
B	**2**	0.04	0.04	0.02	0.10
	3	0.16	0.16	0.08	0.40
	Total	0.40	0.40	0.20	

12. D. Create a table and fill in the values for the probabilities that are given. Using the fact that the variables are independent, the product of row and column totals is the joint probabilities. Complete rows and columns when possible.

		A			
		1	**2**	**3**	**Total**
	1	0.2	0.2	0.4	0.8
B	**2**				
	3				
	Total	0.25	0.25	0.5	

The first value that is filled in is the joint probability at $A = 1$ and $B = 1$. When this row is complete, the entire probability distribution for A may be computed, as 0.25, 0.25, and 0.5 by dividing each of the joint probabilities by 0.8. Choice III is the only one you do not know.

13. B. For independent random variables:

$$E(A - B) = E(A) - E(B)$$

$$Var(A - B) = Var(A) + Var(B)$$

Therefore, simply subtract the expected values but sum the variances.

14. D. In this problem, no information about the dependence or independence of the random variables is given. Therefore, you can compute the mean of the sum, but not the variance or standard deviation.

15. B. Compute the mean and standard deviation of the numbers on each die. For the eight-sided die: $\mu_8 = 4.5$ and $\sigma_8 = 2.3$. For the six-sided die: $\mu_6 = 3.5$ and $\sigma_6 = 1.7$. The outcome on each die is independent of the outcome on the other die. Therefore, these random variables are independent. The mean of the differences is the difference of the means. The standard deviation of the differences is the square root of the sum of the variances. Therefore,

$$\mu_{8-6} = \mu_8 - \mu_6 = 4.5 - 3.5 = 1$$
$$\sigma_{8-6} = \sqrt{\sigma_8^2 + \sigma_6^2} = \sqrt{2.3^2 + 1.7^2} = 2.9$$

Free-Response Question

Directions: Show all work. Indicate clearly the methods you use. You will be graded on method as well as accuracy.

1. You are given two random variables, A and B. The probability distribution is as follows:

A	P(A)
1	0.2
2	0.8

B	P(B)
3	0.4
4	0.6

   a. If you do not know whether the random variables A and B are independent, what can you say about the joint probabilities? Does $P(A = 1, B = 3)$ have a maximum value? What is it? What can you say about $E(A + B)$ and $Var(A + B)$?

   b. If you know that the random variables, A and B, are independent, what can you say about the joint probabilities? Can you determine them? What can you say about $E(A + B)$ and $Var(A + B)$?

Free-Response Answer

1. **a.** Consider the probability distributions.

A	P(A)
1	0.2
2	0.8

B	P(B)
3	0.4
4	0.6

From these tables construct a two-way table of probabilities. Even though all the values are not known, you still can draw conclusions.

	A = 1	A = 2	Total
B = 3			0.4
B = 4			0.6
Total	0.2	0.8	

Since you do not know whether the variables are independent, you cannot determine the joint probabilities, but you do know that they cannot be more than their row and column totals. Thus, the maximum value of $P(A = 1, B = 3)$ is 0.2, since that is the column total. The estimated value of the sum of A and B is the sum of the expected values.

$$E(A + B) = E(A) + E(B)$$
$$= (1)(0.2) + (2)(0.8) + (3)(0.4) + (4)(0.6)$$
$$= 5.4$$

Since you do not know whether the variables are independent, you cannot find the variance of the sum.

b. If the variables are independent, the joint probabilities may be calculated as the product of their respective row and column totals.

	A = 1	A = 2	Total
B = 3	0.08	0.32	0.40
B = 4	0.12	0.48	0.60
Total	0.20	0.80	

The expected value of the sum of the variables may be calculated whether or not the variables are independent, as shown in part **a.** But since the variables are independent, the variances of the sum may now be calculated.

The variance of variable A is 0.25. The variance of variable B is 0.25.

The variance of the sum of the variables is the sum of the individual variances, or $0.25 + 0.25 = 0.50$.

The **bell-shaped** probability distribution is probably the most common of all distributions of **continuous random variables.** This normal random variable has a probability distribution called the **normal distribution.** In the branch of statistics called **inferential statistics,** the normal distribution plays a key role in allowing us the make predictions and to test claims. Normal distributions are all around us. The weights of 10-year-old boys, the diameter of ball bearings being produced by a machine, the net weight of cereal boxes, the amount of water in a particular brand of bottled water, and the IQ of adults are all examples of normally distributed data.

The normal distribution might be thought of as a limiting case of the binomial distribution when the probability of success is 0.5 and the number of trials grows without bound. The illustrations that follow show several binomial distributions with an increasing number of trials. Notice that the distribution is mound-shaped and symmetric. As the number of trials increases, the width of each bar decreases. The stair-step look of the binomial distribution tends toward a smooth, bell-shaped curve.

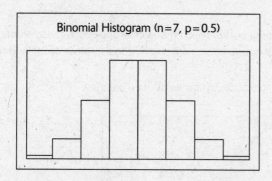

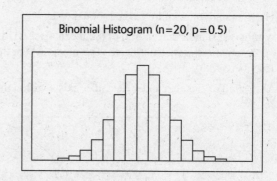

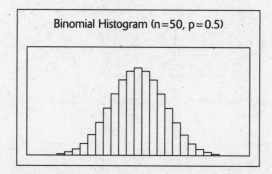

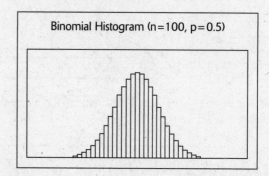

Properties of the Normal Distribution

Unlike discrete random variables, continuous random variables are associated with intervals on the number line. Discrete random variables have a fixed, countable number of possible outcomes. Continuous random variables have an infinite number of possible outcomes. As discussed in the previous chapter, the probability distribution of discrete random variables lists all the possible outcomes of the random variable along with the respective probabilities. A **density curve** describes the probability distribution of continuous random variables. Some features common to all density curves include the following:

The total area under the curve is always equal to one.

The probability of any single event is equal to zero. (Single events correspond to single points or lines, thus, they have no area, and therefore, no probability.)

The probability that an event will occur within a given interval is equal to the area under the curve above that interval.

Probability distributions of several different continuous density curves are used in Statistics. The most common one is the normal probability distribution. This is the same bell-shaped curve used with the Empirical Rule (68%, 95%, 99.7% discussed in an earlier chapter. More precise values are calculated using the normal probability distribution.

The following is the formula for the probability distribution for a normal random variable, x:

$$f(x) = \frac{1}{\sigma\sqrt{2\pi}} e^{-\frac{1}{2}\left(\frac{x-\mu}{\sigma}\right)^2}$$

The use of this formula is cumbersome to find the area in intervals under the curve. Tables of values are produced and provided for this purpose. On the AP Statistics Test, you will be required to be able to read these tables. You also need to know how to use technology tools, such as the TI-83/4, to find these values.

Some characteristics of the normal distribution include the following:

The mean, median, and mode all have the same value.

The curve is bell-shaped and symmetric about a vertical line through the mean.

The curve approaches, but never touches, the x-axis as you move away from the mean.

The area under the entire curve is equal to 1.

Within one standard deviation of the mean, ($\mu \pm \sigma$), the graph curves (opens) downward. Beyond these points, the graph curves (opens) upward. The points where this transition occurs are referred to as **points of inflection.** They occur at ($\mu \pm \sigma$).

Almost all of the area under the curve exists within three standard deviations of the mean ($\mu \pm 3\sigma$).

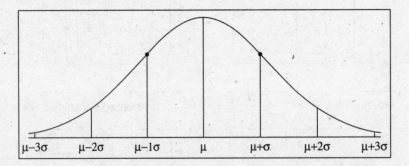

The following two figures show how changing the mean and standard deviation of the normal curve changes the shape of the curve.

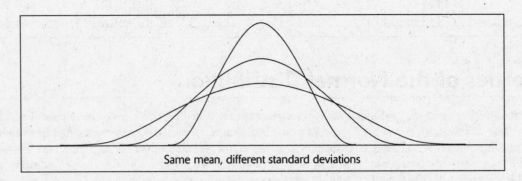

Same mean, different standard deviations

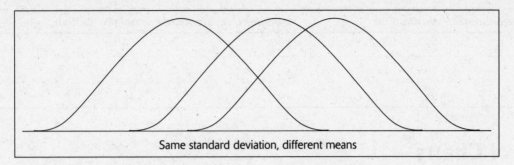

Same standard deviation, different means

The TI-83/4 can draw probability density functions. Here is an example of the normal distribution with three different standard deviations, but the same mean:

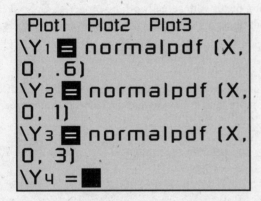

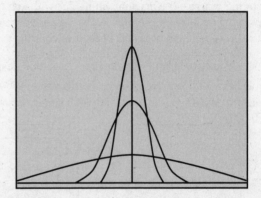

There are countless normal distributions, each having a unique mean and standard deviation. One specific normal distribution is of great interest to us. A standard normal distribution is a normal distribution that has mean $\mu = 0$ and standard deviation $\mu = 1$. The variable z corresponding to this specific distribution is called a **standard normal variable,** or **z-score.**

Any normal distribution x with mean μ and standard deviation σ may be standardized by using the formula $z = \frac{x - \mu}{\sigma}$. After standardization, the area in an interval of the nonstandard normal distribution is the same as the area under the standard normal distribution with respect to corresponding z-scores. The random variable x represents values in normal distributions. The random variable z represents values in the standard normal distribution. *Every normal distribution may be standardized into the standard normal distribution.* You can, therefore, use z-scores to find areas in intervals under any normal curve.

The variable z is a unitless measure. It simply counts the number of standard deviations x is from μ. This is an extremely important fact. It means that you can compare z-scores to each other even when they come from distributions that use different units, different means, and different standard deviations.

Always keep in mind that about 68% of the area under the normal curve lies within one standard deviation of the mean, about 95% lies within two standard deviations of the mean, and about 99.7% lies within three standard deviations of the mean. The fact that such a high percentage of all data lies within three standard deviations of the mean implies that for normally distributed data, excluding outliers, the standard deviation may be approximated as one-sixth of the range of representative data.

The z-score indicates how many standard deviations above or below the mean a point lies. A positive z-score represents positions on the number line greater than the mean, and negative z-scores represent positions on the number line that are less than the mean. The following chart shows the relationship between values of a random variable x from a normal distribution and the corresponding values of the variable z from the corresponding standard normal distribution.

187

x-values from normal distributions	z-values from standard normal distribution
$x < \mu$	$z < 0$
$x > \mu$	$z > 0$
$x = \mu$	$z = 0$

Control Charts

If individual measurements of a process are distributed normally, a control chart can help detect whether the process is *out of control*. It can be an indicator of a machine that needs adjustment or that more attention needs to be spent on a manufacturing process. Is a machine filling jars with jam or filling boxes with cereal working properly? Control charts help in pointing out possible problems. They are not absolute, but rather a warning device. Three warning signals are used to detect whether a process may be out of control.

1. A single measurement lies more than 3 standard deviations from the mean.

   Probability of occurrence: Since approximately 99.7% of normally distributed measurements fall within three standard deviations, the probability of a single occurrence more than three standard deviation from the mean is 0.003.

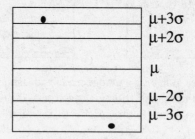

2. A sequence of nine consecutive measurements on the same side of the mean.

   Probability of occurrence: Since 50% of normally distributed measurements lie on each side of the mean, the probability that nine consecutive points will be on the same side of the mean is $0.5^9 = 0.002$. This probability is for each side of the mean, so the value is doubled to 0.004.

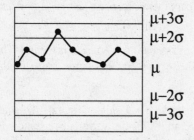 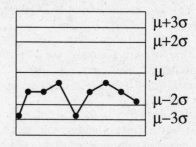

3. At least two of three consecutive measurements lie more than two standard deviations from the mean on the same side of the mean.

   Probability of occurrence: From the Empirical Rule, approximately 2.35% of normally distributed measurements will lie between 2 and 3 standard deviations above the mean. This signal is generated if at least two of three consecutive points lie in this region. Use the binomial distribution to determine the probability of at least two occurrences.

$$\binom{3}{2}(0.0235)^2(.9765)^2 + \binom{3}{3}(0.0235)^2(.9765)^2 = 0.016$$

This probability is doubled to take into account both sides of the mean, giving a probability of occurrence of 0.003.

Using Tables of the Normal Distribution

Tables are used to determine the area under curves to the left of a given point. This corresponds to finding the probability that a value in the distribution will fall to the left of that point. More specifically, the table of standard normal probabilities is for areas under the standard normal distribution. This table is used after x-values have been standardized to z-values (z-scores). You will need to know how to read this table for the AP Statistics Test. You should also be able to use your calculator to obtain the probabilities.

Although tables may be designed in a variety of ways, the table of standard normal probabilities used on the AP Statistics Test lists entries for z and the corresponding probability of lying to the left of (below) z.

A note about notation: In a continuous distribution, the probability of a single point is 0. Therefore, it does not matter whether you use $P(z < k)$ or $P(z \leq k)$; the probabilities are the same. Another way to think about this is to consider a boundary as being a line. Should you include or exclude the line when considering area or probability? Since a line has no width, it has no area and, therefore, does not represent a probability.

EXAMPLE:
Using the standard normal distribution, what is the probability that $z < 1$?

The table of standard normal probabilities consists of two pages. On one page are probabilities to the left of negative z-scores. On the other page are probabilities to the left of positive z-scores. These are two-place tables. The left column indicates the first decimal place of the z-score, and the column header indicates the second decimal place. Reading down the positive z-scores gives a probability of 0.8413 when $z = 1.00$. You would write this as $P(z < 1.00) = 0.8413$. This is a more accurate answer than the one you would get using the Empirical Rule, which would give 0.84. Sketching these graphs is important, especially in the free-response sections of the exam.

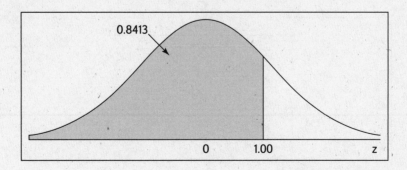

EXAMPLE:

Using the standard normal distribution, find $P(z > -0.73)$.

Looking down the column of negative z-scores, find -0.7 and then move over to the 03 column. The probability to the *left* of this point is 0.2327. This is the complement of what you want. Subtract from 1 to get the correct answer of 0.7673.

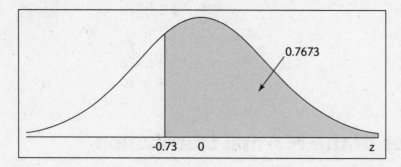

The TI-83/4 calculator graphs the probability density function. Select DISTR DRAW ShadeNorm(lowerbound, upperbound, μ, σ). These two screens show the results of the preceding example ShadeNorm(–99, 1, 0, 1) and this example ShadeNorm(–0.7,99,0,1).

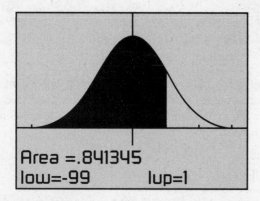 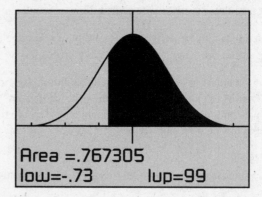

EXAMPLE:

Find the area between z-scores of (-1.43) and (1.88).

To find the probability between two z-scores, find the probability to the left of each using the table and then subtract. The tables shows a probability of 0.9699 to the left of a z-score of 1.88 and a probability of 0.0764 to the left of a z-score of -1.43. Subtract to get the answer of 0.8935.

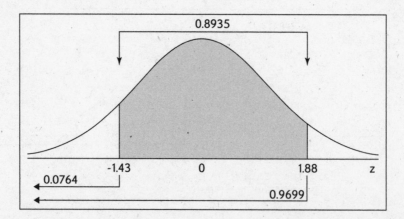

Screenshots from the TI-83/4 are shown here.

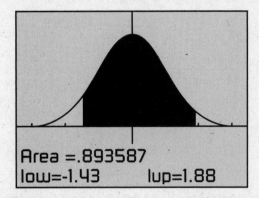

To obtain these results using the TI-83/4 calculator without graphing the function, use the normalcdf(lowerbound, upperbound, μ and σ) function. The calculations for the preceding three examples are

normalcdf(–99, 1, 0, 1)

normalcdf(–1.73, 99, 0, 1)

normalcdf(–1.43, 1.88, 0, 1)

The default values for the mean and standard deviation are 0 and 1, respectively, so they do not have to be included in the preceding formulas.

In the last three examples, you found probabilities based on z-scores. The inverse of this process is to find approximate values of z-scores based on probabilities. Remember, the area given in the table of standard normal probabilities is that which is to the left of the respective z-score.

EXAMPLE:
Find the z-score that has 71.3% of the distribution's area to its left.

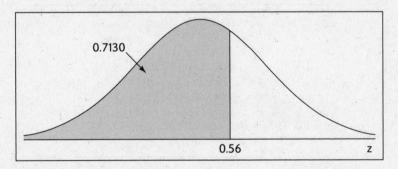

Since the table of values shows probabilities to the left of a given z-score and the probability lies to the left of the z-score in question, simply find 0.7130 as a probability in the interior of the table. You are not looking up by z-score, but rather by probability. If there is no match, find the one that is the closest. In this case, the closest value is 0.7123. This is the probability that corresponds to a z-score of 0.56. This, of course, is an approximate answer. The TI-83/4 can be used to find z-scores based on probability. Select DISTR invNorm(area, μ, σ). The mean and standard deviation have defaults of 0 and 1, respectively.

EXAMPLE:

Find the z-score with an area of 0.9355 to its right.

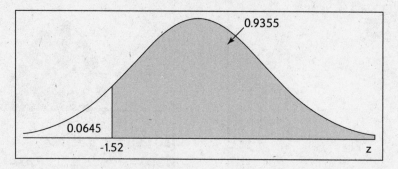

In this problem, the area to the right is given. Table values show probabilities to the left of a given z-score. Therefore, subtract 0.9355 from 1 and then look up the probability of 0.0645. The value of 0.0643 is the closest, and it corresponds to a z-score of –1.52. To calculate the value using the TI-83/4, select DISTR invNorm(0.0645,0,1) or just invNorm(0.0645) since the defaults of $\mu = 0$ and $\sigma = 1$ are defaults.

EXAMPLE:

Find the z-score for which 82% of the distribution's area lies between –z and z.

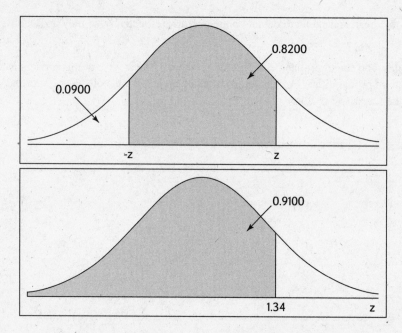

This problem is different since the area in question does not extend to the left indefinitely. Table values show probabilities to the left of a given z-score. There is more than 82% of the distribution area to the left of z. Since the distribution is symmetric, there must be 18% (100% – 82%) outside the interval. This area is equally divided in each tail of the distribution. Therefore, the value to look up in the table is (0.8200 + .0900), or 0.9100. The closest value in the table is 0.9099. This corresponds to a z-score of 1.34. To calculate the value using the TI-83/4, select DISTR invNorm(0.9100,0,1) or just invNorm(0.9100) since the defaults of $\mu = 0$ and $\sigma = 1$ are defaults.

The Normal Distribution as a Model for Measurements, Including Solving for the Mean and Standard Deviation

Whenever the normal distribution is being used as a model to solve a problem, a rough sketch of the normal curve should be drawn marking in any critical values and probabilities. Marking and labeling both the x-value and the z-value should be done clearly. A convenient way of showing the relationship between the x-value and the z-value is to indicate both beneath the curve. Shade in the area of the graph representing what you are looking for. For free-response questions, be sure to write the equation, show the substitutions, and solve, making clear what your final answer is. (Usually, it is best to restate the final answer in sentence form.)

Problems require you to find different missing variables. All the following examples use the formula that relates four important values. The following four equations are versions of the same formula.

$$z = \frac{x - \mu}{\sigma}$$
$$x = z\sigma + \mu$$
$$\mu = x - z\sigma$$
$$\sigma = \frac{x - \mu}{z}$$

You may need to calculate any one of the four variables given the other three. If you know the probability to the left of a certain point, you can find the value of z.

EXAMPLE:
The average cruising fuel consumption of a jet aircraft is 3380 gallons per hour. If fuel consumption per hour is normally distributed with a standard deviation of 250 gallons per hour, what is the probability the cruising fuel consumption is

  a. less than 3100 gallons per hour?

  b. more than 3900 gallons per hour?

  c. between 3400 and 3700 gallons per hour?

  a. To find the probability of using less than 3100: Draw a sketch of the normal curve. Mark in the mean fuel consumption and the value in question, 3100. Shade in the part of the distribution you are interested in finding. In this case, it is the area to the left of 3100. Calculate a z-score for the value of 3100:
  $z = \frac{x - \mu}{\sigma} = \frac{3100 - 3380}{250} = -1.12$. Look up this z-score in the table of standard normal probabilities.
  Fill in appropriate values in the sketch. The corresponding probability is 0.1314.

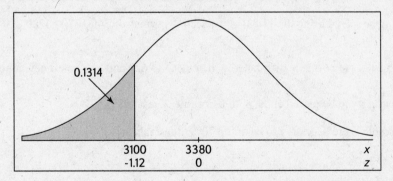

  This problem may be solved using the TI-83/4 by selecting normalcdf(-99999,3100,3380,250).

  b. To find the probability of using more than 3900: Draw a sketch of the normal curve. Mark in the mean fuel consumption and the value in question, 3900. Shade in the part of the distribution you are interested in finding. In this case, it is the area to the right of 3900. Calculate a z-score for the value of 3900: $z = \frac{x - \mu}{\sigma} = \frac{3900 - 3380}{250} = 2.08$.

  Look up this z-score in the table of standard normal probabilities. The probability corresponding to this z-score is 0.9812. This represents the area to the left of the z-score of 2.08. You are interested in the area to the right. This is the complement. Subtract from 1 to give the correct answer. Fill in appropriate values in the sketch. The corresponding probability is 0.0188.

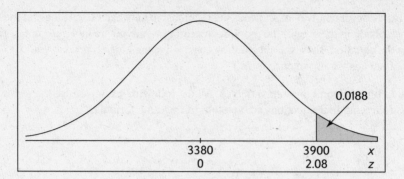

This problem may be solved using the TI-83/4 by selecting normalcdf(3900,99999,3380,250).

c. To find the probability of using between 3400 and 3700: Draw a sketch of the normal curve. Mark in the mean fuel consumption and the values in question, 3400 and 3700. Shade in the part of the distribution you are interested in finding; in this case, between 3400 and 3700. Calculate the z-scores for both 3400 and 3700:

$$z = \frac{x - \mu}{\sigma} = \frac{3700 - 3380}{250} = 1.28 \text{ and } \sigma = \frac{x - \mu}{z} = \frac{3400 - 3380}{250} = 0.08.$$

Look up these z-scores in the table of standard normal probabilities. Subtract these probabilities to obtain the probability of being between the two values. The probability corresponding to a z-score of 1.28 is 0.8997. The probability corresponding to a z-score of 0.08 is 0.5319. Subtract to get the answer of 0.3678.

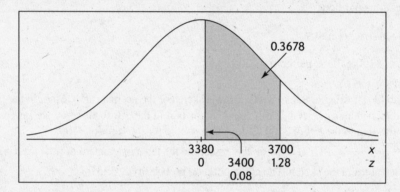

This problem may be solved using the TI-83/4 by selecting normalcdf(3400,3700,3380,250).

EXAMPLE:
The scores received on a test are normally distributed with a mean of 620 and a standard deviation of 124.

a. What score is necessary to be placed at the 85th percentile of test takers?

b. What is the minimum score necessary to be in top 70% of test takers?

c. What is the IQR of this data?

a. To find score for 85th percentile: Draw a sketch of the normal curve. Mark the mean. The 85th percentile is to the right of the mean. Position the variable x to the right of the mean. Eighty-five percent of the distribution's area is to the left of this point. Shade this region and label it. Look up 0.8500 in the table of standard normal probabilities. It corresponds to a z-score of 1.04. Label the 85th percentile with this z-score. Solve for x. $x = z\sigma + \mu = (1.04)(124) + 620 = 748.96$. The score necessary to be placed at the 85th percentile is 749.

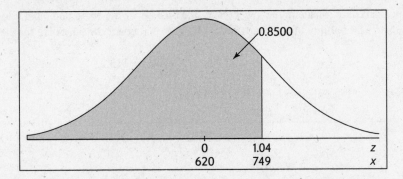

This problem may be solved using the TI-83/4 by selecting invNorm(0.85,620,124)

b. To find the minimum score to be in the top 70%: Draw a sketch of the normal curve. Mark the mean. Mark a point to the left of the mean that has 70% of the area of the distribution to its right. Shade in this portion of the graph. It is important to show this accurately in free-response questions. If 70% lies to the right of the unknown score, then 30% lies to the left. The table of probabilities always list probabilities to the left. Look up 0.3000 in the table of standard normal probabilities. It corresponds to a z-score of -0.52. Label the unknown point with the z-score. Solve for x. $x = z\sigma + \mu = (-0.52)(124) + 620 = 555.52$. The minimum score is 556.

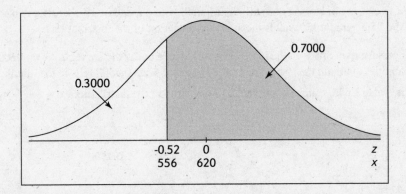

This problem may be solved using the TI-83/4 by selecting invNorm(0.30,620,124). (The calculator actually indicates it should be 555. This is due to round off error in selecting the z-value from the table.)

c. To find the IQR: The interquartile range stretches from the 25th percentile to the 75th percentile. Use the procedure, outlined in part **a,** twice. Subtract to get the IQR.

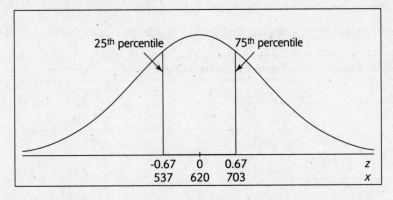

The interquartile range is equal to Q3 − Q1 = 703 − 537 = 166.

EXAMPLE:
The life expectancy of a projector bulb is normally distributed with a standard deviation of 12.3 hours. If 7% of these types of bulbs last less than 95 hours, what is the average life expectance of these bulbs?

Draw a sketch of the normal curve. Shade in the lower 7% of the area under the curve and label it as 95. Determine the z-score that corresponds to a probability of 0.0700. It is −1.48. Label that under the 95. Solve for the mean.

$$\mu = x - z\sigma = 95 - (-1.48)(12.3) = 113.2$$

The average life expectancy of the projector bulbs is 113.2 hours.

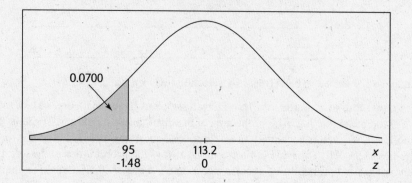

EXAMPLE:

The average weight of two-year-old boys is normally distributed with a mean of 12.6 kg. If a two-year-old boy who weighs 15.2 kg. is at the 95th percentile, what is the standard deviation of the distribution?

Draw a sketch of the normal curve. Shade in the lower 95% of the area under the curve. Look up 0.9500 in the table of standard normal probabilities to obtain the z-score of 1.645. Note that since 0.9500 falls in the middle between 0.9495 and 0.9505, you use the value 1.645. Calculate the standard deviation of the distribution: $\sigma = \dfrac{x - \mu}{z} = \dfrac{15.2 - 12.6}{1.645} = 1.58$.

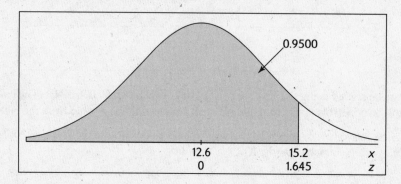

Certain probabilities and z-scores occur with great frequency in problems. These are summarized in the following table.

Probability (Area under curve)	Relative position to z-score	z-score
0.8000	is left of	0.84
0.9000	is left of	1.28
0.9500	is left of	1.645
0.9900	is left of	2.32
0.8000	is right of	−0.84
0.9000	is right of	−1.28
0.9500	is right of	−1.645
0.9900	is right of	−2.32

Probability (Area under curve)	Relative position to z-score	z-score
0.8000	is between	−1.28 and 1.28
0.9000	is between	−1.645 and 1.645
0.9500	is between	−1.96 and 1.96
0.9900	is between	−2.576 and 2.576
0.6826	is between	−1 and 1
0.9544	is between	−2 and 2
0.9975	is between	−3 and 3

The Normal Approximation to the Binomial

The binomial distribution is a discrete distribution. The probability of each value of the random variable is calculated with the binomial formula. If a problem involves a few different values of the random variable, using the binomial formula repeatedly is reasonable. For example, if a task is successfully completed 72% of the time, determine the probability of at least 6 successes out of 8 attempts. It is reasonable to use the binomial formula to solve this problem since it only has to be used three times, for $x = 6$, 7, and 8. However, if the number of trials is large, the number of binomial calculations needed to answer a question could be excessive. For example, if a task is successfully completed 72% of the time, determine the probability of at least 600 successes out of 800 attempts. In this case, it is not practical to use the binomial formula to answer the question since it would have to be used 201 times. It is better to use the normal distribution to approximate the binomial distribution. This is referred to as the normal approximation to the binomial.

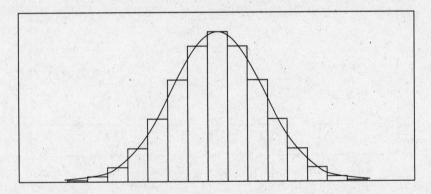

Under what conditions will the binomial distribution be approximately normally distributed? If the probability of success is 0.5, then the binomial is normally distributed for most values of n, even small ones. If the probability of success is close to 0 or 1, the binomial is skewed for small values of n but is more normally distributed as n grows larger. Consider the following two histograms of the binomial distribution.

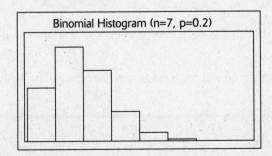

Binomial Histogram (n=7, p=0.2)

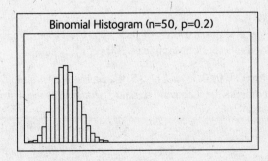

Binomial Histogram (n=50, p=0.2)

Both are binomial distributions with a probability of success of $p = 0.2$. When $n = 7$, the distribution is definitely not mound-shaped and symmetric. When $n = 50$, the distribution is approximately normal.

If $np > 5$ and $nq > 5$ (some authors use 10) then the binomial variable is approximately normally distributed with $\mu = np$ and $\sigma = \sqrt{npq}$. The variable, q, is used in place of $(1 - p)$ by some authors.

Since the binomial distribution is discrete, it can be represented by a histogram. The probability of each value of the random variable is the area of each bar in the histogram. The width of each bar is 1 and the midpoint of each bar is the value of the random variable. If you use a continuous distribution, such as the normal distribution, to approximate the binomial distribution, it is necessary to make an adjustment. You must move 0.5 units either to the left or to the right of the midpoint to include the entire bar of the histogram in the calculation. This adjustment is called a **correction for continuity.**

EXAMPLE:

If a task is successfully completed 72% of the time, determine the probability of at least 600 successes out of 800 attempts.

To use the normal approximation to the binomial, first verify that $np > 5$ and $nq > 5$. Since 28% of 800 is clearly greater than 5, you may proceed. Calculate the mean and standard deviation of the distribution.

$$\mu = np = (800)(0.72) = 576$$
$$\sigma = \sqrt{npq} = \sqrt{(800)(0.72)(0.28)} = 12.7$$

Since you are interested in at least 600 successes, the bar representing exactly 600 successes must be included. Using the correction for continuity, the continuous variable in the normal distribution needs to begin at 599.5. If the problem had stated "greater than 600 successes," then you would have used 600.5 instead. Using this value for x, proceed with the calculation of the normal probability.

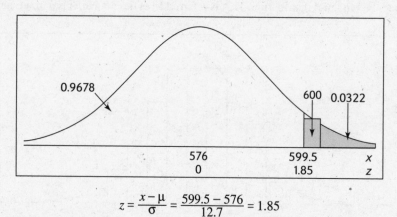

$$z = \frac{x - \mu}{\sigma} = \frac{599.5 - 576}{12.7} = 1.85$$

This z-score corresponds to a probability of 0.9678. This represents the probability for less than 600 successes. Subtract from 1 to get the correct answer of 0.0322.

Compare this value with the more accurate value of 0.0311 obtained from the TI-83/4 using 1–binomcdf(800,0.72,599).

EXAMPLE:

In the general population 38% have type O+ blood. What is the probability of finding more than 100 people with type O+ blood in a random sample of 300 people?

Since $np = (300)(0.38) = 114 > 5$, the problem is suitable for using the normal approximation to the binomial for solution. First, compute the mean and standard deviation of the distribution.

$$\mu = np = (300)(0.38) = 114$$
$$\sigma = \sqrt{npq} = \sqrt{(300)(0.38)(0.62)} = 8.4$$

Since the problem asked for "more than 100," exclude the bar valued at 100 and begin at 100.5.

$$z = \frac{x - \mu}{\sigma} = \frac{100.5 - 114}{8.4} = -1.61$$

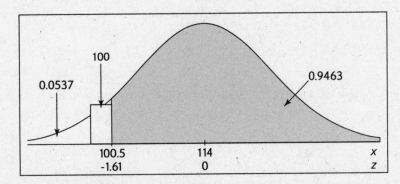

This z-score corresponds to a probability of 0.0537. This represents the probability for less than or equal to 100 successes. Subtract from 1 to get the correct answer of 0.9463.

Compare this value with the more accurate value of 0.9468 obtained from the TI-83/4 using 1–binomcdf(300,0.38,100).

Review Questions and Answers

Multiple Choice Questions

Directions: Solve each of the following problems. Decide which is the best of the choices given.

1. Which of the following are true about the normal distribution?

 I. The total area under the standard normal curve is equal to 1.
 II. The total area under a nonstandard normal curve is equal to 1.
 III. Every normal distribution can be standardized.

 A. I only
 B. III only
 C. I and II
 D. I and III
 E. I, II, and III

2. Which of the following are true about the normal distribution?

 I. The standard deviation gets smaller as z increases.
 II. Approximately 68% of the area under a normal curve lies within one variance of the mean.
 III. Normal distributions are asymmetric about the mean.

 A. I and II
 B. I and III
 C. II and III
 D. All of the statements are true.
 E. None of the statements is true.

3. What is the probability that a randomly selected member of a normally distributed population will lie more than 1.8 standard deviations from the mean?

    A. 0.0359

    B. 0.0718

    C. 0.1841

    D. 0.8159

    E. 0.9641

4. A standardized test has $\mu = 100$ and $\sigma = 250$. What score would be necessary to score at the 85th percentile?

    A. 740

    B. 1040

    C. 1250

    D. 1260

    E. 1900

5. Which of the following are true about the normal distribution?

    I.   It is symmetric about the mean; the mean, median, and mode are all the same; more than 90% of the distribution is within 2 standard deviations of the mean.

    II. The normal density curve is defined by its mean and standard deviation and nothing else; there is no largest or smallest data value.

    III. An interval x units wide and centered about the mean represents more data values than any other interval x units wide.

    A. I only

    B. I and II

    C. I and III

    D. II and III

    E. I, II, and III

6. Using a normal distribution, find two positive z-scores such that the z-scores differ by 0.10, and the probabilities to their left differ by 0.01. What is the larger of the two z-scores?

    A. 0.705

    B. 1.615

    C. 1.715

    D. 1.960

    E. 2.760

7. In a normal distribution with $\mu = 4$ and $\sigma = 1$, where would the points of inflection be located?

    A. $z = \pm 1$

    B. $z = 4 \pm 1$

    C. $z = 1 \pm 4$

    D. $z = 4 \pm 4$

    E. None of the above is a correct response to the question.

8. The ERA of starting pitchers is normally distributed with a mean of 3.82 and a standard deviation of 1.14. What proportion of pitchers have ERAs between 3 and 4?

   A. 0.24
   B. 0.33
   C. 0.56
   D. 0.72
   E. 0.88

9. You are given a very large normal distribution with $\mu = 200$ and $\sigma = 85$. A sample of 500 is drawn from the population. How many would you expect to have values between 150 and 250?

   A. 0.7224
   B. 139
   C. 222
   D. 361
   E. 372

10. Given the graph of a normal distribution, what happens to the shape of the curve if μ increases and σ decreases?

    A. The curve will move to the right and get taller.
    B. The curve will move to the right and get shorter.
    C. The curve will move to the left and get taller.
    D. The curve will move to the left and get shorter.
    E. Cannot tell since the distribution is not standardized.

11. Which of the following are true about the normal distribution?

    I.   The area in the range of $z = -2$ to $z = -1$ is less than half of the area in the range of $z = 0$ to $z = 1$.
    II.   The area to the left of $z = 2$ is equal to the area to the right of $z = -2$.
    III. If $z = -1$ represents the 40th percentile, then $z = -2$ represents the 30th percentile.

    A. II only
    B. I and II
    C. I and III
    D. II and III
    E. I, II, and III

12. Jack scored 82 on a test in which $\mu = 76$ and $\sigma = 7$. Jill scored 85 on a test in which $\mu = 78$ and $\sigma = 8$. If both sets of scores are normally distributed, who scored better on their test relative to the rest of their class?

    A. Jack, since his z-score was higher
    B. Jack, since the standard deviation was smaller
    C. Jill, since her z-score was higher
    D. Jill, since the standard deviation is greater
    E. Cannot tell since the distributions are not compatible

13. What is the difference in percentiles associated with the z-scores of $z = -2.34$ and $z = 2.34$?

    A. 50%
    B. 86%
    C. 96%
    D. 98%
    E. 99%

Multiple Choice Answers

1. **E.** All the statements are true. The total area under any normal curve is equal to one. Converting values in a nonstandard normal curve to z-scores allows for the standardization of any normal distribution.

2. **E.** None of the statements is true. The standard deviation of a distribution does not change as you determine different z-scores. There is 68% of the area under a normal distribution within 1 standard deviation of the mean, not the variance. Normal distributions are symmetric, not asymmetric.

3. **B.** The z-score indicates how many standard deviations a value is away from the mean. Look up $z = -1.80$ in the table. This gives 0.0359, the area in the left tail. Double it. The total area (probability) beyond 1.8 standard deviations from the mean is 0.0718.

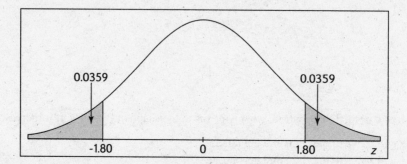

4. **D.** A score at the 85th percentile means that there is 85% of the area of the curve to its left. Look up 0.8500 in the table of standard normal probabilities. It gives a corresponding z-score of 1.04. Solve using $x = z\sigma + \mu = (1.04)(250) + 1000 = 1260$.

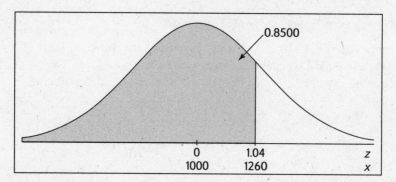

5. **E.** All the statements are true.

6. **C.** This is an exercise in table reading. Look down the table of positive z-scores looking for two that differ by 0.1 and whose corresponding probabilities differ by 0.0100. Z-scores of 1.61 and 1.71 differ by only 0.0101, and z-scores of 1.62 and 1.72 differ by only 0.00199. Split the difference and arrive at 1.715 as the larger of the two z-scores.

7. **A.** In a normal curve, the points of inflection, also known as transition points, where the curve changes from opening upward to opening downward to opening upward again. These points of inflection occur at $\mu \pm \sigma$ for any normal distribution. This corresponds to $z = \pm 1$.

8. **B.** First calculate the z-scores for the ERAs of 3 and 4: $z_4 = \frac{x - \mu}{\sigma} = \frac{4 - 3.82}{1.14} = 0.16$ and $z_3 = \frac{x - \mu}{\sigma} = \frac{3 - 3.82}{1.14} = -0.72$. Look up these two z-scores in the table of standard normal probabilities and subtract to get the desired result: $0.5636 - 0.2358 = 0.3278$.

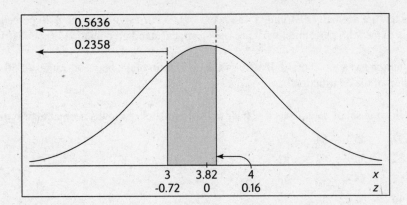

9. **C.** First calculate the z-scores for each value: $z_{250} = \frac{x - \mu}{\sigma} = \frac{250 - 200}{85} = 0.59$ and $z_{150} = \frac{x - \mu}{\sigma} = \frac{150 - 200}{85} = -0.59$.

Look up these two z-scores in the table of standard normal probabilities and subtract to get the desired result: $0.7224 - 0.2776 = 0.4448$. Multiply this probability by 500 to get the number of values between 150 and 250: $(500)(0.4448) = 222.4$.

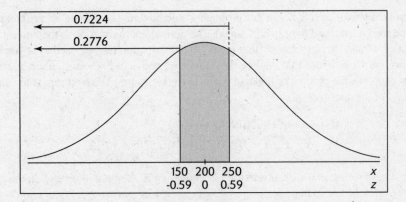

10. **A.** Increasing the mean of a distribution will shift the mean to the right. Decreasing the standard deviation decreases the spread making the distribution more compact. This will increase the area closer to the mean, making the curve taller.

11. **B.** Choice I is true. See the Empirical Rule diagram in Question 20. The interval from -2 to -1 contains approximately 13.5% of the distribution, and the interval from 0 to 1 contains approximately 34%. Choice II is correct by the symmetry of the normal curve. Choice III is not correct. The normal curve is not linear, that is, not proportional.

12. **C.** Relative strength in the population is best compared with the z-score. After all, that is the purpose of the z-score—to standardize distributions so that comparisons can be made. Calculate each z-score: $z_{82} = \frac{x - \mu}{\sigma} = \frac{82 - 76}{7} = 0.857$ and $z_{85} = \frac{x - \mu}{\sigma} = \frac{85 - 78}{8} = 0.875$. Since Jill's score corresponds to a z-score that is higher than Jack's, Jill did better relative to the rest of the test takers in her class.

13. **D.** Look up each z-score. Percentiles are the probabilities to the left of the given values. The table of standard normal probabilities gives the probabilities. Subtract the probabilities: $0.9904 - 0.0096 = 0.9808 = 98.08\%$.

Free-Response Questions

Directions: Show all work. Indicate clearly the methods you use. You will be graded on method as well as accuracy.

1. In the game of roulette, the probability that a spin will result in an odd number being selected is 0.474. What is the probability of getting at least 400 odd numbers in 800 spins? Use normal approximation to the binomial to solve.

2. The results of a test are normally distributed. If a score of 624 corresponds to the 80th percentile, and a score of 710 corresponds to the 90th percentile, what are the mean and standard deviation of the distribution?

3. A normal distribution has a mean of 40. If 10% of the distribution falls between values of 50 and 60, what is the standard deviation of the distribution?

4. Consider the following set of data. Does it appear to approximately follow a normal distribution? Why?

45	31	37	55	54	56
48	54	52	55	52	51
49	46	62	38	45	48
47	46	40	61	50	58
46	35	36	59	50	48
39	48	51	52	43	45

Free-Response Answers

1. To use the binomial distribution directly in this problem would be time-consuming. Approximately 400 equations would have to be worked out, and their results added. The normal approximation to the binomial is the proper alternative. First, you must check to see whether the normal distribution may be used as an approximation to the binomial. The two basic conditions that must be met are $np > 5$ and $nq > 5$. (Some authors prefer 10 as a minimum.) In this case, it is clear that the product of 800 and 0.474 is greater than 5. The next step is to calculate the mean and standard deviation of the distribution.

$$\mu = np = (800)(0.474) = 379.2$$
$$\sigma = \sqrt{npq} = \sqrt{(800)(0.474)(0.526)} = 14.123$$

Sketch a normal curve filling in the mean and the bar equal to 400. You are interested in the area of the bar plus all the area to the right. Shade in that area.

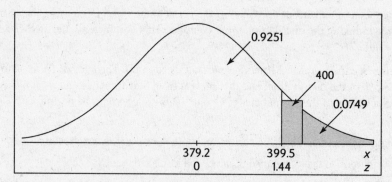

Calculate the z-score for 399.5 and look up the probability in the table of standard normal probabilities. Subtract from 1 to get the required result of 0.0749.

This is very close to the answer obtained using the distribution function in the TI-83/4:
$1-\text{binomcdf}(800,0.474,399) = 0.0754$.

2. In this problem you have a normal distribution, but you do not know its mean or standard deviation. The value of 624 is at the 80th percentile and the value of 710 is at the 90th percentile. Using this information, you can determine the z-scores for these values.

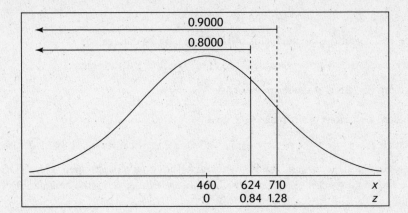

Look up 0.8000 and 0.9000 in the table of standard normal probabilities. The z-scores are 0.84 and 1.28, respectively. Set up two equations using these values. Solve $z = \frac{x - \mu}{\sigma}$ for the mean and standard deviation: $\sigma = \frac{x - \mu}{z}$ and $\mu = x - z\sigma$.

Choose a variable to solve for first, say μ. Substitute in the first equation and solve. $\sigma = \frac{x - \mu}{z} = \frac{710 - \mu}{1.28} = \frac{624 - \mu}{0.84}$

$$(0.84)(710 - \mu) = (1.28)(624 - \mu)$$
$$596.4 - 0.84\mu = 798.72 - 1.28\mu$$
$$1.28\mu - 0.84\mu = 798.72 - 596.4$$
$$0.44\mu = 202.32$$
$$\mu = 459.81$$
$$\mu = 460$$

Then use the solution of the mean to solve for the standard deviation.

$$\sigma = \frac{x - \mu}{z} = \frac{710 - 460}{1.28} = \frac{624 - 460}{0.84} = 195$$

3. This is a table reading problem. First set up the relationships that are given.

$$\sigma = \frac{x - \mu}{z} = \frac{60 - 40}{z_{60}} = \frac{50 - 40}{z_{50}}$$

Determine the relationship between the two z-scores.

$$\frac{60 - 40}{z_{60}} = \frac{50 - 40}{z_{50}}$$
$$\frac{20}{z_{60}} = \frac{10}{z_{50}}$$
$$20z_{50} = 10z_{60}$$
$$2z_{50} = z_{60}$$

You now know that one z-score is twice the other, and their corresponding probabilities differ by 0.1000. You also know that the z-scores are positive since both represent numbers larger than the mean. Here is where table reading comes in. You must search the table of standard normal probabilities to find two such z-scores. You will find the values to be $z = 1.25$ and $z = 2.50$. The next task is to solve for the standard deviation.

$$\sigma = \frac{x - \mu}{z} = \frac{60 - 40}{2.50} = \frac{50 - 40}{1.25} = 8$$

4. To see whether this set of data approximates a normal distribution, you need to analyze the data. Enter the values into L1 in your TI-83/4 calculator. Determine the mean and standard deviation of the data. Use STAT CALC 1-VarStats. Sort the data for easy counting of values using STAT SortA(L1). Check to see whether the data follows the Empirical Rule. What percent of the data values are within one standard deviation of the mean? How about two standard deviations?

The mean of this data set is 48.1, and the standard deviation is 7.3.

For +/– one standard deviation, the interval is (40.8, 55.4) with 24 data values.

For +/– two standard deviations, the interval is (33.1, 62.7) with 35 data values.

Within one standard deviation of the mean you have $\frac{24}{36} = 67\%$.

Within two standard deviations of the mean you have $\frac{35}{36} = 97\%$.

These values match very closely the percentage given in the Empirical Rule of 68% and 95%.

Next, plot a histogram of the data and look for symmetry. Turn on a plot and then select ZOOM ZoomStat. You can also set the window settings manually with Xmin and Xmax being the boundaries of the plot and Xscl as the class width.

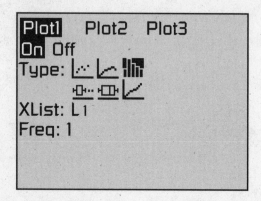
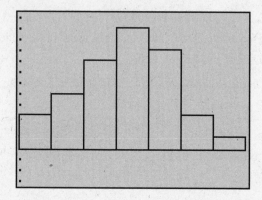

This data does look symmetric and mound-shaped. Next you can do a *normal probability plot*. This graph plots each observation in the data set versus the corresponding quantile z of the standard normal distribution. If the plotted points lie close to a straight line, then the plot indicates that the data are normal. To use this plot, change the StatPlot from a histogram to the normal probability plot as shown.

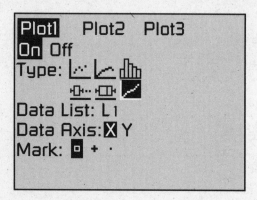
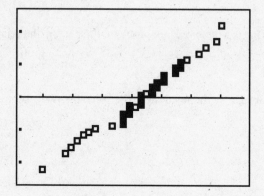

From the preceding calculations and distribution plots, you can conclude that the data set does approximately follow a normal distribution.

Anticipating Patterns: Sampling Distributions

A population is a collection of all outcomes, responses, counts, or measurements that are of interest. A *parameter* is a numerical description of a population characteristic.

The mean height of all students who attend a high school would be a population parameter.

The mean weight of all dogs of a certain breed would be a population parameter.

The standard deviation of the diameter of ball bearings produced by a machine would be a population parameter.

The proportion of left-handed high school students in the state of California would be a population parameter.

Population *parameters* are fixed quantities. To calculate a population parameter exactly would require measurements of all members of the population. This is usually difficult or even impossible due to a number of factors, including the size of the population, cost, time limitations, or unavailability of population members.

A sample is a subset of a population. The size of a sample is usually very small when compared to the size of the population from which it was drawn. A *statistic* is a numerical description of a sample characteristic.

The mean height of 30 randomly selected students at a high school would be a sample statistic.

The standard deviation of 40 randomly selected ball bearings produced by a machine would be a sample statistic.

The proportion of 35 randomly selected high school students in the state of California would be a sample statistic.

Sample statistics are not fixed in value; their value depends on the sample that is selected.

A **sampling distribution** is the probability distribution of a sample statistic that is formed from all possible values of the statistic computed from a sample of size n.

The following example illustrates a sampling distribution. It uses a population of limited size so that all possible values of the sample statistic may be calculated.

EXAMPLE:
Determine the sampling distribution of the mean of the two numbers that result from rolling two dice. What is the mean and standard deviation of the sampling distribution?

This is equivalent to finding the average of each possible roll of a pair of dice.

Die #1

		1	2	3	4	5	6
	1	1.0	1.5	2.0	2.5	3.0	3.5
	2	1.5	2.0	2.5	3.0	3.5	4.0
	3	2.0	2.5	3.0	3.5	4.0	4.5
Die #2	4	2.5	3.0	3.5	4.0	4.5	5.0
	5	3.0	3.5	4.0	4.5	5.0	5.5
	6	3.5	4.0	4.5	5.0	5.5	6.0

The probability distribution is

x	1.0	1.5	2.0	2.5	3.0	3.5	4.0	4.5	5.0	5.5	6.0
P(x)	0.028	0.056	0.083	0.111	0.139	0.167	0.139	0.111	0.083	0.056	0.028

The mean and standard deviation on this sampling distribution are $\mu = 3.5$ and $\sigma = 1.208$. [TI-83/4: Enter the values of x in L1. Enter the probabilities in L2. Select STAT CALC 1-VarStats L1, L2. (The calculator displays the mean and standard deviation.)]

The following figures illustrate the tendency of the sampling distribution's shape to approach the shape of a normal distribution as the sample size increases. Even with small sizes, the change in shape is evident. The first figure shows the sampling distribution of choosing samples of size 1 from the digits 1 to 6. It is a uniform distribution. It is the distribution obtained from rolling a single die over and over. The second figure illustrates the shape of the distribution discussed previously, which consists of all of the averages of pairs of digits chosen from 1 to 6. This is the distribution obtained by averaging the outcomes of rolling a pair of dice over and over. The third figure illustrates the distribution of rolling 3 dice and averaging the three outcomes. Notice how the shape, even with a sample size of only 3, is beginning to look normal.

Single Die: $n = 1$

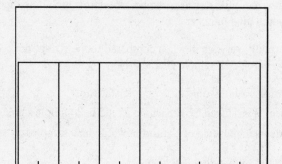

Mean of Two Dice: $n = 2$

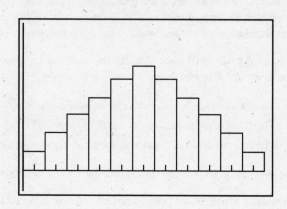

Mean of Three Dice: $n = 3$

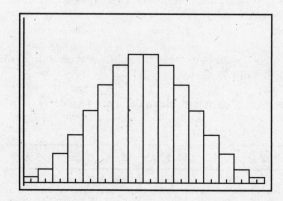

The study of *inferential statistics* uses sample statistics $\left(\bar{x},\ s,\ \text{and}\ \hat{p}\right)$ to make inferences about population parameters (μ, σ, and ρ). You estimate the mean of a population by considering the mean of a randomly selected representative sample from the population. You estimate a population proportion by considering the proportion of an event in a randomly selected representative sample from the population. In order to evaluate the reliability of the sample statistic, you need to know the probability distribution for the statistic you are using. The sample statistic that is being used to estimate the corresponding population parameter is called a **point estimate.** You want the sampling distribution to be centered over the value of the parameter you want to estimate. The statistic is **unbiased** if the mean of the sampling distribution is equal to the parameter it is intended to estimate.

Sampling Distributions of a Sample Proportion

The proportion of a population having a particular characteristic is called the **population proportion** and is denoted by p. If you want to estimate the value of p, collect a random sample from the population and calculate the corresponding **sample proportion,** which is called $\hat{p}$. A specific sample may produce a value of $\hat{p}$ that is some distance away from p. As repeated samples are taken, you can reasonably expect the majority of corresponding $\hat{p}$ samples to fall close to p; as the difference between the $\hat{p}$ values and p increases (the farther the $\hat{p}$ values get from p), the frequency of their occurrence decreases. Sampling distributions behave much like binomial distributions. As the sample size n increases, the shape of the sampling distribution approximates a normal distribution.

To find a proportion in a sample, divide the number of successes by the sample size. This is equivalent to the probability of success. If p represents the population proportion, n represents the sample size, and x represents the number successes, then $\hat{p} = \frac{x}{n}$ is the sample proportion, and $\hat{p}$ is called a point estimate for p.

Consider the formulas for the mean and standard deviation of the binomial distribution: $\mu_x = np$ and $\sigma_x = \sqrt{np(1-p)}$. Since proportions are calculated by dividing successes by sample size, equivalent formulas for the mean and standard deviation of the distribution of sample proportions are

$$\mu_{\hat{p}} = \frac{np}{n} = p \text{ and } \sigma_{\hat{p}} = \frac{\sqrt{np(1-p)}}{n} = \sqrt{\frac{np(1-p)}{n^2}} = \sqrt{\frac{p(1-p)}{n}}$$

Dividing by n does not change the fact that if n is sufficiently large, this distribution will be approximately normal. What is sufficiently large? The same general rule applies here as with normal approximation to the binomial. Both $np > 5$ and $n(1-p) > 5$ must be true. Values greater than 5 (some authors like 10) will provide more accurate results.

Note on notation: The following are sometimes used to represent the binomial distribution, normal distribution, and if n is sufficiently large, the distribution of sample proportions: $B(n,p)$, $N(\mu,\sigma)$, and $N\left(p, \sqrt{\frac{p(1-p)}{n}}\right)$.

Properties of the Sampling Distribution $\hat{p}$

1. The mean of the sampling distribution is equal to the population proportion and is called an unbiased point estimate of p:

$$\mu_{\hat{p}} = p$$

2. The standard deviation of the sampling distribution is the square root of the quotient of $p(1-p)$ and the sample size:

$$\sigma_{\hat{p}} = \sqrt{\frac{p(1-p)}{n}}.$$

EXAMPLE:

If a coin is tossed 40 times, what is the probability of getting at least 55% heads?

The probability of tossing a head on a single toss is 0.5, so $p = 0.5$. First check to make sure that both $np > 5$ and $n(1-p) > 5$. $np = (40)(.5) = 20$ and $n(1-p) = (40)(.5) = 20$. The distribution is approximately normally distributed.

$$p = 0.5$$

$$\sigma_{\hat{p}} = \sqrt{\frac{p(1-p)}{n}} = \sqrt{\frac{(0.5)(1-0.5)}{40}} = 0.079$$

$$z = \frac{\hat{p} - p}{\sigma_{\hat{p}}} = \frac{0.55 - 0.5}{0.079} = 0.63$$

Look up 0.63 in the table of standard normal probabilities. It corresponds to a probability of 0.7357. This represents the probability of less than 55%. Subtract from 1 to get $1 - 0.7357 = 0.2643$.

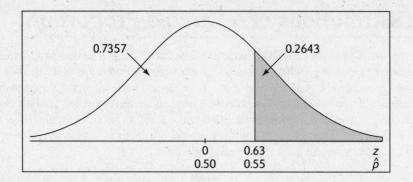

EXAMPLE:

According to a research study, 42% of U.S. households receive at least 4 magazines per month in the mail. If a random sample of 250 households is taken, what is the probability that between 40% and 50% receive at least 4 magazines per month in the mail?

Both np and $n(1 - p)$ are greater than 5. The distribution of sample proportions will be approximately normally distributed.

$$p = 0.42$$

$$\sigma_{\hat{p}} = \sqrt{\frac{p(1-p)}{n}} = \sqrt{\frac{(0.42)(1-0.42)}{250}} = 0.0312$$

$$z_{50} = \frac{\hat{p} - p}{\sigma_{\hat{p}}} = \frac{0.50 - 0.42}{0.0312} = 2.56$$

$$z_{40} = \frac{\hat{p} - p}{\sigma_{\hat{p}}} = \frac{0.40 - 0.42}{0.0312} = -0.64$$

Look up 2.56 and –0.64 in the table of standard normal probabilities. Subtract the results.

$$0.9948 - 0.2611 = 0.7337$$

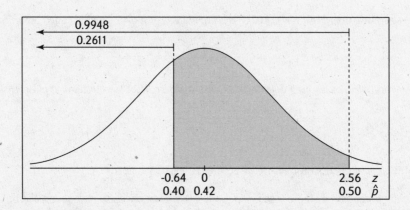

Sampling Distributions of a Sample Mean

Suppose that you want to determine an estimate for the mean, μ, of a population. You do not know what kind of distribution the population consists of. If you select a random sample from the population and compute the sample mean, $\bar{x}$, you will have a point estimate for the population mean. Larger sample sizes would produce better estimates. If a distribution is formed of all possible values of $\bar{x}$, which were computed from samples of size n taken from a population with mean μ and standard deviation σ, the resulting distribution would be a **sampling distribution of sample means.** To find the mean of a sample, the sample members are added, and then the sum is divided by n. Since variances add in a similar way—that is, the variance of a sum is the sum of the variances, $\sigma_{\bar{x}}^2 = \frac{n\sigma^2}{n^2} = \frac{\sigma^2}{n}$—the standard deviation of the sampling distribution is the square root of the variance: $\sigma_{\bar{x}} = \frac{\sigma}{\sqrt{n}}$.

When samples are selected from a population, and the population is very large (if sampling is done with replacement, the population is infinite), the resulting change in the population standard deviation is not significant. If, on the other hand, the sample size, n, is more than 5% of a finite population size, N, then there is a finite number of samples; the change in the population standard deviation is significant and should be accounted for. The use of a **finite correction factor,** $\sqrt{\frac{N-n}{N-1}}$, should be applied to adjust $\sigma_{\bar{x}}$. Therefore, if n is more than 5% of N, then $\sigma_{\bar{x}} = \frac{\sigma}{\sqrt{n}}\sqrt{\frac{N-n}{N-1}}$.

Properties of the Sampling Distribution $\overline{x}$

1. The mean of the sampling distribution equals the mean of the population:

$$\mu_{\bar{x}} = \mu$$

2. The standard deviation of the sampling distribution equals the standard deviation of the population divided by the square root of the sample size:

$$\sigma_{\bar{x}} = \frac{\sigma}{\sqrt{n}}$$

EXAMPLE:

The average life expectancy of a lightbulb is normally distributed with a mean of 4000 hours and a standard deviation of 300 hours. What is the probability that the average life of 20 such lightbulbs will be less than 3800 hours?

First determine the mean and standard deviation of the sampling distribution.

$$\mu_{\bar{x}} = \mu = 4000 \text{ and } \sigma_{\bar{x}} = \frac{\sigma}{\sqrt{n}} = \frac{300}{\sqrt{20}} = 67.082$$

Calculate a z-score for the value of 3500: $z = \frac{\bar{x} - \mu_{\bar{x}}}{\sigma_{\bar{x}}} = \frac{3800 - 4000}{67.082} = -2.98$.

Look up -2.98 in the table of standard normal probabilities. The probability that the average life of 20 randomly selected bulbs is 0.0014.

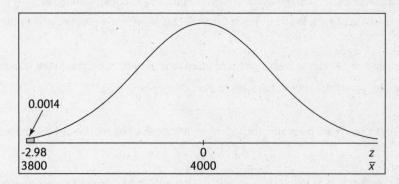

(*Note:* In this example, you are given a normally distributed population from which to choose your sample. If you do not know that the population is normal, a sample of size 20 is not adequate to assume a normally distributed sampling distribution.)

EXAMPLE:
Consider a population with a mean of 32 and a standard deviation of 7. Random samples of size 15 are selected from the population. What is the mean and standard deviation of the sampling distribution?

The normality of the population is not known; therefore, it is unclear whether the sampling distribution is normally distributed. However, the mean and standard deviation of the sampling distribution can be calculated.

$$\mu_{\bar{x}} = \mu = 32 \text{ and } \sigma_{\bar{x}} = \frac{\sigma}{\sqrt{n}} = \frac{7}{\sqrt{15}} = 1.807$$

Central Limit Theorem

The **Central Limit Theorem** is arguably the most important theorem in statistics. The branch of statistics known as inferential statistics relies heavily on this theorem. When you make inferences about a population mean based on information from a sample, you must know the relationship between the population from which your sample is taken and the sampling distribution of sample means. The Central Limit Theorem describes that relationship.

In order to use the normal distribution as a model for a sampling distribution of sample means, the sampling distribution must be normally distributed. But how do you know whether it is normally distributed? Two main factors that influence the shape of a sampling distribution are the shape of the population distribution from which the samples are taken and the sample size. The shape of the population plays a larger role in this determination. If the population from which the samples are drawn is normal, then samples of any size have a normal sampling distribution. If the population from which the samples are drawn is not normal, or is not known to be normal, then the shape of the sampling distribution will probably resemble the population itself. Sample size can overcome this problem. If the sample size is large enough (30 is usually considered the minimum sample size), then the sampling distribution of sample means will be approximately normal even if the population from which they are drawn is not.

Properties of the Central Limit Theorem

1. If repeated samples of size n, where $n \geq 30$, are selected from ANY population with mean μ and standard deviation σ, then the sampling distribution of sample means will approximate a normal distribution. As the sample size increases, the approximation improves.

2. If the population from which the samples are drawn is normally distributed, then the sampling distribution of sample means will be normally distributed for any sample size.

3. The mean of a sampling distribution of sample means is equal to the population mean: $\mu_{\bar{x}} = \mu$.

4. The sampling distribution of sample means has a variance that is inversely proportional to the sample size: $\sigma_{\bar{x}}^2 = \frac{\sigma^2}{n}$.

5. The sampling distribution of sample means has a standard deviation that is equal to the standard deviation of the population divided by the square root of the sample size: $\sigma_{\bar{x}} = \frac{\sigma}{\sqrt{n}}$.

EXAMPLE:
The heights of 19-year-old women are normally distributed with a mean of 64 inches and a standard deviation of 2.7 inches.

a. If one 19-year-old woman is selected at random, what is the probability that she is less than 63 inches tall?

b. If a random sample of ten 19-year-old women is selected , what is the probability that the mean height, $\bar{x}$, of the sample is less than 63 inches?

c. Compare the results.

a. This is a direct application of using the normal distribution, since you are given that the population is normally distributed. The standard deviation is 2.7. Calculate a z-score for the height of 63 inches:

$z = \dfrac{x - \mu}{\sigma} = \dfrac{63 - 64}{2.7} = -0.37$. Look up the z-score in the table of standard normal probabilities. The corresponding probability of 0.3557 is the answer. [TI-83/4: normalcdf(-999,63,64,2.7)]

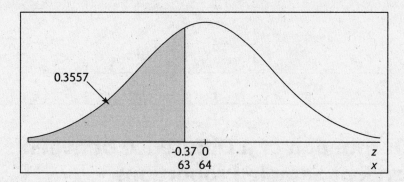

b. Since the sample is selected from a population that is normally distributed, the sampling distribution of sample means will be normal, even with a sample size of less than 30. The standard deviation of this sampling distribution of sample means is $\sigma_{\bar{x}} = \dfrac{\sigma}{\sqrt{n}} = \dfrac{2.7}{\sqrt{10}} = 0.854$. Calculate a z-score for the height of 63 inches:

$z = \dfrac{\bar{x} - \mu}{\sigma_{\bar{x}}} = \dfrac{63 - 64}{0.854} = -1.17$. The corresponding probability is 0.1210. [TI-83/4: (normalcdf(−999,63,64,2.7/$\sqrt{10}$)]

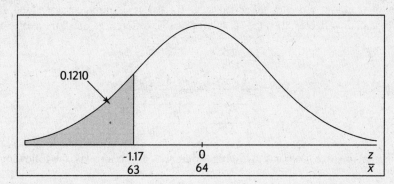

c. The mean of a random sample is more likely to be closer to the actual mean of the population than is a single selection. As the sample size increases, the standard deviation of the sampling distribution decreases. A smaller standard deviation produces a larger z-score.

EXAMPLE:

Let x be a random variable that represents the cholesterol level in 40-year-old men. If x has a distribution with $\mu = 224$ and $\sigma = 44$, what is the probability that a random sample of 75 40-year-old men would have a mean between 215 and 230?

Since the sample size is greater than 30, the sampling distribution of sample means will be approximately normally distributed even if the population from which it was drawn is not normal. Calculate a z-score for the levels of 215 and 230. Mark these z-scores on the sketch. Look up the probabilities in the table of standard normal probabilities.

$$z_{230} = \dfrac{\bar{x} - \mu}{\dfrac{\sigma}{\sqrt{n}}} = \dfrac{230 - 224}{\dfrac{44}{\sqrt{75}}} = 1.18 \qquad z_{215} = \dfrac{\bar{x} - \mu}{\dfrac{\sigma}{\sqrt{n}}} = \dfrac{215 - 224}{\dfrac{44}{\sqrt{75}}} = -1.77$$

Subtract the corresponding probabilities to give: $0.8810 - 0.0384 = 0.8426$. [TI-83/4: (normalcdf(215, 230, 224, 44/$\sqrt{75}$)]

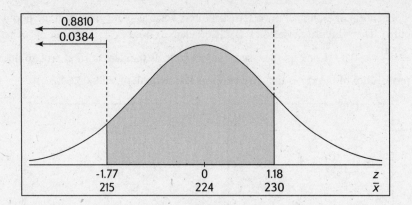

Sampling Distribution of a Difference between Two Independent Sample Proportions

Many times, it is not the individual population proportions that matter, it is the difference between them that is more critical. For example, if two machines are compared based on the percentage of faulty parts they produce, it is the difference in these proportions that is important. If two political candidates are being compared based on their popularity, it may be the difference in their popularity that is significant.

You have seen that when two random variables are added or subtracted, their variances are added. If σ_1^2 and σ_2^2 represent the variances of two random variables, then the set of all possible differences make up a distribution of sample differences where

$$\sigma_d^2 = \sigma_1^2 + \sigma_2^2$$

$$\sigma_d^2 = \frac{p_1(1-p_1)}{n_1} + \frac{p_2(1-p_2)}{n_2}$$

$$\sigma_d = \sqrt{\frac{p_1(1-p_1)}{n_1} + \frac{p_2(1-p_2)}{n_2}}$$

To use the normal distribution to solve problems involving differences of proportions, the following conditions must be true:

1. The samples must be independent.
2. The samples must be large enough to use a normal sampling distribution.

$$(n_1 p_1 \geq 5, n_1(1-p_1) \geq 5, n_2 p_2 \geq 5, \text{ and } n_2(1-p_2) \geq 5)$$

Provided that these two conditions are met, the sampling distribution for the differences between the sample proportions, $\hat{p}_1 - \hat{p}_2$, is approximately normal with

$$\mu_{\hat{p}_1 - \hat{p}_2} = p_1 - p_2 \text{ and } \sigma_{\hat{p}_1 - \hat{p}_2} = \sqrt{\frac{p_1(1-p_1)}{n_1} + \frac{p_2(1-p_2)}{n_2}}.$$

The z-score may be computed by

$$z = \frac{\left(\hat{p}_1 - \hat{p}_2\right) - \left(p_1 - p_2\right)}{\sqrt{\frac{p_1(1-p_1)}{n_1} + \frac{p_2(1-p_2)}{n_2}}}$$

EXAMPLE:
Suppose that 53% of State A's residents are senior citizens and 40% of State B's residents are senior citizens. If a random sample of 60 residents from State A and an independent random sample of 50 residents from State B is taken, what is the probability that the difference in the percentages of senior citizens in the samples is at least 10%?

Calculate the difference in the department's proportions: $p_1 - p_2 = 0.53 - 0.40 = 0.13$.

Calculate the standard deviation of the sampling distribution of the difference of the proportions:

$$\sigma_{\hat{p}_1 - \hat{p}_2} = \sqrt{\frac{p_1(1-p_1)}{n_1} + \frac{p_2(1-p_2)}{n_2}} = \sqrt{\frac{(0.53)(0.47)}{60} + \frac{(0.4)(0.6)}{50}} = 0.095$$

Calculate the value of z:

$$z = \frac{\left(\hat{p}_1 - \hat{p}_2\right) - \left(p_1 - p_2\right)}{\sqrt{\frac{p_1(1-p_1)}{n_1} + \frac{p_2(1-p_2)}{n_2}}} = \frac{0.10 - 0.13}{0.095} = -0.32$$

Look up −0.32 in the table of standard normal probabilities and obtain 0.3745. Subtract from 1 to get $1 - 0.3745 = 0.6255$.

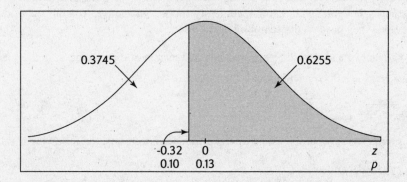

EXAMPLE:

Studies have shown that 18% of the cereal boxes sold by manufacturer A are underweight and 8% of the cereal boxes sold by manufacturer B are underweight. A reporter is going to test 150 boxes produced by manufacturer A and 175 boxes produced by manufacturer B. Before the test begins, he wants to make a prediction of the difference in percentages of underweight boxes from each manufacturer. The reporter wants to be 95% certain of his claim. What is the minimum difference the reporter should predict?

The mean of the sampling distribution is $p_1 - p_2 = 0.18 - 0.08 = 0.10$. The standard deviation is

$$\sigma_{\hat{p}_1 - \hat{p}_2} = \sqrt{\frac{p_1(1-p_1)}{n_1} + \frac{p_2(1-p_2)}{n_2}} = \sqrt{\frac{(0.18)(0.82)}{150} + \frac{(0.08)(0.92)}{175}} = 0.037$$

The z-score with 95% of the distribution to its right is −1.645. The formula for the z-score is $z = \frac{\left(\hat{p}_1 - \hat{p}_2\right) - \left(p_1 - p_2\right)}{\sigma_{\hat{p}_1 - \hat{p}_2}}$. Solving for the differences in percentages gives $\hat{p}_1 - \hat{p}_2 = z\sigma_{\hat{p}_1 - \hat{p}_2} + \left(p_1 - p_2\right) = (-1.645)(0.037) + 0.10 = 0.039$. The reporter can be 95% sure that the differences in percentages from these samples will be at least 3.9%.

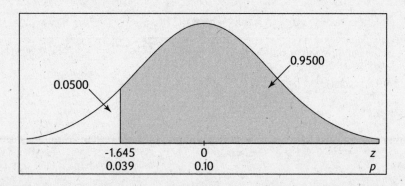

Sampling Distribution of a Difference between Two Independent Sample Means

Comparisons between the means of populations is common in statistics. Are the average salaries of teachers in California higher than those of teachers in Montana? Who studies longer for college exams, males or females? Do brand A tires last longer than brand B tires? Who loses more weight, low-carb dieters or low-fat dieters? Which of two models of automobile can stop more quickly? All of these questions require comparing the means of two populations. This involves looking at the differences in the means of samples taken from the two populations in question.

If you want to determine the difference in weights of two types of tomatoes, you could select two independent samples, one from each type of tomato. You could average the weights in each sample and find their difference. What would a difference of 2 ounces tell you? You cannot assume that you have collected two "perfect" samples in which the sample means are exactly equal to the population means. The difference obtained from your samples is only one difference in a sampling distribution full of differences. You do know that the mean of the sampling distribution reflects the true mean of the population differences, but you do not know specifically about your sample. You must consider the variance of each sample and what effect they have on the sampling distribution.

You do know that the variance of a sum or difference is equal to the sum of the variances. In this case, you are referring to differences. You have $\sigma_{\bar{x}_1 - \bar{x}_2}^2 = \sigma_{\bar{x}_1}^2 + \sigma_{\bar{x}_2}^2$ where $\sigma_{\bar{x}_1}^2 = \dfrac{\sigma_1^2}{n_1}$ and $\sigma_{\bar{x}_2}^2 = \dfrac{\sigma_2^2}{n_2}$.

Therefore, $\sigma_{\bar{x}_1 - \bar{x}_2} = \sqrt{\sigma_{\bar{x}_1}^2 + \sigma_{\bar{x}_2}^2} = \sqrt{\dfrac{\sigma_1^2}{n_1} + \dfrac{\sigma_2^2}{n_2}}$.

To use the normal distribution to solve problems involving differences of means, the following conditions must be true:

1. The samples must be independent.
2. The samples must be large enough to use a normal sampling distribution, or the populations from which any size samples are selected must be normally distributed.

If these two conditions exist, the sampling distribution for the differences between the sample means, $\bar{x}_1 - \bar{x}_2$, is normal with $\mu_{\bar{x}_1 - \bar{x}_2} = \mu_1 - \mu_2$ and $\sigma_{\bar{x}_1 - \bar{x}_2} = \sqrt{\dfrac{\sigma_1^2}{n_1} + \dfrac{\sigma_2^2}{n_2}}$.

The z-score may be computed by

$$z = \frac{(\bar{x}_1 - \bar{x}_2) - (\mu_1 - \mu_2)}{\sqrt{\dfrac{\sigma_1^2}{n_1} + \dfrac{\sigma_2^2}{n_2}}}$$

EXAMPLE:
The mean burning time for a Brand X candle is 96.4 minutes with a standard deviation of 6.2 minutes. The mean burning time for a Brand Y candle is 68.8 minutes with a standard deviation of 5.4 minutes. The distributions of burning times of Brand X and Brand Y candles are normally distributed. If independent random samples of 15 Brand X candles and 20 Brand Y candles are tested, what is the probability that the difference in average burning times between the sample of Brand X candles and the sample of Brand Y candles will be less than 25 minutes?

The difference in the population means is $\mu_1 - \mu_2 = 96.4 - 68.8 = 27.6$.

The standard deviation of the sampling distribution is $\sigma_{\bar{x}_1 - \bar{x}_2} = \sqrt{\dfrac{\sigma_1^2}{n_1} + \dfrac{\sigma_2^2}{n_2}} = \sqrt{\dfrac{6.2^2}{15} + \dfrac{5.4^2}{20}} = 2.005$.

The z-score is $z = \dfrac{(\bar{x}_1 - \bar{x}_2) - (\mu_1 - \mu_2)}{\sqrt{\dfrac{\sigma_1^2}{n_1} + \dfrac{\sigma_2^2}{n_2}}} = \dfrac{25 - 27.6}{2.005} = -1.30$.

Therefore, the probability that the difference in mean burning times will be less than 25 minutes is 0.0968.

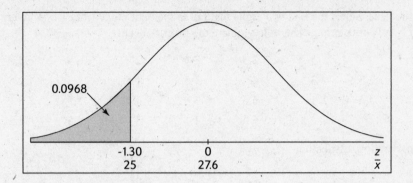

EXAMPLE:

The average salary of a teacher in California is $45,945 with a standard deviation of $1211. The average salary of a teacher in Arizona is $41,819 with a standard deviation of $1184. The salaries of teachers in these two states are normally distributed. A random sample of 225 teachers in California and an independent random sample of 150 teachers in Arizona are taken. With a 99% certainty, what would be the smallest difference in salaries in these two samples?

The difference in the population means is $\mu_1 - \mu_2 = 45,945 - 41,819 = 4126$.

The standard deviation of the sampling distribution is $\sigma_{\bar{x}_1 - \bar{x}_2} = \sqrt{\dfrac{\sigma_1^2}{n_1} + \dfrac{\sigma_2^2}{n_2}} = \sqrt{\dfrac{1211^2}{225} + \dfrac{1184^2}{150}} = 125.95$.

Since you are looking for the smallest difference, you must find a z-score where there is 99% of the distribution area to its right. Therefore, there would be only 1% to its left. Look up 0.0100 in the table of standard normal probabilities. The z-score is –2.33. Solving for the difference in sample means: $\bar{x}_1 - \bar{x}_2 = z\sigma_{\bar{x}_1 - \bar{x}_2} + (\mu_1 - \mu_2) = (-2.33)(125.95) + 4126 = 3832.5$. So, with 99% certainty, the smallest difference in sample means you can expect is approximately $3833.

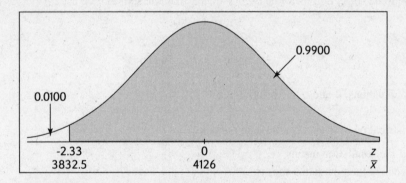

Simulation of Sampling Distributions

A sampling distribution consists of the results of all possible samples of size n taken from the population. The probability of where a particular sample might fall in the distribution has been covered in this chapter. You can get a good idea of what a sampling distribution might look like by looking at repeated samples taken from the population. You can use simulation to help produce a random sample of samples.

EXAMPLE:

Simulate the sampling distribution of the mean of the two numbers that result from rolling two dice. Use the following random digit table to simulate 40 samples. Create a probability distribution of the results.

36146	15570	28593	42089	99282	59640	15323	97054	39916	05321
21549	18432	73720	52218	02789	81003	49092	79044	50912	08388
87334	50174	30962	23607	88691	29294	87179	45443	51370	69555
92043	59814	60673	56569	22035	43311	56013	62846	69030	47559
47681	72704	49759	76359	12525	32143	15882	36916	08097	90578

217

Begin on row one of the table. Select the first two digits that fall in the digit range from 1 to 6. Average them and record the result. If a digit is 7, 8, 9, or 0, skip it. The following are the first 40 means:

4.5	2.5	3.5	5	3.5	3.5	2	3.5	5	3
2.5	4	3.5	3.5	4	1.5	1.5	4.5	2.5	2.5
2.5	3.5	1.5	1.5	3.5	3	4.5	1.5	3	3.5
3	3.5	4	2.5	6	1.5	3	2.5	4.5	3.5

The following is the probability distribution:

x	1.0	1.5	2.0	2.5	3.0	3.5	4.0	4.5	5.0	5.5	6.0
f	0	6	1	7	5	11	3	4	2	0	1
$P(x)$	0.000	0.150	0.025	0.175	0.125	0.275	0.075	0.100	0.050	0.000	0.025

Review Questions and Answers

Multiple Choice Questions

Directions: Solve each of the following problems. Decide which is the best of the choices given.

1. When should the finite correction factor be used and what statistic should it be used for?

   A. $N > 20n$, μ
   B. $N > 20n$, σ
   C. $N < 20n$, μ
   D. $N < 20n$, σ
   E. All finite populations, μ and σ

2. The sampling distribution of $\bar{x}_1 - \bar{x}_2$ has a mean equal to

   A. The sum of the population means.
   B. The difference of the population means.
   C. The average of the population means.
   D. The larger of the population means.
   E. None of the above is correct.

3. The sampling distribution of $\bar{x}_1 - \bar{x}_2$ has a standard deviation equal to

   A. The sum of the population standard deviations.
   B. The difference of the population standard deviations.
   C. The average of the population standard deviations.
   D. The larger of the population standard deviations.
   E. None of the above is correct.

4. Which of the following are true about an unbiased estimate?

   I.   If the sampling distribution of a sample statistic has a mean equal to the population parameter it is estimating, the statistic is said to be an unbiased estimate of the parameter.

   II. If the sampling distribution of a sample statistic has a standard deviation equal to the population parameter it is estimating, the statistic is said to be an unbiased estimate of the parameter.

   III. If the sampling distribution of a sample statistic has a variance equal to the population parameter it is estimating, the statistic is said to be an unbiased estimate of the parameter.

   A. I only
   B. II only
   C. III only
   D. I and II
   E. I and III

5. Which of the following are true?

   I.   A sample whose mean is not equal to its population mean may be used as an unbiased estimate of the population parameter since its sampling distribution is unbiased.

   II. A sample whose proportion is not equal to its population proportion may be used as an unbiased estimate of the population parameter since its sampling distribution is unbiased.

   III. A sample whose variance is not equal to its population variance may be used as an unbiased estimate of the population parameter since its sampling distribution is unbiased.

   A. I only
   B. I and II
   C. I and III
   D. I, II, and III
   E. None of the above is a true statement.

6. Which of the following statements is false?

   A. As sample size increases, the variability of the sample decreases, and it becomes a better predictor of a population statistic.

   B. The mean of a sampling distribution is an unbiased estimate of the population parameter it is estimating, even if individual samples from the sampling distribution have statistics far from the population parameters.

   C. The standard deviation of a sampling distribution varies directly as the standard deviation of the population and inversely as the square root of the sample size.

   D. Population size has less of an effect on variance than does sample size.

   E. The sampling distribution of $\hat{p}$ has a standard deviation equal to $\sqrt{\dfrac{p(1-p)}{n}}$.

7. Which of the following are true?

   I.   The sampling distribution of $\bar{x}$ is normal if the population has a normal distribution.

   II. The population will have a normal distribution if the sampling distribution of $\bar{x}$ is normal.

   III. If a population distribution is not normal, a sampling distribution from that population is approximately normal if the sample size is large enough.

   A. I only
   B. II only
   C. I and III
   D. II and III
   E. I, II, and III

8. Which of the following are true?

    I.   If a population is not normally distributed, $\mu_{\bar{x}} = \mu$ and $\sigma_{\bar{x}} \frac{\sigma}{\sqrt{n}}$.

    II. A sampling distribution consists of a set of all sized samples taken from a population.

    III. In all sampling distributions, $\mu_{\bar{x}} = \mu$, $\sigma_{\bar{x}} \frac{\sigma}{\sqrt{n}}$, all samples making up the sampling distribution must be the same size.

    A. I only
    B. III only
    C. I and II
    D. I and III
    E. II and III

9. A sampling distribution is formed from samples of size 9 taken from a population with $\mu = 81$ and $\sigma = 36$. What is the mean and standard deviation of the sampling distribution?

    A. 9, 6
    B. 81, 4
    C. 9, 12
    D. 81, 12
    E. 9, 4

10. A population that is bimodal and is skewed to the left has a mean of 120 and a standard deviation of 32. What is the probability that a sample of size 60 will have a mean less than 110?

    A. 0.0059
    B. 0.0078
    C. 0.0102
    D. 0.3783
    E. Cannot be determined since the population is not normal

11. A town has a population of 20,000 residents. Sixty percent of the 800 people in a random sample of residents stated that they voted in a recent election. What is $\mu_{\hat{p}}$ and $\sigma_{\hat{p}}$?

    A. 0.6, 0.0173
    B. 0.48, 0.0173
    C. 0.6, 0.0184
    D. 0.48, 0.0184
    E. Cannot be determined from the information given

12. Fifteen percent of adults are left-handed. In a random sample of 60 adults, what is the probability that more than 12 are left-handed?

    A. 0.0287
    B. 0.1379
    C. 0.1524
    D. 0.2266
    E. 0.4042

13. Thirty-one percent of motorists in the state drive domestic cars. In a random sample of 150 motorists, what is the probability that between 40 and 50 drive domestic cars?

    A. 0.36
    B. 0.41
    C. 0.57
    D. 0.68
    E. 0.74

14. Which of the following are correct notations for means and standard deviations of sampling distributions?

    I. $\mu_{\bar{x}} = \mu$, $\sigma_{\hat{p}} = \sqrt{\dfrac{p(1-p)}{n}}$, $\mu_{\hat{p}} = p$

    II. $\sigma_{\hat{p}} = \sqrt{np(1-p)}$, $\mu_{\hat{p}} = p$, $\mu_{\bar{x}} = np$

    III. $\mu_{\hat{p}} = p$, $\sigma_{\bar{x}} = \dfrac{\sigma}{\sqrt{n}}$, $\sigma_{\hat{p}} = \sqrt{\dfrac{p(1-p)}{n}}$

    A. I only
    B. I and II
    C. I and III
    D. II and III
    E. I, II, and III

15. Suppose that 75% of computer users have made a purchase online. In a random sample of 200 computer users, what is the probability that less than 65% have made a purchase online?

    A. 0.0005
    B. 0.3707
    C. 0.4602
    D. 0.6293
    E. 0.9995

16. A school district is comparing the average GPA of students at two of its schools. The average GPA of students at school A is 2.23 with a standard deviation of 0.12. The average GPA of students at school B is 2.14 with a standard deviation of 0.07. In a random sample of 35 student GPAs from school A and a random sample of 40 student GPAs from school B, what is the probability that the difference between the average of the school A sample and the average of the school B sample will be less than 10%?

    A. 0.43
    B. 0.53
    C. 0.67
    D. 0.74
    E. 0.76

17. An airline has two flights, Flight A and Flight B, leaving LAX each morning for a nonstop flight to IAD. Flight A is on time 80% of the time, and Flight B is on time 75% of the time. A simple random sample is taken of 75 Flight A departures and a simple random sample is taken of 65 Flight B departures. What is the probability that the percentage of on time flights in the two samples will be within 10% of each other?

    A. 0.0174
    B. 0.2420
    C. 0.7404
    D. 0.7580
    E. 0.9826

Multiple Choice Answers

1. D. The finite correction factor applies to standard deviations when the size of a sample exceeds 5% of the size of a finite population. The finite correction factor is $\sqrt{\dfrac{N-n}{N-1}}$. So, if a population is less than 20 times the sample size, then $\sigma_{\bar{x}} = \dfrac{\sigma}{\sqrt{n}} \sqrt{\dfrac{N-n}{N-1}}$.

2. B. The sampling distribution of a difference of means is the difference in the means.

3. E. The sampling distribution of a difference of variances is the sum of the variances, not the standard deviations.

4. A. Bias refers to measures of center, such as mean, not variance or standard deviation.

5. A. Bias refers to measures of center, such as mean, not variance or standard deviation.

6. A. Populations have parameters, samples have statistics.

7. C. A sampling distribution taken from a normally distributed population will be normal even with very small sample sizes. If a population is known to have a nonnormal distribution, or if you do not know the shape of the population, then the Central Limit Theorem requires sample sizes of at least 30 to guarantee approximately normal sampling distributions.

8. D. Choice I is true for all populations, normal or not. Choice II is false since a sampling distribution is made up of all possible samples of a fixed size drawn from a population, not variable sizes. Choice III is true.

9. B. The mean of a sampling distribution is equal to the mean of the population. Therefore, the mean of the sampling distribution is 81. The standard deviation of a sampling distribution is equal to the standard deviation of the population divided by the square root of the sample size. Therefore, the standard deviation of the sampling distribution is 12.

10. B. Since this has a large sample, the Central Limit Theorem applies and the sampling distribution will be normal no matter what the shape of the population is. The standard deviation of the sampling distribution will be the standard deviation of the population divided by the square root of the sample size: $\sigma_{\bar{x}} = \dfrac{\sigma}{\sqrt{n}} = \dfrac{32}{\sqrt{60}} = 4.1312$. Calculate the z-score: $z = \dfrac{\bar{x} - \mu}{\sigma_{\bar{x}}} = \dfrac{110 - 120}{4.1312} = -2.42$. Look up -2.42 in the table of standard normal probabilities to obtain 0.0078. Therefore, the probability that a sample will have a mean less than 110 is 0.0078. Many students carry out the computation for the z-score in one step: $z = \dfrac{\bar{x} - \mu}{\dfrac{\sigma}{\sqrt{n}}} = \dfrac{110 - 120}{\dfrac{32}{\sqrt{60}}} = -2.42$

This calculation may be checked in the TI-83/4 [normalcdf(-E99,110,120,32/$\sqrt{60}$)].

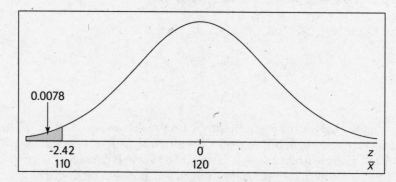

11. A. The proportion of the sampling distribution will be the same as the proportion of the population, or $\mu_{\hat{p}} = 0.60$. The standard deviation is $\sigma_{\hat{p}} = \sqrt{\dfrac{p(1-p)}{n}} = \sqrt{\dfrac{(0.6)(0.4)}{800}} = 0.0173$.

12. B. First, calculate the sample proportion: $\hat{p} = \frac{x}{n} = \frac{12}{60} = 0.20$. Next, calculate the standard deviation of the sampling distribution: $\sigma_{\hat{p}} = \sqrt{\frac{p(1-p)}{n}} = \sqrt{\frac{(0.15)(0.85)}{60}} = 0.046$. Determine the z-score: $z = \frac{\hat{p} - p}{\sigma_{\hat{p}}} = \frac{0.20 - 0.15}{0.046} = 1.09$. Look up the value of z in the table of standard normal probabilities. This represents the area to the left of z. You are interested in the area to the right. Subtract from 1 giving: $1 - 0.8621 = 0.1379$. This problem could be checked in the TI-83/4 [normalcdf(0.20,E99,0.15,0.046)]. Note that there will usually be a slight difference in results using the 2-place table of standard normal probabilities and the more accurate calculator. Both methods should yield an answer suitable for use on the AP Statistics Test. This problem could also be solved as a binomial distribution problem with the answer differing quite a bit from the previous approach. The reason, of course, is that the sample size is small. [1 − binomcdf(60, 0.15, 12)]

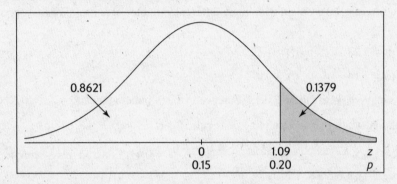

13. C. First, calculate the sample proportions: $\hat{p} = \frac{x}{n} = \frac{40}{150} = 0.267$ and $\hat{p} = \frac{x}{n} = \frac{50}{150} = 0.333$. Next, calculate the standard deviation of the sampling distribution: $\sigma_{\hat{p}} = \sqrt{\frac{p(1-p)}{n}} = \sqrt{\frac{(0.15)(0.85)}{60}} = 0.046$. Determine the two z values: $z = \frac{\hat{p} - p}{\sigma_{\hat{p}}} = \frac{0.267 - 0.31}{0.0378} = -1.14$ and $z = \frac{\hat{p} - p}{\sigma_{\hat{p}}} = \frac{0.33 - 0.31}{0.0378} = 0.53$. Look up the probabilities to the left of these z-scores in the table of standard normal probabilities and then subtract to find the probability between them: $0.7019 - 0.1271 = 0.5748$.

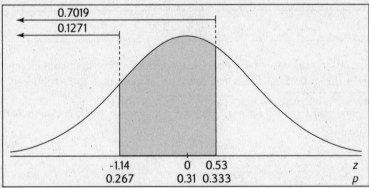

14. C. All the formulas are correct in choices I and III. In choice II, the first and third formulas are not correct.

15. A. The sampling distribution will be approximately normal since both np and $n(1 - p)$ are greater than 5 (or 10, as some authors prefer). The mean of the sampling distribution will be the same as the population proportion, 0.75. Therefore, $\mu_{\hat{p}} = \mu = 0.75$. The standard deviation is $\sigma_{\hat{p}} = \sqrt{\frac{p(1-p)}{n}} = \sqrt{\frac{(0.75)(0.25)}{200}} = 0.0306$. Calculate the z-score: $z = \frac{\hat{p} - p}{\sigma_{\hat{p}}} = \frac{0.65 - 0.75}{0.0306} = -3.27$. Look up the z-score in the table of standard normal probabilities to get 0.0005. There is a very small chance that the probability will be less than 65%.

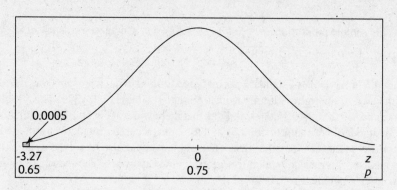

16. C. When solving a long word problem with many different variables, it is useful to first summarize the values of the required variables.

$n_A = 35$ $\mu_A = 2.23$ $\sigma_A = 1.12$

$n_B = 40$ $\mu_B = 2.14$ $\sigma_B = 0.07$

The mean of the sampling distribution is the difference in the population means: $\mu_{A-B} = \mu_A - \mu_B = 2.23 - 2.14$
$= 0.09$. The standard deviation of the sampling distribution is $\sigma_{\bar{x}_A - \bar{x}_B} = \sqrt{\dfrac{\sigma_A^2}{n_A} + \dfrac{\sigma_B^2}{n_B}} = \sqrt{\dfrac{0.12^2}{35} + \dfrac{0.07^2}{40}} = 0.023$.
Calculate the z-score: $z = \dfrac{(\bar{x}_A - \bar{x}_B) - (\mu_A - \mu_B)}{\sigma_{\bar{x}_A - \bar{x}_B}} = \dfrac{0.10 - 0.09}{0.023} = 0.43$. Look up this z-score in the table of standard normal probabilities to get 0.6664.

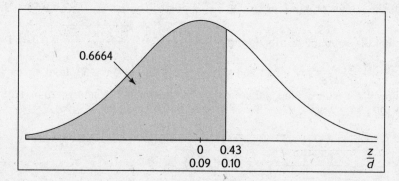

17. E. The distribution of differences has a mean equal to the differences of the population proportions:
$\mu_{\hat{p}_A - \hat{p}_B} = p_A - p_B = 0.80 - 0.75 = 0.05$. The standard deviation of the sampling distribution is
$\sigma_{\hat{p}_A - \hat{p}_B} = \sqrt{\dfrac{p_A(1 - p_A)}{n_A} + \dfrac{p_B(1 - p_B)}{n_B}} = \sqrt{\dfrac{(0.80)(0.20)}{75} + \dfrac{(0.75)(0.25)}{65}} = 0.071$. Calculate two z-scores, one for
$+10\%$ and the other for -10%.

$$z_{10} = \dfrac{\left(\hat{p}_A - \hat{p}_B\right) - \left(p_A - p_B\right)}{\sigma_{\hat{p}_A - \hat{p}_B}} = \dfrac{0.10 - 0.05}{0.071} = 0.70$$

$$z_{-10} = \dfrac{\left(\hat{p}_A - \hat{p}_B\right) - \left(p_A - p_B\right)}{\sigma_{\hat{p}_A - \hat{p}_B}} = \dfrac{-0.10 - 0.05}{0.071} = -2.11$$

Look up both z-scores in the table of standard normal probabilities and subtract to get $0.7580 - 0.0174 = 0.7404$.

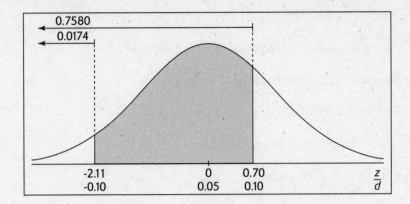

Free-Response Questions

Directions: Show all work. Indicate clearly the methods you use. You will be graded on method as well as accuracy.

1. Discuss the differences or similarities between a sampling distribution of size 5 and a simple random sample of size 5.

2. The average weight of a chicken egg is 2.15 ounces with a standard deviation of 0.12 ounces. You obtain a random sample of 40 chicken eggs.

   a. What are the mean and standard deviation of the sampling distribution of size 40?

   b. What is the probability that the mean weight of this 40-egg sample is less than 2.10 ounces?

3. Using the population of fish in a lake as an example, explain what is meant by a sampling distribution of size 5 of the weights of the fish in the lake. Discuss the shape of the sampling distribution.

4. The distribution of salaries of teachers in a community college is skewed left, with most teachers earning near the maximum of the pay scale. What would a sampling distribution of size 2 look like? How about size 5? How about size 50?

5. In a sample of 180, what is the probability of getting more than 50 percent green from a very large population consisting of 45 percent green?

6. In the game of roulette, there are 38 slots where the ball can land. There are 18 red slots, 18 black slots, and 2 green slots. A $1 bet on red wins $1 if the ball lands in a red slot and is lost if the ball lands in a black or green slot. Show that the expected win per $1 bet placed on red is $–0.0526. You can expect to lose $0.0526 each time you make a $1 bet. What is the probability that, after twenty $1 bets on red, you are even or ahead?

7. You are given a population comprised of 5 numbers: 3, 6, 9, 15, and 24. Find all samples of size 3 that may be selected from this population, and list them.

   a. Find the mean of each sample of 3.

   b. Find the mean of the sample means.

   c. Find the standard deviation of the sample means.

   d. Find the population mean.

   e. Find the population standard deviation.

f. Compare the mean of the sample means (b) with the population mean (d).

g. Compare the standard deviation of the sample means (c) with $\dfrac{\sigma}{\sqrt{n}}\sqrt{\dfrac{N-n}{N-1}}$.

h. Discuss the use of the finite correction factor: $\sqrt{\dfrac{N-n}{N-1}}$.

i. Find the proportion of numbers in the population that are multiples of 6.

j. Find the proportion of multiples of 6 in each sample.

k. Find the mean of the sample proportions.

l. Find the standard deviation of the sample proportions.

m. Compare the mean of the sample proportions (k) with the population proportion of multiples of 6 (i).

n. Compare the standard deviation of the sample proportions (l) with $\sqrt{\dfrac{p(1-p)}{n}}\sqrt{\dfrac{N-n}{N-1}}$.

Free-Response Answers

1. If 5 members are selected from a population in such a way that each and every set of 5 members in the population has an equal probability of being selected, then the sample of 5 members is a simple random sample. In a sampling distribution of size 5, every possible sample of size 5 from the population is averaged, and the result becomes part of the sampling distribution. The similarity is the inclusive nature of both the simple random sample as well as the sampling distribution. A sampling distribution consists of taking all possible simple random samples from a population.

2. Given $\mu = 2.15$, $\sigma = 0.12$, and $n = 40$.

a. The mean of the sampling distribution is the same as the mean of the population: $\mu_x = \mu = 2.15$. The standard deviation of the sampling distribution is the standard deviation of the population divided by the square root of the sample size: $\sigma_{\bar{x}} = \dfrac{\sigma}{\sqrt{n}} = \dfrac{0.12}{\sqrt{40}} = 0.019$.

b. To find $P(\bar{x} < 2.10)$, calculate the z-score at 2.10: $z = \dfrac{2.10 - 2.15}{0.019}$. Look up this z-score in the table of standard normal probabilities to obtain 0.0043.

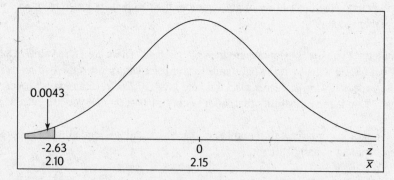

3. A sampling distribution of fish weights of size 5 is made up of the mean weights all possible samples of 5 fish in the lake. The mean of the sampling distribution will be the same as the mean of all fish in the lake. The standard deviation of the sampling distribution will be equal to the standard deviation of all the fish in the lake divided by the square root of the sample size, 5. The distribution will probably be mound-shaped, but without knowing the shape of the population, you do not know the shape of the sampling distribution. If the weights of fish in the lake were known to be normally distributed, then the sampling distribution would be normal also. If the sample size of the sampling distribution was at least 30, then it would be normal even if the population of all fish weights was not normal. This follows from the Central Limit Theorem.

4. You are given a population that is not normally distributed. In order for a sampling distribution to be normally distributed, a sample size of at least 30 is required, according to the Central Limit Theorem. Sampling distributions of less than 30 tend to look similar to the populations from which they are selected. So, for sample sizes of 2 and 5, the sampling distributions would probably be mound-shaped and skewed left, with the sample of size 2 showing more of a skew. However, the sample of size 50 would be approximately normally distributed. In all cases, the sampling distribution would have a mean equal to that of the population and a standard deviation equal to the standard deviation of the population divided by the square root of the sample size.

5. From the statement of the problem, $n = 180$ and $p = 0.45$. A sampling distribution of size 180 would have a mean of all sample proportions equal to the population proportion: $\mu_{\hat{p}} = p = 0.45$. The standard deviation of the sampling distribution would be $\sigma_{\hat{p}} = \sqrt{\dfrac{p(1-p)}{n}} = \sqrt{\dfrac{(0.45)(0.55)}{180}} = 0.037$. Find the z-score for a specific sample with a proportion of 0.50: $z = \dfrac{\hat{p} - p}{\sigma_{\hat{p}}} = \dfrac{0.50 - 0.45}{0.037} = 1.35$. Look up this z-score in the table of standard normal probabilities. Subtract from 1 giving $1 - 0.9115 = 0.0885$.

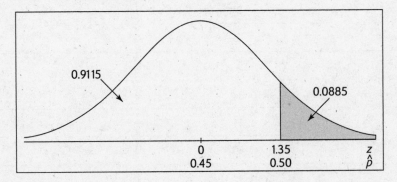

6. To calculate the expected value of a payout, construct a probability distribution. The values are either a +1 if you win and −1 if you lose. The probabilities are 18/38 that you win and 20/38 that you will lose.

x	1	−1
$P(x)$	$\dfrac{18}{38} = 0.4737$	$\dfrac{20}{38} = 0.5263$

The expected value is the sum of the products of value of the variable and the probability of getting that value: $\mu = E(x) = (1)(0.4737) + (-1)(0.5263) = -0.0526$. The variance is $\sigma^2 = (1 - (-0.0526))^2(0.4737) + (-1 - (-0.0526))^2(0.5263) = 0.9972$, and the standard deviation is $\sigma = \sqrt{\sigma^2} = \sqrt{0.9972} = 0.9986$.

(TI-83/4 – You may determine these values by entering 1 and −1 in L1 and the probabilities in L2. Then select STAT CALC 1-VarStats.)

The sampling distribution will have a standard deviation of $\sigma_{\bar{x}} = \dfrac{\sigma}{\sqrt{n}} = \dfrac{0.9986}{\sqrt{20}} = 0.2233$. Since you are interested in breaking even, calculate the z-score for $\mu_{\bar{x}} = 0$. $z = \dfrac{\mu_{\bar{x}} - \mu}{\sigma_{\bar{x}}} = \dfrac{0 - (-0.0526)}{0.2233} = 0.24$. Look up this z-score in the table of standard normal probabilities.

Subtract from 1 to obtain $1 - 0.5948 = 0.4052$. [TI-83/4 – You may determine the probability by entering (normalcdf(0,E99,-0.0526, 0.9986/$\sqrt{20}$)]

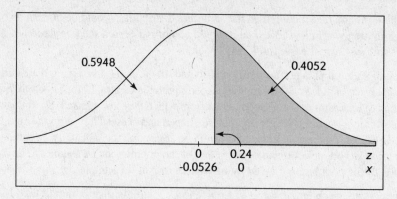

7. There are 10 ways of choosing samples of size 3. This chart lists the samples, the mean of the samples, and the proportion of numbers in the set that are multiples of 6, along with totals and means.

Sample	Sample Mean	Sample Proportion of Multiples of 6
3, 6, 9	6	$\frac{1}{3}$
3, 6, 15	8	$\frac{1}{3}$
3, 6, 24	11	$\frac{2}{3}$
3, 9, 15	9	$\frac{0}{3}$
3, 9, 24	12	$\frac{1}{3}$
3, 15, 24	14	$\frac{1}{3}$
6, 9, 15	10	$\frac{1}{3}$
6, 9, 24	13	$\frac{2}{3}$
6, 15, 24	15	$\frac{2}{3}$
9, 15, 24	16	$\frac{1}{3}$
Means of sample means and sample proportions	$\mu_{\bar{x}} = \frac{114}{10} = 11.4$	$\mu_{\hat{p}} = \frac{4}{10} = 0.4$
Standard deviation of sample means and sample proportions	$\sigma_{\bar{x}} = 3.04$	$\sigma_{\hat{p}} = 0.2$

The mean of the population is $\mu = \dfrac{3+6+9+15+24}{5} = \dfrac{57}{5} = 11.4$.

The standard deviation of the population is $\sigma = 7.446$. (The standard deviation for the set of sample means as well as the standard deviation for the population was obtained by placing the respective values into lists in the calculator and using 1-VarStats.)

The mean of the population and the mean of the sample means are both 11.4. They are equal in value. Divide the population standard deviation by the square root of the sample size and multiply by the finite correction factor, and the result will equal the standard deviation of the sample means.

$$\sigma_{\bar{x}} = \frac{\sigma}{\sqrt{n}}\sqrt{\frac{N-n}{N-1}} = \frac{7.446}{\sqrt{3}}\sqrt{\frac{5-3}{5-1}} = 3.04$$

The finite correction factor, $\sqrt{\dfrac{N-n}{N-1}}$, needs to be applied to standard deviations whenever a sample size is more than 5% of the population size. In this case, the sample size (3) was 60 percent of the population size (5).

$$\sigma_{\hat{p}} = \sqrt{\frac{p(1-p)}{n}}\sqrt{\frac{N-n}{N-1}} = \sqrt{\frac{(0.4)(0.6)}{3}}\sqrt{\frac{5-3}{5-1}} = 0.2$$

Statistical Inference: Confidence Intervals

Descriptive statistics is the branch of statistics that involves the organization and display of data. Inferential statistics is the branch of statistics that involves using a sample to draw conclusions and generalizations about a population. The first part of inferential statistics is **estimation,** in which sample data are used to estimate the value of unknown population parameters such as mean, μ; standard deviation, σ; and proportion, ρ.

Any sample you choose from a population is part of a sampling distribution. When the population from which the samples are drawn is normally distributed, the sampling distribution of sample means is also normal. If the sample size is sufficiently large, the sampling distribution of sample means is approximately normal regardless of the shape of the population from which the sample is drawn. The mean of a sampling distribution of sample means, $\bar{x}$, is equal to the population mean, μ. The standard deviation of $\bar{x}$ is $\frac{\sigma}{\sqrt{n}}$.

Is it possible that the sample you choose from a population will be the "perfect" sample and have a mean exactly equal to the mean of the population? It is possible, but not likely. Since the mean of the sampling distribution is clustered around the mean of the population, it is more likely that the mean of your sample will be close to the population mean rather than far away from it. You use the properties of sampling distributions to establish intervals within which you believe a population parameter will lie and to establish rules for assessing that likelihood.

The Meaning of a Confidence Interval

In the previous chapter, using the properties of sampling distributions, you determined the probability that the mean of a sample would lie within a given distance of the mean of the population. You now reverse the process. You determine an interval about a sample mean (or proportion) within which you establish the likelihood that the population mean (proportion) will lie. The interval is called a **confidence interval,** and the likelihood it contains the population parameter is called the **confidence level.** The statistic of interest in your sample is a single value estimate, the **point estimate,** of the population parameter. For example, the most unbiased point estimate for the population mean would be the mean of the sample.

The general format for a confidence interval is

$$\text{statistic} \pm (\text{critical value}) \cdot (\text{standard deviation of statistic})$$

or

$$\text{estimate} \pm \text{margin of error}$$

The estimate comes from your sample—either the sample mean or the sample proportion. The critical value is a z-score based on the level of confidence. The standard deviation of statistic is really an estimated population standard deviation.

The following is a summary of the types of confidence intervals that are discussed in this chapter. This chapter discusses only confidence intervals based on large samples ($n \geq 30$) or the fact that the populations from which the samples are drawn are known to be normal. In other words, the conditions of the central limit theorem apply. Situations in which the central limit theorem does not apply, such as the use of small samples, are discussed in the last chapter of this text.

Population Parameter	Sample Estimate	Conditions for Use	Formula
mean μ	$\overline{x}$	Simple Random Sample	$\overline{x} \pm z_c \dfrac{s}{\sqrt{n}}$
proportion ρ	$\hat{p}$	Simple Random Sample $n\hat{p} \geq 5, n\left(1 - \hat{p}\right) \geq 5$	$\hat{p} \pm z_c \sqrt{\dfrac{\hat{p}\left(1 - \hat{p}\right)}{n}}$
difference of means $\mu_1 - \mu_2$	$\overline{x}_1 - \overline{x}_2$	Independent Simple Random Samples	$\left(\overline{x}_1 - \overline{x}_2\right) \pm z_c \sqrt{\dfrac{s_1^2}{n_1} + \dfrac{s_2^2}{n_2}}$
difference of proportions $\rho_1 - \rho_2$	$\hat{p}_1 - \hat{p}_2$	Independent Simple Random Samples $n_1 \hat{p}_1 \geq 5,\ n_1\left(1 - \hat{p}_1\right) \geq 5,$ $n_2 \hat{p}_2 \geq 5,\ n_2\left(1 - \hat{p}_2\right) \geq 5$	$\left(\hat{p}_1 - \hat{p}_2\right) \pm z_c \sqrt{\dfrac{\hat{p}_1\left(1 - \hat{p}_1\right)}{n_1} + \dfrac{\hat{p}_2\left(1 - \hat{p}_2\right)}{n_2}}$

Statisticians do not like to be wrong. Therefore, common confidence levels include 99%, 95%, and 90%, but any confidence level may be established. The confidence level, c, is the probability that the confidence interval contains the population parameter. It is NOT the probability that the population parameter is in the confidence interval. It is either in the interval, or it is not. For example, a 99% confidence interval will contain the actual population parameter 99% of the time. This is a very important distinction. If you want to be more confident of your prediction, you must increase the size of your confidence interval. The size of the confidence interval also depends of the size of the sample that is used to make the prediction. Larger samples provide more accurate information and can reduce the size of confidence intervals.

How Are z-Scores Determined for Confidence Intervals?

The confidence level, c, is the area under the standard normal curve between the **critical values,** $-z_c$ and z_c. The area outside the interval is $1 - c$. Half of this area is in each tail of the distribution. Different values of c produce different z-scores.

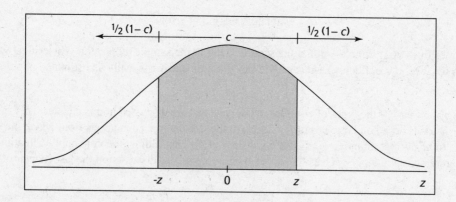

EXAMPLE:

Determine the z-score for a 95% confidence interval.

Since the area between $-z_c$ and z_c is 0.9500, there is $1 - 0.9500 = 0.0500$ outside the interval. Divide this in half, giving 0.0250 in each tail of the distribution. When you look up a z-score in the table of standard normal probabilities, you must include all area to the left of the z-score. In this case, look up 0.9750. The corresponding z-score is $z = 1.96$.

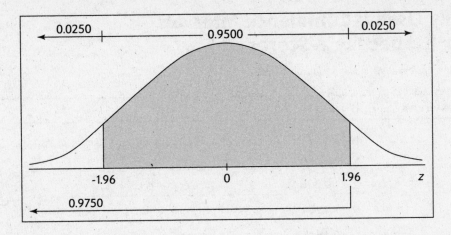

EXAMPLE:
Determine the z-score for a 99% confidence interval.

Since the area between $-z_c$ and z_c is 0.9900, there is $1 - 0.9900 = 0.0100$ outside the interval. Divide this in half, giving 0.0050 in each tail of the distribution. When you look up a z-score in the table of standard normal probabilities, you must include all area to the left of the z-score. In this case, look up 0.9950. The corresponding z-score is $z = 2.576$.

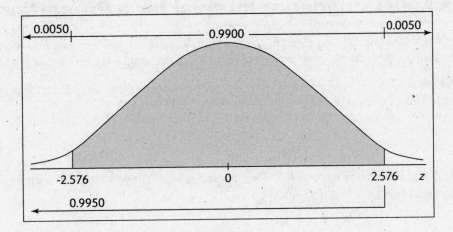

EXAMPLE:
What c-confidence interval corresponds to a z-score of $z = 2.17$?

Look up the z-score in the table of standard normal probabilities to obtain an area to the left of $z = 2.17$, which is 0.9850. This is the area to the left of z. Subtract from 1 to obtain the area in the right tail of the distribution: $1 - 0.9850 = 0.0150$. This is the area in each tail of the distribution of the confidence interval. Therefore, there is $2(0.0150) = 0.0300$ in the two tails of the distribution. This leaves 0.9700 between $-z_c$ and z_c. This corresponds to a 97% confidence interval.

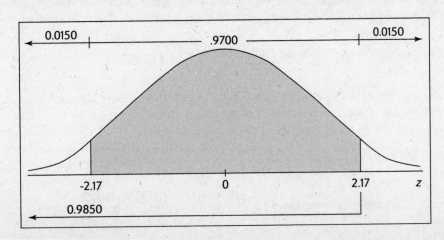

Commonly Used c-Confidence Intervals and Their Respective z-Scores

The most common are $c = 0.90$, $c = 0.95$, and $c = 0.99$.

c-Confidence Intervals	z-Score
$c = 0.999$	$z = 3.291$
$c = 0.99$	$z = 2.576$
$c = 0.98$	$z = 2.326$
$c = 0.95$	$z = 1.960$
$c = 0.90$	$z = 1.645$
$c = 0.80$	$z = 1.282$
$c = 0.50$	$z = 0.674$

Large Sample Confidence Interval for a Proportion

(*Note:* The material in this section relies on one of these conditions: Samples are sufficiently large so that the sampling distributions will be approximately normal; or the populations from which the samples are drawn are known to be normal.)

You want to estimate the population proportion, p, using information from a sample taken from the population. The point estimate for p is the proportion of successes in a sample and is denoted as

$$\hat{p} = \frac{x}{n}$$

where x is the number of successes in the sample and n is the sample size. The point estimate for the number of failures is $1 - \hat{p}$. (The proportion of failures is also denoted by $\hat{q}$.)

EXAMPLE:

You are interested in determining the number of defective switches in a large shipment. You randomly choose 250 switches from the shipment and find that 32 are defective. Based on your sample, what would be a point estimate for the population proportion of defective switches?

The point estimate would be $\hat{p} = \frac{x}{n} = \frac{32}{250} = 0.128$.

The standard deviation of a sampling distribution of sample proportions is $\sigma_{\hat{p}} = \sqrt{\frac{p(1-p)}{n}}$, where p is the population proportion in question and n is the sample size. If you do not know the population proportion, p, and want to estimate it using a sample from the sampling distribution, then you substitute $\hat{p}$ for p. Since this is an approximation, it is usually referred to as the standard error instead of the standard deviation: $\sigma_{\hat{p}} \approx \sqrt{\frac{\hat{p}(1-\hat{p})}{n}}$.

EXAMPLE:

You want to estimate the proportion of elementary school teachers who hold master's degrees. You randomly choose 400 elementary school teachers and determine that 21 of them hold master's degrees. What would be your point estimate for the proportion of all elementary teachers who hold master's degrees? What would be the standard deviation?

The point estimate would be $\hat{p} = \frac{x}{n} = \frac{21}{400} = 0.0525$

The standard deviation (standard error) would be $\sigma_{\hat{p}} \approx \sqrt{\frac{\hat{p}(1-\hat{p})}{n}} = \sqrt{\frac{(0.0525)(0.9475)}{400}} = 0.011$.

A c-confidence interval for the population proportion p is given by

$$\hat{p} - E < p < \hat{p} + E \text{ where } E = z_c\,\sigma_{\hat{p}} = z_c\sqrt{\frac{\hat{p}\left(1 - \hat{p}\right)}{n}}$$

The value of E is known as the **error of estimate.** The value of E is also known as the **margin of error.**

EXAMPLE:
You want to estimate the proportion of residents in your county who are in favor of a change in county election policy. You take a simple random sample of 240 residents and find that 182 are in favor. Determine a 95% confidence interval for the proportion of county residents who are in favor of the change.

The z-score that corresponds to a 95% confidence interval is $z = 1.96$. Find the sample proportion of residents in favor of the change: $\hat{p} = \frac{x}{n} = \frac{182}{240} = 0.758$. Find the error of estimate:

$$\sigma_{\hat{p}} = \sqrt{\frac{\hat{p}\left(1 - \hat{p}\right)}{n}} = \sqrt{\frac{(0.758)(0.242)}{240}} = 0.0276$$

$$E = z_c\sqrt{\frac{\hat{p}\left(1 - \hat{p}\right)}{n}} = (1.96)\sqrt{\frac{(0.758)(0.242)}{240}} = 0.054$$

Add E to and subtract E from the point estimate:

$$\hat{p} - z_c\,\sigma_{\hat{p}} < p < \hat{p} + z_c\,\sigma_{\hat{p}}$$
$$\hat{p} - E < p < \hat{p} + E$$
$$0.758 - 0.054 < p < 0.758 + 0.054$$
$$0.704 < p < 0.812$$

This interval may be written in interval notation: (0.704, 0.812). You say, "I am 95% sure that the proportion of county residents who are in favor of the change is between 70.4% and 81.2%." [TI-83/4–This problem may be solved by selecting CALC TESTS 1-PropZInt and entering the appropriate data.]

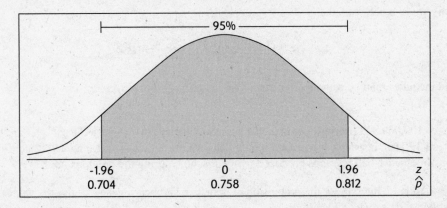

After determining a confidence interval, you may find that the margin of error is too large for your purpose. Consider the last example. The margin of error is more than 5%. How can the margin of error be reduced? Consider the possibilities. One way to reduce the margin of error is to consider a lower confidence level. Reducing the confidence level from 95% ($z = 1.96$) to 90% ($z = 1.645$) would reduce the margin of error from 5.4% to 4.5%. The reduction in the confidence level is usually not desirable. You have no control over the proportion obtained in the sample. You do have control over the sample size. Increasing the sample size would reduce the standard deviation of the sampling distribution and, thus, decrease the margin of error.

Solving the equation for the margin of error for n gives a formula to determine the sample size necessary to obtain any specific margin of error.

$$n = \left(\hat{p}\right)\left(1 - \hat{p}\right)\left(\frac{z_c}{E}\right)^2$$

In this formula, $\hat{p}$ is the proportion obtained from a **preliminary sample**; z_c is the z-score for your particular confidence level, and E is the required margin of error.

EXAMPLE:

After surveying 240 county residents about their feelings toward changes in election policy, you find that 75.8% were in favor. Using a 95% confidence level, the margin of error in this survey was more than 5%; you need to reduce it to 3%. How many more residents need to be included in the survey to reduce the margin of error to 3%?

Substitute the proper values in the formula for n and solve:

$$x = \left(\hat{p}\right)\left(1 - \hat{p}\right)\left(\frac{z_c}{E}\right)^2 = (0.758)(0.242)\left(\frac{1.96}{0.03}\right)^2 = 783$$

Since 240 have already been included in the preliminary data, 543 additional residents should be surveyed and added to the preliminary results. You should calculate a new margin of error since increasing the sample size will probably change the value of $\hat{p}$ slightly and could result in a margin of error greater than 3%. Most statisticians will survey a few more than required so that they can avoid repeated surveys.

What happens if you do not have a preliminary study? What if you want to determine how large the sample size should be, and you do not have a value of $\hat{p}$ to use in the formula for n? The answer is to use the maximum possible value for the product of $\hat{p}$ and $(1 - \hat{p})$. If two positive fractions add up to 1, the maximum value of their product is 0.25. Therefore, if no preliminary sample is available, the formula for n is changed.

$$n = (0.25)\left(\frac{z_c}{E}\right)^2 \text{ or } n = \left(\frac{z_c}{2E}\right)^2$$

This gives a worst-case value for the sample size.

EXAMPLE:

You need to poll voters to determine whether they favor a ballot proposition. You need a 95% confidence level and a margin of error of 3% or less. How many voters should you include in the study?

Since a preliminary study is not available:

$$n = (0.25)\left(\frac{z_c}{E}\right)^2 = (0.25)\left(\frac{1.96}{0.03}\right)^2 = 1068$$

Your study should include a random sample of at least 1068 voters.

EXAMPLE:

A machine produces 100,000 ball bearings per hour. To maintain quality control, periodic samples are taken and analyzed. In a sample of 120 ball bearings, it was determined that 15% were defective. Using a 99% confidence level, determine a range of defective ball bearings produced by the machine during the previous hour.

First, determine a confidence interval for the proportion of defective ball bearings. Next, use the values in the interval to determine the number of defective ball bearings.

Find the margin of error:

$$\sigma_{\hat{p}} = \sqrt{\frac{\hat{p}\left(1 - \hat{p}\right)}{n}} = \sqrt{\frac{(0.15)(0.85)}{120}} = 0.0326$$

$$E = z_c\sqrt{\frac{\hat{p}\left(1 - \hat{p}\right)}{n}} = (2.576)\sqrt{\frac{(0.15)(0.85)}{120}} = 0.084$$

The 99% confidence interval is $\hat{p} \pm E$, or 0.15 ± 0.084, or $(0.066, 0.234)$.

Multiply each percentage by the number of ball bearings produced per hour.

$$(100,000)(0.066) = 6600 \text{ and } (100,000)(0.234) = 23400.$$

Therefore, the range of defective ball bearings produced the previous hour is (6600, 23400). [TI-83/4 – Use (.15)(120) = 18 for x. Select STAT TESTS 1-PropZInt x:18 n:120 C-Level:0.99 Calculate Display (0.066, 0.234)]

EXAMPLE:
Ellen has observed 700 cars at an intersection and noted that 45% did not make a complete stop. She stated to a newspaper reporter that "With a margin of error of 2%, 45% of all cars do not stop at the intersection." What confidence level did Ellen use in her study?

Start with formula for the margin of error. Substitute the values for E, n, and $\hat{p}$, and solve for the z-score.

$$\sigma_{\hat{p}} = \sqrt{\frac{\hat{p}\left(1 - \hat{p}\right)}{n}} = \sqrt{\frac{(0.45)(0.55)}{700}} = 0.188$$

$$E = z_c \sqrt{\frac{\hat{p}\left(1 - \hat{p}\right)}{n}} = z_c \sqrt{\frac{(0.45)(0.55)}{700}}$$

$$0.02 = z_c(0.0188)$$

$$z_c = 1.06$$

Look up the z-score of 1.06 in the table of standard normal probabilities to obtain the probability to the left of the z-score. The value is 0.8554. Subtract this value from 1 to obtain the probability in the right tail of the distribution, 0.1446. Double it and then subtract from 1 to give the confidence level of 71.08%.

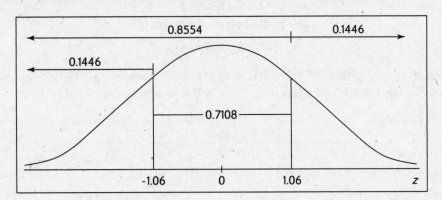

Large Sample Confidence Interval for a Mean

(*Note:* The material in this section relies on one of these conditons: Samples are sufficiently large so that the sampling distributions will be approximately normal; or the populations from which the samples are drawn are known to be normal.)

You want to estimate the population mean, μ, using information from a sample taken from the population.

The mean of a sampling distribution of sample means is equal to the population mean. That is, $\mu_{\bar{x}} = \mu$.

The standard deviation of a sampling distribution of sample means is $\sigma_{\bar{x}} = \frac{\sigma}{\sqrt{n}}$, where σ is the population standard deviation and n is the sample size. If you do not know the population standard deviation, σ, you estimate it using a sample from the sampling distribution and substitute s for σ. Since this is an approximation, it is usually referred to as the

235

standard error instead of the standard deviation: $\sigma_{\bar{x}} \approx \dfrac{s}{\sqrt{n}}$. Since the value of the population standard deviation is approximated by the sample standard deviation, some authors argue that a more relaxed distribution should be used in place of the normal distribution. (This distribution, known as the *t*-distribution, is covered in the last chapter.) The exercises in this section use the sample standard deviation as a suitable substitute for the population standard deviation.

The point estimate for μ is the mean of the sample, $\bar{x}$. You use this point estimate as the center of a confidence interval.

A *c*-confidence interval for the population mean, μ, is given by

$$\bar{x} - E < \mu < \bar{x} + E \text{ where } E = z_c \sigma_{\bar{x}} = z_c \frac{s}{\sqrt{n}}$$

The value of E is referred to as the **error of estimate** or the **margin of error.**

EXAMPLE:

A quality control supervisor wants to check of the accuracy of one of the machines that is filling bottles with syrup. He selects a simple random sample of 45 bottles and carefully measures the contents. The sample had a mean of 33.2 ounces with a standard deviation of 2.1 ounces. Construct a 95% confidence interval for the average amount of syrup this machine is placing in the bottles.

Use the mean of the sample, $\bar{x}$, as the point estimate for the population mean, μ. The *z*-score that corresponds to a 95% confidence level is $z = 1.96$. Use the standard deviation of the sample, s, as an estimate for the population standard deviation, σ. Calculate the margin of error.

$$E = z_c \sigma_x = z_c \frac{s}{\sqrt{n}} = (1.96)\frac{2.1}{\sqrt{45}} = 0.614$$

Calculate the confidence interval for μ.

$$\bar{x} - E < \mu < \bar{x} + E$$
$$33.2 - 0.614 < \mu < 33.2 + 0.614$$
$$32.586 < \mu < 33.814$$

You are 95% sure that the interval from 32.586 ounces to 33.814 ounces contains the population mean. [TI-83/4: Select STAT TESTS ZInterval Inpt:Stats σ:2.1 $\bar{x}$:33.2 n:45 C-Level:0.95 Calculate Display: (32.586,33.814)]

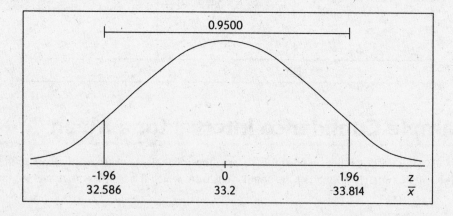

EXAMPLE:

In 32 random samples of fields of wheat, the mean yield was 34.5 bushels per acre with a standard deviation of 9.7 bushels per acre. Construct 95% and 90% confidence intervals for the population mean and compare the results.

Use the mean of the sample, $\bar{x}$, and the point estimate for the population mean, μ. The *z*-score that corresponds to a 95% confidence level is $z = 1.96$, and the *z*-score that corresponds to a 90% confidence level is $z = 1.645$. Use the standard deviation of the sample, s, as an estimate for the population standard deviation, σ. Calculate the margin of error.

For the 95% confidence interval:

$$E = z_c \sigma_{\bar{x}} = z_c \frac{s}{\sqrt{n}} = (1.96) \frac{9.7}{\sqrt{32}} = 3.361$$

Calculate the confidence interval for μ.

$$\bar{x} - E < \mu < \bar{x} + E$$
$$34.5 - 3.361 < \mu < 34.5 + 3.361$$
$$31.139 < \mu < 37.861$$

For the 90% confidence interval:

$$E = z_c \sigma_{\bar{x}} = z_c \frac{s}{\sqrt{n}} = (1.645) \frac{9.7}{\sqrt{32}} = 2.821$$

$$\bar{x} - E < \mu < \bar{x} + E$$
$$34.5 - 2.821 < \mu < 34.5 + 2.821$$
$$31.679 < \mu < 37.321$$

[TI-83/4: Select STAT TESTS ZInterval Inpt:Stats σ:9.7 $\bar{x}$:34.5 n:32 C-Level:0.95 Calculate Display: (31.139, 37.861)]

[TI-83/4: Select STAT TESTS ZInterval Inpt:Stats σ:9.7 $\bar{x}$:34.5 n:32 C-Level:0.90 Calculate Display: (31.68, 37.32)]

The interval that corresponds to the lower confidence level (90%) is smaller than the interval that corresponds to the higher confidence level (95%). The means are the same. Reducing the confidence level uses a lower value for the z-score and, therefore, produces a smaller margin of error.

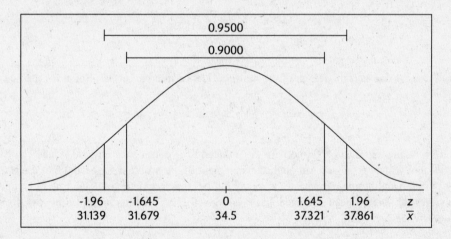

After determining a confidence interval, you may find that the margin of error is too large for your purpose. Consider the last example. The margin of error for the 95% confidence interval is greater than 3. How can the margin of error be reduced? Consider the possibilities. One way to reduce the margin of error is to consider a lower confidence level. Reducing the confidence level from 95% ($z = 1.96$) to 90% ($z = 1.645$) reduces the margin of error from 3.361 to 2.821. The reduction in the confidence level is usually not desirable. You have no control over the standard deviation obtained in the sample. You do have control over the sample size. Increasing the sample size would reduce the standard deviation of the sampling distribution and, thus, decrease the margin of error.

Solving the margin of error equation for n gives a formula to determine the sample size necessary to obtain any specific margin of error. (*Note:* The use of this formula requires a value of s. This value comes from a preliminary sample but may also be available from past experience. There is no worst-case maximum value as there was with proportions.)

$$n = \left(\frac{z_c s}{E} \right)^2$$

In this formula, s is the standard deviation obtained from a preliminary sample; z_c is the z-score for your particular confidence level, and E is the required margin of error.

In the previous example, you were given $\bar{x} = 34.5$, $s = 9.7$, and $n = 32$. The 95% confidence interval contained a margin of error of $E = 3.361$. If the sample standard deviation stays the same (and it probably will not) and you maintain a 95% level of confidence, what sample size would be required to reduce the margin of error to 2?

$$n = \left(\frac{z_c s}{E}\right)^2 = \left(\frac{(1.96)(9.7)}{2}\right)^2 = 90.4$$

So, a sample size of about 91 should produce a margin of error of only 2. In the initial study, a sample size of 32 was used. If an additional 59 (the difference between how many you need and how many you have already sampled) were combined with the initial sample, a new sample mean and standard deviation should be computed. If the sample standard deviation did not increase (smaller is okay), then the new confidence interval will have a margin of error of less than 2.

EXAMPLE:
A 95% confidence interval for a sample size of 184 is $44.5 < \mu < 45.5$. By approximately how many does the sample size need to be increased in order to reduce the 95% confidence interval to $44.8 < \mu < 45.2$? (Assume that the sample standard deviation remains the same after the increase in sample size.)

Determine the margin of error for the original interval. Since the confidence interval is determined by adding the margin of error to the sample mean and subtracting the margin of error from the sample mean, the margin of error is one-half the length of the interval. So, the margin of error for the original interval is 0.5. Use this information to determine the sample standard deviation for the original sample of 184:

$$E = z_c \frac{s}{\sqrt{n}}$$

$$0.5 = (1.96)\left(\frac{s}{\sqrt{184}}\right)$$

$$s = 3.46$$

The new margin of error is one-half the length of the new confidence interval, or 0.2. Solve for the new sample size:

$$n = \left(\frac{z_c s}{E}\right)^2 = \left(\frac{(1.96)(3.46)}{0.2}\right)^2 = 1149.75$$

The sample size must be increased to 1150 to obtain the reduced 95% confidence interval. Since 184 have already been included, 966 additional will be required. Although the statement of the problem suggested that the standard deviation of the new larger sample would remain the same, this may not be true. Recalculate the margin of error and confidence interval after the larger sample has been collected. [TI-83/4: STAT TESTS ZInterval Inpt:Stats σ:3.46 $\bar{x}$:45 n:1150 C-Level:0.95 Calculate Display (44.8, 45.2)]

EXAMPLE:
A random sample of 44 bags of sugar had a mean weight of 82 ounces with a standard deviation of 2.9 ounces. Find a 90% confidence interval for the weight of all bags of sugar. If the sample size had been 200 instead of 44, the margin of error would have been reduced by how much?

Method 1

The standard deviation of the sample is used as an approximation to the standard deviation of the population. The standard deviation of the sampling distribution is $\sigma_{\bar{x}} = \frac{s}{\sqrt{n}} = \frac{2.9}{\sqrt{44}} = 0.437$. The z-score for a 90% level of confidence is 1.645. The confidence interval is

$$\text{statistic} \pm (\text{critical value}) \cdot (\text{standard deviation of statistic})$$

$$\bar{x} \pm z_c \sigma_{\bar{x}}$$

$$82 \pm (1.645)(0.437)$$

$$(81.28, 82.72)$$

Method 2

Find the margin of error, and then add it to, and subtract it from, the sample mean.

$$E = z_c \frac{s}{\sqrt{n}} = (1.645) \frac{2.9}{\sqrt{44}} = 0.719$$

$$\bar{x} - E < \mu < \bar{x} + E$$

$$82 - 0.719 < \mu < 82 + 0.719$$

$$81.281 < \mu < 82.719$$

[TI-83/4: Select STAT TESTS ZInterval Inpt: Stats σ:2.9 $\bar{x}$:82 n:44 C-Level:0.90 Calculate Display (81.281, 82.719)]

An increased sample size of 200 produces a smaller margin of error:

$$E = z_c \frac{s}{\sqrt{n}} = (1.645) \frac{2.9}{\sqrt{200}} = 0.337$$

The difference is 0.719 − 0.337 = 0.382.

EXAMPLE:

From a population of 3,240,000 elementary school children in the state, a random sample of 60 indicated that they watch an average of 2.8 hours of television per day with a standard deviation of 0.8 hours. Using a 99% level of confidence, determine a range for the total number of hours watched per day by all the elementary school children in the state.

Calculate the margin of error for the 99% confidence interval. Determine the interval of hours watched per day per child. Multiply the minimum and maximum value in the interval by the population size.

$$E = z_c \frac{s}{\sqrt{n}} = (2.576) \frac{0.8}{\sqrt{60}} = 0.266$$

$$\bar{x} - E < \mu < \bar{x} + E$$

$$2.8 - 0.266 < \mu < 2.8 + 0.266$$

$$2.534 < \mu < 3.066$$

$$(3240000)(2.534) = 8210160$$

$$(3240000)(3.066) = 9933840$$

The range of total hours of television watched per day by elementary school children in the state is (8210160, 9933840).

The first part of the problem may be verified in the calculator. [TI-83/4: Select STAT TESTS ZInterval Inpt: Stats σ:0.8 $\bar{x}$:2.8 n:60 C-Level:0.99 Calculate Display (2.534, 3.066)]

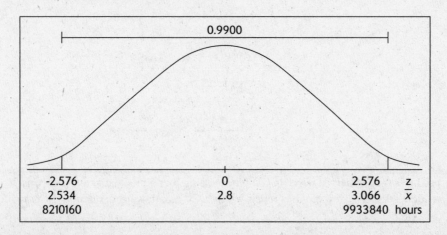

EXAMPLE:

A random sample of 75 bags of gravel weighed an average of 136 pounds with a standard deviation of 5.41 pounds. What confidence level would have to be used to produce a confidence interval with a margin of error of 1 pound?

Start with the formula for the margin of error. Solve for the z-score. Look up the z-score to get the area (probability) to its left. Subtract from 1 to get the area in the right tail of the curve. Double that difference. Subtract the doubled amount from 1 to get the confidence level.

$$E = z_c \frac{s}{\sqrt{n}}$$

$$1 = z_c \frac{5.41}{\sqrt{75}}$$

$$z_c = 1.60$$

The area to the left of a z-score of 1.60 is 0.9452.

$$1 - 0.9452 = 0.0548$$

$$(0.0548)(2) = 0.1096$$

$$1 - 0.1096 = 0.8904$$

The confidence level is 89.04%.

Large Sample Confidence Interval for a Difference between Two Proportions

The point estimate for the difference of two proportions, $p_1 - p_2$, is $\hat{p}_1 - \hat{p}_2$.

The variance of the difference of two proportions in the sampling distribution for $\hat{p}_1 - \hat{p}_2$ is the sum of the variances.

The standard deviation of the differences is the square root of the sum of the variances.

$$\sigma_{\hat{p}_1 - \hat{p}_2} = \sqrt{\frac{\hat{p}_1\left(1 - \hat{p}_1\right)}{n_1} + \frac{\hat{p}_2\left(1 - \hat{p}_2\right)}{n_2}}$$

The margin of error is $E = z_c \, \sigma_{\hat{p}_1 - \hat{p}_2} = z_c \sqrt{\dfrac{\hat{p}_1\left(1 - \hat{p}_1\right)}{n_1} + \dfrac{\hat{p}_2\left(1 - \hat{p}_2\right)}{n_2}}$

The c-confidence interval for the difference of population proportions is

$$\left(\hat{p}_1 - \hat{p}_2\right) - E < p_1 - p_2 < \left(\hat{p}_1 - \hat{p}_2\right) + E$$

$$\left(\hat{p}_1 - \hat{p}_2\right) \pm E$$

$$\left(\hat{p}_1 - \hat{p}_2\right) \pm z_c \, \sigma_{\hat{p}_1 - \hat{p}_2}$$

$$\left(\hat{p}_1 - \hat{p}_2\right) \pm z_c \sqrt{\frac{\hat{p}_1\left(1 - \hat{p}_1\right)}{n_1} + \frac{\hat{p}_2\left(1 - \hat{p}_2\right)}{n_2}}$$

EXAMPLE:

A large company produces two models of portable CD players, a high-end model and a less expensive low-end model. A CD player is considered defective if it requires repair within a 24-month warranty period. In a random sample of 165 low-end models, 77 were considered defective. In a random sample of 120 high-end models, 13 were considered defective. Determine a 95% confidence interval for the difference between the percentage of defective low-end players and the percentage of defective high-end players.

In problems dealing with several sets of values, it is important to list them before trying to make the substitutions into the appropriate formula. For the free-response questions, you should show the formulas and then carefully make the substitutions showing all your work.

low-end	high-end
$n_1 = 165$	$n_2 = 120$
$x_1 = 77$	$x_2 = 13$

Determine the respective proportions:

$$p_1 = \frac{x_1}{n_1} = \frac{77}{165} = 0.467 \qquad p_2 = \frac{x_2}{n_2} = \frac{13}{120} = 0.108$$

Determine the margin of error:

$$E = z_c \sqrt{\frac{\hat{p}_1\left(1 - \hat{p}_1\right)}{n_1} + \frac{\hat{p}_2\left(1 - \hat{p}_2\right)}{n_2}} = (1.96)\sqrt{\frac{(0.467)(0.533)}{165} + \frac{(0.108)(0.892)}{120}} = 0.094$$

Determine the confidence interval:

$$\left(\hat{p}_1 - \hat{p}_2\right) - E < p_1 - p_2 < \left(\hat{p}_1 - \hat{p}_2\right) + E$$
$$(0.467 - 0.108) - 0.094 < p_1 - p_2 < (0.467 - 0.108) + 0.094$$
$$0.256 < p_1 - p_2 < 0.453$$

The company is 95% sure that the difference between the percentage of defective low-end players and the percentage of defective high-end players is between 26.5% and 45.3%. This is a large interval with a margin of error of greater than 9%. Increasing the size of the samples considerably would reduce the margin of error.

[TI-83/4: Select STAT TESTS 2-PropZInt x1:77 n1:165 x2:13 n2:120 C-Level: 0.95 Calculate Display (0.264, 0.453)]

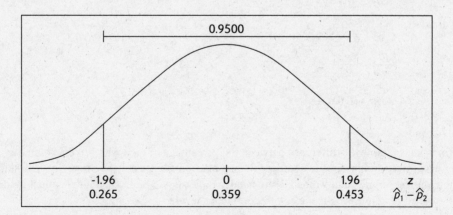

EXAMPLE:
An ice cream store owner is interested in knowing the difference between the percentage of men who like strawberry ice cream and the percentage of women who like strawberry ice cream. In a random sample of 250 men, 48% said they like strawberry ice cream. In a random sample of 300 women, 31% said they like strawberry ice cream. Using a 90% confidence interval, determine the difference between the percentage of men who like strawberry ice cream and the percentage of women who like strawberry ice cream.

Given:

Men	Women
$n_1 = 250$	$n_2 = 300$
$p_1 = 0.48$	$p_2 = 0.31$

Determine the margin of error:

$$E = z_c \sqrt{\frac{\hat{p}_1\left(1 - \hat{p}_1\right)}{n_1} + \frac{\hat{p}_2\left(1 - \hat{p}_2\right)}{n_2}} = (1.645) \sqrt{\frac{(0.48)(0.52)}{250} + \frac{(0.31)(0.69)}{300}} = 0.068$$

Determine the confidence interval:

$$\left(\hat{p}_1 - \hat{p}_2\right) - E < p_1 - p_2 < \left(\hat{p}_1 - \hat{p}_2\right) + E$$
$$(0.48 - 0.31) - 0.068 < p_1 - p_2 < (0.48 - 0.31) + 0.068$$
$$0.102 < p_1 - p_2 < 0.238$$

The ice cream store owner can be 90% sure that the difference between the percentage of men who like strawberry ice cream and the percentage of women who like strawberry ice cream is between 10.2% and 23.8%. The margin of error is almost 7%. Increasing the size of the samples would reduce the margin of error.

[TI-83/4: Select STAT TESTS 2-PropZInt x1:120 n1:250 x2:93 n2:300 C-Level: 0.90 Calculate Display (0.102, 0.238)]

To determine the sample sizes necessary to reduce the margin of error to any given level, solve the equation for the margin of error for n with the following modifications:

Let both sample sizes equal the same value.

Use a worst-case relationship where both $\hat{p}$ and $(1-\hat{p})$ equal 0.5.

$$E = z_c \sqrt{\frac{\hat{p}_1\left(1 - \hat{p}_1\right)}{n_1} + \frac{\hat{p}_2\left(1 - \hat{p}_2\right)}{n_2}} = z_c \sqrt{\frac{(0.5)(0.5)}{n} + \frac{(0.5)(0.5)}{n}}$$
$$E = z_c \sqrt{\frac{0.5}{n}}$$
$$\frac{E}{z_c} = \sqrt{\frac{0.5}{n}}$$
$$\left(\frac{E}{z_c}\right)^2 = \frac{0.5}{n}$$
$$n = (0.5)\left(\frac{z_c}{E}\right)^2$$

EXAMPLE:

An advertising firm wants to know the difference between the percentage of men who drive foreign cars and the percentage of women who drive foreign cars. The study will take place in a large metropolitan city. The statistician wants to question the same number of men and women. How many people should be in each independent random sample to maintain a margin of error of at most 3% using a 95% confidence level?

Substitute 3% for the margin of error and 1.96 for the z-score and solve for n:

$$n = (0.5)\left(\frac{z_c}{E}\right)^2 = (0.5)\left(\frac{1.96}{0.03}\right)^2 = 2134.2$$

Each sample should contain at least 2135 people.

Large Sample Confidence Interval for a Difference between Two Means

The point estimate for the difference of two means, $\mu_1 - \mu_2$, is $\overline{x}_1 - \overline{x}_2$.

The variance of the difference of two means in the sampling distribution for $\overline{x}_1 - \overline{x}_2$ is the sum of the variances.

The standard deviation of the differences is the square root of the sum of the variances.

The exercises in this section use the sample standard deviation as a suitable substitute for the population standard deviation.

$$\sigma_{\overline{x}_1 - \overline{x}_2} = \sqrt{\frac{\sigma_1^2}{n_1} + \frac{\sigma_2^2}{n_2}} \approx \sqrt{\frac{s_1^2}{n_1} + \frac{s_2^2}{n_2}}$$

The margin of error is $E = z_c \, \sigma_{\overline{x}_1 - \overline{x}_2} = z_c \sqrt{\frac{s_1^2}{n_1} + \frac{s_2^2}{n_2}}$.

The c-confidence interval for the difference of population proportions is

$$\left(\overline{x}_1 - \overline{x}_2\right) - E < \mu_1 - \mu_2 < \left(\overline{x}_1 - \overline{x}_2\right) + E$$
$$\left(\overline{x}_1 - \overline{x}_2\right) \pm E$$
$$\left(\overline{x}_1 - \overline{x}_2\right) \pm z_c \, \sigma_{\overline{x}_1 - \overline{x}_2}$$
$$\left(\overline{x}_1 - \overline{x}_2\right) \pm z_c \sqrt{\frac{s_1^2}{n_1} + \frac{s_2^2}{n_2}}$$

EXAMPLE:

A city traffic engineer is studying traffic flow through two intersections. At the first intersection, in a 50-hour study, an average of 634 cars per hour crossed the intersection with a standard deviation of 94 cars per hour. At the second intersection, in a 45-hour study, an average of 540 cars per hour crossed the intersection with a standard deviation of 68 cars per hour. Using a 90% level of confidence, find a confidence interval for the difference in the hourly averages at these two intersections.

In problems dealing with several sets of values, it is important to list them before trying to make the substitutions into the appropriate formula. For the free-response questions, you should show the formulas and then carefully make the substitutions showing all your work.

1st Intersection	2nd Intersection
$n_1 = 50$	$n_2 = 45$
$\overline{x}_1 = 634$	$\overline{x}_2 = 540$
$s_1 = 94$	$s_2 = 68$

First, determine the margin of error:

$$E = z_c \sqrt{\frac{s_1^2}{n_1} + \frac{s_2^2}{n_2}} = (1.645)\sqrt{\frac{94^2}{50} + \frac{68^2}{45}} = 27.5$$

Next, determine the confidence interval:

$$\left(\overline{x}_1 - \overline{x}_2\right) - E < \mu_1 - \mu_2 < \left(\overline{x}_1 - \overline{x}_2\right) + E$$
$$(634 - 540) - 27.5 < \mu_1 - \mu_2 < (634 - 540) + 27.5$$
$$66.5 < \mu_1 - \mu_2 < 121.5$$

The traffic engineer can be 90% sure that the difference in traffic flow at the two intersections is between 66 and 122 cars per hour.

[TI-83/4: Select STAT TESTS 2-SampZInt Inpt:Stats σ_1:94 σ_2:68 $\overline{x1}$:634 n1:50 $\overline{x2}$:540 n2:45 C-Level:0.90 Calculate Display (66.5, 121.5)]

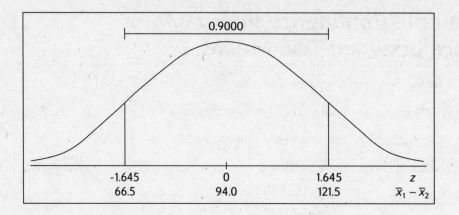

EXAMPLE:

How much cheaper is it to buy a digital camera online than it is to buy it in a local camera store? A digital camera model was priced at a random selection of 32 traditional camera stores, where the average price of the camera was $232.35 with a standard deviation of $33.40. The same camera model was priced at a random selection of 44 online retailers, where the average price of the camera model was $189.78 with a standard deviation of $21.15. Find a 95% confidence interval for the difference in price between the traditional camera stores and the online retailers.

Traditional	Online
$n_1 = 32$	$n_2 = 44$
$\bar{x}_1 = \$232.35$	$\bar{x}_2 = \$189.78$
$s_1 = \$33.40$	$s_2 = \$21.15$

First, determine the margin of error:

$$E = z_c \sqrt{\frac{s_1^2}{n_1} + \frac{s_2^2}{n_2}} = (1.96)\sqrt{\frac{33.40^2}{32} + \frac{21.15^2}{44}} = \$13.15$$

Next, determine the confidence interval:

$$\left(\bar{x}_1 - \bar{x}_2\right) - E < \mu_1 - \mu_2 < \left(\bar{x}_1 - \bar{x}_2\right) + E$$
$$(\$232.35 - \$189.78) - \$13.15 < \mu_1 - \mu_2 < (\$232.35 - \$189.78) + \$13.15$$
$$\$29.95 < \mu_1 - \mu_2 < \$55.72$$

You can be 95% sure that the difference in camera price between the traditional camera store and the online retailers is between $29.42 and $55.72.

[TI-83/4: Select STAT TESTS 2-SampZInt Inpt:Stats σ_1:33.40 σ_2:21.15 x1:232.35 n1:32 x2:189.78 n2:44 C-Level:0.95 Calculate Display (29.418, 55.722)]

After determining a confidence interval, you may find that the margin of error is too large for your purpose. Consider the last example. The margin of error for the 95% confidence interval is greater than $13.00. How can the margin of error be reduced? Consider the possibilities. One way to reduce the margin of error is to consider a lower confidence level. Reducing the confidence level from 95% ($z = 1.96$) to 90% ($z = 1.645$) reduces the margin of error from $13.15 to $11.04. The reduction in the confidence level is usually not desirable. You have no control over the standard deviations obtained in the sample. You do have control over the sample sizes. Increasing the sample sizes would reduce the standard deviations of the sampling distribution and, thus, decrease the margin of error.

Solving the margin of error equation for n gives a formula to determine the sample size necessary to obtain any specific margin of error. (*Note:* The use of this formula requires values of s. These values come from preliminary samples, but may also be available from past experience. There is no worst-case maximum value as there was with proportions.)

$$E = z_c \sqrt{\frac{s_1^2}{n_1} + \frac{s_2^2}{n_2}}$$

Let $n_1 = n_2 = n$ and solve for n:

$$n = \left(s_1^2 + s_2^2\right)\left(\frac{z_c}{E}\right)^2$$

In this formula, s_1 and s_2 are the standard deviations obtained from preliminary samples; z_c is the z-score for our particular level of confidence, and E is the required margin of error.

EXAMPLE:

A company is comparing production rates between an old machine and a new one. The old machine operates with a standard deviation of 34.3 parts per hour. The new machine operates with a standard deviation of 21.6 parts per hour. Using a 95% confidence level, how large should the samples from each machine be to determine the difference in production rates accurate to plus or minus 5 parts per hour?

Using a critical z-score of 1.96 and a margin of error of 5, solve for n, the sample size for each machine.

$$n = \left(s_1^2 + s_2^2\right)\left(\frac{z_c}{E}\right)^2 = \left(34.3^2 + 21.6^2\right)\left(\frac{1.96}{5}\right)^2 = 252.5$$

Approximately 253 samples should be taken for each machine. [TI-83/4–This answer may be verified using an arbitrary value for the sample average rate. Use the same value for each machine, for example, 200. Select STAT TESTS 2-SampZInt Inpt: Stats σ_1:34.3 σ_2:21.6 x1:200 n1:253 x2:200 n2:253 C-Level:0.95 Calculate Display (–4.995, 4.997)]

Review Questions and Answers

Multiple Choice Questions

Directions: Solve each of the following problems. Decide which is the best of the choices given.

1. It has been calculated that a 99% confidence interval for the difference between two population means is (12.4, 19.3). Which of the following are true?

  I.   The probability that the real difference is between 12.4 and 19.3 is 0.99.
  II. There is a 1% chance that the real difference is less that 12.4 and a 1% chance that the real difference is greater than 19.3.
  III. We are 99% confident that the real difference in population means is between 12.4 and 19.3.

  A. I only
  B. III only
  C. I and II
  D. I and III
  E. I, II, and III

2. If a 95% confidence interval for the circumference of trees in a forest ranges from 7.4 feet to 9.1 feet, which of the following statements is true?

  A. There is a 95% chance that the real population mean is between 7.4 feet and 9.1 feet.
  B. You can be 95% confident that all trees in the forest have circumferences between 7.4 feet and 9.1 feet.
  C. If numerous samples of a certain size are drawn from the population and a confidence interval was constructed from each sample, 95% of the confidence intervals would contain the true population mean.
  D. From all trees in the forest, 95% have circumferences between 7.4 feet and 9.1 feet.
  E. None of the above is a true statement.

3. Which of the following statements about sample size are true?

  I.   If you halve the sample size, you double the margin of error.
  II. Increasing the sample size will increase the level of confidence.
  III. When finding confidence intervals for differences in population means, equal-sized samples provide better results than samples of a different size.

  A. I only
  B. II only
  C. III only
  D. Two of the above are true statements.
  E. None of the above is a true statement.

4. Using a random sample of 125 adults, it was discovered that their reflex time for a specific task was 0.94 seconds with a standard deviation of 0.08 seconds. Let the sample standard deviation be a suitable approximation for the population standard deviation. Construct a 95% confidence interval for the population mean reflex time.

  A. (0.922, 0.958)
  B. (0.926, 0.954)
  C. (0.928, 0.952)
  D. (0.930, 0.950)
  E. (0.935, 0.945)

5. Using a random sample of 125 adults, it was discovered that their reflex time for a specific task was 0.94 seconds with a standard deviation of 0.08 seconds. Let the sample standard deviation be a suitable approximation for the population standard deviation. Using a 99% confidence level, how many more adults must be studied to result in a margin of error of 0.01 seconds?

  A. 121
  B. 246
  C. 300
  D. 425
  E. No more are needed. The preliminary sample provides a sufficient number.

For problems 6–7: The following data was collected from 30 college students as to the number of miles they drive, one way, to college.

7	9	6	18	24	9	17	16	32	24
17	34	18	18	45	24	29	30	16	19
6	26	9	17	30	17	2	19	24	4

(Use the standard deviation of this data as a suitable substitute for σ.)

6. What would be the margin of error for a 95% confidence interval?

  A. 3.00
  B. 3.44
  C. 3.57
  D. 3.72
  E. 4.70

7. How many more students need to be surveyed to bring the margin of error down to 2?

    A. 30

    B. 46

    C. 66

    D. 96

    E. 124

8. In a survey of 80 elementary school-age children, 42 said they bring their lunch to school. Construct a 99% confidence interval for the percentage of elementary school age children who bring their lunch to school.

    A. (0.350, 0.700)

    B. (0.361, 0.689)

    C. (0.381, 0.669)

    D. (0.416, 0.634)

    E. (0.433, 0.617)

9. A survey of 320 newspaper readers revealed that 63% of them drink milk on a regular basis. What confidence level was used if the margin of error was 3%?

    A. 71.4%

    B. 73.3%

    C. 87.0%

    D. 88.6%

    E. 94.2%

10. In a clinical study of 375 patients who took a drug to lower their cholesterol level, 12 complained of leg cramps. If the drug is administered to 85,000 patients, determine a 95% confidence interval for the number of patients who will experience leg cramps while taking the medication.

    A. 2720 ± 1271

    B. 2720 ± 1513

    C. 2720 ± 1724

    D. 2720 ± 1990

    E. 2720 ± 2044

11. How large does a sample need to be to estimate a population proportion within 1.5% if you are using a 90% level of confidence?

    A. 1504

    B. 2134

    C. 3007

    D. 4268

    E. 6013

12. In a random sample of 80 college math textbooks, the average number of pages was 762 with a standard deviation of 122. With what level of confidence could you state that the average number of pages is between 732 and 792?

    A. 95.4%

    B. 96.8%

    C. 97.2%

    D. 98.4%

    E. 98.6%

13. In a random sample of 160 teenage girls, 45% said they like broccoli. In a random sample of 220 teenage boys, 28% said they like broccoli. Construct a 95% confidence interval for the difference between the percentages of teenage girls and boys who like broccoli.

    A. 17% ± 7.9%

    B. 17% ± 9.7%

    C. 36.5% ± 7.9%

    D. 36.5% ± 9.7%

    E. 36.5% ± 8.8%

14. An auto manufacturer installs one of two different engines in its SUV. A random sample of 64 SUVs with the 6-cylinder engine were tested and had an average fuel consumption of 21.4 miles per gallon with a standard deviation of 4.1 miles per gallon. A random sample of 54 SUVs with an 8-cylinder engine were tested and had an average fuel consumption of 19.4 miles per gallon with a standard deviation of 3.9 miles per gallon. Construct a 99% confidence interval for the difference in fuel consumption between the two types of engines.

    A. (0.1, 3.9)

    B. (0.6, 3.4)

    C. (0.8, 3.2)

    D. (1.1, 2.9)

    E. (1.3, 2.7)

15. Two manufacturers sell boxes of cereal with a net weight listed as 28 ounces. A testing company wants to determine the difference in average weight in the two brands of cereal. The same number of boxes of each brand of cereal will be tested. A preliminary study has shown that the standard deviation in weight for each brand is 0.28 ounces. How many boxes of each cereal must be included in the study to be 95% sure of being within 0.1 ounces of the actual difference in average weight?

    A. 43

    B. 61

    C. 64

    D. 74

    E. 105

16. How large a sample would you need if you want the calculation of the population proportion to be within 2% of the correct percentage using a 90% level of confidence? What if you used a preliminary estimate of the population proportion of 19%?

    A. 1068, 657

    B. 1264, 812

    C. 1692, 1042

    D. 2416, 1478

    E. 4147, 2554

Multiple Choice Answers

  1. B. There is a 99% chance your interval will contain the difference. You do not say there is a 99% chance the difference is in the interval.

  2. C. You do not assign a probability or chance that a population parameter is in the confidence interval. You say the confidence interval has a chance of containing the population parameter.

3. E. For single samples means, the margin of error is inversely proportional to the square root of the sample size. A similar relationship exists for sample proportions and differences of means and proportions. Changing the sample size has no effect on the confidence level. Confidence is set by the statistician. When finding confidence intervals for differences, the fact that the sample sizes are the same or different does not impact the interval's accuracy. The actual size of the samples does. The formulas may be simplified if the sample sizes are the same but that does not improve accuracy.

4. B. Calculate the margin of error: $E = z_c \dfrac{s}{\sqrt{n}} = (1.96)\dfrac{0.08}{\sqrt{125}} = 0.014$.

Calculate the confidence interval: $\bar{x} \pm E = 0.940 \pm 0.014 = (0.926, 0.954)$.

5. C. First calculate the sample size necessary to provide the required accuracy:

$$n = \left(\frac{z_c s}{E}\right)^2 = \left(\frac{(2.576)(0.08)}{0.01}\right) = 425$$

This is the sample size necessary. You already have 125 samples. Therefore, subtract 125 from 425 to get 300.

6. C. Enter the 30 numbers into a list in the calculator and determine the sample mean and the sample standard deviation: $\bar{x} = 18.867$ and $s = 9.989$.

Calculate the margin of error:

$$E = z_c \frac{s}{\sqrt{n}} = (1.96)\frac{9.989}{\sqrt{30}} = 3.575$$

7. C. Calculate the sample size necessary to provide the required accuracy.

$$n = \left(\frac{z_c s}{E}\right)^2 = \left(\frac{(1.96)(8.989)}{2}\right) = 95.8.$$ Round up to 96. Subtract the 30 from the original sample, leaving an additional 66 required to reduce the margin of error to 2.

8. C. Calculate the margin of error:

$$E = z_c \sqrt{\frac{\hat{p}\left(1 - \hat{p}\right)}{n}} = (2.576)\sqrt{\frac{(0.525)(0.475)}{80}} = 0.144$$

The required confidence interval is $\hat{p} \pm E = 0.525 \pm 0.144 = (0.381, 0.669)$.

9. B. Start with the formula for the margin of error:

$$E = z_c \sqrt{\frac{\hat{p}\left(1 - \hat{p}\right)}{n}}$$

$$0.03 = z_c \sqrt{\frac{(0.63)(0.37)}{320}}$$

$$0.03 = z_c(0.027)$$

$$\frac{0.03}{0.027} = z_c$$

$$z_c = 1.11$$

Look up the z-score in the table of standard normal probabilities. The value 0.8665 represents the area to the left of this z-score. Subtract from 1 to obtain the probability in the right tail, 0.1335. Double that value to get 0.2670. Subtract from 1 to get the confidence interval's probability of 0.7330 or 73.3%.

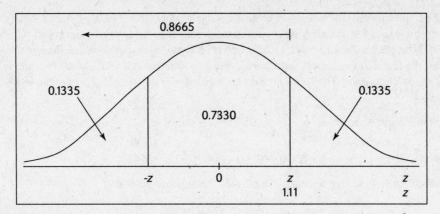

10. B. Calculate the point estimate: $\hat{p} = \dfrac{x}{n} = \dfrac{12}{375} = 0.032$.

Calculate the margin of error:

$$E = z_c \sqrt{\frac{\hat{p}\left(1 - \hat{p}\right)}{n}} = (1.96)\sqrt{\frac{(0.032)(0.968)}{375}} = 0.178$$

Multiply the values of $\hat{p}$ and E by 85,000.

$$(0.032)(85000) = 2720$$
$$(0.0178)(85000) = 1513$$

The required confidence interval is 2720 ± 1513.

11. C. Since a preliminary estimate is not known, use the worst-case value for the product of $\left(\hat{p}\right)\left(1 - \hat{p}\right) = 0.25$.

Calculate the required sample size:

$$n = \hat{p}\left(1 - \hat{p}\right)\left(\frac{z_c}{E}\right)^2 = (0.25)\left(\frac{1.645}{0.015}\right)^2 = 3007$$

12. C. The length of the confidence interval is $792 - 732 = 60$. The length of the interval (60) is equal to $2E$. Therefore, $E = 30$. Use the formula for the margin of error and solve for the z-score.

$$E = z_c \frac{s}{\sqrt{n}}$$

$$30 = z_c \frac{122}{\sqrt{80}}$$

$$z_c = 2.20$$

Look up the z-score 2.20 in the table of standard normal probabilities. This value of 0.9861 represents the data to the left of the z-score. Subtract from 1. This gives 0.0139, which is the probability in the right tail of the distribution. There is an equal amount in the left tail of the distribution. This leaves a confidence interval of 0.9722, or 97.2%.

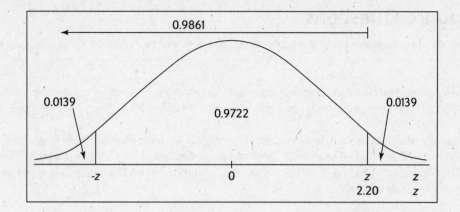

13. B. Calculate the margin of error using the values of $\hat{p}$ and sample size from both samples:

$$E = z_c \sqrt{\frac{\hat{p}_1\left(1 - \hat{p}_1\right)}{n_1} + \frac{\hat{p}_2\left(1 - \hat{p}_2\right)}{n_2}}$$

$$= 1.96 \sqrt{\frac{(0.45)(0.55)}{160} + \frac{(0.28)(0.72)}{220}} = 0.097$$

Calculate the confidence interval. The center of the confidence interval is the difference in the sample proportions: $0.45 - 0.28 = 0.17$. The confidence interval is the center, plus and minus the margin of error: $17\% \pm 9.7\%$.

14. A. Calculate the margin of error using the values of the standard deviation and sample size from both samples:

$$E = z_c \sqrt{\frac{s_1^2}{n_1} + \frac{s_2^2}{n_2}} = 2.576 \sqrt{\frac{4.1^2}{64} + \frac{3.9^2}{54}} = 1.9$$

Calculate the confidence interval:

$$\left(\overline{x}_1 - \overline{x}_2\right) - E < \mu_1 - \mu_2 < \left(\overline{x}_1 - \overline{x}_2\right) + E$$
$$(21.4 - 19.4) - 1.9 < \mu_1 - \mu_2 < (21.4 - 19.4) + 1.9$$
$$0.1 < \mu_1 - \mu_2 < 3.9$$

This result may be written in interval notation: $(0.1, 3.9)$.

15. B. Using the fact that the sample sizes are the same, solve the formula for the margin of error for the sample size:

$$n = \left(s_1^2 + s_2^2\right)\left(\frac{z_c}{E}\right)^2 = \left(0.28^2 + 0.28^2\right)\left(\frac{1.96}{0.1}\right)^2 = 60.2$$

Round the value for the sample size up to the next whole number, 61.

16. C. Since a preliminary estimate is not known, use the worst-case value for the product of $\left(\hat{p}\right)\left(1 - \hat{p}\right) = 0.25$.

Calculate the required sample size:

$$n - \hat{p}\left(1 - \hat{p}\right)\left(\frac{z_c}{E}\right)^2 = (0.25)\left(\frac{1.645}{0.02}\right)^2 = 1691.3$$

This rounds up to 1692.

The sample size may be reduced with data from a preliminary study. If an estimate of 19% is used, the sample size changes.

$$n = \hat{p}\left(1 - \hat{p}\right)\left(\frac{z_c}{E}\right)^2 = (0.19)(0.81)\left(\frac{1.645}{0.02}\right)^2 = 1041.1$$

This rounds up to 1042.

Free-Response Questions

Directions: Show all work. Indicate clearly the methods you use. You will be graded on method as well as accuracy.

1. A newspaper reported that based on a random sample of 500 reporters, 34% of all reporters had advanced college degrees. No other details about the study were provided. How would you interpret this information?

2. A travel company conducted a study to determine the average hotel room rate in a large resort area. A random selection was made of 38 hotels. The average room rate for a standard room with two double beds was $173.40, with a standard deviation of $31.65. Construct 90%, 95%, and 99% confidence intervals and compare to the state's average room rate of $162.

3. A study was conducted to see what percent of 15-year-old boys and girls like to read mysteries. The table that follows summarizes the results.

Do You Like to Read Mysteries?		
	YES	**NO**
Girls	25	154
Boys	25	247

Calculate point estimates separately for the girls and the boys in the study. Compare. Construct a 95% confidence interval for the difference in percentage between girls and boys. Comment on the results.

4. A professor at a large state college has been teaching statistics for many years. She tells her classes that she thinks females generally score higher on statistics tests than do males. This caused such a debate among the faculty that they decided to conduct a study. Thirty-five female and 32 male students are randomly selected from the several hundred students who take statistics classes each year. A common test is administered to these students. The following chart summarizes the results of the study.

	$\bar{x}$	s	n
Females	71.2	3.9	35
Males	68.9	3.5	32

Construct individual 95% confidence intervals for the females and for the males. Comment on the confidence intervals. Construct a 95% confidence interval for the difference in the averages between the females and the males. Comment on how this compares to the individual confidence intervals.

Free-Response Answers

1. If this was a well-designed and well-conducted study, some assumptions may be made.

   If the study used a 95% confidence level, which is typical, you can calculate the margin of error:

   $$E = z_c \sqrt{\frac{\hat{p}\left(1 - \hat{p}\right)}{n}} = 1.96 \sqrt{\frac{(0.34)(0.66)}{500}} = 0.042.$$ With a 95% confidence level, the margin of error is 4.2%. Therefore, you can interpret the results as follows: "We are 95% confident that the percentage of reporters who hold advanced college degrees is between 29.8% and 38.2%."

   If the study used a 3% margin of error, which is typical, you can calculate the confidence level.

$$E = z_c \sqrt{\frac{\hat{p}\left(1 - \hat{p}\right)}{n}}$$

$$0.03 = z_c \sqrt{\frac{(0.34)(0.66)}{500}}$$

$$0.03 = z_c(0.0212)$$

$$z_c = 1.415$$

Looking up this value in the table of standard normal probabilities, gives a probability of 0.9214 to the left of z. Subtract from 1, giving 0.0786. This is the area in the right tail of the curve. Double it to get the area in both tails of 0.1572. Subtract from 1 to get the confidence level of approximately 84%. Therefore, you can interpret the results as follows: "We are 84% confident that the percentage of reporters who hold advanced college degrees is between 31% and 37%."

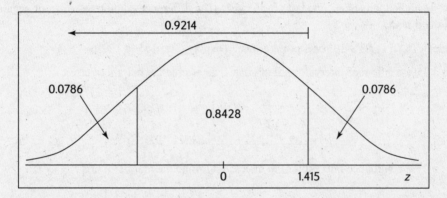

2. A 90%, 95%, and 99% confidence interval may be constructed from the data. Determine the margin of error and confidence interval for each level of confidence.

$$E_{90} = z_c \frac{s}{\sqrt{n}} = 1.645 \left(\frac{31.65}{\sqrt{38}}\right) = 8.45$$

$$\$173.40 \pm \$8.45 = (\$164.95, \$181.85)$$

$$E_{95} = z_c \frac{s}{\sqrt{n}} = 1.96 \left(\frac{31.65}{\sqrt{38}}\right) = 10.06$$

$$\$173.40 \pm \$10.06 = (\$163.34, \$183.46)$$

$$E_{99} = z_c \frac{s}{\sqrt{n}} = 2.576 \left(\frac{31.65}{\sqrt{38}}\right) = 13.23$$

$$\$173.40 \pm \$13.23 = (\$160.17, \$186.63)$$

As the confidence level increases from 90% to 95% to 99%, the confidence interval increases in size. If you use either the 90% or the 95% confidence level, you are confident that the room rates in this resort area are higher than the state average of $162. But, if you use a 99% confidence interval, then the state's average of $162 is included in the interval, so you cannot say that the average rate in this resort area is higher than the state average. [TI-83/4: Select STAT TESTS ZInterval Enter Data C-Level: 99 Display (160.16, 186.63)]

3. The point estimate for the percentage of girls who like to read mysteries is $\hat{p}_g = \frac{x}{n} = \frac{25}{179} = 0.140$ and the percentage of boys who like to read mysteries is $\hat{p}_b = \frac{x}{n} = \frac{25}{272} = 0.092$. From the individual percentages determined here, it appears that the percentage of girls who like to read mysteries is about 4% higher than that of boys. If you think about the fact that 14 is about 50% larger than 9, you might conclude that 50% more girls than boys like to read mysteries. This could be very misleading. Consider a 95% confidence interval for the difference in percentages between the girls and the boys. Calculate the margin of error:

$$E = z_c \sqrt{\frac{\hat{p}_g\left(1 - \hat{p}_g\right)}{n_g} + \frac{\hat{p}_b\left(1 - \hat{p}_b\right)}{n_b}}$$

$$= 1.96 \sqrt{\frac{(0.140)(0.860)}{179} + \frac{(0.092)(0.908)}{272}} = 0.061$$

Construct the confidence interval:

$$\left(\hat{p}_g - \hat{p}_b\right) - E < p_g - p_b \leq \left(\hat{p}_g - \hat{p}_b\right) + E$$

$$(0.140 - 0.092) - 0.061 \leq p_g - p_b \leq (0.140 - 0.092) + 0.061$$

$$-0.013 \leq p_g - p_b \leq 0.109$$

The confidence interval contains the value of ZERO. This means that, at a 95% level of confidence, you cannot tell who has the higher percentage, the boys or the girls. The difference could be positive or negative. They are in a **statistical dead heat.**

[TI-83/4: Select STAT TESTS 2-PropZInt Enter Data Display (−0.0135, 0.109)]

4. To construct a 95% confidence interval for the females, determine the margin of error.

$$E_F = z_c \frac{s}{\sqrt{n}} = 1.96\left(\frac{3.9}{\sqrt{35}}\right) = 1.292$$

$$71.2 \pm 1.292 = (69.908, 72.492)$$

To construct a 95% confidence interval for the males, determine the margin of error.

$$E_M = z_c \frac{s}{\sqrt{n}} = 1.96\left(\frac{3.5}{\sqrt{32}}\right) = 1.213$$

$$68.9 \pm 1.213 = (67.687, 70.113)$$

The individual confidence intervals overlap. From this observation you could conclude that although the female average was more than 2 points higher than the average of the males, since the confidence intervals overlap, it is possible that the male average is higher.

Now construct a confidence interval for the difference in the means.

Calculate the margin of error:

$$E = z_c \sqrt{\frac{s_F^2}{n_F} + \frac{s_M^2}{n_M}} = 1.96 \sqrt{\frac{3.9^2}{35} + \frac{3.5^2}{32}} = 1.772$$

$$(71.2 - 68.9) \pm 1.772 = (0.528, 4.072)$$

The confidence interval for the difference does not contain zero. So, even though the individual confidence intervals overlapped, providing no useful information, the confidence interval for the differences did show that, "at a 95% level of confidence, the average score for females on the exam is higher than that of males."

[TI-83/4: Select STAT TESTS 2-SampZInt Inpt:Stats Enter Data Display (0.528, 4.072)]

Statistical Inference: Tests of Significance

Statistical inference involves answering questions about a population based on information obtained from a sample taken from the population. There are two main types of inference. The first is estimation, in which you make estimates of population parameters by establishing confidence intervals based on a sample from the population. The second is decision making concerning the value of a population parameter. Making decisions about the value of a population parameter involves **hypothesis testing**, a procedure in which samples are used to determine the likelihood that a claim about a population parameter is true.

When do the data from a sample cast doubt on the validity of a claim? If a manufacturer claims that the average net weight of its boxes of cereal is 33 ounces, when would you doubt the claim? If a random sample of 40 boxes of cereal had an average net weight of 32.5 ounces, would this indicate the claim was too high? Probably not, since that difference could be caused by the randomness of the sample. What if the sample average was 32 ounces? 31 ounces? 30 ounces? At what point would the difference between the claimed average and the sample average be great enough for you the think that it could be caused by something other than the randomness of the sample? Hypothesis testing helps answer these questions.

There is a link between creating a confidence interval and testing a hypothesis. If a confidence interval actually contains the claimed value, then you have no reason to believe that the claim is wrong, since the variability of the sample could result in any value in the confidence interval. If, on the other hand, the entire confidence interval is on one side of the claimed value and does not contain the claimed value, then you would have reason to doubt the claim. Any result that is unlikely to have occurred by chance is called **statistically significant.** Hypothesis testing, like the creation of confidence intervals, attempts to determine the likelihood that a claimed population parameter is true.

EXAMPLE:
Suppose a manufacturer claims that the average life of a certain type of lightbulb is 900 hours. A random sample of 100 of these bulbs has a mean life of 875 hours with a standard deviation of 75 hours. Does this sample data cast doubt on the manufacturer's claim?

Assume that the manufacturer's claim is correct. How likely would it be to obtain this kind of sample? Using the Central Limit Theorem, a sampling distribution with its mean of 900 and a standard deviation of $\dfrac{75}{\sqrt{100}} = 7.5$ would be approximately normal. A sample from this distribution with a mean of 875 would be more than 3 standard deviations to the left of the mean. The likelihood of this happening is less than 0.0004. So, either you happened to obtain a highly unlikely sample, or the claim of the manufacturer is not true.

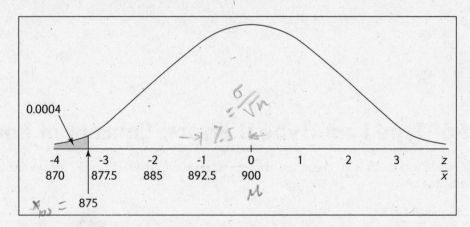

Logic of Significance Testing, Null and Alternative Hypotheses

A claim is a hypothesis. Testing a hypothesis requires creating two hypotheses; one that represents the claim and the other that represents the complement of the claim. Since each hypothesis is the complement of the other, one must be true, and the other must be false. The hypothesis that contains a statement of equality is the **null hypothesis.** The complementary hypothesis, is the **alternate hypothesis,** which contains a statement of inequality. Depending on how the claim is phrased, either hypothesis may be the claim.

Two Types of Hypotheses

The null hypothesis, referred to as H_0, is a statistical hypothesis that contains a statement of equality: $=$, $\leq$, or $\geq$.

The alternate hypothesis, referred to as H_a, is the complement of the null hypothesis and contains a statement of inequality: $\neq$, $>$, or $<$.

Claims usually involve population means or population proportions, but variances and standard deviations may also be tested. For tests involving one sample, the population mean or population proportion is compared to a constant value, such as k. Common one-sample tests include

$H_0{:}\mu = k$	$H_0{:}\mu \leq k$	$H_0{:}\mu \geq k$	$H_0{:}p = k$	$H_0{:}p \leq k$	$H_0{:}p \geq k$
$H_a{:}\mu \neq k$	$H_a{:}\mu > k$	$H_a{:}\mu < k$	$H_a{:}p \neq k$	$H_a{:}p > k$	$H_a{:}p < k$

For tests involving two samples, the population means or population proportions are compared to each other. Common two-sample tests include

$H_0{:}\mu_1 = \mu_2$	$H_0{:}\mu_1 \leq \mu_2$	$H_0{:}\mu_1 \geq \mu_2$	$H_0{:}p_1 = p_2$	$H_0{:}p_1 \leq p_2$	$H_0{:}p_1 \geq p_2$
$H_a{:}\mu_1 \neq \mu_2$	$H_a{:}\mu_1 > \mu_2$	$H_a{:}\mu_1 < \mu_2$	$H_a{:}p_1 \neq p_2$	$H_a{:}p_1 > p_2$	$H_a{:}p_1 < p_2$

EXAMPLE:
Write null and alternate hypotheses using these verbal statements:

   A.   The average weight is greater than 45 pounds.
   B.   The average height is at least 16 inches.
   C.   Eighteen percent of the switches are defective.

A. $H_0{:}\mu \leq 45$
  $H_a{:}\mu > 45$ Claim

B. $H_0{:}\mu \geq 16$ Claim
  $H_a{:}\mu < 16$

C. $H_0{:}p = 0.18$ Claim
  $H_a{:}p \neq 0.18$

Concept of Type I and Type II Errors; Concept of Power

It does not matter which hypothesis is the claim; you always test the null hypothesis. The test always involves one of two possible results. You either

A. reject the null hypothesis, or

B. fail to reject the null hypothesis.

Notice that the complement of "reject" is "fail to reject." You do not "accept" the null hypothesis. This is similar to the results of a criminal trial. A defendant is either "guilty" or "not guilty." He is not "innocent."

A sample does not provide a complete and accurate picture of a population. Only a complete census of a population produces complete information. If the sample happens to be the "perfect sample," providing a mirror image of the population parameters, then you could be sure that decisions based on the sample were right. However, samples are not perfect. Whenever you base decisions on samples, errors can and will occur.

Consider the experiment of tossing a coin with the claim that it is a fair coin. If the coin is fair, one with equal probabilities for heads and tails, tossing it 50 times should result in approximately 25 heads and 25 tails. If you toss the coin 50 times and end up with 22 heads and 28 tails, would you be surprised? Would you still think that this was a fair coin? Getting heads 22 times out of 50 seems reasonable, even with a fair coin. The fact that heads occurred a little less than half of the time could be due to the randomness of the coin flips. What if you toss the coin 50 times and end up with 12 heads and 38 tails? Would you still think that this coin was fair? Since the probability of getting 12 heads out of 50 tosses with a fair coin is so very unlikely, 0.0001, you would probably reject the claim that the coin was fair. Can you be 100% sure that the coin is not fair? No. It is possible to get 12 heads out of 50 tosses with a fair coin, just not very likely. The coin could still be fair.

When decisions are made about claims using data from samples, you must accept the fact that errors will be made. You might reject the null hypothesis when, in reality, it was actually true. You might fail to reject the null hypothesis when, in reality, it was actually false.

If you reject the null hypothesis, H_0, when it is actually true, you are committing a **type I error**. If you fail to reject the null hypothesis, H_0, when it is actually false, you are committing a **type II error**.

Decision	H_0 Is Actually True	H_0 Is Actually False
Fail to reject H_0	Correct decision	Type II error
Reject H_0	Type I error	Correct decision

EXAMPLE:

In a court of law, a defendant is considered not guilty until "proven" guilty. Enough significant evidence must be presented to return a guilty decision. What kind of errors could occur? Which type of error is "better" and which type is "worse"?

Null Hypothesis: Not Guilty

Alternate Hypothesis: Guilty

Decision	Defendant Is Not Guilty	Defendant Is Guilty
Verdict of Not Guilty	Correct decision	Type II error
Verdict of Guilty	Type I error	Correct decision

No error is desirable, but if an error is made, a type II error is better than a type I error.

EXAMPLE:

Medical tests are routinely run on patients. Decisions are made based on the test results. Which type of error is "better" and which type is "worse"?

Null Hypothesis: Patient does not have an ailment

Alternate Hypothesis: Patient does have an ailment

Decision	Patient has no ailment	Patient has ailment
Do not treat for ailment	Correct decision	Type II error
Treat for ailment	Type I error	Correct decision

No error is desirable, but if an error is made, a type I error is better than a type II error.

The probability of making a type I error is called the **significance level** and is denoted by the Greek letter, α (alpha). The significance level should be chosen before data is collected. The probability of making a type II error is denoted by the Greek letter, β (beta). The quantity $1-\beta$ is called the **power of the test** and represents the probability of rejecting the null hypothesis when it is actually false, in other words, making the correct decision by rejecting the null hypothesis. The power of the test is the probability on not making a type II error.

Any value of α may be chosen, although statisticians usually choose small values. Common values for α include

$$\alpha = 0.01 - \text{willingness to make a type I error 1\% of the time}$$
$$\alpha = 0.05 - \text{willingness to make a type I error 5\% of the time}$$
$$\alpha = 0.10 - \text{willingness to make a type I error 10\% of the time}$$

The person performing the test chooses the significance level α. How much power you get from a test depends on the significance level. The value of β is very difficult or impossible to calculate. The calculation of the value of β is beyond the scope of the AP Statistics Test, but you need to know what it means.

The power of a test (the probability of rejecting the null hypothesis when it is false) increases as the significance level also increases. A test performed at $\alpha = 0.10$ has more power than a test performed at $\alpha = 0.05$. Increasing the significance level, α, to increase the power can be counterproductive, since it increases the risk of making a type I error. Decreasing α also decreases the probability of rejecting the null hypothesis. This reduces the power of the test, which increases the probability of making a type II error, β. Choosing α properly requires finding a balance appropriate for the situation.

Decision	H_0 Is Actually True	H_0 Is Actually False
Fail to reject H_0	Correct decision	Type II error, β
Reject H_0	Type I error, α	Correct decision, $1 - \beta$

One-Sided and Two-Sided Tests

After determining the null and alternate hypotheses, you obtain random sample data from the population. You calculate sample statistics, such as mean and standard deviation, and compare the values to the parameter in the null hypothesis to determine the type of test you use. These sample statistics are called **test statistics.** You decide whether or not to reject the null hypothesis by determining whether the test statistic falls within a range of values called the rejection region of the sampling distribution.

A **rejection region,** or critical region, of a sampling distribution is the range of values for which the null hypothesis is not likely. If the test statistic falls within this region, you reject the null hypothesis. A **critical value** separates the rejection region from the nonrejection region. The type and location of the rejection region(s) depends on the statement of the null and alternate hypotheses.

Three Types of Hypothesis Tests

In the following diagrams, z_0 is the critical value, and α is the significance level. The shaded area is the rejection region. The total shaded area is equal to α.

If the alternate hypothesis, H_a, contains a less-than symbol ($<$), then the hypothesis test is a **left-tailed test:** $H_a : \mu < k$.

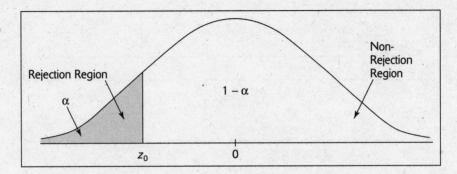

If the alternate hypothesis, H_a, contains a greater-than symbol ($>$), then the hypothesis test is a **right-tailed test:** $H_a : \mu > k$.

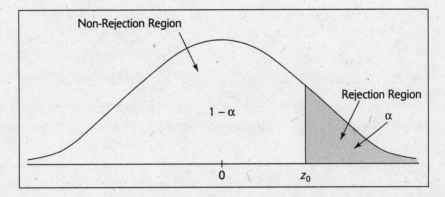

If the alternate hypothesis, H_a, contains a not-equal-to symbol ($\neq$), then the hypothesis test is a **two-tailed test:** $H_a : \mu \neq k$.

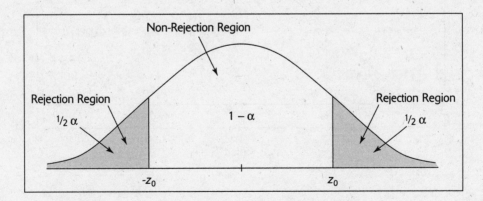

Decision Rules Based on the Rejection Region and the Value of *z*

From the sample data, calculate the standardized test statistic, z. If the standardized test statistic is located in the rejection region (shaded area, α), then reject H_0. If the standardized test statistic is not located in the rejection region, then fail to reject H_0. Failure to reject the null hypothesis does not mean you accept the null hypothesis as true; you just did not have enough statistically significant data to reject it.

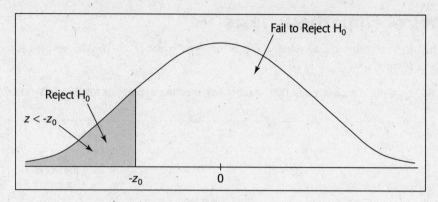

Left-Tailed Test

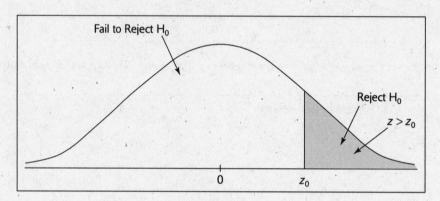

Right-Tailed Test

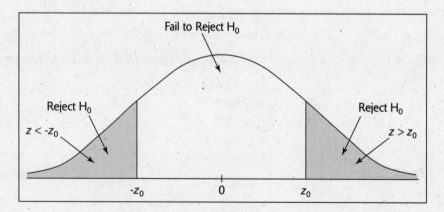

Two-Tailed Test

p-Value

The ***p*-value** of a hypothesis test is the probability of observing a sample statistic with a value as extreme or more extreme than the one determined from the sample data, assuming that the null hypothesis is true.

To determine the *p*-value, compute the test statistic, z. If the alternate hypothesis contains

- a less-than symbol, the *p*-value is the area to the left of z.
- a greater-than symbol, the *p*-value is the area to the right of z.
- a not-equal-to symbol, the *p*-value is twice the area to the right of $|z|$.

Decision Rule Based on *p*-Value

If *p*-value $\leq \alpha$, then reject H_0.

If *p*-value $> \alpha$, then fail to reject H_0.

The *p*-value tells you down to what level of α your data is statistically significant, which then allows you to reject the null hypothesis. For example, a *p*-value of 0.0234 tells you that you can reject the null hypothesis with α values of 0.10, 0.05, 0.04, 0.03, and fail to reject at α levels of 0.02, 0.01, and so on.

EXAMPLE:

The *z*-statistic calculated from a random sample is 1.71. The alternate hypothesis contains a greater-than symbol. Under what significance levels would you be able to reject the null hypothesis?

The easiest way to calculate the area to the right of a *z*-score of 1.71 is to look up −1.71 in the table of standard normal probabilities. You get 0.0436. This is the *p*-value. This means that you may reject the null hypothesis with any α value larger than 0.0436, such as $\alpha = 0.05$, $\alpha = 0.07$, or $\alpha = 0.10$. You would fail to reject the null hypothesis for any α value less than 0.0436, such as $\alpha = 0.04$, $\alpha = 0.02$, or $\alpha = 0.01$.

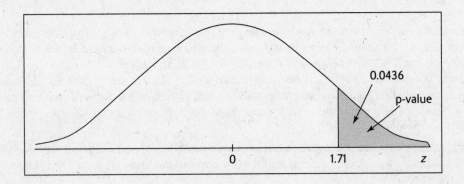

EXAMPLE:

Jamie claims to be able to throw a baseball an average of 90 miles per hour. Jamie threw the baseball 35 times with an average speed of 88.2 miles per hour and standard deviation of 5.2 miles per hour. If these speeds are approximately normally distributed and you use 5.2 as the population standard deviation, at what significance level would you start to believe that the results were caused by more than just chance? Is this result statistically significant at $\alpha = 0.05$? Is this result statistically significant at $\alpha = 0.01$?

Calculate the *z*-score for a sample mean of 88.2 miles per hour assuming the null hypothesis, that Jamie's average is 90 miles per hour, is true.

$$z_{882} = \frac{\bar{x} - \mu}{\frac{s}{\sqrt{n}}} = \frac{88.2 - 90}{\frac{5.2}{\sqrt{35}}} = -2.05$$

Look up −2.05 in the table of standard normal probabilities to determine that the probability of an average that is less than 88.2 is 0.0202. Therefore, $P(\bar{x} < 88.5) = 0.0202$. This represents the *p*-value. This data would be significant at any $\alpha \geq 0.0202$. You would reject the null hypothesis at $\alpha = 0.05$ but fail to reject the null hypothesis at $\alpha = 0.01$. In other words, if you were willing to make a type I error 5% (or 4% or 3%) of the time, you would reject the null hypothesis that Jamie averages 90 miles per hour. If you were willing to make a type I error only 1% (or 2%) of the time, you would fail to reject the null hypothesis.

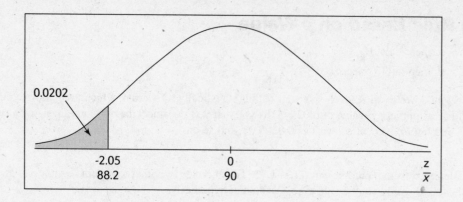

Hypothesis Testing Process

There are five specific components to the hypothesis testing process. To receive full credit on free-response questions, all five must be present in your answer.

A. You must state the null and alternate hypotheses using the correct notation. The null hypothesis always contains the statement of equality. The alternate hypothesis always contains a statement of inequality. For example: $H_0:\mu = 25$ (may also be written $H_0:\mu \le 25$ or $H_0:\mu \ge 25$ depending on H_a), $H_0:\mu_1 = \mu_2$, $H_a:\mu > 7$, $H_a:\mu < \mu_2$, $H_0:\mu_1 - \mu_2 \le 0$, or $H_a:p_1 - p_2 < 0$. You do not need to define standard symbols such as $H_0:$, μ, σ, and α. You must be specific in the use of symbols. For example: "Let μ_1 represent the population mean weight of a jelly bean." You may assume that all symbols presented on the formula sheets are accurate and defined. Be sure to reference any symbols for populations and samples in the problem.

B. The testing procedure and the test statistic must be clearly listed. Use proper statistical form. Listing the formulas will identify the procedure. A clear statement of the procedure is also acceptable, such as: "Use a two-sample z-test for proportions."

C. You must identify and check any assumptions you are making. The actual format and values of the assumptions are less important than the fact that you know that there are assumptions that must be checked and verified. For example, you know that to use the normal distribution to solve a problem involving proportions, both np and $n(1 - p)$ must be greater than 5 (or 10). State it and verify it. Stating the assumption is not enough; it must be checked. In some situations, the normality of a population is needed. You may use a graph of the data, such as a boxplot, to show that the data is not skewed and does not contains outliers.

D. You must use correct mechanics. Show intermediate steps; do not leave out what you think are "unnecessary" steps. Be sure the steps in the process are clear and organized. Use correct values for test statistics, levels of significance, and p-values. Make sure that they are all identified properly.

E. You must use test statistics to arrive at the correct conclusion. Use either the p-value approach or the rejection region approach. Be sure to link these approaches to your conclusion. For example, "Since the test statistic falls in the rejection region, you reject the null hypothesis that the average height is 67 inches," or "Since the p-value is greater than α, you conclude that your sample data is not significant at $\alpha = 0.01$." If confidence intervals are used to make inferences, be sure to use the correct confidence interval statement.

Since the p-value gives you information about under what significance levels you would reject or fail to reject the null hypothesis, it can be used as your primary decision-making source. The TI-83/4 calculator does not ask for nor give values of α. The results give the test statistic and the p-value. It is up to you to interpret the p-value in the context of the problem. Drawing a picture of the rejection region and labeling the critical value(s) as well as labeling the test statistic help you visualize the results. Using one of these techniques is essential; using both is preferred.

Large Sample Test for a Proportion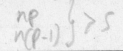

$np \atop n(p-1)$ $\}> 5$

To use the normal distribution in a test for a proportion using a single large sample, the following condition is required:

$np > 5$ and $n(p - 1) > 5$ must be true. (Some authors require at least 10.)

The accuracy of the results improve as the products increase in value. Sample size is not the only factor. You could use a sample size of 50, but if the proportion, p, is quite small, you will not get accurate results.

EXAMPLE:

A researcher has estimated that at most 49% of American adults skip breakfast on weekdays. Using a random sample of 280 American adults, 55% said they skip breakfast on weekdays. Is there enough evidence to reject the null hypothesis at a 1% significance level ($\alpha = 0.01$)?

$X_{280} = 0.55 \qquad p = 0.49$

State the null and alternate hypotheses.

$H_0: p \leq 0.49$ Claim

$H_a: p > 0.49$

Verify that the sample size and proportion values are appropriate for using the normal distribution.

$$np = (280)(0.55) = 154 > 5$$
$$n(1 - p) = (280)(0.45) = 126 > 5$$

Using the claimed value of 49% in the calculation of the standard deviation, find the z-score of the test statistic.

$$z_{0.55} = \frac{\hat{p} - p}{\sqrt{\frac{p(1-p)}{n}}} = \frac{0.55 - 0.49}{\sqrt{\frac{(0.49)(0.51)}{280}}} = 2.01$$

$\sigma = \sqrt{\frac{p(1-p)}{n}}$

p-Value Based Solution

Since this is a one-tail test, the area (probability) beyond $z = 2.01$ is 0.0222. The p-value represents the probability of attaining a value at least as improbable as the test statistic. Therefore, the p-value = 0.0222. Your data is significant down to the 2.22% level of significance. This means that at a 1% significance level you fail to reject H_0 since you do not have enough significant data to reject it. You fail to reject H_0 whenever the p-value > α. Since the claim is in the null hypothesis, you are unable to reject the claim. You would be able to reject H_0 whenever the p-value $\leq \alpha$. You would reject H_0 if $\alpha = 0.03$. You do not have enough evidence to reject the claim that at most 49% of Americans skip breakfast.

Rejection Region Based Solution

This is a right-tail test. The alternate hypothesis determines the type of test and points in the direction of the test. The z-score that corresponds to a significance level of $\alpha = 0.01$ in a one-tail test is $z_0 = 2.326$. This is the critical value (you use a "sub zero" to indicate a critical value) that marks the beginning of the rejection region. Any test statistic beyond this point will be in the rejection region and would indicate that the test data is significant. A test statistic in the rejection region is evidence to reject the null hypothesis. Your test statistic ($z = 2.01$) is not in the rejection region. Therefore, the data in your sample is not significant, and you fail to reject H_0. You are unable to reject the claim. You do not have enough evidence to reject the claim that at most 49% of Americans skip breakfast. [TI-83/4–Select STAT TESTS 1-PropZTest po:0.49 x:154 n:280 prop >po Calculate Display z=2.01 p=0.0223)]

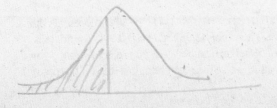

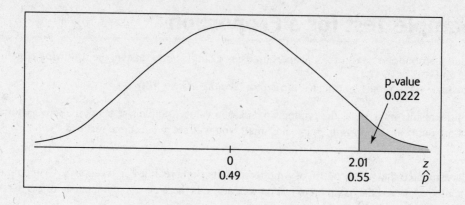

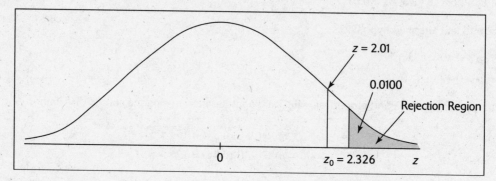

EXAMPLE:

A government agency claimed that 60% of Americans agree that oil exploration in our national parks is necessary. You want to test this claim. In a survey of 1945 Americans, 1215 said they agree with the claim. Using $\alpha = 0.05$, can you reject the claim?

State the null and alternate hypotheses.

$H_0:p = 0.60$ Claim

$H_a:p \neq 0.60$

Verify that the sample size and proportion values are appropriate for using the normal distribution:

$$np = (1945)(0.60) = 1167 > 5$$
$$n(1 - p) = (1945)(0.40) = 778 > 5$$

Calculate the test statistic:

$$\hat{p} = \frac{x}{n} = \frac{1215}{1945} = 0.625$$

Using the claimed value of 60% in the calculation of the standard deviation, find the z-score of the test statistic:

$$z_{0.625} = \frac{\hat{p} - p}{\sqrt{\frac{p(1 - p)}{n}}} = \frac{0.625 - 0.60}{\sqrt{\frac{(0.60)(0.40)}{1945}}} = 2.25$$

p-Value Based Solution

Since this is a two-tail test, the area (probability) beyond $z = 2.25$ is $(2)(0.0122) = (0.0244)$. The p-value represents the probability of attaining a value at least as improbable as the test statistic. Therefore, the p-value = 0.0244. Your data is significant down to the 2.44% level of significance. This means that at a 5% significance level, you reject H_0 since you do have enough significant data to reject it. You reject H_0 whenever the p-value $\leq \alpha$. Since the claim is in the null hypothesis, you are able to reject the claim. You would be unable to reject H_0 whenever the p-value $> \alpha$. You would fail to reject H_0 if $\alpha = 0.01$. You have enough evidence to reject the claim that 60% of Americans agree that oil exploration in our national parks is necessary.

Rejection Region Based Solution

This is a two-tail test. The alternate hypothesis determines the type of test. The z-score that corresponds to a significance level of $\alpha = 0.05$ in a two tail test is $z_0 = 1.96$. (If $\alpha = 0.05$, then the 5% is split, half in each tail. So you actually look up 0.025 to find the z-score.) This is the critical value (you use a "sub zero" to indicate a critical value) that marks the beginning of the rejection regions. Any test statistic beyond this point in either tail will be in the rejection region and would indicate that the test data is more significant than the required significance level. A test statistic in the rejection region is evidence to reject the null hypothesis. Your test statistic ($z = 2.25$) is in the rejection region. Therefore, the data in your sample is significant, and you reject H_0. You are able to reject the claim. You have enough evidence to reject the claim that 60% of Americans agree that oil exploration in our national parks is necessary. [TI-83/4–Select STAT TESTS 1-PropZTest po:0.60 x:1215 n:1945 prop ≠ po Calculate Display z = 2.22 p = 0.0263)–Note slight differences due to round-off error]

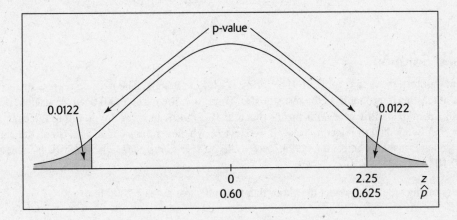

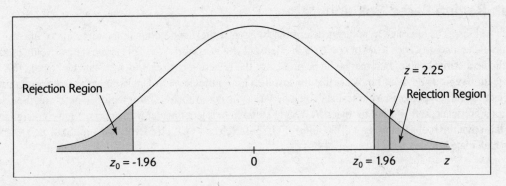

Large Sample Test for a Mean

To use the normal distribution to test the mean, the following condition is required:

The sample must be large (n ≥ 30), or the population must be known to be normal with known σ.

The test statistic is the sample mean, $\bar{x}$. When the sample is large, the sample standard deviation, s, may be used as an approximation for the population standard deviation, σ.

$$z = \frac{\bar{x} - \mu}{\frac{\sigma}{\sqrt{n}}} \approx \frac{\bar{x} - \mu}{\frac{s}{\sqrt{n}}}$$

EXAMPLE:

A manufacturer of lightbulbs claims that their bulbs have an average life of at least 2000 hours. A random sample of 40 lightbulbs has an average life of 1980 hours with a standard deviation of 85 hours. Do you have enough evidence to reject the manufacturer's claim? Use $\alpha = 0.05$.

State the null and alternate hypotheses.

$H_0: \mu \geq 2000$ Claim

$H_a: \mu < 2000$

Verify that the sample size is large enough to use the normal distribution:

$$n = 40 > 30$$

Using the sample value of the standard deviation, find the z-score of the test statistic:

$$z_{1980} = \frac{\bar{x} - \mu}{\frac{s}{\sqrt{n}}} = \frac{1980 - 2000}{\frac{85}{\sqrt{40}}} = -1.49$$

p-Value Based Solution

Since this is a one-tail test, the area (probability) beyond $z = -1.49$ is 0.0681. The *p*-value represents the probability of attaining a value at least as improbable as the test statistic. Therefore, the *p*-value = 0.0681. Your data is significant down to the 6.81% level of significance. This means that at a 5% significance level, you fail to reject H_0 since you do not have enough significant data to reject it. You fail to reject H_0 whenever the *p*-value > α. Since the claim is in the null hypothesis, you are unable to reject the claim. You would be able to reject H_0 whenever the *p*-value $\leq \alpha$. You would reject H_0 if $\alpha = 0.10$.

You do not have enough evidence to reject the claim that the bulbs last at least 2000 hours.

Rejection Region Based Solution

This is a left-tail test. The alternate hypothesis determines the type of test and points in the direction of the test. The z-score that corresponds to a significance level of $\alpha = 0.05$ in a left-tail test is $z_0 = -1.645$. This is the critical value (you use a "sub zero" to indicate a critical value) that marks the beginning of the rejection region. Any test statistic beyond this point will be in the rejection region and would indicate that the test data is significant. A test statistic in the rejection region is evidence to reject the null hypothesis. Your test statistic ($z = -1.49$) is not in the rejection region. Therefore, the data in your sample is not significant, and you fail to reject H_0. You are unable to reject the claim. You do not have enough evidence to reject the claim that the bulbs last at least 2000 hours. [TI-83/4–Select STAT TESTS Z-Test Inpt:Stats μ:2000 σ:85 $\bar{x}$:1980 n:40 $\mu < \mu_0$ Calculate Display z = –1.49 p = 0.0684)]

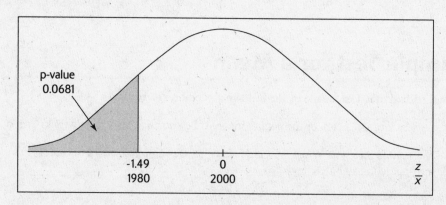

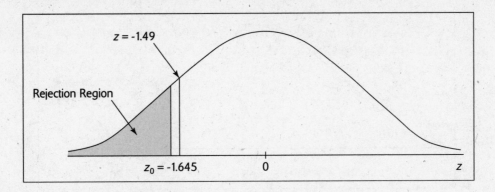

EXAMPLE:

A fancy restaurant claims that the average caffeine content in 1 cup of its special coffee mixtures is 65 milligrams. You want to test this claim. Using a random sample of 60 cups of coffee, you determine that the average caffeine content per cup is 70 milligrams with a standard deviation of 18 milligrams. Use $\alpha = 0.05$.

State the null and alternate hypotheses.

$H_0{:}\mu = 65$ Claim

$H_a{:}\mu \neq 65$

Verify that the sample size is large enough to use the normal distribution:

$$n = 60 \geq 30$$

Using the sample value of the standard deviation, find the z-score of the test statistic:

$$z_{70} = \frac{\bar{x} - \mu}{\frac{s}{\sqrt{n}}} = \frac{70 - 65}{\frac{18}{\sqrt{60}}} = 2.15$$

p-Value Based Solution

Since this is a two-tail test, the area (probability) beyond $z = 2.15$ is $(2)(0.0158) = (0.0316)$. The *p*-value represents the probability of attaining a value at least as improbable as the test statistic. Therefore, the *p*-value $= 0.0316$. Your data is significant down to the 3.16% level of significance. This means that at a 5% significance level you reject H_0 since you have enough significant data to reject it. You reject H_0 whenever the *p*-value $\leq \alpha$. Since the claim is in the null hypothesis, you are able to reject the claim. You would be unable to reject H_0 whenever the *p*-value $> \alpha$. You would not reject H_0 if $\alpha = 0.01$. You have enough evidence to reject the claim that the average caffeine content in 1 cup of its special coffee mixtures is 65 milligrams.

Rejection Region Based Solution

This is a two-tail test. The alternate hypothesis determines the type of test. The z-score that corresponds to a significance level of $\alpha = 0.05$ in a two-tail test is $z_0 = 1.96$. (If $\alpha = 0.05$, then the 5% is split, half in each tail. So you actually look up 0.025 to find the z-score.) This is the critical value (you use a "sub zero" to indicate a critical value) that marks the beginning of the rejection region. Any test statistic beyond this point will be in the rejection region and would indicate that the test data is significant. A test statistic in the rejection region is evidence to reject the null hypothesis. Your test statistic ($z = 2.15$) is in the rejection region. Therefore, the data in your sample is significant, and you reject H_0. You are able to reject the claim. You have enough evidence to reject the claim that the average caffeine content in 1 cup of its special coffee mixtures is 65 milligrams. [TI-83/4–Select STAT TESTS Z-Test Inpt:Stats μ:65 σ:18 $\bar{x}$:70 n:60 $\mu \neq \mu_0$ Calculate Display z =2.15 p=0.0314)]

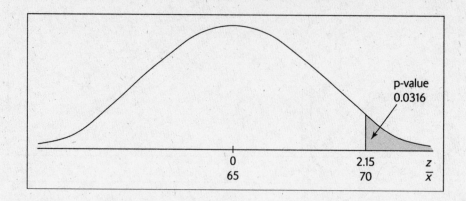

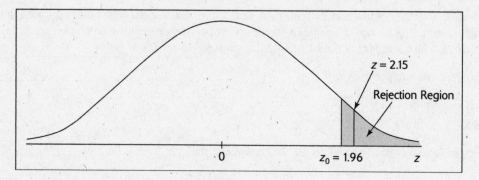

Large Sample Test for a Difference between Two Proportions

To test the difference between 2 proportions using the normal distribution, the following conditions are required:

A. The samples must be independent (unrelated).

B. The samples must be large enough so that the normal sampling distribution may be used. This requires the following (some authors require 10 instead of 5):

$$n_1 p_1 \geq 5 \qquad n_1(1 - p_1) \geq 5 \qquad n_2 p_2 \geq 5 \qquad n_1(1 - p_1) \geq 5$$

If these conditions are met, then the sampling distribution of the differences between the proportions, $\hat{p}_1 - \hat{p}_2$, is normally distributed. The mean of this distribution will be

$$\mu_{\hat{p}_1 - \hat{p}_2} = p_1 - p_2$$

The standard error of this distribution will be

$$\sigma_{\hat{p}_1 - \hat{p}_2} = \sqrt{\frac{p_1(1 - p_1)}{n_1} + \frac{p_2(1 - p_2)}{n_2}}$$

The population proportions, p_1 and p_2, are needed to calculate the standard error. Since the null hypothesis implies equality between the proportions, a weighted average of the population proportions may be substituted. The weighted average is $\hat{p} = \frac{x_1 + x_2}{n_1 + n_2}$. Using the weighted average, you simplify the standard error:

$$\sigma_{\hat{p}_1 - \hat{p}_2} = \sqrt{\hat{p}(1 - \hat{p})\left(\frac{1}{n_1} + \frac{1}{n_2}\right)}$$

The weighted mean, $\hat{p}$, could be used to determine whether the normal distribution can be used. That is,

$$n_1\hat{p} \geq 5 \qquad n_1\left(1 - \hat{p}\right) \geq 5 \qquad n_2\hat{p} \geq 5 \qquad n_2\left(1 - \hat{p}\right) \geq 5$$

The calculation of the z-score for a difference of proportions is

$$z = \frac{\left(\hat{p}_1 - \hat{p}_2\right) - \left(p_1 - p_2\right)}{\sqrt{\hat{p}\left(1 - \hat{p}\right)\left(\frac{1}{n_1} + \frac{1}{n_2}\right)}} \quad \text{where} \quad \hat{p} = \frac{x_1 + x_2}{n_1 + n_2}$$

EXAMPLE:

The following table shows the results of a study of dropout rates for students in college algebra classes at a private university. Use a 1% test for significance to determine whether there a difference in dropout rates between male and female students.

	1 - Male	2 - Female
Dropped out of class	114	77
Finished the class	323	321
Total	437	398

State the null and alternate hypotheses.

$H_0 : p_1 - p_2 = 0 \qquad$ Claim

$H_a : p_1 - p_2 \neq 0$

Calculate the sample statistics for the proportions.

$$\hat{p}_1 = \frac{x_1}{n_1} = \frac{114}{437} = 0.261 \qquad \hat{p}_2 = \frac{x_2}{n_2} = \frac{77}{398} = 0.193$$

Verify that the sample size and proportion values are appropriate for using the normal distribution:

$$n_1 p_1 = (437)(0.261) = 114 > 5$$
$$n_1(1 - p_1) = (437)(0.739) = 323 > 5$$
$$n_2 p_2 = (398)(0.193) = 77 > 5$$
$$n_2(1 - p_2) = (398)(0.807) = 321 > 5$$

Find the z-score of the test statistic:

$$\hat{p} = \frac{x_1 + x_2}{n_1 + n_2} = \frac{114 + 77}{437 + 398} = \frac{191}{835} = 0.229$$

$$z = \frac{\left(\hat{p}_1 - \hat{p}_2\right) - \left(p_1 - p_2\right)}{\sqrt{\hat{p}\left(1 - \hat{p}\right)\left(\frac{1}{n_1} + \frac{1}{n_2}\right)}} = \frac{(0.261 - 0.193) - 0}{\sqrt{(0.229)(0.771)\left(\frac{1}{437} + \frac{1}{398}\right)}} = 2.34$$

p-Value Based Solution

Since this is a two-tail test, the area (probability) beyond $z = 2.34$ is $(2)(0.0096) = (0.0192)$. The p-value represents the probability of attaining a value at least as improbable as the test statistic. Therefore, the p-value $= 0.0192$. Your data is significant down to the 1.92% level of significance. This means that at a 1% significance level you fail to reject H_0 since you do not have enough significant data to reject it. You fail to reject H_0 whenever the p-value $> \alpha$. Since the claim is in the null hypothesis, you are unable to reject the claim. You would be able to reject H_0 whenever the p-value $\leq \alpha$. You would reject H_0 if $\alpha = 0.05$. You do not have enough evidence to reject the claim that the dropout rates are the same.

Rejection Region Based Solution

This is a two-tail test. The alternate hypothesis determines the type of test. The z-score that corresponds to a significance level of $\alpha = 0.01$ in a two tail test is $z_0 = 2.576$. (If $\alpha = 0.01$, then the 1% is split, half in each tail. So you actually look up 0.005 to find the z-score.) This is the critical value (you use a "sub zero" to indicate a critical value) that marks the beginning of the rejection regions. Any test statistic beyond this point in either tail will be in the rejection region and would indicate that the test data is significant. A test statistic in the rejection region is evidence to reject the null hypothesis. Your test statistic ($z = 2.34$) is not in the rejection region. Therefore, the data in your sample is not significant, and you fail to reject H_0. You are unable to reject the claim. You do not have enough evidence to reject the claim that the dropout rates are the same. [TI-83/4–Select STAT TESTS 2-PropZTest x1:114 n1:437 x2:77 n2:398 $p_1 \neq p_2$ Calculate Display z = 2.32 p = 0.0206)–Note slight differences due to round-off error]

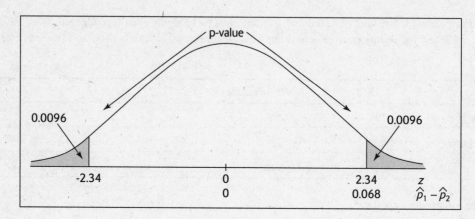

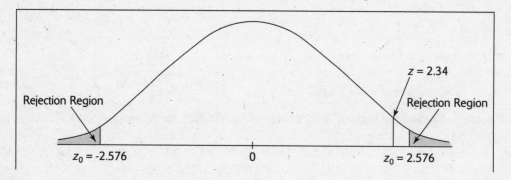

EXAMPLE:

In a 1990 survey of 1840 adults, 1045 said that their primary source of news was print media. In a 2000 survey of 1260 adults, 686 said that their primary source of news was print media. At a 5% significance level, can you support the claim that the percentage of adults getting most of their news from print media had decreased from 1990 to 2000?

State the null and alternate hypotheses.

$H_0: p_1 - p_2 \leq 0$

$H_a: p_1 - p_2 > 0$ Claim

Calculate the sample statistics for the proportions:

$$\hat{p}_1 = \frac{x_1}{n_1} = \frac{1045}{1840} = 0.568 \qquad \hat{p}_2 = \frac{x_2}{n_2} = \frac{676}{1260} = 0.544$$

Verify that the sample size and proportion values are appropriate for using the normal distribution:

$$n_1 p_1 = (1840)(0.568) = 1045 > 5$$
$$n_1(1 - p_1) = (1840)(0.432) = 795 > 5$$
$$n_2 p_2 = (1260)(0.544) = 676 > 5$$
$$n_2(1 - p_2) = (1260)(0.456) = 575 > 5$$

Find the z-score of the test statistic:

$$\hat{p} = \frac{x_1 + x_2}{n_1 + n_2} = \frac{1045 + 676}{1840 + 1260} = \frac{1721}{3100} = 0.555$$

$$z = \frac{\left(\hat{p}_1 - \hat{p}_2\right) - \left(p_1 - p_2\right)}{\sqrt{\hat{p}\left(1 - \hat{p}\right)\left(\frac{1}{n_1} + \frac{1}{n_2}\right)}} = \frac{(0.568 - 0.544) - 0}{\sqrt{(0.555)(0.445)\left(\frac{1}{1840} + \frac{1}{1260}\right)}} = 1.32$$

p-Value Based Solution

Since this is a one-tail test, the area (probability) beyond $z = 1.32$ is 0.0934. The p-value represents the probability of attaining a value at least as improbable as the test statistic. Therefore, the p-value = 0.0934. Your data is significant down to the 9.34% level of significance. This means that at a 5% significance level you fail to reject H_0 since you do not have enough significant data to reject it. You fail to reject H_0 whenever the p-value > α. Since the claim is in the alternate hypothesis, you are unable to support the claim. You would be able to reject H_0 whenever the p-value $\leq \alpha$. You would reject H_0 if $\alpha = 0.10$. You do not have enough evidence to support the claim that the percentage of adults who get most of their news from print media has decreased.

Rejection Region Based Solution

This is a right-tail test. The alternate hypothesis determines the type of test. The z-score that corresponds to a significance level of $\alpha = 0.05$ in a one-tail test is $z_0 = 1.645$. This is the critical value (you use a "sub zero" to indicate a critical value) that marks the beginning of the rejection region. Any test statistic beyond this point in the tail will be in the rejection region and would indicate that the test data is significant. A test statistic in the rejection region is evidence to reject the null hypothesis. Your test statistic ($z = 1.32$) is not in the rejection region. Therefore, the data in your sample is not significant, and you fail to reject H_0. You are unable to support the claim. You do not have enough evidence to support the claim that the percentage of adults who get most of their news from print media has decreased. [TI-83/4–Select STAT TESTS 2-PropZTest x1:1045 n1:1840 x2:686 n2:1260 $p_1 > p_2$ Calculate Display z=1.29 p=0.0979)–Note slight differences due to round-off error]

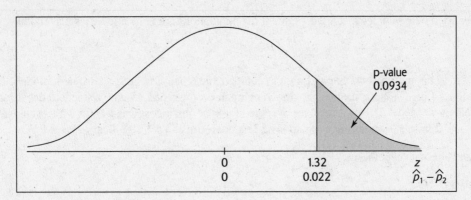

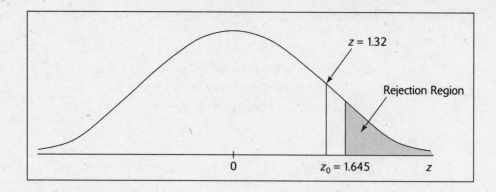

Large Sample Test for a Difference between Two Means— Independent Samples (Unpaired) $n_1, n_2 > 30$

The following conditions are required to test the difference between two means using the normal distribution:

A. The samples must be independent (unrelated).

B. Each sample must be large ($n_1 \geq 30$, $n_2 \geq 30$).

If these conditions are met, then the sampling distribution of the differences between the means, $\bar{x}_1 - \bar{x}_2$, will be approximately normally distributed. The mean of this distribution will be

$$\mu_{\bar{x}_1 - \bar{x}_2} = \mu_1 - \mu_2$$

When both samples are large, the sample standard deviations may be used as approximations of the population standard deviations. The standard error of this distribution will be

$$\sigma_{\bar{x}_1 - \bar{x}_2} = \sqrt{\frac{\sigma_1^2}{n_1} + \frac{\sigma_2^2}{n_2}} \approx \sqrt{\frac{s_1^2}{n_1} + \frac{s_2^2}{n_2}}$$

The standardized test statistic is

$$z = \frac{(\bar{x}_1 - \bar{x}_2) - (\mu_1 - \mu_2)}{\sqrt{\frac{s_1^2}{n_1} + \frac{s_2^2}{n_2}}}$$

This test may be used with samples that are not large if the populations are known to be normal and have known standard deviations.

EXAMPLE:

You are interested in buying a dishwasher and want to compare the repair costs of two different models. In a random sample of 38 Model 1 dishwashers, the average first-year repair cost was $85.45 with a standard deviation of $17.92. In a random sample of 45 Model 2 dishwashers, the average first-year repair cost was $77.25 with a standard deviation of $9.88. Does Model 2 have a lower average repair cost? Test the claim at a 5% significance level.

State the null and alternate hypotheses.

$H_0: \mu_1 - \mu_2 \leq 0$

$H_a: \mu_1 - \mu_2 > 0$ Claim

Verify that the sample size is large enough to use the normal distribution:

$$n_1 = 38 \geq 30$$
$$n_2 = 45 \geq 30$$

Using the sample value of the standard deviation, find the z-score of the test statistic:

$$z = \frac{(\bar{x}_1 - \bar{x}_2) - (\mu_1 - \mu_2)}{\sqrt{\frac{s_1^2}{n_1} + \frac{s_2^2}{n_2}}} = \frac{(85.45 - 77.25) - 0}{\sqrt{\frac{17.92^2}{38} + \frac{9.88^2}{45}}} = 2.52$$

p-Value Based Solution

Since this is a one-tail test, the area (probability) beyond $z = 2.52$ is 0.0059. The p-value represents the probability of attaining a value at least as improbable as the test statistic. Therefore, the p-value = 0.0059. Your data is significant down to the 0.59% level of significance. This means that at a 5% significance level you reject H_0 since you do have enough significant data to reject it. You reject H_0 whenever the p-value $\leq \alpha$. Since the claim is in the alternate hypothesis, you are able to support the claim. You would be unable to reject H_0 whenever the p-value $> \alpha$. You would fail to reject H_0 if $\alpha = 0.005$.

You do have enough evidence to support the claim that Model 2 has a lower average first-year repair cost.

Rejection Region Based Solution

This is a right-tail test. The alternate hypothesis determines the type of test and points in the direction of the test. The z-score that corresponds to a significance level of $\alpha = 0.05$ in a right-tail test is $z_0 = 1.645$. This is the critical value (you use a "sub zero" to indicate a critical value) that marks the beginning of the rejection region. Any test statistic beyond this point will be in the rejection region and would indicate that the test data is significant. A test statistic in the rejection region is evidence to reject the null hypothesis. Your test statistic ($z = 2.52$) is in the rejection region. Therefore, the data in your sample is significant, and you reject H_0. You are able to support the claim. You do have enough evidence to support the claim that Model 2 has a lower average first-year repair cost. [TI-83/4–Select STAT TESTS 2-SampZTest Inpt:Stats σ_1:17.92 σ_2:9.88 $\bar{x}1$:85.45 n1:38 $\bar{x}2$:77.25 n2:45$\mu1 > \mu2$ Calculate Display z = 2.52 p = 0.0059)]

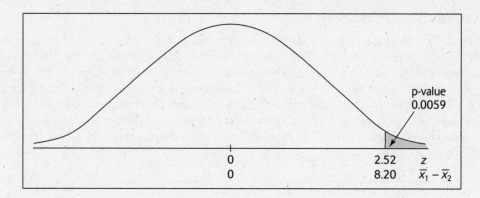

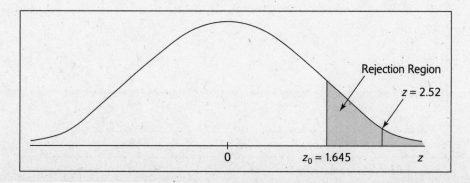

EXAMPLE:

The average score for 65 females students taking the SAT is 578 with a standard deviation of 9.8. The average score for 52 male students taking the SAT is 575 with a standard deviation of 7.7. Based on these samples, do male and female students have SAT scores that are equal? Use $\alpha = 0.10$.

Let sample 1 represent the female students and sample 2 represent the male students.

State the null and alternate hypotheses.

$H_0: \mu_1 - \mu_2 = 0$ Claim

$H_a: \mu_1 - \mu_2 \neq 0$

Verify that the sample size is large enough to use the normal distribution:

$$n_1 = 65 \geq 30$$
$$n_2 = 52 \geq 30$$

Using the sample value of the standard deviation, find the z-score of the test statistic:

$$z = \frac{(\bar{x}_1 - \bar{x}_2) - (\mu_1 - \mu_2)}{\sqrt{\frac{s_1^2}{n_1} + \frac{s_2^2}{n_2}}} = \frac{(578 - 575) - 0}{\sqrt{\frac{9.8^2}{65} + \frac{7.7^2}{52}}} = 1.85$$

p-Value Based Solution

Since this is a two-tail test, the area (probability) beyond $z = 1.85$ is $(2)(0.0322) = (0.0644)$. The *p*-value represents the probability of attaining a value at least as improbable as the test statistic. Therefore, the *p*-value = 0.0644. Your data is significant down to the 6.44% level of significance. This means that at a 10% significance level, you reject H_0 since you do have enough significant data to reject it. You reject H_0 whenever the *p*-value $\leq \alpha$. Since the claim is in the null hypothesis, you are able to reject the claim. You would be unable to reject H_0 whenever the *p*-value $> \alpha$. You would fail to reject H_0 if $\alpha = 0.05$. You do have enough evidence to reject the claim that male and female students have the same SAT score. (Even with only a 3-point difference in score, the difference was significant at the 10% level.)

Rejection Region Based Solution

This is a two-tail test. The alternate hypothesis determines the type of test. The z-score that corresponds to a significance level of $\alpha = 0.10$ in a two-tail test is $z_0 = 1.645$. This is the critical value (you use a "sub zero" to indicate a critical value) that marks the beginning of the rejection regions. Any test statistic beyond this point will be in the rejection region and would indicate that the test data is significant. A test statistic in the rejection region is evidence to reject the null hypothesis. Your test statistic ($z = 1.85$) is in the rejection region. Therefore, the data in our sample is significant, and you reject H_0. You are able to reject the claim. You do have enough evidence to reject the claim that male and female students have the same SAT score. [TI-83/4–Select STAT TESTS 2-SampZTest Inpt:Stats σ_1:9.8 σ_2:7.7 $\bar{x}$1:578 n1:65 $\bar{x}$2:575 n2:52μ1 $\neq \mu$2 Calculate Display z = 1.85 p = 0.0637)]

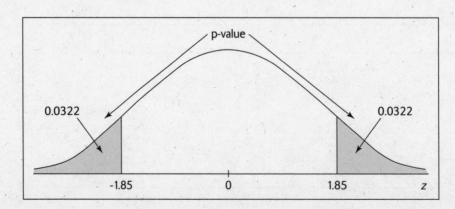

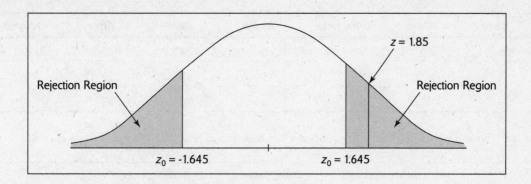

Large Sample Test for a Difference between Two Means— Dependent Samples (Paired)

Two samples are independent if the sample from one population is not related in any way to the sample from the other population. Two samples are dependent if there is a correspondence between the members of the two samples. Another name for dependent samples is paired samples. A **before-and-after test** is a common example of using paired, dependent samples. The samples are dependent since the members of the samples are the same, just tested under different conditions or different times.

A difference test should not be used on two dependent samples. Inaccurate results may lead to the wrong conclusion. This example illustrates the problem that may arise by using the wrong test.

EXAMPLE:

The average scores of 30 golfers using an executive course were recorded. All the golfers were given a set of golf clubs with a new and improved design. The golfers practiced with the new clubs for six months, and their new average scores were also recorded. The "before and after" scores for each of the 30 golfers are listed in the chart that follows along with the difference in their scores. Using a 5% significance level, is there significant evidence to support the claim that the scores of the golfers improved after using the new clubs? (In golf, lower scores are better.)

Golfer	Before	After	Difference	Golfer	Before	After	Difference
1	70	66	4	16	78	82	−4
2	60	60	2	17	64	66	−2
3	79	82	−3	18	74	66	8
4	71	63	8	19	61	66	−5
5	62	67	−5	20	60	52	8
6	72	70	2	21	66	70	−4
7	78	77	1	22	60	53	7
8	78	80	−2	23	71	65	6
9	77	71	6	24	66	60	6
10	67	62	5	25	65	70	−5
11	70	65	5	26	68	63	5
12	73	78	−5	27	61	66	−5

(continued)

Golfer	Before	After	Difference	Golfer	Before	After	Difference
13	61	59	2	28	78	77	1
14	60	54	6	29	65	59	6
15	74	69	5	30	78	70	8

The means and standard deviations for the before scores, the after scores, and the differences are as follows:

	Before Scores	After Scores	Differences
Mean $\bar{x}$	68.967	66.933	2.033
Standard Deviation s	6.610	8.056	4.789

If a two sample difference test is performed on the before and after scores:

State the null and alternate hypotheses.

$H_0: \mu_1 - \mu_2 \leq 0$

$H_a: \mu_1 - \mu_2 > 0$ Claim

Verify that the sample size is large enough to use the normal distribution:

$$n_1 = 30 \geq 30$$
$$n_2 = 30 \geq 30$$

The standardized statistic is $z = 1.07$ with a p-value of 0.14. Your data is significant down to the 14% level of significance. This means that at a 5% significance level you would fail to reject H_0 since you do not have enough significant data to reject it. Since the claim is in the alternate hypothesis, you are unable to support the claim.

On the other hand, if a one-sample test is performed on the differences:

State the null and alternate hypotheses.

$H_0: \mu \leq 0$

$H_a: \mu > 0$ Claim

Verify that the sample size is large enough to use the normal distribution:

$$n = 30 \geq 30$$

The standardized statistic is $z = 2.33$ with a p-value of 0.01. Your data is significant down to the 1% level of significance. This means that at a 5% significance level you would reject H_0 since you do have enough significant data to reject it. Since the claim is in the alternate hypothesis, you are able to support the claim.

It is clear that for dependent data, the use of a two-sample difference test does not give valid results. The use of a one-sample test for the mean is the correct choice for dependent samples.

Chi-Square Test for Goodness of Fit

How do you determine whether two distributions are similar? For example, has the breakdown of political affiliation changed on a college campus over the last 10 years? Or, is the distribution of grades (A, B, C, D, and F) given by a particular instructor the same as the overall distribution on campus? To answer these types of questions, use the **Chi-Square Distribution,** denoted by χ^2.

Some distributions are made up of categories of data. The binomial distribution consists of two categories, success and failure. The results of an experiment with more than two possible outcomes may be divided into categories, each with its own frequency, thus forming a frequency distribution. How would one compare the frequency distribution for political affiliation among local college students with the national average? The solution is a **chi-square goodness-of-fit test.**

A chi-square goodness-of-fit test is an inferential test that shows whether or not a frequency distribution fits an expected, or claimed, distribution.

Characteristics of the Chi-Square Distribution

A. The chi-square distribution is not symmetric.

B. The shape of the chi-square distribution depends on the degrees of freedom.

C. As the number of degrees of freedom increases, the shape of the chi-square distribution becomes more symmetric.

D. All values of the chi-square distribution are non-negative, $\chi^2 \geq 0$.

The χ^2 Distribution

First, state the null and alternate hypotheses for the goodness-of-fit test. The null hypothesis, H_0, is a statement that the frequency distribution fits a specified distribution. The alternate hypothesis, H_a, is a statement that the frequency distribution does not fit a specified distribution. To calculate the test statistic for the chi-square goodness-of-fit test, you must determine two sets of values, the observed frequencies and the expected frequencies.

The **observed frequency,** O, of a category is the frequency (count or value) of the category that is observed in the sample data.

The **expected frequency,** E, of a category is a calculated frequency (count or value) obtained assuming that the null hypothesis is true. The expected frequency in a category is the product of the sample size, n, and the assumed probability for that category $(E_i = np_i)$.

EXAMPLE:

A candy manufacturer states that their candy packages contain 40% red, 25% green, 15% blue, 10% brown, and 10% yellow candies. In a package of 240 candies, what is the expected number of each color of candy?

For each of the five categories, multiply the sample size, 240, by each respective percentage to get the expected count of each color of candy.

Category	$E_i = np_i$
Red	$(240)(0.40) = 96$
Green	$(240)(0.25) = 60$
Blue	$(240)(0.15) = 36$
Brown	$(240)(0.10) = 24$
Yellow	$(240)(0.10) = 24$

To use the chi-square goodness-of-fit test, the following conditions must be met:

A. All observed data are obtained using a random sample.

B. All the expected frequencies are greater than or equal to 1.

C. No more than 20% of the expected frequencies are less than 5. (Some authors require each expected frequency to be greater than or equal to 5.)

The sampling distribution for the goodness-of-fit test is a chi-square distribution with $k - 1$ degrees of freedom, where k is the number of categories. The test statistic is

$$\chi^2 = \sum \frac{(\text{observed} - \text{expected})^2}{\text{expected}} = \sum \frac{(O - E)^2}{E}$$

where E is the expected frequency (count) of each category and O is the observed frequency (count) of each category.

Null and alternate hypotheses:

H_0:Observed frequencies fit expected frequencies.

H_a:Observed frequencies do not fit expected frequencies.

If the observed and expected frequencies are close in value, then the chi-square test statistic, χ^2, will be close to zero. If there is a large difference between the observed frequencies and the expected frequencies, the difference between O and E will be large, resulting in a large value of χ^2. A large value of χ^2 will result in rejecting the null hypothesis. A small value of χ^2 will result in failing to reject the null hypothesis. The critical value of χ^2, which depends on the significance level and the degrees of freedom, is the value beyond which the null hypothesis is rejected. The chi-square goodness-of-fit test is a right-tail test.

EXAMPLE:

A candy manufacturer states that their candy packages contain 40% red, 25% green, 15% blue, 10% brown, and 10% yellow candies. In a package of 240 candies, you find 82 red, 74 green, 30 blue, 18 brown, and 34 yellow candies. Using a 5% significance level, does the distribution in this package fit the one stated by the manufacturer?

The expected frequencies were calculated in the previous example.

State the null and alternate hypotheses:

H_0:Observed frequencies fit expected frequencies.   Claim

H_a:Observed frequencies do not fit expected frequencies.

Check to make sure the basic conditions of the goodness-of-fit test have been met.

Calculate the test statistic, χ^2:

$$\chi^2 = \sum \frac{(O-E)^2}{E} = \frac{(84-96)^2}{96} + \frac{(74-60)^2}{60} + \frac{(30-36)^2}{36} + \frac{(18-24)^2}{24} + \frac{(34-24)^2}{24} = 11.433$$

Determine the degrees of freedom. Since there are five categories, the expected value of four are free to be chosen and the fifth is a calculated amount. Therefore, the number of degrees of freedom is $k - 1 = 5 - 1 = 4$. This problem specified a 5% significance level, which represents the (right) tail probability. In the table of critical values for χ^2, on the line marked 4 degrees of freedom and in the column marked tail probability 0.05, find the critical value of $\chi^2 = 9.49$. Any value larger than $\chi^2 = 9.49$ lies in the rejection region. Since $11.433 > 9.49$, the data is significant, and you reject the null hypothesis that the distribution in your package fits the distribution stated by the manufacturer.

Consider the critical value of χ^2 if $\alpha = 0.01$. In this case, the critical value of $\chi^2 = 13.28$. So, if the significance level was 1%, you would fail to reject the null hypothesis, and you could support the manufacturer's claimed distribution.

Learn these two techniques on the TI-83/4 calculator. They are time-savers.

[TI-83/4–Enter observed values into L1, expected into L2. Move to the title of L3 and enter (L1-L2)^2/L2 Calculate 1-VarStats L3. Read the chi-square value as sum of x.] [TI-83/4–The p-value may be calculated as follows: Select DIST χ^2 cdf(11.433,E99,4) Display 0.022]

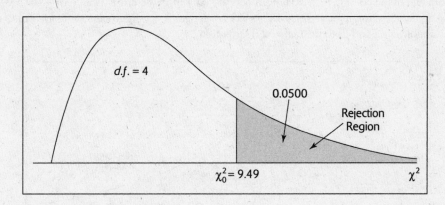

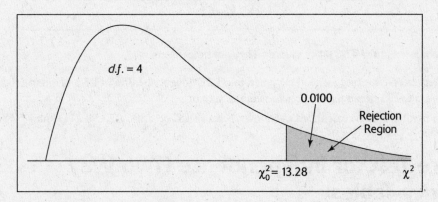

EXAMPLE:

Your school newspaper reported that 62% of students favored a fee increase to help pay for a student lounge, 28% were opposed, and 10% voiced no opinion. You think that these numbers are not accurate, and you take your own random survey. Your survey results included 17 who were in favor, 11 who were opposed, and 4 who voiced no opinion. Do your survey results match those published in the school newspaper? Use a 5% significance level.

State the null and alternate hypotheses:

H_0:Observed frequencies fit expected frequencies.   Claim

H_a:Observed frequencies do not fit expected frequencies.

Check to make sure that the basic conditions of the goodness-of-fit test have been met.

Calculate the expected values and the value of χ^2.

Observed (O)	Expected (E)	O − E	(O − E)²	(O − E)² / E
17	(32)(0.62)=19.84	−2.84	8.07	0.41
11	(32)(0.28)=8.96	2.04	4.16	0.46
4	(32)(0.10)=3.20	0.80	0.64	0.20
$\Sigma O = 32$				$\chi^2 = \Sigma \dfrac{(O-E)^2}{E}$ $= 1.07$

Determine the degrees of freedom. The number of degrees of freedom is $k - 1 = 3 - 1 = 2$. This problem specified a 5% significance level. This represents the (right) tail probability. In the table of critical values for χ^2, on the line marked 2 degrees of freedom and in the column marked tail probability 0.05, find the critical value of $\chi_0^2 = 5.99$. Any value larger than 5.99 lies in the rejection region. Since $1.07 < 5.99$, the data is not significant, and you fail to reject the null hypothesis that the sample is a good fit to the claimed distribution.

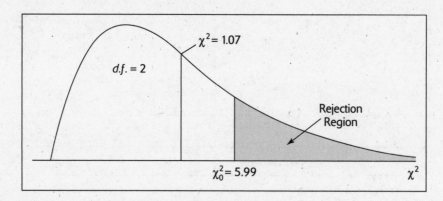

Learn these two techniques of the TI-83/4 calculator. They are time-savers.

[TI-83/4–Enter observed values into L1, expected into L2. Move to the title of L3 and enter (L1-L2)^2/L2 Calculate 1-VarStats L3. Read the chi-square value as sum of x.]

[TI-83/4–The p-value may be calculated as follows: Select DIST χ^2 cdf(1.07,E99,2) Display 0.586]

Chi-Square Test for Independence (Two Way Contingency Tables)

Many tests involve independent variables. There are times that a researcher is not sure whether two variables are dependent or independent. A **chi-square test for independence** is a test that determines whether two variables are dependent or independent within a stated level of significance. In order to perform a chi-square test for independence, organize your data in a contingency table.

An **r x c contingency table**, or **two-way table**, contains the joint observed frequencies of two variables in cells arranged in *r* rows and *c* columns. The number of rows in the table is the number of categories for the *r* variable. The number of columns in the table is the number of categories for the *c* variable. Marginal totals may be included in the table.

The following contingency table shows the observed frequencies—frequencies obtained from a sample—for a class of students. The two variables illustrated are gender and class.

OBSERVED FREQUENCIES

		Class				
		Freshman	**Junior**	**Sophomore**	**Senior**	**TOTAL**
Gender	**Male**	12	17	13	10	52
	Female	5	22	25	14	66
	TOTAL	17	39	38	24	118

This two-way table has two rows, the categories for gender, and four columns, the categories for class. It is a 2×4 contingency table. The marginal totals are the sums of the rows (52 and 66) and columns (17, 39, 38, and 24). The grand total (118), or sample size, is the sum of the row and column totals.

The preceding table shows the joint frequencies of the two variables, gender and class. But are these two variables independent? Is there some relationship between the two variables? To answer these questions, you need to determine how close the values in this table of observed frequencies are to what they should be if the variables are truly independent.

To see whether the variables gender and class are independent requires creating a table of expected frequencies. These are the frequencies of what the observed frequencies should be if the variables gender and class are completely independent. How do you compute the expected values? If the variables in question are independent, the expected value in a cell is the product of the row total for the cell and the column total for the cell, divided by the sample size. That is, the expected value of a cell E_{rc} in row *r* and column *c*, is

$$E_{r,c} = \frac{(\text{sum of row } r)(\text{sum of column } c)}{\text{sample size}}$$

Start with the table of observed frequencies. Create a new table with the same row and column totals. Use the preceding formula to fill in the expected frequencies.

OBSERVED FREQUENCIES

		Class				
		Freshman	**Junior**	**Sophomore**	**Senior**	**TOTAL**
Gender	**Male**	12	17	13	10	52
	Female	5	22	25	14	66
	TOTAL	17	39	38	24	118

EXPECTED FREQUENCIES

		Class				
		Freshman	*Junior*	*Sophomore*	*Senior*	**TOTAL**
Gender	*Male*	7.5	17.2	16.7	10.6	52
	Female	9.5	21.8	21.3	13.4	66
	TOTAL	17	39	38	24	118

To use the chi-square test for independence, the following conditions must be met:

A. All observed data are obtained using a random sample.

B. All the expected frequencies are greater than or equal to 1.

C. No more than 20% of the expected frequencies are less than 5. (Some authors require each expected frequency to be greater than or equal to 5.)

The sampling distribution for the independence test is a chi-square distribution with $(r-1)(c-1)$ degrees of freedom, where r and c are the number of rows and the number of columns, respectively. The test statistic is

$$\chi^2 = \sum \frac{(\text{observed} - \text{expected})^2}{\text{expected}} = \sum \frac{(O-E)^2}{E}$$

where E is the expected frequency (count) of each category and O is the observed frequency (count) of each category.

Null and alternate hypotheses:

H_0: Variables are independent.
H_a: Variables are dependent.

Use the values from the observed and expected frequency tables to fill in this chart.

Observed (O)	Expected (E)	O – E	(O – E)²	(O – E)²/E
12	7.5	4.5	20.3	2.7
17	17.2	−0.2	0.0	0.0
13	16.7	−3.7	13.7	0.8
10	10.6	−0.6	0.4	0.0
5	9.5	−4.5	20.3	2.1
22	21.8	0.2	0.0	0.0
25	21.3	3.7	13.7	0.6
14	13.4	0.6	0.4	0.0
$\Sigma O = 118$				$\chi^2 = \sum \frac{(O-E)^2}{E}$ $= 6.2$

What does a χ^2 of 6.2 mean? For this table, the degrees of freedom is calculated by multiplying $(r-1)(c-1) = (2-1)(4-1) = 3$. In the table of critical values for the chi-square distribution, using the row for 3 degrees of freedom, you see that the tail probability is approximately 0.10 or a 10% significance level. This means that if you are running a 5% significance test, you would fail to reject the null hypothesis and conclude that the variables are independent at a 5% significance level.

If the observed and expected frequencies are close in value, then the chi-square test statistic, χ^2, will be close to zero. If there is a large difference between the observed frequencies and the expected frequencies, the difference between O and E will be large, resulting in a large value of χ^2. A large value of χ^2 will result in rejecting the null hypothesis. A small value of χ^2 will result in failing to reject the null hypothesis. The critical value of χ^2, which depends on the significance level and the degrees of freedom, is the value beyond which the null hypothesis is rejected. The chi-square test for independence is a right-tail test.

EXAMPLE:
Following are results of an experiment using a random sample of patients with an acid-reflux condition. Some received an active ingredient while others received a placebo. The results of the study are shown in the following table. Using $\alpha = .05$, are these variables related?

	Treatment	
	Active Drug	**Placebo**
Result **No Improvement**	108	140
Improvement	70	50

Add marginal totals to the table and calculate the expected frequencies.

OBSERVED FREQUENCIES

		Treatment		
		Active Drug	**Placebo**	**TOTAL**
Result	**No Improvement**	108	140	248
	Improvement	70	50	120
	TOTAL	178	190	368

EXPECTED FREQUENCIES

		Treatment		
		Active Drug	**Placebo**	**TOTAL**
Result	**No Improvement**	120	128	248
	Improvement	58	62	120
	TOTAL	178	190	368

State the null and alternate hypotheses:

H_0: The treatment and result are independent.

H_a: The treatment and result are dependent.

Check to make sure that the basic conditions of the goodness-of-fit test have been met.

Calculate the test statistic, χ^2.

$$\chi^2 = \sum \frac{(O-E)^2}{E} = \frac{(108-120)^2}{120} + \frac{(140-128)^2}{128} + \frac{(70-58)^2}{58} + \frac{(50-62)^2}{62} = 7.13$$

The degrees of freedom for this contingency table is $(2-1)(2-1) = 1$.

The critical value of χ^2 from the table of values for a 5% test is $\chi_0^2 = 3.84$. Your test statistic is greater than the critical value and, therefore, in the rejection region. You reject the null hypothesis, concluding that the treatment and the result are dependent—the drug provided better results than did the placebo. [TI-83/4—Chi-test for independence—Enter the observed in a matrix. Use the χ^2-test under STAT TESTS—Enter appropriate matrices]

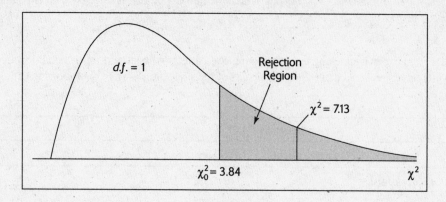

Chi-Square Test for Homogeneity of Proportions

You use a **chi-square test for homogeneity of proportions** to test the claim that several proportions are equal when samples are taken from different populations. After sampling several populations for the same characteristic, you test whether the proportions in each category are the same using the same technique as for chi-square tests for independence. The null and alternate hypotheses are

H_0: The proportions are equal.

H_a: At least one of the proportions is different from the others.

EXAMPLE:

Three machines are producing stencils. Periodically, the machines malfunction. The results of a random sample of stencils produced by each machine are listed in the table by the quantity of stencils with partial punches or no punches at all. Are the proportions for stencils with partial punches or no punches the same for all three machines? Use a 5% test for homogeneity of proportions.

	Machine A	Machine B	Machine C	TOTAL
Partial Punch	70	100	45	215
No Punch	85	160	42	287
TOTAL	155	260	87	402

These values are the observed frequencies. Calculate the expected frequencies.

OBSERVED FREQUENCIES				
	Machine A	Machine B	Machine C	TOTAL
Partial Punch	70	100	45	215
No Punch	85	160	42	287
TOTAL	155	260	87	402

EXPECTED FREQUENCIES			
	Machine A	*Machine B*	*Machine C*	*TOTAL*
Partial Punch	66.4	111.4	37.3	215
No Punch	88.6	148.6	49.7	287
TOTAL	155	260	87	402

$$\chi^2 = \sum \frac{(O-E)^2}{E} = \frac{(70-66.4)^2}{66.4} + \frac{(109-111.4)^2}{111.4} + \frac{(45-37.3)^2}{37.3}$$
$$+ \frac{(85-88.6)^2}{88.6} + \frac{(160-148.6)^2}{148.6} + \frac{(42-49.7)^2}{49.7} = 5.2$$

State the hypotheses:

H_0: The proportions are equal.

H_a: At least one of the proportions is different from the others.

Make sure that the conditions for the test for independence are met. The number of degrees of freedom is $(2-1)(3-1) = 2$. Look up the critical value for χ^2. Using 2 degrees of freedom and 5% significance gives a critical value of $\chi_0^2 = 5.99$. Any value larger than this critical value would be significant. The value of the χ^2 test statistic in this case is 5.2, which is not in the rejection region. Therefore, you fail to reject the null hypothesis. At a 5% significance level, the proportions are the same.

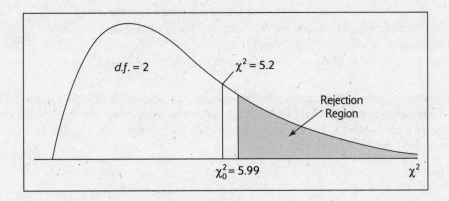

Review Questions and Answers

Multiple Choice Questions

Directions: Solve each of the following problems. Decide which is the best of the choices given.

1. The meaning of "the p-value is statistically significant" is:

    A. The result is probably due to random variation.
    B. The null hypothesis should not be rejected.
    C. The result is probably not due to random variation.
    D. The significance level is less than the p-value.
    E. The claim is true.

2. After completing an experiment, you determine that the p-value of your test data is 0.0842. How should you interpret this finding?

    A. The data exhibits strong statistical significance.

    B. The data exhibits statistical significance.

    C. The data exhibits weak statistical significance.

    D. The data exhibits little or no statistical significance.

    E. You cannot use the p-value without referring to the value of α.

3. Three hundred ninety-five students were each asked to toss a coin 100 times and record the outcomes. The students then were asked to determine the p-value of their results. Four students reported p-values that were less than 0.01. How should you interpret these results?

    A. The 4 students who reported p-values less than 0.01 were not accurate in their calculations.

    B. There is strong statistical evidence that some students are lucky.

    C. The results are as expected. One percent of the students should have results that appear to be beyond what one would expect due to random chance.

    D. The results are surprising. In a sample of only 395, you would expect no p-value less than 0.01.

    E. The results are surprising. In a sample of 395, you would expect 40 of the p-values to be less than 0.01.

4. You manage a casino. Your policy is to use a 2% significance level to suspect cheating. A gambler's play exhibits a p-value of 0.01. What is your reaction to these findings?

    A. The gambler is one-half as likely to cheat as the casino standards.

    B. The gambler is not very lucky, considering the low p-value.

    C. Based on the casino's significance level, the gambler is probably not cheating.

    D. Based on the casino's significance level, the gambler is twice as likely to be cheating than the casino standards allow.

    E. The gambler is 28% more likely to be cheating than the casino standards allow.

5. A researcher is doing a survey for a company involving customer satisfaction with the company's service department. The researcher used $\alpha = 0.01$ for the study. After tabulating the results, the researcher finds that the data produce a p-value of 0.04. The researcher reports that his findings are not significant. What can the researcher do to make the data significant?

    A. Lower α.

    B. Raise α.

    C. Lower the p-value.

    D. Raise the p-value.

    E. You cannot make data more significant.

6. A population is normal with a mean of 80 and a standard deviation of 12. A simple random sample of 50 is selected from the population. The sample mean is 78. What is the p-value if you are conducting a one-tail test?

    A. 0.1190

    B. 0.4325

    C. 0.5675

    D. 0.8810

    E. The p-value cannot be determined without a significance level.

7. Which of the following techniques may be used to test a hypothesis?

    I.   Determine how the p-value relates to α.

    II. Determine whether the assumed value is in a calculated confidence interval.

    III. Determine whether the test statistic is in the rejection region.

    A. III only

    B. I and II

    C. I and III

    D. II and III

    E. I, II, and III

8. You are performing a hypothesis test with $\alpha = 0.05$. You have determined that your data is significant at this level. Which of the following statements are true?

    I.   You may reject H_a at a 10% significance level.

    II. You must support H_0 at a 1% significance level.

    III. You may reject H_0 at a 10% significance level.

    A. III only

    B. I and II

    C. I and III

    D. II and III

    E. None of the statements is true.

9. Which of the following is not a required step in hypothesis testing?

    A. Stating the null and alternate hypotheses.

    B. Verifying the validity of using the test procedure.

    C. Calculating the value of the test statistic.

    D. Stating a conclusion in the context of the given situation.

    E. All the above are required steps in hypothesis testing.

10. You want to test the claim that less than 60% of the cars in the parking lot at your college are foreign. You collect a random sample of 300 cars and find that 161 are foreign. What is the z-score and the p-value for this test?

    A. −2.23, 0.013

    B. −1.71, 0.044

    C. −1.40, 0.081

    D. 1.71, 0.044

    E. 2.23, 0.013

11. Which of the following conditions are required for testing a population proportion?

    I.   The sample should be small relative to the population.

    II. Both $np \geq 5$ and $n(1-p) \geq 5$.

    III. Sample size should be at least 30.

    IV. The population is approximately normal.

    A. I and II

    B. I and III

    C. II and III

    D. II and IV

    E. III and IV

12. Which of the following are true statements?

   I.   A small p-value implies weak evidence against the null hypothesis.

   II. The p-value is the probability that the null hypothesis is true.

   III. To reject the null hypothesis, it must be false.

   A. I only

   B. II only

   C. III only

   D. Two of the above are true statements.

   E. None of the above is a true statement.

13. A study of islands in the South Pacific claimed that the average daytime high temperature year-round is 81 degrees with a standard deviation of 3 degrees. To test this claim, you will take a random sample of 50 daily high temperatures from records listing temperatures over the past 5 year period. If the average is not within 1 degree of the claimed temperature, you will reject the claim. What is the probability that you will make a type I error?

   A. $0.00 < \alpha < 0.01$

   B. $0.01 < \alpha < 0.02$

   C. $0.02 < \alpha < 0.03$

   D. $0.03 < \alpha < 0.04$

   E. $0.04 < \alpha < 0.05$

14. One brand of vacuum cleaner claims to have the same annual repair costs as its competitor. You plan a hypothesis test to determine the validity of the claim. If you sample the repair costs of 40 of each type of vacuum and find a difference in repair costs to be more than \$5, you plan on rejecting the claim that the repair costs are the same. If the standard deviation of repair costs for each brand is \$12, what is the probability that you reject the claim when it is really true?

   A. 0.0204

   B. 0.0408

   C. 0.0628

   D. 0.0844

   E. Not enough information is provided to answer the question.

15. A survey about the proportion of people who smoke found that of 3500 Californians, 21.6% smoked and of 3500 New Yorkers, 24.1% smoked. At $\alpha = 0.01$, can you conclude that the percentage of people who smoke is the same in both states?

   A. Yes, because the p-value < 0.01.

   B. Yes, because the p-value > 0.01.

   C. Yes, because you can reject the null hypothesis.

   D. No, because the p-value < 0.01.

   E. No, because the p-value > 0.01.

16. A casino suspects that a die it has been using in a casino game may not be fair. The die is rolled 300 times. The table that follows shows the number of times each side landed face up. Test the claim, at a 10% significance level, that the die is fair. What is the value of the test statistic and what is your conclusion?

Number	1	2	3	4	5	6
Frequency	42	57	54	41	62	44

    A. 7.8, fail to reject the null hypothesis
    B. 7.8, reject the null hypothesis
    C. 9.8, fail to reject the null hypothesis
    D. 9.8, reject the null hypothesis
    E. 13.6, reject the null hypothesis

17. A survey was taken to determine whether political party affiliation is related to voters' feelings about a school bond issue. The following table shows the results of a survey of 800 voters. Is there evidence of a relationship between political party affiliation and opinion at a 5% significance level?

Opinion	Republican	Democrat	Independent
In Favor	160	85	70
Opposed	130	75	90
No Opinion	110	40	40

    A. Yes, but not at 10%.
    B. Yes, but not at 1%.
    C. No, but there is at 10%.
    D. No, but there is at 1%.
    E. Relationships do not show up at a 5% significance level.

Multiple Choice Answers

    1. C. Data is said to be significant if the significance level is greater than the p-value. A given p-value may be statistically significant in one case, but not in another; it depends on the significance level stated in the problem.

    2. C. Since you are not given a significance level to compare against, use the following guidelines. A p-value less than 0.01 indicates strong statistical significance. A p-value between 0.01 and 0.05 indicates moderate statistical significance. A p-value between 0.05 and 0.10 indicates weak statistical significance. A p-value greater than 0.10 indicates little or no real statistical significance.

    3. C. If you perform a statistical test 100 times at a 1% level of significance, you would expect that 1%, or 1, of your trials will produce data more extreme than the critical value. This experiment was performed approximately 400 times. Having four trials beyond the critical value is expected at a 1% significance level.

    4. D. A 2% significance level implies that you expect 2% of the data to be more extreme than the critical value. A p-value representing a 1% significance level implies only 1% of the data will be more extreme. Since 1% is half of 2%, the gambler is twice as likely to be cheating than the casino standards allow.

    5. E. Data either is or is not significant. Changing the requirements for rejecting a null hypothesis may change the results of the hypothesis test, but does not change the significance of the data.

    6. A. In this problem you are given the population standard deviation to be used in the formula for the z-score:
$$z = \frac{\bar{x} - \mu}{\frac{\sigma}{\sqrt{n}}} = \frac{82 - 80}{\frac{12}{\sqrt{50}}} = 1.18.$$ Look up the z-score of -1.18 in the table of standard normal probabilities (it is easier

than subtracting from 1) to obtain 0.1190. This is the probability of getting a value greater than $z = 1.18$ by chance alone. [TI-83/4–STAT TESTS Z-Test μ0:80 σ:12 x̄:82 n:50 μ > μ₀ Calculate]

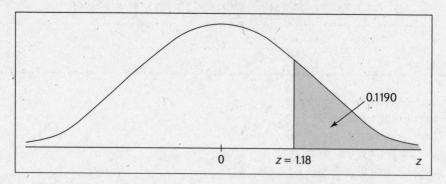

7. E. All three represent suitable techniques to test a hypothesis. Choice II should be used in a two-tail test since, in that case, the significance level α is the complement of the confidence level c.

8. A. Choice I is false since you do not reject claims in the alternate hypothesis. Choice II is false since you do not support claims in the null hypothesis. Choice III is true because data significant at a 5% level will be significant at any level above 5%.

9. E. All four steps, A–D, are required for a complete answer when testing a hypothesis.

10. A. First verify that the normal distribution is appropriate for this problem. Make sure that basic conditions are met: $np > 5$, $n(1 - p) > 5$.

Calculate $\hat{p}$ and the z-score:

$$\hat{p} = \frac{x}{n} = \frac{161}{300} = 0.537 \qquad z = \frac{\hat{p} - p}{\sqrt{\dfrac{p(1-p)}{n}}} = \frac{0.537 - 0.60}{\sqrt{\dfrac{(0.6)(0.4)}{300}}} = -2.23$$

This yields a p-value of 0.0129. The correct answer choice is A. [TI-83/4–STAT CALC 1-PropZTest p0:0.6 x:161 n:300 prop < p0 Calculate]

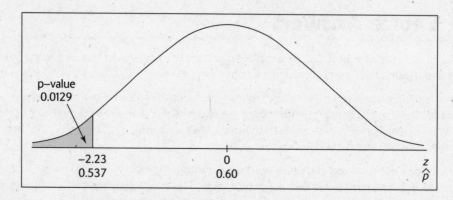

11. A. Choices I and II are required. Choice III is not required since the test is for proportions, not means. Choice IV is not required if the sample size is large enough.

12. E. Choice I is false since a small p-value implies strong evidence against the null hypothesis. Choice II is false since the p-value is the probability of making a type I error. Choice III is false since you may make an error and reject the null hypothesis even if it is true.

13. B. This is a two-sided test. You want to determine α, the probability of making a type I error.

First state the hypotheses:

$H_0: \mu = 81$

$H_a: \mu \neq 81$

This is a large sample, so using the normal distribution is appropriate. Calculate the z-score:

$$z = \frac{\bar{x} - \mu}{\frac{s}{\sqrt{n}}} = \frac{80 - 81}{\frac{3}{\sqrt{50}}} = -2.36$$

The probability to the left of this z-score represents one half of α. Look up −2.36 in the table of standard normal probabilities. Multiply by 2. This gives $\alpha = (2)(0.0091) = 0.0182$. This is the required probability. [TI-83/4–STAT TESTS Z-Test $\mu 0{:}81$ $\sigma{:}3$ $\bar{x}{:}80$ $n{:}50$ $\mu = \mu_0$ Calculate]

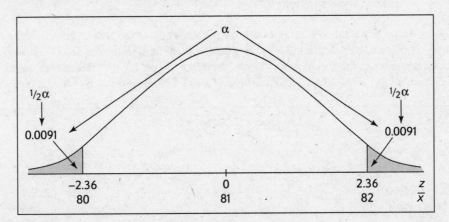

14. C. This is a two-sample difference test of the means. Even though the test is two-sided, you can calculate the z-score on each side separately.

First state the hypotheses:

$H_0: \mu_1 - \mu_2 = 0$

$H_a: \mu_1 - \mu_2 \neq 0$

Both samples are large, so using the normal distribution is appropriate. Calculate the z-score:

$$z = \frac{\bar{x}_1 - \bar{x}_2}{\sqrt{\frac{\sigma_1^2}{n_1} + \frac{\sigma_2^2}{n_2}}} = \frac{-5}{\sqrt{\frac{12^2}{40} + \frac{12^2}{40}}} = -1.86$$

Look up this value in the table of standard normal probabilities. Multiply by two giving $\alpha = 2(0.0314) = 0.0628$. [TI-83/4–STAT TESTS 2-SampZTest $\sigma 1{:}12$ $\sigma 2{:}12$ $\bar{x}1{:}0$ $n1{:}40$ $\bar{x}2{:}5$ $n2{:}40$ $\mu \neq \mu_0$ Calculate]

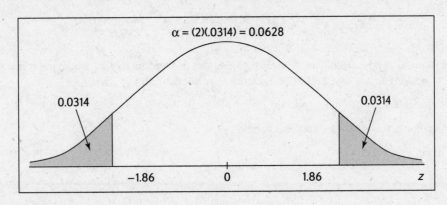

15. B. The claim is that the percentage of smokers in the two states is the same. Equality is always stated in the null hypothesis. Choice C is not correct since rejecting the null hypothesis would reject the claim.

State the null and alternate hypotheses.

$H_0: p_1 - p_2 = 0$

$H_a: p_1 - p_2 \neq 0$

Calculate the z-score:

$$z = \frac{\hat{p}_1 - \hat{p}_2}{\sqrt{\dfrac{\hat{p}_1\left(1 - \hat{p}_1\right)}{n_1} + \dfrac{\hat{p}_2\left(1 - \hat{p}_2\right)}{n_2}}} = \frac{0.216 - 0.241}{\sqrt{\dfrac{(0.216)(0.784)}{3500} + \dfrac{(0.241)(0.759)}{3500}}} = -2.49$$

Determine the p-value. Since this is a two-tail test, the p-value is twice the area to the left of the z-score. The p-value = (2)(0.0064) = 0.0128. Since the p-value is greater than the significance level α, you do not have sufficient evidence to reject the null hypothesis. You, therefore, do not have evidence to reject the claim that the proportions are equal. [TI-83/4–STAT TESTS 2-PropZTest x1:756 n1:3500 x2:844 n2:3500 p1 ≠ p2 Calculate]

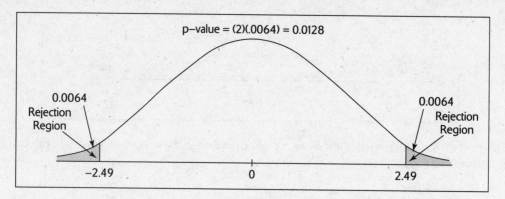

p–value = (2)(.0064) = 0.0128

0.0064
Rejection
Region

0.0064
Rejection
Region

−2.49   0   2.49

16. A. This is a chi-square goodness-of-fit test. If the die is fair, each value would have an equal chance of occurring. Out of 300 rolls, you would expect that each number would occur 50 times. These are the expected values. State the hypotheses.

H_0: The observed values fit the expected values.

H_a: The observed values do not fit the expected values.

Calculate the chi-square statistic:

$$\chi^2 = \sum \frac{(O - E)^2}{E} = \frac{(42 - 50)^2}{50} + \frac{(57 - 50)^2}{50} + \frac{(54 - 50)^2}{50}$$
$$+ \frac{(41 - 50)^2}{50} + \frac{(62 - 50)^2}{50} + \frac{(44 - 50)^2}{50} = 7.8$$

The critical value for a 10% significance level and 5 degrees of freedom is 9.24. Since the test statistic is less than the critical value, you do not have sufficient evidence to reject the null hypothesis.

17. B. This is a chi-square test for independence.

Add row and column totals and determine expected values.

OBSERVED VALUES

Opinion	Republican	Democrat	Independent	TOTAL
In Favor	160	85	70	315
Opposed	130	75	90	295
No Opinion	110	40	40	190
TOTAL	400	200	200	800

EXPECTED VALUES

Opinion	Republican	Democrat	Independent	TOTAL
In Favor	157.5	78.75	78.75	315
Opposed	147.5	73.75	73.75	295
No Opinion	95	47.5	47.5	190
TOTAL	400	200	200	800

Determine the test statistic:

$$\chi^2 = \sum \frac{(O-E)^2}{E} = \frac{(160-157.5)^2}{157.5} + \frac{(85-78.75)^2}{78.75} + \frac{(70-78.75)^2}{78.75}$$
$$+ \frac{(130-147.5)^2}{147.5} + \frac{(75-73.75)^2}{73.75} + \frac{(90-73.75)^2}{73.75}$$
$$+ \frac{(110-95)^2}{95} + \frac{(40-47.5)^2}{47.5} + \frac{(40-47.5)^2}{47.5} = 11.92$$

The critical value for a 5% significance level and 4 degrees of freedom is 9.49. Since the test statistic is greater than the critical value, you fall in the rejection region and have sufficient evidence to reject the null hypothesis. The critical value for a 1% test is 13.28. You do not have enough evidence to reject the null hypothesis at a 1% level. [TI-83/4–For the chi-square test for independence: Enter the observed values in a 3×3 matrix. Select STAT TESTS χ^2-Test. The expected values appear in the second matrix.]

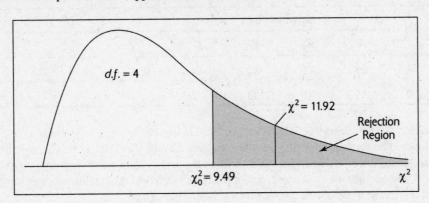

293

Free-Response Questions

Directions: Show all work. Indicate clearly the methods you use. You will be graded on method as well as accuracy.

1. Logan is doing a project for his local city planning department in which he tests the claim that the city's housing project contains family units of average size. A random sample of 80 homes in the project shows a sample mean of 3.4 people per family unit with a sample standard deviation of 1.4 people. Construct a hypothesis test to determine whether the average size of family units in the housing project is different from the national average of 3.8. Use $\alpha = 0.01$.

2. To test the claim that a new special coating helps prevent cavities, 40 young children had their teeth cleaned and coated with the coating, and another 31 young children had their teeth cleaned but received no special coating. One year later, the children whose teeth were given the special coating had an average of 1.6 cavities with a sample standard deviation of 0.9. The children who received no coating had an average of 2.2 cavities with a sample standard deviation of 1.2. Is the claim supported at the 1% level? What is the p-value, and what does it tell you?

3. A random sample of 512 union carpenters showed that 38 had been laid off at least once in the last three years. An independent random sample of 654 nonunion carpenters showed that 67 had been laid off at least once in the last three years. Does this data indicate that the proportion of carpenters who have experienced recent layoffs is greater for the nonunion members than for the union members? Use a 5% significance level. What is the significance of the p-value?

4. Each semester at a Midwestern college, students rate their professors on a scale from 0 to 5. Data from the last 10 years is tabulated with the following results.

			Student Rating			
	0	1	2	3	4	5
# of Students	38	330	832	1382	950	308

The college president had some knowledge about statistics and commented that the distribution seemed to follow a binomial distribution. Since the highest value occurred for a ranking of 3, the president guessed that the value of p is probably 0.6. Use a goodness-of-fit test to test this claim at a 5% significance level.

5. The chi-square test of homogeneity of proportions and the chi-square test for independence use similar techniques. Using the following table, calculate the χ^2 statistic and interpret in the context of each kind of test.

		Variable I			
		W	X	Y	Z
Variable II	A	25	25	30	40
	B	35	75	50	120

6. A random sample of 32 students was selected to take part in a study on the effectiveness of a lecture about test-taking techniques. The students were given similar tests before and after the lecture. Their scores on both tests are listed in the following table. What is your opinion about the results? Perform two types of hypothesis tests. First, perform a two-sample difference test. Next, perform a one-sample test on the differences. Compare the results and comment on the use of these two types of tests for this kind of data.

Student															
1	**2**	**3**	**4**	**5**	**6**	**7**	**8**	**9**	**10**	**11**	**12**	**13**	**14**	**15**	**16**
Before Lecture 62	90	84	69	60	85	82	68	85	89	78	81	63	72	77	83
After Lecture 63	95	90	68	60	89	80	65	81	95	86	82	63	72	83	88

Student															
17	**18**	**19**	**20**	**21**	**22**	**23**	**24**	**25**	**26**	**27**	**28**	**29**	**30**	**31**	**32**
Before Lecture 70	71	86	83	62	64	71	83	72	79	74	73	69	70	60	70
After Lecture 80	71	93	86	68	60	72	89	79	89	84	75	73	67	55	66

Free-Response Answers

1. This is a one-sample test of a mean using a large sample.

   First state the hypotheses:

   $H_0: \mu = 3.8$

   $H_a: \mu \neq 3.8$ Claim

   This is a large sample, so using the normal distribution is appropriate. Calculate the z-score:

   $$z = \frac{\bar{x} - \mu}{\frac{s}{\sqrt{n}}} = \frac{3.4 - 3.8}{\frac{1.4}{\sqrt{80}}} = -2.555$$

   Since this is a two-sided test, the area to the left of the z-score must be doubled to obtain the p-value of (2)(0.0053) = 0.0106. Although the data is very significant, this z-score is not quite in the rejection region, which begins at –2.576. It is not significant enough to reject at the 1% level of significance. Clearly, it is significant enough to reject the null hypothesis at the 5% level. At a 1% significance level you fail to reject the null hypothesis that the average number of people per housing unit is equal to 3.8. You cannot support the claim that the average in not equal to 3.8.

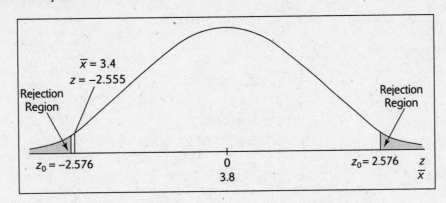

2. This is a two-sample test of the difference of two means. The samples are independent, and the sample sizes are large, so this is the appropriate test to use.

First state the hypotheses:

$H_0: \mu_1 - \mu_2 \geq 0$

$H_a: \mu_1 - \mu_2 < 0$

Calculate the z-score:

$$z = \frac{(\bar{x}_1 - \bar{x}_2) - (\mu_1 - \mu_2)}{\sqrt{\frac{s_1^2}{n_1} + \frac{s_2^2}{n_2}}} = \frac{(1.6 - 2.2) - 0}{\sqrt{\frac{0.9^2}{40} + \frac{1.2^2}{31}}} = -2.323$$

This value is very close to the critical value of the z-score for 1%, which is −2.326. Although it is close, it does not fall in the rejection region. You fail to reject (barely) the null hypothesis. This data is very significant. The p-value is the probability of obtaining a value as extreme or more extreme due to chance alone. The p-value of 0.0102 is so close to $\alpha = 0.01$ that the data should be looked at again. The experiment might be repeated with a new sample to verify the significance at this level. Under the given conditions, you must fail to reject the null hypothesis. You cannot support the claim at the 1% level.

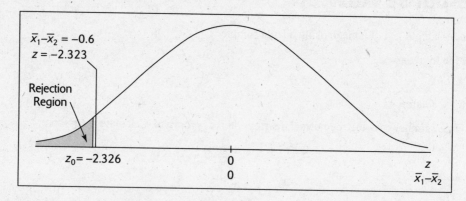

3. This is a two-sample test for a difference of two proportions.

The normal distribution is appropriate since $n_1 p_1 \geq 5$, $n_2 p_2 \geq 5$, $n_1(1 - p_1) \geq 5$, and $n_2(1 - p_2) \geq 5$. Some authors require 10 instead of 5, but clearly the products are greater than 10 also.

First state the hypotheses:

$H_0: p_1 - p_2 \geq 0$

$H_a: p_1 - p_2 < 0$

Calculate the sample proportion:

$$\hat{p}_1 = \frac{x_1}{n_1} = \frac{38}{512} = 0.074$$

$$\hat{p}_2 = \frac{x_2}{n_2} = \frac{67}{654} = 0.102$$

$$\hat{p} = \frac{x_1 + x_2}{n_1 + n_2} = \frac{38 + 67}{512 + 654} = 0.090$$

Calculate the z-score:

$$z = \frac{(\hat{p}_1 - \hat{p}_2) - (p_1 - p_2)}{\sqrt{\hat{p}(1 - \hat{p})\left(\frac{1}{n_1} + \frac{1}{n_2}\right)}} = \frac{(0.074 - 0.102) - 0}{\sqrt{(0.09)(0.91)\left(\frac{1}{512} + \frac{1}{654}\right)}} = -1.66$$

The critical value of the z-score for a 5% significance level is −1.645. The value of −1.66 is in the rejection region (barely) and, therefore, you may reject the null hypothesis at the 5% level of significance. Look up the z-score of −1.66 to obtain the p-value of 0.0486. Thus, the p-value < α.

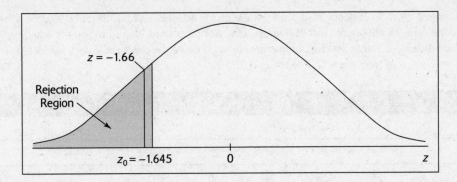

4. A goodness-of-fit test determines how good one distribution "fits" another distribution. The sum of the observed values is the sample size.

$$\Sigma O = 38 + 330 + 832 + 1382 + 950 + 308 = 3840$$

The binomial probabilities for the six expected values may be found using the binomial formula, $P(x) = \binom{n}{x} p^x (1-p)^{n-x}$, where $n = 5$, $p = 0.6$, and $x = 0, 1, 2, 3, 4,$ and 5. The TI-83/4 calculator may also be used to determine these probabilities. Select DISTR binompdf(5, 0.6), and the result will be all six probabilities. Multiply these by the sample size of 3840. This may be done in one step by selecting binompdf(5, 0.6)*3840. Calculate the required chi-square statistic.

$$\chi^2 = \Sigma \frac{(O-E)^2}{E} = \frac{(38-39)^2}{39} + \frac{(330-295)^2}{295} + \frac{(832-885)^2}{885}$$
$$+ \frac{(1382-1327)^2}{1327} + \frac{(950-995)^2}{995} + \frac{(308-299)^2}{299} = 11.9$$

This value of the chi-square statistic may be found using the TI-83/4 directly. Enter the six observed values into L1. Select DISTR binompdf(5,0.6)*3840 STO L2. This places the expected values in L2. Select STAT EDIT and in the title of L3 enter (L1-L2)^2/L2. Select STAT CALC 1-VarsStats L3. Read the value of the chi-square statistic as $\Sigma x = 11.9$.

State the hypotheses:

H_0: The observed values fit a binomial distribution.

H_a: The observed values do not fit a binomial distribution.

The value of each cell is at least 5, so the chi-square test may be used. Using 5 degrees of freedom, the critical value for a 5% significance level is 11.07. The calculated chi-square value of 11.9 is greater than 11.07. This means that at a 5% significance level, you may reject the null hypothesis. You fail to reject the null hypothesis at the 1% level.

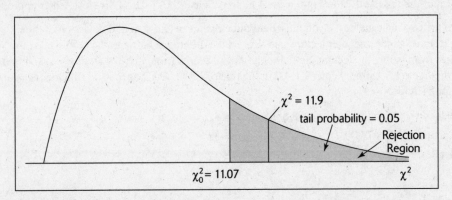

5. A chi-square test for independence is used to test the independence of two different categorical variables using the same population. A chi-square test of homogeneity of proportions is used to test the equality of proportions of one categorical variable across several populations. First compute the expected values and determine the chi-square statistic. The degrees of freedom is $(r-1)(c-1) = 3$.

Observed Variables

		Variable I				
		W	X	Y	Z	Total
	A	25	25	30	40	120
Variable II	B	35	75	50	120	280
	Total	60	100	80	160	400

Expected Variables

		Variable I				
		W	X	Y	Z	Total
	A	18	30	24	48	120
Variable II	B	42	70	56	112	280
	Total	60	100	80	160	400

$$\chi^2 = \sum \frac{(O-E)^2}{E} = \frac{(25-18)^2}{18} + \frac{(25-30)^2}{30} + \frac{(30-24)^2}{24} + \frac{(40-48)^2}{48}$$
$$+ \frac{(35-42)^2}{42} + \frac{(75-70)^2}{70} + \frac{(50-56)^2}{56} + \frac{(120-112)^2}{112} = 9.1$$

In a chi-square test for independence, you are testing the independence of variable I and variable II. You can conclude that the data is significant at the 5% level since the calculated chi-square statistic of 9.1 is greater than the critical value of 7.8. Thus, the variables are dependent. The data is not significant at the 1% level since 9.1 is less than the critical value of 11.3.

In a chi-square test for homogeneity of proportions, you test the equality of the proportion of variable II across the four populations of variable I. You conclude that at a 5% significance level, at least one of the proportions is different than the other three. At a 1% significance level, you cannot conclude that at least one of the proportions is different than the other three.

[TI-83/4–Enter the observed values into a 2×4 matrix. Select STAT TESTS χ^2-test. Enter appropriate matrices.]

6. To perform the two indicated tests, you must determine the mean and standard deviation of three samples of data: the before lecture sample, the after lecture sample, and the difference between the before and after samples. Enter the 32 scores from before the lecture into L1; enter the 32 scores from after the lecture into L2; find the differences; and place them into L3. (Simply enter L1–L2 in the title of L3.) Use 1-Var Stats to find the mean and standard deviation for each list.

Before the lecture: $\bar{x}_b = 75.53$ $s_b = 8.85$ $n_b = 32$

After the lecture: $\bar{x}_a = 77.09$ $s_a = 11.39$ $n_a = 32$

Difference (B –A): $\bar{x}_d = -2.56$ $s_d = 4.49$ $n_d = 32$

Since the lecture is designed to help students improve their scores, the claim is that the difference between before and after scores will be negative.

State the hypotheses:

$H_0: \mu_b - \mu_a \geq 0$

$H_a: \mu_b - \mu_a < 0$ Claim

Determine the z-score for the two-sample difference test between the before and after scores.

$$z_{b-a} = \frac{(\bar{x}_b - \bar{x}_a) - (\mu_b - \mu_a)}{\sqrt{\frac{s_b^2}{n_b} + \frac{s_a^2}{n_a}}} = \frac{(74.53 - 77.09) - 0}{\sqrt{\frac{8.85^2}{32} + \frac{11.39^2}{32}}} = -1.00$$

This z-score corresponds to a p-value of 0.1587. This data is significant only down to a 15.87% level. This means you fail to reject the null hypothesis at all significance levels less than 15.87%. Using this difference test would indicate that the lecture does not help students improve their scores.

Determine the z-score for a one-sample test on the differences between the before and after scores.

$$z_d = \frac{\mu_d - 0}{\frac{s_d}{\sqrt{n_d}}} = \frac{-2.56}{\frac{4.49}{\sqrt{32}}} = -3.23$$

This z-score corresponds to a p-value of 0.0006. This data is significant all the way down to a 0.06% level. This is very significant data. This means you reject the null hypothesis at all levels down to 0.06%. Using a significance test on the differences would indicate that the lecture is very helpful to students.

Why is there a difference in the conclusions for the two tests? The answer is simple. The before-and-after samples are dependent. They represent the same sample of students. To use a difference test, the samples must be independent. The correct test to use is the one-sample test on the differences where the lecture was shown to be very helpful for students.

Statistical Inference: Special Case of Normally Distributed Data

Sample size plays a significant role in estimation and inference. As sample size increases, so does the accuracy of your inferences. Under ideal conditions, all samples would be very large. Due to cost, time, or availability constraints, obtaining large samples may not be possible. Officials of a company that is exploring for oil by digging test wells may have data from only a handful of test sites. Researchers may be looking at eggs of an endangered species of bird where they can obtain only a small sample for study. Health officials who are studying the effects of a medication may only have a few subjects on which to base their inferences.

t-Distribution

For samples of size 30 or larger, you use the Central Limit Theorem to justify using the sample standard deviation, *s*, as a suitable approximation to the population standard deviation, σ. When sample sizes are less than 30, the normal distribution should not be used since *s* is not a suitable substitute for σ. To avoid making this error, use a distribution called **Student's t-distribution** instead of the normal distribution when your samples are small. The **t-distribution** was formulated by William Gosset in 1908. He was a statistician for the Guinness Brewing Company in Dublin. He needed to make inferences about barley varieties using small samples. He recognized the problem of substituting the sample standard deviation for the population standard deviation with small samples and developed a distribution based on small sample sizes.

The *t*-distribution is defined by

$$t = \frac{\bar{x} - \mu}{\frac{s}{\sqrt{n}}}$$

where $\bar{x}$ is the mean of a random sample of *n* repeated measurements, μ is the population mean, and *s* is the sample standard deviation. This distribution looks just like the one for

$$z = \frac{\bar{x} - \mu}{\frac{\sigma}{\sqrt{n}}}$$

except that the σ is used in place of *s*.

The methods of inference using the normal distribution with large samples may still be applied to small samples; instead of using the normal distribution, however, you will use the *t*-distribution. If repeated samples of size *n* are drawn from a population, you get a set of *t* values that form the *t*-distribution with a slightly different shape for each value of *n*.

The shape of the *t*-distribution depends only on *n* provided that the population from which the sample is drawn is normal or approximately normal. Therefore, whenever the *t*-distribution is used, it is assumed that the distribution of the *x* variable is normal.

In summary, to use the *t*-distribution, the following conditions must be met:

The population from which we draw the sample must be approximately normal, or the sample must be at least 30.

The sample drawn from the population must be a simple random sample.

The table of probabilities for the *t*-distribution is arranged in rows corresponding to a number called the degrees of freedom. You use *d.f.* as an abbreviation for degrees of freedom. The distribution is different for each value of the sample size, *n*. The degrees of freedom of a distribution is one less than the sample size. That is, *d.f.* = *n* –1.

As the sample size increases, the t-distribution approaches the normal distribution. The normal distribution and the t-distribution are almost identical when the sample size exceeds 30. Many tables for the t-distribution only list degrees of freedom to 29. Some extend the table to more than 30. The table used for the AP Statistics Test, Table B in the appendix, actually lists $d.f.$ up to 1000.

The following figure shows how the shape of the t-distribution changes as the degrees of freedom decreases.

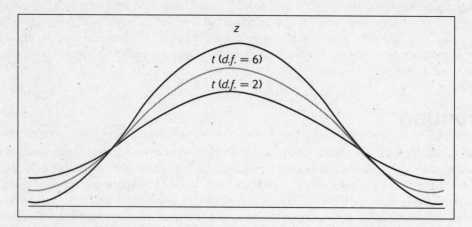

Using the TI-83/4 calculator, you can graph the t-distribution for different degrees of freedom. A graph of the normal distribution would be approximately the same as graphing the t-distribution using 30 degrees of freedom.

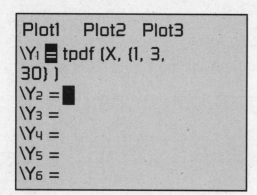 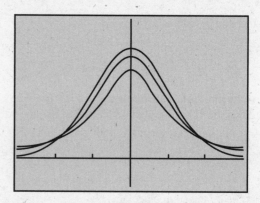

For a given critical value of t, the tail area, and, therefore, the probability, is greater than the corresponding tail area for the z distribution.

EXAMPLE:

Compare the approximate tail probabilities for critical value of $z_0 = 2.3$ and $t_0 = 2.3$ with 3 degrees of freedom.

The critical value of $z_0 = 2.3$ corresponds to a tail probability of approximately 0.01. The critical value of $t_0 = 2.3$ with 3 degrees of freedom corresponds to a tail probability of approximately 0.05. As the critical values increase, the t-distribution does not approach the horizontal axis as rapidly as does the normal distribution.

The table of values for the t-distribution (Table B) only lists critical values for a few specific tail probabilities. Therefore, when using this table to look up tail probabilities when you are given critical values, only a range of tail probabilities can be determined. Note the difference in format between the z-table and the t-table. In the z-table, probabilities correspond to the area to the left of the z-value. In the t-table, probabilities correspond to the area to the right of the t-value. (The terms z-score and z-value are interchangeable, and the term t-value refers to a value in the t-table.)

EXAMPLE:

What is the tail probability for the t-distribution using 15 degrees of freedom and a critical value of $t_0 = 1.45$?

Using the t-table and looking at the row marked $d.f. = 15$, you see that the tail probability that corresponds to a critical value of 1.45 is between 0.05 and 0.10. [Using the TI-83/4 calculator, select DISTR tcdf(lowerbound,upperbound,df)=tcdf(1.45,E99,15) = 0.0838.]

EXAMPLE:

Using a sample size of 15, what is the t-value that corresponds to tail probabilities of 0.01, 0.05, and 0.10?

A sample size of 15 corresponds to 14 degrees of freedom. Using the line marked 14 degrees of freedom and the column corresponding to a tail probability of 0.01 gives a t-value of 2.624. Similarly the t-values for probabilities of 0.05 and 0.10 are $t = 1.761$ and $t = 1.345$, respectively.

The t-distribution is the distribution of choice with small sample sizes. Most researchers do not think about using the t-distribution when sample sizes are large. They automatically use the normal distribution. In reality, you usually do not know the value of σ. Therefore, the t-distribution should be used in many cases even when the sample size is large. The problem, of course, is accuracy. The table of t-values is very limited. Each row of the table corresponds to an entire distribution of values, and you are forced to make rough approximations when it comes to probabilities. Results like "It is between 5% and 10%" are common. The introduction of technology tools, like the TI-83/4, make using the t-distribution more user-friendly and accurate.

Whenever you want to use a statistical procedure, you must make sure that all the conditions for its use are met. The conditions for using the t-distribution have been refined over the years. Most statisticians agree on the following basic conditions based on sample size:

Sample Size	Conditions Required to Use the t-Distribution
$n \leq 15$	The sample should not contain outliers and should not exhibit skewness; or, the population should be normal or very close to normal.
$15 < n < 40$	The sample should not contain outliers and should exhibit little skewness; or, the population should be normal or very close to normal.
$n \geq 40$	(No restrictions are placed on the sample or population.)

Single Sample t-Procedures

The t-distribution should be used for both confidence intervals and hypothesis testing when the sample size is small.

EXAMPLE:

The mean length of a random sample of 12 trout from Lake Catchmore is $\bar{x} = 14.3$ inches with a standard deviation of $s = 1.5$ inches. Compute a 90% confidence interval for the length of all trout in Lake Catchmore.

Since the sample size is small, and the population standard deviation is not known, the t-distribution is appropriate if there are no outliers in the sample and the sample is not skewed. In the t-table, look up the critical t-value in the row marked $d.f. = n - 1 = 11$ degrees of freedom and the column marked (at the bottom of the column) 90% confidence. The error of the estimate is $E = t_c \dfrac{s}{\sqrt{n}} = 1.796 \dfrac{1.5}{\sqrt{12}} = 0.778$. The confidence interval is $\bar{x} \pm E = 14.3 \pm 0.778 = (13.5, 15.1)$.

Therefore, you are 90% confident that the mean length of all the trout is between 13.5 inches and 15.1 inches. [TI-83/4—Select STAT TESTS TInterval Inpt: Stats $\bar{x}$:14.3 sx:1.5 n:12 C-Level: 0.90 Calculate Display (13.5, 15.1)]

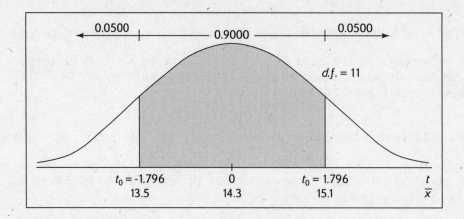

EXAMPLE:

Chuck works as a waiter at a fancy restaurant and has been asked by his boss to determine his average tip when he serves a party of 10. Chuck rarely gets to serve that many people in one group, but manages to collect a sample of size 6. If the six tips were $24.00, $32.50, $40.00, $28.50, $35.00, and $26.00, what would be a 95% confidence interval for his average tip for a party of 10?

Enter the six values into a list and compute the sample mean and standard deviation of $\bar{x} = \$31.00$ and $s = \$5.99$. In the t-table, look up the critical t-value in the row marked $d.f. = n - 1 = 5$ degrees of freedom and the column marked (at the bottom of the column) 95% confidence. The error of the estimate is $E = t_c \frac{s}{\sqrt{n}} = 2.571 \frac{5.99}{\sqrt{6}} = 6.29$. The confidence interval is $\bar{x} \pm E = \$31.00 \pm \$6.29 = (\$24.71, \$37.29)$. Therefore, he can be 95% confident that his average tip is between $24.71 and $37.29. [TI-83/4 – Select STAT TESTS TInterval Inpt: Stats $\bar{x}$:31.00 sx:5.99 n:6 C-Level: 0.95 Calculate Display (24.71, 37.29) or Select STAT TESTS TInterval Inpt: Data Choose appropriate list and confidence interval]

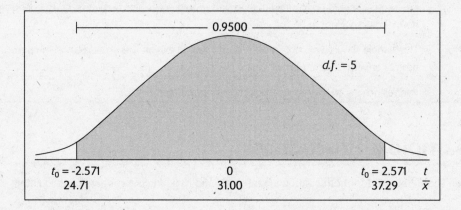

EXAMPLE:

You work for an appliance repair store and have read in a service bulletin that the average repair cost of a certain model of television is not more than $75. You think it is more than that. You find that a random sample of 7 of this model of television has an average repair cost of $89.45 with a standard deviation of 13.55. Test your claim that the average cost is more than $75 at a 5% level of significance.

The hypotheses are

$$H_0: \mu \leq 75$$

$$H_a: \mu > 75$$

Determine the t-score. Since this is a 5% test, in the t-table, use the column marked 0.05 and the row marked $d.f. = n - 1 = 6$ to get a critical value of 1.943. At this point, there are three ways to look at the problem.

Rejection Region Method

Determine the t-score from your sample: $t = \dfrac{\bar{x} - \mu}{\frac{s}{\sqrt{n}}} = \dfrac{89.45 - 75}{\frac{13.55}{\sqrt{7}}} = 2.82$. Since 2.82 is greater than the critical value of

1.943, reject the null hypothesis and conclude that the average repair costs is more than \$75.

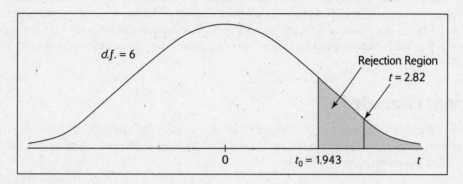

Critical Value Method

Using the critical value, find the maximum value of the repair that would be within the allowable variation. The critical value of t tells you how many standard deviations above the mean would be the point where the higher repair costs are probably due to something other than random variation of the sample. Find $\mu + t_c \dfrac{s}{\sqrt{n}} = 75 + 1.943 \dfrac{13.55}{\sqrt{7}} = 84.95$. Since your average of \$89.45 is greater than the \$84.95, you reject the null hypothesis and conclude that the average cost is greater than \$75.

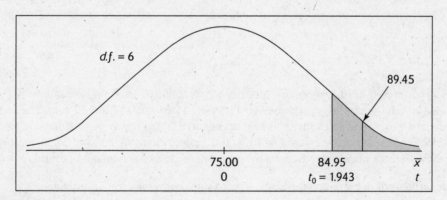

p-value Method

The t-table is not detailed enough to determine the p-value with any degree of accuracy. Determine the t-score from your sample: $t = \dfrac{\bar{x} - \mu}{\frac{s}{\sqrt{n}}} = \dfrac{89.45 - 75}{\frac{13.55}{\sqrt{7}}} = 2.82$. If you try to look up this value in the t-table on the row marked $d.f. = 6$,

you see that the value of 2.82 lies between 2.612 and 3.143. These critical values correspond to tail probabilities of 0.02 and 0.01, respectively. Therefore, you can conclude that the p-value is between 0.01 and 0.02. Using a technology tool, such as the TI-83/4, you get a more accurate value of 0.0151. This p-value shows that the data is very significant. There is only a 1.5%chance you would make a type I error if you reject the null hypothesis. [TI-83/4–Select STAT TESTS T-Test Inpt:Stats μ_0:75 $\bar{x}$:89.45 sx:13.55 n:7 $\mu > \mu_0$ Calculate Display t=2.82 p-value=0.0151]

Two Sample *t*-Procedures (Independent and Matched Pairs)

Matched Pairs

Matched pair tests include tests in which the two samples are related in some way. A popular use of matched pair tests is before-and-after tests. In this type of test, data is collected from a random sample of test subjects, the test subjects undergo some procedure, and data is again collected from the same subjects. Two-sample test procedures are not appropriate here since the samples are dependent, not independent. Instead, a one-sample testing procedure on the differences should be performed.

Independent Samples

A two-sample *t*-test should be used to test the differences between the means of two populations using a random sample from each proportion if at least one of the sample sizes is less than 30. Both populations must be normally distributed to use this procedure. The standardized test statistic is

$$t = \frac{(\overline{x}_1 - \overline{x}_2) - (\mu_1 - \mu_2)}{\sigma_{\overline{x}_1 - \overline{x}_2}}$$

If the population variances are known to be equal (which does not happen often), then $d.f. = n_1 + n_2 - 2$ and

$$\sigma_{\overline{x}_1 - \overline{x}_2} = \sqrt{\frac{(n_1 - 1)s_1^2 + (n_2 - 1)s_2^2}{n_1 + n_2 - 2}} \sqrt{\frac{1}{n_1} + \frac{1}{n_2}}$$

If the population variances are not equal (or you do not know if they are equal), then $d.f.$ is the smaller of $n_1 - 1$ and $n_2 - 1$ and

$$\sigma_{\overline{x}_1 - \overline{x}_2} = \sqrt{\frac{s_1^2}{n_1} + \frac{s_2^2}{n_2}}$$

EXAMPLE:

A testing company is performing crash tests on two models of automobile to determine the amount of damage that each sustains in a low-speed crash. The test was performed on 12 Model 1 cars and 14 Model 2 cars. The average damage sustained by the Model 1 cars was $7840 with a standard deviation of $378. The average damage sustained by the Model 2 cars was $6790 with a standard deviation of $324. If the population variances are equal, what is a 95% confidence interval for the difference in damage sustained by these two models of automobiles in this type of crash test?

When problems are written out in paragraph form, it is wise to summarize the given information.

$$n_1 = 12 \qquad \overline{x}_1 = 7840 \qquad s_1 = 378$$
$$n_2 = 14 \qquad \overline{x}_2 = 6790 \qquad s_2 = 324$$

Since the population variances are equal, the standard deviation of the differences is

$$\sigma_{\overline{x}_1 - \overline{x}_2} = \sqrt{\frac{(n_1 - 1)s_1^2 + (n_2 - 1)s_2^2}{n_1 + n_2 - 2}} \sqrt{\frac{1}{n_1} + \frac{1}{n_2}}$$
$$= \sqrt{\frac{(11)(378^2) + (13)(324^2)}{24}} \sqrt{\frac{1}{12} + \frac{1}{14}} = 137.605$$

The critical *t*-scores for 95% confidence and $d.f. = 24$ is ±2.064.

The confidence interval is

$$\left(\mu_1 - \mu_2\right) = \left(\overline{x}_1 - \overline{x}_2\right) \pm t_c \, \sigma_{\overline{x}_1 - \overline{x}_2} = \left(7840 - 6790\right) \pm \left(2.064\right)\left(137.605\right)$$
$$= 1050 \pm 284.02 = \left(765.98, 1334.02\right)$$

You conclude with 95%confidence that the difference in average repair costs for these two models is between \$766 and \$1334. [TI-83/4 – Select STAT TESTS 2-SampTInt Inpt:Stats $\overline{x}$1:7840 sx1:378 n1:12 $\overline{x}$2:6790 sx2:324 n2:14 C-Level:0.05 Pooled Yes Calculate Display (766, 1334)]

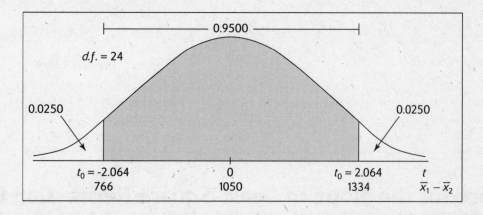

EXAMPLE:
A fish and game expert claims that condor eggs from Northern California weigh more than condor eggs from Southern California. To test this claim, he weighed a random sample of eight Northern California condor eggs. The average weight was 23.2 ounces with a standard deviation of 1.2 ounces. He weighed another random sample of six Southern California condor eggs. Their average weight was 22.3 ounces with a standard deviation of 1.1 ounces. Is the fish and game expert's claim justified at a 5% significance level? Assume that the populations have equal variances.

Summarize the given information.

$n_1 = 8$	$\overline{x}_1 = 23.2$	$s_1 = 1.2$	Northern California
$n_2 = 6$	$\overline{x}_2 = 22.3$	$s_2 = 1.1$	Southern California

The hypotheses are

$$H_0 : \mu_1 \leq \mu_2$$
$$H_a : \mu_1 > \mu_2$$

Since the population variances are equal, the standard deviation of the differences is

$$\sigma_{\overline{x}_1 - \overline{x}_2} = \sqrt{\frac{(n_1 - 1)s_1^2 + (n_2 - 1)s_2^2}{n_1 + n_2 - 2}} \sqrt{\frac{1}{n_1} + \frac{1}{n_2}}$$
$$= \sqrt{\frac{(7)(1.2^2) + (5)(1.1^2)}{12}} \sqrt{\frac{1}{8} + \frac{1}{6}} = 0.626$$

To find the critical t-value, look up a tail probability of 0.05 and $d.f. = 12$. You obtain a critical t-value of 1.782.

Calculate the t-score of the sample data:

$$t = \frac{\left(\overline{x}_1 - \overline{x}_2\right) - \left(\mu_1 - \mu_2\right)}{\sigma_{\overline{x}_1 - \overline{x}_2}} = \frac{(23.2 - 22.3) - 0}{0.626} = 1.438$$

307

This value of the t-score is not in the critical region. You fail to reject the null hypothesis and conclude that the fish and game expert's claim is not justified. From the TI-83/4 example that follows, you see that the p-value is 0.088. Therefore, this claim is not justified at a 5% significance level but would be at a 10% significance level. [TI-83/4 Select STAT TESTS 2-SampTTest Inpt:Stats $\bar{x}$1:23.2 sx1:1.2 n1:8 $\bar{x}$2:22.3 sx2:1.1 n2:6 $\mu_1 \geq \mu_2$ Pooled:Yes Calculate Display t=1.737 p=0.088]

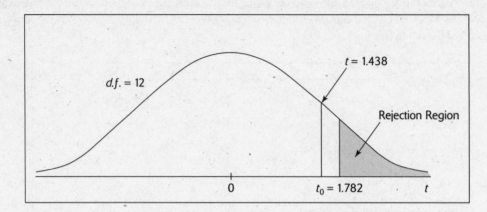

Inference for the Slope of Least-Square Regression Line

When bivariate data exhibits a linear correlation, the least-squares line may be used to make predictions based on the bivariate data. The equation for the least-squares line is

$$\hat{y} = b_0 + b_1 x$$

where b_1 is the slope of the regression line and is an estimate of the true slope of the population β.

The **standard error of estimate** is denoted by s and is the standard deviation of the observed y-values about the predicted $\hat{y}$ values. It is an estimate for σ, the standard deviation of the residuals. The value of s is given by

$$s = \sqrt{\frac{\sum\left(y_i - \hat{y}_i\right)^2}{n-2}}$$

The standard error of the slope is given by

$$s_{b_1} = \frac{s}{\sqrt{\sum\left(x_i - \bar{x}\right)^2}} = \frac{\sqrt{\dfrac{\sum\left(y_i - \hat{y}_i\right)^2}{n-2}}}{\sqrt{\sum\left(x_i - \bar{x}\right)^2}}$$

You equate linear correlation with the slope of the regression line. That is, if the slope is zero, there is no linear relationship between the variables.

Use technology tools—such as Minitab or a calculator such as the TI-83/4—to find these values. When a linear regression is performed in the calculator, it finds the value of s along with the value of the slope and y-intercept of the regression line. The value of $\sqrt{\sum\left(x_i - \bar{x}\right)^2}$ is the same as $s_x\sqrt{n-1}$.

Technology is used to help construct confidence intervals for the true slope of regression lines and to test hypotheses concerning the slope. You should be able to read a Minitab output and use the information it provides. Consider the following relationship between the golf scores of 10 golfers both before and after using a new set of clubs.

Before using new clubs	62	90	84	69	60	85	82	68	85	89
After using new clubs	63	95	90	68	60	89	80	65	81	95

The Minitab output for this regression is as follows:

The regression equation is

After = −11.0 + 1.16 Before

Predictor	Coef	StDev	T	P
Constant	−10.961	8.096	−1.35	0.213
Before	1.1571	0.1036	11.17	0.000

$S = 3.547$ R-Sq = 94.0%   R-Sq(adj) = 93.2%

In the "Predictor" column, the "Constant" is the y-intercept and the "Before" is the slope.

In the "Coef" column, the values of the y-intercept and slope of the regression line are given.

Disregard the "Constant" values in the other three columns.

In the "StDev" column, the "Before" value is the standard error of the slope, s_{b_1}.

In the "T" or "Tratio" column, the "Before" value is the t statistic, $t = \dfrac{b_1}{s_{b_1}}$ with $d.f. = n - 2$.

In the "P" column, the "Before" value is the p-value for a two-sided test.

In the bottom row, "S" is the standard error of the residuals, $S = \sqrt{\dfrac{\sum\left(y_i - \hat{y}_i\right)}{n - 2}}$.

In the bottom row, "R-Sq" is the value of the coefficient of determination, r^2.

The TI-83/4 can produce all of the preceding information. Enter values of the "Before" scores into L1 and the "After" scores into L2. Select STAT TESTS and select LinRegTTest. If you placed data in lists other than L1 and L2, enter the appropriate lists. Set Freq:1 and choose ≠ as the test relationship and Calculate.

"t" is the t statistic.

"p" is the p-value.

"df" is the degrees of freedom.

"a" is the constant coefficient.

"b" is the slope.

"S" is the standard error of the residuals.

"r^2" is the coefficient of determination.

The only value not directly available is the standard error of the slope, s_{b_1}. This can be found by solving $t = \dfrac{b_1}{s_{b_1}}$ for s_{b_1} giving $s_{b_1} = \dfrac{b_1}{t}$.

In this example, $s_{b_1} = \dfrac{b_1}{t} = \dfrac{1.157}{11.169} = 0.1036$.

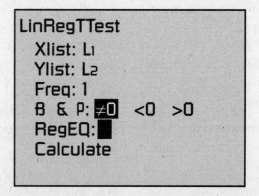

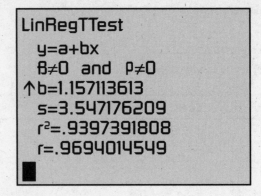

EXAMPLE:

The following table shows the relationship between stride length and height of adult males. Find the equation of the least-squares regression line based on this sample and compute a 90% confidence interval for the slope of the actual regression line for the population.

Height (in)	72	70	71	68	66	71	66	67	65
Stride (in)	33	31	31	28	28	30	28	27	27

Use a technology tool (Minitab, TI-83/4, and so on) to find the equation of the regression line:

$$\hat{y} = b_0 + b_1 x = -21.4 + 0.740x$$

Obtain the following values (on the TI-3/4 perform a LinRegTTest to get s and find the standard deviation of the heights):

$$s_x = 2.6$$

$$s = 0.917$$

$$s_{b_1} = \frac{\sqrt{\frac{\sum\left(y_i - \hat{y}_i\right)^2}{n-2}}}{\sqrt{\sum\left(x_i - \overline{x}\right)^2}} = \frac{s}{s_x\sqrt{n-1}} = \frac{0.917}{2.6\sqrt{8}} = 0.125$$

There are $9 - 2 = 7$ degrees of freedom in this example. A 90% confidence interval has 5% of the area of the distribution in each tail. Look up the critical t-value in the row marked $d.f.=7$ and the column marked 0.05 tail probability to give 1.895.

The confidence interval for the slope is

$$b_1 \pm (t)(s_{b_1}) = (1.895)(0.125) = 0.740 \pm 0.237 = (0.503, 0.997)$$

EXAMPLE:

Using the data from the previous example, test the hypothesis that there is no linear relationship between height and stride length.

First state the hypotheses:

$$H_0 : \beta = 0$$
$$H_a : \beta \neq 0$$

The t-value may be calculated as $t = \dfrac{b_1}{s_{b_1}} = \dfrac{0.740}{0.125} = 5.92$.

It may also be found by performing a LinRegTTest using the TI-83/4 calculator.

Using 7 degrees of freedom, look up the critical t-values for various tail probabilities. The t-value from this data indicates that the data is significant down below the 0.1% level. In fact, it is off the chart. Your data is very significant, and you easily reject the null hypothesis and conclude that there is strong linear correlation between height and stride length.

Review Questions and Answers

Multiple Choice Questions

Directions: Solve each of the following problems. Decide which is the best of the choices given.

1. Which of the following are true statements?

    I.   The shape of the t-distributions changes as the sample size decreases.
    II. The t-distributions are mound-shaped and symmetric.
    III. The t-distributions may be used wherever the z-distribution is appropriate.

    A. I only
    B. I and II
    C. I and III
    D. II and III
    E. I, II, and III

2. Which of the following are true statements?

    I.   The area under the curve of the t-distribution between ± 1 standard deviation is greater when $d.f. = 5$ than when $d.f. = 10$.
    II. There is less area in the tails, beyond ± 3 standard deviations, of the t-distribution when $d.f. = 5$ than when $d.f. = 10$.
    III. For a given α, the critical t-value increases as $d.f.$ decreases.

    A. I only
    B. II only
    C. III only
    D. I and II
    E. I, II, and III

3. Which of the following is a false statement?

    A. When using the t-distribution with $n < 30$, you assume that the parent distribution is normal.
    B. When using the t-distribution with $n < 30$, you assume that samples are simple random samples.
    C. When using the t-distribution with $n \leq 15$, you assume that $\sigma = s$.
    D. When using the t-distribution with $n \leq 15$, no outliers or skewness are allowed in the sample.
    E. When using the t-distribution for inferences with two-sample procedures, $d.f. = n - 1$.

4. Which of the following are conditions for using the *t*-distribution for small sample difference tests?

    I.   Samples must be independent.

    II.   Samples must be drawn from normal populations.

    III.   Samples must be of equal size.

    A. I only

    B. II only

    C. I and II

    D. I and III

    E. I, II, and III

5. When a sample size of 12 is used to perform a two-sided test for the mean, a *t*-value of 2.1 is significant to what level?

    A. Between 0.5% and 1%

    B. Between 1% and 2.5%

    C. Between 2.5% and 5%

    D. Between 5% and 10%

    E. Between 10% and 15%

6. Using a sample size of 25, what is the critical *t*-value for a 95% confidence interval?

    A. 1.708

    B. 1.711

    C. 2.060

    D. 2.064

    E. 2.172

7. A town dug seven test wells until they reached water. The average depth was 174 feet with a standard deviation of 9 feet. Establish a 90% confidence interval for the depth of water in this area.

    A. 174 ± 4.9

    B. 174 ± 6.4

    C. 174 ± 6.6

    D. 174 ± 7.1

    E. 174 ± 13.4

8. A gasoline additive is being tested to determine the amount of improvement that can be expected in gas mileage. Twelve cars are randomly selected to be included in the study. The results are given below. Construct a 95% confidence interval for the improvement in gas mileage.

Before Additive	17	22	23	19	18	19	24	23	19	22	21	20
After Additive	19	22	25	21	24	21	24	25	21	25	22	21

    A. 1.92 ± 0.80

    B. 1.92 ± 0.81

    C. 1.92 ± 0.88

    D. 1.92 ± 0.98

    E. 1.92 ± 0.99

9. A computer repair facility claims that an average repair for a personal computer is less than $145. To test this claim, you randomly select eight computers delivered for repair. The average repair cost is $138 with a standard deviation of $12. What is the p-value?

    A. $0.001 < p\text{-value} < 0.01$

    B. $0.01 < p\text{-value} < 0.025$

    C. $0.025 < p\text{-value} < 0.05$

    D. $0.05 < p\text{-value} < 0.10$

    E. $0.10 < p\text{-value} < 0.20$

10. A random sample of 10 trees had a mean height of 37 feet with a standard deviation of 8 feet. What is the maximum claimed average height of this kind of tree that would not be rejected as being too tall at a 10% confidence level?

    A.   39.9 feet

    B.   40.2 feet

    C.   40.5 feet

    D.   40.8 feet

    E.   50.1 feet

11. Two long jumpers are having a discussion. Jamie claims she can jump farther than Katie. They each jump eight times and record their distances. To test the claim that Jamie jumps farther, they determine the p-value. What is the p-value? Assume that the population variances are different.

Jamie's Jumps (in ft.)	19	17	18	21	20	19	21	20
Katie's Jumps (in ft.)	18	18	17	21	21	18	20	18

    A. $0.001 < p\text{-value} < 0.01$

    B. $0.01 < p\text{-value} < 0.05$

    C. $0.05 < p\text{-value} < 0.10$

    D. $0.10 < p\text{-value} < 0.20$

    E. $p\text{-value} > 0.20$

    E. $16.07 \pm 1.11\%$

12. The following table represents the size (in 100s of square feet) of homes and their recent selling prices (in $1000). Determine a 95% confidence interval for the rise in selling price per 100 square foot increase in square footage of the home.

Square feet (100s)	29	23	34	22	24	28
Price ($1000s)	671	524	796	620	610	740

    A. 18.85 ± 10.94

    B. 18.85 ± 13.19

    C. 18.85 ± 14.24

    D. 157.3 ± 10.94

    E. 157.3 ± 14.24

Multiple Choice Answers

1. **E.** The shape of the t-distribution depends on the degrees of freedom. The t-distribution is flatter than the normal distribution but it is mound-shaped and symmetric. Since the shape of the t-distribution approaches the normal as the degrees of freedom increase, in cases where the normal is appropriate, the t-distribution will give the same results.

2. **C.** Choices I and II are false since the opposite of each is true. As the degrees of freedom increases, the height of the t-distribution increases in the center. [TI-83/4–Select DISTR tcdf(–1,1,5)=0.637 and tcdf(–1,1,10)=0.659.] Choice III is true.

3. **C.** When using the t-distribution, use s as a suitable approximation for σ. Do not assume that they are equal.

4. **C.** Equal size samples are not necessary for two sample tests. The other two choices are conditions for using the t-distribution.

5. **D.** Look in the t-table on the line marked 11 degrees of freedom. Find the two values between which 2.1 resides. Move up to the top to determine the tail probability. Since this is a two-sided test, double the tail probabilities.

6. **D.** Look in the t-table on the line marked 24 degrees of freedom. The chart lists confidence intervals at the bottom. Find 95% confidence. The intersection is the critical t-value of 2.064. Since it is a two-sided test, there will be 2.5% of the total probability in each tail. A 95% confidence is in the same column as a 2.5% tail probability.

7. **C.** Calculate the standard error as $\sigma_{\bar{x}} = \frac{s}{\sqrt{n}} = \frac{9}{\sqrt{7}} = 3.4$. Look up the critical t-value of 1.943. The confidence interval is

$$\bar{x} \pm t_c \sigma_{\bar{x}} = 174 \pm (1.943)(3.4) = 174 \pm 6.6.$$

[TI-83/4–Select TInterval, enter appropriate values, and read interval.]

8. **E.** This is a problem involving two dependent samples. A two-sample test is not appropriate in this case. Determine the differences and treat them as one sample. Determine the mean and standard deviation of this sample (set of differences). For example, on the TI-83/4 enter the 12 differences into a list and calculate one variable statistics giving $\bar{x} = 1.917$ and $s = 1.564$. Calculate the standard error as $\sigma_{\bar{x}} = \frac{s}{\sqrt{n}} = \frac{1.564}{\sqrt{12}} = 0.451$. Look up the critical t-value of 2.201. The confidence interval is

$$\bar{x} \pm t_c \sigma_{\bar{x}} = 1.917 \pm (2.201)(0.451) = 1.917 \pm 0.99.$$

[TI-83/4–Select TInterval, enter appropriate values, and read interval.]

9. **D.** To calculate the t-value of the data, first calculate the standard error as $\sigma_{\bar{x}} = \frac{s}{\sqrt{n}} = \frac{12}{\sqrt{8}} = 4.243$. Then calculate $t = \frac{\bar{x} - \mu}{\sigma_{\bar{x}}} = \frac{138 - 145}{4.243} = -1.65$. Look in the t-table on the line marked 11 degrees of freedom. Find the two numbers between which 1.65 resides. (The table lists only positive values. You must remember that this is a left-tail test. The tail probabilities will be the same no matter which side you are on.) Move up to the line marked with the tail probabilities. Since this is a one-sided claim, the two tail probabilities are the bound of the significance of the data. Therefore, the p-value is between 5% and 10%.

10. **C.** First calculate the standard error as $\sigma_{\bar{x}} = \frac{s}{\sqrt{n}} = \frac{8}{\sqrt{10}} = 2.53$. Look in the t-table on the line marked 9 degrees of freedom. In the column marked as 0.10 tail probability (10% significance) read the critical t-value of 1.383. Solve the equation for the t-statistic for the population mean.

$$t = \frac{\bar{x} - \mu}{\sigma_{\bar{x}}}$$

$$1.383 = \frac{37 - \mu}{2.53}$$

$$\mu = 37 + (1.383)(2.53) = 40.5$$

11. **E.** Calculate the sample mean and sample standard deviation of the two samples. For example, on the TI-83/4 enter the eight jumps for Jamie into a list and calculate one variable statistics giving $\bar{x}_1 = 19.375$ and $s_1 = 1.407$. Repeat for Katie's jumps giving $\bar{x}_2 = 18.875$ and $s_2 = 1.55$.

Calculate the standard error as

$$\sigma_{\bar{x}_1 - \bar{x}_2} = \sqrt{\frac{s_1^2}{n_1} + \frac{s_2^2}{n_2}} = \sqrt{\frac{1.407^2}{8} + \frac{1.55^2}{8}} = 0.74$$

Calculate the *t*-value as

$$t = \frac{(\bar{x}_1 - \bar{x}_2) - (\mu_1 - \mu_2)}{\sigma_{\bar{x}_1 - \bar{x}_2}} = \frac{(19.375 - 18.875) - 0}{0.74} = 0.67$$

Look in the *t*-table on the line marked 7 degrees of freedom. The *t*-value of 0.67 is off the chart, with a tail area larger than 0.25. This is not significant data, so the jumpers should conclude that Jamie does not jump farther than Katie.

[TI-83/4–Select 2-SampTTest, enter appropriate values, and read the *p*-value.]

12. **C.** Enter the six pairs of numbers into lists in a technology tool such as the TI-83/4. Perform a LinRegTTest. Obtain the values of the slope of the regression line, $b_1 = 18.85$, and the value of the standard error of the residuals, $s = 52.147$. Perform 1-VarStats on the *x*-values (square footage) and obtain their standard deviation, $s_x = 4.546$. Calculate the standard error of the slope, $s_{b_1} = \dfrac{s}{s_x\sqrt{n-1}} = \dfrac{52.147}{4.546\sqrt{5}} = 5.13$. Look up the critical *t*-value in the *t*-table on the line marked 4 degrees of freedom and 95% confidence of 2.776. The confidence interval is

$$b_1 \pm t_c \, s_{b_1} = 18.85 \pm (2.776)(5.13) = 18.85 \pm 14.24$$

Free-Response Questions

Directions: Show all work. Indicate clearly the methods you use. You will be graded on method as well as accuracy.

1. An auto manufacturer claims that the mean gas mileage of their subcompact model is 39 mpg. You believe that the mean mileage is actually less than that. You decide to test your claim. You obtain a random sample of 5 of this model car and find that the cars get 37, 39, 36, 40, and 36 mpg respectively. What is your conclusion? Assume that the parent population is normally distributed.

2. A company needs to purchase new machines for its manufacturing plant. Two different brands meet their overall specifications. To test the operating speeds of these two brands, a random sample of seven brand A machines and seven brand B machines are obtained. Each machine is tested. The seven brand A machines produced 76, 82, 72, 77, 77, 76, and 75 components per minute. The seven brand B machines produced 78, 78, 76, 81, 78, 78, and 77 components per minute. The plant foreman believes that brand B is the faster of the two. Test his claim. Is the difference significant? Assume that the parent populations are normally distributed.

3. A company that specializes in test preparation claims that if students take their SAT prep class, their scores will improve by at least 85 points. To test this claim, a statistician took a random selection of five students who took the company's course. Their scores, both before and after taking the prep class, are listed. Is the claim justified? Assume that the parent populations are normally distributed.

SAT Score Before Prep	1320	1260	1120	1210	1130
SAT Score After Prep	1410	1340	1210	1280	1180

Free-Response Answers

1. State the hypotheses:

$$H_0 : \mu \geq 39$$
$$H_a : \mu < 39$$

Since the sample size is small and the parent population is normal, a hypothesis test using the t-distribution is appropriate. Determine the mean and standard deviation of the sample as $\bar{x} = 37.6$ and $s = 1.817$. Calculate the standard error as $\sigma_{\bar{x}} = \dfrac{s}{\sqrt{n}} = \dfrac{1.817}{\sqrt{5}} = 0.813$. Then calculate $t = \dfrac{\bar{x} - \mu}{\sigma_{\bar{x}}} = \dfrac{37.6 - 39}{0.813} = -1.72$. Look in the t-table on the line marked 4 degrees of freedom. Find the two numbers that 1.72 is between. (The table lists only positive values. You must remember that this is a left-tail test. The tail probabilities will be the same no matter which side you are on.) Move up to the line marked with the tail probabilities. The critical t-value for a 0.10 tail probability is 1.533. The critical t-value for a 0.05 tail probability is 2.132. The t-value of 1.72 lies between them. Since this is a one-sided claim, the tail probabilities of 5% and 10% are the bounds of the data's significance. Therefore, the p-value is between 5% and 10%. This data is moderately significant. You could reject the null hypothesis (that the cars get at least 39 mpg) at a 10% significance level but not at a 5% significance level. [TI-83/4 – Select STAT TESTS T-Test $\mu 0$:39 $\bar{x}$:37.6 sx:1.817 n:5 $\mu < \mu_0$ Calculate Display t= –1.72 p=0.08]

2. State the hypotheses:

$$H_0 : \mu_A - \mu_B \geq 0$$
$$H_a : \mu_A - \mu_B \leq 0$$

Since the sample size is small and the parent population is normal, a hypothesis test using the t-distribution is appropriate. Calculate the sample mean and sample standard deviation of the two samples. For example, on the TI-83/4 enter the seven rates for brand A into a list and calculate one variable statistics giving $\bar{x}_A = 76.4$ and $s_A = 2.99$. Repeat for brand B giving $\bar{x}_B = 78$ and $s_B = 1.53$.

In this problem you are not told whether the variances of the two populations are equal. You can solve the problem both ways.

If variances are equal:

Calculate the standard error as

$$\sigma_{\bar{x}_A - \bar{x}_B} = \sqrt{\frac{(n_A - 1)s_A^2 + (n_B - 1)s_B^2}{n_A + n_B - 2}} \sqrt{\frac{1}{n_A} + \frac{1}{n_B}}$$
$$= \sqrt{\frac{(6)(2.99^2) + (6)(1.53^2)}{12}} \sqrt{\frac{1}{7} + \frac{1}{7}} = 1.269$$

Calculate the t-value as

$$t = \frac{(\bar{x}_A - \bar{x}_B) - (\mu_A - \mu_B)}{\sigma_{\bar{x}_A - \bar{x}_B}} = \frac{(76.4 - 78) - 0}{1.269} = -1.26$$

If variances are not equal:

Calculate the standard error as

$$\sigma_{\bar{x}_A - \bar{x}_B} = \sqrt{\frac{s_A^2}{n_A} + \frac{s_B^2}{n_B}} = \sqrt{\frac{2.99^2}{7} + \frac{1.53^2}{7}} = 1.269$$

Calculate the t-value as

$$t = \frac{(\bar{x}_A - \bar{x}_B) - (\mu_A - \mu_B)}{\sigma_{\bar{x}_A - \bar{x}_B}} = \frac{(76.4 - 78) - 0}{1.269} = -1.26$$

The t-values with variances equal or unequal are the same but will be looked up on different lines of the t-table. Look up the positive value in the t-table. The t-value of 1.26 on the line marked 12 degrees of freedom falls between tail probabilities of 0.10 and 0.15. The t-value of 1.26 on the line marked 6 degrees of freedom also falls between tail probabilities of 0.10 and 0.15. In either case, the p-value is between 0.10 and 0.15. This indicates that data is not very significant, and the null hypothesis should not be rejected. The claim by the foreman that brand B is faster is not justified. [TI-83/4–Select STAT TESTS 2-SampTTest Inpt:Data $\bar{x}$1:76.4 sx1:2.99 n1:7 $\bar{x}$ 2:78 xs2:1.53 n2:7 $\mu_1 < \mu_2$ Pooled:Yes Calculate Display t = –1.26 p = 0.116]

3. This is a dependent sample test. Although there are two samples, they are not independent. Therefore, a one-sample test should be run of the differences in the scores. Subtract each pair of scores to get the following: 90, 80, 90, 70, and 50. Enter the five differences into a list and calculate their mean and standard deviation as $\bar{x} = 76$ and $s = 16.73$.

State the hypotheses:

$$H_0 : \mu \geq 85 \text{ claim}$$
$$H_a : \mu < 85$$

Calculate the standard error as $\sigma_{\bar{x}} = \dfrac{s}{\sqrt{n}} = \dfrac{16.73}{\sqrt{5}} = 7.48$. Then calculate $t = \dfrac{\bar{x} - \mu}{\sigma_{\bar{x}}} = \dfrac{76 - 85}{7.48} = -1.20$.

Look in the t-table on the line marked 4 degrees of freedom. Find the two numbers that 1.20 is between. (The table lists only positive values. You must remember that this is a left-tail test. The tail probabilities will be the same no matter which side you are on.) You find that 1.20 is approximately the same as 1.19, which represents a tail probability of 0.15. This data is not significant. Therefore, you should fail to reject the null hypothesis of the prep company. You conclude that you cannot reject the claim by the testing company that the test scores improve by at least 85 points. [TI-83/4–Select STAT TESTS T-Test μ 0:85 $\bar{x}$:76 sx:16.73 n:5 $\mu < \mu_0$ Calculate Display $t = -1.20$ $p = 0.148$]

PART III

AP STATISTICS PRACTICE TESTS

For an additional practice test, go to **http://www.cliffsnotes.com/go/APStatistics.**

Section I

Time: 1 hour and 30 minutes   Number of questions: 40   Percent of total grade: 50%

Directions: Solve each problem. Decide which is the best of the answer choices given.

1. Two measures, x and y, were taken and yielded the least-squares regression line $\hat{y} = 18.8 + 3.45x$. The following is a plot of the residuals for the regression analysis:

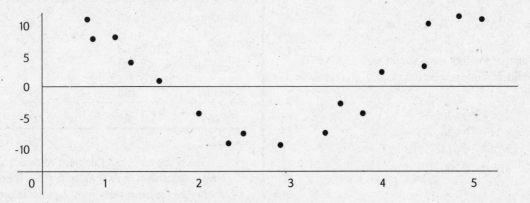

Which of the following statements is supported by this information?

A. There is a strong, direct linear relationship between x and y.

B. There is a strong, inverse linear relationship between x and y.

C. There is a linear relationship between x and y, but it cannot be determined whether the relationship is direct or inverse from the information given.

D. There is a strong relationship between x and y, but the relationship is nonlinear.

E. There is no strong relationship between x and y.

GO ON TO THE NEXT PAGE

2. The manager of a wildlife reserve is doing a study comparing the heights and weights of brown bears. Eleven bears were captured and measured, and it was determined that there was a strong linear relationship between the heights and weights of the bears. The results of the regression analysis are given here:

Regression Equation:

Weight = −165.97 + 8.249 Height

Predictor	Coef	Stdev	t-ratio	p
Constant	−165.9666	43.01989	−3.8579	0.004
Height	8.248695	0.44689	18.4579	0.000

S = 20.43   R-sq = 97.4

Which of the following would represent a 95% confidence interval for the slope of the regression line?

A. 8.249 ± 0.876
B. 8.249 ± 0.936
C. 8.249 ± 1.011
D. -165.97 ± 84.319
E. -165.97 ± 97.311

3. A Las Vegas Hotel and Casino typically has 16,500 customers per year. Among these customers, 11,300 will actually enter the casino, and approximately 85% of those will actually play the casino games. If a random sample of 200 customers is taken, what is the expected number of customers who will play the casino games?

A. 85
B. 116
C. 137
D. 144
E. 170

4. Calmatom is a drug taken for stomach disorders. However, one of the possible side effects is an increase in heart rate. Several patients with stomach disorders, who were given Calmatom, had their heart rates (in beats per minute) tested before taking the drug and then taken exactly one hour after. This is the data observed.

Patient Name	Heart Rate Before	Heart Rate After
Brockington	88	89
Hunter	90	97
Lane	79	81
Bowman	91	99
Lueck	77	79
Goodman	80	84
Withrow	88	98
Himes	80	78

What is the number of degrees of freedom associated with the appropriate t-test for testing whether the heart rates for the patients actually increase, with the use of Calmatom?

A. 2
B. 7
C. 8
D. 15
E. 16

5. Suppose that a medical school has determined that only about 45% of applicants will be accepted for admission. Suppose that this proportion is approximately true over the long run. What would be the expected number of people admitted to the medical school, if 960 apply?

A. 194
B. 432
C. 450
D. 528
E. 550

6. Which of the following is a requirement for choosing a *t*-test, rather than a *z*-test, when testing a claim concerning a population mean?

A. The sample is not a simple random sample.

B. The sample size is less than 30.

C. The underlying population is only approximately normally distributed.

D. The population mean is unknown.

E. The population standard deviation is unknown.

7. A wildlife reserve contains a population of deer. Suppose that the state's Department of Natural Resources wants to estimate the total number of deer in the reserve. Two plans are proposed:

Plan I:

   a. Select 100 deer at random.

   b. Place red tags on the deer and release them into the population.

   c. One week later, select 100 deer at random again.

   d. Determine the proportion of deer in the new sample with red tags, divide 100 by this proportion.

Plan II:

   a. Measure the total area of the wildlife reserve in square miles.

   b. Collect all deer in a randomly selected 1 square mile region.

   c. Multiply this number by the total number of square miles of the reserve.

On the basis of the information given, which of the two plans should be selected to give the best estimate of the number of deer in the wildlife reserve?

A. Choose Plan I over Plan II.

B. Choose Plan II over Plan I.

C. Choose either plan, since both will provide equally accurate results.

D. Choose neither plan, since neither will provide an accurate estimate.

E. The plans cannot be evaluated from the information given.

8. It has been shown that students who are successful in high school algebra courses also tend to have higher grade-point averages when they attend college. Which statement best describes the proper relationship between a student's high school algebra grades and college grade-point average?

A. The factors have a cause-and-effect relationship.

B. The factors are directly correlated, but not necessarily by a cause-and-effect relationship

C. The factors are inversely correlated, but not necessarily by a cause-and-effect relationship.

D. One factor has a confounding effect on the other.

E. Any relationship between the two factors is coincidental.

9. Suppose that Pacific Stereo wants to estimate their average amount of gross income per day. In observing their sales for 38 consecutive days, their average gross income was $12,317, with a sample standard deviation over these 38 days being $2,959. Which would be a 95% confidence interval for their average gross daily income?

A. $11,344 < \mu < $13,290

B. $11,014 < \mu < $13,620

C. $11,376 < \mu < $13,258

D. $11,330 < \mu < $13,304

E. $11,345 < \mu < $13,289

10. The heights of adult Somoke trees are normally distributed with a mean height 20.2 feet and a population standard deviation 6.5 feet. A tree that is in the 95th percentile among all Somoke trees will have what approximate height?

A. 32.9 feet

B. 9.5 feet

C. 28.5 feet

D. 30.9 feet

E. 7.5 feet

GO ON TO THE NEXT PAGE

11. A dentist has a "treasure chest" that contains the following items:

15 orange tigers	25 gold tigers
10 orange rings	5 gold rings
10 red fire engines	20 red rings

At the end of each visit, the dentist allows each child to take a random item from the "treasure chest." Find the probability that a child chooses a ring, given that the item is something orange.

A. 0.4000
B. 0.2857
C. 0.1176
D. 0.5882
E. 0.3333

12. Heather has a very important exam to take in the morning. Since she wants to be sure to that she will wake up in time, she sets two alarm clocks. One has a .95 probability that it will ring, and the other has a .98 probability that it will ring. She sets both clocks. What is the probability that at least one of the alarm clocks will wake her up?

A. 0.9025
B. 0.9310
C. 0.9604
D. 0.9800
E. 0.9990

13. Suppose that a slot machine requires that you pay 5 cents to play. It gives payouts based on the number of cherries that appear. The following table describes how the machine gives winnings.

PAYOUT				
Number of Cherries	3	2	1	0
Amount Machine Pays	$1.00	0.25	0.05	0
Probability	.01	.02	.10	.87

What profit should a person expect to make per play on this machine?

A. $1.00
B. $0.065
C. 0
D. –$0.0235
E. –$0.03

14. Karl receives the results on his standardized NEDT scores. The results on his Verbal section indicate that he finished in the 90th percentile. Which of the following is the best description of what this means?

A. Karl got 90% of the questions correct.
B. Karl finished in the top 90% of all those taking the test.
C. Karl finished in the bottom 90% of all those taking the test.
D. Ninety percent of all those taking the test scored greater than Karl.
E. Ninety percent of all those taking the test scored lower than Karl.

15. The following boxplots summarize two data sets, A and B.

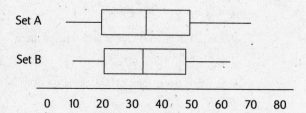

Which of the following statements *must* be true?

A. Set A has a higher standard deviation than Set B.
B. Set A has a higher mean than Set B.
C. Set A contains an outlier.
D. Set A has a higher interquartile range than Set B.
E. Set A has more data points than Set B.

16. Which of the following is the best description of a "random sample?"

A. Each member of the population is equally likely to be chosen in the sample.
B. Each stratum of the population will be represented in the sample.
C. The sample contains a large number of values.
D. It is not known ahead of time which values will be chosen in the sample.
E. The values in the sample do not follow any recognizable patterns.

17. An engine additive is being tested to see whether it can effectively increase gas mileage for a number of vehicles. Twenty assorted vehicles had their gas mileage, in miles per gallon, measured. Then, the engine additive was placed into each of the engines, and the gas mileage was measured again. Let μ_A be the mean gas mileage of the vehicles without the engine additive, and let μ_B be the mean gas mileage of the vehicles with the engine additive. The 99% confidence interval for the true mean difference between the two means is (2 mpg, 5 mpg). Which of the following statements is the best interpretation of this confidence interval?

A. With probability 0.99, the interval (2 , 5) contains the true difference $\mu_B - \mu_A$.
B. μ_B is approximately equal to 5 mpg, and μ_A is approximately equal to 2 mpg.
C. $\mu_B - \mu_A$ is approximately equal to 3.
D. $\mu_B > \mu_A$ with probability 0.99.
E. It is likely that the difference $\mu_B - \mu_A$ will exceed 5.

18. The manager of the Arizona Silver Mine has indicated that the standardized z-score for their total yearly output of silver, in relation to all other Silver Mines in the country, is -2.50. Which of the following is the best interpretation of the meaning of this z-score?

A. The Arizona mine produces 2.50 tons less silver than all other mines in the country.
B. All other mines produce 2.50 times as much silver as the Arizona mine does.
C. The Arizona mine's production is in the bottom 2.5% of all mines in the country.
D. The Arizona mine's production is 2.50 standard deviations below the national average.
E. The Arizona mine's production is 2.50 times as much as the national average.

19. Suppose that a college professor is going to be teaching a course in a large lecture hall. In order to describe the composition of the students by class, the professor has assigned Freshmen as 1s, Sophomores as 2s, Juniors as 3s, and Seniors as 4s. If the class consists of 110 Freshmen, 60 Sophomores, 30 Juniors, and 20 Seniors, which of the following measurements would give the professor the best indicator of the typical student in the class?

A. Mean
B. Median
C. Mode
D. Range
E. Standard deviation

20. Suppose that a solid-state company is manufacturing a brand of power strips that is supposed to have a particular mean wattage. Furthermore, the power strips should be stable, meaning that all the power strips should have approximately the same wattage. If a sample of 100 power strips is measured, which measurement, taken from the sample, would give the best indicator of the stability of the brand of power strips?

A. Mean
B. Median
C. Mode
D. Range
E. Standard deviation

21. Ed has two coins that his friends suspect are weighted. He tosses the coins 200 times, and these are the results:

Number of Heads	0	1	2
Times Occurred	34	95	71

Based on the results, which are the most likely probabilities for the coins?

A. P(Head) = .25 P(Tail) = .75
B. P(Head) = .40 P(Tail) = .60
C. P(Head) = .50 P(Tail) = .50
D. P(Head) = .60 P(Tail) = .40
E. P(Head) = .75 P(Tail) = .25

GO ON TO THE NEXT PAGE

22. Suppose that a breed of tigers has been observed over several years. Let X = the number of tiger cubs in a tiger birth. Probabilities have been estimated and are given in the following probability distribution:

X = number of tiger cubs	1	2	3	4	5	6
Probability	0.02	0.11	0.34	0.31	0.21	0.01

Based on these probabilities, what is the expected number of tiger cubs in a birth?

A. 3.61
B. 3.5
C. 3.49
D. 3
E. 1

23. The back-to-back stem-and-leaf plots compare the ages of players with two Minor League baseball teams.

Stockton Ports		Waffletown Syrups
	0	
	0	
	1	
98887	1	88999
443322110	2	0011344
987555	2	556689
410	3	0113
8	3	67

Which of the following statements is NOT justified by the data?

A. Waffletown has more players over 30 than Stockton does.
B. The range of ages for both teams is the same.
C. Stockton's players tend to be slightly younger than Waffletown's players.
D. Waffletown has a higher median age than Stockton.
E. Stockton has more players in their 20s than Waffletown does.

24. A sample of 40 batteries is taken from a case of 400. Thirty-seven of the batteries in the sample are good, and three are defective. Let p = the probability that a battery in the case is still good. Which of the following is NOT a possible value for p?

A. 0.5000
B. 0.7500
C. 0.9000
D. 0.9250
E. 1.0000

25. Suppose that the chart that follows represents a probability distribution for X.

X	0	1	2	3	4	5
Probability	0.15	x	x	$2x$	0.25	0.20

What is the value of x?

A. 0.05
B. 0.10
C. 0.15
D. 0.20
E. 0.40

26. A random sample of 35 plumber jobs produced a sample mean of 87.7 minutes per job, with a sample standard deviation of 24.4 minutes. Which of the following is an approximate 95% confidence interval for the true mean time required for a plumber job?

A. 87.7 ± 8.08 minutes
B. 87.7 ± 8.37 minutes
C. 87.7 ± 8.38 minutes
D. 87.7 ± 47.80 minutes
E. 87.7 ± 49.58 minutes

27. The weights for a population of monkeys from the area of Kampuchea follow a normal distribution with mean 42 pounds, and a standard deviation of 17 pounds. The weights for a population of monkeys from the Zanzibar area follow a normal distribution with a mean of 15 pounds, and a standard deviation of 3 pounds. A monkey from Kampuchea has been measured to be 44 pounds, and a Zanzibar monkey has been measured to be 19 pounds. Which of the following statements best describes the comparison between the two sample monkeys?

A. The Kampuchea monkey is heavier for its breed than the Zanzibar monkey is for its breed.

B. The Zanzibar monkey is heavier for its breed than the Kampuchea monkey is for its breed.

C. The monkeys are about equally heavy for their respective breeds.

D. There is no basis for comparison, since the monkeys come from different breeds.

E. There is not enough information to compare, since the population sizes are unknown.

28. Suppose that Basketball Jones has an approximate 0.85 probability of making a free throw successfully. If Basketball Jones attempts 100 free throws, what is the approximate probability that he will make at least 90 out of 100 successfully?

A. .1500
B. .1038
C. .0808
D. .0618
E. .0444

29. Suppose that there is a strong linear relationship between the weight of a tiger, and the tiger's maximum running speed. A least-squares fit computed from a sample of tigers yielded the following estimated relationship between the maximum speed, in miles per hour, and weight in pounds:

$$\hat{y} = 101.6 - 0.153x \qquad 150 < x < 350$$

What is the estimated change in speed for an increase in 20 pounds in weight?

A. A decrease of 20 miles per hour
B. A decrease of 3 miles per hour
C. A decrease of 0.15 miles per hour
D. An increase of 3 miles per hour
E. An increase of 6 miles per hour

30. A candidate is seeking election as a delegate for a district representing four counties. The candidate's staff wants to take a random sample of 100 voters, in order to estimate the proportion of support the candidate has in the district. Which of the following methods will best produce a simple random sample?

A. Use random numbers to select 25 voters from each of the four counties.

B. Select the first 100 names on a voter registration list for the district.

C. Use random numbers to select 100 voters from a voter registration list for the district.

D. From the voter registration list, select every 10th name listed, until 100 are selected.

E. Send volunteers to street corners and select 100 people from the streets.

31. Suppose that, from a sample of 200 college students, each student's grade point average and parents' income level was compared. The correlation coefficient was measured to be $r = 0.27719$. Which of the following is the best description of the meaning of this correlation coefficient?

A. There is a strong, direct linear correlation between grade point average and parents' income level.

B. There is a weak, direct linear correlation between grade point average and parents' income level.

C. There is no correlation between grade point average and parents' income level.

D. There is a weak, inverse correlation between grade point average and parents' income level.

E. There is a strong, inverse correlation between grade point average and parents' income level.

GO ON TO THE NEXT PAGE

32. Suppose that there is a strong linear relationship between the height of a tree and its number of leaves. A least-squares fit from a sample of 1000 trees produced the following relationship:

$$\hat{y} = -116.7 + 50.2x \qquad 15 < x < 35$$

where x represents the height in feet, and y represents the number of leaves.

Based on this model, the predicted number of leaves for a two-foot-tall tree is negative 16 leaves. What is the best explanation for why the answer was negative, an impossible result?

A. The number of leaves is considered to be approximately zero in this case.

B. There is always variation in the result, so a negative value could be observed.

C. A two-foot-tall tree is not within the range of data the line was based on, so the prediction is invalid.

D. The relationship between height and number of leaves is not truly linear, so the results are invalid.

E. There was an error made in the computation of the original least-squares line.

33. In a test of a null hypothesis $H_0: \mu = 45$ against the alternate hypothesis $H_a: \mu > 45$, the sample produced a sample mean of 51.1. The p-value of the test statistic was 0.029. Which of the following is the best description of the meaning of the p-value in this case?

A. The sample mean will be greater than 45 2.9% of the time.

B. The sample mean will exceed 51.1 2.9% of the time.

C. There is a 0.029 probability that rejecting the null hypothesis is the correct decision.

D. There is a 0.029 probability that the sample mean would be 45, if the true mean was 51.1.

E. There is a 0.029 probability that the sample mean would exceed 51.1, if the true mean was 45.

34. Suppose that a population of pigs has a mean weight 290 pounds, with a standard deviation 75 pounds. A sample of 225 pigs is taken at random. The average weight of the pigs in the sample would follow which distribution?

A. Normally distributed with mean 290 pounds and standard deviation 75 pounds.

B. Normally distributed with mean 290 pounds and standard deviation 5 pounds.

C. Approximately normally distributed with mean 290 pounds and standard deviation 75 pounds.

D. Approximately normally distributed with mean 290 pounds and standard deviation 5 pounds.

E. The distribution cannot be determined from the information given.

35. The life span of a genus of insect has been found to follow a normal distribution. In a large sample of insects measured, it was found that 20% of the insects lived for less than 30.3 hours, and 5% of the insects lived for more than 67.6 hours. What are the mean and standard deviation for this population of insects?

A. $\mu = 41.5$ hours $\sigma = 13.3$ hours
B. $\mu = 41.5$ hours $\sigma = 14.5$ hours
C. $\mu = 42.9$ hours $\sigma = 15.0$ hours
D. $\mu = 48.9$ hours $\sigma = 9.5$ hours
E. $\mu = 48.9$ hours $\sigma = 22.1$ hours

36. An automobile manufacturer wants to create a 95% confidence interval for the mean gas mileage of their new GRX, in miles per gallon. In a pilot sample, the company has determined that the standard deviation in the gas mileage is $\sigma = 4.5$ miles per gallon. If they require that the margin of error for their confidence interval is no more than 0.5 miles per gallon, how many GRX automobiles should be tested?

A. 8
B. 18
C. 78
D. 220
E. 312

37. In testing the effectiveness of a new drug for gastric disorders, the laboratory wants to test whether the proportion of people experiencing side effects while taking the drug exceeds 10%. The drug was given to 360 subjects, and 47 of them reported that they experienced significant side effects. What is the approximate *p*-value related to the results of this test?

    A. 0.0266
    B. 0.0533
    C. 0.1306
    D. 0.4734
    E. 0.9734

38. Senator Feingold, while running for re-election as U.S. Senator, wants to estimate the percentage of support that he has in a closely contested county. In a poll of 650 voters from that county, 308 indicated that they would vote for Senator Feingold. Which of the following is a 90% confidence interval for the true percentage of support for Senator Feingold in this county?

    A. 44.9% to 49.9%
    B. 44.2% to 50.6%
    C. 43.5% to 51.2%
    D. 42.8% to 51.9%
    E. 42.3% to 52.4%

39. A trucking company wants to estimate the weight load capacity of a particular brand of their flatbed trucks. In measuring 13 of their trucks, the average load capacity was 2646 pounds, with a sample standard deviation 845 pounds. A *t*-interval was computed to be:

    2017.7 pounds to 3274.3 pounds

What confidence level does this interval represent?

    A. 80%
    B. 90%
    C. 95%
    D. 98%
    E. 99%

40. Suppose that an algebra class is being taught in a large lecture hall. Throughout the course of the semester, approximately 20% of the students tend to be absent on any given day. The professor wants to design a simulation to estimate the probabilities of having all five of five randomly selected students being present on a given day. Which of the following assignments of the digits 0 through 9 would be most appropriate for modeling the behavior of the students, using a random number table?

    A. Assign "0, 1, 2, 3, 4, 5, 6, and 7" as being absent, and "8 and 9" as being present.
    B. Assign "0, 1, and 2" as being absent, and "3, 4, 5, 6, 7, 8, and 9" as being present.
    C. Assign "0 and 1" as being absent, and "2, 3, 4, 5, 6, 7, 8, and 9" as being present.
    D. Assign "0, 1, 2, 3, 4, and 5" as being present, and "6, 7, 8, and 9" as being absent.
    E. Assign "0, 1, and 2" as being present, and "3, 4, 5, 6, 7, 8, and 9" as being absent.

Section II

Time: 1 hour and 30 minutes   Number of questions: 6   Percent of total grade: 50%

Part A

Questions 1–5   Spend about 65 minutes on this part of the exam.   Percent of Section II grade: 75%

Show all your work. Clearly indicate the methods you use—you will be graded on the correctness of your methods as well as the accuracy of your results and explanation.

1. A competitive university requires that students take a specialized series of standardized tests for admission to their graduate program. This series of tests consists of four parts: Mathematics, Verbal Skills, Logical Analysis, and Science Knowledge. The standardized scores for these four parts are constructed to follow a normal distribution with the following means and standard deviations. Assume that the scores for each part occur independently.

Test Part	Mean	Standard Deviation
Mathematics	400	100
Verbal Skills	500	150
Logical Analysis	300	75
Science Knowledge	400	100

   a. For general admission, the university requires that students take all four parts, and consideration will be based upon the sum of the four parts. What are the mean and standard deviation of this sum?

   b. If the university wants to consider only the top 25% of all applicants on this series of tests, what minimum total score should be considered acceptable?

   c. Suppose that the mathematics department, for admission to a mathematics specific major, requires that students score at least 600 on the mathematics portion, or at least 500 on both the mathematics and science knowledge portions, what approximate percentage of applicants will the mathematics department accept?

   d. Suppose that a group of 45 students from a highly regarded high school, who are now students at this university, are taking this series of tests. What would be an appropriate test to see whether students, in general, from this high school score above average on these tests?

2. The managers of a wildlife reserve want to estimate the total population of deer living in the reserve. To accomplish this, the managers have captured 100 deer at random, tagged them, and released the deer back into the population. One week later, 100 random deer have again been captured.

   a. Describe how the second sample of deer can be used to estimate the total population of the deer in the reserve.

   b. How might a confidence interval for population size be computed?

   c. What are some possible factors that may affect the randomness of the samples taken?

3. A pharmaceutical company wants to compare dosages of a new aspirin formulation with the amount of time it takes for patients to receive relief from headaches. Various dosages were given to patients, and the time at which the patients reported relief was recorded. Regression analysis was done, whereby x represented the dosage in milligrams, and y represented the time to relief in minutes. The following is the results of the study:

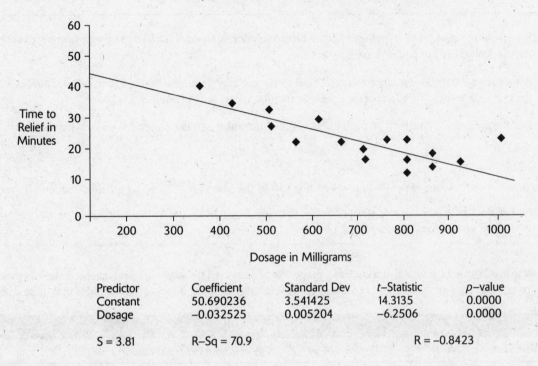

Scatterplot of Data with Least-Squares Regression Line

Predictor	Coefficient	Standard Dev	t–Statistic	p–value
Constant	50.690236	3.541425	14.3135	0.0000
Dosage	–0.032525	0.005204	–6.2506	0.0000

$S = 3.81$ $R–Sq = 70.9$ $R = –0.8423$

a. From the information given, what is the equation of the least-squares regression line relating time to relief and dosage? Define any variables used.

b. What is the correlation coefficient relating time to relief and dosage? Interpret the meaning of this value.

c. What is the predicted time to relief for a patient given a dosage of 500 milligrams of aspirin? From the scatterplot, what might the residuals be for the patients actually given this dosage? What are some possible explanations for these residuals?

d. If a patient is given a dosage of 2000 milligrams, the time to relief is a negative value, which is not possible. Explain why this occurs.

4. For a campaign for Congress, candidate Neumann is deciding whether to run extra ads in certain counties. His staff already feels that he has spent enough money running ads in Walworth County but is still deciding whether to run ads in Ozaukee County. To make this decision, they plan to estimate the percentage of support that candidate Neumann has in both counties, and whether there is very strong evidence that the support is lower in Ozaukee County than in Walworth County; then they will run extra ads in Ozaukee County.

a. What would be an appropriate hypothesis test, and level of significance, for this study?

b. From a poll of 500 voters in Walworth County, candidate Neumann had the support of 272. From a poll of 400 voters in Ozaukee County, candidate Neumann has the support of 204. What conclusions can be made from this data?

c. What are some practical reasons for not taking larger sample sizes for these polls?

GO ON TO THE NEXT PAGE

5. The Norton Candy Company is producing a new brand of candy called Dorks, which come in bags of 50, in colors red, orange, yellow, green, and purple. They desire that the colors be equally distributed, so they sample several bags. This was the distribution of the colors:

Red	Orange	Yellow	Green	Purple
72	65	98	74	91

a. Based on the appropriate hypothesis test, is there evidence, at the $\alpha = 0.05$ level of significance, to conclude that the colors are not equally distributed?

b. An additional color is introduced, and 80 blue Dorks are added to the sample. Again, is there now evidence, at the $\alpha = 0.05$ level of significance, to conclude that the colors are not equally distributed?

c. Did the conclusion change with the addition of the blue color into the sample? Why or why not?

Part B

Question 6   Spend about 25 minutes on this part of the exam.   Percent of Section II grade: 25%

Directions for Part B: Allow additional time for this part. Clearly indicate the methods that you use and give clear explanations for all your results.

6. A statistics instructor claims that a student's grade can be impacted by where the student sits in the classroom. The instructor teaches four classes, and at the end of the semester, has placed the students' grades into these categories:

Final Grades			
	A–B	C–D	F–W (W = withdrew from course)
Sat in Front	24	17	8
Sat in Middle	19	20	10
Sat in Back	11	26	14

a. Based on this data, is there evidence to suggest that a student's grade is impacted by their positioning in the classroom?

b. In order to examine more closely the impact of seating position on grades, the instructor reconstructed the chart to show all possible grades:

Final Grades						
	A	B	C	D	F	W
Sat in Front	16	8	12	5	7	1
Sat in Middle	7	12	11	9	8	2
Sat in Back	1	10	7	19	9	5

Based on this reconstructed chart, is there evidence to suggest that a student's grade is impacted by their positioning in the classroom?

c. What are some other ways the instructor could have subdivided the categories? How may the defining of categories impact the outcome of a test comparing the effect of one variable on another?

Section 1 Answers

1. **D.** Since the pattern of the residuals exhibits an approximate parabolic shape, the relationship between x and y would not be linear. However, because of the parabolic shape, the variables x and y may be fit by a quadratic relationship, which is nonlinear.

2. **C.** The slope of the regression line is $b_1 = 8.249$. From the regression results, the standard deviation of the slope is $s_{b_1} = 0.44689$ found in the chart as "stdev" for Height. With degrees of freedom = (sample size – 2) = (11 – 2) = 9, the 95% confidence interval would be $(8.249) \pm (2.262)(0.44689) = 8.249 \pm 1.011$.

3. **B.** The ratio of people who enter the casino is 11300/16500. Among those, there is a 0.85 probability that a person would play a casino game. Therefore, the expected number of people, out of a random sample of 200, who would play a casino game, would be (200)(11300/16500)(0.85), or approximately 116.

4. **B.** For a paired t-test, the degrees of freedom is the number of pairs, minus 1. There are eight people being tested, creating eight pairs of values. The degrees of freedom is 7.

5. **B.** Counting the number of successful applicants out of a total number of applicants would be a binomial random variable, in this case, with probability of success p = 0.45. The expected number of successes, out of a sample of size $n = 960$ would be $np = (960)(0.45) = 432$.

6. **E.** The only condition listed that is a requirement for using the t-test, over a z-test, is that the true standard deviation is not known. Being a simple random sample would actually be preferred in either case, so *not* being a simple random sample would not be a requirement. Having a sample size under 30 is not required, since t-test is preferable for any sample size, if standard deviation is not known. Being only approximately normal is not a requirement, since the t-distribution applies when the underlying population is normal, but the standard deviation is unknown. Knowing the population mean does not apply in this case.

7. **A.** Plan I is the superior plan, because both the initial selection of the deer, and the second selection, are based on random samples from the population. Plan II lacks randomness, because only the one square mile region is taken at random. This process would not take into consideration factors, such as terrain, that may affect the distribution of the deer over the region, whereby the deer would not be randomly chosen into the samples.

8. **B.** The factors are correlated, directly, since it is indicated that higher grades in high school algebra correspond to higher college grade-point averages. However, a cause-and-effect relationship is likely not in place, since it would not be the algebra grades, themselves, that cause the college grades. Rather, both grade measurements would have a causal relationship with a third factor, the quality of the student.

9. **A.** The 95% t-interval, with 37 degrees of freedom, would have the construction $12317 \pm (2.026)(2959/\sqrt{38})$. Therefore, the interval would be [11344 , 13290].

10. **D.** A tree whose height is at the 95th percentile would be approximately the cutoff for the highest 5% of all trees. The z-score representing the cutoff for the highest 5% is 1.645, or 1.645 standard deviations above the mean. In this case, the tree height would be approximately 20.2 + (1.645)(6.5) = 30.9 feet.

11. **A.** To find the conditional probability of an item being a ring, given that the item is orange, use the formula $P(\text{ring and orange})/P(\text{orange})$. The $P(\text{ring and orange}) = 10/85$, and the $P(\text{orange}) = 25/85$. Therefore, the conditional probability $P(\text{ring} \mid \text{orange}) = (10/85)/(25/85) = 0.4$.

12. **E.** To find the probability that at least one of the alarm clocks will ring can be found by using the complement rule. The $P(\text{at least one alarm clock will ring}) = 1 - P(\text{neither will ring})$. Since the probabilities that each clock will fail to ring is 0.05 and 0.02, the $P(\text{at least one alarm clock will ring}) = 1 - (0.05)(0.02) = 0.9990$.

13. **E.** The "profit," or the amount of money that would be made after the nickel is paid, would follow this distribution: $P(\text{profit} = 0.95) = 0.01$, $P(\text{profit} = 0.20) = 0.02$, $P(\text{profit} = 0) = 0.10$, and $P(\text{profit} = \text{negative } 0.05) = 0.87$. The expected value of a random variable would follow the formula $E(X) = \Sigma\, x P(X = x) = (0.95)(0.01) + (0.20)(0.02) + (0.00)(0.10) + (-0.05)(0.87) = -0.03$.

14. **E.** The percentile associated with a score represents how many whole percent of all scores lie below that score. Therefore, if a score is in the 90th percentile, this means that 90% of all other scores are below that score.

15. D. The center box for Set A is wider than the center box for Set B, indicating a greater interquartile range for Set A. Other statements concerning the exact mean, standard deviation, set size, or presence of outliers cannot be justified, since the exact distribution of actual data points cannot be determined from the boxplot alone.

16. A. The definition of "random sample" is that each possible sample of size n is equally likely to be chosen as the sample of size n. Therefore, if a sample is random, each member of the population is equally likely to be included in the sample. A random sample does not need to have any particular size, nor does the random sample guarantee that each stratum of the population will be represented or that the values will follow any pattern.

17. A. The interval [2 mpg , 5 mpg] is given as a 99% confidence interval for the difference in the true means, μ_A and μ_B. Thus, by the definition of confidence interval, there is a 99% probability that the difference $\mu_B - \mu_A$ is contained within the interval [2 mpg , 5 mpg].

18. D. The given z-score –2.50 means that the observed value lay 2.5 standard deviations below the population mean. Thus, the correct interpretation is that the output of the Arizona mine was 2.5 standard deviations below the national average.

19. C. The goal in this case was to best represent the typical student in the large class. The typical student, which made up the largest portion of the class, was a Freshman. By assigning values 1, 2, 3, and 4 to the students, the mode, the value which appears most often, would indicate that the Freshmen make up the greatest portion of the class.

20. E. Standard deviation gives a measure of the amount of variation in the values in either a sample or a population. In this case, the standard deviation would give a measure of the amount of variation in the wattages in the sample of power strips. Low variation would indicate that the values are, on the whole, close to the mean. Therefore, standard deviation would be the best indicator of stability.

21. D. With $P(\text{Head}) = 0.60$ and $P(\text{Tail}) = 0.40$, $P(\text{no heads out of two}) = (0.40)(0.40) = 0.16$, $P(\text{one head out of two}) = 2(0.60)(0.40) = 0.48$, and $P(\text{two heads out of two}) = (0.60)(0.60) = 0.36$. These probabilities would produce these expected values for 200 trials of $(200)(0.16) = 32$, $(200)(0.48) = 96$, and $(200)(0.36) = 72$, respectively.

22. A. To compute the expected value, use the formula $E(X) = \Sigma x P(X = x)$, which in this case would be $(1)(0.02) + (2)(0.11) + (3)(0.34) + (4)(0.31) + (5)(0.21) + (6)(0.01) = 3.61$.

23. B. The only statement that is not true is the claim that the ranges are equal. The range for Stockton is $(38 - 17) = 21$, and the range for Waffletown is $(37 - 18) = 19$. The other statements are true. Waffletown has 5 players over 30, and Stockton has 4 players over 30. The ages of the Stockton players, if compared in order, are equal, or lower than each corresponding age of the Waffletown players, with the exception of only the oldest player. The median age for Waffletown is 24.5, and the median age for Stockton is 23.5. Stockton has 9 players in their 20s, and Waffletown has 7.

24. E. The exact probability cannot be determined. However, since the population is finite, and the sample has proven that failures exist in the population, the probability of batteries in the population being good cannot be 1.

25. B. The probabilities for a discrete probability distribution must add up to 1. Therefore, it must be the case that $0.15 + x + x + 2x + 0.25 + 0.20 = 1$. Solving equation, $x = 0.10$.

26. A. The 95% t-interval, with 34 degrees of freedom, would have the construction $87.7 \pm (2.032)(24.4/\sqrt{35})$. Therefore, the interval would be 87.7 ± 8.38.

27. B. In order to compare values from different populations, z-scores are computed. The z-score for the Kampuchea monkey is $z = (44 - 42)/(17) = 0.12$. The z-score for the Zanzibar monkey is $z = (19 - 15)/3 = 1.33$. Therefore, since the Zanzibar monkey has the higher z-score, the Zanzibar monkey would be considered as larger for its breed.

28. B. Using normal approximation to binomial, $\mu = np = (100)(0.85) = 85$, and $\sigma = \sqrt{npq} = \sqrt{(100)(0.85)(0.15)} = 3.570714$. To estimate the probability of the number of successes being at least 90, the z-score is computed for 89.5, applying the proper "continuity correction." The z-score for 89.5 is $z = (89.5 - 85)/(3.570714) = 1.26$. The approximate probability of exceeding a z-score of 1.26 is 0.1038.

29. B. The slope of the regression line, in this case, is -0.153, which represents a decrease of 0.153 in the value of y for each increase in one unit of x. Therefore, if x is increased by 20 pounds, the speed, y, would be decreased by $(0.153)(20)$ or approximately 3 mph.

30. C. To produce a simple random sample, all values in the population must be equally likely to be chosen into the sample. Therefore, a random process should be implemented that selects values from the population, as one single, nonstratified group. Using random numbers to select voters from a voter registration list would best produce a random sample from the entire population. Selecting 25 voters from four counties would produce a stratified sample, whereas selecting the first 100 voters on a list is not a random process. Selecting every 10th voter on a list is a systematic process that is not random, and selecting voters from street corners eliminates a large number of voters from the possibility of selection.

31. B. The computed correlation coefficient is $r = 0.27719$. Since r is non-zero, some correlation is indicated. Since r is positive, the correlation is direct. Since r is closer to 0 than to 1, the correlation is weak.

32. C. It is indicated that the regression equation is valid for values—in this case, heights of trees—within the interval $[15, 35]$. This indicates that the least-squares regression line was based on values in a sample whose x-values were within this interval. This regression line would be unreliable, and predictions would be invalid for values outside this range of values. In using the regression line to predict the number of leaves for a tree that is 2 feet tall, the prediction is invalid, since 2 feet is outside the range of data where the least-squares regression line was fit.

33. E. The *p-value* of a test statistic represents the level of a test at which the null hypothesis would be rejected, if the null hypothesis was true. In this case, then, there would be a 0.029 probability of observing a sample mean of 51.1, if the true mean was 45.0.

34. D. The exact underlying distribution of the weights of the pigs is not known. However, by the Central Limit Theorem, if the sample size is 30 or greater, the sample mean, x, would follow an approximate normal distribution, with mean μ, and standard deviation $\sigma/\sqrt{n}$. Therefore, with sample size 225, the sample average would follow an approximate normal distribution with mean 290 pounds, and standard deviation $75/\sqrt{225} = 5$ pounds.

35. C. The value 30.3 hours represents the cutoff for the bottom 20%, or the value that lies 0.841 standard deviation below the mean. The value 67.6 hours represents the cutoff for the top 5%, or the value that lies 1.645 standard deviations above the mean. Thus, the following two equations would be true: $\mu - 0.841\sigma = 30.3$ and $\mu + 1.645\sigma = 67.6$. Solving the two equations for μ and σ, would give the result $\mu = 42.9$ and $\sigma = 15.0$.

36. E. With an estimated population standard deviation $\sigma = 4.5$ mpg, in order to create a 95% confidence interval for mean, with error no greater than 0.5 mpg, the following formula should be used: $n \geq (z\sigma/E)^2$. Thus, the minimum sample size would be $n \geq [(1.960)(4.5)/(0.5)]^2 = 311.1696$. Therefore, the minimum sample size would be 312.

37. A. The observed proportion in this sample was 47/360. This is being tested against the claim that the true proportion is 0.10. The *z*-statistic for a test of proportion would be $z = \left(\hat{p} - p\right)/\sqrt{pq/n}$. In this case, $z = (47/360 - 0.10)/\sqrt{(0.10)(0.90)/360} = 1.93$. The p-value, or probability of exceeding $z = 1.93$, is 0.0266.

38. B. The observed proportion in this sample was $308/650 = 0.4738$. The corresponding 90% confidence interval for the true population proportion would be $0.4738 \pm (1.645)/\sqrt{(0.4738)(0.5262)/650}$, or 0.4738 ± 0.0322.

39. D. This *t*-interval for population mean is of the form $2646 \pm E$, where $E = 628.3$, and the degrees of freedom is 12. The error term is $E = ts/\sqrt{n} = t(845)/\sqrt{13} = 628.3$. Solving for t, the t-value, for 12 degrees of freedom, is 2.681, which corresponds to 0.01 area on the tail of the t-distribution, or a 98% confidence level.

40. C. In order to simulate a process whereby 20% of students are absent, and 80% of students are present, assign two of the random digits to represent "absent" and eight of the random digits to represent "present." Assigning 0 and 1 to represent "absent" and the remainder of the digits as "present" will accomplish this.

Section II Answers

1a. The mean of the sum of four random variables is $\mu_1 + \mu_2 + \mu_3 + \mu_4 = 400 + 500 + 300 + 400 = 1600$. The variance of the sum of four random variables is $\sigma_1^2 + \sigma_2^2 + \sigma_3^2 + \sigma_4^2 = 100^2 + 150^2 + 75^2 + 100^2 = 48125$. Therefore, the standard deviation of the sum is $\sqrt{48125} = 219.374$.

1b. The minimum value that lies in the highest 25% would be approximately $z = 0.674$ deviation above the mean, since the scores are normally distributed. Therefore, the minimum value would be approximately $1600 + (0.674)(219.374) = 1747.858$, or a minimum score of 1748.

1c. If X is the score on the mathematics part, and Y is the score on the science part, the probability can be found by finding $P(X > 600, \text{ or } X > 500 \text{ and } Y > 500) = P(X > 600) + P(X > 500 \text{ and } Y > 500) - P(X > 600, \text{ and } X > 500 \text{ and } Y > 500) = P(X > 600) + P(X > 500)P(Y > 500) - P(X > 600)P(Y > 500)$, since X and Y are independent. $P(X > 600) = P(z > (600-400)/100 = 2) = 0.0228$. $P(X > 500) = P(z > (500-400)/100 = 1) = 0.1587$. $P(Y > 500) = P(z > (500-400)/100 = 1) = 0.1587$. Therefore, $P(X > 600, \text{ or } X > 500 \text{ and } Y > 500) = (0.0228) + (0.1587)(0.1587) - (0.0228)(0.1587) = 0.0444$.

1d. Since the sum of the scores is normally distributed, and the standard deviation is known, it is appropriate to perform a hypothesis test using z. Moreover, since it is desired that evidence be found in favor of the group of students who perform above average, this claim should be the alternate claim. Thus, the test should be set up with H_o: $\mu = 1600$ and H_a: $\mu > 1600$, and the sample average, x, can be taken from the 45 students in the group. The test statistic would be the z-value, computed with the known standard deviation of 219.374, so that $z = (x - 1600)/(219.374/\sqrt{45})$. Depending on the α-level of significance that is used, the critical value would be $z > z_\alpha$, or the upper-tail p-value can be used.

2a. Assuming that both samples of deer are taken randomly, the population size can be estimated from the proportion of tagged deer in the second sample. Since each of the 100 deer in the first sample was tagged and then released into the population, it is reasonable to assume that the larger the actual population, the lower the proportion should be of deer in the second sample that are tagged. The first sample represents 100 total tagged deer out of the entire population, and the second sample represents a proportion of tagged deer out of 100 taken from the entire population. If x = the number of tagged deer in the second sample, and N = total population size, then the ratios should be proportionate within randomness as $(100/N) = (x/100)$. Solving for N, an estimate for N would be $N = (10,000/x)$.

2b. If $p = x/100$ is an estimate for the proportion of deer, out of 100, that will be tagged, provided that conditions for normality hold, namely that $np \geq 5$ and $n(1 - p) \geq 5$, a confidence interval for the proportion can be computed as $[p_1, p_2]$, where $p_1 = p - z\sqrt{(p(1-p)/100}$ and $p_2 = p + z\sqrt{(p(1-p)/100}$ depending on the level of confidence desired. Since the estimate of N is $N = (10,000/x) = 100/p$, the confidence interval for N would be $(100/p_2) < N < (100/p_1)$.

2c. A number of possible answers can be given, but those affecting randomness should involve those factors that prevent each individual deer from being equally likely to be chosen into the sample. Some examples may include terrain of the territory that prevents access to all areas where deer may be, the varying agility in deer which may prevent some from being easily captured, the ages of deer such as infant deer or elderly deer being unavailable in easily accessible locations, the time of year whereby weather conditions may affect the availability or accessibility of deer, or the fact that other outside sources may cause deer to exit or enter the territory such as wandering off, immigration, or hunting.

3a. From the regression results, $\hat{y} = 50.690236 - 0.032525x$, where $\hat{y}$ = the predicted time to relief from headache, and x = the dosage of the aspirin in milligrams.

3b. The correlation coefficient is $r = -0.8423$. Since the absolute value is near 1, the relationship is a fairly strong linear relationship. Since the value is negative, the relationship is an inverse one, implying that increases in x, the dosage, will tend to result in a decrease in y, the time to relief.

3c. The predicted time to relief for the patient with dosage $x = 500$ mg would be $\hat{y} = 50.690236 - (0.032525)(500) = 34.427736$ minutes, or approximately 34.4 minutes. At 500, there is one value 2–3 units above the regression line and one value 2–3 units below. The residuals would be positive 2–3, and another negative 2–3. This implies that one patient took 2–3 minutes longer than predicted to receive the relief, and the other took 2–3 minutes less to receive relief. Possible explanations may vary, but they may include the patients' weight, age, rate of metabolism, internal susceptibility to the drug, or personal immune system in terms of healing the headache regardless of the drug. In other words, the dosage, x, is only one of many possible predictors of the time of relief, y.

3d. The predicted time for $x = 2000$ mg dosage is $\hat{y} = 50.690236 - (0.032525)(2000) = -14.359764$. Note that the range of data from which the least-squares regression line was fit was 350 to 1000. Based on the strong linear fit as indicated by the correlation coefficient, the data is approximately linear within the range of data. The regression line has not been fit to data points outside this range, and, therefore, it is invalid to assume that the relationship will remain linear outside this range. Since 2000 is well outside the range of data, a prediction based on the current regression line is invalid and unreliable.

4a. Since it is desired to see whether the proportion in Ozaukee County is lower than the proportion in Walworth County, construct the test whereby H_o: $p_1 = p_2$ and H_a: $p_1 < p_2$, with $p_1 =$ proportion in Ozaukee and $p_2 =$ proportion in Walworth. Since it is desired that there be very strong evidence, the level of significance, α, should be very low; for instance, set $\alpha = 0.01$ or lower.

4b. Based on the hypothesis set up given previously, the estimated proportion for Ozaukee is $\hat{p}_1 = 204/400 = 0.510$, and the estimated proportion for Walworth is $\hat{p}_2 = 272/500 = 0.544$. The pooled proportion is $p = 476/900 = 0.5288889$, resulting in a z-test statistic of $z = (0.510 - 0.544)/\sqrt{((0.529)(0.471)/400 + (0.529)(0.471)/500)} = -1.015$. At the $\alpha = 0.01$ level of significance, since z is not less than -2.326, there is not sufficient evidence to conclude that candidate Neumann's proportion of support in Ozaukee is less than his proportion of support in Walworth County. Therefore, his campaign staff should not spend money running the additional ads in Ozaukee County.

4c. There are various reasons for not taking larger sample sizes, the most common being cost. There are also other concerns, such as lack of availability of resources, time constraints, or lack of staff to be able to generate larger sample sizes. Also, in campaigns, access to voter registration lists, which are necessary for generating truly random samples, may be constrained.

5a. The appropriate hypothesis test would be a χ^2-Goodness of Fit Test, whereby the null hypothesis is H_o: The colors are equally distributed, and the alternate hypothesis is H_a:. The colors are not equally distributed. The total sample size is $n = 400$, so the expected values for each category would be 80. The χ^2-test statistic is $\chi^2 = \Sigma (O - E)^2/E = (72 - 80)^2/80 + (65 - 80)^2/80 + (98 - 80)^2/80 + (74 - 80)^2/80 + (91 - 80)^2/80 = 9.625$. With the level of significance $\alpha = 0.05$, and degrees of freedom = number of categories $- 1 = 4$, since the χ^2 statistic exceeds the value 9.488, there is evidence that the colors are not equally distributed.

5b. With 80 additional blue Dorks added to the sample, the new sample size becomes $n = 480$, but with one additional category, the expected values for each category remains 80. The χ^2-test statistic for this test is also $\chi^2 = (72 - 80)^2/80 + (65 - 80)^2/80 + (98 - 80)^2/80 + (74 - 80)^2/80 + (91 - 80)^2/80 + (80 - 80)^2/80 = 9.625$. However, with level of significance $\alpha = 0.05$, and degrees of freedom = number of categories $- 1 = 5$, since the χ^2 statistic does not exceed the value 11.071, there is no longer sufficient evidence, in this case, to conclude that the colors are not equally distributed.

5c. Yes, the conclusion did change with the addition of the new category, blue. Although the χ^2-test statistic was the same in both cases, the critical value for rejection increased, with the addition of one more category, and thus one more degree of freedom. Practically speaking, the overall fit to "equally distributed" did become better, since the new category, blue, had exactly 80 items, which was exactly equal to the expected value of 80 per category.

6a. The appropriate test is a χ^2-Test of Independence, whereby the null hypothesis is H_o: Grade is independent of Seating Position, and the alternate hypothesis is H_a: Grade is not independent of Seating Position. By applying the two-way computation of expected values, the matrix of expected values would be

	A–B	C–D	F–W
Sat in Front	17.76	20.72	10.52
Sat in Middle	17.76	20.72	10.52
Sat in Back	18.48	21.56	10.95

with sample size $n = 149$. The corresponding χ^2-test statistic is $\chi^2 = \Sigma (O - E)^2/E = 8.394$, which has a corresponding p-value of 0.0782. Also, with degrees of freedom = (number of rows $- 1$)(number of columns $- 1$) = 4, the critical value cutoffs for levels $\alpha = 0.10$, $\alpha = 0.05$, and $\alpha = 0.01$ would be 7.779, 9.488, and 13.277, respectively. Rejection of the null hypothesis would only occur for level $\alpha = 0.10$, which would indicate that there is some evidence, but not strong evidence, to show that a student's grade is impacted by position in the classroom.

6b. Again, applying the χ^2-Test of Independence, the two-way computation of expected values produces this matrix of expected values:

	A	B	C	D	F	W
Sat in Front	7.89	9.87	9.87	10.85	7.89	2.63
Sat in Middle	7.89	9.87	9.87	10.85	7.89	2.63
Sat in Back	8.21	10.27	10.27	11.30	8.21	2.74

The corresponding χ^2-test statistic in this case is $\chi^2 = 29.155$, which has a corresponding p-value of 0.0012. With degrees of freedom = (number of rows − 1)(number of columns − 1) = 10, the critical value cutoffs for levels $\alpha = 0.10$, $\alpha = 0.05$, and $\alpha = 0.01$ would be 15.987, 18.307, and 23.209, respectively. Rejection of the null hypothesis would occur at each of these levels, which indicates strong evidence that a student's grade is, indeed, impacted by position in the classroom.

6c. The instructor could have also subdivided positioning into other categories, such as "sits on right side," "sits on left side," and "sits in middle." There are also other considerations, such as "moved around" and "sat in one place." The category of grades could have been redone, so as not to include "Ws" among the grades at all, or possibly kept "F–W" as a category, while still separating the individual grades into individual categories. As shown by the two tests in this problem, the defining of categories can have a dramatic impact on the outcome of a test. Dividing data into too few categories can hide differences that may exist within those categories themselves, thus giving the appearance that a dependent variable is not affected by an independent variable, when in fact, it is. However, dividing data into too many categories can have a similar effect in that the differences between subdivisions can be distinct and numerous, but become minute, whereby a high "degrees of freedom" will result in failing to reject a null hypothesis when the test statistic is compared to a critical value.

Practice Test 2

Section I

Time: 1 hour and 30 minutes   Number of questions: 40   Percent of total grade: 50%

Directions: Solve each problem. Decide which is the best of the answer choices given.

---

1. Two measures, x and y, were taken, and yielded the least-squares regression line $\hat{y} = 25.56 - 7.76x$. The following is a plot of the residuals for the regression analysis:

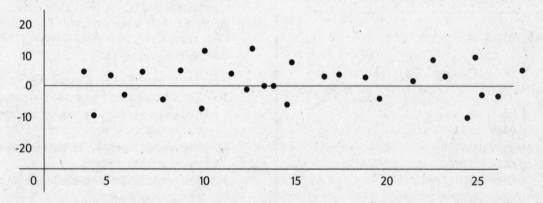

Which of the following statements is supported by this information?

A. There is a strong, direct linear relationship between x and y.

B. There is a strong, inverse linear relationship between x and y.

C. There is a linear relationship between x and y, but it cannot be determined whether the relationship is direct or inverse from the information given.

D. There is a strong relationship between x and y, but the relationship is nonlinear.

E. There is no strong relationship between x and y.

GO ON TO THE NEXT PAGE

2. Slippery Stone College desires to study the relationship between an applicant's SAT score and score on the foreign language placement exam. Sixteen applicants were included in the sample, and it was determined that there was a linear relationship between the SAT scores and the placement exam scores. The results of the regression analysis are given here:

Regression Equation:

Foreign = 23.715 + 0.0489 SAT

Predictor	Coef	Stdev	t-ratio	p
Constant	23.715133	0.290305	81.6904	0.000
SAT	0.0489032	0.007954	6.1477	0.000

S = 8.370   R-sq = 70.3

Which of the following would represent a 95% confidence interval for the slope of the regression line?

A. 0.0489 ± 0.0140
B. 0.0489 ± 0.0156
C. 0.0489 ± 0.0168
D. 0.0489 ± 0.0171
E. 0.0489 ± 0.6227

3. Suppose that the correlation between a set of scores X and a set of scores Y is equal to 0.65. If the scores are reversed, so that the X scores become the Y scores, and the Y scores become the X scores, what would the new correlation between the scores be?

A. -0.65
B. -0.35
C. 0.00
D. 0.35
E. 0.65

4. Suppose that a set of scores on a standardized test is normally distributed, with mean 170, and standard deviation 50. If the professor for the course divides all scores by 2, what would be the new mean and standard deviation of the set of scores?

A. Mean 170   Standard deviation 50
B. Mean 170   Standard deviation 25
C. Mean 85   Standard deviation 50
D. Mean 85   Standard deviation 35.35
E. Mean 85   Standard deviation 25

5. A test has been given in a trigonometry class of 35 students. The mean on the test was 81, with a median of 77, and standard deviation 16. The teacher indicated that there was one outlier among the scores. If the teacher removes the outlier from the list of scores, which of the following statements would be true?

A. The mean and median would both go up.
B. The mean and median would both go down.
C. The mean would go up, but the median would stay the same.
D. The median would go up, but the mean would stay the same.
E. The result cannot be determined from the information given.

6. Suppose that a fishing company wants to create a 95% confidence interval for the mean number of fish that are caught by their fishing boats each day. A sample of 100 boats was measured, and the observed confidence interval was

1033 fish to 1357 fish

Another sample of boats is taken, but with a sample size 200. What effect will this have on the confidence interval?

A. The new confidence interval will be approximately the same.
B. The new confidence interval will have a higher confidence level.
C. The new confidence interval will be narrower.
D. The new confidence interval will be wider.
E. The new confidence interval will have approximately the same width, but the center of the interval will be higher.

7. A large monkey house at a zoo has a population of 950 monkeys. The weights of the monkeys follow an approximate normal distribution with mean 37 pounds and standard deviation 11 pounds. Approximately how many monkeys would be in the range of 26 pounds to 48 pounds?

   A. 425
   B. 645
   C. 855
   D. 900
   E. 945

8. Suppose that a newspaper in Wisconsin wants to take a statewide survey concerning issues regarding state budgetary issues. The newspaper creates a sample by randomly selecting 50 people from each county in the state. Which of the following terms best describes the type of sample that is being created?

   A. A simple random sample
   B. A convenience sample
   C. A stratified sample
   D. A systematic sample
   E. A cluster sample

9. Suppose that the night before a national election, the host of a radio show asked callers to call his program and indicate which of the candidates they would vote for. At the end of the program, the radio show host indicated that, based on his survey, a certain candidate would likely win. However, on election day, the candidate lost. Which of the following is the most likely explanation for why the radio show's survey was wrong?

   A. The survey was voluntary, and only those who wanted to participate did.
   B. The question to the callers was slanted, producing incorrect results.
   C. A large number of callers lied in their responses.
   D. The survey was accurate, but many people changed their minds when they voted.
   E. The sample size was too small.

10. The following two-way contingency table represents results from a test as to whether taking an MCSE study course has a positive effect on students wanting to pass the MCSE server test.

	Passed Test	Failed Test
Took MCSE study course	57	23
Did not take MCSE study course	61	77

If the null hypothesis is that the MCSE study course has no effect on whether students pass the test, which of the following values gives the expected number of people, taking the MCSE study course, who would pass the test?

   A. 18
   B. 43
   C. 57
   D. 59
   E. 118

11. A dietician has developed a new diet called the Life Science Diet, which is claimed to reduce LDL cholesterol levels for those who use the diet. The dietician wants to test the diet by sampling a random group of 25 people. The dietician will measure the LDL cholesterol levels of each of the 25 people and then measure their cholesterol levels after people in the sample have used the Life Science Diet for eight weeks. Which of the following tests would be most appropriate for this study?

   A. t-test of one sample
   B. z-test of two independent samples
   C. t-test of two independent samples
   D. t-test of paired data
   E. chi-square test of independence

GO ON TO THE NEXT PAGE

12. A geologist takes a simple random sample from a population and creates a 90% z-interval for the population mean. The width of the interval is 6 feet. The geologist has determined that the interval is too wide. Which of the following procedures will make the interval narrower?

   A.   Increase the confidence level from 90 to 95.

   B.   Create a *t*-interval instead of a *z*-interval.

   C.   Take a stratified sample instead of a simple random sample.

   D.   Take a pilot sample in order to better estimate the population standard deviation first.

   E.   Increase the sample size.

13. A mining company wants to test a claim concerning the mean weight of their silver nuggets. They are testing the null hypothesis that the true mean is 3 ounces, against the alternate hypothesis that the mean is less than 3 ounces. The *p*-value for the hypothesis test was determined to be 0.023. Which of the following is a correct interpretation of this *p*-value?

   A.   The null hypothesis would be rejected at a 0.05 level, but not at a 0.01 level.

   B.   The null hypothesis would be rejected at a 0.01 level, but not at a 0.05 level.

   C.   The null hypothesis would be rejected at both the 0.05 and 0.01 levels.

   D.   The null hypothesis would not be rejected at either the 0.05 or 0.01 levels.

   E.   The null hypothesis would only be rejected if the test was a two-tail test.

14. At a college football game, several thousand colored balloons have been released into the stadium at halftime. In a sample of 150 of these balloons, it was determined that 34 of them were popped. Which of the following is a 90% confidence interval for the true proportion of balloons in the stadium that were popped?

   A.   0.160 to 0.294

   B.   0.170 to 0.283

   C.   0.173 to 0.287

   D.   0.182 to 0.270

   E.   0.196 to 0.264

15. The television station WVTV wants to determine whether men and women watch the same amount of television, on the average, per day. In order to test this claim, the station, by means of a television ad, has asked volunteers to respond to a survey regarding how much time they spend watching television. On hundred seventy-three women responded to the ad, and 214 men responded to the ad. The mean time for each of the two groups was computed and a *t*-test statistic was computed, comparing two independent samples. Which of the following changes is necessary to make the test more accurate?

   A.   The test should have been done with a *z*-statistic instead of a *t*-statistic.

   B.   Equal sample sizes should have been taken.

   C.   The sample sizes should have been larger.

   D.   The samples should have been taken by a random process, and not by a voluntary procedure.

   E.   The test should have been done as a paired *t*-test.

16. A least-squares regression line was computed that relates the number of hours studied for an exam and the score the student earns on the exam. The equation of the line is

$$\hat{y} = 51.7 + 3.47x$$

where *x* represents the number of hours studied for the exam, and *y* represents the score on the exam. Based on this predicted relationship, approximately how many hours should a student study, if the student wants to get at least an 85 on the exam?

   A.   3

   B.   10

   C.   14

   D.   39

   E.   347

17. Which of the following statements are NOT true about the standard normal distribution?

    I.   The standard normal distribution is symmetric.

    II. The standard normal distribution has mean 0 and standard deviation 1.

    III. The area under the standard normal curve, for any nonzero interval, is positive, and no more than 1.

    A. I only
    B. II only
    C. I and II only
    D. I and III only
    E. I, II, and III are all true.

18. Suppose that p is the probability that a certain California town will experience a cataclysmic earthquake during the course of any given year. What would be the value of p, if the probability of a cataclysmic earthquake NOT occurring in the space of 100 years is approximately 0.5?

    A. approximately 0
    B. 0.001
    C. 0.005
    D. 0.007
    E. 0.993

19. The following two-way contingency table represents a test of whether passing a college entrance exam is independent of the year of the high school student.

	Passed Exam	*Failed Exam*
Freshman	4	17
Sophomore	8	11
Junior	22	9
Senior	40	6

Which of the following is the degrees of freedom for this test?

    A. 2
    B. 3
    C. 4
    D. 7
    E. 8

20. A least-squares regression line is computed, relating a college graduate's grade point average and the graduate's starting yearly salary upon first employment. The equation of the line is

$$\hat{y} = -10769 + 13855x$$

where x represents grade point average, and y represents yearly salary in dollars. A student with a grade point average of 3.19 had a starting salary of \$27000. Which of the following is the residual, in dollars, for this student?

    A. −33428
    B. −6428
    C. −3376
    D. 6428
    E. 33428

21. The manager of an auto dealership wishes to test whether five brands of automobiles are equally popular among customers. During the course of a week, sales of the five brands followed this chart:

Secord	*Alto*	*Lionel*	*Tahoe*	*Zenith*
23	17	21	29	10

What is the value of the χ^2 test statistic for the appropriate goodness-of-fit test?

    A. 1.300
    B. 1.665
    C. 10.000
    D. 13.761
    E. 110.000

GO ON TO THE NEXT PAGE

22. In a study of the effect of volunteerism, the incidence of juvenile delinquency was observed to be higher among 7th and 8th grade children who were not involved in volunteer activities. As part of an effort to reduce juvenile delinquency among 7th and 8th grade children, such children who were involved in a crime were required to join a volunteer activity. However, the incidence of juvenile delinquency was not reduced among these children. Which of the following is the most likely explanation for the error in the expectation that the volunteer activities would reduce the delinquency?

   A. The differences between boys and girls involved in delinquency was not considered.

   B. There was a correlation between volunteer activities and low delinquency, but the correlation was not strong.

   C. There were confounding factors among the children involved in the delinquency.

   D. It was assumed that the volunteer activities were the cause of low delinquency, not merely a factor that was correlated to low delinquency.

   E. Another sample of children might reveal that juvenile delinquency is actually higher among the children who are involved in volunteer activities.

23. Suppose that event A and event B are independent events. Which of the following statements is NOT true?

   A. The events cannot be mutually exclusive.

   B. $P(A \text{ and } B) = P(A) \cdot P(B)$.

   C. If event A occurs, the probability of event B occurring does not change.

   D. $P(A \text{ or } B) = P(A) + P(B)$.

   E. The conditional probability of event A, given B, is equal to the probability of event A.

24. A research company desires to test the effect of a drug meant to reduce the effect of migraine headaches. Two groups are tested. One group is given the drug, and the patients are instructed to indicate whether they feel relief from the drug. Another group is given a placebo, a fake pill, and also instructed to indicate whether they feel relief. The test is done as a double-blind study. What is meant by saying that the study is "double blind?"

   A. Neither group knows whether they are receiving the actual drug or the placebo.

   B. Neither the patient nor the doctor administering the pill knows whether the pill is the actual drug or the placebo.

   C. Not only do the patients not know whether the pill is the actual drug or the placebo, but they also do not know why they are taking a pill.

   D. It is not known how many of the patients are taking actual drugs or the placebos.

   E. Patients are blindfolded while they are given one of the pills.

25. A zoologist is testing a claim concerning the mean weights of a breed of toads. The null hypothesis is that the true mean weight of the toads is 60 grams. The alternate hypothesis is that the weights are actually less than 60 grams. From an appropriate sample of toads, the p-value computed from the study was 0.034. If the alternate hypothesis was that the weights of the toads were not equal to 60 grams, what would be the p-value as computed from the same sample of toads?

   A. –0.034

   B. 0.017

   C. 0.034

   D. 0.068

   E. 0.966

26. An entomologist takes a sample of a certain breed of insect and computes a 95% confidence interval for the mean life span of the insect. The interval is

44.6 hours to 55.1 hours

Which of the following is the best explanation for the meaning of "95% confidence?"

A. There is a 0.95 probability that the true mean will fall within this interval.
B. There is a 0.95 probability that this interval contains, within it, the true mean.
C. Ninety-five percent of all insects of this breed have life spans within this interval.
D. There is a 0.95 probability that a sample mean of life spans will fall within this interval.
E. There is a 0.95 probability that the true standard deviation will fall within this interval.

27. An orchard of maple trees produces sap for manufacturing maple syrup. The daily sap output of the trees follows a normal distribution, with a mean of 4.7 quarts and a standard deviation of 1.8 quarts. What is the minimum amount of sap that must be produced by a tree, in order to be in the highest 1% of productive trees?

A. 0.51 quarts
B. 7.01 quarts
C. 7.66 quarts
D. 8.89 quarts
E. 9.34 quarts

28. Suppose that event A and event B are two independent events. The probability of event A is 0.2, while the probability of event B is 0.3. What is the probability of either event A or event B occurring?

A. 0.06
B. 0.44
C. 0.50
D. 0.60
E. 0.94

29. A random sample of 400 one-bedroom apartments in a suburban area is taken. A 95% confidence interval for the mean monthly rent of one-bedroom apartments was computed as

$576 to $614

Is it possible to use this confidence interval to test the null hypothesis H_o: $\mu = \$500$ against the alternate hypothesis H_a: $\mu > \$500$ at a level of significance $\alpha = 0.01$?

A. No, since it is not known whether the rents are normally distributed.
B. No, since the true value of σ is unknown.
C. No, since a 95% confidence interval cannot be compared to a 0.01 level of significance.
D. Yes, and the test would result in rejecting the null hypothesis.
E. Yes, and the test would result in not rejecting the null hypothesis.

30. Suppose that a random sample of two values is taken from the population $\{1, 3, 4, 8\}$. If the sample is taken without replacement, then the samples have mean $\mu_{\bar{x}} = 4$ and standard deviation $\sigma_{\bar{x}} = 1.472$. If the sample is taken with replacement, how would the mean $\mu_{\bar{x}}$ and standard deviation $\sigma_{\bar{x}}$ differ?

A. $\mu_{\bar{x}}$ and $\sigma_{\bar{x}}$ would both stay the same.
B. $\mu_{\bar{x}}$ would increase and $\sigma_{\bar{x}}$ would stay the same.
C. $\mu_{\bar{x}}$ would stay the same and $\sigma_{\bar{x}}$ would increase.
D. $\mu_{\bar{x}}$ and $\sigma_{\bar{x}}$ would both increase.
E. $\mu_{\bar{x}}$ would stay the same and $\sigma_{\bar{x}}$ would decrease.

31. A group of representatives to a student government consists of 4 men and 1 woman. Two of the students are chosen at random. What is the probability that the two students will include the woman?

A. 0.10
B. 0.32
C. 0.40
D. 0.50
E. 0.84

GO ON TO THE NEXT PAGE

32. A continental congress consists of 14 members, with 1 representative from each of the 13 colonies, except for Virginia, which has two. A president and vice president are chosen at random. What is the probability that the president and vice president are not the two Virginians together?

   A. 0.7252
   B. 0.8622
   C. 0.9286
   D. 0.9890
   E. 0.9945

33. The Badger Oil Company desires to estimate the mean density of the crude oil being taken from a newly discovered well. A randomly selected sample of 250 quarts of oil is measured. Although it is not known whether the density of the quarts of oil would follow a normal distribution, an analysis of the sample of 250 quarts indicates that the population follows an approximate normal distribution. Which of the following is a justification for constructing a z-confidence interval for the mean density of the quarts of oil?

   A. Any confidence interval for mean can be done with a z-interval.
   B. All that is required for a z-interval is that the underlying population be approximately normal.
   C. Since the sample size is large enough, t-values are approximately equal to z-values.
   D. The true standard deviation is unknown.
   E. Provided that the measurements for oil density are converted to z-scores, a z-interval can be used.

34. For a standardized exam, a test is done whereby the null hypothesis is $H_o: \mu = 80$ and the alternate hypothesis is $H_a: \mu > 80$. The test is being done with a level of significance $\alpha = 0.01$. Which is the best explanation of the meaning of this level of significance?

   A. There is a 0.01 probability of observing a sample mean greater than 80.
   B. There is a 0.01 probability of rejecting the null hypothesis when the true mean is 80.
   C. There is a 0.01 probability of not rejecting the null hypothesis when the true mean actually is greater than 80.
   D. There is a 0.01 probability of rejecting the null hypothesis under any circumstances.
   E. There is a 0.01 probability of observing a sample mean exactly equal to 80.

35. For a hypothesis test of proportion, the null hypothesis is $H_o: p = 0.75$ and the alternate hypothesis is $H_a: p > 0.75$. The test is being done with a level of significance $\alpha = 0.05$. If the level of significance is changed to $\alpha = 0.02$, which of the following statements is true?

   A. The test with the 0.02 level of significance requires a larger sample size.
   B. The test with the 0.02 level of significance will result in rejections of the null hypothesis more often.
   C. The test with the 0.02 level of significance will have a smaller critical value in its rejection region.
   D. A rejection at the 0.02 level of significance implies weaker evidence against the null hypothesis.
   E. A rejection at the 0.02 level of significance implies stronger evidence against the null hypothesis.

36. A bag contains four cards, numbered 1, 2, 3, and 4. Two cards are chosen at random, and X represents the average of the two numbers on the cards. Which of the following is the probability that X is equal to 2.5?

   A. $\dfrac{1}{16}$
   B. $\dfrac{1}{8}$
   C. $\dfrac{1}{6}$
   D. $\dfrac{1}{3}$
   E. $\dfrac{1}{2}$

37. The Moseby Tool Company is testing the stress tolerance of a certain type of steel. By applying pressure to a sample of 80 steel sheets, they have created the following *t*-interval for the mean amount of pressure that the sheets of steel are able to endure before breakage, in pounds per square inch:

467 psi to 648 psi

However, upon examining the data, it has been determined that the sample contains an outlier. If the outlier is removed from the sample, and the *t*-interval is recomputed, which of the following statements must be true about the new interval?

A. The sample mean, which is the center of the interval, will be smaller.

B. The confidence level of the interval will be greater.

C. The interval will be narrower.

D. The interval will be wider.

E. The upper limit of the interval will be greater.

38. A simple random sample from a set of data is taken for the purpose of creating a 95% confidence interval for the population mean. Both a *t*-interval and a *z*-interval are created. Which of the following statements is true about the difference between a *t*-interval and a *z*-interval?

A. The *t*-interval will be wider than the *z*-interval.

B. The *t*-interval will have a greater sample size than the *z*-interval.

C. The *t*-interval will have a lower confidence level than the *z*-interval.

D. The *t*-interval will use the sample standard deviation, *s,* and the *z*-interval will use the population standard deviation, σ.

E. The *t*-interval will be less accurate than the *z*-interval.

39. An infrared communication device has a 35% probability of sending a signal successfully. If 10 signals are sent, what is the approximate probability that at least 8 of the signals are sent successfully?

A. 0.0005

B. 0.0043

C. 0.0048

D. 0.2616

E. 0.9952

40. A biology lab wants to compare the mean life span of a species of horsefly with the mean life span of a species of boll weevil. The test that they have constructed has a null hypothesis H_o: $\mu_1 = \mu_2$ and an alternate hypothesis H_a: $\mu_1 > \mu_2$. In a sample of 60 horseflies, the sample mean was 37.7 days, with a sample standard deviation 11.1 days. In a sample of 50 boll weevils, the sample mean was 34.2 days, with a sample standard deviation 8.8 days. If it is assumed that the two species will have different population standard deviations, which of the following would be the appropriate *t*-statistic for this test?

A. −1.173

B. 0.785

C. 1.522

D. 1.806

E. 1.844

Practice Test 2

STOP

347

Section II

Time: 1 hour and 30 minutes   Number of questions: 6   Percent of total grade: 50%

Part A

Questions 1–5   Spend about 65 minutes on this part of the exam.   Percent of Section II grade: 75%

Show all your work. Clearly indicate the methods you use—you will be graded on the correctness of your methods as well as the accuracy of your results and explanation.

1. Four biologists are working on a study estimating the mean life span of a species of insect. Each has agreed to take a separate sample and has computed a confidence interval for the mean, in hours. They have met, and these are their results:

Abraham	[138.8 days, 159.5 days]
Barnett	[135.6 days, 155.4 days]
Kamron	[140.7 days, 149.9 days]
Millicent	[127.7 days, 164.8 days]

   a. Describe the possible reasons for the differences in the interval estimates given by the biologists, especially those that result in different widths of intervals.

   b. Suppose that the interval computed by Barnett was a 95% confidence interval. Describe what is meant by "95% confidence."

   c. Suppose that the biologists have determined that the standard deviation in the life spans of the insects is $\sigma = 28$ days. If they desire to create a 95% confidence interval that is only one unit wide, how many insects should be included in a sample? If each biologist computes such an interval, will they each arrive at the same answer?

2. A pharmaceutical company wants to study the effects of a new medication intended to reduce LDL cholesterol levels. To achieve this, they will begin with a sample of 100 patients whose LDL cholesterol levels are approximately 150. They want to compare the mean LDL cholesterol levels of patients who have used the medication for six weeks with the mean LDL cholesterol levels of patients who have not.

   a. How can the study be constructed as a t-test, comparing means of independent samples?

   b. How can the study be constructed as a paired t-test?

   c. Which of these two tests can be constructed as a double-blind study? Please explain how.

3. Suppose that President George W. Bush desires to compare the percentage of support that he has among voters in Wisconsin with the percentage of support among voters in Michigan. In a poll of 500 voters in Wisconsin, he had the support of 258 of them. In a poll of 600 voters in Michigan, he had the support of 302 of them.

   a. Why is it valid to perform a z-test comparing data that follows binomial distributions?

   b. If President Bush's staff wants to test, at an $\alpha = 0.05$ level of significance, whether the proportions are equal, against the alternate claim that the proportions are not equal, what conclusion is made?

   c. Why is it not valid to perform the same z-test comparing the proportion of support President Bush has among voters in Wisconsin with the proportion of support Senator Kerry has among voters in Wisconsin?

4. A university is conducting a study of the sleep patterns of their students, and the claim is made that students who go to sleep earlier sleep more than those who go to sleep late. Group A consists of students who regularly go to sleep before 11 P.M., while Group B consists of students who regularly go to sleep after 1 A.M. The students in these groups were observed for one week, and the total number of hours of sleep were recorded. These were the results:

	Number	*Sample Mean*	*Sample Standard Deviation*
Group A	24	52.4	8.8
Group B	35	47.8	9.8

a. Assuming that μ_1 = the mean amount of sleep for students who go to sleep early, and μ_2 = the mean amount of sleep for students who go to sleep late, what are the results of the hypothesis test, with a level of significance of $\alpha = 0.05$, that has null hypothesis H_o: $\mu_1 = \mu_2$ and alternate hypothesis H_a: $\mu_1 > \mu_2$?

b. How do the results of this test change if the alternate hypothesis is H_a: $\mu_1 \neq \mu_2$?

c. What is the *p*-value for the test statistic computed in part **a**? What is the meaning of this *p*-value?

5. The coach of a high school girls basketball team wants to see if there is a correlation between the heights of his players and the average points per game that they score. The following is the scatterplot and regression results for the twelve players:

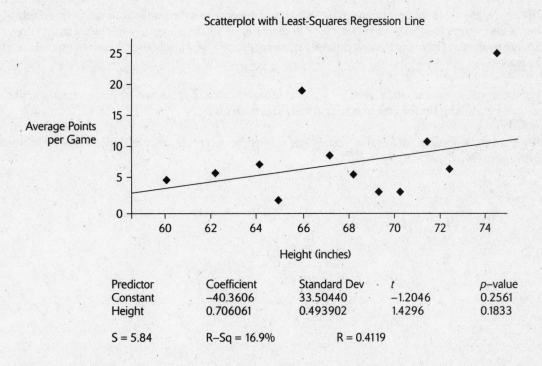

Scatterplot with Least-Squares Regression Line

Predictor	Coefficient	Standard Dev	t	*p*–value
Constant	−40.3606	33.50440	−1.2046	0.2561
Height	0.706061	0.493902	1.4296	0.1833

S = 5.84   R–Sq = 16.9%   R = 0.4119

a. From the information given, what is the equation of the least-squares regression line relating average points per game and height? Define any variables used.

b. What is the correlation coefficient relating average points per game with height? Interpret the meaning of this value.

GO ON TO THE NEXT PAGE

c. Describe what is meant by the residuals of the scatterplot.

d. How are the residuals related to the correlation coefficient?

e. Based on the information given, would the player's height be a good predictor of her average points per game? Explain.

Part B

Question 6   Spend about 25 minutes on this part of the exam.   Percent of Section II grade: 25%

Directions for Part B: Allow additional time for this part. Clearly indicate the methods that you use, and give clear explanations for all your results.

6. A statistics instructor teaches two courses, one in the morning and one in the afternoon. He has given a midterm exam to both classes, and these were the results:

Class	Number	Mean	Standard Deviation
9:00 class	34	81.45	16.779
1:00 class	29	77.60	15.844

a. Noting that the mean for the morning class was higher, suppose that the instructor wants to determine whether this is evidence to conclude that students tend to score higher, on the average, in morning classes than in afternoon classes. How may the instructor set up an appropriate hypothesis test? What assumptions need to be made?

b. Is there evidence to conclude, at an $\alpha = 0.01$ level of significance, that the true mean for students in the morning class is higher than the true mean for the afternoon class?

c. What are some possible confounding factors that may affect the conclusion that students tend to do better in morning classes than in afternoon classes?

Section I Answers

1. **B.** Because of the random pattern of the points in the graph that appear to fit the zero line fairly closely, the relationship would be linear. Furthermore, since it is given that the slope of the least-squares regression line is negative, the linear relationship is inverse as well.

2. **D.** The slope of the regression line is $b_1 = 0.0489$. From the regression results, the standard deviation of the slope is $s_{b_1} = 0.007954$ found in the chart as "stdev" for SAT. With degrees of freedom = (sample size – 2) = (16 – 2) = 14, the 95% confidence interval would be $(0.0489) \pm (2.145)(0.007954) = 0.0489 \pm 0.0171$.

3. **E.** The correlation between two sets of data is the same, regardless of which set is called X and which set is called Y.

4. **E.** Since each value in the set is divided by 2, the mean and standard deviation would both be divided by 2. With the original mean being 170 and standard deviation being 50, the new mean and standard deviation would be 85 and 25, respectively.

5. **E.** First, since no maximum possible score was given, it is not known whether the outlier was an extremely high value or low value. However, if it is known whether the outlier is a low value, its removal would cause the mean to increase, but the median could possibly stay the same, or go up with the removal of the lowest value of the set. If it is known whether the outlier is a high value, its removal would cause the mean to decrease, but the median could possibly stay the same, or go down with the removal of the highest value of the set. Therefore, the exact behavior of the mean and median cannot be determined from the information given.

6. **C.** The confidence interval for the mean is of the form $\bar{x} \pm E$, where $E = ts/\sqrt{n}$ if the population standard deviation is unknown, or $E = z\sigma/\sqrt{n}$ if the population standard deviation is known. If the sample size was increased from 100 to 200, and a new 95% confidence interval is computed, the confidence level would stay the same; the new $\bar{x}$ may be slightly higher or lower, but since the error term, E, includes division by $\sqrt{n}$, the width of the interval would be significantly smaller. Thus, the confidence interval would be much narrower.

7. **B.** Since 11 pounds is the population standard deviation, the interval [26 pounds , 48 pounds] would represent a range of one standard deviation from the population mean of 37 pounds. By the empirical rule for large populations, approximately 68% of all values in the population would lie within one standard deviation of the mean. In this case 68% of 950 monkeys would be (0.68)(950) = 646 monkeys.

8. **C.** A stratified sample involves dividing the population into a number of subsets called strata, and taking a simple random sample from each stratum. In this case, the strata are the counties of the state.

9. **A.** The most likely explanation for the difference between the poll results and the actual election results is the fact that those who participated in the poll were only those who chose to be included in the sample. This is the issue of voluntary sampling. Although the other responses are all possible explanations for the difference in the results, they would unlikely be causes of great differences. It is possible that the question was slanted, but the actual question is not given and, therefore, cannot be assumed. Lying in the responses is possible, but would likely not account for great differences in the results. Also, respondents changing their minds might account for some difference, but likely not a great difference in the results. Last, it is likely, from the context, that the sample size was sufficient to produce publishable results.

10. **B.** In order to create a table of expected values for a two-way test of independence, each corresponding entry in the table is computed by this formula: Expected Value = (row total)(column total)/(n), where n equals the grand total of all values in the chart. Thus, the expected value corresponding to those who took the MCSE study course and passed the test is equal to (80)(118)/(218) = 43, rounded to the nearest whole number.

11. **D.** This hypothesis test would involve sampling a group of 25 people, measuring their LDL levels and then measuring the LDL levels of the same group of people after using the diet. Since the two samples of data are not independent, and of the same sample size, they should be treated as paired data. Since it is the same group of people that are tested twice, a paired t-test is the most appropriate method of performing a test comparing two means.

12. E. The z-interval that has been computed is of the form $\bar{x} \pm E$, where $E = z\sigma/\sqrt{n}$. Therefore, increasing the value of n would decrease the value of E, thus making the confidence interval narrower. Increasing the confidence level would actually increase the z-value for the interval, increase the value of E, and make the interval wider. Similarly, corresponding t-values are also greater than z-values, and thus increase the value of E. Taking stratified samples would likely not have a significant impact on the width of the interval, and pilot samples to estimate the population standard deviation would be unnecessary, since the population standard deviation is either already known or sufficiently estimated, since the z-interval has been created.

13. A. Since the p-value indicates the level of a test at which rejection of the null hypothesis would occur, with p-value 0.023, rejection would occur at α-level 0.05, but not at α-level 0.01.

14. B. The observed proportion in this sample was $34/150 = 0.2267$. The corresponding 90% confidence interval for the true population proportion would be $0.2267 \pm (1.645)\sqrt{(0.2267)(0.7733)/(150)}$, or 0.2267 ± 0.0562.

15. D. The most likely cause of inaccuracies would be attributed to the process being a voluntary process, whereby samples consisted of only those who wanted to be included. Sampling by a random process would give most accurate results. Taking equal sample sizes is not necessary, nor would a paired t-test be done, since the samples would be considered independent. Also, while taking larger sample sizes would increase accuracy, the sample sizes are already large. Computing the test statistic as a z, instead of a t would not affect the accuracy of the sample, but only change the criteria for rejecting a null hypothesis.

16. B. If a student is predicted to score $\hat{y} = 85$ on the test, based on the least-squares regression line $\hat{y} = 51.7 + 3.47x$, determining the estimated number of hours studied, x, involves solving the equation $85 = 51.7 + 3.47$ for x. The value is $x = 9.59$, or approximately 10 hours.

17. E. The normal distribution is symmetric for any mean and standard deviation. The standard normal, in particular, has mean 0 and standard deviation 1. The area under the normal curve, for any nonzero interval, represents a probability, which is a value between 0 and 1. All three statements are true.

18. D. If p equals the probability of a cataclysmic earthquake occurring in a year, then the probability of a cataclysmic earthquake not occurring in a year is $1 - p$. Therefore, the probability that a cataclysmic earthquake not occurring for a period of 100 years is $(1 - p)^{100}$. If $(1 - p)^{100} = 0.5$, then the value of p would be approximately 0.007.

19. B. The degrees of freedom for a two-way test of independence is (number of rows $- 1$)(number of columns $- 1$) or $(3)(1) = 3$.

20. B. The predicted starting salary for a student with grade-point average 3.19, according to this least-squares regression line, would be $\hat{y} = -10769 + (13855)(3.19) = 33428$. The residual for a value of x is defined to be the difference between the actual observed y-value, and the predicted y-value. In this case, the residual for the value $x = 3.19$ is $y - \hat{y} = 27000 - 33428 = -6428$.

21. C. Since the null hypothesis is that the five brands of automobiles are equally preferred, with a sample size $n = 100$, the expected values would be 20 for each brand. The formula for the χ^2-test statistic is $\Sigma (O - E)^2/E = (23 - 20)^2/20 + (17 - 20)^2/20 + (21 - 20)^2/20 + (29 - 20)^2/20 + (10 - 20)^2/20 = 10.000$.

22. D. It was originally noted that there was an inverse relationship between the rate of involvement in volunteer activities and the rate of delinquency among this group of children. Therefore, it was assumed that if children who had a high rate of delinquency were placed in voluntary activities, their rate of delinquency would be reduced. However, this was based on the assumption that there was a cause-and-effect relationship between volunteer activities and delinquency. In reality, since the children placed in the volunteer activities did not have a reduction in delinquency, it showed that volunteer activities were not the cause of low delinquency, but merely that the high volunteer rate and low delinquency were only correlated, being caused by a third factor, namely the type of children who would be involved in both. Differences between boys and girls would not account for the difference, nor would necessarily examining other factors. Observing other samples could possibly produce differing results but may not explain the failure of placing children into volunteer activities as an attempt to lower delinquency rates.

23. D. In this case, if event A and event B are independent events, $P(A \text{ or } B) = P(A) + P(B) - P(A \text{ and } B)$, and $P(A \text{ and } B)$ will be some nonzero number in all cases, unless either event A or event B is the empty set. It is true to say that the events cannot be mutually exclusive, since this would imply that if one of the events occurs, the other cannot possibly occur. It is also true to say that $P(A \text{ and } B) = P(A)P(B)$ if the events are independent. To say that if one event occurs, the probability of the other event occurring does not change is the definition of independent events, and the given statement of conditional probability is another way of making this same statement.

24. B. In a study to measure the effect of a drug, the effects are compared to a control group, which measures the natural behavior of a condition without medication, in this case, that of migraine headaches. In order to reduce the psychological bias of patients who know they are receiving medication, the members of the control group are given a placebo, or fake pill. To further reduce this bias, the study is a blind study, whereby the patients do not know whether the pill they are given is the real medication or the placebo. Moreover, in a double-blind study, neither the patient nor the doctor administering the pill knows whether the pill is the real medication or the placebo. This is meant to eliminate any unintended clues the doctor may give to the patient to indicate whether the medication is real or not.

25. D. The p-value of a test statistic, in a one-tail test of mean, is the level of test at which rejection of the null hypothesis would occur. This is the equivalent to the probability of being more extreme than the test statistic on one tail of the normal curve. If the test is a two-tail test of mean, the rejection region would become a two-tail rejection region on the normal curve, with equal critical values on either end of the normal curve. This is equivalent to the probability of being more extreme than the test statistic on either tail of the normal curve. Since the normal curve is symmetric, the p-value in the two-tail case is found by doubling the p-value from the one-tail case. The two-tail p-value is $2(0.034) = 0.068$.

26. B. A confidence interval is computed based on a random sample of values from the population and will vary from sample to sample. However, a 95% confidence interval, in the case of mean, is constructed so that there is a 0.95 probability that the interval will contain, within it, the true population mean μ. Moreover, since the population mean μ is a parameter, it remains fixed, regardless of which values are taken into the sample, so it is not correct to say that there is a 0.95 probability that the population mean μ will fall within the confidence interval.

27. D. The cutoff for the highest 1% lies at a z-score of 2.326 standard deviations above the mean. In this case, the value in quarts would be $4.7 + (2.326)(1.8) = 8.89$ quarts.

28. B. Since event A and event B are independent events, $P(A \text{ and } B) = P(A)P(B) = (0.2)(0.3) = 0.06$. Thus, $P(A \text{ or } B) = P(A) + P(B) - P(A \text{ and } B) = 0.2 + 0.3 - 0.06 = 0.44$.

29. D. Since the sample size is given as $n = 400$, the sample mean and sample standard deviation can be determined from the 95% confidence interval $[576, 614]$. The sample mean is the center of the confidence interval, 595. Then, since the interval is of the form $595 \pm E$, where $E = (1.960)s/\sqrt{400} = 19$, solving for s, s is approximately equal to 193.88. Therefore, a t-test statistic can be computed as $t = (595 - 500)/(193.88/\sqrt{400}) = 9.80$. Since the critical value for this hypothesis test, at an α-level 0.01, is 2.326, the results of the test would be to reject the null hypothesis.

30. C. With replacement, the possible samples of size 2 are $\{1,1\}$, $\{1,3\}$, $\{1,4\}$, $\{1,8\}$, $\{3,1\}$, $\{3,3\}$, $\{3,4\}$, $\{3,8\}$, $\{4,1\}$, $\{4,3\}$, $\{4,4\}$, $\{4,8\}$, $\{8,1\}$, $\{8,3\}$, $\{8,4\}$, and $\{8,8\}$ yielding possible sample means 1, 2, 2.5, 4.5, 2, 3, 3.5, 5.5, 2.5, 3.5, 4, 6, 4.5, 5.5, 6, and 8. For these possible samples, $\mu_x = 4$ and $\sigma_x = 1.80$.

31. C. In this situation, $P(1 \text{ man, } 1 \text{ woman}) = ({}_4C_1)({}_1C_1)/({}_5C_2) = (4)(1)/(10) = 0.40$.

32. D. The total possible pairs of president and vice president among 14 members would be permutations, since the order matters, given by $(14)(13) = 182$. The total number of possible pairs, without the two Virginians together, would be $182 - 2 = 180$. Therefore, the probability that the president, vice president pair does not consist of the two Virginians together is $180/182 = 0.9890$.

33. C. For large sample sizes, which correspond to larger degrees of freedom, the t-distribution becomes approximately equal to the standard normal (z) distribution. Therefore, even if the true standard deviation is unknown, the construction of a z-confidence interval will be approximately equal to a t-confidence interval, when the sample size is large. In this case, the sample size is $n = 250$, so it is justified to use the z-value to create the confidence interval. However, it is not true that any confidence interval for mean can be created with the z-score, nor is having the underlying population being approximately normal sufficient for using the z-score. The true standard deviation being unknown is actually an indicator that t should be used, while values should not be converted to z-scores when creating a confidence interval for mean.

34. B. The level of significance of a hypothesis test, α, is defined to be the probability of Type I error, which is the probability of rejecting the null hypothesis, when the null hypothesis is true. Therefore, if $\alpha = 0.01$, there is a 0.01 probability of rejecting the null hypothesis, which is the claim that the true mean $\mu = 80$.

35. E. The level of significance of a test, α, represents the probability that the null hypothesis is rejected, when the null hypothesis is, in actuality, true. Therefore, if the null hypothesis is rejected at an $\alpha = 0.05$ level, there is no more than a 0.05 probability that the null hypothesis is true. However, if the null hypothesis is rejected at an $\alpha = 0.02$ level, there is no more than a 0.02 probability that the null hypothesis is true. Thus, if the null hypothesis is rejected at a lower level of α, the null hypothesis is shown to be less likely to be true. This would suggest that rejection at a level $\alpha = 0.02$ provides stronger evidence against the null hypothesis than rejection at the $\alpha = 0.05$ level.

36. D. If two cards are chosen randomly from a set of four, without replacement, the total number of possible pairs would be given by $_4C_2 = 6$. There are two pairs that result in an average of 2.5, $\{1,4\}$ and $\{2,3\}$. Therefore, the probability that the average of the cards is 2.5 is $2/6 = 1/3$.

37. C. It is not known whether the outlier is an extreme high value or an extreme low value. However, if there is one outlier and it is removed from the sample, the value that is the greatest distance from the sample mean would be removed. This would have the effect of reducing the value of s, the sample standard deviation. Since the confidence interval for mean is of the form $x \pm E$, where $E = ts/\sqrt{n}$, a reduction in the value of s would result in a reduction in the value of E, and thus, the confidence interval would become narrower. Again, since it is not known whether the outlier is a high value or low value, it is unknown what affect its removal would have on the sample mean or the upper limit of the interval.

38. A. For any fixed level of confidence and for any degrees of freedom, the value of t is greater than the value of z, implying that the t-interval would be wider than the z-interval. Note also that the confidence level is the same, if both intervals were computed as 95% confidence intervals, and that z-intervals can be computed when the true standard deviation is not known, when large samples are involved. Moreover, t-intervals tend to be more accurate than z-intervals, not less.

39. C. If X is the number of signals that are successfully received out of 10, then $P(X \geq 8) = P(X = 8) + P(X = 9) + P(X = 10) = (_{10}C_8)(0.35)^8(0.65)^2 + (_{10}C_9)(0.35)^9(0.65)^1 + (_{10}C_{10})(0.35)^{10}(0.65)^0 = 0.0048$.

40. E. The test statistic for the difference of two means, with large independent samples, with the assumption that the true standard deviations are not equal (standard deviations not pooled) is given by $t = (\overline{x}_1 - \overline{x}_2)/\sqrt{(s_1)^2/n_1 + (s_2)^2/n_2} = (37.7 - 34.2)/\sqrt{(11.1)^2/60 + (8.8)^2/50} = 1.844 = 1.844$.

Section II Answers

1a. The form of the confidence interval for mean is $\overline{x} \pm ts/\sqrt{n}$, which includes four factors that could differ from sample to sample. The intervals will likely have different centers because each sample will likely have different sample means, $\overline{x}$. Also, each sample will likely have different sample standard deviations, s. However, the two factors that will most greatly contribute to the differences in width are the t-value and sample size n. The t-value is determined by the degrees of freedom (sample size $- 1$) and the confidence level that is used, whereby higher confidence levels will result in wider intervals. Higher sample sizes result in narrower intervals. A fifth possible factor could be whether the interval was computed as a z-interval instead of a t-interval.

1b. If the interval [135.6 days , 155.4 days] is a 95% confidence interval, this means that the interval was constructed so that there is a 0.95 probability that the true mean, μ, is contained within this interval. It is important to note that it is the interval that is random and will vary from sample to sample, not the mean, μ, which is fixed, although unknown.

1c. If it is assumed that the true standard deviation is known, and to be $\sigma = 28$, a z-interval will be created. Moreover, if it is desired that the width of the interval is only one unit wide, the margin of error is to be no more than $E = 0.5$. Since the z-value for a 95% confidence interval is 1.960, the minimum sample size would be $n \geq ((1.960)(28)/(0.5))^2 = 12047.2576$ or a minimum of 12,048 insects. Although the width of four separate intervals will be the same, with equal sample sizes and confidence levels, it is still possible to compute different sample means, so the intervals may still differ.

2a. The study comparing two means of independent samples can be done by randomly dividing the group of 100 patients into two samples of 50 patients each. One group can be prescribed the medication for six weeks, and the sample mean and sample standard deviation of the LDL cholesterol levels can be computed. The other group can be given a placebo for six weeks, and the sample mean and standard deviation are computed from this group. A hypothesis test can be done for a preselected level of significance, with $H_o: \mu_1 = \mu_2$ and $H_a: \mu_1 < \mu_2$. The t-statistic can be computed for this data, with the assumption that the population standard deviations are not equal and can be compared to a t-critical value, or the p-value can be computed.

2b. The test can be constructed as a paired t-test by measuring the LDL cholesterol levels of all 100 patients at the end of a six-week period without any medications at all, and then at the end of another six-week period after being prescribed the medication. The differences between the corresponding LDL cholesterol levels before using the medication, and after the six weeks on the medication, are computed. The appropriate t-statistic for paired data can be computed, and either compared to a critical value based on a preselected level of significance, or converted to a p-value.

2c. The test of two independent samples can be done as a double-blind study whereby both the individual patients and the attendants administering the pills are unaware of whether each patient is in the medicated group or the placebo group. There is no such blindness in the paired test, since all the patients are being tested as a placebo group, first, followed by a medicated group, second. It is not possible to have patients medicated first, since such medication may have an effect on the cholesterol levels of these patients as they are being tested afterward.

3a. By the Central Limit Theorem, for large sample sizes, the binomial distribution is approximately normal with mean $\mu = np$ and $\sigma = \sqrt{npq}$. Specifically, for comparing two proportions, the distribution of the difference $\hat{p}_1 - \hat{p}_2$ is approximately normal, with mean $p_1 - p_2$ and standard deviation $\sqrt{\left(\dfrac{\overline{pq}}{p_1} + \dfrac{\overline{pq}}{p_2}\right)}$ where $\overline{p}$ is the pooled proportion between the two samples, provided that $n_1 \hat{p}_1 \hat{q}_1 \geq 10$ and $n_2 \hat{p}_2 \hat{q}_2 \geq 10$. With $\hat{p}_1 = 258/500 = 0.516$ and $\hat{p}_2 = 302/600 = 0.50333$, it holds that $n_1 \hat{p}_1 \hat{q}_1 = 124.872$ and $n_2 \hat{p}_2 \hat{q}_2 = 150$, implying that the conditions for sufficiently large sample size hold.

3b. With the pooled proportion being $\overline{p} = 560/1100 = 0.509091$, the test statistic for the z-test is $z = (0.516 - 0.503)/\sqrt{(0.509)(0.491)/(500) + (0.509)(0.491)/(600)} = 0.429$. At the $\alpha = 0.05$ level of significance, the rejection region is $z > 1.960$ or $z < -1.960$. Therefore, the null hypothesis, $H_o: p_1 = p_2$, is not rejected, meaning that there is not sufficient evidence to conclude that the proportions of support that George W. Bush has in Wisconsin and in Michigan are not equal.

3c. The reason it is not valid to perform the same z-test to compare the proportion of support Bush has in Wisconsin with the proportion of support Kerry has in Wisconsin, is that the two proportions are not independent. The two-sample z-test of proportion assumes that the two proportions come from independent samples.

4a. Under the assumption that the population standard deviations are not equal, the nonpooled t-statistic comparing two population means is $t = 1.883$. The corresponding degrees of freedom is 52, whereby the rejection region for a one-tail upper test, with level of significance $\alpha = 0.05$ is $t > 1.675$. The conclusion is that the null hypothesis, $H_o: \mu_1 = \mu_2$, is rejected in favor of the conclusion that $\mu_1 > \mu_2$. Therefore, there is evidence to conclude that the mean hours of sleep per week for those who go to sleep early is greater than the mean hours of sleep per week for those who go to sleep late.

4b. If the alternate hypothesis is that $\mu_1 \neq \mu_2$, the test statistic remains the same as $t = 1.883$, and the degrees of freedom also remains the same with a value of 52, but the two-tailed rejection region, with a level of significance $\alpha = 0.05$ becomes $t > 2.007$ and $t < -2.007$. The conclusion is that the null hypothesis, $H_o: \mu_1 = \mu_2$, is not rejected, implying that there is not sufficient evidence to conclude that the mean hours of sleep per week for those who go to sleep early is not equal to the mean hours of sleep per week for those who go to sleep late.

4c. The *p*-value corresponding to the one-tail test statistic computed in part **a** is 0.0326. The definition of *p*-value is the level of significance at which the null hypothesis would be rejected for that test statistic. In other words, if the null hypothesis was true, the probability of observing a *t*-value of 1.883 or greater is approximately 0.0326, implying that the level of Type I error for any test with this level of significance is 0.0326. Rejection of the null hypothesis would occur, then, for levels of $\alpha \geq 0.0326$.

5a. The equation of the least-squares regression line is $\hat{y} = -40.3606 + 0.706061x$, where $\hat{y}$ = the predicted average points per game, and x = the player's height in inches.

5b. The correlation coefficient is 0.4119. Since the value is positive, the relationship between height and points per game is direct. However, since the magnitude of the number is only about 0.4, the relationship is a moderately weak relationship. Although some relationship exists, the relationship is not strong.

5c. The definition of residual for each individual value, *x*, in this case height in inches, is the difference between the actual observed value and the predicted value from the regression line, $y - \hat{y}$. On the scatterplot, the residuals are illustrated as the distance each actual point, (x, y), is away from the least-squares regression line.

5d. Since the residuals represent the distance each individual point is away from the least-squares regression line, if the overall magnitude of the residuals is low, this would indicate a generally strong fit of the points to the regression line. If the overall magnitude of the residuals is high, the points are not fitting the regression line well. Therefore, if the overall magnitude of the residuals is low, this would result in a correlation coefficient that is close, in magnitude, to 1, indicating a strong linear relationship between *x* and *y*. High overall residuals would result in a value of the correlation coefficient, *r*, being closer to 0, representing a weak linear relationship between *x* and *y*.

5e. Based on the regression results given, the correlation between height and average points per game is not strong. Therefore, using a least-squares regression line would not provide accurate results, if height alone is used to predict average points per game. Height could only be used to provide accurate predictions for average points per game if some higher order curve is used that provides a strong fit between height and average points per game.

6a. In order to determine whether the samples provide evidence that students score, on the average, higher in the morning class than in the afternoon class, a hypothesis test can be set up whereby the null hypothesis is $H_o: \mu_1 = \mu_2$ and the alternate hypothesis is $H_a: \mu_1 > \mu_2$. The assumption should be made that the two samples are independent samples, and either a predetermined level of significance, α, should be chosen, or the *p*-value for the results can be computed. Furthermore, if it is figured that the standard deviations for the scores of two groups are also unknown, it should also be decided whether to assume whether the standard deviations are equal or not equal. If both groups are being given the same exam, it could be assumed that the standard deviations will be equal. However, even if the groups are being given the same exam, it could also be assumed that the standard deviations are not equal, figuring that the distributions of the scores between the two classes could still be different, with consequent different standard deviations.

6b. If it is assumed that the scores of the two groups are independent, with equal standard deviations, the pooled *t*-statistic is $t = 0.931$, with degrees of freedom 61, and corresponding *p*-value 0.1777. If it is assumed that the scores of the two groups are independent, with unequal standard deviations, the nonpooled *t*-statistic is $t = 0.936$, with degrees of freedom 60, and corresponding *p-value* 0.1766. In either case, the null hypothesis, $H_o: \mu_1 = \mu_2$ is not rejected, at level of significance $\alpha = 0.01$, implying that there is not significant evidence to show that students will tend to score higher, on the average, on tests in the morning, than in the afternoon.

6c. The purpose of the original test is to see whether students tend to score higher on one test rather than on another, where the difference is the time of day. Confounding factors may be simply the quality of the students in the two classes, regardless of the time of day. Other confounding factors may be whether the teacher or whether the test itself differs based on the time of day. In addition, other factors need to be considered, such as what rooms the tests are being given in, or how much time is being allotted.

Practice Test 3

Section I

Time: 1 hour and 30 minutes   Number of questions: 40   Percent of total grade: 50%

Directions: Solve each problem. Decide which is the best of the answer choices given.

1. Two measures, x and y, were taken, and the correlation and least-squares regression line were computed. The following is a plot of the residuals for the regression analysis:

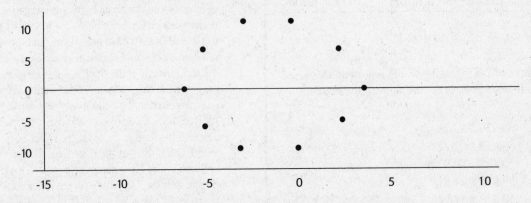

Which of the following is the most likely value for the correlation coefficient, r?

A. −0.90
B. −0.50
C. 0
D. 0.50
E. 0.90

GO ON TO THE NEXT PAGE

2. Mathematics majors at Wisconsin State College are taking the GRE. Among 21 of these students, the number of math courses taken by each was compared to the student's GRE score, and it was determined that there was a linear relationship between the number of math courses and GRE scores. The results of the regression analysis are given here:

Regression Equation:

GRE = 812.988 + 50.479 Courses

Predictor	Coef	Stdev	t-ratio	p
Constant	812.98763	70.73298	11.4938	0.000
Courses	50.478786	3.347518	15.0795	0.000

S = 120.37   R-sq = 92.3

Which of the following would represent a 99% confidence interval for the slope of the regression line?

A. 50.479 ± 8.623
B. 50.479 ± 9.577
C. 50.479 ± 10.971
D. 50.479 ± 11.017
E. 50.479 ± 12.988

3. In a hypothesis test for proportion, the null hypothesis is H_0: $p = 0.7$ and the alternate hypothesis is H_a: $p < 0.7$. The z-test statistic is computed, and is $z = -1.676$. For which levels of the test would rejection of the null hypothesis occur?

A. Reject for $\alpha = 0.10$, $\alpha = 0.05$, and for $\alpha = 0.01$.
B. Reject for $\alpha = 0.10$ and $\alpha = 0.05$, but not for $\alpha = 0.01$.
C. Reject for $\alpha = 0.10$, but not for $\alpha = 0.05$ nor $\alpha = 0.01$.
D. Do not reject for $\alpha = 0.10$, $\alpha = 0.05$, or $\alpha = 0.01$.
E. Cannot be determined from information given.

4. A case of 400 batteries contains 10 defective batteries. Ten batteries are chosen at random. If X represents the number of batteries that are defective, which of the following is the most probable value of X?

A. 0
B. 1
C. 2
D. 3
E. 4

5. On the first Saturday of every month of summer, Dandelion Park has a game in front of their roller coaster, which has 100 plastic ducks in water, each with a colored dot on its belly, submerged underwater so it cannot be seen. One of the ducks has a gold dot, 10 have green dots, and the rest have red dots. Each child under 12 is allowed to choose a duck at random. If the duck has a green dot, the child may ride the roller coaster for 25 cents. If the duck has the gold dot, the child may ride the roller coaster for free. If the duck has a red dot, no discount is given. If the regular price for the roller coaster is $1.50, and if 40% of the roller coaster riders are children under 12, what is the expected average price that is paid for a ride on the roller coaster?

A. $0.625
B. $1.360
C. $1.375
D. $1.444
E. $1.500

Questions 6 and 7 refer to the following information:

A vending machine contains the following items:

10 blue marbles	15 blue rings
5 gold marbles	20 white rings
15 white marbles	1 gold ring

6. One item is taken randomly from the vending machine. What is the approximate probability that the item is either a ring or something gold?

A. 0.015
B. 0.049
C. 0.545
D. 0.621
E. 0.636

7. Two items are taken from the vending machine. What is the approximate probability that the items are two blue marbles in a row?

   A. 0.021
   B. 0.023
   C. 0.152
   D. 0.203
   E. 0.303

8. The Chicago Cubs are playing the Milwaukee Brewers on a Saturday. Sammy Sosa is a very good player, who plays for the Chicago Cubs. On this particular Saturday, Sammy Sosa may or may not play. Of the following pairs of events, which pair would be events that are neither independent nor mutually exclusive?

   A. Event A = "The Chicago Cubs defeat the Milwaukee Brewers."
      Event B = "The Milwaukee Brewers defeat the Chicago Cubs."
   B. Event A = "The Chicago Cubs defeat the Milwaukee Brewers."
      Event B = "The New York Yankees defeat the Baltimore Orioles."
   C. Event A = "Sammy Sosa plays in the game that day."
      Event B = "Sammy Sosa does not play in the game that day."
   D. Event A = "The New York Yankees defeat the Baltimore Orioles."
      Event B = "Sammy Sosa does not play in the game that day."
   E. Event A = "Sammy Sosa plays in the game that day."
      Event B = "The Chicago Cubs defeat the Milwaukee Brewers."

9. A random sample of 20 scores on a 300-question multiple choice test had a sample mean of 162, with a sample standard deviation of 49. Which of the following is an approximate 95% confidence interval for the true mean score on this test?

   A. 162 ± 10.96
   B. 162 ± 18.95
   C. 162 ± 21.47
   D. 162 ± 22.93
   E. 162 ± 23.09

10. A least-squares regression line is computed, relating the number of hours that a 10-year-old child exercises per week, and the child's standing heart rate, in beats per minute. The equation of the line is

$$\hat{y} = 99.1 - 1.923x$$

where x represents the number of hours exercising per week and y represents the standing heart rate. Based on this estimated relationship, by approximately how many hours per week would a 10-year-old child have to increase exercising per week, in order to lower the standing heart rate by 5 beats per minute?

   A. 0.4 hours
   B. 2.6 hours
   C. 4.3 hours
   D. 9.6 hours
   E. 48.9 hours

11. Leigha took a standardized math exam, and her grade report indicated that her score was in the 89th percentile. Which of the following is the best interpretation of the meaning of this percentile?

   A. She got 89% of the problems correct.
   B. Eighty-nine percent of all those taking the exam had scores below hers.
   C. Eighty-nine percent of all those taking the exam had scores above hers.
   D. Only 89% of those taking the exam received passing scores.
   E. There was an 89% probability that her score was above the mean on the exam.

12. The null hypothesis for a test was $H_0: \mu = 16$ feet, with an alternate hypothesis $H_a: \mu > 16$ feet. A random sample produces a p-value for this test of 0.023. Which of the following statements would NOT be true about this hypothesis test?

   A. The null hypothesis would be rejected at a level $\alpha = 0.05$.
   B. The null hypothesis would not be rejected at a level $\alpha = 0.01$.
   C. If the alternate hypothesis was $H_a: \mu < 16$ feet, the null hypothesis would not be rejected at a level $\alpha = 0.05$.
   D. If the test was a two-tail test instead of a one-tail test, the null hypothesis would not be rejected at a level $\alpha = 0.05$.
   E. The sample mean was greater than 16 feet.

GO ON TO THE NEXT PAGE

13. The weekly milk output of a population of Guernsey cows is normally distributed with population mean $\mu = 40$ quarts and standard deviation $\sigma = 12$ quarts. A sample of 36 cows is taken, and the sample mean $\bar{x}$ is computed. What is the mean and standard deviation of $\bar{x}$?

   A. $\mu_{\bar{x}} = 40$ quarts, $\sigma_{\bar{x}} = 12$ quarts
   B. $\mu_{\bar{x}} = 40$ quarts, $\sigma_{\bar{x}} = 2$ quarts
   C. $\mu_{\bar{x}} = 40$ quarts, $\sigma_{\bar{x}} = {}^1/_3$ quart
   D. $\mu_{\bar{x}} = 6\frac{2}{3}$ quarts, $\sigma_{\bar{x}} = 12$ quarts
   E. $\mu_{\bar{x}} = 6\frac{2}{3}$ quarts, $\sigma_{\bar{x}} = 2$ quarts

14. The students in a large school district are taking a standardized geography exam that is constructed to have a standard deviation $\sigma = 20$. The school district wants to create a 99% confidence interval for the true mean score on this exam, for the students in their district. They also desire that the width of the interval be no greater than five units wide. Approximately how many students in the district should be sampled in order to create this confidence interval?

   A. 25
   B. 110
   C. 250
   D. 350
   E. 425

15. Suppose that a prestigious law school, as a policy, accepts only a percentage of applicants for admission. Let p represent that percentage. If 80 random applicants were polled, and 28 of those applicants indicated that they were accepted to the college, what would be a 90% confidence interval for p?

   A. 0.3500 ± 0.0047
   B. 0.3500 ± 0.0533
   C. 0.3500 ± 0.0694
   D. 0.3500 ± 0.0877
   E. 0.3500 ± 0.1045

16. Samantha has taken the first two exams in her Calculus class. She scored 78 on the first exam and 84 on the second exam. The class average on the first exam was 70, with a standard deviation of 10. The class average on the second exam was 75, with a standard deviation 17. Which statement describes how well Samantha did on the two exams, relative to the rest of the class?

   A. Samantha did better on the first exam.
   B. Samantha did better on the second exam.
   C. Samantha did equally well on both exams.
   D. How well she did cannot be determined, because the sample size is not given.
   E. How well she did cannot be determined, because it is not known whether the sample sizes were the same on both exams.

17. Suppose that the distribution of a set of values has a population mean of 76 and a standard deviation 14. If 6 is subtracted from each score and then each score is divided by 2, what will be the new mean and standard deviation of the set of values?

   A. Mean = 76; standard deviation = 14
   B. Mean = 70; standard deviation = 14
   C. Mean = 70; standard deviation = 7
   D. Mean = 35; standard deviation = 14
   E. Mean = 35; standard deviation = 7

18. Suppose that it has been determined that 16% of all homes with washing machines have Brand A, while 12% of all homes with washing machines have Brand B. Also, 2% of homes with washing machines have both brands. If six homes that have washing machines are selected at random, what is the approximate probability that none of these homes will have either Brand A or B?

   A. 0.003
   B. 0.139
   C. 0.164
   D. 0.260
   E. 0.740

19. A biologist wants to test whether two subspecies of beetles have the same life span. The biologist takes samples of size 200 from each population. The sample mean of the life spans of Beetle X was 45.8 days, with standard deviation 16.6 days. The sample mean of the life spans of Beetle Y was 41.1 days, with standard deviation 13.3 days. An appropriate *t*-test statistic was computed, under the assumption that the populations would have different population standard deviations. What is the value of this *t*-test statistic?

A. 2.209
B. 2.223
C. 3.125
D. 3.716
E. 4.419

20. A bag contains 400 marbles. The colors of the marbles follow this distribution:

Color	Red	Blue	White	Silver	Black
Percentage	0.20	0.25	0.30	0.05	0.20

If two marbles are simultaneously selected from the bag, what is the approximate probability that they are both blue?

A. 0.0620
B. 0.0625
C. 0.0750
D. 0.4375
E. 0.5000

21. Bill is a contestant on a game show called Auto Club! whereby he has the chance to win a new Lexus. The room has 16 celebrities, one of which holds the keys to the Lexus. Bill is allowed to choose 5 of the celebrities, and if he chooses the one holding the key, he wins the Lexus. What is the probability that Bill will win the Lexus?

A. 0.0030
B. 0.0367
C. 0.3125
D. 0.4495
E. 0.6875

22. Out of all students who take the NMSQT, 20% of those taking the test will be granted scholarships. If 80 random students in high school take the test, what is the approximate probability that at least 20 of them will be granted scholarships?

A. 0.1038
B. 0.1314
C. 0.1635
D. 0.5000
E. 0.6635

23. Gregory is a sixth grader who is learning how to play basketball. In order to estimate his probability of making a single free throw, he has attempted 150 sets of 3 free throws and recorded how many times he has made none of the three, one of the three, two of the three, and all three of the three. These were the results:

Number of made free throws	0	1	2	3
Times occurred	5	30	64	51

Based on this data, which of the following values would be the most likely probability of Gregory making a free throw on a single attempt?

A. 0.30
B. 0.50
C. 0.60
D. 0.70
E. 0.80

24. Suppose that the chart that follows represents a probability distribution for X.

X	1	2	3	4	5	6	7
Probability	x	x	0.15	3x	0.25	0.10	0.05

What is the value of *x*?

A. 0.05
B. 0.09
C. 0.15
D. 0.22
E. 0.55

GO ON TO THE NEXT PAGE

25. Jessica has taken the first three exams in a chemistry class. Her scores were, in order, 81, 84, and 88. The class mean for exam one was 81, with standard deviation 16. The class mean for exam two was 80, with standard deviation 16. The class mean for exam three was 86, with standard deviation 8. Which of the following statements best describes how she did on each exam, relative to the rest of the class?

    A. She did equally well on all three exams.

    B. She did best on exam three, and worst on exam one.

    C. She did best on exam three, and worst on exam two.

    D. She did equally well on exams two and three, but worst on exam one.

    E. She did equally well on exams two and three, but best on exam one.

26. A trigonometry class has 30 students, all of whom have taken each of the class's three exams. The mean on exam one was 78, with standard deviation 17. The mean on exam two was 83, with standard deviation 14. The mean on exam three was 73, with standard deviation 20. The final grade in the course, for each student, is the average of the three grades. What is the mean and standard deviation of the final grades?

    A. Mean 78 and standard deviation 9.92

    B. Mean 78 and standard deviation 17

    C. Mean 78 and standard deviation 17.18

    D. Mean 83 and standard deviation 17

    E. Mean 83 and standard deviation 20

27. Suppose that, from a sample of 200 graduates from Green Valley College, final grade-point averages and starting salaries are compared for each student. The correlation coefficient was computed to be $r = -0.191$. Which of the following statements best represents the meaning of this value?

    A. There is a strong, direct linear relationship between grade point average and starting salary.

    B. There is a weak, direct linear relationship between grade point average and starting salary.

    C. There is no linear relationship between grade point average and starting salary.

    D. There is a weak, inverse linear relationship between grade point average and starting salary.

    E. There is a strong, inverse linear relationship between grade point average and starting salary.

28. About 106,000 people attended the Reagan funeral at the Reagan Library. If the total amount of time people spent in line followed a normal distribution, with mean 6.5 hours, and standard deviation 0.85 hours, approximately how many people spent more than 8 hours in line?

    A. 650

    B. 4150

    C. 5700

    D. 11,000

    E. 16,950

29. You encounter a woman who has one of her children with her, and the child is a girl. The woman tells you that she has one other child. Assuming that the probability that a childbirth results in having a girl is exactly 50%, what is the probability that the woman's other child is also a girl?

    A. 0.2000

    B. 0.3333

    C. 0.4000

    D. 0.5000

    E. 0.6667

30. Scores on a standardized test are structured to follow a normal distribution with mean $\mu = 400$. If approximately 15% of all scores exceed 582, which of the following values would be the standard deviation of these test scores?

A. 75
B. 125
C. 150
D. 175
E. 250

31. North Beaver Dam wants to estimate the mean daily energy output of their dam in gigawatts per day. In a pilot sample, the owners of the dam have estimated that the standard deviation of their daily outputs is $\sigma = 16.7$. If they want to create a 90% confidence interval for the mean daily outputs, and that interval should be accurate within 2 gigawatts, for how many days should the dam be observed?

A. 14 days
B. 115 days
C. 189 days
D. 268 days
E. 755 days

32. A Vegas game, which requires 25 cents per play, has been programmed to give payouts according to this probability distribution:

Payout (dollars)	0.00	1.00	5.00	10.00
Probability	0.93	0.04	0.02	0.01

What is the expected average profit per play for this Vegas game?

A. $-0.20
B. $-0.01
C. $0.02
D. $0.24
E. $1.29

33. The Motor Wrench automotive company wants to estimate the mean life span of their auto batteries. After sampling 79 batteries, a 95% confidence interval was computed to be [289 hours, 297 hours]. However, the sample of battery life spans contained one extremely low value. If this low value is removed from the sample, and the interval is recomputed, which of the following will be true?

I. The width of the interval will be decreased.
II. The center of the interval will be decreased.
III. The error of the interval will be decreased.

A. I only
B. II only
C. I and II only
D. I and III only
E. I, II, and III

34. A random sample of 2000 high school boys were asked the question, "Do you shower every time you use the gymnasium?" The results were that 1945 said "yes," 53 said "no," and 2 refused to answer. However, when observers were placed in high school locker rooms, the percent of high school boys who took showers was only about 73%. Which of the following is the most likely reason for the difference in the results between the verbal survey and the observational survey?

A. The survey was voluntary, and only those who wanted to answer in the verbal survey did.
B. The sample size for the verbal survey was too small.
C. The verbal survey question was sensitive, and respondents did not answer honestly.
D. The verbal survey question was slanted, and caused dishonest results.
E. The difference can be attributed to random chance.

35. The Harmon advertising company wants to test the effectiveness of one of their television spots aired on Channel 10. In a poll of 1000 Channel 10 viewers, 224 indicated that they recalled seeing the television ad. Which of the following would be a 99% confidence interval for the true proportion of Channel 10 viewers who remembered seeing the ad?

   A. [0.190 , 0.258]
   B. [0.198 , 0.250]
   C. [0.202 , 0.246]
   D. [0.206 , 0.242]
   E. [0.211 , 0.237]

36. A botanist has determined that there is a strong linear correlation between the life spans of a certain species of toads and their adult weights. The least-squares regression line representing the relationship between the life span of a toad in days, y, and the weight in ounces, x, is given by the following equation:

$$\hat{y} = 173.3 - 1.65x \qquad 50 < x < 90$$

If the life span of the toad is estimated to be 60 days, what is the weight of the toad.

   A. 46.8 ounces
   B. 68.7 ounces
   C. 71.2 ounces
   D. 74.3 ounces
   E. 99.0 ounces

37. Which of the following statements is true about the t-distribution in relation to the standard normal curve?

   I. The t-distribution is wider than the standard normal curve for every degrees of freedom.
   II. As the degrees of freedom increases, the t-distribution approaches the standard normal curve.
   III. The t-distribution has a higher median value than the standard normal curve.

   A. I only
   B. II only
   C. I and II only
   D. I and III only
   E. I, II, and III

38. Suppose that event A and event B are mutually exclusive events. Which of the following statements is not true?

   A. $P(A \text{ or } B) = P(A) + P(B)$
   B. $P(A \text{ and } B) = 0$
   C. $P(A \mid B) = 0$
   D. If event A occurs, the probability of event B does not change.
   E. Events A and B are not independent.

39. The flight times for a league of competitive hang gliders follows a normal distribution with mean $\mu = 26.8$ minutes and standard deviation of 6.4 minutes. What is the minimum flight time a hang glider must have in order to be in the highest 1%?

   A. 11.9 minutes
   B. 33.2 minutes
   C. 39.3 minutes
   D. 41.7 minutes
   E. 43.3 minutes

40. The Bango market research company wants to perform a taste test to determine whether random customers prefer Koala Cola or Poopsie. Workers performing the survey present customers with two 6 ounce glasses, labeled "Cola A" and "Cola B." After consuming each glass of cola, the customer indicates which of the two colas is preferred. The test is constructed as a double-blind study. Which of the following statements best describes the meaning of "double blind?"

   A. The customer does not know the identity of either Cola A or Cola B.
   B. The customer wears a blindfold while testing the colas.
   C. In addition to not knowing which cola is which, the customers do not know why they are tasting the colas.
   D. The customers do not know what the total sample size is.
   E. Neither the customer nor the worker conducting the survey knows which cola is which.

Section II

Time: 1 hour and 30 minutes   Number of questions: 6   Percent of total grade: 50%

Part A

Questions 1–5   Spend about 65 minutes on this part of the exam.   Percent of Section II grade: 75%

Show all your work. Clearly indicate the methods you use—you will be graded on the correctness of your methods as well as the accuracy of your results and explanation.

1. An entrance exam for admission to a public service training program is being given to two groups of applicants. It has been claimed that the test was not fair and that the test discriminated against one of the groups. The following chart shows the results of the test:

	Pass	Fail
Group I	44	17
Group II	18	13

   a. Describe an appropriate hypothesis test that would test the claim that the entrance exam discriminated against one of the groups.

   b. Based on the data, and the appropriate hypothesis test, with a level of significance $\alpha = 0.05$, what can be concluded from the given sample?

   c. If it is concluded that the results on the test are significantly different for Groups I and II, what other conclusions can be made, other than that the test discriminated against one of the groups?

2. As part of training for the Air Force, trainees are given tests of hand-eye coordination. It has been observed that, with the advent of video games, scores on these hand-eye coordination tests have improved dramatically. The following is a chart of the mean score on a particular coordination test, as it has been given over the span of 30 years:

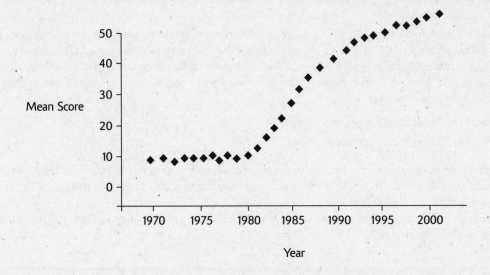

GO ON TO THE NEXT PAGE

a. Describe the trend of the scores, in relation to year, as it is shown in the graph.

b. Estimate what year video games may have begun to influence the scores on the coordination tests and what years video games became overwhelmingly influential. Justify your answers by citing information from the graph.

c. What type of data might be collected and analyzed in order to further investigate the claim that the presence of video games is related to scores on these hand-eye coordination tests?

3. A shipping plant has employed five workers to process boxes for shipment. The workers have been measured in terms of how many boxes they are able to process per hour. It has been determined that their box processing abilities each follow a normal distribution with the following means and standard deviations:

Worker	Mean	Standard Deviation
Baker	60.7	10.7
Collins	60.4	11.8
Harris	56.1	8.4
Jones	51.3	7.7
Thomas	43.2	12.9

a. Working together, and assuming that each worker processes boxes independently, how many boxes will the total crew be able to process per hour?

b. If their minimum work requirement is processing 225 boxes per hour, what percentage of hours will see the crew meet their requirement?

c. Suppose that Harris is sick one day. What is the probability that the crew will meet their requirement of 225 boxes during any given hour?

d. During a high demand month, the work requirement increases to 250 boxes per hour. Should the plant hire another worker? Explain your answer.

4. Suppose that Tri-City College has an exam that applicants must pass to be considered for admission. It has been claimed that version 1 of the exam was too difficult and that too many students were failing the exam. The college rewrote the exam so that version 2 would see an increase greater than 10% in the number of applicants passing the exam. A sample of previous applicants taking version 1 was compared to a sample of new applicants taking version 2, and these were the results:

Version 1: 223 out of 467 applicants passed.

Version 2: 107 out of 158 applicants passed.

a. What would be the appropriate hypothesis test to test whether there is an increase of at least 10% in students passing the exam with version 2? What assumptions need to be made for the test to be valid?

b. Based on the data and a level of significance $\alpha = 0.05$, did the reconstruction of the test from version 1 to version 2 achieve its goal?

5. A botanist is studying the relationship between the trunk circumference of a species of tree and the number of leaves it has. The scatterplot and regression results are given here:

Scatterplot with Least-Squares Regression Line

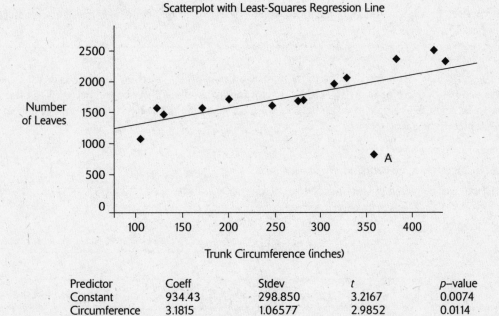

Predictor	Coeff	Stdev	t	p–value
Constant	934.43	298.850	3.2167	0.0074
Circumference	3.1815	1.06577	2.9852	0.0114

S = 363.09   R–Sq = 42.6%   R = 0.6528

a. What is the equation of the least squares regression line relating number of leaves with the trunk circumference in inches? Define any variables used.

b. If the point A, as shown in the scatterplot, represents a tree with trunk circumference 350 inches, and number of leaves 980, what is the residual for this data point?

c. If the data point A is removed from the sample, what effect will this have on the correlation coefficient, *r?* Explain.

GO ON TO THE NEXT PAGE

Part B

Question 6   Spend about 25 minutes on this part of the exam.   Percent of Section II grade: 25%

Directions for Part B: Allow additional time for this part. Clearly indicate the methods that you use and give clear explanations for all your results.

6. The manager of a work crew has the majority of his workers working overtime hours. It is desired that the average number of overtime hours worked by employees not significantly exceed 5 per week. During the course of one week, a random sample of 40 employees was taken, and the following represents the results in the sample, and a boxplot of the data:

Number of workers: 40

Sample mean of overtime hours: 9.55

Sample standard deviation of overtime hours: 9.459

Boxplot

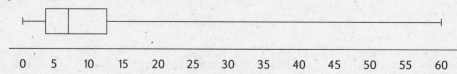

   a. What would be the appropriate hypothesis test used to see whether there is evidence that the true mean number of overtime hours exceeds 5 hours?

   b. At a level of significance $\alpha = 0.01$, does the evidence show that the true mean number of overtime hours exceeds 5 hours?

   c. How might the examination of a boxplot of data offer additional information regarding the number of overtime hours?

   d. Based on the boxplot, how might removing a value from the sample have an effect on the results of a hypothesis test of mean?

Section I Answers

1. **C.** Because of the near circular shape of the residual plot, the relationship is shown to be a very close nonlinear relationship. Furthermore, with residuals lying in a near symmetric pattern above and below the zero line, the strength of linear relationship would be approximately 0.

2. **B.** The slope of the regression line is $b_1 = 50.479$. From the regression results, the standard deviation of the slope is $s_{b_1} = 3.347518$ found in the chart as "stdev" for Courses. With degrees of freedom = (sample size − 2) = (21 − 2) = 19, the 99% confidence interval would be $(50.479) \pm (2.861)(3.347518) = 50.479 \pm 9.577$.

3. **B.** Critical values for z-tests of levels $\alpha = 0.10$, $\alpha = 0.05$, and $\alpha = 0.01$ are $z = -1.282$, $z = -1.645$, and $z = -2.326$, respectively. Thus, for a test statistic $z = -1.676$, rejection of the null hypothesis would occur for α-levels 0.10 and 0.05, but not for 0.01.

4. **A.** For the case of batteries, 10 are defective and 390 are good. If X is the number of defective batteries out of 10 chosen at random, the $P(X = 0) = (_{390}C_{10})(_{10}C_0)/(_{400}C_{10}) = 0.774$. The probabilities for X = 1, 2, 3, and 4 would be, at most 0.226, so X = 0 has the greatest probability.

5. **D.** For a roller coaster rider to qualify for a lower price, the rider must be a child under 12. The probability that a rider is under 12 is 0.40. In turn, the probability that the rider under 12 qualifies for the 25 cent rate is 0.10, and the probability that the rider qualifies for the free ride is 0.01. Thus, the probability that a rider rides for free is $(0.40)(0.01) = 0.004$, and the probability that a rider rides for 25 cents is $(0.40)(0.10) = 0.04$. The probability that a rider rides for full price is 0.956. The expected average price of riders on the roller coaster is $E(X) = \Sigma xP(X = x) = (1.50)(0.956) + (0.25)(0.04) + (0.00)(0.004) = \$1.444$.

6. **D.** The $P(\text{Ring or Gold}) = P(\text{Ring}) + P(\text{Gold}) - P(\text{Ring and Gold}) = 36/66 + 6/66 - 1/66 = 0.621$

7. **A.** $P(\text{Blue Marble, Blue Marble}) = (10/66)(9/65) = 0.021$.

8. **E.** The events "Chicago Cubs defeat Milwaukee Brewers" and "Milwaukee Brewers defeat Chicago Cubs" are mutually exclusive since they cannot both occur at same time. The events "Chicago Cubs defeat Milwaukee Brewers" and "New York Yankees defeat Baltimore Orioles" are independent events, since one result occurring does not change the probability of other result occurring. The events "Sammy Sosa play in the game that day" and "Sammy Sosa does not play in the game that day" are mutually exclusive since the events cannot both occur. The events "New York Yankees defeat Baltimore Orioles" and "Sammy Sosa does not play in the game that day" are independent events, since one event occurring does not change the probability of the other occurring, noting that Sammy Sosa is the player for the Chicago Cubs. The events "Sammy Sosa plays in the game that day" and "Chicago Cubs defeat the Milwaukee Brewers" are neither mutually exclusive, nor independent, since the events can both occur, and if Sammy Sosa does play for the Chicago Cubs, that would affect their probability of defeating the Milwaukee Brewers.

9. **D.** The 95% t-interval, with 19 degrees of freedom, would have the construction $162 \pm (2.093)(49/\sqrt{20})$. Therefore, the interval would be 162 ± 22.93.

10. **B.** The relationship between hours exercising and heart rate is inverse, since the slope of the least-squares regression line is negative. Furthermore, the value −1.923 indicates that, for each increase in one unit of x, or an increasing of one hour exercising, the predicted heart rate, y, would be reduced by 1.923 bpm. Therefore, in order to reduce the predicted heart rate by 5 bpm, it is necessary to increase the hours exercising by $5/1.923 = 2.6$ hours.

11. **B.** The percentile associated with a score represents how many whole percent of all scores lie below that score. Therefore, if a score is in the 89th percentile, this means that 89% of all other scores are below that score.

12. **D.** Since the p-value of the test statistic is 0.023, and since $0.01 < 0.023 < 0.05$, the null hypothesis would be rejected for $\alpha = 0.05$, but not for $\alpha = 0.01$. If the test is reversed, so that the alternate hypothesis was $H_a: \mu < 16$, the new p-value would become $\alpha = 1 - 0.023 = 0.977$, and thus the null hypothesis would not be rejected for $\alpha = 0.05$. With a p-value 0.023, together with the alternate hypothesis $H_a: \mu > 16$, this implies that the test statistic, either z or t, would be positive, and that the sample mean was greater than 16. However, with a one-tail p-value of 0.023, the two-tail p-value would become $2(0.023) = 0.046$, and the null hypothesis would be rejected at level $\alpha = 0.05$.

13. **B.** If the underlying population of values has mean μ and standard deviation σ, then the distribution of the sample mean, taken from a random sample, size n, would have mean μ and standard deviation $\sigma/\sqrt{n}$. In this case, the sample mean would have mean 40 and standard deviation $12/\sqrt{36} = 2$.

14. **E.** It is desired that the width of the interval be no more than five units wide. Since the interval is of the form $x \pm E$, the maximum error would be $E = 2.5$. With the population standard deviation $\sigma = 20$, in order to create a 99% confidence interval for mean, with error no greater than 2.5, the following formula should be used: $n \geq (z\sigma/E)^2$. Thus, the minimum sample size would be $n \geq [(2.576)(20)/(2.5)]^2 = 424.68$. Therefore, the minimum sample size would be 425.

15. **D.** The observed proportion in this sample was $28/80 = 0.35$. The corresponding 90% confidence interval for the true population proportion would be $0.35 \pm (1.645)\sqrt{(0.35)(0.65)/80}$, or 0.3500 ± 0.0877.

16. **A.** In order to compare scores with the performance of the rest of the class, z-scores should be computed. The z-score for the first exam was $z = (78 - 70)/(10) = 0.80$. The z-score for the second exam was $z = (84 - 75)/(17) = 0.53$. In comparing z-scores, Samantha did better on the first exam.

17. **E.** The original data set has population mean $\mu = 76$ and standard deviation $\sigma = 14$. When 6 is subtracted from each value, the mean is reduced to 70, but the standard deviation remains the same. However, when each value is then divided by 2, both the mean and standard deviation are divided by 2. The final mean and standard deviation are 35 and 7, respectively.

18. **C.** It is given that $P(\text{Brand A}) = 0.16$, $P(\text{Brand B}) = 0.12$, and $P(\text{Brand A and Brand B}) = 0.02$. Therefore, the $P(\text{Brand A or Brand B}) = P(\text{Brand A}) + P(\text{Brand B}) - P(\text{Brand A and Brand B}) = 0.16 + 0.12 - 0.02 = 0.26$. Then, the $P(\text{neither Brand A nor Brand B}) = 1 - 0.26 = 0.74$. Finally, the probability that 0 out of 6 homes would have "neither Brand A nor Brand B" would be $(0.74)^6 =$ approximately 0.164.

19. **C.** The test statistic for difference of two means, with large independent samples, with the assumption that the true standard deviations are not equal (standard deviations not pooled) is given by $t = (x_1 - x_2)/\sqrt{(s_1)^2/n_1 + (s_2)^2/n_2} = (45.8 - 41.1)/\sqrt{(16.6)^2/200 + (13.3)^2/200} = 3.125$.

20. **A.** With a population size $N = 400$, the distribution of the colored marbles would be red = 80, blue = 100, white = 120, silver = 20, and black = 80. If two marbles are chosen simultaneously, without replacement, then, the probability of two blue would be $(100/400)(99/399) = 0.0620$. This probability can also be computed by the formula $({}_{100}C_2)({}_{300}C_0)/({}_{400}C_2) = 0.0620$.

21. **C.** With 16 people to choose from, and 1 holding the key, the probability that Bill chooses the person who has the key, in five tries, can be found by computing $1 - P(\text{Bill does not choose the person with the key})$, which is equal to $1 - (15/16)(14/15)(13/14)(12/13)(11/12) = 1 - 11/16 = 0.3125$.

22. **C.** Using the normal approximation to binomial, the mean would be $\mu = np = (80)(0.20) = 16$, with standard deviation $\sigma = \sqrt{npq} = \sqrt{(80)(0.20)(0.80)} = 3.57771$. With the proper continuity correction, the appropriate z-score would be $z = (19.5 - 16)/(3.57771) = 0.98$. The approximate probability of exceeding a z-score of 0.98 is 0.1635.

23. **D.** If the probability of making one free throw is 0.70, and X is the number of free throws made out of 3, the $P(X = 0) = (0.30)^3 = 0.027$, the $P(X = 1) = 3(0.70)(0.30)^2 = 0.189$, the $P(X = 2) = 3(0.70)^2(0.30) = 0.441$, and the $P(X = 3) = (0.70)^3 = 0.343$. Therefore, the expected values, for 150 sets, would be 4.05, 28.35, 66.15, and 51.45, respectively. These values are close to the observed values. Moreover, if p is the probability of making a free throw, it can be estimated by setting $p^3 = (51/150)$, whereby $p = 0.698$.

24. **B.** For any probability distribution, the sum of all probabilities is 1. Therefore, solving for x in the equation $x + x + 0.15 + 3x + 0.25 + 0.10 + 0.05 = 1$ yields $5x = 0.45$, or $x = 0.09$.

25. **D.** For exam one, her z-score was $z = (81 - 81)/16 = 0$. For exam two, her z-score was $z = (84 - 80)/16 = 0.25$. For exam three, her z-score was $z = (88 - 86)/8 = 0.25$. Therefore, she did equally well on exams two and three, but not as well, or worse, on exam one.

26. C. The mean for the average of three random variables would be $(\mu_1 + \mu_2 + \mu_3)/3 = (78 + 83 + 73)/3 = 78$. The standard deviation for the average of three random variables would be $\sqrt{\sigma_1^2 + \sigma_2^2 + \sigma_3^2}/3 = \sqrt{17^2 + 14^2 + 20^2}/3 = 17.18$.

27. D. A negative correlation coefficient represents an inverse linear relationship. The fact that the value is close to, but not equal to, zero represents a weak linear relationship.

28. B. The z-score for the value 8 is $z = (8 - 6.5)/(0.85) = 1.76$. The probability of exceeding $z = 1.76$ on the normal distribution is 0.0392. Therefore, the expected number would be approximately $(106{,}000)(0.0392) = 4155$.

29. B. Assuming that the probability of having a girl is 0.50, then for two children, $P(\text{no girls}) = 0.25$, $P(\text{one boy, one girl, either order}) = 0.50$, and $P(\text{two girls}) = 0.25$. So, if it is known that the woman has one girl, then, finding the probability that the other child is a girl is equivalent to finding the conditional probability, $P(\text{two girls} \mid \text{at least one girl}) = (0.25)/(0.75) = 0.3333$, realizing that the probability of at least one girl is $0.50 + 0.25 = 0.75$.

30. D. The z-score representing the cutoff for the highest 15% on the normal curve is approximately 1.04. Therefore, if the cutoff for the highest 15%, in this case, is $582 - 400 = 182$, then the standard deviation can be found by solving the equation $(1.04)(\sigma) = 182$, or approximately 175.

31. C. To say that the interval is accurate within 2 gigawatts is to say that the error term in the confidence interval, given by the form $\bar{x} \pm E$, is $E = 2$. The minimum sample size for a 90% confidence interval, with $\sigma = 16.7$, is given by the formula $n \geq (z\sigma/E)^2 = ((1.645)(16.7)/(2))^2 = 188.67$, or 189.

32. B. The actual profits for this game are -0.25, 0.75, 4.75, and 9.75, with probabilities 0.93, 0.04, 0.02, and 0.01, respectively. Therefore, the expected value is given by $\Sigma(x)(\text{probability of } x) = (-0.25)(0.93) + (0.75)(0.04) + (4.75)(0.02) + (9.75)(0.01) = -0.01$.

33. E. If an extremely low value is removed from a data set, the standard deviation will be reduced, and thus the error term in the confidence interval, where $E = ts/\sqrt{n}$ will be reduced, and consequently the width of the interval will be reduced. Furthermore, with the removal of this low value, the sample mean, which is the center of the interval, will be reduced. All three statements are true.

34. C. The most likely cause for the difference in the results is the sensitivity of the question, asking people to answer a question regarding their hygiene. The sample size was large, 2000, and since only 2 refused to answer, the voluntary nature of the survey was not a factor. The question was not slanted, as it was a simple "yes" or "no" question, and a difference of well over 20% in large samples cannot be attributed to random chance.

35. A. The observed sample proportion was $224/1000 = 0.224$. The 99% confidence interval would be given by $p \pm z\sqrt{p(1-p)/n} = (0.224) \pm 2.576\sqrt{(0.224)(0.776)/(1000)} = 0.224 \pm 0.034$.

36. E. To determine the weight of the toad, x, solve the equation $60 = 173.3 - 1.65x$. Therefore, $x = 68.7$.

37. C. The t-distribution is wider than the standard normal curve for every degrees of freedom, but as the degrees of freedom increases, the t-distribution becomes narrower and approaches the standard normal. However, the median for both curves is 0.

38. D. If events A and B are mutually exclusive, this means that if one event occurs, the other cannot possibly occur. Therefore, the $P(\text{A and B}) = 0$, also implying that $P(\text{A or B}) = P(\text{A}) + P(\text{B})$. Furthermore, this also means that the conditional probability $P(\text{A} \mid \text{B}) = 0$, and that since if one event occurs, the probability of the other event becomes 0, the events are not independent. This also means that to say if one event occurs, the probability of the other event does not change is false, since the probability becomes 0.

39. D. For a value to lie in the highest 1%, the value must exceed the z-score 2.326. Therefore, the minimum such flight time would be $26.8 + (2.326)(6.4) = 41.7$.

40. E. The term "double blind" refers to the fact that neither the person taking the test nor the person administering the test knows the identity of the items, in this case the identity of the cola brands being tested.

Section II Answers

1a. An appropriate hypothesis test would be a two-way test of independence, whereby the expected chart is computed showing the expected results if passing the exam was independent of Groups I and II. The null hypothesis is that passing the exam is independent of group, and the alternate hypothesis is that passing the exam is not independent of group. The χ^2 test statistic is computed as $\Sigma (O - E)^2/E$, whereby the degrees of freedom is 1, and, depending on the level of significance, the χ^2 statistic is compared to a particular critical value or a p-value can be computed.

1b. The expected values for this data would be

	Pass	*Fail*
Group I	41.109	19.891
Group II	20.891	10.109

The χ^2 test statistic is 1.851, whereby, compared with a critical value of 3.841, corresponding to a level of significance $\alpha = 0.05$, and degrees of freedom 1, the null hypothesis is not rejected. There is not evidence to conclude that passing the exam is influenced by group membership. Furthermore, the p-value associated with this test statistic is 0.1737, indicating the same result.

1c. If it had been concluded that passing the exam was affected by group membership, the construction of the exam as discriminating against one of the groups can be an explanation. However, it could also be an explanation that the exam is not discriminatory, but that one of the groups is either less prepared or less able to pass this exam. It is also possible that there are confounding factors that result in one group having a higher percentage of passing the exam, such as location of the exam, ability to provide information about the exam, or other circumstances surrounding the taking of the exam.

2a. The trends of the scores, according to the graph, are that mean scores remained steady at approximately 10 during the years 1970 to 1980. Then, scores began to rise at a rapid pace between the years 1980 and 1985, going from an average of about 10 to an average of about 30. After 1985, the scores still continued to rise, but at a less rapid pace, seeming to level off near an average of about 50 by the year 2000.

2b. It appears that video games may have begun to become a factor in the early 1980s, as the year 1981 showed the first visible increase in the average scores. At approximately 1990, video games appeared to have a dramatic influence, as the scores increased rapidly up to 1990, going significantly above 40 and beginning to level off, showing that some great level of influence had been reached.

2c. There are many possible ways that data can be collected and analyzed to show the effect of video games on hand-eye coordination tests. One way may be to perform a test of two means, whereby the average of a sample of scores before the advent of video games, 1975 for example, can be compared with the average of a sample of scores afterward, 1985 for example. This test, however, may be subject to numerous confounding factors. Another possibility is to perform a regression analysis that compares the number of people with video games during that year, in millions, perhaps, with the corresponding average score on the hand-eye coordination tests during that year. Even a very direct comparison of means can be done, comparing the mean score on coordination tests among a sample of people who play video games, with the mean scores on coordination tests among a sample of people who do not play video games.

3a. The mean of the sum of five independent random variables is $\mu_1 + \mu_2 + \mu_3 + \mu_4 + \mu_5 = 271.7$ boxes per hour.

3b. Furthermore, since the five random variables are normally distributed, the sum is also normally distributed, whereby the variance of the sum is $\sigma_1^2 + \sigma_2^2 + \sigma_3^2 + \sigma_4^2 + \sigma_5^2 = 10.7^2 + 11.8^2 + 8.4^2 + 7.7^2 + 12.9^2 = 549.99$. The standard deviation of the sum is $\sqrt{549.99} = 23.4519$. The probability of the sum exceeding 225 is the probability of exceeding $z = (225 - 271.7)/(23.4519) = -1.991$ or a probability of approximately 0.9768. In other words, the crew will achieve their goal in about 97.7% of their hours.

3c. With Harris missing from the group, the mean of the sum of the remaining four is $\mu_1 + \mu_2 + \mu_4 + \mu_5 = 215.6$ boxes per hour, with standard deviation $\sqrt{\sigma_1^2 + \sigma_2^2 + \sigma_4^2 + \sigma_5^2} = \sqrt{10.7^2 + 11.8^2 + 7.7^2 + 12.9^2} = \sqrt{479.43} = 21.8959$. The probability of this sum exceeding 225 is the probability of exceeding $z = (225 - 215.6)/(21.8959) = 0.4293$ or a probability of approximately 0.3339.

3d. The probability of the full work crew exceeding 250 boxes per hour is the probability of exceeding $z = (250 - 271.1)/(23.4519) = -0.9253$, or a probability of 0.8224. If it is considered unacceptable for the crew to fail to meet their goal nearly 18% of the time, yes, the company should hire an additional worker.

4a. An appropriate hypothesis test to see whether there is evidence that more than 10% additional students will pass the exam could be done as a comparison of two independent proportions. If p_1 represents the proportion of students who pass version 1, and p_2 represents the proportion of students who pass version 2, then, if it is desired that the difference in the proportions exceeds 10%, the null hypothesis could be set up as H_0: $p_2 - p_1 \leq 0.10$ with alternate hypothesis H_a: $p_2 - p_1 > 0.10$. It needs to be assumed that the two proportions are independent, whereby the same students are not taking both versions of the exam, and that the sample sizes are sufficiently large, so that a z-test can be performed.

4b. The observed proportion for version 1 is $\hat{p}_1 = 223/467$, the observed proportion for version 2 is $\hat{p}_2 = 107/158$, and the pooled proportion is $\bar{p} = 330/625 = 0.528$. The test statistic corresponding to this hypothesis test is $z = ((107/158) - (223/467) - 0.10)/\sqrt{(0.528)(0.472)/467 + (0.528)(0.472)/158} = 2.170$. At a level of significance $\alpha = 0.05$, compared to critical value $z = 1.645$, the null hypothesis is rejected. There is evidence that the proportion of applicants who take version 2 exceeds 10% more than the proportion of applicants who take Version 1.

5a. The equation of the least-squares regression line relating the number of leaves with trunk circumference is $\hat{y} = 934.43 + 3.1815x$, where $\hat{y}$ is the predicted number of leaves the tree has, and x is the trunk circumference in inches.

5b. The residual for a data point is the difference between the actual observed value and the predicted value, $y - \hat{y}$. The predicted number of leaves, based on the regression equation, would be $\hat{y} = 934.43 + (3.1815)(350) = 2047.955$, or approximately 2048 leaves. The residual is $980 - 2048 = -1068$.

5c. The point A, whose value is (350, 980), clearly has the largest residual in magnitude and appears to be an extreme outlier. The correlation coefficient for the overall data set is 0.6528, indicating a moderate direct linear correlation between trunk circumference and number of leaves. However, it does appear that the data points appear to lie in an approximate straight line, with the exception of point A. Removal of point A would leave a set whose points fit a straight line much more closely, indicating a much higher strength of linear correlation. The new correlation coefficient, r, with point A removed from the set, will be much closer to 1, possibly 0.8 or 0.9.

6a. The appropriate hypothesis test for whether the true mean exceeds 5 hours would be a t-test of one sample, since the population standard deviation is unknown. Since it is desired to determine whether there is evidence that the mean exceeds 5 hours, the null hypothesis would be H_0: $\mu = 5$ hours, tested against the alternate hypothesis H_a: $\mu > 5$ hours. The t-statistic would be computed as $t = \dfrac{(\bar{x} - 5)}{\left(\dfrac{s}{\sqrt{n}}\right)}$, and compared to a t-critical value, depending on the level of significance of the test.

6b. The t-statistic is $t = (9.55 - 5)/(9.459/\sqrt{40}) = 3.042$. With degrees of freedom $40 - 1 = 39$, and level of significance $\alpha = 0.01$, the rejection region is $t > 2.426$. There is evidence, then, that the true mean number of overtime hours exceeds 5.

6c. The boxplot shows that the median number of hours is 5, with definite skewness to the right. First, the lower half of the data is between 0 and 5, and the third quartile is within the range 5 to 10. The fourth quartile is spread throughout the range 10 to 60. This may indicate that there are large data points, significantly higher than the mean, evenly spread throughout the 10 to 60 range. It may also indicate that, although there are values somewhat above the mean of 9.55 and the median of 5, there may be only one extreme outlier at approximately 60. The exact nature of the points within each quartile cannot be determined from the boxplot alone. However, there seems to be large data points that are dramatically affecting the results of the hypothesis test.

6d. Removal of a single point from the center of the data may have little impact on the results of a hypothesis test. However, the removal of an extreme outlier, for instance an extremely large value in the set, may have one of two effects on the outcome of a hypothesis test. Removal of a lone large outlier will result in a drop in the sample mean, which could result in a drop of the test statistic, t, significant enough to result in failure to reject the null hypothesis, whereas it was rejected previously. However, it is possible for the t-statistic to actually increase with the removal of a lone extremely high value. Removal of an extremely large value could result in a moderate, or slight decrease in the sample mean, $\bar{x}$. However, the removal may also result in a dramatic decrease in the sample standard deviation, whereby the value whose greatest distance from the mean was removed. The overall t-statistic, with a relatively small decrease in the sample mean, relative to a major decrease in the sample standard deviation, could actually increase, possibly resulting in the rejection of a null hypothesis that was previously not rejected.

Section I

Time: 1 hour and 30 minutes　　　　　Number of questions: 40　　　　　Percent of total grade: 50%

Directions: Solve each problem. Decide which is the best of the answer choices given.

1. Two measures, x and y, were taken, and the correlation and least-squares regression line were computed. The following is a plot of the residuals for the regression analysis:

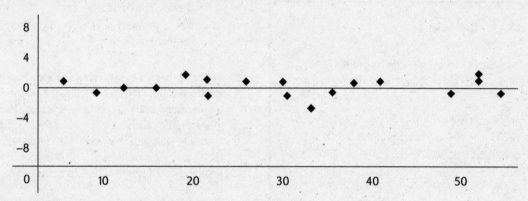

   Which of the following is the most likely value for the correlation coefficient, r?

   A.　−0.50
   B.　0
   C.　0.10
   D.　0.50
   E.　0.95

GO ON TO THE NEXT PAGE

2. A forestry study has determined that there is a linear relationship between the trunk circumference of a maple tree and its number of leaves. From a sample of 25 maple trees, the number of leaves was compared to its trunk circumference in centimeters. The results of the regression analysis are given here:

Regression Equation:

Leaves = 230.504 + 6.201 Trunk

Predictor	Coef	Stdev	t-ratio	p
Constant	230.50445	68.7333	3.3536	0.003
Trunk	6.2010127	0.34487	17.9806	0.000

S = 108.43   R-sq = 93.4

Which of the following would represent a 99% confidence interval for the slope of the regression line?

A. 6.201 ± 0.888
B. 6.201 ± 0.968
C. 6.201 ± 1.135
D. 6.201 ± 1.176
E. 6.201 ± 4.337

3. Of the following statements concerning the normal distribution, which of the following are true?

I.   The normal curve is symmetric.
II. The mean of the normal curve is 0.
III. The area under the entire normal curve is 1.

A. I only
B. II only
C. III only
D. I and III only
E. All three statements are true.

4. Sunset Hills farms is harvesting and packing bales of hay for delivery to other farms. The weights of the bales follow some non-normal distribution with mean $\mu = 1500$ pounds and standard deviation $\sigma = 40$ pounds. If 400 bales are randomly selected, what would be the probability distribution of the averages of the weights $\bar{x}$?

A. Normal, with mean 1500 and standard deviation 40
B. Normal, with mean 1500 and standard deviation 2
C. Approximately normal with mean 1500 and standard deviation 40
D. Approximately normal with mean 1500 and standard deviation 2
E. Approximately normal with mean 1500 and standard deviation 0.1

5. Suppose that the producers of Gooey Peanut Butter want to estimate the mean amount of fat in a 16-ounce jar. In a randomly selected sample of 500 jars, the mean amount was 165.6 grams, with a sample standard deviation 38.8 grams. Which of the following would be a 90% confidence interval for the mean amount of fat, in grams, for a 16-ounce jar?

A. 165.6 ± 0.1
B. 165.6 ± 2.2
C. 165.6 ± 2.9
D. 165.6 ± 3.4
E. 165.6 ± 63.8

6. Suppose that a New Jersey testing service has created a standardized test for assessing the reading and computing skills of 8th graders. The test consists of a reading part, which is structured to have a mean of 200 and a standard deviation of 50. It also has a mathematics part, which is structured to have a mean of 100 and a standard deviation of 20. Students take both parts of the test and are given a final score that is the sum of both parts together. What would be the standard deviation of the final student scores?

A. 11.54
B. 30
C. 53.85
D. 70
E. 300

7. Suppose that the probability of event A is 0.4, the probability of event B is 0.3, and the probability of events A and B both occurring is 0.2. Which of the following represents the relationship between events A and B?

A. The events are independent.

B. The events are mutually exclusive.

C. The events are both independent and mutually exclusive.

D. The events are neither independent nor mutually exclusive.

E. The relationship between the two events cannot be determined from the information given.

8. Suppose that among moviegoers to the Cedurburg Metroplex, 70% of them have seen the movie *Titanic*. Furthermore, among those who have seen *Titanic*, 60% of those have seen the movie at least a second time. If 600 people at the Cedurburg Metroplex are chosen at random, what would be the expected number of people who have seen *Titanic* more than once?

A. 60

B. 216

C. 252

D. 294

E. 360

9. One of the important issues of the early 1990s was whether the president of the United States should have the line-item veto, which allows the president to veto selected parts of a bill, rather than only being allowed to veto, or approve, the entire bill as it is. A polling service wanted to gauge the opinions of the general public concerning whether the President should be given this right. Approximately 10,000 people were randomly selected, and asked the question "Should the president be given the line-item veto, in order to eliminate government waste?" The results of the survey showed that approximately 84% of the public supported the line-item veto. However, when other polling services polled the public concerning this issue, the support for the line- item veto was only about 50%. Which is the most likely reason why the support in this survey was so much higher than what other surveys showed?

A. The survey was done with a loaded question.

B. There was a bias in the way the sample was chosen.

C. The question was sensitive, and people answered dishonestly.

D. The sample size was too small, in relation to the size of the population.

E. The difference in the results can be attributed to random chance.

10. Suppose that the success rate in a college algebra class is 85%, meaning that approximately 85% of students who finish the course receive a C or better. A professor wants to simulate the probability distribution of these college algebra students by using colored marbles and selecting them at random. He has a bag that consists of 1 blue marble, 2 green marbles, and 25 red marbles. Which of the following marble assignments would best simulate the 85% probability?

A. Assign the green marbles as "failure" and all other marbles as "success."

B. Assign the green marbles as "failure," 10 red marbles as "success," and discard the other marbles.

C. Assign the blue marble as "failure," 8 red marbles as "success," and discard the other marbles.

D. Assign the green marbles as "failure," 11 red marbles as "success," and discard the other marbles.

E. Assign the blue marble as "failure," the green marble as "failure," 17 red marbles as "success," and discard the other marbles.

GO ON TO THE NEXT PAGE

11. Suppose that a study has been done, whereby the age of a species of tree is estimated by measuring the circumference of its trunk. The following least-squares regression line has been created that relates the circumference, x, in inches, with the age of the tree, y, in years.

$$\hat{y} = -34.97 + 0.848x \text{ for } 50 < x < 500$$

If a tree has been estimated to be 240 years old, what was the measured trunk circumference?

A. 168 inches
B. 238 inches
C. 242 inches
D. 275 inches
E. 324 inches

12. Crosswhite Lumber company wants to test whether one brand of boards is stronger than another brand of boards. The company structures a test whereby the mean amount of weight that can be withstood by a random sample of boards from Brand X is compared with the mean of a random sample from Brand Y. The alternate hypothesis of their test is that the mean for Brand X is greater than the mean for Brand Y. The results of their test produce a p-value of 0.023. If the predetermined level of significance of the test was $\alpha = 0.05$, what would be the company's conclusion concerning the strength of the boards?

A. There is evidence to conclude that Brand X is stronger than Brand Y.
B. There is not enough evidence to conclude that Brand X is stronger than Brand Y.
C. There is enough evidence to conclude that Brand Y is stronger than Brand X.
D. There is not enough evidence to conclude that Brand Y is stronger than Brand X.
E. There is enough evidence to conclude that the strengths of Brand X and Brand Y are equal.

13. The null hypothesis of a test is $H_o: \mu = 70$, and the alternate hypothesis is $H_a: \mu > 70$. A sample has been taken, and based on the results, Type I error has been committed. Which of the following best describes a scenario in which this occurred?

A. The sample mean was observed to be near 70, but the true mean was greater than 70.
B. The sample mean was observed to be significantly greater than 70, but the true mean was 70.
C. The sample mean was observed to be significantly less than 70, but the true mean was 70.
D. The sample mean was observed to be significantly greater than 70, and the true mean was greater than 70.
E. The sample mean was observed to be near 70, and the true mean was 70.

14. Which of the following statements is not true about the t-distribution?

A. The t-distribution is symmetric.
B. The t-distribution is wider than the normal distribution.
C. As the number of degrees of freedom increases, the t-distribution becomes approximately normal.
D. The total area under the t-distribution is 1.
E. As the degrees of freedom increases, the t-distribution becomes wider.

15. The following two-way contingency table represents a test of whether the college entrance is independent of the type of high school a student has attended.

School Type			
	Urban	*Suburban*	*Rural*
Four-Year College	24	46	29
Two-Year College	31	41	19
Did not attend	40	23	57

Based on this data, approximately how many urban students would be expected to attend a four-year college?

A. 24
B. 30
C. 32
D. 33
E. 34

16. Suppose that Rosanna's is a restaurant chain that has a number of locations throughout several states. Each of their restaurants is approximately the same size, and some of their restaurants allow smoking but others do not. The owner of the Rosanna's chain wants to determine whether allowing smoking has an effect on the yearly income of the location. In order to test whether there is a difference between the yearly income of smoking locations and nonsmoking locations, which of the following would be the most appropriate test?

A. A *t*-test of one sample
B. A *t*-test of two independent samples
C. A paired *t*-test
D. A χ^2 goodness-of-fit test
E. A χ^2 test of independence

17. A mortgage company gathers data concerning applications for mortgage and has determined that each month, the percentage of applicants for a new mortgage who are approved is approximately 67%, with a margin of error 5%. Which of the following statements best describes the meaning of "margin of error 5%"?

A. The difference between the estimated proportion and the true proportion is likely to be no more than 5%.
B. Among those who are approved for a mortgage, 5% will later be denied the mortgage.
C. It is likely that 5% of applicants who were counted as "approved" have been counted in error.
D. Approximately 5% of applicants have been neither approved nor denied.
E. It is likely that the measured 67% will go down by 5% in the future.

18. Super Saver shopping center wants to measure the buying patterns of their customers. Specifically, they want to estimate the mean amount of money spent by customers each visit. To accomplish this, they record the amount of money spent by every customer over the course of one week. Which term best describes this type of study?

A. Census
B. Cluster sample
C. Random sample
D. Stratified sample
E. Systematic sample

19. Nicole is a sixth grade student who has taken the DAT. Her results indicate that her mathematics score has placed her in the 88th percentile. Which of the following statements is the best description of what this means?

A. She got exactly 88 questions correct.
B. She got 88% of the questions correct.
C. Her score was in the top 88% of all those taking the test.
D. Eighty-eight percent of all people taking the test had scores above hers.
E. Eighty-eight percent of all people taking the test had scores below hers.

GO ON TO THE NEXT PAGE

20. Suppose Graph I gives the scatterplot relating data set X with data set Y, and Graph II gives the scatterplot relating data set G with data set H. The correlation coefficient relating data set X and data set Y is 0.958, and the correlation coefficient relating data set G and data set H is – 0.944. Which of the following statements will most likely describe the difference between Graph I and Graph II?

   A. The patterns of the points in both graphs will actually be similar.

   B. The points in Graph I will lie in an approximate straight line, whereas the points in Graph II will be very scattered.

   C. The points in Graph I will lie in an approximate straight line with positive slope, whereas the points in Graph II will lie in an approximate straight line with negative slope.

   D. The points in Graph I will lie in an approximate straight line, whereas the points in Graph II will lie in an approximate circle.

   E. The pattern of the points in both graphs will be very scattered, whereby the patterns cannot be compared.

21. Mrs. Bush has given a writing test to her 12th grade class. She announces to her class that the mean score was 85, with standard deviation 16, but that there was one extremely low score. If she removes the low score, what effect will this have on the mean and standard deviation?

   A. The mean and standard deviation will both increase.

   B. The mean and standard deviation will both decrease.

   C. The mean will increase and the standard deviation will decrease.

   D. The mean will decrease and the standard deviation will increase.

   E. The mean will increase and the standard deviation will stay the same.

22. Suppose that a data set contains exactly one outlier. If the outlier is removed from the data set, some of the data set's measurements will be effected. Which of the following statements is not necessarily true?

   A. The range will decrease.

   B. The standard deviation will decrease.

   C. The size of the data set will decrease.

   D. The interquartile range will decrease.

   E. The variance will decrease.

23. Kelly has taken the first two exams in a Statistics class. Her score on exam one was 81, and her score on exam two was 78. The scores for the entire class on exam one had a mean of 84, with standard deviation 15. The scores for the entire class on exam two had a mean of 75, with standard deviation 12. Which of the following statements is not true?

   A. Kelly's score on exam one was higher than her score on exam two.

   B. In relation to the rest of the class, Kelly did better on exam two than on exam one.

   C. Both of Kelly's scores were equally close to the class average for both exams.

   D. In terms of the computed z-scores, both of Kelly's scores were equally close to the class average for both exams.

   E. Neither of Kelly's scores would be considered outliers in relation to the rest of the class.

24. Students at Onizuka High School are taking a standardized test that is constructed to have a standard deviation $\sigma = 50$. The average among 143 seniors who took the exam was 173.5. The average among 128 juniors who took the exam was 161.4. A test is done to compare the true mean between seniors and juniors on this exam. If the alternate hypothesis is that the mean for seniors is greater than the mean for juniors, what is the value of the z-statistic for this test, based on the sample data given?

   A. 1.424

   B. 1.711

   C. 1.989

   D. 2.738

   E. 2.894

25. The Happy Nappy Candy Company produces a brand of candy called Dum-Dums. Dum-Dums come in several colors, and the company desires that the colors be distributed equally in the bags. In order to test whether the colors are equally distributed, a sample is taken, with the following observed frequencies.

Red	Blue	Green	Yellow	White	Pink	Orange	Purple
24	27	31	44	19	22	29	20

What is the value of the χ^2 test statistic for the appropriate goodness-of-fit test?

A. 1.704
B. 5.750
C. 14.552
D. 16.889
E. 232.889

26. The Midwestern Testing Company has created a standardized exam that is constructed to have a standard deviation of 75. They want to estimate the mean score for students actually taking the exam. They desire to create a 95% confidence interval for the true mean score and that the width of the interval should be only one unit wide. To create the confidence interval with these specifications, how many students should be selected into the sample?

A. 294
B. 15,221
C. 21,609
D. 60,886
E. 86,436

27. An Olympic archer has a 65% probability of hitting a bulls-eye on a shot. If this archer attempts seven shots at the target, what is the probability of making at least six out of seven attempts?

A. 0.158
B. 0.234
C. 0.453
D. 0.793
E. 0.842

28. Emily and Christy are lab partners in a biology class. They are collecting data in order to test whether the mean weight of a species of insect is 50 mg. They have measured 80 insects and computed the sample mean and sample standard deviation. Emily determines that the p-value for a one-tail hypothesis test is 0.045 and rejects the claim that the mean is 50 mg. However, Christy considers the test to be a two-tail hypothesis test, and decides not to reject the claim that the mean is 50 mg. Both students have used the same level of significance, α, for each of their tests. Which of the following is a possible value for α?

A. 0.005
B. 0.01
C. 0.025
D. 0.05
E. 0.10

29. Tri-County Graphics company has printed a set of magazines for national distribution. However, after the printing was completed, a member of the quality control division indicated that printing errors were found in several of the copies he looked at. The printing manager is concerned that the magazines may need to be reprinted, and wants to estimate the proportion of magazines that have printing errors. A sample of 500 magazines is taken at random, and 84 were found to have printing errors. Which of the following is a 95% confidence interval for the true proportion of magazines that have errors?

A. [0.125 , 0.211]
B. [0.135 , 0.201]
C. [0.141 , 0.196]
D. [0.151 , 0.185]
E. [0.167 , 0.169]

GO ON TO THE NEXT PAGE

30. The mean life span of a species of bacteria is to be estimated in hours. A sample of 100 bacteria are measured, and, based on the sample mean and sample standard deviation, a 95% t-confidence interval is computed to be [5.65 hours , 6.41 hours]. However, the scientist doing the study desires that the interval be narrower. Which of the following would decrease the width of the interval?

   I.   Recompute the interval as a z-interval.
   II. Recompute the interval with a lower confidence level.
   III. Increase the sample size.

   A. I only
   B. II only
   C. III only
   D. II and III only
   E. I, II, and III

31. The following two-way contingency table is meant to test whether there is a relationship between the type of housing a student has and the student's mode of travel to class.

Type of Housing			
	House	**Apartment**	**Dormitory**
Walk	12	44	155
Bicycle/ Skateboard	26	38	108
Bus	35	64	7
Car	168	119	3

What would be the degrees of freedom for the appropriate χ^2 test of independence?

   A. 6
   B. 8
   C. 9
   D. 12
   E. 778

32. During the course of the 2004 Democratic Presidential Primary, a state poll indicates that the level of support for the candidates follows these percentages:

   John Kerry 35%   Dick Gephardt 10%
   John Edwards 25%   Joe Lieberman 5%
   Howard Dean 20%   Al Sharpton 5%

A local television station wants to test whether these percentages are accurate, and takes a poll of randomly selected Democratic voters, and arrives at these results:

   John Kerry 710   Dick Gephardt 212
   John Edwards 468   Joe Lieberman 104
   Howard Dean 428   Al Sharpton 78

Which of the following is the χ^2 test statistic for the appropriate goodness-of-fit test?

   A. 0.468
   B. 5.870
   C. 9.871
   D. 10.208
   E. 11.199

33. A 100-point history test is given to two classes, one at 7:30 and the other at 10:00. The following is a back-to-back stem-and-leaf plot of the scores in the two classes.

7:30 class		10:00 class
7	5	5
8	6	79
98521	7	00147889
887544200	8	11346678899
83110	9	0359

Which of the following statements is not justified by the data?

   A. The 10:00 class has a larger sample size than the 7:30 class.
   B. The 10:00 class has a higher median than the 7:30 class.
   C. The 10:00 class has a higher maximum value than the 7:30 class.
   D. The 10:00 class has a higher range than the 7:30 class.
   E. The 10:00 class has more values in the 80–89 range than the 7:30 class.

34. The state of Illinois wants to estimate the mean household income of homeowners in the state. Moreover, to ensure that all parts of the state have been represented in the sample, 50 homes have been randomly selected from every county in the state. The sample mean is then computed from the large sample of all these homes that have been selected. Which of the following terms best describes this type of sampling?

   A. Census
   B. Simple random sample
   C. Cluster sample
   D. Systematic random sample
   E. Stratified sample

Questions 35 and 36 refer to the following information:

A vending machine contains these items, dispensing items randomly, one at a time:

16 red charms	7 gold charms	22 red marbles
8 gold marbles	24 red rings	3 gold rings

35. If one item is drawn from the vending machine, what is the probability that the item is either a ring or something gold?

   A. 0.0375
   B. 0.2250
   C. 0.5250
   D. 0.5625
   E. 0.9625

36. If three items are consecutively drawn from the machine, without replacement, what is the approximate probability that the items are all charms?

   A. 0.0207
   B. 0.0216
   C. 0.0238
   D. 0.2875
   E. 0.8625

37. A group of patients at a psychologist's office have taken a questionnaire evaluating stress level. These were the scores on that test:

31	34	35	37	37	37	37	37	37
37	37	38	38	38	38	39	39	40

Which of the following measurements could the value 37 not represent?

   A. Q_1
   B. Q_3
   C. Mean
   D. Median
   E. Mode

38. A small college has several professors in the Chemistry and Biology departments. The number of years of experience for the professors in the departments are to be compared:

Chemistry	1	1	4	5	8	15	22
Biology	0	1	2	5	6	8	17

For which of these measurements does the Chemistry department have the larger value?

   I. Range
   II. Standard deviation
   III. Interquartile range

   A. I only
   B. II only
   C. III only
   D. I and II only
   E. I, II, and III

39. The weights of Porker's Pride pigs follow a normal distribution with mean $\mu = 315$ pounds and standard deviation $\sigma = 65$ pounds. A sample of 60 pigs is taken at random. What is the approximate probability that the sample average, $\bar{x}$, will exceed 330 pounds?

   A. 0.0000
   B. 0.0367
   C. 0.1093
   D. 0.4090
   E. 0.4633

GO ON TO THE NEXT PAGE

40. A study is done to test whether students who are able to speak multiple languages also have higher scores on the English portion of the SAT. A nationwide sample of randomly selected students is taken, and among 1000 students who were multilingual, the average score on the English portion of the SAT was 493. However, among 3000 students who spoke only one language, the average score on the English portion was 512. The research group conducting the study was surprised by the results, since they expected the multilingual students to have the higher sample mean. Which of the following is the most likely cause of the results being different than what was expected?

    A.   The sample sizes were too small.

    B.   The sample sizes were not equal.

    C.   There was a bias in the way the samples were taken.

    D.   There was a confounding factor that affected the results.

    E.   The difference in the results could be attributable to random chance.

Section II

Time: 1 hour and 30 minutes   Number of questions: 6   Percent of total grade: 50%

Part A

Questions 1–5   Spend about 65 minutes on this part of the exam.   Percent of Section II grade: 75%

Show all your work. Clearly indicate the methods you use—you will be graded on the correctness of your methods as well as the accuracy of your results and explanation.

1. A zoologist is studying the relationship between the weight of a tiger and the tiger's maximum speed. A random sample of tigers was measured, and the scatterplot and regression results are given here:

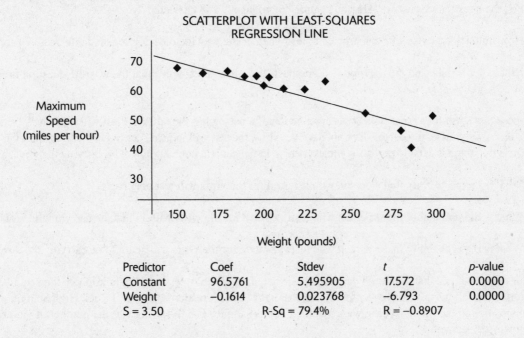

SCATTERPLOT WITH LEAST-SQUARES REGRESSION LINE

Predictor	Coef	Stdev	t	p-value
Constant	96.5761	5.495905	17.572	0.0000
Weight	–0.1614	0.023768	–6.793	0.0000
S = 3.50		R-Sq = 79.4%	R = –0.8907	

a. What is the equation of the least-squares regression line relating the maximum speed in miles per hour with weight in pounds? Define any variables used.

b. Is the relationship between maximum speed and weight direct or inverse? What are three ways that this can be determined from the information given?

c. What is the predicted maximum speed for a 650 pound tiger? Explain why the result does not make sense.

GO ON TO THE NEXT PAGE

2. An automall is made up of six dealers. The manager of the automall wants to test the claim that the six dealers are equally popular. The number of auto sales are recorded for one week, and these were the results:

Nissan 47   Audi 34   Saturn 51   Ford 26   Toyota 29   Honda 35

a. Perform the appropriate goodness-of-fit test, at level of significance $\alpha = 0.05$. Is there sufficient evidence to conclude that the auto dealers are not equally popular?

b. What is meant by saying that the test is performed at an $\alpha = 0.05$ level of significance?

c. What are the results of the test if the level of significance is changed to $\alpha = 0.01$?

3. A small county has been asked to vote whether to approve a millage for school funding. In one sample of 400 voters, the question was asked "Do you support the millage?" 252 answered "yes." In another sample of 300 voters, the question was asked "Are you against the millage?" 148 answered "yes."

a. How might a hypothesis be constructed to test whether the way the question is asked affects how people vote?

b. Based on the data, and the appropriate hypothesis test, is there evidence that the way the question is asked affects how people vote?

4. Suppose that a test for a virus is 98 % accurate, in that if a person has the virus, the test will indicate "positive" with 0.98 probability. Also, if a person does not have the virus, the test will indicate "negative" with 0.98 probability. Also suppose that there is a 0.004 probability that a person in the general population will be carrying the virus.

a. What is the probability that a person who is tested for the virus will test positive?

b. What is the probability that a person who tests positive for the virus will, in fact, be carrying the virus?

c. What is the probability that a person who tests negative for the virus will actually be carrying the virus?

5. It has been assumed that with each year of experience, high school wrestlers should improve their number of victories the following year. To test this claim, the eight senior wrestlers at Mineral Rock High School, who also wrestled in their junior years, were included in this sample. The following was the number of victories each wrestler gained:

Wrestler	Junior Year	Senior Year
Shaw	10	15
Peterson	21	28
Miller	8	11
Wilson	14	13
Brooks	27	30
Baker	20	22
O'Brien	7	18
Smith	11	13

a. Which type of hypothesis is most appropriate for this study?

b. Is there evidence, at an $\alpha = 0.05$ level of significance, to support the claim that wrestlers will average more victories in their senior year than in their junior year?

Part B

Question 6 — Spend about 25 minutes on this part of the exam. — Percent of Section II grade: 25%

Directions for Part B: Allow additional time for this part. Clearly indicate the methods that you use and give clear explanations for all your results.

6. Suppose that over the past several years, the land value for standard one-acre lots in a particular town have steadily increased. However, the selling prices for such homes have been corrected, based on the interest rate. For a typical one-acre lot, these have been the land values, selling prices, and interest rates for a four-year period:

Month	Jul. 00	Jan. 01	Jul. 01	Jan. 02	Jul. 02	Jan. 03	Jul. 03	Jan. 04
Land Value (dollars)	36,000	38,000	41,500	43,000	44,500	46,000	47,000	47,500
Interest Rate (%)	7.25	6.75	6.50	6.25	6.00	5.75	5.25	5.75
Selling Price (dollars)	34,000	37,500	41,000	43,000	45,500	48,500	51,500	50,000

a. If it is noted that land values are steadily increasing, how may an equation be created relating land value to the progression of six-month time periods?

b. Which provides a stronger relationship, the correlation between time period and land value or the correlation between interest rate and selling price? Justify your answer.

c. Suppose that interest rate acts as a correction factor, modifying land values to result in a selling price. How may the correction to land value, resulting in selling price, be related to interest rate? Find the equation of a regression line relating this correction factor to interest rate.

d. Supposing that the interest rate in July 2004 is 5.50, and based on the projection of what the land value will be in July 2004, predict how much the selling price of one-acre of land would be, to the nearest dollar.

Section I Answers

1. E. Since the plot of the residuals exhibits a random pattern that appears to fit the zero line closely, this is evidence that there is a strong linear relationship between x and y, whereby the correlation coefficient would be close to 1 in magnitude.

2. B. The slope of the regression line is $b_1 = 6.201$. From the regression results, the standard deviation of the slope is $s_{b_1} = 0.34487$ found in the chart as "stdev" for Trunk. With degrees of freedom = (sample size − 2) = (25 − 2) = 23, the 99% confidence interval would be $(6.201) \pm (2.807)(0.34487) = 6.201 \pm 0.968$.

3. D. The normal distribution, represented by the normal curve, is symmetric, and since it is a probability density function, the total area under the curve is 1. However, the mean is not necessarily 0. Various normal curves could have any real value for mean. Some curves, such as the standard normal, will have mean 0.

4. D. Since the underlying distribution is non-normal, the distribution of the sample mean will not be normal. However, by the Central Limit Theorem, the distribution of the sample mean will be approximately normal, since the sample size is greater than 30. Moreover, the mean of the sample mean is equal to the population mean, in this case 1500. Also, the standard deviation of the sample mean is $\sigma/\sqrt{n}$, which would be 2.

5. C. The confidence interval for mean would be given by $x \pm ts/\sqrt{n}$ (since the sample size is large, the t-value would be approximately equal to the z-value). For a 90% confidence interval, the form would be $165.6 \pm (1.646)(38.8/\sqrt{500}) = 165.6 \pm 2.9$.

6. C. If the standard deviation for two random variables is known, the standard deviation for the sum of the random variables can be found by finding the sum of the variances. The variance of the sum of two random variables is given by $(\sigma_1)^2 + (\sigma_2)^2$. Therefore, the variance of the sum would be 2500 + 400, and the standard deviation would be found by taking the square root, or 53.85

7. D. If two random variables, A and B, are independent, then $P(A \text{ and } B) = P(A)P(B)$. Since $P(A \text{ and } B)$ is not equal to $P(A)P(B)$ in this case, the events are not independent. If two random variables are mutually exclusive, $P(A \text{ and } B) = 0$. Since $P(A \text{ and } B)$ is nonzero in this case, the two random variables are not mutually exclusive.

8. C. The probability that a person has both seen *Titanic* and seen the movie more than once would be $(0.7)(0.6) = 0.42$. Therefore, the expected value would be $(600)(0.42) = 252$.

9. A. Since the question is "Should the president have the line-item veto, in order to eliminate government waste?" instead of simply reading "Should the president have the line-item veto?" it is likely that the wording of the question would skew the results. There would be no issue with the sample itself, since it was a large sample, and it was taken randomly. Furthermore, the question is likely not sensitive enough to affect the results, and a difference of about 30% would not be attributable to chance.

10. E. The objective is to create a simulation whereby the probability of success is 85%, and the probability of failure is 15%. Seventeen marbles denoted as "success" and 3 marbles denoted as "failure" would create the proper ratios, in this case, 17 out of 20 and 3 out of 20.

11. C. In order to determine the trunk circumference, x, corresponding to the tree age, $y = 240$, the value 240 should be substituted for $\hat{y}$ in the least-squares line. Solving the equation for x would give $x = 242$.

12. A. In comparing the strength of the two brands of boards, strength is represented by the mean amount weight the boards can withstand. A higher mean weight corresponds to a stronger board. The test is structured so that rejection of the null hypothesis implies that the mean for Brand X is higher than the mean for Brand Y. With a p-value of 0.023, which is less than the test level $\alpha = 0.05$, the null hypothesis is rejected, in favor of concluding that the mean for Brand X is greater than the mean for Brand Y, meaning that Brand X is stronger than Brand Y.

13. B. Type I error is defined as the error of rejecting the null hypothesis, when the null hypothesis is actually true. In this case, if the sample mean was observed to be significantly greater than 70, the null hypothesis would be rejected. In turn, if the true mean was 70, Type I error would have then occurred.

14. E. The t-distribution is represented by a probability curve that is symmetric. Since its curve is a probability density function, the area under the curve is 1. The curve is wider than the normal curve but approaches the normal curve as its degrees of freedom increases. However, as the degrees of freedom increases, the t-distribution gets gradually narrower as it approaches the normal curve, not wider.

15. **B.** To create a table of expected values for a two-way test of independence, each corresponding entry in the table is computed by this formula: Expected Value = (row total)(column total)/(n), where n equals the grand total of all values in the chart. Therefore, the expected value corresponding to urban students who attend a four-year college would be equal to (99)(95)/(310) = 30, rounded to the nearest whole number.

16. **B.** In order to test whether smoking has an effect on the yearly income of the restaurants, the difference can be observed by comparing the mean of a sample of smoking locations and the mean of a sample of nonsmoking locations. The samples would be independent, and, therefore, the appropriate test would be a t-test of two independent samples.

17. **A.** The statement that the "error" is 5% represents the error in a confidence interval for proportion, in this case in the form 0.67 ± 0.05. Therefore, there is a high probability that the true proportion would be contained within this interval, within 0.05 of the sample proportion 0.67.

18. **B.** The best term to describe this sample would be a cluster sample, since all observations are made from a randomly selected portion of the population, specifically one week of customers. It is not a census, since it is not data collected from all customers who have ever or will enter the store. It is not a random sample, nor a systematic sample, since the study collects all customers for the week, but not for any other week. Moreover, there is no stratification of the population that has been done.

19. **E.** The percentile associated with a score represents how many whole percent of all scores lie below that score. Therefore, if a score is in the 88th percentile, this means that 88% of all other scores are below that score.

20. **C.** If two factors are related by a correlation that is a value close to positive 1, there is a strong, direct relationship, and, therefore, the points in the scatterplot will lie in an approximately straight line with positive slope. If two factors are related by a correlation that is a value close to negative 1, there is a strong, inverse relationship, and, therefore, the points in the scatterplot will lie in an approximately straight line with negative slope.

21. **C.** If the lowest value of a data set is removed, the mean of the set will increase. Furthermore, if this lowest score is the only outlier, it will be the value that is the greatest distance from the mean. If it is removed from the data set, with all other values being closer to the mean, the standard deviation will be decreased.

22. **D.** If one of the outermost values of a data set is removed, the range will be decreased. Furthermore, if the value is the only outlier, it will be the value that is the greatest distance from the mean. If it is removed from the data set, with all other values being closer to the mean, both the standard deviation and the variance will be decreased. Also, with the removal of any single value, the size of the set is reduced by 1. However, it is not necessarily true that the interquartile range will be decreased, since this value is based on the difference between Q_3 and Q_1, which may still stay the same, even with the removal of an outermost point.

23. **D.** Kelly's raw score on exam one was higher than her raw score on exam two. However, in relation to the class, her score on exam two was above the class mean while her score on exam one was below the class mean. Both scores were three units away from the mean. However, the z-score for exam one was -0.2, while the z-score for exam two was 0.25. Since both of her scores were within one standard deviation of the mean, neither would be considered outliers.

24. **B.** With the standard deviation known to be $\sigma = 50$, the z-statistic would be computed. The formula for comparing two means would be $z = (x_1 - x_2)/(\sigma/\sqrt{\frac{1}{n_1} + \frac{1}{n_2}}) = (173.5 - 161.4)/(50/\sqrt{\frac{1}{143} + \frac{1}{128}}) = 1.711$.

25. **D.** Since the null hypothesis is that the eight colors occur equally, with a sample size $n = 216$, the expected values for each color would be 27. The formula for the χ^2-test statistic is $\Sigma (O - E)^2/E = (24 - 27)^2/27 + (27 - 27)^2/27 + (31 - 27)^2/27 + (44 - 27)^2/27 + (19 - 27)^2/27 + (22 - 27)^2/27 + (29 - 27)^2/27 + (20 - 27)^2/27 = 16.889$.

26. **E.** It is desired that the width of the interval be no more than one unit wide. Since the interval is to be of the form $x \pm E$, the maximum error would be $E = 0.5$. With the population standard deviation $\sigma = 50$, in order to create a 95% confidence interval for mean, with error no greater than 0.5, the following formula should be used: $n \geq (z\sigma/E)^2$. Therefore, the minimum sample size would be $n \geq [(1.960)(75)/(0.5)]^2 = 86436$.

27. B. The probability of making "at least six" would be the probability of exactly six added to the probability of exactly seven. This would be $(_7C_6)(0.65^6)(0.35^1) + (_7C_7)(0.65^7)(0.35^0) = 0.234$.

28. D. If the level of significance is α, then a rejection of the null hypothesis in a one-tail test would occur if the one-tail p-value is less than α. With a p-value 0.045, rejection would occur for values $\alpha = 0.10$ and 0.05. However, if the test is two-tail, the one-tail p-value is doubled, and becomes 0.090, in which case, the values of α for which the null hypothesis would not be rejected are 0.05, 0.025, 0.01, and 0.005. Therefore, for $\alpha = 0.05$, the null hypothesis is rejected in the one-tail case, but not rejected in the two-tail case.

29. B. The observed sample proportion is $84/500 = 0.168$. The 95% confidence interval would be of the form $0.168 \pm (1.960)\left(\sqrt{\dfrac{(0.168)(0.832)}{(500)}}\right)$. The lower and upper values are 0.135 and 0.201, respectively.

30. E. A t-confidence interval for mean is of the form $x \pm ts/\sqrt{n}$. Decreasing the confidence level would reduce the value of t, and thus make the interval narrower. Increasing the sample size would also reduce the width of the interval. Also, since the t-value is larger than the z-value for any confidence level, and for any degrees of freedom, computing the interval as a z-interval would also result in a narrower interval.

31. A. The degrees of freedom for a two-way test of independence is (number of rows – 1)(number of columns – 1). Therefore, the degrees of freedom is $(3)(2) = 6$.

32. C. In this goodness-of-fit test, the claim that the candidates follow specified percentages, and thus the counts within each category should also follow these percentages within a sample. With a total sample size of $n = 2000$, the expected values would be: Kerry 700, Edwards 500, Dean 400, Gephardt 200, Lieberman 100, and Sharpton 100. The formula for the χ^2-test statistic is $\Sigma (O - E)^2/E = (710 - 700)^2/700 + (468 - 500)^2/500 + (428 - 400)^2/400 + (212 - 200)^2/200 + (104 - 100)^2/100 + (78 - 100)^2/100 = 9.871$.

33. B. Based on the data from the stem-and-leaf plots, the sample size is 26 for the 10:00 class and 21 for the 7:30 class. The maximum value is 99 for the 10:00 class and 98 for the 7:30 class. The range is 44 for the 10:00 class and 41 for the 7:30 class. The 10:00 class has 11 values in the 80–89 range, and the 7:30 class has 9. However, the median in the 10:00 class is 82, but the median in the 7:30 class is 84.

34. E. This sample was formed by dividing the population into a number of categories and drawing a random sample from each category. Such categories are called *strata*, and this type of sample is called a stratified sample.

35. C. For two events A and B, the $P(A \text{ or } B) = P(A) + P(B) - P(A \text{ and } B)$. In this case, $P(\text{ring or gold}) = P(\text{ring}) + P(\text{gold}) - P(\text{ring and gold}) = 27/80 + 18/80 - 3/80 = 42/80 = 0.5250$.

36. B. The probability of drawing three charms in a row, without replacement, would be $(23/80)(22/79)(21/78) = 0.0216$.

37. B. For this set, the mean, median, and mode are all 37. Furthermore, the first quartile cutoff is $Q_1 = 37$. However, the third quartile cutoff is $Q_3 = 38$.

38. E. For the chemistry set, the range is 21, the standard deviation is $\sigma = 7.25$, and the interquartile range is $IQR = 14$. For the biology set, the range is 17, the standard deviation is $\sigma = 5.37$, and the interquartile range is $IQR = 7$. The chemistry set has larger values for all three measurements.

39. B. By the Central Limit Theorem, the sample average, x, would follow a normal distribution with mean 315 and standard deviation $\sigma/\sqrt{n} = 65/\sqrt{60}$. Therefore, the z-score corresponding to a sample average of 330 would be approximately $z = 1.79$. The probability of exceeding this z-value would be 0.367.

40. D. In this study, the mean SAT scores of multilingual students is compared to the mean SAT scores of students who speak only English. Note that the SAT score that is examined is, specifically, the English portion. It is likely that there are other factors related to a student being multilingual that may also affect the outcome on an English test. For instance, many multilingual students may be foreign students or have English as their second language. Such factors may cause a student to have lower scores on an English test. Therefore, the most likely cause of the difference in the scores would be confounding factors. Bias is not an issue, since the samples were chosen randomly, and in comparing independent samples, the sample sizes do not need to be the same. The samples were large, and the difference in the observed means is significant enough not to be attributable to random chance.

Section II Answers

1a. The equation of the least-squares regression line relating maximum speed of a tiger with the tiger's weight is $\hat{y} = 96.5761 - 0.1614x$, where $\hat{y}$ is the predicted speed in miles per hour, and x is the weight in pounds.

1b. The relationship between the speed and the weight is inverse. The three ways this can be determined are by the pattern of the points in the scatterplot; the correlation coefficient, r; and the slope of the regression equation, b_0. Since the pattern of the points is generally downward, from left to right, this implies that as the weight increases, the speed decreases. This is also indicated by the slope of the regression line, $b_0 = -0.1614$, which denotes a downward slant in the regression line, and specifically, that for each increase in 1 pound of weight, the predicted speed of the tiger will decrease by 0.1614 miles per hour. Thirdly, the correlation coefficient, r, is -0.8907, indicating that the relationship between speed and weight is strong and inverse.

1c. The predicted speed for $x = 650$ pounds is $\hat{y} = 96.5761 - (0.1614)(650) = -8.3339$ miles per hour. The negative value does not make sense. Note that the range of data from which the least-squares regression line was calculated extended from approximately 150 pounds to 300 pounds. The correlation coefficient indicated a strong linear correlation between weight and speed, but only for values within the range of data. The regression line has not been fit to data points outside this range, and, therefore, it is not valid to assume that the relationship will remain linear for values considerably outside this range. Since 650 pounds is considerably outside this range of data, a prediction based on this regression line would be considered invalid and unreliable.

2a. The null hypothesis, H_0: The auto dealers are equally popular is being tested against the alternate hypothesis, H_a: The auto dealers are not equally popular. The total number of values in the sample is 222, implying that the expected values would be 37 for each dealer. The χ^2 test statistic would be computed as $\Sigma (O - E)^2/E = (47 - 37)^2/37 + (34 - 37)^2/37 + (51 - 37)^2/37 + (26 - 37)^2/37 + (29 - 37)^2/37 + (35 - 37)^2/37 = 13.351$. At an $\alpha = 0.05$ level of significance, the rejection region would be $\chi^2 > 11.071$, with the degrees of freedom categories $- 1 = 5$. Based on this test, there is sufficient evidence to conclude that the auto dealers are not equally popular.

2b. The level of significance, α, of a test, is the probability of Type I error, which is the probability of rejecting the null hypothesis when the null hypothesis is, in fact, true. In this case, it is unlikely to observe six identical numbers of sales for each dealer, even if the dealers are equally popular. However, it should be expected that the observations be close to equal. With the level of significance, $\alpha = 0.05$, there is only a 0.05 probability of, by randomness alone, observing sales that are so far apart that the conclusion would be that the dealers are not equally popular, when, in fact, they are.

2c. When the level of significance is changed to $\alpha = 0.01$, the criteria for rejecting is changed to a rejection region $\chi^2 > 15.086$. In this case, with stronger evidence required to reject the claim that the auto dealers are not equally popular, the claim is not rejected.

3a. To test whether there is a difference in the proportion of support for the millage, based on how the question is asked, a test comparing two proportions can be used. If $p_1 =$ the proportion of affirmative responses when asked "Do you support the millage?," and if $p_2 =$ the proportion of affirmative responses when asked "Are you against the millage?," the null hypothesis would be H_0: $p_1 = p_2$, tested against the alternate hypothesis H_a: $p_1 \neq p_2$. For this sample, the observed proportion of affirmative votes in the first case is $\hat{p}_1 = 252/400$, and the observed proportion of affirmative votes in favor of the millage is $\hat{p}_2 = 152/300$.

3b. Assuming that the two samples were independent samples, together with the pooled proportion being $\bar{p} = 404/700 = 0.57714$, the z statistic is computed to be $z = 3.269$, with corresponding two-tailed p-value 0.00108. Except for the most extremely low levels of significance, α, the null hypothesis would be rejected, implying that there is strong evidence to conclude that the way the question is asked will have a definite impact on how respondents vote on the millage.

4a. It is given that P(tests positive | has virus) = 0.98, implying that P(tests negative | has virus) = 0.02. It is also given that P(tests negative | does not have virus) = 0.98, which also implies that P(tests positive | has virus) = 0.02. Since the probability that a person has the virus is 0.004, the probability that the person does not have the virus is 0.996. This implies that P(tests positive) = P(tests positive and has virus) + P(tests positive and does not have virus) = $(0.98)(0.004) + (0.02)(0.996) = 0.00392 + 0.01992 = 0.02384$. A two-way table may also be used.

4b. The conditional probability $P(\text{has virus} \mid \text{tests positive}) = P(\text{has virus and tests positive})/P(\text{tests positive}) = (0.00392)/(0.02384) = 0.1644$

4c. The probability of the person testing negative is $P(\text{tests negative}) = P(\text{tests negative and does not have virus}) + P(\text{tests negative and has virus}) = (0.98)(0.996) + (0.02)(0.004) = 0.97608 + 0.00008 = 0.97616$. Thus, the conditional probability $P(\text{has virus} \mid \text{tests negative}) = P(\text{has virus and tests negative})/P(\text{tests negative}) = (0.00008)/(0.97616) = 0.00008195$.

5a. Since the tests are paired, dependent data, any of the tests comparing means with independent samples would not apply. The appropriate test would be a paired t-test whereby the null hypothesis is $H_o: \mu_1 = \mu_2$, tested against the alternate hypothesis $H_a: \mu_1 < \mu_2$, where μ_1 = mean wins in junior year and μ_2 = mean wins in senior year.

5b. To compute the t-test statistic for the paired t-test, the $\Sigma d = -32$, and the $\Sigma d^2 = 222$. With the number of pairs $n = 8$, the test statistic is $t = (-32/8)/\sqrt{\dfrac{\left[\dfrac{222 - (-32)^2}{8}\right]}{56}} = -3.087$. With degrees of freedom $n - 1 = 7$, and level of significance $\alpha = 0.05$, the rejection region is $t < -1.895$. Therefore, the null hypothesis is rejected, indicating that there is sufficient evidence to conclude that wrestlers have fewer mean victories in junior year than in senior year. In other words, the mean wins in senior year is greater.

6a. The land value for each six-month time period can be related to the time period by numbering each time period as 1, 2, 3, 4, 5, 6, 7, and 8, respectively. The correlation coefficient relating the time periods, x, with the land values in dollars, y, is $r = 0.9745$, and the regression line, relating the land value to the time period is $\hat{y} = 35410.71429 + 1672.619048x$.

6b. The correlation between interest rate, x, and selling price in dollars, y, is $r = -0.9869$. Although the correlation is negative, it shows a stronger strength of relationship than that of time period and land value, although the relationship is inverse.

6c. The correction factor between land value and selling price would be the difference between selling price and land value, noting that when the interest rate is higher, the selling price is a bit lower than land value, and when the interest rate is lower, the selling price is a bit higher than land value. The corresponding differences are -2000, -500, -500, 0, $+1000$, $+2500$, $+4500$, and $+2500$. If x is the interest rate and y is the difference, the correlation is computed as -0.9718, which is a strong inverse relationship. The regression line relating the difference, the correction factor, $\hat{y}$, in dollars, to interest rate, x, is $y = 20859.89011 - 3219.78022x$.

6d. First, to predict the land value in July 2004, set $x = 9$ in the regression equation from part **a**. The predicted land value is $\hat{y} = 35410.71429 + (1672.619048)(9) = 50,464.29$ dollars. To find the corresponding correction factor, for the interest rate 5.50 %, set $x = 5.50$ in the regression equation from part **c**. Therefore, the predicted correction is $\hat{y} = 20859.89011 - (3219.78022)(5.50) = 3151.09$. Thus, the projected selling price in July 2004, to the nearest dollar, is $53,615.

Practice Test 5

Section I

Time: 1 hour and 30 minutes   Number of questions: 40   Percent of total grade: 50%

Directions: Solve each problem. Decide which is the best of the answer choices given.

1. A group of 20 students took the second exam in a mathematics class. The instructor of the course wanted to determine whether there was a strong linear relationship between the students' scores on Exam 2 and the students' scores on Exam 1. Also, the instructor wanted to determine whether there was a strong linear relationship between the students' scores on Exam 2 and the number of hours studied for that exam. In both cases, the instructor computed the least-squares regression line and examined the plot of residuals.

PLOT I

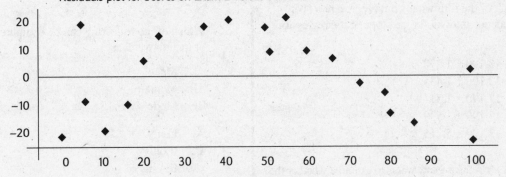

PLOT II

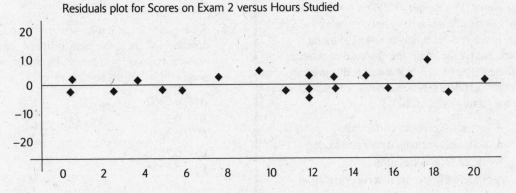

Which of the following statements is best supported by the two plots?

A. There is a linear relationship exhibited in Plot I, but not for Plot II.
B. There is a linear relationship exhibited in Plot II, but not for Plot I.
C. There is a linear relationship exhibited in both Plot I and Plot II.
D. Neither Plot I nor Plot II exhibits a linear relationship.
E. The relationship cannot be determined by these residual plots.

GO ON TO THE NEXT PAGE

2. Western Fish Beach has observed that there is a strong linear relationship between the day's high temperature in Fahrenheit and the total number of visitors to their beach, as observed for temperatures above 60 degrees. During the course of 20 consecutive days, the high temperature and number of visitors was recorded and the least-squares regression line was computed. The results of the regression analysis are given here:

Regression Equation:

Visitors = −858.05 + 13.19 Temperature

Predictor	Coef	Stdev	t-ratio	p
Constant	−858.0508	58.94052	−14.5579	0.000
Temperature	13.189891	0.732367	18.0088	0.000

S = 27.20   R-sq = 94.7

Which of the following would represent a 90% confidence interval for the slope of the regression line?

   A. 13.190 ± 1.270
   B. 13.190 ± 1.435
   C. 13.190 ± 1.511
   D. 13.190 ± 1.539
   E. 13.190 ± 5.215

3. The Electric Company wants to examine whether the household income levels of homes in their district are related to the average monthly electric bills of those homes. In a sample of 200 randomly selected homes, with x denoting the yearly household income of the home and y denoting the average monthly electric bill for the home, the observed correlation coefficient was $r = 0.716$. What does this indicate about the correlation between household income and average monthly electric bills?

   A.   A very strong, direct correlation
   B.   A moderately strong, direct correlation
   C.   Weak, or little correlation
   D.   A moderately strong, inverse correlation
   E.   A very strong, inverse correlation

4. The Sylmar Oil Company has determined that there is a strong correlation between the amount of money used to fund a drilling location and the amount of oil produced by the location in barrels. The following least-squares regression line was computed, relating the yearly amount of oil produced in barrels, y, and the amount of money used to fund the location in dollars, x.

$$\hat{y} = 20411 + 0.02488x$$
$$1{,}000{,}000 < x < 5{,}000{,}000$$

Their Pine Desert location was funded for $1,500,000 and produced 62,400 barrels of oil. What is the residual corresponding to this value?

   A.   −37320
   B.   −4669
   C.   4669
   D.   37320
   E.   57731

5. Which of the following can be computed for a set of qualitative data?

   I.   Mean
   II.   Median
   III.   Mode

   A.   I only
   B.   II only
   C.   III only
   D.   II and III only
   E.   None of these

6. A case of 600 lightbulbs contains 16 bulbs that are defective. What is the probability of selecting 10 bulbs at random, without replacement, and have none of those bulbs be defective?

   A.   0.5462
   B.   0.7333
   C.   0.7616
   D.   0.7632
   E.   0.9733

7. The manager of Shea Stadium receives several cases of stadium lightbulbs every day, and each case contains 240 lightbulbs. Over the course of time, she has determined that approximately 85% of the cases arrive containing at least one defective bulb. Based on this estimate, what is the approximate probability that any one bulb will be defective?

    A. 0.0000
    B. 0.0007
    C. 0.0035
    D. 0.0079
    E. 0.1500

8. A professional photographer is using a very sensitive type of bulb meant for outdoor use at night. However, because of the bulb's sensitivity, there is only a 0.80 probability that the bulb will actually light, if turned on. Then, if the bulb is on, it will stay lit for only a limited number of minutes before it fades out. The number of minutes it will stay lit, if it does light, follows a normal distribution with mean $\mu = 16$ minutes and standard deviation $\sigma = 4.8$ minutes. If the photographer requires 10 minutes to complete a specific project with the bulb, what is the probability that he will not be able to with the bulb?

    A. 0.0845
    B. 0.1056
    C. 0.2845
    D. 0.3056
    E. 0.3320

9. A professor is teaching an evening algebra class that has only eight students. Two tests have been given in the course, and the professor has computed the correlation coefficient, relating the Test I scores, x, with the Test II scores, y, as well as determining the least-squares regression line. These were the results:

$$r = 0.7196$$

$$\hat{y} = 28.77 + 0.647x$$

$$50 < x < 100$$

The professor noted that Anna's score on Test II was unusual, noting that the residual for her score was 15. The next highest residual for any other student was 4.5. If the professor removes Anna's scores from the data sets, what effect will this have on the correlation coefficient?

    A. The value of r will become closer to 1.
    B. The value of r will decrease in magnitude somewhat.
    C. There will be little or no change in the value of r.
    D. The value of r will become negative.
    E. The value of r will become close to 0.

10. Craig is enrolled in a trigonometry course and has received his score on the uniform midterm exam. His score on the midterm was 114, and the professor has indicated that his z-score was 0.78. What is the best interpretation of the meaning of this z-score?

    A. He got 78% of the problems on the test correct.
    B. Seventy-eight percent of all students taking the exam had scores below his.
    C. Seventy-eight percent of all students taking the exam had scores above his.
    D. His score was 0.78 IQR above the median of all scores.
    E. His score was 0.78 standard deviation above the mean of all scores.

GO ON TO THE NEXT PAGE

Practice Test 5

11. Coastal College wants to determine whether smoking has decreased on campus over the past five years. According to a survey done five years previously, among 400 randomly selected students, 123 were smokers. The survey is done again in the present day, and among 600 randomly selected students, 155 were smokers. If the null hypothesis is that the proportion of smokers is the same, tested against the alternate hypothesis that the proportion has decreased, what would be the value of the appropriate z-statistic for this test?

    A. 0.845
    B. 1.433
    C. 1.700
    D. 2.158
    E. 2.949

12. A card game is used with a small set of five cards, numbered 1, 2, 3, 4, and 5. If three cards are drawn at a time, with replacement, and this is done three times in a row, what is the probability that at least one of the three times, the card with the "1" is drawn?

    A. 0.216
    B. 0.600
    C. 0.784
    D. 0.800
    E. 0.936

13. Suppose that it is determined that there is a strong correlation between temperature and the rate at which a population of bacteria will reproduce. For each experiment, a population of 100 cells is placed in a container, and the container is kept at a constant temperature for 24 hours. Then the number of cells is counted. A least-squares regression line is computed, relating the temperature, x, in Fahrenheit, with the final number of cells, y, at the end of the 24-hour period:

    $$\hat{y} = 117 + 3.446x$$
    $$90 < x < 180$$

    Based on this relationship, if the temperature is increased by 5 degrees Fahrenheit, what effect will this have on the total number of cells at the end of the 24-hour period?

    A. The number will increase by about 2 cells.
    B. The number will increase by about 5 cells.
    C. The number will increase by about 17 cells.
    D. The number will increase by about 134 cells.
    E. The number will increase by about 585 cells.

14. A die is tossed. Let A represent the event of the result being a 1. Let B represent the event of the result being a 1, 3, or 5. Which of the following would describe the relationship between the events A and B?

    A. The events are independent.
    B. The events are mutually exclusive.
    C. The events are both independent and mutually exclusive.
    D. The events are neither independent nor mutually exclusive.
    E. The relationship cannot be determined from the information given.

15. Suppose that Winona Farms is the largest producer of turkeys for sale throughout the world. It has been determined that their population of turkeys has a mean weight of $\mu = 112$ pounds, with a standard deviation of $\sigma = 28$ pounds. Based on these measurements, approximately what percent of Winona Farms turkeys would have a weight greater than 140 pounds, but less than 168 pounds?

    A. 2.5%
    B. 11%
    C. 13.5%
    D. 16%
    E. 27%

16. An investor wants to purchase stock on the NYSE. It is desired that the stock be very stable, meaning that the price of the stock remain approximately the same from day to day, with very little change. If the investor decides to track a number of stocks to observe stability, before purchasing, which measurement would be most appropriate to compute?

    A. Range
    B. Mean
    C. Mode
    D. Midrange
    E. Standard deviation

17. The butcher at a grocery store wants to observe how many days, on the average, packages of hamburger meat will stay fresh in the display case. He sets up a test, whereby the null hypothesis is that the mean number of days is $\mu = 4.0$ days, tested against the alternate hypothesis that the mean is actually less than 4.0, or $\mu < 4.0$ days. After observing a sample of 90 packages of hamburger meat for a number of days, he arrives at a p-value of 0.833 for this test. What would this p-value lead him to conclude?

A. There is very strong evidence to conclude that the mean is less than 4.0 days.

B. There is some evidence to conclude that the mean is less than 4.0 days.

C. The mean is less than 4.0 days, but there is not enough evidence to reject the null hypothesis.

D. The mean is approximately equal to 4.0 days.

E. The mean is actually greater than 4.0 days.

18. A binomial experiment, which has the probability of success for one trial $p = 0.63$, is being observed, and 70 trials are preformed. Binomial probabilities for various outcomes can be computed. However, they can also be computed using another distribution. In this case, which distribution could be used to approximate this particular distribution?

A. Uniform distribution with mean 44.1

B. Geometric distribution with $p = 0.63$

C. χ^2 distribution with 69 degrees of freedom

D. t-distribution with 69 degrees of freedom

E. Normal distribution with mean 44.1

19. The null hypothesis of a test is $H_o: \mu = 250$, and the alternate hypothesis is $H_a: \mu < 250$. A sample has been taken and based on the results, a Type II error has been committed. Which of the following best describes a scenario in which this occurred?

A. The sample mean was observed to be near 250, but the true mean was less than 250.

B. The sample mean was observed to be significantly greater than 250, but the true mean was 250.

C. The sample mean was observed to be significantly less than 250, but the true mean was 250.

D. The sample mean was observed to be significantly less than 250, and the true mean was less than 250.

E. The sample mean was observed to be near 250, and the true mean was 250.

20. A data set contains 20 values. Among these 20 values, it has one outlier. If the outlier is removed from the data set, which of the following measurements must change?

  I.   Mean
  II. Median
  III. Interquartile range

A. I only

B. II only

C. III only

D. I and III only

E. I, II, and III

21. A professor of a philosophy class announces that he determines grades based on the student's z-score on each exam, relative to the rest of the class. His scale is given as follows:

A—above 1.5

B—between 0.5 and 1.5

C—between –0.5 and 0.5

D—between –1.5 and –0.5

F—below –1.5

If his class consists of 220 students, based on this scale, approximately how many students would receive an A on any given test?

A. 5

B. 15

C. 35

D. 53

E. 68

22. A standardized test for admission to a Lifeguard Training program in California is given to both California residents and out-of-state applicants. In the most recent pool of applicants, the results are given in a two-way chart.

Resident Status		
	California	*Out-of-state*
Pass	48	22
Fail	17	13

If these results are used to test whether passing the test is affected by one's resident status, what would be the value of the appropriate χ^2 test of independence?

A. 0.253
B. 1.308
C. 2.577
D. 3.018
E. 16.871

23. Suppose that a school wants to determine the average amount of money students spend every year on school supplies. Which of the following procedures of collecting data would provide the most accurate results?

A. Census
B. Simple random sample
C. Cluster sample
D. Stratified sample
E. Systematic random sample

24. A Pennsylvania polling service wants to conduct a telephone survey in which people are simply asked whether they have ever cheated on their federal tax forms. However, it is clearly believed that respondents will rarely answer honestly, because of the illegality of cheating on taxes. Therefore, some adjustments to the procedure have been proposed, in order to preserve the anonymity of the respondents.

Plan I "Yes" would refer to having cheated on taxes, while "No" would refer to not having cheated. However, before responding, the respondent is asked to toss a coin. If the coin is a head, the respondent is to simply answer "Yes." At the end of the survey, final results will be adjusted based on the probability of "head" being 0.50.

Plan II "Yes" would refer to having cheated on taxes, while "No" would refer to not having cheated. Instruct respondents not to answer over the phone, but to simply write "Yes" or "No" on a piece of paper and mail the response to an address given, providing no return address, in order to preserve anonymity.

If a large number of people are included in the survey, which of the following plans would provide accurate results?

A. Plan I only.
B. Plan II only.
C. Both Plan I and Plan II would provide accurate results.
D. Neither Plan I nor Plan II would provide accurate results.
E. It cannot be determined which would provide accurate results based on the information given.

25. The St. Casimir Church carnival has a game whereby children pay 25 cents to draw a marble from a large jar. The jar contains 100 marbles, of which 4 are silver, 1 is gold, and the remaining marbles are white. If a silver marble is drawn, the child wins 1 dollar. If the gold marble is drawn, the child wins 10 dollars. If a white marble is drawn, the child wins nothing. What is the expected amount of winnings for this game, per play?

A. A loss of 11 cents per play.
B. A loss of 6 cents per play.
C. The game is even.
D. A gain of 9 cents per play.
E. A gain of 14 cents per play.

26. For a set of exam scores, the mean was 68, and the standard deviation was 12. If 10 points is added to every test score, what will be the new mean and standard deviation of the exam scores?

   A. Mean 68 and standard deviation 12
   B. Mean 78 and standard deviation 12
   C. Mean 68 and standard deviation 15.16
   D. Mean 78 and standard deviation 15.16
   E. Mean 78 and standard deviation 22

27. Suppose that events A and B are independent events. Also, the $P(A) = 0.34$ and the $P(B) = 0.15$. What would be the $P(A \text{ or } B)$?

   A. 0.051
   B. 0.241
   C. 0.439
   D. 0.490
   E. 0.541

28. A hotel desires that the temperature of their party ballroom be 72 degrees Fahrenheit at all times. In order to test whether this is the case, the hotel manager decides to take temperature measurements at 40 random times during the course of the week and then to use the sample mean and sample deviation to test a claim concerning the true mean temperature of the ballroom. Which of the following would be the most appropriate null and alternate hypothesis for this test?

   A. H_o: $\mu = 72$ degrees, H_a: $\mu > 72$ degrees
   B. H_o: $\mu = 72$ degrees, H_a: $\mu < 72$ degrees
   C. H_o: $\mu = 72$ degrees, H_a: $\mu \neq 72$ degrees
   D. H_o: $\mu \leq 72$ degrees, H_a: $\mu > 72$ degrees
   E. H_o: $\mu \geq 72$ degrees, H_a: $\mu < 72$ degrees

29. The Soft Light Electric Company is producing 40-watt lightbulbs. To test whether the bulbs are being produced correctly, the production manager has sampled 200 random 40-watt bulbs in order to test the null hypothesis that the mean wattage is $\mu = 40$ watts against the alternate hypothesis that the mean wattage is not equal to 40 watts. The sample mean was determined to be 40.117 watts, with a sample standard deviation 0.966. What is the p-value of the appropriate test statistic?

   A. 0.0441
   B. 0.0478
   C. 0.0883
   D. 0.1211
   E. 0.4558

30. A professor of a physics class has given an exam to a class of 20 students. The output for the exam is determined, and the various sample measurements have been announced to the class. However, the professor discovers that one of the exams was graded in error and decides to remove the exam score from the data set. Which of the following measurements must change if the score is removed from the set?

   I. Mean
   II. Median
   III. Standard deviation

   A. I only
   B. II only
   C. III only
   D. I and III only
   E. None of these

31. Suppose that the ABC polling agency conducts a poll as to whether there is sufficient state funding for the functioning of hospitals. Surveys are distributed to random patients at a number of hospitals in the state, simply asking respondents to answer "yes" if the state funding for hospitals should be increased or "no" if state funding for hospitals does not need to be increased. Among approximately 12,000 people polled, about 82% of the respondents indicated "yes." However, when other polling services presented similar surveys to the general public, the percent of respondents indicating "yes" was always between 40% and 50%. Which of the following statements is the most likely reason for the unusually high results found by the ABC polling agency?

   A. The sample size was too small.
   B. Due to the sensitivity of the question, many respondents answered dishonestly.
   C. There was a bias in the sample, in that only hospital patients were being surveyed.
   D. The survey was voluntary, and the sample only included those who chose to respond.
   E. The difference in the results can be attributed to random chance.

GO ON TO THE NEXT PAGE

Questions 32 and 33 refer to the following information:

Brown High School has a small group of students who have taken the SAT but did poorly. The school's counselor has asked these students to enroll in a Retry study course and then to take the SAT a second time. These were the results:

	First SAT score	SAT score after Retry course
Amy A.	685	710
Brian B.	720	780
Colleen C.	785	815
David D.	800	800
Ed E.	810	825
Francine F.	840	810
Gerry G.	870	940

32. What would be the degrees of freedom for the appropriate paired t-test?

    A. 5
    B. 6
    C. 7
    D. 13
    E. 14

33. What would be the value of the t-test statistic for the appropriate paired t-test?

    A. −0.710
    B. −1.014
    C. −1.273
    D. −1.532
    E. −1.878

34. Caliente Casino has a game whereby players toss three dice and gain a payoff if the sum of the toss is 10. However, on Tuesday evenings, if the toss is a triple, meaning that the three dice are the same—for example, all three 1s—the player is allowed to toss again. What effect does this have on the player winning?

    A. The probability will increase by 0.025.
    B. The probability will increase by about 0.003.
    C. The probability will stay the same.
    D. The probability will decrease by about 0.003.
    E. The probability will decrease by 0.025

35. Suppose that the Republican Party in Wisconsin wants to estimate the proportion of voters who support President Bush in the election. They want to poll 1000 random voters. Which of the following procedures will best produce a simple random sample of registered voters in Wisconsin?

    A. Use a random number generator to select 1000 voters from a voter registration list.
    B. Use a random number generator to select 1000 telephone numbers from the statewide phonebook.
    C. Select every 100th name from a voter registration list until 1000 names are selected.
    D. Select 13 random voters from each of the 79 counties in Wisconsin.
    E. Place volunteers at 20 random locations in the state and have each select 50 random people.

36. Suppose that the manager of a hotel is testing whether the hotel ballroom is being kept at a constant 72 degrees throughout the entire day and night. The manager decides to take temperature measurements every 15 minutes for an entire week. One of the hotel workers informs the manager that the sample the manager is taking is not random. The manager responds "close enough." Which of the following are aspects of this sample that make it not random?

    I. Not every possible time of day has an equal likelihood of being chosen.
    II. There may be a bias, in that some times that exhibit temperature changes may not be chosen.
    III. Some times are automatically included in the sample, by design.

    A. I only
    B. II only
    C. III only
    D. I and III only
    E. I, II, and III

37. Suppose that 65% of all entrants to Valley Park are children under 12. One of their most popular rides is the Wild Mouse, which is restricted to children under 12, and on any given day, 85% of children under 12 will ride the Wild Mouse. If on one particular day, 8,700 total people have come to Valley Park, based on the percentages given, approximately how many people will ride the Wild Mouse that day?

   A. 3676
   B. 4807
   C. 5655
   D. 6286
   E. 7395

38. Suppose that CD Shack wants to estimate how long, on the average, a walk-in customer remains in the store. Thirty-nine random customers are observed, and the sample mean was 8.77 minutes, with a sample standard deviation 3.45 minutes. Which of the following would be a 99% confidence interval for the true mean time a walk-in customer will remain in the store?

   A. 7.25 minutes $< \mu <$ 10.29 minutes
   B. 7.27 minutes $< \mu <$ 10.27 minutes
   C. 7.43 minutes $< \mu <$ 10.11 minutes
   D. 7.65 minutes $< \mu <$ 9.89 minutes
   E. 8.22 minutes $< \mu <$ 9.32 minutes

39. The game between the Conquistadors and the Cougars is tied 108–108 as time has run out. However, on the final play of the game, the Cougars have committed a foul, and Basketball Jones, the best player for the Conquistadors, will shoot three free throws. However, Jones has difficulty with free throws, and only has a 0.62 probability of making a free throw. If the Conquistadors only need him to make one of the three free throws, what is the probability that the Conquistadors will win the game without going into overtime?

   A. 0.2383
   B. 0.2686
   C. 0.6200
   D. 0.7617
   E. 0.9451

40. For population control, a small country has passed a law that families are allowed to have only one son, but may have as many daughters as they wish. If every family has children until they have a son, regardless of how many daughters they have in the process, and if the probability of having a son is exactly 50% for any childbirth, how many daughters, on the average, will families in this nation have?

   A. 0.5 daughters
   B. 1 daughter
   C. 2 daughters
   D. 5 daughters
   E. The mean number of daughters will be infinite.

Section II

Time: 1 hour and 30 minutes   Number of questions: 6   Percent of total grade: 50%

Part A

Questions 1–5   Spend about 65 minutes on this part of the exam.   Percent of Section II grade: 75%

Show all your work. Clearly indicate the methods you use—you will be graded on the correctness of your methods as well as the accuracy of your results and explanation.

1. The following shows a cumulative frequency chart for the distribution of scores on a 10-question intelligence test

Score	Number
0	2
1	6
2	13
3	28
4	44
5	62
6	89
7	129
8	178
9	266
10	298

   a. What is the median of the scores?

   b. What is the interquartile range of the scores?

   c. What is the mean of the scores?

   d. Does it appear that the scores are approximately normally distributed? Explain.

2. It is often believed that a candidate for president benefits from a post-convention bounce. Specifically, after the political party's convention, that party's candidate usually rises temporarily in the polls. Suppose that before the convention, a random poll was taken, and Candidate Rice had the support of 643 out of 1200 voters. After the convention for Candidate Rice's party, another random poll was taken, and the poll showed the support of 878 out of 1500 voters.

   a. How should an hypothesis test be constructed to see whether there is evidence that Candidate Rice was the beneficiary of a post-convention bounce?

   b. Is there evidence, at an $\alpha = 0.01$ level of significance, to show that Candidate Rice did go up significantly in the polls after the convention?

   c. How might a study be done to show that the post-convention bounce is only temporary?

3. A new type of fertilizer is being used that is meant to increase the mean overall weight of beans produced by bean plants over a six-week period. In order to test the efficacy of the fertilizer, the results need to be compared to bean plants grown with previous fertilizer. The bean plants are to be grown in a garden as shown in the following diagram. However, it is believed that the direction of the sun will also have an effect on the way the bean plants grow.

EAST

$$\begin{array}{cccc} \circ & \circ & \circ & \circ \\ \circ & \circ & \circ & \circ \\ \circ & \circ & \circ & \circ \end{array}$$

WEST

Describe how an experiment may be constructed that compares the effectiveness of the new fertilizer with the old fertilizer and also accounts for the effect of the direction of the sun on the growth of the plants.

4. The life span of radio batteries follows a normal distribution with mean $\mu = 45$ hours and standard deviation $\sigma = 10$ hours. However, 5% of all batteries are defective and will not function at all.

a. If a random battery is placed into a radio, what is the probability that the battery will function for more than 60 hours?

b. If a radio requires two batteries to function and two random batteries are placed into it, what is the probability that the radio will function for at least 30 hours?

c. If a radio takes two batteries, but it only requires that at least one be functioning, what is the probability that the radio will function for at least 55 hours?

5. The instructor of a mathematics class has collected data to see whether there is a correlation between the number of absences a student has and the student's score on the final exam. The following is the scatterplot of the absences and the final exam scores, with the regression results:

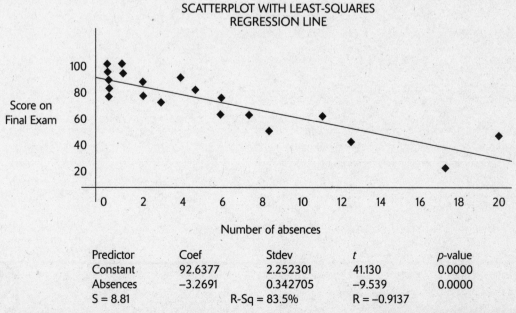

SCATTERPLOT WITH LEAST-SQUARES
REGRESSION LINE

Predictor	Coef	Stdev	t	p-value
Constant	92.6377	2.252301	41.130	0.0000
Absences	−3.2691	0.342705	−9.539	0.0000
S = 8.81		R-Sq = 83.5%	R = −0.9137	

GO ON TO THE NEXT PAGE

a. What is the equation of the least-squares regression line relating score on final exam with number of absences? Define any variables used.

b. What would be a 95% confidence interval for the slope of the regression line, b_o?

c. What is the correlation coefficient relating score on final exam with number of absences? Explain the meaning of this value.

d. What is the predicted score on the final exam for a student who had exactly nine absences?

Part B

Question 6   Spend about 25 minutes on this part of the exam.   Percent of Section II grade: 25%

Directions for Part B: Allow additional time for this part. Clearly indicate the methods that you use and give clear explanations for all your results.

6. During the course of the 2000 election, it was desired to test whether the proportion of support held by the four major candidates was Bush 47%, Gore 47%, Nader 5%, and Buchanan 1%. A sample of 5000 random voters was taken, and the results were Bush 2410, Gore 2335, Nader 241, Buchanan 14.

a. At an $\alpha = 0.05$ level of significance, is there evidence to show that the candidates do not follow these percentages?

b. In many analyses of elections, it is desired to compare how the two major candidates would compare, without the third-party candidates included. How may a test be done to compare Bush and Gore, without the two other candidates? What factors need to be considered?

c. Discounting the voters who supported Nader and Buchanan, is there evidence, at an $\alpha = 0.05$ level of significance, to show whether the support for Bush and Gore is not equal?

d. How would the results from part **c** change if it is assumed that if Nader and Buchanan are removed from the election, all the Nader voters would vote for Gore, and all the Buchanan voters would vote for Bush?

Section I Answers

1. **B.** Since Plot I exhibits a parabolic pattern, the relationship is nonlinear. However, since Plot II shows a pattern that appears random, but generally fits the zero line well, the relationship is linear.

2. **A.** The slope of the regression line is $b_1 = 13.190$. From the regression results, the standard deviation of the slope is $s_{b1} = 0.732367$ found in the chart as "stdev" for Temperature. With degrees of freedom = (sample size – 2) = (20 – 2) = 18, the 90% confidence interval would be $(13.190) \pm (1.734)(0.732367) = 13.190 \pm 1.270$.

3. **B.** Since the correlation coefficient $r = 0.716$ is a positive value, the correlation is direct. Furthermore, since the value is closer to 1 than to 0, the correlation is strong. However, it would not be considered very strong, since it is not extremely close to 1. For instance, a value of $r = 0.95$ would be considered to represent a very strong correlation.

4. **C.** The residual for a data point is the difference between the observed value and the predicted value, as computed from the least-squares regression line. The predicted value for $x = 1,500,000$ dollars would be $\hat{y} = 20411 + (0.02488)(1500000) = 57731$. The residual would be given by $62400 - 57731 = 4669$.

5. **C.** Since qualitative data is non-numerical, it is not possible to compute a mean or median. However, modes can be determined, since, even if the data is non-numerical, it can be computed how many of each observation has occurred, and consequently, which observation has occurred the most number of times.

6. **C.** Since the case of 600 bulbs contains 16 defective bulbs, 584 bulbs would be good. The probability of randomly selecting a group of 10 good bulbs would be given by $(_{584}C_{10})/(_{600}C_{10}) = 0.7616$.

7. **D.** Since it is indicated that the probability of a case of bulbs containing at least one defective bulb is 0.85, the probability that the case contains no defective bulbs is 0.15. This means that if p represents the probability that a bulb is good, then, for a case of 240 bulbs, $p^{240} = 0.15$. This implies that p is about equal to 0.9921, which is the probability that a bulb is good. Therefore, the probability that a bulb is defective would be $1 - 0.9921 = 0.0079$.

8. **C.** If the photographer is unable to complete the project, this means that either the bulb did not light, or the bulb did light but lasted for less than 10 minutes. Since the probability that the bulb does light is 0.80, the probability that it does not light would be 0.20. Still, if the bulb does light, the probability that it lasts for less than 10 minutes must be considered. The life of a lit bulb follows a normal distribution, and the z-score for 10 minutes would be $z = (10 - 16)/(4.8) = -1.25$. The probability that the life is less than 10 minutes, for a bulb that actually lights, would be the probability of observing a z-score less than -1.25, or 0.1056. So, the probability that a bulb lights and then lasts for less than 10 minutes is $(0.80)(0.1056) = 0.0845$. Thus, the total probability of the bulb being unavailable for the required 10 minutes would be $0.2000 + 0.0845 = 0.2845$.

9. **A.** It is observed that one value has a very high residual in relation to all other points in the data set. This means that one point was a significantly greater distance from the least-squares regression line than all the other points. Therefore, if this one point is removed, the remaining points in the data set would be those that are comparatively closer to lying in a straight line. Since the correlation coefficient, r, represents strength of linear relationship, or how close to a straight line the points are, the data set would exhibit a stronger linear relationship, and thus a larger value for r.

10. **E.** The z-score for a value is defined to be the number of standard deviations that the value lies above or below the mean. In this case, a z-score of 0.78 indicates that the value was 0.78 standard deviation above the mean of the data set.

11. **C.** For the sample data, the observed proportion for 5 years ago is $\hat{p}_1 = 123/400 = 0.3075$, and the observed proportion for the present day is $\hat{p}_{2()} = 155/600 = 0.258333$. The pooled proportion is $\bar{p} = 278/1000 = 0.278$.

The test statistic would be $z = \left(\hat{p}_1 - \hat{p}_2\right) / \sqrt{(\bar{p})(1-\bar{p})/(n_1) + (\bar{p})(1-\bar{p})/(n_2)} =$

$(0.3075 - 0.2583)/\sqrt{(0.278)(0.722)/(400) + (0.278)(0.722)/(600)} = 1.700$.

12. E. The probability that the 1 card is not selected in a single drawing is given by $(_4C_3)/(_5C_3) = 0.4$. The probability that the 1 card is not selected for three drawings in a row would be $(0.4)^3 = 0.064$. Therefore, the probability of the 1 card being drawn at least once out of three drawings would be $1 - 0.064 = 0.936$.

13. C. The slope of the least-squares regression line is given to be 3.446. This indicates that, for each increase of one degree Fahrenheit, the final population of cells would be increased by an estimated 3.446 cells. Therefore, for an increase of 5 degrees, the estimated increase in the population of cells would be $(3.446)(5) = 17.23$, or approximately 17 cells.

14. D. Since it is possible for event A and event B to both occur, specifically, if the 1 is rolled, the events cannot be mutually exclusive. Furthermore, since, if event B does not occur, namely that neither a 1, 3, nor 5 is rolled, this would preclude event A from occurring, so the events are not independent, either.

15. C. The value 168 lies exactly two standard deviations above the mean, and 140 lies exactly one standard deviation above the mean. Based on the Empirical Rule for large data sets, approximately 95% of all measurements are within two standard deviations of the mean, whereas approximately 68% of all measurements are within one standard deviation of the mean. Therefore, approximately 27% of all measurements would be within one and two standard deviations of the mean either above or below. This would mean that the percentage of the data lying within one and two standard deviations above the mean would be approximately 13.5%.

16. E. Standard deviation is an indicator of the amount of variation from the mean and would be used to show whether stock prices have a large amount of variation or not.

17. E. Since the p-value of a test represents the level of test at which rejection of the null hypothesis would occur, in the lower-tail case, a p-value that is greater than 0.5 would indicate that the rejection region cutoff would have to be a value greater than the mean. Therefore, it can be concluded that the sample mean was greater than the mean, producing a positive value for z, or for t in either case, resulting in a p-value greater than 0.5.

18. E. By the Central Limit Theorem, for large values of n, the binomial distribution can be approximated by the normal distribution, with mean $np = (70)(0.63) = 44.1$.

19. A. Type II error is defined as the error of failing to reject the null hypothesis when the null hypothesis is actually false. In this case, if the sample mean was observed to be close to 250, the null hypothesis would not be rejected. In turn, if the true mean was actually less than 250, as indicated by the alternate hypothesis, Type II error would then have occurred.

20. A. If the most extreme value of a data set is removed, the value of the mean will either increase, or decrease, depending on whether the outlier was a high value or a low value. However, it is still possible for the median to remain unchanged. Furthermore, it is also possible for the quartile cutoffs Q_1 and Q_3 to remain the same as well, whereby the interquartile range is the difference in these two values.

21. B. Based on the normal distribution, the probability of having a z-score exceed 1.5 is 0.0668. Therefore, the approximate number of students with z-scores exceeding 1.5 would be $(220)(0.0668) = 14.696$.

22. B. For this two-way contingency chart, the expected values would be

	California	*Out-of-State*
Pass	45.5	24.5
Fail	19.5	10.5

The χ^2-test statistic would be $\Sigma (O - E)^2/E = (48-45.5)^2/45.5 + (22-24.5)^2/24.5 + (17-19.5)^2/19.5 + (13-10.5)^2/10.5 = 1.308$.

23. A. Since a census is a collection of all data in a population, it would provide the most exact results for any study.

24. A. Plan I would provide effective results, since it would preserve the anonymity of the respondents, as well as include the responses of everyone who was polled. Furthermore, since the sample is large, an adjustment to the results, based on the probability of heads being 0.5 would maintain the accuracy of the results. Plan II, although preserving the anonymity of the respondents, would fail in that the actual results would be based on a voluntary sample. The results would only include respondents who chose to mail their results in.

25. **A.** Since 25 cents is paid for each play, the amount of money won for drawing a gold marble would be 9.75, for a silver marble 0.75, and for a white marble a loss of 0.25. Therefore, if X represents the amount of winning for each play, the expected value for the game would be given by $\Sigma (x)P(X = x) = (9.75)(0.01) + (0.75)(0.04) + (-0.25)(0.95) = -0.11$, or a loss of 11 cents per play.

26. **B.** Adding 10 to every value in a data set would result in the mean of the set being increased by 10. However, since the same value is added to every value in the set, the standard deviation would not change.

27. **C.** If events A and B are independent, the $P(A \text{ and } B) = P(A)P(B) = (0.34)(0.15) = 0.051$. Therefore, $P(A \text{ or } B) = P(A) + P(B) - P(A \text{ and } B) = 0.34 + 0.15 - 0.051 = 0.439$.

28. **C.** The objective is to test whether the average temperature of the ballroom is 72 degrees. Failure would occur if the average is either too high or too low. Therefore, the null hypothesis should be $\mu = 72$ degrees, tested against the alternate hypothesis $\mu \neq 72$ degrees.

29. **C.** The value of the test statistic is $t = (\bar{x} - \mu)/(s/\sqrt{n}) = (40.117 - 40)/(0.966/\sqrt{200}) = 1.7129$. The probability of the t-value exceeding 1.7129 is approximately 0.04415. However, since the test is a two-tail test, this value is doubled, so that the p-value becomes 0.0883.

30. **E.** It is possible to remove one value from a set of 20 values, and have the mean, median, and standard deviation all remain the same. For example, if all 20 values are 86s, the mean and median would both be 86, with standard deviation 0. Removal of one of the 86s would still leave the same three measurements for the set.

31. **C.** The most likely cause of error in the results is that the poll was only taken of hospital patients, who would likely have much different opinions about hospital funding than would the rest of the population. The other statements given would likely not cause skewed results. The sample size was large, and the question was not overly sensitive. Moreover, there was no indication that the survey was voluntary, nor could a difference in more than 30% be likely attributable to random chance.

32. **B.** The degrees of freedom for a paired t-test is given by (number of pairs $- 1$) $= 7 - 1 = 6$.

33. **E.** Use the calculator to find the mean and standard deviation of the differences as $\bar{d} = -24.2857$ and $S = 34.2087$. Therefore, $t = \bar{d}/(s/\sqrt{n}) = (-24.2857)/(34.2087/\sqrt{7}) = -1.878$.

34. **B.** The probability of having the sum of three dice equal exactly 10 is $27/216 = 0.125$. The probability of getting a second roll and winning is $(6/216)(27/216) = .00347$.

35. **A.** A simple random sample would be produced by randomly selecting 1000 names from the entire voter population as a whole. Selecting telephone numbers excludes those without telephone numbers, while selecting every 100th name would produce a systematic, not random sample. Selecting a number of voters from each county, or based on the selections of 20 volunteers would produce stratified, not random samples.

36. **E.** The definition of random sample means that every member of the population has an equal likelihood of being chosen. This means that every time should be equally likely to be chosen, which does not occur. Furthermore, many times are excluded from the sample, and some times are included by design, by the fact that only times that occur each 15 minutes are included. All three statements work against randomness.

37. **B.** The estimated number of people who will ride the Wild Mouse will be $(8700)(0.65)(0.85) = 4806.75$.

38. **B.** The confidence interval for mean, with true standard deviation unknown, is given by $\bar{x} \pm ts/\sqrt{n}$. The 99% interval, with 38 degrees of freedom, would be $8.77 \pm (2.712)(3.45)/\sqrt{39}$, or 8.77 ± 1.50.

39. **E.** Since the probability of making one free throw is 0.62, the probability of not making a free throw is 0.38. Therefore, the probability of making at least one out of three can be found by computing $1 - P(\text{making none out of three}) = 1 - (0.38)^3 = 1 - 0.054872 = 0.945128$.

40. **B.** The probability of the family having no daughters and one son is 0.50. For one daughter then one son, it is 0.25; for two daughters then one son, it is 0.125; or, for each number of daughters, x, the probability is $(0.50)^{x+1}$. The expected value would be the infinite sum of all $x = 0, 1, 2, 3, \ldots$, given by $\Sigma x(0.50)^{x+1}$. Assuming all families will have children until they have a son, this sum converges on 1.

Section II Answers

1a. Since the total number of values is 298, the median would be between the 149th and 150th values. Since there are 129 values 7 and below, and 178 values 8 and below, these values fall in the 8 category. The median is 8.

1b. The interquartile range is the difference between the third quartile cutoff Q_3, and the first quartile cutoff Q_1. Q_1 is the median of the lower 149 values, or the 75th value. Since 62 values are 5 and below, and 89 values are 6 and below, Q_1 is 6. Q_3 is the median of the upper 149 values, or the 224th value. Since there are 178 values 8 and below, and 266 values 9 and below, Q_3 is 9. Therefore, the interquartile range, IQR, is $Q_3 - Q_1 = 9 - 6 = 3$.

1c. Rewriting the chart as actual values, the direct frequency chart would be

x	0	1	2	3	4	5	6	7	8	9	10
f_x	2	4	7	15	16	18	27	40	49	88	32

The sum of all the values is $\Sigma x \cdot f_x = 2163$, and $n = 298$. Therefore, the mean is $\bar{x} = 7.258$.

1d. The scores do not appear to be normally distributed, mainly because the scores appear to be skewed to the left.

2a. If it is desired to see whether a candidate has a post-convention bounce, a test of two proportions can be done, whereby p_1 = proportion of voters before the convention, and p_2 = proportion of voters after the convention. Since it is desired to find evidence as to whether the proportion went up after the convention, the null hypothesis would be $H_o: p_1 = p_2$, with alternate hypothesis $H_a: p_1 < p_2$. Provided that the sample sizes are sufficiently large, the test can be done as a z-test.

2b. The candidate's observed proportion before the convention is $\hat{p}_1 = 643/1200$, and the candidate's observed proportion after the convention is $\hat{p}_2 = 878/1500$. With the pooled proportion, $\bar{p} = 1521/2700 = 0.5633333$, the z-test statistic is $z = ((643/1200 - 878/1500))/\sqrt{(0.5633)(0.4367)/1200 + (0.5633)(0.4367)/1500} = -2.577$. Based on the $\alpha = 0.01$ level of significance, the rejection region is $z < -2.326$, resulting in rejection of the null hypothesis. Therefore, there is evidence to show that the candidate's proportion of voter support before the convention was less than the proportion after the convention, implying that the candidate did benefit from the post-convention bounce. You can also use the 2-PropZ Test in the calculator.

2c. In order to test whether the post-convention bounce is temporary, various tests of two proportions can be done. The proportion of support immediately after the convention can be compared to the proportion of support four weeks, six weeks, eight weeks, or any specified time period after the convention. Another possible way is to test whether the candidate returns to the proportion of support that the candidate had previous to the convention. This can be done by comparing the proportion of support prior to the convention to the proportion of support some number of weeks after the convention, and see whether they are approximately the same.

3. The effect of the sun can be considered to differ depending on whether the plants are positioned in the row facing the east, the row facing the west, or the row in the middle. Since each row contains four clusters, two of the clusters can be selected to be given the new fertilizer, and the other two can be given the old fertilizer. Then there are several possibilities for comparing the groups with the new fertilizer with the groups with the old fertilizer. Considering the groups to be independent samples, likely assuming that the standard deviations are unknown and not equal, if μ_1 is the mean weight of beans produced by a plant with new fertilizer, and μ_2 is the mean weight of beans produced by a plant with old fertilizer, a hypothesis can be set up with null hypothesis $H_o: \mu_1 = \mu_2$, and alternate hypothesis $H_a: \mu_1 > \mu_2$. It is possible to group all plants with new fertilizer into one sample, and all plants with old fertilizer into the other sample, since the positioning of all plants have been equally distributed among positions in the garden. It is also possible to perform three separate hypothesis tests, comparing the means for subgroups within the east group, within the middle group, and within the west group.

4a. Since there is a 0.05 probability that a battery will not function at all, there is a 0.95 probability that a battery will have a positive life span. If a battery does function, the probability that it will function for more than 60 hours is the probability of exceeding $z = (60 - 45)/(10) = 1.5$ on the normal distribution, which is 0.0668. Therefore, the probability of exceeding 60 hours, for any battery, is $(0.95)(0.0668) = 0.0635$.

4b. The probability that one battery that functions at all will function for at least 30 hours is the probability of exceeding $z = (30 - 45)/(10) = -1.5$ on the normal distribution, which is 0.9332. The probability for any battery functioning for at least 30 hours is $(0.95)(0.9332) = 0.88654$. The probability of two independent batteries functioning for at least 30 hours is $(0.88654)(0.88654) = 0.7860$.

4c. The probability that one battery that functions at all will function for at least 55 hours is the probability of exceeding $z = (55 - 45)/(10) = 1.0$ on the normal distribution, which is 0.1587. The probability for any battery functioning for at least 55 hours is $(0.95)(0.1587) = 0.150765$. The probability of at least one out of two independent batteries functioning for at least 55 hours is $1 -$ (the probability both fail before 55 hours) $= 1 - (0.849235)(0.849235) = 0.2788$.

5a. The equation of the least-squares regression line relating score on final exam with number of absences is $\hat{y} = 92.6377 - 3.2691x$, where $\hat{y}$ is the score on the final exam, and x is the number of absences.

5b. The slope of the regression line is $b_o = -3.2691$, and the standard deviation of the slope is 0.342705. The degrees of freedom is $n - 2$, where n is the sample size, which must be determined by counting the number of points in the scatterplot, which is 20. The t-value, for a 95% confidence interval, with 18 degrees of freedom, is 2.101. Therefore, the confidence interval would be $-3.2691 \pm (2.101)(0.342705)$, or $[-3.9891, -2.5491]$.

5c. The correlation coefficient relating score on final exam with number of absences is -0.9137. Since the value is, in magnitude, close to 1, there is a strong linear correlation between score and absences. Furthermore, since the value is negative, the relationship is inverse, implying that as the number of absences increases, the score on final exam will tend to decrease, and when the number of absences is lower, the score on final exam will tend to be higher.

5d. Using the regression equation, if the number of absences is $x = 9$, then, the predicted score on the final exam will be $\hat{y} = 92.6377 - (3.2691)(9) = 63.2158$, or a score of approximately 63.

6a. Based on a total sample size of 5000, the expected totals for each candidate, according to the percentages, would be Bush 2350, Gore 2350, Nader 250, and Buchanan 50. Since it is desired to see whether there is evidence that the candidates do not follow these percentages, the appropriate χ^2 test statistic would be computed as $\Sigma (O - E)^2 / E = (2410 - 2350)^2/2350 + (2335 - 2350)^2/2350 + (241 - 250)^2/250 + (14 - 50)^2/50 = 27.872$. At an $\alpha = 0.05$ level of significance, and degrees of freedom-number of categories $- 1 = 4 - 1 = 3$, the rejection region would be $\chi^2 > 7.815$. Based on this test, there is sufficient evidence to conclude that the candidates do not follow these percentages.

6b. A similar hypothesis test can be done whereby the degrees of freedom is only 1, since there are two categories, being Bush 50% and Gore 50%. The issues involve what to do with the voters who would have voted for Nader or Buchanan. These voters could simply be discounted, and the sample could be modified to contain only voters who choose Bush or Gore. The sample could also be done, whereby voters who indicate Nader or Buchanan must be asked the additional question, "Whom would you vote for, if you could not vote for Nader or Buchanan?" If a sample could not be redone, then the margin of error in the analysis would involve the Nader and Buchanan voters who might otherwise skew the results between Bush and Gore.

6c. If the sample is modified so as not to contain the Nader and Buchanan voters, the sample simply becomes Bush 2410 and Gore 2335, with sample size $n = 4745$, with expected values Bush 2372.5 and Gore 2372.5, whereby the new null hypothesis is that the percentages are Bush 50% and Gore 50%. The χ^2 test statistic would become $\Sigma (O - E)^2/E = (2410 - 2372.5)^2/2372.5 + (2335 - 2372.5)^2/2372.5 = 1.185$. At an $\alpha = 0.05$ level of significance, and degrees of freedom-number of categories $- 1 = 2 - 1 = 1$, the rejection region would be $\chi^2 > 3.841$. Therefore, there is not sufficient evidence to conclude that the two candidates do not have equal percentages of support.

6d. If the previous test is done, and it is assumed that all Nader voters would vote for Gore, and all Buchanan voters would vote for Bush, the sample size remains $n = 5000$, with expected values Bush 5000 and Gore 5000, with new observed frequencies Bush 2424 and Gore 2576. With this sample, the χ^2 test statistic will become $\Sigma (O - E)^2/E = (2424 - 2500)^2/2500 + (2576 - 2500)^2/2500 = 2.310$. At an $\alpha = 0.05$ level of significance, with degrees of freedom 1, the rejection region is still $\chi^2 > 3.841$. Therefore, there is still not sufficient evidence to conclude that the two candidates would not have equal percentages of support.

Practice Test 6

Section I

Time: 1 hour and 30 minutes   Number of questions: 40   Percent of total grade: 50%

Directions: Solve each problem. Decide which is the best of the answer choices given.

1. Two measures, x and y, were taken, and yielded the least-squares regression line $\hat{y} = 54.49 + 4.48x$. The following is a plot of the residuals for the regression analysis:

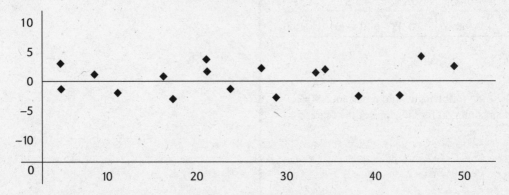

Which of the following statements is supported by this information?

A. There is a strong, direct linear relationship between x and y.
B. There is a strong, inverse linear relationship between x and y.
C. There is a linear relationship between x and y, but it cannot be determined whether the relationship is direct or inverse from the information given.
D. There is a strong relationship between x and y, but the relationship is nonlinear.
E. There is no strong relationship between x and y.

GO ON TO THE NEXT PAGE

2. The Erickson Oil Company has found oil on their Northern Arizona Site. They have determined that there is a linear relationship between the number of well towers they place on the site, and the amount of oil, in barrels, that they are able to collect in a week. For 17 consecutive weeks, they activated a number of wells, and recorded the amount of oil that was collected. The results of their regression analysis are given here:

Regression Equation:

Barrels = 177.74 + 406.92 Towers

Predictor	Coef	Stdev	t-ratio	p
Constant	177.74404	110.042	1.6152	0.127
Towers	406.91892	13.0813	31.1070	0.000

S = 251.62   R-sq = 98.5

Which of the following would represent a 90% confidence interval for the slope of the regression line?

A. 177.74 ± 181.02
B. 177.74 ± 192.90
C. 406.92 ± 22.93
D. 406.92 ± 27.88
E. 406.92 ± 64.97

3. Three coins have been tossed. It is revealed that two of the coins are heads. Assuming that the coins are fair, meaning that the probability of both heads and tails is 0.50, what is the probability that the unrevealed coin is a head?

A.   0.125
B.   0.250
C.   0.333
D.   0.500
E.   0.750

4. The following boxplots summarize two data sets, A and B.

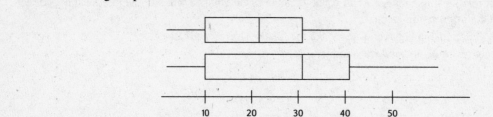

Which of the following statements is not justified by the plots?

A.   The median for Set A is less than the median for Set B.
B.   The range for Set A is less than the range for Set B.
C.   The IQR for Set A is less than the IQR for Set B.
D.   The maximum value for Set A is less than the maximum value for Set B.
E.   The sample size for Set A is less than the sample size for Set B.

5. Data set G is summarized by this boxplot:

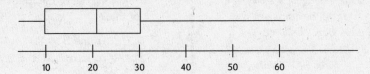

Which of the following must be true about the data set G?

A. The majority of the data points are greater than 30.

B. The data set contains a value at 20.

C. There are fewer points between 55 and 60 than between 0 and 5.

D. The IQR is less than the width of the fourth quartile.

E. The data set contains an outlier.

6. A polling service wants to conduct a survey of voter preferences within a county. The population of almost all of the county is comprised of four ethnic groups. The polling service wants to ensure that each of the four ethnic groups is well represented in the sample. Which type of sample would best achieve this goal?

A. Simple random sample

B. Cluster sample

C. Stratified sample

D. Convenience sample

E. Systematic random sample

Questions 7 and 8 refer to the following information:

It is determined that there is a strong linear correlation between the sale price and the number of skirts sold at Feingold's Department Store. The least-squares regression line relating the sale price, x, in dollars, and the number sold in a week, y, is given by:

$$\hat{y} = 124.8 - 5.63x$$

$$8 < x < 20$$

7. If the sale price is set at $12.50, approximately how many skirts would be sold in one week?

A. 20

B. 54

C. 88

D. 124

E. 195

8. During the course of one week, 71 skirts were sold, during which time the sale price was $11. What is the residual for this data measurement?

A. −8.13

B. −1.44

C. 1.44

D. 8.13

E. 9.56

9. Which of the following statements is true about a χ^2-distribution with k-degrees of freedom.

I. $P(\chi^2 < x) > 0$ only if $x > 0$.

II. The mean of the χ^2-distribution is equal to k.

III. As k increases, $P(\chi^2 < c)$ decreases for any fixed, positive value of c.

A. I only

B. II only

C. I and II only

D. II and III only

E. I, II, and III

GO ON TO THE NEXT PAGE

Practice Test 6

413

10. The owner of the Tiger Oaks Auto Mall believes that each of the five dealers is equally successful in making auto sales. During the course of one week, the following sales were observed:

Toys Audi	Mel's Ford	A-1 Chevy	Max 1 Lexus	Whitehorse Auto
23	22	30	28	34

Which of the following would be the value of the χ^2 statistic for the goodness-of-fit test, testing the null hypothesis that the auto dealers are equally preferred?

A. 0.715
B. 0.739
C. 3.620
D. 3.687
E. 5.480

11. A two-way test of independence is done, whereby the corresponding contingency table contains three rows and four columns. Based on the data collected, the χ^2 statistic for this test is 17.333. Which of the following values would be the lowest level of significance, α, at which rejection of the null hypothesis would occur?

A. 0.005
B. 0.01
C. 0.025
D. 0.05
E. 0.10

12. Suppose A and B are two events whereby the $P(A \text{ and } B) > 0$. Which of the following statements cannot be true?

A. A and B are mutually exclusive events.
B. A and B are independent events.
C. $P(A \text{ or } B) = P(A) + P(B) - P(A \text{ and } B)$.
D. $P(A \text{ and } B) = P(A) \cdot P(B)$.
E. A and B are neither independent nor mutually exclusive.

13. Suppose that A, B, and C are independent events. Which of the following statements is not true?

A. $P(A \text{ and } B \text{ and } C) = P(A) \cdot P(B) \cdot P(C)$
B. $P(A \text{ and } B) = P(A) \cdot P(B)$
C. $P(A \text{ or } C) = P(A) + P(C) - P(A) \cdot P(C)$
D. $P(B \mid C) = P(B)$
E. $P(A \text{ or } B \text{ or } C) = P(A) + P(B) + P(C) - P(A) \cdot P(B) \cdot P(C)$

14. Suppose that A and B are mutually exclusive events. Which of the following statements is not true?

A. $P(A \text{ and } B) = 0$.
B. If A occurs, $P(B) = 0$.
C. $P(A \mid B) = 0$.
D. $P(A \text{ or } B) = P(A) + P(B)$
E. If B does not occur, $P(A) = 1$

15. Dyno-Gen is a genetics lab that produces a genetically altered strain of bacteria for drain cleaners. For each bacteria cell that is produced and lives, the life span of the cell follows a normal distribution with mean $\mu = 140$ hours and standard deviation $\sigma = 45$ hours. However, for each cell that is produced, there is a 0.30 probability that the cell will not live at all. If 2000 cells are produced, approximately how many cells, on the average, would live beyond 200 hours?

A. 55
B. 128
C. 182
D. 224
E. 600

16. Carl's Trucking Company needs to estimate the mean weight of shipments of coal. A pilot sample is taken, and the weights of the shipments were figured to have a standard deviation of 13.8 tons. If the company wants to have an estimate of the mean within 1 ton of the true mean, with 99% confidence, how many shipments should be included in the sample?

A. 36
B. 731
C. 1030
D. 1264
E. 5055

17. The following is a cumulative frequency histogram of scores on a uniform mathematics final at PCU.

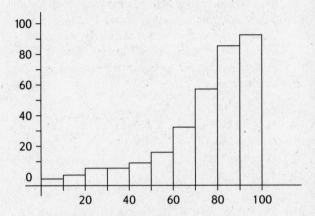

Which of the following statements is true?

A. The median is less than 60.
B. The distribution of the scores is approximately uniform.
C. Among each interval of 10, the most number of students scored in the 90s.
D. The majority of scores were above 80.
E. There was no score in the 30s.

18. In a sample of 84 employees at a large corporation, a 95% confidence interval for the mean yearly wages for the employees was computed to be [$18,855, $24,117]. This information is used to test the null hypothesis that the true mean income is $\mu = \$24,000$ against the alternate hypothesis that $\mu < \$24,000$. Which of the following conclusions could be made?

A. There is not enough evidence to conclude that $\mu < 24,000$ for any level, α, less than 0.10.
B. There is enough evidence to conclude that $\mu < 24,000$ for $\alpha = 0.10$, but not for $\alpha = 0.05$.
C. There is enough evidence to conclude that $\mu < 24,000$ for $\alpha = 0.05$, but not for $\alpha = 0.01$.
D. There is enough evidence to conclude that $\mu < 24,000$ for $\alpha = 0.01$.
E. A conclusion cannot be made from the information given.

19. Suppose that a particular state issues license plates that consist of three letters, followed by three digits. Charlie wants to request that the state issue him a vanity plate with his initials and birthdate, so that it reads "CMB 714." If 1,267,110 license plates have already been issued randomly, what is the probability that the plate Charlie has requested is already being used?

A. Approximately 0
B. 0.0041
C. 0.0721
D. 0.1128
E. 0.1267

20. A class consists of 24 women and 17 men. Five people in the class are going to be chosen at random for a class project. What is the probability that the group will consist of at least 1 woman and 1 man?

A. 0.0005
B. 0.0650
C. 0.3173
D. 0.6827
E. 0.9350

21. Four cards are numbered {1, 2, 3, 4} and two cards are chosen at random. Which of the following would be the distribution of the sample average?

A.	$\bar{x}$	1.5	2	2.5	3	3.5
	Probability	1/5	1/5	1/5	1/5	1/5
B.	$\bar{x}$	1.5	2	2.5	3	3.5
	Probability	1/6	1/6	1/3	1/6	1/6
C.	$\bar{x}$	1.5	2	2.5	3	3.5
	Probability	1/7	2/7	1/7	2/7	1/7
D.	$\bar{x}$	1.5	2	2.5	3	3.5
	Probability	1/10	1/5	2/5	1/5	1/10
E.	$\bar{x}$	1.5	2	2.5	3	3.5
	Probability	1/8	1/4	1/4	1/4	1/8

22. Which of the following is not a condition for using the t-distribution instead of the standard normal when computing a confidence interval for mean?

A. The underlying population is normal or near normal.
B. The population standard deviation is not known.
C. The sample size is small.
D. The sample contains no outliers.
E. All of these are conditions for using the t-distribution.

GO ON TO THE NEXT PAGE

23. From a sample of size $n = 100$, a 95% confidence interval for the mean is computed to be [21, 27]. Which of the following statements best describes the meaning of this interval?

   A. There is a 95% probability that this interval contains the true mean.

   B. Ninety-five percent of all data in the sample is within this interval.

   C. This interval would likely contain 95% of all the data in the population.

   D. If another sample is taken, there is a 95% probability that the sample mean would be in this interval.

   E. There is a 95% probability that all the data within the sample would be contained within this interval.

24. A biotech company wants to test the effects of two rat poisons, labeled C and D. Rat poison C is given to a sample of 40 rats at their laboratory in Florida, and rat poison D is given to a sample of 60 rats at their laboratory in Pennsylvania. The proportion of rats given poison C that died within one hour was 0.725, while the proportion of rats given poison D that died within one hour was 0.80. The company then concludes that the poison labeled D is more effective. Why was this experiment not well designed?

   A. The sample sizes for the two groups were not the same.

   B. The sample sizes were not large enough.

   C. It was inappropriate to compute proportions when comparing the success rate for the two groups.

   D. Since the groups were tested in different labs, the possibility of confounding factors was overlooked.

   E. The study was not done as a double-blind study.

25. A professor is using a piece of sensitive AV equipment that requires 4 batteries. In order for the piece of equipment to function, all 4 batteries must be functioning. The professor has been given 4 batteries from the supply chief who has selected them at random from a box of 100. However, the box of 100 contains 3 dead batteries. What is the probability that the AV equipment will not function?

   A. 0.0300

   B. 0.1147

   C. 0.1164

   D. 0.8853

   E. 0.8836

26. The Braveland Conference consists of 14 high schools. Two of these high schools are crosstown rivals Brookfield Central and Brookfield East. For the wrestling season, nine meets will take place, whereby the teams are paired at random, so that no pair of high schools will meet more than once. What is the probability that rivals Brookfield Central and Brookfield East will not meet?

   A. 0.0714

   B. 0.2857

   C. 0.3077

   D. 0.6923

   E. 0.7143

27. A state high school mathematics competition has a final round consisting of two questions. Historically, 68% of the finalists would get at least one of the questions right, and 28% of the finalists would get both questions right. Based on these percentages, if there are 400 finalists, about how many total questions are expected to be done correctly?

   A. 112

   B. 224

   C. 272

   D. 384

   E. 496

28. The random variable X is represented by the following probability density function:

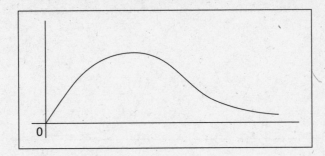

Which of the following is not a possibility for this curve?

A. This curve could represent a χ^2 distribution.

B. This curve is symmetric.

C. $X \geq 0$ for every value of X.

D. The probability that X is contained in any negative interval is 0.

E. For samples of size n taken from this distribution, the sample average, $\bar{x}$, could be estimated by the normal distribution for large values of n.

29. The following stem-and-leaf plot shows the scores for a 60-question geography test.

```
0 | 7
1 | 68
2 | 5899
3 | 013359
4 | 001124577899
5 | 111135678
6 | 0
```

Which of the following statements is not justified by this plot?

A. The median is 42.

B. The mode is 51.

C. The category with the most number of scores is 40–49.

D. There was 1 perfect score on the test.

E. The IQR is 22.

30. Rachel and Ashley are two students in a Statistics class who arrive to class independently. For Friday classes, there is a 0.70 probability that Rachel will come to class, while there is a 0.40 probability that Ashley will come to class. For a Friday class, what is the probability that at least one of them will be there?

A. 0.28

B. 0.54

C. 0.70

D. 0.82

E. 1.10

31. Matthew was told by his doctor that his LDL cholesterol level is too high, and that the z-score for his reading was 1.75. If LDL readings in the population follow a normal distribution with mean $\mu = 85$ and standard deviation $\sigma = 32$, what was Matthew's LDL reading?

A. 29

B. 117

C. 125

D. 141

E. 148

GO ON TO THE NEXT PAGE

32. This curve represents a normal distribution with mean μ and standard deviation σ.

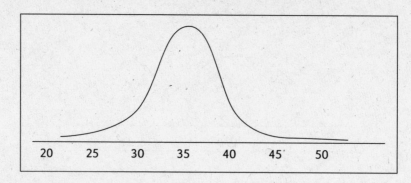

Which of the following is the most likely value for σ?

A. 2
B. 5
C. 10
D. 16
E. 25

33. During the course of the 2004 election, a polling service surveys 1000 random voters in Oklahoma, and 585 of those polled indicated that they would vote for George W. Bush. Therefore, the sample proportion is 0.585. However, the polling service knows that there will be variation in this proportion each time a different sample is be taken. Which of the following is an estimate of the standard deviation in the sample proportion, $\hat{p}$?

A. 0.0131
B. 0.0156
C. 0.0184
D. 0.0242
E. 0.4927

34. The following boxplot represents a sample of 100 values taken from a normal population with mean μ and standard deviation σ:

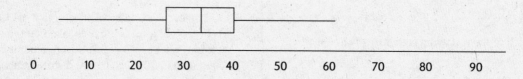

Which of the following are the most likely values for μ and σ?

A. μ = 24   σ = 8
B. μ = 24   σ = 12
C. μ = 32   σ = 8
D. μ = 32   σ = 12
E. μ = 40   σ = 16

35. A professor, teaching two algebra courses, gives an exam to both classes. Among 24 students in the early class, the average on the exam was 84. Among 32 students in the late class, the average on the exam was 76. What would the average be if both classes were combined together?

    A. 78.0
    B. 79.4
    C. 80.0
    D. 80.6
    E. 82.0

36. The following scatterplot represents a set of values Y plotted against a set of values X:

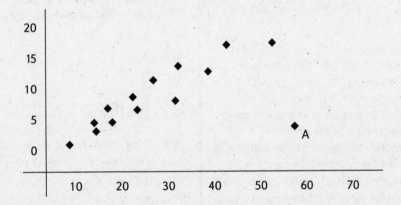

The correlation coefficient representing the relationship between X and Y is $r = 0.627$. If point A is removed from the plot, what effect will this have on the correlation coefficient r?

    A. The value r will increase.
    B. The value r will decrease, but remain positive.
    C. The value r will become 0.
    D. The value r will become negative.
    E. The value r will stay the same.

GO ON TO THE NEXT PAGE

37. The following curve represents a probability density function for a normally distributed random variable X:

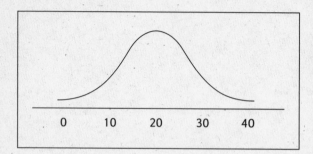

If Y is the random variable given by Y = X/2, how will the density function for Y compare with the density function for X.

A. The density function for Y will be shifted to the right, but the shape will stay the same.

B. The density function for Y will be shifted to the left, but the shape will stay the same.

C. The density function for Y will be narrower, but the center will stay the same.

D. The density function for Y will be shifted to the right, and the curve will be narrower.

E. The density function for Y will be shifted to the left, and the curve will be narrower.

38. The Chamber of Commerce in the City of Rock Bay wants to estimate the typical income level for the town's residents. To accomplish this, the Chamber plans on taking a simple random sample of size 100 from the yearly incomes of the residents. However, the Chamber is aware that there are several residents who have extremely high incomes that may skew the results of their survey. Which procedure would produce an accurate measure of the typical income level while preserving the simple random sample?

A. Remove the wealthy residents from the population, take the sample, and compute the mean.

B. Take the sample, remove any wealthy residents that appear in the sample, and compute the mean.

C. Take the sample as it is, and compute the mean.

D. Take the sample as it is, and compute the mode.

E. Take the sample as it is, and compute the median.

Questions 39 and 40 refer to the following information:

A survey of 200 high school juniors and seniors was taken to see whether there is a difference between the two classes as to whether students drive to school.

	Drive to School	Does Not Drive to School
Juniors	24	56
Seniors	45	75

39. What would be the degrees of freedom for the corresponding two-way test of independence?

A. 1
B. 2
C. 3
D. 4
E. 199

40. What would be the value of the χ^2 statistic for the corresponding two-way test of independence?

A. 0.764
B. 1.195
C. 1.232
D. 8.504
E. 27.24

Section II

Time: 1 hour and 30 minutes   Number of questions: 6   Percent of total grade: 50%

Part A

Questions 1–5   Spend about 65 minutes on this part of the exam.   Percent of Section II grade: 75%

Show all your work. Clearly indicate the methods you use—you will be graded on the correctness of your methods as well as the accuracy of your results and explanation.

1. A biologist is trying to determine whether the catch yield in a fishing area that was contaminated by the runoff after a fire is better now than it was before the fire. Some fisherman say it is actually better after the fire than before the fire. Data was available for the area covering a four-year period before the fire. In a random sample of 178 fishing reports in the region before the fire, the average catch per day was 5.8 trout with a sample standard deviation of 1.8 trout. A random sample of 145 fishing reports two years after the fire showed an average catch per day of 6.9 trout with a sample standard deviation of 2.2.

    a. For each sample, what is the population? Are the samples independent or dependent? Explain.

    b. Construct a 95% confidence interval for the difference of the population means. Explain its meaning.

2. A testing company wants to study the effectiveness of a newly developed vitamin supplement to promote improved memory skills. One hundred participants are randomly selected to participate. The subjects will be given a test to determine their basic skill level.

    a. How can the study be constructed as a t-test, comparing means of independent samples?

    b. How can the study be constructed as a paired t-test?

    c. Which of these two tests can be constructed as a double-blind study? Please explain how.

3. The life of a certain type of lightbulb follows a normal distribution with mean $\mu = 1000$ hours and standard deviation $\sigma = 140$ hours. Eight percent of all the bulbs are broken in shipment and are defective.

    a. If a random bulb is placed into a lamp, what is the probability that the bulb will function for more than 1200 hours?

    b. If a lamp requires two functioning bulbs with both bulbs working properly, and two random bulbs are placed into the lamp, what is the probability that the lamp will work properly for at least 1100 hours?

    c. If a lamp accepts two bulbs, but it requires that at least one be operating properly, what is the probability that after placing two randomly selected bulbs in the lamp that the lamp will work properly for at least 1100 hours?

4. You need to choose 20 random subjects for an experiment. The experiment involves determining the probability that at least three of the subjects selected are left-handed. You know that 15% of the general population is left-handed. You are given a bag, 25 black marbles, and 25 red marbles. The marbles are indistinguishable, except for color. Using the bag with some or all of the marbles, design a procedure to simulate the selection of the 20 subjects for the experiment.

GO ON TO THE NEXT PAGE

5. Ten friends named *a, b, c, d, e, f, g, h, k,* and *m* buy 10 movie tickets, all in adjacent seats in a theater.

a. How many ways can these 10 friends sit down in these 10 adjacent seats?

b. If *d* and *g* are really good friends and want to sit next to each other, how many ways can these 10 friends sit down in these 10 adjacent seats?

c. If *a, b,* and *c,* are really good friends and want to sit in three adjacent seats, how many ways can these 10 friends sit down in these 10 adjacent seats?

d. If these 10 friends randomly sit down in the 10 adjacent seats, what is the probability that *g* and *k* will not be sitting next to each other.

Part B

Question 6   Spend about 25 minutes on this part of the exam.   Percent of Section II grade: 25%

Directions for Part B: Allow additional time for this part. Clearly indicate the methods that you use and give clear explanations for all your results.

6. A teacher is interested in what role gender plays in learning course material in her classes. She recorded and calculated the grades separately for boys and for girls. Here are the results:

Gender	Number	Mean	Standard Deviation
Female	28	71.2	8.3
Male	38	67.7	7.7

a. Noting that the mean for female students was higher, suppose that the instructor wants to determine whether this is evidence to conclude that female students tend to score higher, on the average, than male students. How might the instructor set up an appropriate hypothesis test? What assumptions need to be made?

b. Is there evidence to conclude, at an $\alpha = 0.01$ level of significance, that the true mean for female students is higher than the true mean for male students?

c. What are some possible confounding factors that might affect the conclusion that female students tend to do better than male students?

Section I Answers

1. **A.** Because of the random pattern of the points in the graph, which appear to fit the zero line fairly closely, the relationship would be linear. Furthermore, since it is given that the slope of the least-squares regression line is positive, the linear relationship is direct as well.

2. **C.** The slope of the regression line is $b_1 = 406.92$. From the regression results, the standard deviation of the slope is $s_{b_1} = 13.0813$ found in the chart as "stdev" for Towers. With degrees of freedom = (sample size – 2) = (17 – 2) = 15, the 90% confidence interval would be $(406.92) \pm (1.753)(13.0813) = 406.92 \pm 22.93$.

3. **B.** Since it is not known which of the three coins is the unrevealed coin, the conditional probability is computed as P(three heads | at least two are heads) = (1/8)/(4/8) = 1/4 = 0.250.

4. **E.** The median for Set A is 20, which is less than the median for Set B, 30. The range for Set A is 40, which is less than the range for Set B, which is over 50. The IQR for Set A is 20, which is less than the IQR for Set B, 30. The maximum value for Set A is 40, which is less than the maximum value for Set B, over 50. The sample size for a set cannot be determined from a boxplot alone.

5. **D.** Since approximately 25% of the scores are above Q_3, the majority of the scores cannot be above 30. The data set does not necessarily contain a value at 20, since the median could be the average of two values in the center of the data set. It is not necessarily true that there are fewer points in the range [55, 60] than within [0, 5], as it is possible to have a concentration of points in one small portion of a quartile. Also, a wide fourth quartile does not necessarily imply an outlier, as data values may be equally spread through the wide quartile. However, the IQR is 20, while the width of the fourth quartile is 30.

6. **C.** If it is desired that distinct groups be represented in a sample, a stratified sample should be taken, since a stratified sample involves dividing the population into distinct groups, called strata, and taking a random subsample from each.

7. **B.** To determine the predicted number of skirts, $\hat{y}$, that would be sold at $x = 12.50$, solve the equation $\hat{y} = 124.8 - (5.63)(12.50)$ for $\hat{y}$. The value is $\hat{y} = 54.425$.

8. **D.** The estimated value, $\hat{y}$, for $x = 11$ would be $\hat{y} = 124.8 - (5.63)(11) = 62.87$. The residual is the difference between the observed value and the predicted value, or $y - \hat{y} = 71 - 62.87 = 8.13$.

9. **E.** Since the χ^2 distribution has positive values only, the probability that χ^2 is less than x can only be positive if x is a positive value. Also, since the χ^2-curve becomes wider as the degrees of freedom increases, the left-tail areas will decrease, implying that the probability that χ^2 is less than a fixed positive value will also decrease. Lastly, the mean of the χ^2 distribution is equal to the degrees of freedom.

10. **C.** The value of the χ^2 statistic for a goodness-of-fit test is given by the formula $\chi^2 = \Sigma(O - E)^2/E$. The expected values for each category, in this case, would be the average of the sample size 137/5 = 27.4, since it is claimed that the categories should be equal. Therefore, the χ^2 statistic would be computed as $(23 - 27.4)^2/27.4 + (22 - 27.4)^2/27.4 + (30 - 27.4)^2/27.4 + (28 - 27.4)^2/27.4 + (34 - 27.4)^2/27.4 = 3.620$.

11. **B.** The degrees of freedom for a two-way test of independence is (number of rows – 1)(number of columns – 1) = (2)(3) = 6. The χ^2 upper-tail cutoff for 6 degrees of freedom, for $\alpha = 0.01$, is 16.812, so rejection of the null hypothesis would occur for the α values of 0.01 and higher. However, the cutoff for $\alpha = 0.005$ is 18.548, whereby rejection of the null hypothesis would not occur.

12. **A.** If the P(A and B) > 0, this implies that both events can occur at the same time, so they cannot be mutually exclusive. However, it is possible that P(A and B) = P(A)P(B) > 0, so the events could be independent. Also, P(A or B) = P(A) + P(B) – P(A and B) for any events A and B. Still, it is possible that the two events, though having a positive intersection, are not independent.

13. **E.** If A, B, and C are independent events, then P(A and B and C) = P(A)P(B)P(C). Furthermore, A and B would also, as a pair, be independent events, so that P(A and B) = P(A)P(B). Also, P(A or C) = P(A) + P(C) – P(A and C) for any two events A and C. Independence between any two events also implies that if one event occurs, the probability of the other event occurring would not change, so that the statement P(B | C) = P(B) would be true. However, P(A or B or C) = P(A) + P(B) + P(C) – P(A and B) – P(A and C) – P(B and C) + P(A and B and C) by Bayes's Theorem.

14. E. If A and B are mutually exclusive events, this means that both events cannot occur at the same time. Therefore, $P(A \text{ and } B) = 0$, and if A occurs, $P(B) = 0$. Also, this would mean that, by conditional probability, $P(A \mid B) = 0$, since if B occurs, $P(A) = 0$. Then, for addition rule $P(A \text{ or } B) = P(A) + P(B) - P(A \text{ and } B)$ would become $P(A \text{ or } B) = P(A) + P(B)$. However, it is not true that if B does not occur, then A must occur, unless A and B are complements of each other.

15. B. The z-score for a living cell to exceed a life span of 200 hours is $z = (200 - 140)/(45) = 1.333$. The probability of exceeding a z-score of 1.333 is 0.0912. However, since there is only a 0.70 probability that a cell will live at all, the probability that a cell's life exceeds 200 is $(0.70)(0.0912) = 0.06384$. Therefore, the expected number of cells that will exceed a life span of 200 would be $(2000)(0.06384) = 127.68$.

16. D. It is desired that the estimate be made with an error no greater than 1 ton, with a confidence level 0.99. The minimum sample size would be $n \geq (z\sigma/E)^2 = ((2.576)(13.8)/1)^2 = 1263.717$.

17. E. The median cannot be less than 60, since the height of the category ending at 60 is less than 50%. Since there is variation in the changes in the heights of the categories from one category to the next, the distribution is not uniform. The percentage of scores in the 90s would not be determined by the height of the category at 90, but by the change between the category ending at 90 and the category beginning at 90, which is not the greatest change. Since the category which ends at 80 is above 50%, it is not true that the majority of scores are above 80. However, since the height of the category that ends at 30 and that which begins at 30 are the same, this implies that there was no change from the 20s category and the 30s category, meaning that there were no scores in the 30s.

18. C. The confidence interval is of the form $x \pm E$, where $x = 21,486$ and $E = 2631$. Since this is a 95% confidence interval, with t-value approximately 1.990, this would imply that since $E = ts/\sqrt{n}$ the term $s/\sqrt{n} = 2631/1.990 = 1322.11$. Therefore, if the claim is that $\mu = 24,000$, this would imply that the corresponding t-statistic would be $t = (21,486 - 24,000)/1322.11 = -1.902$. Tested against the claim that $\mu < 24,000$, for 83 degrees of freedom, the lower-tail critical values for $\alpha = 0.05$ and $\alpha = 0.01$ would be approximately 1.664 and 2.374, respectively. Therefore, rejection of the null hypothesis would occur for $\alpha = 0.05$, but not for $\alpha = 0.01$.

19. C. The total number of license plates consisting of three letters and three digits would be $(26)(26)(26)(10)(10)(10) = 17,576,000$. Therefore, the probability that one plate is among the ones already issued would be $1,267,110/17,576,000 = 0.0721$.

20. E. The total number of possible groups of 5, taken from 41 total people would be $_{41}C_5 = 749,398$. The number of groups that consist of only women would be $_{24}C_5 = 42,504$, and the number of groups that consist of only men would be $_{17}C_5 = 6188$. Therefore, the number of groups consisting of at least one woman and one man would exclude these two possibilities and be $749,398 - (42,504 + 6188) = 700,706$. The probability of at least one woman and one man would be $(700,706)/(749,398) = 0.9350$.

21. B. The possible samples of two would be $\{1,2\}, \{1,3\}, \{1,4\}, \{2,3\}, \{2,4\}, \{3,4\}$, producing sample means of 1.5, 2, 2.5, 2.5, 3, and 3.5, respectively. Therefore, the probabilities for each value would be 1/6 for each possible value, except for 2.5, which would be $2/6 = 1/3$.

22. D. In order to use the t-distribution, the underlying population must be normal or near normal, and the population standard deviation must be unknown. Also, for large sample sizes, the standard normal can be used, so small sample size also becomes a consideration when using t. However, the presence of outliers in the sample is not a consideration when using the t-distribution.

23. A. The 95% confidence interval is constructed so that there is a 95% probability that the interval will contain, within in, the true mean μ.

24. D. For a test comparing two proportions, the sample sizes do not need to be the same, nor are 40 and 60 small samples. It is appropriate to compare proportions, if success rates are to be compared. The issue of double blind would not enter, since the rats are unaware of any substance they are taking. However, there is the possibility that the location and, thus, the surroundings, care, or even the breeds being tested could become confounding factors that may affect the results.

25. C. The probability that all four of the batteries chosen are among the 97 good batteries would be $(_{97}C_4)/(_{100}C_4) = (3,464,840)/(3,921,225) = 0.8836$. Therefore, the probability that at least one of the batteries is bad is $1 - 0.8836 = 0.1164$.

26. C. For either team, 9 opponents will be chosen, without duplication, from among the 13 other teams in the conference. Since the teams are being chosen randomly, the probability that the rival will be among the teams that are not chosen would be 4/13 = 0.3077.

27. D. The probability that a finalist gets two questions right is 0.28. The probability that a finalist gets exactly one question right would be 0.68 − 0.28 = 0.40. Therefore, the expected number right for each finalist would be (1)(0.40) + (2)(0.28) = 0.96. So, the expected total questions right would be (400)(0.96) = 384.

28. B. For every value of X, X ≥ 0, since the curve is everywhere to the right of 0. Furthermore, since X cannot be negative, the probability that X lies in a negative interval is 0. This curve could represent a χ^2 distribution, and, by the Central Limit Theorem, sample averages, $\bar{x}$, from any distribution will follow an approximate normal curve for sample sizes large enough. The curve is not symmetric.

29. E. The median is 42 and the mode is 51. The category 40–49 does contain the most number of values, and there is a value of 60 in the chart. However, $Q_1 = 31$ and $Q_3 = 51$, so the IQR = 20.

30. D. Since Rachel and Ashley both arrive independently, the probability that neither of them arrive would be (1 − 0.7) (1 − 0.4) = (0.3)(0.6) = 0.18. Therefore, the probability that at least one of them arrives is 1 − 0.18 = 0.82.

31. D. Since z-score represents how many standard deviations above or below the mean the value is, the LDL reading would be 85 + (1.75)(32) = 141.

32. B. The mean of the curve appears to be approximately 35. Noting that for a normal distribution, 68% of all values will lie within one standard deviation of the mean, and the majority of the curve lies in the range [30, 40], it appears that the standard deviation would be, most likely, 5.

33. B. The standard deviation of a sample proportion, p, is $\sqrt{\dfrac{p(1-p)}{n}}$, where p is the true population proportion. In this case, the true population proportion is not known, so, using the estimated p, the estimated standard deviation would be $\sqrt{\dfrac{(0.585)(1-0.585)}{(1000)}} = 0.0156$.

34. C. The median of the sample is approximately 32. Since the mean and median of a normal distribution are equal, the sample median would be approximately the sample mean. The second and third quartiles, shown by the width of the box, appears to go from about [26, 39], which would represent 50% of the data. For a normal distribution, approximately 68% of the data would be within one standard deviation of the mean. Therefore, slightly beyond these boundaries would show the standard deviation to be approximately 8.

35. B. The weighted average between these two means would be given by $(n_1 x_1 + n_2 x_2)/(n_1 + n_2) = ((24)(84) + (32)(76))/(24 + 32) = 79.4$.

36. A. The points in the scatterplot appear to be close to lying in a straight line, with the exception of point A. The removal of one lone point that lies significantly away from the line of best fit would imply that the remaining points would lie close to a straight line, and, thus, the value of r would be significantly closer to 1.

37. E. The mean of the distribution is approximately 20, so dividing the random variable by 2 would result in the new mean being approximately 10, so the curve would shift to the left. Also, dividing the random variable by 2 would result in the standard deviation being reduced by a factor of 2 as well, so the curve would become narrower.

38. E. Removal of the wealthy residents would result in the sample no longer being a simple random sample, so the sample needs to be taken as it is. Simply computing the mean would allow the possibility of the wealthy residents skewing the measurement. The mode would be irrelevant, as it only computes the measurement that occurs most often. However, the median would reduce the effect of any unusually high measurements in the sample, as they would only be counted as the highest values, but not change the values that are in the middle of the data.

39. A. The degrees of freedom for a two-way contingency table is given by (number of rows − 1) (number of columns − 1) = (1)(1) = 1.

40. B. The expected values, as computed by the formula (row total)(column total)/(grand total) would be, correspondingly, juniors 27.6 and 52.4 and seniors 41.4 and 78.6. The χ^2 test statistic would be given by the formula $\Sigma(O - E)^2/E = (24 - 27.6)^2/27.6 + (56 - 52.4)^2/52.4 + (45 - 41.4)^2/41.4 + (75 - 78.6)^2/78.6 = 1.195$.

Section II Answers

1a. The population for the first sample is the number of trout that were caught per day by fisherman in the area before the fire. The population for the second sample is the number of trout that were caught per day by fisherman in the area after the fire. There was no attempt to pair the samples from the two populations. They are independent samples.

1b. Both samples are large, so using the z-distribution is appropriate. The critical value for z is 1.96. The confidence interval for the difference in population means is $(\bar{x}_1 - \bar{x}_2) \pm z\sqrt{s_1^2/n_1 + s_2^2/n_2}$. Substituting the values from the collected samples gives $(5.8 - 6.9) \pm 1.96\sqrt{(1.8)^2/178 + (2.2)^2/145}$. This gives an interval of -1.1 ± 0.445, which gives $[-1.545, -0.655]$. This interval shows an increase in catch after the fire. Since the entire interval is on the same side of zero, you can be 95% sure that there was an increase in catch yield from before the fire to after the fire.

2a. The study comparing two means of independent samples can be done by randomly dividing the group of 100 participants into two samples of 50 subjects each. One group can be given the vitamins for 10 weeks, and the sample mean and sample standard deviation of their basic memory skills can be computed. The other group can be given a placebo for 10 weeks, and the sample mean and standard deviation is computed from this group. A hypothesis test can be done for a preselected level of significance, with $H_o: \mu_1 = \mu_2$ and $H_a: \mu_1 > \mu_2$. The t-statistic can be computed for this data, with the assumption that the population standard deviations are not equal and can be compared to a t-critical value, or the *p-value* can be computed.

2b. The test can be constructed as a paired t-test by measuring the basic memory skills of all 100 patients at the end of a 10-week period without taking the vitamins during that period, and then at the end of another 10-week period after being given the vitamins. The differences between memory skill levels before using the vitamins and after the 10 weeks using the vitamins then can be computed. The appropriate t-statistic for paired data can be computed and either compared to a critical value based on a preselected level of significance or converted to a *p-value*.

2c. The test of two independent samples can be done as a double-blind study whereby both the individual subjects and the researchers are unaware of whether each subject is in the vitamins group or the placebo group. There is no such blindness in the paired test, since all the subjects are being tested as a placebo group, first, followed by a vitamin group.

3a. Since there is a 0.08 probability that a bulb will not work, there is a 0.92 probability that a bulb will work. If a bulb does work, the probability that it will work for more than 1200 hours is the probability of exceeding $z = (1200 - 1000)/(140) = 1.23$ on the normal distribution, which is 0.0764. Therefore, the probability of exceeding 1200 hours, for any bulb, is $(0.92)(0.0764) = 0.0703$.

3b. The probability that one bulb that works at all will last for at least 1100 hours is the probability of exceeding $z = (1100 - 1000)/(140) = 0.714$ on the normal distribution, which is 0.238. The probability for any bulb functioning for at least 1100 hours is $(0.92)(0.238) = 0.219$. The probability of two independent bulbs functioning for at least 1100 hours is $(0.219)(0.219) = 0.048$.

3c. The probability that one bulb that works at all will last for at least 1100 hours is the probability of exceeding $z = (1100 - 1000)/(140) = 0.714$ on the normal distribution, which is 0.238. The probability for any bulb lasting for at least 1100 hours is $(0.92)(0.238) = 0.219$. The probability of at least one out of two independent bulbs lasting for at least 1100 hours is $1 - $ (the probability both fail before 1100 hours) $= 1 - (0.781)(0.781) = 0.39$.

4. Since the population is very large compared to the sample being selected, using a procedure that involves replacing the marbles in the bag after each selection is appropriate. You need to place in the bag a population of marbles that represents left-handed people in the general population. Since 15% of the population is left-handed, placing 15% of one color marble and 85% of the other color marble would duplicate the correct percentages. If the white marbles represent right-handed people and the black marbles represent left-handed people, place 17 white marbles and 3 black marbles in the bag. This way, 15% of the marbles in the bag will be black. Mix up the marbles in the bag. Select a random marble and record what color it is. Place the marble back in the bag. Repeat 19 more times. The number of black marbles selected out of the 20 trials would simulate the selection of left-handed people from the general population.

5a. This is a permutations problem. Order makes a difference. There are 10 choices for who sits in the first seat. There are then 9 choices for who sits in the next seat, and so on. The number of ways the 10 friends can sit down in the 10 adjacent seats is $(10)(9)(8)(7)(6)(5)(4)(3)(2)(1) = 10! = 3628800$ ways.

5b. If 2 of the 10 friends want to sit next to each other, then they have to move as a group of 2. Therefore, there are only 9 groups to choose from. For each of these arrangements, you can arrange the two friends two different ways. Therefore, the total number of ways the 10 friends can sit down in these 10 adjacent seats so that d and g are sitting next to each other is $9!2! = 725760$.

5c. If 3 of the 10 friends want to sit next to each other, then they have to move as a group of 3. Therefore, there are only 8 groups to choose from. For each of these arrangements, you can arrange the 3 friends in 3! different ways. Therefore, the total number of ways the 10 friends can sit down in these 10 adjacent seats so that a, b, and c, are sitting next to each other is $8!3! = 241920$.

5d. Probability is defined as the ratio of favorable to total possible events. Therefore, if these 10 friends sit down randomly in these 10 adjacent seats, the probability that 2 specific friends will be sitting next to each other is the ratio of the number of ways 2 can sit next to each other and the total number of arrangements possible. Therefore, the probability is $725760/3628800 = 0.2$. Subtract from 1 to get the probability of not sitting next to each other, that is, 0.8.

6a. In order to determine whether the samples provide evidence that female students score, on the average, higher than male students, a hypothesis test can be set up whereby the null hypothesis is $H_o: \mu_1 = \mu_2$ and the alternate hypothesis is $H_a: \mu_1 > \mu_2$. The assumption should be made that the two samples are independent samples, and either a predetermined level of significance, α, should be chosen, or the *p-value* for the results can be computed. If both groups are being given the same exams, it could be assumed that the standard deviations will be equal. However, even if the groups are being given the same exams, it could also be assumed that the standard deviations or the populations are not equal, figuring that the distributions of the scores between the two classes could be different, with different standard deviations.

6b. If it is assumed that the scores of the two groups are independent, with equal standard deviations, using a technology tool, the pooled t-statistic is $t = 1.766$, with degrees of freedom 64, and corresponding p-value 0.0411. If it is assumed that the scores of the two groups are independent, with unequal standard deviations, the nonpooled t-statistic is $t = 1.746$, with degrees of freedom 56, and corresponding p-value 0.0432. In either case, the null hypothesis, $H_o: \mu_1 = \mu_2$ is not rejected, at level of significance $\alpha = 0.01$, implying that there is not significant evidence to show that female students score higher than male students. If the significance level is relaxed to 5%, then the results are significant and the null hypothesis could be rejected.

6c. The purpose of the original test is to see whether one group of students tends to score higher on tests than another group, where the difference is gender. Confounding factors might be simply the quality of the students in the classes, regardless of gender. Other confounding factors might be whether the teacher relates better to one gender than another. The subject also might be of greater interest to one gender than the other.

Practice Test 7

Section I

Directions: Solve each problem. Decide which is the best of the answer choices given.

1. During the course of the 2000 Presidential Election, the *Zogby Poll* reports that in a poll of 600 randomly selected "likely voters" in the state of Washington, 47% of those polled indicated that they supported Al Gore for President. The *Zogby Poll* reports that Al Gore's current support in Washington is 47%, with a margin of error 3%. Which of the following statements best describes the meaning of "margin of error 3%?"

   A. About 3% of those polled are expected to change their minds by election time.
   B. About 3% of those polled indicated that they will vote for Al Gore, but were not sure.
   C. The difference between the sample proportion, and the true population proportion is likely to be no more than 3%.
   D. It is estimated that about 3% of those polled lied in their responses.
   E. Three percent of those polled gave no preference in their response.

2. A telemarketer is given a commission of $3.00 for each successful sales call. The number of sales calls that will result in a sale (and a commission for the telemarketer) in each hour follows this probability distribution:

Number of Sales	0	1	2	3	4	5	6
Probability	0.25	0.20	0.20	0.15	0.10	0.05	0.05

   If the telemarketer works an 8-hour day, what is the expected total commission that the telemarketer should receive in a day?

   A. $6.00
   B. $9.00
   C. $24.00
   D. $48.00
   E. $72.00

3. Greg believes that digits in Social Security numbers do not have a true mean of 4.5, because he does not believe that each of the digits occur with equal probability, but rather are based on date of birth, and other considerations. In order to estimate the true mean, he has taken a sample of 20 random Social Security digits, and used these values to create a 95% t-confidence interval for the mean. Why is Greg's computation of the t-interval not appropriate in this case?

   A. Since the true standard deviation is not known, the t-distribution cannot be used.
   B. Since the sample size is small, the t-distribution cannot be used.
   C. Since the population of digits is not normally or near normally distributed, the t-distribution cannot be used.
   D. Computation of a t-interval requires a higher confidence level than 95%.
   E. Computation of a t-interval requires a sample size of at least 30.

GO ON TO THE NEXT PAGE

4. Suppose that Ben Wallace is a "75% free throw shooter," meaning that the probability that he makes a free throw is 0.75. Which of the following statements is the best interpretation of the meaning of the probability being 0.75?

   A. He has made 75% of all the free throws he has attempted in the past.
   B. Out of 100 free throws, he will make 75 of them.
   C. If he attempts 10 free throws, he should make 7 or 8 of them.
   D. Out of all the free throws he attempts in his life, he will make 75% of them.
   E. If he attempts one free throw, there is a 0.75 likelihood that he will make that one free throw.

5. Suppose that Rolling Canyons College has an admission standard for admission to their mathematics graduate program, whereby they only accept applicants whose GRE scores on the quantitative portion exceed 675. If the GRE scores on the quantitative portion are constructed to follow a normal distribution with mean $\mu = 500$ and standard deviation $\sigma = 100$, approximately what percent of all those who take the quantitative portion of the GRE would qualify for admission to this mathematics program?

   A. Less than 1%
   B. 4%
   C. 8%
   D. 13%
   E. 45%

6. Tri-City Graphics Company has three large printing machines. The probability that one of them blacks out during the course of an hour is 0.02. If a black-out occurs, the contracted cost for the electrician to repair it is $200. What is the expected average cost per 24-hour period for Tri-City Graphics for these electrician repairs?

   A. $48
   B. $96
   C. $230
   D. $288
   E. $600

7. A random sample of 40 trout is taken from a lake. The sample mean for the lengths of the trout was 21.2 inches, with sample standard deviation 5.9 inches. Which of the following would be a 90% confidence interval for the true mean length of the trout in the lake?

   A. 21.2 ± 0.93
   B. 21.2 ± 1.22
   C. 21.2 ± 1.53
   D. 21.2 ± 1.57
   E. 21.2 ± 5.90

8. The Ontiveros Pool Company has observed that pool construction jobs can be completed in a shorter time if more workers are used and that there was a strong linear relationship between the number of workers and the time of completion, in hours. For a sample of 27 pool construction jobs, the results of the regression analysis are given here:

   Regression Equation:

   Time = 141.57 – 6.724 Workers

Predictor	Coef	Stdev	t-ratio	p
Constant	141.56994	6.26140	22.6099	0.000
Workers	–6.724680	0.54940	–12.2401	0.000

   S = 15.41   R-sq = 85.7

   Which of the following would represent a 95% confidence interval for the slope of the regression line?

   A. -6.725 ± 0.616
   B. -6.725 ± 0.938
   C. -6.725 ± 1.077
   D. -6.725 ± 1.127
   E. -6.725 ± 1.132

9. A preservative company manufactures a preservative meant to ensure that fish, if packaged according to the directions, should remain fresh for an average of six days. A fish market, in deciding whether to use the preservative, wants to test the claim. Which of the following hypothesis tests would be most appropriate?

   A. $H_o: \mu = 6$ days, $H_a: \mu > 6$ days
   B. $H_o: \mu = 6$ days, $H_a: \mu \neq 6$ days
   C. $H_o: \mu = 6$ days, $H_a: \mu < 6$ days
   D. $H_o: \mu \leq 6$ days, $H_a: \mu > 6$ days
   E. $H_o: \mu \neq 6$ days, $H_a: \mu = 6$ days

10. Ashley is enrolled in a biology class. She scored 85 on all three exams. However, the class mean on Exam I was 77, with standard deviation 16. The class mean on Exam II was 75 with standard 20. The class mean on Exam III was 72, with standard deviation 15. Which of the statements that follows best describes how well Ashley did on the three exams, in relation to the rest of the class?

A. She did best on Exam III, and worst on Exam I.

B. She did best on Exam I, and worst on Exam III.

C. She did equally well on Exam I and Exam II, but better on Exam III.

D. She did equally well on Exam I and Exam II, but worse on Exam III.

E. She did equally well on all three exams.

11. In a physics class, Melvina and Amanda were performing a hypothesis test concerning the mean amount of static electricity in a capacitor. Both students arrived at the same test statistic, but Melvina's result was to reject the null hypothesis, while Amanda's result was not to reject the null hypothesis. Which of the following is NOT a possible explanation for why the students had difference conclusions?

A. Melvina was testing at an $\alpha = 0.05$ level, but Amanda was testing at an $\alpha = 0.01$ level.

B. Melvina was performing a one-tail test, but Amanda was performing a two-tail test.

C. Melvina considered the test statistic to be z, while Amanda considered the test statistic to be t.

D. Melvina performed an upper-tail test, while Amanda performed a lower-tail test.

E. Melvina computed the p-value of the test statistic, while Amanda compared the test statistic to the corresponding critical value in the chart.

12. An electrical supply company produces a brand of lightbulbs. One type of lightbulb is their 75-watt bulb. In order to test whether their lightbulbs have been created to give the correct wattage, 200 bulbs are sampled. What would be the appropriate null and alternate hypotheses for this test?

A. H_o: $\mu = 75$ watts, H_a: $\mu > 75$ watts

B. H_o: $\mu = 75$ watts, H_a: $\mu < 75$ watts

C. H_o: $\mu = 75$ watts, H_a: $\mu \neq 75$ watts

D. H_o: $\mu \leq 75$ watts, H_a: $\mu > 75$ watts

E. H_o: $\mu \geq 75$ watts, H_a: $\mu < 75$ watts

13. The lengths of Wooten brand foot-long hot dogs follow a normal distribution with mean $\mu = 12.00$ inches, and standard deviation $\sigma = 0.13$ inches. The manager of the production plant has decided to discard all hot dogs that are among the 5% shortest hot dogs, and not include them in packaging. What is the cutoff length at which a short hot dog is to be discarded?

A. 11.74 inches

B. 11.79 inches

C. 11.83 inches

D. 11.87 inches

E. 12.21 inches

14. Suppose that Event A and Event B are independent events. Which of the following statements is not true?

A. $P(A \text{ and } B) = P(A) \cdot P(B)$

B. $P(A \mid B) = P(A)$

C. $P(B \mid A) = P(B)$

D. $P(A \text{ or } B) = P(A) + P(B)$

E. If A occurs, then the probability that B occurs does not change.

GO ON TO THE NEXT PAGE

15. Borham's Drugstore has 18 locations. The district manager wants to determine whether there is a linear relationship between the location's yearly income and the amount of its internal budget. Also, the manager wanted to determine whether there is a linear relationship between the location's yearly income and the size of the store in square feet. In both cases, the manager computed the least-squares regression line and examined the plot of residuals.

PLOT I

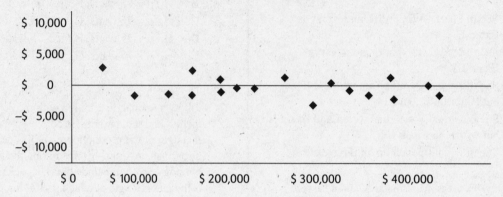

PLOT II

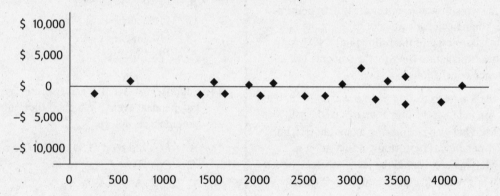

Which of the following statements is best supported by the two plots?

A. There is a linear relationship exhibited in Plot I, but not for Plot II.

B. There is a linear relationship exhibited in Plot II, but not for Plot I.

C. There is a linear relationship exhibited in both Plot I and Plot II.

D. Neither Plot I nor Plot II exhibits a linear relationship.

E. The relationship cannot be determined by these residual plots.

16. Suppose that Event A and Event B are mutually exclusive events. Which of the following statements is not true?

   A. $P(A \text{ and } B) = 0$
   B. $P(A \mid B) = 0$
   C. $P(B \mid A) = 0$
   D. $P(A \text{ or } B) = P(A) + P(B)$
   E. $P(A) = 1 - P(B)$

17. Jessica has taken the first three exams in an algebra class. She scored 90 on all three exams. For Exam I, the class mean was 85 with standard deviation 10. For Exam II, the class mean was 80 with standard deviation 15. For Exam III, the class mean was 78 with standard deviation 20. Which of the following statements best describes how well Jessica did on these three exams in relation to the rest of the class?

   A. She did equally well on all three exams.
   B. She did equally well on Exam I and Exam II, but better on Exam III.
   C. She did equally well on Exam II and Exam III, but worse on Exam I.
   D. She did best on Exam III and worst on Exam I.
   E. She did best on Exam II and worst on Exam I.

18. A used car dealer is given a commission of $500 per day for each car he sells. The number of cars he sells each day follows this probability distribution:

Cars Sold	0	1	2	3	4
Probability	0.25	0.35	0.20	0.15	0.05

Based on these probabilities, what is the expected average commission that the dealer should receive?

   A. $250
   B. $500
   C. $700
   D. $850
   E. $1000

19. Suppose that random variable X has mean 45 and standard deviation 15, and random variable Y has mean 15 and standard deviation 3. What would be the mean and standard deviation of the random variable $X + Y$?

   A. Mean 30; standard deviation 9
   B. Mean 30; standard deviation 18
   C. Mean 60; standard deviation 9
   D. Mean 60; standard deviation 15.3
   E. Mean 60; standard deviation 18

20. A polling service wants to create a confidence interval for the proportion of support that a candidate has. What is the main reason for taking a large sample size from which the confidence interval will be computed?

   A. To decrease the width of the interval
   B. To increase the confidence level of the interval
   C. To reduce the effect of nonresponse bias
   D. To eliminate the effect of confounding variables
   E. To reduce the effect of untruthful responses

GO ON TO THE NEXT PAGE

21. A DMV test station desires to determine whether people under 18 have a different level of success than people 18 and over in passing the driving test. The following is a two-way contingency chart of a sample of people who attempted the driving test.

	Passed	Did Not Pass
Under 18	145	91
18 and Over	101	63

If a test is done whereby the null hypothesis is that passing the driving test is independent of age, which of the following would represent the expected number of people under 18 who would pass the driving test?

A. $\dfrac{(145)(236)}{400}$

B. $\dfrac{(145)(246)}{400}$

C. $\dfrac{(236)(246)}{400}$

D. $\dfrac{(236)(246)}{145}$

E. $\dfrac{(236+246)}{400}$

22. Which of the following will affect the width of a confidence interval for mean?

I.   The sample size
II. The confidence level that is used
III. Whether the interval is computed as t or z

A. I only
B. II only
C. I and II only
D. I and III only
E. I, II, and III

23. The following boxplots summarize two data sets labeled A and B

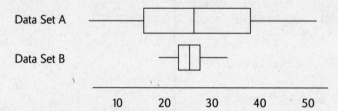

Which of the following is justified by the boxplots?

I.   Data set A contains more values than data set B.
II. Data set A has a wider range than data set B.
III. Data set A has a wider interquartile range than data set B.

A. I only
B. II only
C. I and II only
D. II and III only
E. I, II, and III

24. A member of congress wants to poll voters in his state regarding various national issues. Which of the following methods would be an example of "cluster sampling?"

   A. Use random numbers to select a random sample of 1000 voters from a voter registration list.

   B. Use random numbers to select a random sample of 50 voters from voter registration lists in each of the state's counties.

   C. From the voter registration list, select every 50th name on the list.

   D. Select one random county and poll every registered voter in that county.

   E. Place volunteers in 20 locations throughout the state and have each volunteer question random people for one week.

25. A least-squares regression line was computed that compared the heights, y, in inches for a sample of 50 children, with the ages of the children, x, in months. The regression line was

$$\hat{y} = -1.88 + 0.668x$$
$$48 < x < 84$$

What would be the predicted height for a child who was exactly 6 years old?

   A. 2.1 inches
   B. 38.2 inches
   C. 46.2 inches
   D. 54.8 inches
   E. 110.6 inches

26. A math department in a small high school wants to test the claim that each level of math would typically have an equal number of students. For one particular semester, this was the distribution of students:

Algebra I	Geometry	Algebra II	Trigonometry	Calculus
18	21	25	18	13

What would be the value of the χ^2-statistic related to the null hypothesis that the categories would be equal?

   A. 0.842
   B. 0.908
   C. 3.765
   D. 4.105
   E. 7.818

27. In the 2004 election, George W. Bush is running for re-election as president against the challenger John Kerry. George W. Bush is running with the vice president, Dick Cheney; John Kerry chose John Edwards as his running mate. Which of the following pairs of events are mutually exclusive?

   A. "George W. Bush wins election" and "John Kerry wins election."

   B. "George W. Bush wins election" and "George W. Bush decides to run in election."

   C. "John Kerry wins election" and "John Kerry decides to run in election."

   D. "George W. Bush wins election" and "John Kerry loses election."

   E. "John Kerry wins election" and "John Kerry chose John Edwards as his running mate."

GO ON TO THE NEXT PAGE

28. In a psychological study, a test was performed based on a null hypothesis that $\mu = 175$, tested against the alternate hypothesis that $\mu > 175$. The test was done at a level of significance $\alpha = 0.05$, and the sample statistics yielded a *p*-value of 0.028. However, after the test was done, it was realized that the alternate hypothesis should have been $\mu \neq 175$. What effect does this have on the results?

   A. There is no change in the results. Since $0.028 < 0.05$, the null hypothesis is rejected for both tests.

   B. There is no change in the results. Since $0.028 < 0.05$, the null hypothesis is not rejected for either test.

   C. The results change. Since $2(0.028) > 0.05$, the null hypothesis is rejected, whereas it was not rejected for the alternate hypothesis $\mu > 175$.

   D. The results change. Since $2(0.028) > 0.05$, the null hypothesis is not rejected, whereas it was rejected for the alternate hypothesis $\mu > 175$.

   E. The new results cannot be determined, since the new *p*-value cannot be determined from the information given.

29. The Tri-County Graphics Company is manufacturing a new type of copy machine. The inspection manager wants to estimate the mean amount of time the copier will function before servicing is required and desires to compute a 99% confidence interval for this mean, which is accurate within 1 hour. A pilot study is done, and the standard deviation is estimated to be $\sigma = 30$ hours. How many copy machines should be tested to create the desired confidence interval?

   A. 78

   B. 155

   C. 4870

   D. 5973

   E. 23,889

30. The following is the graph of a normal probability curve:

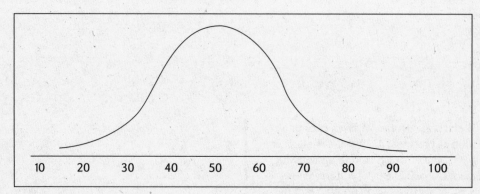

Which of the following is the most likely value for the standard deviation of this distribution?

   A. 5

   B. 10

   C. 15

   D. 20

   E. 30

31. A population of cows has a mean weight of $\mu = 650$ pounds. The weights are also normally distributed with standard deviation $\sigma = 160$. If a sample of 400 cows is taken, what would be the mean and standard deviation of the sample average, $\bar{x}$?

   A.   Mean 32.5; standard deviation 8
   B.   Mean 32.5; standard deviation 160
   C.   Mean 650; standard deviation 0.4
   D.   Mean 650; standard deviation 8
   E.   Mean 650; standard deviation 160

32. A forester has measured a sample of maple trees and found that there is a strong linear relationship between the tree's trunk circumference, x, in inches, and the yearly amount of sap, y, the tree produces in quarts. A least-squares regression line was computed to be $\hat{y} = -37.61 + 0.55x$. Which of the following statements best describes the meaning of the slope of this regression line?

   A.   For each increase of one inch in trunk circumference, the tree will produce an estimated 0.55 quarts of sap.
   B.   For each additional quart of sap the tree produces, the tree is estimated to be 0.55 inch more around in trunk circumference.
   C.   For each increase of one inch in trunk circumference, the tree will produce an estimated 1/0.55 quarts of sap.
   D.   For each increase of one inch in trunk circumference, the tree will produce an estimated 37.61 quarts of sap.
   E.   For each increase of 0.55 inch in trunk circumference, the tree will produce an estimated 37.61 quarts of sap.

33. A contestant on a game show has the opportunity to win a new car. Six cars are on the stage, and the contestant is given the key to one of the cars. The contestant chooses one of the cars, and if the key works, the contestant wins the car. If the contestant does not win, the contestant would again be given a key to one of the six cars, and the winning car may be the same one. If the customer is allowed three chances, what is the probability that the contestant will win one of the cars?

   A.   0.1667
   B.   0.4213
   C.   0.5000
   D.   0.5787
   E.   0.8333

34. For a particular hypothesis test, the null hypothesis is $H_o: \mu = 40$, the alternate hypothesis is $H_a: \mu > 40$, and the level of significance is $\alpha = 0.05$. Which of the following statements best describes the meaning of the power of the test, $1 - \beta$?

   A. $1 - \beta$ = probability of Type II error
   B. $1 - \beta$ = the complement of the probability of rejecting H_o when $\mu = 40$.
   C. $1 - \beta$ = the complement of the probability of not rejecting H_o when $\mu = 40$.
   D. $1 - \beta$ = the complement of the probability of rejecting H_o when $\mu > 40$.
   E. $1 - \beta$ = the complement of the probability of not rejecting H_o when $\mu > 40$.

35. A sample is taken from a normal distribution, and a 90% confidence interval for the mean is created to be [40, 60]. Which of the following statements best describes the meaning of this interval?

   A.   Ninety percent of the sample values are within the interval [40, 60].
   B.   Ninety percent of the values in the population are contained within the interval [40, 60].
   C.   The population mean is 50.
   D.   If additional samples are taken, 90% of the sample means will fall within the interval [40, 60].
   E.   There is a 0.90 probability that the interval [40, 60] contains the true population mean.

36. During a certain time of the year on any given day, there is a 0.60 probability that the island of Kauai will experience rain. If 90 days during this time of year are observed, what is the approximate probability that Kauai will experience at least 60 days of rain?

   A.   0.0000
   B.   0.0595
   C.   0.0808
   D.   0.0985
   E.   0.1190

GO ON TO THE NEXT PAGE

37. A student is a geography class wanted to compare the mean size of states in the United States with the mean size of the provinces of Canada. The student took the average land area of all 50 states of the United States and the average land area of all 10 provinces of Canada and computed a *t*-statistic for a test comparing means from two independent samples. Which of the following can be valid reasons for stating that the student's procedure was an inappropriate approach in this context?

   I.   Since the distributions of the land areas are not normally distributed, it is invalid to use the *t*-distribution.

   II. Since all the states and provinces are taken in the sample, a hypothesis test is not necessary, since the population means are known.

   III. The land areas of the states and provinces are not independent.

   A.   I only
   B.   II only
   C.   I and II only
   D.   I and III only
   E.   I, II, and III

38. Which of the following is an advantage of using a stratified sample instead of a simple random sample?

   A.   In a stratified sample, each member of the population is equally likely to be chosen in the sample.
   B.   In a stratified sample, certain groups of interest are guaranteed to be represented in the sample.
   C.   A stratified sample can be done with a smaller sample size.
   D.   A stratified sample is easier to create than a simple random sample.
   E.   Significance tests cannot be done with a simple random sample.

39. Gasotrek is an engine additive that is meant to improve gasoline mileage for automobiles. In order to test whether there is evidence that Gasotrek is effective, the gas mileage for a sample of 200 automobiles is measured, and then the gas mileage is measured for each with Gasotrek added. If μ_1 is the true mean gas mileage of automobiles with no additive, and μ_2 is the true mean gas mileage of automobiles with Gasotrek, what would be the most appropriate null and alternate hypotheses for this study?

   A. $H_o: \mu_2 - \mu_1 = 0$ $H_a: \mu_2 - \mu_1 > 0$
   B. $H_o: \mu_2 - \mu_1 = 0$ $H_a: \mu_2 - \mu_1 \neq 0$
   C. $H_o: \mu_2 - \mu_1 = 0$ $H_a: \mu_2 - \mu_1 < 0$
   D. $H_o: \mu_2 - \mu_1 > 0$ $H_a: \mu_2 - \mu_1 = 0$
   E. $H_o: \mu_2 - \mu_1 < 0$ $H_a: \mu_2 - \mu_1 = 0$

40. Crestor is a medication used to lower the LDL cholesterol level of patients using it. A sample of patients were prescribed Crestor and instructed to use it for six weeks. Their LDL cholesterol levels were measured before the six weeks and again at the end of the six weeks. These were the results:

Patient	LDL before the six weeks	LDL after the six weeks
Porter	172	88
Scott	219	158
Garcia	128	78
Auerbach	133	101
Money	214	176
May	294	166
Lahoud	108	101
Briggs	328	156
Colborn	122	51

What is the degrees of freedom for the appropriate paired *t*-test associated with this data?

   A.   2
   B.   7
   C.   8
   D.   9
   E.   17

Section II

Time: 1 hour and 30 minutes   Number of questions: 6   Percent of total grade: 50%

Part A

Questions 1–5   Spend about 65 minutes on this part of the exam.   Percent of Section II grade: 75%

Show all your work. Clearly indicate the methods you use—you will be graded on the correctness of your methods as well as the accuracy of your results and explanation.

1. The department head of a mathematics department has taken data from the instructors in the department to observe the correlation between the number of homework assignments the instructors give for a course and the average course grade for the students. The following is a plot of the residuals for this study:

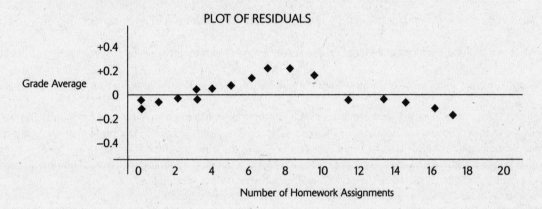

a. Based on the plot of residuals, describe the strength of linear relationship between Number of Homework Assignments and Grade Average. What would be a likely value for the correlation coefficient, *r?* Explain answer.

b. Based on the plot of residuals, describe the effect that Number of Homework Assignments has on student grades.

c. Based on the plot of residuals, about how many homework assignments should an instructor give, to maximize student grade average? Explain answer.

GO ON TO THE NEXT PAGE

2. The Science Division for a state university system has broken down the majors into the following categories:

	Math	*Biology*	*Chemistry*	*Physics*	*Computers*
Men	0.113	0.071	0.065	0.091	0.121
Women	0.127	0.066	0.072	0.099	0.175

Assume that there are no double majors.

a. What is the probability that a student is a chemistry major, given that the student is a woman?

b. What is the probability that a student is a biology major, given that the student is a man?

c. What is the probability that a student is a woman, given that the student is a computers major?

d. What is the probability that a student is a man, given that the student is a biology major?

e. What is the probability that a student is either a woman or a math major?

f. Are the events "man" and "computers major" independent events? Justify your answer.

3. The Data Information Analysis department for a large corporation has to process records for their marketing database. In order to meet the demands of the company, the 71 employees of the Data Information Analysis department need to average 60 records per day. If it is shown that this department is averaging fewer than 60 records per day, the department will be put on formal report. On one particular day, the total number of records processed was 4024, and the standard deviation among the records was computed to be 9.855.

a. Describe an appropriate hypothesis test that the company would use to determine whether to put the Data Information Analysis department on report.

b. Based on the information given in the sample, what conclusion would the company make regarding whether to put the Data Information Analysis department on report?

c. What is the p-value associated with the data given in this sample in relation to the appropriate hypothesis test? How might the manager of the Data Information Analysis department explain the p-value so as not to be put on report?

4. Suppose that the Braxton School of Law wants to design an entrance exam for admission. They want to design the exam at the proper level of difficulty so as to screen out less qualified applicants yet allow well-qualified applicants to pass. To achieve this goal, they desire that the passing rate be approximately 60%. In their first year of requiring the entrance exam, 109 out of 157 applicants passed the exam.

a. Describe an appropriate hypothesis test that would test whether the entrance exam has been set at the proper level of difficulty.

b. Based on the data and a level of significance $\alpha = 0.05$, is there evidence to show that the entrance exam has not been set at the proper level of difficulty?

c. Does the exam need to be modified? If so, how?

5. A maternity study wants to determine whether there is evidence that childbirths occur with greater frequency during certain times of the year, as opposed to being balanced throughout the year. To conduct this study, a hospital in Ames, Iowa, has been chosen, and the number of births during the year were recorded in this chart:

January	44
February	41
March	43
April	52
May	55
June	47
July	52
August	61
September	66
October	64
November	58
December	53

a. Describe an appropriate hypothesis test for a study that would use this data.

b. Is there enough evidence, at an $\alpha = 0.05$ level of significance, to conclude that childbirths do not occur equally throughout the year?

c. What are some confounding factors that may have affected this study?

GO ON TO THE NEXT PAGE

Part B

Question 6   Spend about 25 minutes on this part of the exam.   Percent of Section II grade: 25%

Directions for Part B: Allow additional time for this part. Clearly indicate the methods that you use and give clear explanations for all your results.

6. Suppose that it has been estimated that the weights for a population of New World Capuchin monkeys follow an approximate normal distribution, with mean $\mu = 11$ kilograms, and standard deviation $\sigma = 2.5$ kilograms. From a sample of 100 Capuchin monkeys, the sample mean was 12.15 kilograms, with sample standard deviation 2.168 kilograms. Furthermore, a boxplot of the sample data follows:

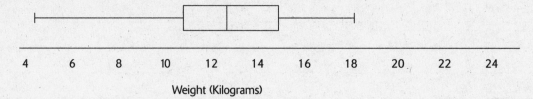

Weight (Kilograms)

a. It is indicated that the population of the monkey weights follows an "approximate normal distribution." What are some realistic factors that prevent these weights from following a true normal distribution?

b. Describe two ways, from the information given, that outliers can be detected in the sample data set. Which of the two ways has indicated that the data set contains an outlier?

c. It was estimated that the true mean for the population is $\mu = 11$ kilograms. Describe a way that this estimate can be tested. Discuss whether a t-test or a z-test should be used.

d. Is there evidence, at an $\alpha = 0.05$ level of significance, that the estimate of $\mu = 11$ kilograms was not an accurate estimate?

e. What is the p-value for the test statistic computed in part **d**? What assumptions may affect the calculation of the p-value?

Section I Answers

1. **C.** The statement that the "error" is 3% represents the error in a confidence interval for proportion, in this case in the form $.47 \pm 0.03$. Therefore, there is a high probability that the true proportion would be contained within this interval—in other words, within .03 of the sample proportion .47.

2. **D.** The expected number of successful calls per hour for the telemarketer is computed by the formula $E(X) = \Sigma x \cdot P(X = x) = (0)(0.25) + (1)(0.20) + (2)(0.20) + (3)(0.15) + (4)(0.10) + (5)(0.05) + (6)(0.05) = 2$. Therefore, the expected commission, for each 8-hour day, at a payment of \$3 for each successful call is $(8)(3)(2) = \$48$.

3. **C.** It is appropriate to compute t-intervals when the sample size is small and when the population standard deviation is unknown. However, for the t-distribution to apply, the assumption is made that the underlying population is normal or near normal. Since Social Security digits are uniform, or near-uniform random variables, and not near-normal, the t-distribution would not apply.

4. **E.** Probability is a value that represents the likelihood that a single event will occur. It has nothing to do with what has been observed, or what will be observed. Therefore, probability 0.75 means that there is a 0.75 likelihood that a single event will occur.

5. **B.** To qualify, the score must be at least 675. The z-score corresponding to 675 would be given by $z = (675 - 500)/(100) = 1.75$. The probability of exceeding $z = 1.75$ in the normal distribution is 0.0401, or approximately 4%.

6. **D.** If the probability of a blackout occurring in 1 hour is 0.02, with the cost of a blackout being \$200, the expected value of the cost for 1 hour is \$4. Therefore, the expected cost for a 24-hour period for one machine is $(4)(24) = \$96$, as the machine may break down more than once. So, for three machines, the expected value would be $(3)(96) = \$288$.

7. **D.** The degrees of freedom is 39. The 90% confidence interval would be of the form $x \pm ts/\sqrt{n} = 21.2 \pm (1.685)(5.9)/\sqrt{40} = 21.2 \pm 1.57$.

8. **E.** The slope of the regression line is $b_1 = -6.725$. From the regression results, the standard deviation of the slope is $s_{b_1} = 0.54940$ found in the chart as "stdev" for Workers. With degrees of freedom $= (\text{sample size} - 2) = (27 - 2) = 25$, the 95% confidence interval would be $(-6.725) \pm (2.060)(0.54940) = -6.725 \pm 1.132$.

9. **C.** The objective is to test whether the average amount of time that fish will last will be six days. If the fish lasts more than six days, the preservative is still successful. Failure of the preservative would occur if the average was less than six days. Therefore, the null hypothesis should be $\mu = 6$ days, tested against the alternate hypothesis $\mu < 6$ days.

10. **C.** In order to compare scores with the performance of the rest of the class, z-scores should be computed. The z-score for Exam I was $z = (85-77)/(16) = 0.50$. The z-score for Exam II was $z = (85-75)/(20) = 0.50$. The z-score for Exam III was $z = (85-72)/(15) = 0.867$. In comparing z-scores, Ashley did equally well on Exam I and Exam II, but better on Exam III.

11. **E.** It is possible to reject the null hypothesis at $\alpha = 0.05$, but not at $\alpha = 0.01$, if the p-value of the test statistic is a value between 0.05 and 0.01. It is possible to reject the null hypothesis for a one-tail test of level α, but not a two-tail test of level α, if the p-value of the one-tail test is less than α, but greater than $\alpha/2$. It is possible to reject the null hypothesis as a z-test, but not as a t-test, if the value of the standardized test statistic exceeds the critical z-value, but not the corresponding critical t-value, which is possible since the critical t-value is always greater than the corresponding z-value for any degrees of freedom. It is possible reject the null hypothesis for an upper-tail test, but not the lower-tail test, provided the test statistic is an extreme positive value. However, if the process and level of a test are the same, computing a p-value and comparing the test statistic to the appropriate critical value would produce the same result.

12. **C.** The objective is to test whether the average wattage of the lightbulbs is 75 watts. Failure would occur if the average is either too high or too low. Therefore, the null hypothesis should be $\mu = 75$ watts, tested against the alternate hypothesis $\mu \neq 75$ watts.

13. B. The cutoff for the bottom 5%, for a normal distribution, would be 1.645 standard deviations below the mean. Therefore, the cutoff for the bottom 5% would be $12.00 - (1.645)(0.13) = 11.79$ inches.

14. D. If two events are independent, this implies that if one event occurs, the probability of the other event does not change. This also implies that the conditional probabilities $P(A \mid B) = P(A)$ and $P(B \mid A) = P(B)$ are the case. Also, for independent events, $P(A \text{ and } B) = P(A)P(B)$. However, $P(A \text{ or } B) = P(A) + P(B) - P(A \text{ and } B)$, provided $P(A \text{ and } B)$ is nonzero. Since $P(A \text{ and } B) = P(A)P(B)$, $P(A \text{ and } B)$ can only be 0 if either $P(A)$ or $P(B)$ is 0.

15. C. For both plots, the points appear to be randomly placed, while approximately fitting the zero line. Therefore, both plots exhibit relationships that are linear.

16. E. If two events are mutually exclusive, both events cannot occur at the same time, or equivalently $P(A \text{ and } B) = 0$. Also, this would imply that the conditional probabilities, $P(A \mid B)$ and $P(B \mid A)$ would both be 0. Moreover, since $P(A \text{ and } B) = 0$, $P(A \text{ or } B) = P(A) + P(B) - P(A \text{ and } B) = P(A) + P(B)$. However, it is not necessarily true that $P(A) = 1 - P(B)$ unless A and B are complements of each other.

17. E. For Exam I, her z-score was $(90 - 85)/10 = 0.5$. For Exam II, her z-score was $(90 - 80)/15 = 0.667$. For Exam III, her z-score was $(90 - 78)/20 = 0.6$. Based on the z-scores, her best exam was Exam II, and her worst was Exam I.

18. C. The expected number of sales per day is $(0)(0.25) + (1)(0.35) + (2)(0.20) + (3)(0.15) + (4)(0.05) = 1.4$. Therefore, at \$500 per sale, the expected commission would be $(500)(1.4) = \$700$.

19. D. The mean of the sum of two random variables would be the sum of the respective means, or $45 + 15 = 60$. In terms of the standard deviation of the sum of two random variables, the variance of the sum is the sum of the two variances. Therefore, the variance of the sum would be $15^2 + 3^2 = 234$. The standard deviation would be $\sqrt{234}$, which is approximately 15.3.

20. A. Since the formula for a confidence interval for proportion is given by $p \pm z \sqrt{\dfrac{(p)(1-p)}{n}}$, the main purpose of a large sample size is to create an interval that has a low margin of error, whereby the interval would have a narrow width.

21. C. The expected value for a value in a two-way contingency chart is found by (row total)(column total)/(grand total) $= (236)(246)/(400)$.

22. E. Since a confidence interval for mean is of the form $x \pm z\sigma/\sqrt{n}$, or $x \pm ts/\sqrt{n}$, the width of the interval will be affected by the magnitude of the sample size, n, as well as by the confidence level, which determines the value of z or t that is used. Furthermore, since t values are larger than z values, whether or not the interval is computed as z or t will also affect the width.

23. D. The boxplot for data set A is wider, overall, indicating a wider range. Also, the "box" portion of the boxplot for data set A is wider, indicating a wider interquartile range, or IQR. However, boxplots do not indicate the sample sizes for the sets they are based upon.

24. D. Cluster sampling is a process whereby a portion of the population is selected, and all values from that portion are taken as the sample. This is achieved in the case whereby a single county is used, in its entirety, as the sample in question.

25. C. To find the predicted height, $\hat{y}$, for a child who is 6 years old, or equivalently, 72 months old, solve the regression equation $\hat{y} = -1.88 + (0.668)(72)$, giving 46.2.

26. D. The null hypothesis, in this case, is that the categories are equal. Therefore, the expected value for each category is 19. The χ^2 test statistic is given by $\chi^2 = \Sigma (O - E)^2/E = (18 - 19)^2/19 + (21 - 19)^2/19 + (25 - 19)^2/19 + (18 - 19)^2/19 + (13 - 19)^2/19 = 4.105$.

27. A. For two events to be mutually exclusive, the events cannot both occur at the same time. Since it is not possible for both George W. Bush and John Kerry to win the election, the events of each winning would be mutually exclusive. For each of the other pairs of events, it is possible for both to occur at the same time.

28. D. For the one-tail test, the p-value was 0.028. Since the p-value was less than the level $\alpha = 0.05$, the null hypothesis is rejected. However, for the two-tail test, the p-value becomes $2(0.028) = 0.056$. Since this p-value is not less than the level $\alpha = 0.05$, the null hypothesis is not rejected.

29. D. To compute the minimum sample size required to create a 99% confidence interval, with error = 1, and estimated $\sigma = 30$, the minimum sample size would be given by $n \geq (z\sigma/E)^2 = ((2.576)(30)/(1))^2 = 5972.1984$, or 5973 copy machines, rounded up to the nearest whole number.

30. B. For this curve, the mean appears to be approximately 50. For the normal distribution, approximately 68% of the area lies within one standard deviation of the mean. Based on the curve, this would be approximately the range 40 to 60, or an estimated standard deviation of 10.

31. D. For a sample of size, n, taken from a normal distribution with mean μ and standard deviation σ, the sample average, $\bar{x}$, will also follow a normal distribution, and have mean μ and standard deviation $\sigma/\sqrt{n}$. Therefore, the mean of the sample average would be 650, and the standard deviation of the sample average would be $160/\sqrt{400} = 8$.

32. A. For a least-squares regression equation $\hat{y} = b_0 + b_1 x$, the meaning of the slope, b_1, is that for each increase in one unit of x, the value of y will be increased by b_1 units, or the effect will be a corresponding decrease if b_1 is negative. Therefore, for each increase of 1 inch in trunk circumference, the sap output of the tree will be increased by 0.55 quarts.

33. B. The probability of winning the car on one attempt is 1/6. Since the key to the winning car is randomly chosen, with replacement, for each attempt, the probability remains 1/6. Therefore, the probability of not winning on a given attempt is 5/6. Therefore, the probability of winning in three attempts is $1 - P(\text{not winning}) = 1 - (5/6)^3 = 0.4213$.

34. E. The power of a test is the complement of the probability of failing to reject a null hypothesis when that null hypothesis is, in actuality, false. Therefore, the power, $1 - \beta$, is the complement of the probability of not rejecting the claim that $\mu = 40$ when the true mean, μ, is greater than 40.

35. E. A 90% confidence interval for population mean is constructed so that there is a 0.90 probability that the interval will contain, within it, the true mean, μ. Therefore, there is a 0.90 probability that the true mean is contained within the interval [40, 60].

36. E. For a binomial distribution with $n = 90$ and $p = 0.60$, the distribution will be approximately normally distributed with mean $\mu = np = (90)(0.60) = 54$ and $\sigma = \sqrt{npq} = \sqrt{(90)(0.60)(0.40)} = 4.64758$. The probability of 60 or more can be estimated by finding the probability of exceeding 59.5 with normal probabilities, by the appropriate continuity correction. The z-score is $z = (59.5 - 54)/(4.64758) = 1.18$. Therefore, the estimated probability is 0.1190. Using $1 - \text{binomial} f(90, 0.6, 59)$ gives 0.1176.

37. E. First, since the size of one of the data sets is 10, and the distribution of the land sizes is likely not normally distributed, the conditions for using the t-distribution are not met. Second, since the entire populations are taken into the samples, the means would be population means, and have no variation. Third, since the two nations are contiguous, sharing borders, it can also be argued that the land sizes of the states and provinces are not independent.

38. B. The main purpose of a stratified sample is to divide the population into groups, called strata, so that each stratum has members represented in the sample. It is the simple random sample that allows each member of the population to have an equal probability of being selected. Both types of samples can be done with any sample size, and significance tests can be done with both. Moreover, it is often that the stratified sample is more difficult to collect.

39. A. If the Gasotrek is considered effective, its mean, μ_2, should be greater than the mean without, μ_1. Therefore, the desired result is that $\mu_2 > \mu_1$. Furthermore, since it is desired that there be evidence in favor of this result, this should be the alternate hypothesis.

40. C. The degrees of freedom for a paired t-test is (number of pairs $- 1$) = $(9 - 1) = 8$.

Section II Answers

1a. Since the plot of residuals follows a fairly distinct nonlinear pattern, this would be an indicator that the original points themselves are following a nonlinear pattern. Specifically, the residuals are exhibiting an approximate parabolic shape, which would be an indicator that the original points are following a fairly strong nonlinear relationship. This would show that the correlation between Number of Homework Assignments and Grade Average is strongly nonlinear, implying that the strength of linear correlation would be very weak, if any at all. This would be shown by a correlation coefficient, r, that is near 0. Possible correlation coefficients could be -0.1, -0.05, 0.05, or 0.1. It is unlikely that the correlation coefficient would be exactly 0, since this would imply that the points follow an exact nonlinear pattern.

1b. Firstly, since the correlation is near 0, it is likely that the regression line is approximately level, whereby the slope of the regression line, b_o, is near 0. With an approximately parabolic relationship between Number of Homework Assignments and Grade Average, it appears that low number of homework assignments and high number of homework assignments leads to the lowest grades. A moderate number of homework assignments would lead to the highest grade averages.

1c. It appears that the highest positive residuals are in the 7 to 8 range. This implies that the grade averages are the highest above the regression line at these points. With the regression line being approximately level, due to the extremely weak strength of linear correlation, it is highly likely that the actual grade averages will be maximized at these points.

2a. $P(\text{Chemistry major} \mid \text{Woman}) = P(\text{Chemistry major and Woman})/P(\text{Woman}) = (0.072)/(0.539) = 0.1336$.

2b. $P(\text{Biology major} \mid \text{Man}) = P(\text{Biology major and Man})/P(\text{Man}) = (0.071)/(0.461) = 0.1540$.

2c. $P(\text{Woman} \mid \text{Computers major}) = P(\text{Woman and Computers major})/P(\text{Computers major}) = (0.175)/(0.296) = 0.5912$.

2d. $P(\text{Man} \mid \text{Biology major}) = P(\text{Man and Biology major})/P(\text{Biology major}) = (0.071)/(0.137) = 0.5182$.

2e. $P(\text{Woman or Math major}) = P(\text{Woman}) + P(\text{Math major}) - P(\text{Woman and Math major}) = (0.539) + (0.240) - (0.127) = 0.6520$.

2f. For events A and B to be independent, it has to hold that $P(A \text{ and } B) = P(A)P(B)$. $P(\text{Man}) = 0.461$, and $P(\text{Computers major}) = 0.296$. $P(\text{Man})P(\text{Computers major}) = (0.461)(0.296) = 0.136456$. However, since $P(\text{Man and Computers major}) = 0.121$, the events "Man" and "Computers major" are not independent events.

3a. Since it is desired to determine whether there is evidence that the department is averaging less than the goal of 60 records per day, the appropriate hypothesis test would be a t-test of one sample, with null hypothesis H_o: $\mu = 60$ records, tested against the alternate hypothesis H_a: $\mu < 60$ records. Since the true standard deviation is unknown, the test statistic would be $t = (x - 60)/(s/\sqrt{n})$, where n, in this case, is 71. The rejection region would be a lower-tail t rejection based on 70 degrees of freedom, and a preselected level of significance, α. If no level, α, has been selected, the p-value can be computed.

3b. Based on the data, the observed sample mean is $\bar{x} = (4024)/(71) = 56.67605$ records per employee. The t-statistic is $t = (56.67605 - 60)/(9.855/\sqrt{71}) = -2.842$. With level of significance $\alpha = 0.01$, and degrees of freedom 70, the t-rejection region would be $t < -2.381$, showing that null hypothesis would be rejected for even a very low level of significance, α. Rejection of the null hypothesis, in this case, would imply that the average is significantly less than 60 records per day, showing evidence that the department is not reaching the specified goal and should be put on report.

3c. The p-value associated with this test statistic is 0.0029. The meaning of this p-value is that there is a 0.0029 probability that the department would have produced this low number of records per employee, by randomness, whereas the true mean is, in actuality, 60 records per day. The manager must explain that, while such an observation would be very rare if the true mean was 60 records per day, it is still possible. The department must have been observed on a bad day, and the manager may request that the department be observed again, with another sample taken.

4a. Since it is desired that the entrance exam have an approximate 60% passing rate, and that the difficulty level be neither too high nor too low, a test of proportion can be done, whereby the null hypothesis is H_o: $p = 0.60$, tested against the alternate hypothesis H_a: $p \neq 0.60$. Since the sample size is large enough, with $npq = (157)(0.60)(0.40) = 37.68 \geq 10$, the test statistic can be $z = (\hat{p} - 0.60)/\sqrt{\frac{(0.60)(0.40)}{n}}$. The corresponding z-rejection region would be two-tailed, with the critical value being determined by a preselected level of significance, α. If no level, α, has been selected, the p-value can be computed. (An alternative method for determining adequate sample size is to make sure both np and $n(1 - p)$ are greater than 5.)

4b. Based on the sample, whereby 109 out of 157 applicants passed the exam, the observed sample proportion was $\hat{p} = 109/157$, producing a z-test statistic $z = ((109/157) - 0.60)/\sqrt{\frac{(0.60)(0.40)}{(157)}} = 2.411$. At an $\alpha = 0.05$ level of significance, the two-tailed rejection region cutoff would be $z > 1.960$ or $z < -1.960$. Therefore, the null hypothesis is rejected, and there is evidence that the true proportion for the passing rate of the entrance exam is not 60%. The exam is not set at the proper difficulty level.

4c. Since the hypothesis test showed that the passing rate for the entrance exam was not 60%, as hoped for, the exam needs to be modified. Furthermore, since the observed proportion, $\hat{p}$, was approximately 69%, the passing rate is also too high. The entrance exam needs to be made more difficult so as to lower the passing rate.

5a. An appropriate hypothesis test would be a χ^2 goodness-of-fit test whereby the null hypothesis is H_o: Childbirths occur equally by month, tested against the alternate hypothesis, H_a: Childbirths do not occur equally by month. Since there are a total of $n = 636$ childbirths in the entire sample, the expected values would be $636/12 = 53$ childbirths per month. A minor adjustment could be made, noting that there are slight differences in the lengths of the months, between 31, 30, 28, or even 29 days. The χ^2-test statistic would be $\Sigma(O - E)^2/E$, where the observed values are those given in the chart, compared with the expected values of 53. The rejection region, depending on the level of significance, α, would be an upper-tail χ^2 rejection, whereby large differences between the observed values and the expected values would result in a larger χ^2 value. The degrees of freedom would be the number of categories $- 1 = 11$, and rejection of the null hypothesis would imply that childbirths do not occur equally by month and are, therefore, not balanced throughout the year.

5b. For this data, the χ^2-test statistic is $\chi^2 = \Sigma(O - E)^2/E = (44 - 53)^2/53 + (41 - 53)^2/53 + (43 - 53)^2/53 + (52 - 53)^2/53 + (55 - 53)^2/53 + (47 - 53)^2/53 + (52 - 53)^2/53 + (61 - 53)^2/53 + (66 - 53)^2/53 + (64 - 53)^2/53 + (58 - 53)^2/53 + (53 - 53)^2/53 = 14.075$. The χ^2-rejection region, based on an $\alpha = 0.05$ level of significance, and 11 degrees of freedom, is $\chi^2 > 19.675$. The conclusion is that the null hypothesis is not rejected, implying that there is not sufficient evidence to show that childbirths do not occur equally by month and, thus, not showing that childbirths do not occur in a balanced fashion throughout the year.

5c. Some confounding factors, besides the minor variation in the lengths of the months, would include location of the city. Cities with different climate patterns may have dramatic differences in the pattern of pregnancies and, thus, childbirths during the course of the year. For example, cities in colder climates, which see distinct changes in seasons, may have different patterns of childbirths throughout the year, whereas warmer climates, with relatively few changes in seasons, may see little variation in childbirths. Another confounding factor may be the location of the hospital, or even the fact that the records are taken from hospital records, which would exclude nonhospital childbirths. Also, the type of city itself may affect the incidence of childbirths during the year, whether the area is urban, rural, suburban, wealthy, or even located in farming areas or industrial regions, all of which may affect the behaviors of the people living in the region.

6a. Realistic factors that may prevent a population of weights from being truly normal may include the fact that even if the population is extremely large, it is still finite, thus not being an infinite population. Also, various spikes and gaps in the actual weights in the population may prevent the weights from following a truly smooth normal curve. Symmetry may be affected, in that weights may be slightly more spread out above the mean, while being less common considerably below the mean, especially as the weight measurements approach 0. Furthermore, it is impossible for the weights to follow a truly normal curve, since the normal curve is infinite in both directions, whereas true weights cannot exist below 0, and extremely large weights, at some point, become no longer possible.

6b. One way an outlier is defined is by the standard deviation. Values that lie more than two standard deviations either above or below the mean are commonly considered outliers. Another way that outliers are detected is by the "fence" method. Based on the interquartile range, IQR, the difference between the third quartile cutoff, Q_3, and the first quartile cutoff, Q_1, a value is considered an outlier if it lies either below the "lower fence" determined by $Q_1 - (1.5)(IQR)$, or above the "upper fence" determined by $Q_3 + (1.5)(IQR)$. Based on the boxplot, it appears that Q_1 is approximately 10.5, and Q_3 is approximately 14.5, implying that the IQR is approximately 4. The lower fence would be $10.5 - 6 = 4.5$, and the upper fence would be $14.5 + 6 = 20.5$. Since the boxplot shows that there is a value just above 4, it appears that this data set contains an outlier, as determined by the "fence" method. Based on the sample mean and standard deviation, two standard deviations below the mean would be $12.15 - 2(2.168) = 7.814$; there clearly is an outlier, again, since there is a value near 4.

6c. The estimated mean can be tested using a t-test of one mean, whereby the null hypothesis is H_o: $\mu = 11$ kilograms, tested against the alternate hypothesis H_a: $\mu \neq 11$ kilograms. The t-test is likely more appropriate, since the test is still whether the distribution has the stated normal distribution. The z-test should only be done if it has been confirmed that the true standard deviation is actually known to be $\sigma = 2.5$ kilograms. It seems, from the context, that the standard deviation is only claimed to be 2.5 and that it has not been confirmed. As a t-test, the test statistic would be $t = (\bar{x} - 12)/(s/\sqrt{n})$, and the rejection region would be a two-tailed rejection region, whose critical value would be determined by the degrees of freedom, in this case, sample size $- 1 = 99$, and a preselected level of significance, α.

6d. Based on the data, the t-test would be $t = (12.15 - 11)/(2.168/\sqrt{100}) = 5.304$. The t-rejection region, based on 99 degrees of freedom, and level $\alpha = 0.05$, would be $t > 1.984$ or $t < -1.984$. Therefore, there is evidence to show that the true mean is not $\mu = 11$ kilograms. Note also, that even if the test is done as a z-test, with $z = (12.15 - 11)/(2.5/\sqrt{100}) = 4.600$, and rejection region $z > 1.960$ or $z < -1.960$, the result is still rejection of the null hypothesis.

6e. Assuming that the test statistic is a t-statistic, the p-value is 6.9×10^{-7} or .0000. If the test statistic is a z-statistic, the p-value is 4.2×10^{-6} or .0000. Although, in both cases, the p-value was negligibly 0, the p-values will differ, depending on whether the statistic is computed against a t-distribution or a standard normal distribution, which are similar but different. Other assumptions that affect the value of the p-value is whether the test is done as a one-tail test or a two-tail test, and whether a sample standard deviation, s, or an assumed true standard deviation, σ, is used in computing the test statistic in the first place.

Glossary

5-number summary minimum value, q1, median, q3, and maximum value for a data set

68-95-99.7 Rule *see* **Empirical Rule**

Alpha the symbol that represents the probability of making a type I error (α)

Alternate hypothesis the complement of the null hypothesis; contains a statement of inequality: $\neq$, $>$, or $<$; denoted by H_a

Back-to-back stemplots two stemplots back-to-back with the same stem, allowing for distribution comparisons

Bar chart a graph in which bars are used to display categories' frequencies

Before-and-after test a t-test for dependent samples or paired differences

Bell-shaped describes a distribution in which values cluster near the center of it, like a normal distribution

Bias the consistent underestimation or overestimation of a true value

Bimodal a characteristic of data that has two modes

Binomial experiment an experiment consisting of a fixed number n observations, that each independently succeed with a probability p or fail with a probability of $1 - p$.

Binomial formula $P(X = k) = \binom{n}{k} p^k (1 - p)^{n-k}$

Binomial probabilities probabilities associated with binomial experiments

Bivariate data involving two variables arranged in pairs

Blinding a procedure in which subjects do not know whether they are receiving the treatment or a placebo

Block a group of subjects with similar characteristics that might affect the outcome of an experiment; part of an experimental structure to compensate for known variables

Blocking a technique of dividing subjects using blocks in experimental design

Box and whisker plot five-number summary in graphical form; each number is indicated on a number line, and a box is drawn encompassing Q1 to Q3; lines called whiskers extend to the maximum and minimum values from Q1 and Q3.

Boxplot *see* **Box and whisker plot**

Categorical data data separated into categories based on nonnumeric characteristics

Census data set from all members of a population

Central Limit Theorem states that a sample mean's sampling distribution approximates normal as the sample size increases

Central tendency the mean, median, and mode of a set of data

Chi-Square Distribution denoted by χ^2

Chi-square goodness-of-fit test an inferential test that shows whether or not a frequency distribution fits an expected, or claimed, distribution

Chi-square test for homogeneity of proportions   used to test the claim that several proportions are equal when samples are taken from different populations

Chi-square test for independence   determines whether two variables are dependent or independent within a stated level of significance

Class boundaries   the point half-way between the midpoints of adjacent classes in a frequency distribution

Class width   the difference between two consecutive lower bounds in a frequency distribution

Coefficient of determination (r^2)   measures how much variation in the response variable is caused by regression on the explanatory variable

Coefficient of variation (CV)   the ratio of the standard deviation and the mean written as a percent

Complementary events   two events whose probabilities add up to 1; $P(E') = 1 - P(E)$

Completely randomized design   a technique used in experimental design in which each subject has the same chance of belonging to the different treatment groups

Conditional probability   the probability of some event occurring, given that some other event has already occurred

Confidence interval   an interval likely to contain a population value given a confidence level; estimate $\pm$ margin of error

Confidence level   probability that the constructed interval will contain the population value

Confounding   results when the effects of two or more variables cannot be distinguished from each other

Contingency table   a table listing outcomes of two categorical variables, one as the row variable and the other as the column variable

Continuous random variable   a random variable with continuous (infinite) data values; takes all values in an interval

Control chart   a chart used to determine whether data is reasonable and whether processes are producing unstable data

Control group   treated identically to all other groups with the exception that they do not receive the actual treatment

Convenience sample   a sample of individuals chosen for ease of selection

Correction for continuity   adjustments made when using continuous data to approximate discrete data

Correlation coefficient (r)   measures the strength of the linear relationship between two quantitative variables;

$$r = \frac{1}{n-1} \sum_{i-1}^{n} \left(\frac{x_i - \overline{x}}{s_x} \right) \left(\frac{y_i - \overline{y}}{s_y} \right)$$

Critical region   *see* **Rejection region**

Critical value   separates the rejection region from the nonrejection region

Cumulative frequency   the sum of the frequencies for all classes less than or equal to a given class

Cumulative frequency chart   a graph of cumulative frequencies of a set of data

Data   information derived from measurements, observations, counts, or responses

Degrees of freedom   number of independent data points in a distribution; $d.f. = n - 1$

Density curve   describes the probability distribution of continuous random variables

Dependent events   a set of events in which the occurrence of one event changes the probability of another event

Descriptive statistics   examining data analytically and graphically; techniques to describe and document data

Deviation   the difference between a value and the mean

Discrete probability distribution   lists each possible value the random variable can assume, along with the probability for that value; the probability for each value of the discrete random variable must be between 0 and 1, inclusive: $0 \le P(x) \le 1$; and the sum of all the probabilities is 1: $\Sigma P(x) = 1$

Discrete random variable   random variable with discrete data values

Dotplot   graph with data values plotted as dots above their corresponding values on a number line

Double blind   experimental design in which neither the subjects nor the experimental administrators know which treatment a subject received

Empirical probability   uses the results of a probability experiment

Empirical Rule   in a normal distribution, about 68% of terms are within one standard deviation of the mean, about 95% are within two, and about 99.7% are within three.

Error of estimate   *see* **Margin of error**

Estimation   sample data are used to estimate the value of unknown population parameters

Event   one or more outcomes and is a subset of the sample space

Expected frequency   a calculated frequency (count or value) obtained assuming that the null hypothesis is true; denoted by E; the product of the sample size, n, and the assumed probability for that category: $(E_i = np_i)$

Expected value   discrete random variable's mean value

Experiment   a researcher imposes and controls one or more treatment variables and measures the responses

Experimental unit   subject in an experiment

Explanatory variable   a variable that explains changes in a response variable; treatment variable; independent variable

Finite correction factor $\sqrt{\dfrac{N-n}{N-1}}$

Five-number summary   *see* **5-number summary**

Frequency distribution   a list of data values with their corresponding frequencies

Geometric distribution   independent observations that succeed at the same probability, p; the number of trials needed until first success is variable of interest

Goodness-of-fit test   *see* **Chi-square goodness-of-fit test**

Homogeneity of proportions   *see* **Chi-square test for homogeneity of proportions**

Hypothesis testing   procedure where samples are used to determine the likelihood that a claim about a population parameter is true

Independent   describes an event whose outcome does not affect another event's outcome; describes a variable that causes, or influences, another variable

Independent events   one event's occurrence does not change the probability of another event's occurrence; $P(A) = P(A|B)$

Inferential statistics   using sample data to make inferences about populations

Influential point   point that dramatically affects the slope and/or y-intercept of the least-squares line

Interquartile range   the third quartile value minus the first quartile value; middle 50% of the data

IQR   *see* **Interquartile range**

Law of large numbers   as the number of times one performs a probability experiment increases, the resulting empirical probability (what did happen) will approach the theoretical probability (what should happen)

Least-squares regression line   the line that minimizes the sum of squared errors from the line

Left-tailed test   hypothesis test to use if the alternate hypothesis, H_a, contains a less-than symbol (<); H_a:$\mu < k$

Level of confidence   *see* **Confidence level**

Lurking variable   a variable that affects the outcome of a study, but is not included in the study

Margin of error   measure of uncertainty in the estimate of a parameter; critical value × standard error

Matched pairs   experimental units paired by a researcher based on a common characteristic

Mean   sum of all values in a dataset divided by the number of values

Mean of a binomial distribution   where n is the number of trials and p is the probability of success, $u_x = np$

Median   the value in the middle of a dataset (if there is an odd number of values) or the average of the two middle values (if there is an even number of values); an equal number of values lies above and below it; also the 50th percentile

Mode   most common value in a dataset

Multiple dotplots   more than one dotplot graphed using the same axis

Multiplication rule for independent events   if event X and event Y are independent, then the probability that they will occur in sequence is the product of their individual probabilities;

$$P(X \text{ and } Y) = P(X \cap Y) = P(X) \cdot P(Y)$$

Mutually exclusive events   events that cannot occur simultaneously; one occurring precludes the other from occurring

Nonresponse bias   stems from subjects who do not reply and are not included in the sample

Normal distribution   distribution of a random variable X so that the area under the curve between a and b is $P(a < X < b)$

Normal probability plot   *see* **Normal quantile plot**

Normal quantile plot   plots each x value versus the corresponding quantile z of the standard normal distribution; a linear relationship indicates that the data is normal

Null hypothesis   a statistical hypothesis that contains a statement of equality: =, ≤, or ≥; denoted by H_0

Observational study   variables are measured without treatments

Observed frequency   the frequency (count or value) of a category that is observed in the sample data; denoted by O

Ogive   *see* **Cumulative frequency plot**

One-tail test   hypothesis test to use if the alternate hypothesis, H_a, contains a less-than sign or a greater-than sign

Ordinal placement   The absolute rank of a number within an ordered data set states how many numbers are larger or smaller than the given number.

Outcome   the result of a single trial

Outlier   a data value far outside the general pattern of the data; values more than $1.5 \times IQR$ above Q3 or below Q1

p-value   probability of observing a sample statistic with a value as extreme or more extreme than the one determined from the sample data, assuming that the null hypothesis is true

Parallel boxplots   several boxplots arranged vertically, allowing one to compare several distributions at once

Parameter   measure describing a population

Percentile   indicates the percentage of values smaller than the given value

Placebo   looks identical to the actual drug, but contains no active ingredient so has no real physical effect

Placebo effect   describes a subject's expectation of an effect from a treatment

Point estimate   the sample statistic being used to estimate the corresponding population parameter

Points of inflection   points where the curve transitions from curving downward to curving upward; occurs at $(\mu \pm \sigma)$

Population   a collection of all the measurements, observations, counts, or responses that you are interested in analyzing

Population proportion   the proportion of a population having a particular characteristic; denoted by p

Power of a test   the probability of rejecting a false null hypothesis $(1 - \beta)$; also the probability on not making a type II error

Prediction interval   *see* **Confidence interval**

Preliminary sample   an initial sample taken from a population and whose statistics are used in additional calculations

Probability distribution   values of a random variable and their corresponding probabilities

Probability experiment   represents some action through which results are collected

Probability of an event   *see* **Theoretical probability**

Q1   first quartile; 25th percentile

Q3   third quartile; 75th percentile

Qualitative data   data divided into categories by nonnumeric characteristics

Quantitative data   data consisting of numbers

Quartiles   25th, 50th, and 75th percentiles of a dataset

r x c contingency table   *see* **Contingency table**

Random sample   each member of the population is equally likely to be selected for inclusion in the sample

Random variable   numerical outcome of a random experiment

Range   difference between maximum and minimum values in a dataset

Regression equation   equation describing a relationship between variables

Regression line   *see* **Least-squares regression line**

Rejection region   the range of values in a sampling distribution in which the null hypothesis is not likely to occur

Relative frequency   frequency of a class divided by the total frequency

Replication   repeating each treatment enough to control for chance variation

Residual   actual value minus predicted value in a regression

Residual plot   a plot of the vertical distance between a predicted value, y, and its actual value

Resistant   not influenced by outliers

Response bias   stems from subjects' inaccurate or untruthful responses

Response variable   measures a study's outcome

Right-tailed test   hypothesis test to use if the alternate hypothesis, H_a, contains a greater-than symbol (>); $H_a : \mu > k$

Sample   a subset or part of a population

Sample proportion   an estimate of population proportion, p, by collecting a random sample from the population and calculating the corresponding statistic; denoted by $\hat{p}$

Sample size   number of items in a sample; usually denoted by n

Sample space   all possible outcomes

Sample survey   collecting data from a representative portion of a population and recording the results

Sampling distribution   probability distribution of a sample statistic that is formed from all possible values of the statistic computed from a sample of size n

Sampling distribution of sample means   a distribution of sample means that is obtained by repeatedly drawing samples of the same size from a population

Scatterplot   graphical representation of a set of ordered pairs; horizontal axis is first element in the pair and vertical axis is second element

Self-selected sample   a sample in which the respondents determine whether they are to be included

Significance level   probability of making a type I error that you are willing to accept; denoted by α

Simple event   An event that consists of a single outcome

Simple random sample   a sample of a given size chosen such that every sample of that size has an equal chance of being selected

Simulation   a mathematical process to approximate a real-life situation; random imitation of a probabilistic situation

Skewed left   asymmetrical distribution with more of a tail on the left than on the right

Skewed right   asymmetrical distribution with more of a tail on the right than on the left

Standard deviation   square root of the variance;

$$s = \sqrt{\frac{\sum (x - \bar{x})^2}{n - 1}}; \ \sigma_x = \sqrt{\text{variance}} = \sqrt{\sigma_x^2}$$

Standard error of estimate   the standard deviation of the observed y-values about the predicted $\hat{y}$ values; denoted by s, where

$$s = \sqrt{\frac{\sum \left(y_i - \hat{y}_i \right)}{n - 2}}$$

Standard error of the slope

$$s_{b_i} = \frac{s}{\sqrt{\sum (x_i - \overline{x})^2}} = \frac{\sqrt{\frac{\sum \left(y_i - \hat{y}_i \right)}{n-2}}}{\sqrt{\sum (x_i - \overline{x})^2}}$$

Standard normal variable   *see* z-**score**

Statistic   measure describing a sample

Statistical dead heat   occurs when confidence intervals overlap or a difference test yields a nonpositive difference

Statistically significant   describes a finding unlikely to occur randomly

Statistics   the science of collecting, organizing, summarizing, analyzing, and interpreting data

Stem and leaf plot   graph that displays data similarly to a histogram, except the data are used as the axis (stem) and "bars" (leaves)

Stemplot   *see* **Stem and leaf plot**

Stratified random sample   sample chosen such that it approximates the same proportion in the population

Subjective probability   based on personal experience, not experimental data

Student's *t*-distribution   *see* *t*-**distribution**

Symmetric   describes data distributed equally above and below the distribution's center

Systematic random sample   probability sample in which each *n*th subject is chosen, where *n* is selected randomly

***t*-distribution**   a distribution based on small sample sizes; defined by

$$t = \frac{\overline{x} - \mu}{\frac{s}{\sqrt{n}}}$$

where $\overline{x}$ is the mean of a random sample of n repeated measurements, μ is the population mean, and s is the sample standard deviation

Test of homogeneity   *see* **Chi-square test for homogeneity of proportions**

Test of independence   *see* **Chi-square test for independence**

Test statistic   sample statistic, such as mean or standard deviation, compared to the parameter in the null hypothesis to determine the type of test we use

Theoretical probability   used when each possible outcome in the sample space is equally likely to occur; what mathematically should happen

Treatment group   a group of subjects given the same treatment in an experiment

Two-tailed test   hypothesis test to use if the alternate hypothesis, H_a, contains a not-equal-to symbol ($\neq$); $H_a{:}\mu \neq k$

Two-way table   *see* **Contingency table**

Type I error   rejecting the null hypothesis when it is actually true

Type II error   failing to reject the null hypothesis when it is actually false

Unbiased estimator   a sample statistic used to estimate the corresponding population parameter

Undercoverage bias   when part of the population is excluded from the sampling process

Uniform distribution   a probability distribution in which all values of the random variable are approximately equally likely to occur

Univariate data   concerns a single variable

Variance   average of the squared deviations from their mean of a set of observations;

$$s^2 = \frac{\sum (x - \bar{x})^2}{n - 1}$$

Voluntary response bias   when people respond to a survey or poll biased toward those with stronger opinions

Wording bias   response bias attributable to a question's phrasing

z-score   indicates how many standard deviations above or below the mean the given value lies

Appendix

Formulas

Descriptive Statistics

$$\bar{x} = \frac{\sum x_i}{n}$$

$$s_x = \sqrt{\frac{1}{n-1}\sum(x_i - \bar{x})^2}$$

$$s_p = \sqrt{\frac{(n_1 - 1)s_1^2 + (n_2 - 1)s_2^2}{(n_1 - 1) + (n_2 - 1)}}$$

$$\hat{y} = b_0 + b_1 x$$

$$b_1 = \frac{\sum(x_i - \bar{x})(y_i - \bar{y})}{\sum(x_i - \bar{x})^2}$$

$$b_0 = \bar{y} - b_1 \bar{x}$$

$$r = \frac{1}{n-1}\sum\left(\frac{x_i - \bar{x}}{s_x}\right)\left(\frac{y_i - \bar{y}}{s_y}\right)$$

$$b_1 = r\frac{s_y}{s_x}$$

$$s_{b_1} = \frac{\sqrt{\dfrac{\sum\left(y_i - \hat{y}_i\right)^2}{n-2}}}{\sqrt{\sum(x_i - \bar{x})^2}}$$

Probability

$$P(A \cup B) = P(A) + P(B) - P(A \cap B)$$

$$P(A|B) = \frac{P(A \cap B)}{P(B)}$$

$$E(X) = \mu_x = \sum x_i p_i$$

$$\text{var}(X) = \sigma_x^2 = \sum(x_i - \mu_x)^2 p_i$$

If X has a binaomial distribution with parameters n and p, then:

$$P(X = k) = \binom{n}{k} p^k (1-p)^{(n-k)}$$

$$\mu_x = np$$

$$\sigma_x = \sqrt{np(1-p)}$$

$$\mu_{\hat{p}} = p$$

$$\sigma_{\hat{p}} = \sqrt{\frac{p(1-p)}{n}}$$

If $\bar{x}$ is the mean of a random sample of size n from an infinite population with mean μ and standard deviation σ, then:

$$\mu_{\bar{x} = \mu}$$

$$\sigma_{\bar{x}} = \frac{\sigma}{\sqrt{n}}$$

Inferential Statistics

Standardized test statistic: $\dfrac{\text{statistic} - \text{parameter}}{\text{standard deviation of the statistic}}$

Confidence interval:

statistic $\pm$ (critical value) $\cdot$ (standard deviation of the statistic)

Single Sample	
Statistic	**Standard Deviation of statistic**
Sample Mean	$\dfrac{\sigma}{\sqrt{n}}$
Sample Proportion	$\sqrt{\dfrac{p(1-p)}{n}}$

Two Sample	
Statistic	**Standard Deviation of statistic**
Difference ($\sigma_1 \neq \sigma_2$) of sample means (unequal variances)	$\sqrt{\dfrac{\sigma_1^2}{n_1} + \dfrac{\sigma_2^2}{n_2}}$
Difference ($\sigma_1 = \sigma_2$) of sample means (equal variances)	$\sigma\sqrt{\dfrac{1}{n_1} + \dfrac{1}{n_2}}$
Difference ($p_1 \neq p_2$) of sample proportions (unequal proportions)	$\sqrt{\dfrac{p_1(1-p_1)}{n_1} + \dfrac{p_2(1-p_2)}{n_2}}$
Difference ($p_1 = p_2$) of sample proportions (equal proportions)	$\sqrt{p(1-p)}\sqrt{\dfrac{1}{n_1} + \dfrac{1}{n_2}}$

Chi-square statistic $= \sum \dfrac{(\text{observed} - \text{expected})^2}{\text{expected}}$

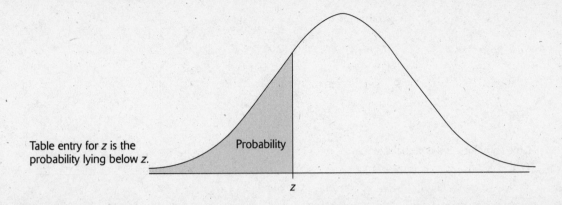

Table entry for z is the probability lying below z.

Probability

z

Table A: Standard Normal Probabilities

z	0.00	0.01	0.02	0.03	0.04	0.05	0.06	0.07	0.08	0.09
-3.4	.0003	.0003	.0003	.0003	.0003	.0003	.0003	.0003	.0003	.0002
-3.3	.0005	.0005	.0005	.0004	.0004	.0004	.0004	.0004	.0004	.0003
-3.2	.0007	.0007	.0006	.0006	.0006	.0006	.0006	.0005	.0005	.0005
-3.1	.0010	.0009	.0009	.0009	.0008	.0008	.0008	.0008	.0007	.0007
-3.0	.0013	.0013	.0013	.0012	.0012	.0011	.0011	.0011	.0010	.0010
-2.9	.0019	.0018	.0018	.0017	.0016	.0016	.0015	.0015	.0014	.0014
-2.8	.0026	.0025	.0024	.0023	.0023	.0022	.0021	.0021	.0020	.0019
-2.7	.0035	.0034	.0033	.0032	.0031	.0030	.0029	.0028	.0027	.0026
-2.6	.0047	.0045	.0044	.0043	.0041	.0040	.0039	.0038	.0037	.0036
-2.5	.0062	.0060	.0059	.0057	.0055	.0054	.0052	.0051	.0049	.0048
-2.4	.0082	.0080	.0078	.0075	.0073	.0071	.0069	.0068	.0066	.0064
-2.3	.0107	.0104	.0102	.0099	.0096	.0094	.0091	.0089	.0087	.0084
-2.2	.0139	.0136	.0132	.0129	.0125	.0122	.0119	.0116	.0113	.0110
-2.1	.0179	.0174	.0170	.0166	.0162	.0158	.0154	.0150	.0146	.0143
-2.0	.0228	.0222	.0217	.0212	.0207	.0202	.0197	.0192	.0188	.0183
-1.9	.0287	.0281	.0274	.0268	.0262	.0256	.0250	.0244	.0239	.0233
-1.8	.0359	.0351	.0344	.0336	.0329	.0322	.0314	.0307	.0301	.0294
-1.7	.0446	.0436	.0427	.0418	.0409	.0401	.0392	.0384	.0375	.0367
-1.6	.0548	.0537	.0526	.0516	.0505	.0495	.0485	.0475	.0465	.0455
-1.5	.0668	.0655	.0643	.0630	.0618	.0606	.0594	.0582	.0571	.0559
-1.4	.0808	.0793	.0778	.0764	.0749	.0735	.0721	.0708	.0694	.0681
-1.3	.0968	.0951	.0934	.0918	.0901	.0885	.0869	.0853	.0838	.0823
-1.2	.1151	.1131	.1112	.1093	.1075	.1056	.1038	.1020	.1003	.0985
-1.1	.1357	.1335	.1314	.1292	.1271	.1251	.1230	.1210	.1190	.1170
-1.0	.1587	.1562	.1539	.1515	.1492	.1469	.1446	.1423	.1401	.1379
-0.9	.1841	.1814	.1788	.1762	.1736	.1711	.1685	.1660	.1635	.1611
-0.8	.2119	.2090	.2061	.2033	.2005	.1977	.1949	.1922	.1894	.1867
-0.7	.2420	.2389	.2358	.2327	.2296	.2266	.2236	.2206	.2177	.2148
-0.6	.2743	.2709	.2676	.2643	.2611	.2578	.2546	.2514	.2483	.2451
-0.5	.3085	.3050	.3015	.2981	.2946	.2912	.2877	.2843	.2810	.2776
-0.4	.3446	.3409	.3372	.3336	.3300	.3264	.3228	.3192	.3156	.3121
-0.3	.3821	.3783	.3745	.3707	.3669	.3632	.3594	.3557	.3520	.3483
-0.2	.4207	.4168	.4129	.4090	.4052	.4013	.3974	.3936	.3897	.3859
-0.1	.4602	.4562	.4522	.4483	.4443	.4404	.4364	.4325	.4286	.4247
-0.0	.5000	.4960	.4920	.4880	.4840	.4801	.4761	.4721	.4681	.4641

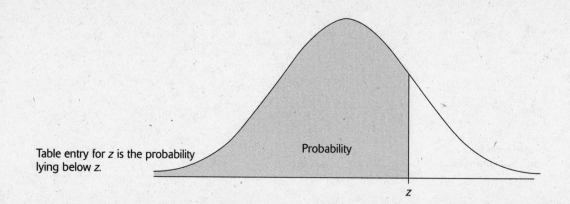

Table entry for z is the probability lying below z.

Probability

z

z	0.00	0.01	0.02	0.03	0.04	0.05	0.06	0.07	0.08	0.09
0.0	.5000	.5040	.5080	.5120	.5160	.5199	.5239	.5279	.5319	.5359
0.1	.5398	.5438	.5478	.5517	.5557	.5596	.5636	.5675	.5714	.5753
0.2	.5793	.5832	.5871	.5910	.5948	.5987	.6026	.6064	.6103	.6141
0.3	.6179	.6217	.6255	.6293	.6331	.6368	.6406	.6443	.6480	.6517
0.4	.6554	.6591	.6628	.6664	.6700	.6736	.6772	.6808	.6844	.6879
0.5	.6915	.6950	.6985	.7019	.7054	.7088	.7123	.7157	.7190	.7224
0.6	.7257	.7291	.7324	.7357	.7389	.7422	.7454	.7486	.7517	.7549
0.7	.7580	.7611	.7642	.7673	.7704	.7734	.7764	.7794	.7823	.7852
0.8	.7881	.7910	.7939	.7967	.7995	.8023	.8051	.8078	.8106	.8133
0.9	.8159	.8186	.8212	.8238	.8264	.8289	.8315	.8340	.8365	.8389
1.0	.8413	.8438	.8461	.8485	.8508	.8531	.8554	.8577	.8599	.8621
1.1	.8643	.8665	.8686	.8708	.8729	.8749	.8770	.8790	.8810	.8830
1.2	.8849	.8869	.8888	.8907	.8925	.8944	.8962	.8980	.8997	.9015
1.3	.9032	.9049	.9066	.9082	.9099	.9115	.9131	.9147	.9162	.9177
1.4	.9192	.9207	.9222	.9236	.9251	.9265	.9279	.9292	.9306	.9319
1.5	.9332	.9345	.9357	.9370	.9382	.9394	.9406	.9418	.9429	.9441
1.6	.9452	.9463	.9474	.9484	.9495	.9505	.9515	.9525	.9535	.9545
1.7	.9554	.9564	.9573	.9582	.9591	.9599	.9608	.9616	.9625	.9633
1.8	.9641	.9649	.9656	.9664	.9671	.9678	.9686	.9693	.9699	.9706
1.9	.9713	.9719	.9726	.9732	.9738	.9744	.9750	.9756	.9761	.9767
2.0	.9772	.9778	.9783	.9788	.9793	.9798	.9803	.9808	.9812	.9817
2.1	.9821	.9826	.9830	.9834	.9838	.9842	.9846	.9850	.9854	.9857
2.2	.9861	.9864	.9868	.9871	.9875	.9878	.9881	.9884	.9887	.9890
2.3	.9893	.9896	.9898	.9901	.9904	.9906	.9909	.9911	.9913	.9916
2.4	.9918	.9920	.9922	.9925	.9927	.9929	.9931	.9932	.9934	.9936
2.5	.9938	.9940	.9941	.9943	.9945	.9946	.9948	.9949	.9951	.9952
2.6	.9953	.9955	.9956	.9957	.9959	.9960	.9961	.9962	.9963	.9964
2.7	.9965	.9966	.9967	.9968	.9969	.9970	.9971	.9972	.9973	.9974
2.8	.9974	.9975	.9976	.9977	.9977	.9978	.9979	.9979	.9980	.9981
2.9	.9981	.9982	.9982	.9983	.9984	.9984	.9985	.9985	.9986	.9986
3.0	.9987	.9987	.9987	.9988	.9988	.9989	.9989	.9989	.9990	.9990
3.1	.9990	.9991	.9991	.9991	.9992	.9992	.9992	.9992	.9993	.9993
3.2	.9993	.9993	.9994	.9994	.9994	.9994	.9994	.9995	.9995	.9995
3.3	.9995	.9995	.9995	.9996	.9996	.9996	.9996	.9996	.9996	.9997
3.4	.9997	.9997	.9997	.9997	.9997	.9997	.9997	.9997	.9997	.9998

Table A *(Continued):* **Standard Normal Probabilities**

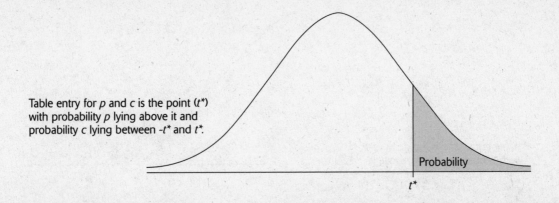

Table entry for p and c is the point (t^*) with probability p lying above it and probability c lying between $-t^*$ and t^*.

Probability

t^*

Table B: t-Distribution Critical Values

					Tail Probability p							
df	.25	.20	.15	.10	.05	.025	.02	.01	.005	.0025	.001	.0005
1	1.000	1.376	1.963	3.078	6.314	12.71	15.89	31.82	63.66	127.3	318.3	636.6
2	.816	1.061	1.386	1.886	2.920	4.303	4.849	6.965	9.925	14.09	22.33	31.60
3	.765	.978	1.250	1.638	2.353	3.182	3.482	4.541	5.841	7.453	10.21	12.92
4	.741	.941	1.190	1.533	2.132	2.776	2.999	3.747	4.604	5.598	7.173	8.610
5	.727	.920	1.156	1.476	2.015	2.571	2.757	3.365	4.032	4.773	5.894	6.869
6	.718	.906	1.134	1.440	1.943	2.447	2.612	3.143	3.707	4.317	5.208	5.959
7	.711	.896	1.119	1.415	1.895	2.365	2.517	2.998	3.499	4.029	4.785	5.408
8	.706	.889	1.108	1.397	1.860	2.306	2.449	2.896	3.355	3.833	4.501	5.041
9	.703	.883	1.100	1.383	1.833	2.262	2.398	2.821	3.250	3.690	4.297	4.781
10	.700	.879	1.093	1.372	1.812	2.228	2.359	2.764	3.169	3.581	4.144	4.587
11	.697	.876	1.088	1.363	1.796	2.201	2.328	2.718	3.106	3.497	4.025	4.437
12	.695	.873	1.083	1.356	1.782	2.179	2.303	2.681	3.055	3.428	3.930	4.318
13	.694	.870	1.079	1.350	1.771	2.160	2.282	2.650	3.012	3.372	3.852	4.221
14	.692	.868	1.076	1.345	1.761	2.145	2.264	2.624	2.977	3.326	3.787	4.140
15	.691	.866	1.074	1.341	1.753	2.131	2.249	2.602	2.947	3.286	3.733	4.073
16	.690	.865	1.071	1.337	1.746	2.120	2.235	2.583	2.921	3.252	3.686	4.015
17	.689	.863	1.069	1.333	1.740	2.110	2.224	2.567	2.898	3.222	3.646	3.965
18	.688	.862	1.067	1.330	1.734	2.101	2.214	2.552	2.878	3.197	3.610	3.922
19	.688	.861	1.066	1.328	1.729	2.093	2.205	2.539	2.861	3.174	3.579	3.883
20	.687	.860	1.064	1.325	1.725	2.086	2.197	2.528	2.845	3.153	3.552	3.850
21	.686	.859	1.063	1.323	1.721	2.080	2.189	2.518	2.831	3.135	3.527	3.819
22	.686	.858	1.061	1.321	1.717	2.074	2.183	2.508	2.819	3.119	3.505	3.792
23	.685	.858	1.060	1.319	1.714	2.069	2.177	2.500	2.807	3.104	3.485	3.768
24	.685	.857	1.059	1.318	1.711	2.064	2.172	2.492	2.797	3.091	3.467	3.745
25	.684	.856	1.058	1.316	1.708	2.060	2.167	2.485	2.787	3.078	3.450	3.725
26	.684	.856	1.058	1.315	1.706	2.056	2.162	2.479	2.779	3.067	3.435	3.707
27	.684	.855	1.057	1.314	1.703	2.052	2.158	2.473	2.771	3.057	3.421	3.689
28	.683	.855	1.056	1.313	1.701	2.048	2.154	2.467	2.763	3.047	3.408	3.674
29	.683	.854	1.055	1.311	1.699	2.045	2.150	2.462	2.756	3.038	3.396	3.660
30	.683	.854	1.055	1.310	1.697	2.042	2.147	2.457	2.750	3.030	3.385	3.646
40	.681	.851	1.050	1.303	1.684	2.021	2.123	2.423	2.704	2.971	3.307	3.551
50	.679	.849	1.047	1.299	1.676	2.009	2.109	2.403	2.678	2.937	3.261	3.496
60	.679	.848	1.045	1.296	1.671	2.000	2.099	2.390	2.660	2.915	3.232	3.460
80	.678	.846	1.043	1.292	1.664	1.990	2.088	2.374	2.639	2.887	3.195	3.416
100	.677	.845	1.042	1.290	1.660	1.984	2.081	2.364	2.626	2.871	3.174	3.390
1000	.675	.842	1.037	1.282	1.646	1.962	2.056	2.330	2.581	2.813	3.098	3.300
∞	.674	.841	1.036	1.282	1.645	1.960	2.054	2.326	2.576	2.807	3.090	3.291
	50%	60%	70%	80%	90%	95%	96%	98%	99%	99.5%	99.8%	99.9%

Confidence Level C

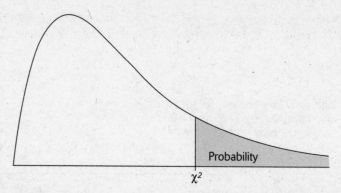

Table entry for p is the point (χ^2) with probability p lying above it.

Probability

χ^2

Table C: χ^2 Critical Values

					Tail probability p						
df	.25	.20	.15	.10	.05	.025	.02	.01	.005	.0025	.001
1	1.32	1.64	2.07	2.71	3.84	5.02	5.41	6.63	7.88	9.14	10.83
2	2.77	3.22	3.79	4.61	5.99	7.38	7.82	9.21	10.60	11.98	13.82
3	4.11	4.64	5.32	6.25	7.81	9.35	9.84	11.34	12.84	14.32	16.27
4	5.39	5.99	6.74	7.78	9.49	11.14	11.67	13.28	14.86	16.42	18.47
5	6.63	7.29	8.12	9.24	11.07	12.83	13.39	15.09	16.75	18.39	20.51
6	7.84	8.56	9.45	10.64	12.59	14.45	15.03	16.81	18.55	20.25	22.46
7	9.04	9.80	10.75	12.02	14.07	16.01	16.62	18.48	20.28	22.04	24.32
8	10.22	11.03	12.03	13.36	15.51	17.53	18.17	20.09	21.95	23.77	26.12
9	11.39	12.24	13.29	14.68	16.92	19.02	19.68	21.67	23.59	25.46	27.88
10	12.55	13.44	14.53	15.99	18.31	20.48	21.16	23.21	25.19	27.11	29.59
11	13.70	14.63	15.77	17.28	19.68	21.92	22.62	24.73	26.76	28.73	31.26
12	14.85	15.81	16.99	18.55	21.03	23.34	24.05	26.22	28.30	30.32	32.91
13	15.98	16.98	18.20	19.81	22.36	24.74	25.47	27.69	29.82	31.88	34.53
14	17.12	18.15	19.41	21.06	23.68	26.12	26.87	29.14	31.32	33.43	36.12
15	18.25	19.31	20.60	22.31	25.00	27.49	28.26	30.58	32.80	34.95	37.70
16	19.37	20.47	21.79	23.54	26.30	28.85	29.63	32.00	34.27	36.46	39.25
17	20.49	21.61	22.98	24.77	27.59	30.19	31.00	33.41	35.72	37.95	40.79
18	21.60	22.76	24.16	25.99	28.87	31.53	32.35	34.81	37.16	39.42	42.31
19	22.72	23.90	25.33	27.20	30.14	32.85	33.69	36.19	38.58	40.88	43.82
20	23.83	25.04	26.50	28.41	31.41	34.17	35.02	37.57	40.00	42.34	45.31
21	24.93	26.17	27.66	29.62	32.67	35.48	36.34	38.93	41.40	43.77	46.80
22	26.04	27.30	28.82	30.81	33.92	36.78	37.66	40.29	42.80	45.20	48.27
23	27.14	28.43	29.98	32.01	35.17	38.08	38.97	41.64	44.18	46.62	49.73
24	28.24	29.55	31.13	33.20	36.42	39.36	40.27	42.98	45.56	48.03	51.18
25	29.34	30.68	32.28	34.38	37.65	40.65	41.57	44.31	46.93	49.44	52.62
26	30.43	31.79	33.43	35.56	38.89	41.92	42.86	45.64	48.29	50.83	54.05
27	31.53	32.91	34.57	36.74	40.11	43.19	44.14	46.96	49.65	52.22	55.48
28	32.62	34.03	35.71	37.92	41.34	44.46	45.42	48.28	50.99	53.59	56.89
29	33.71	35.14	36.85	39.09	42.56	45.72	46.69	49.59	52.34	54.97	58.30
30	34.80	36.25	37.99	40.26	43.77	46.98	47.96	50.89	53.67	56.33	59.70
40	45.62	47.27	49.24	51.81	55.76	59.34	60.44	63.69	66.77	69.70	73.40
50	56.33	58.16	60.35	63.17	67.50	71.42	72.61	76.15	79.49	82.66	86.66
60	66.98	68.97	71.34	74.40	79.08	83.30	84.58	88.38	91.95	95.34	99.61
80	88.13	90.41	93.11	96.58	101.88	106.63	108.07	112.33	116.32	120.10	124.84
100	109.14	111.67	114.66	118.50	124.34	129.56	131.14	135.81	140.17	144.29	149.45

Table D: Random Numbers

64008	53414	01655	79912	46035	39601	50907	85446	95301	72912
38876	97993	15892	98056	36015	31884	56869	37649	74476	51288
31474	26432	12514	30698	06794	53181	12376	67850	78770	25616
27326	05149	90164	31581	84697	38431	59073	84576	50261	38251
95080	91626	83031	68704	67917	37290	46619	70411	28197	49498
08576	41812	65247	15330	79002	07963	33308	47339	46699	60569
49346	77904	21637	25881	07493	12082	87223	39398	50584	11106
54702	96954	15323	10465	01192	35566	22266	99111	95032	40085
54182	97220	26313	49572	74548	59711	48766	58003	74719	43114
52333	44782	32443	45181	48601	32562	18900	45767	06887	60729
86543	46312	57131	05919	54431	95915	02923	31982	22630	76692
62014	13460	18412	48028	13613	19020	22245	89360	29316	41446
62492	68398	63398	58743	44747	88602	88924	45342	25478	46626
62568	44635	85048	82247	76317	39477	33275	21360	03409	09924
05370	85058	85028	81815	32335	84892	48857	54041	61953	71226
23121	98406	71651	09568	93301	32953	58344	25775	63727	90160
87093	65257	11376	46645	22060	76527	94110	80613	21856	71424
86027	99398	13250	55119	45005	21543	01573	76034	52234	20968
49996	39264	39904	21677	11195	72008	16446	38393	87239	95513
56058	72575	88216	92709	24289	66318	36098	41769	38992	62544
67359	57619	03495	50566	31278	05933	93350	11563	87049	37880
47436	93229	25591	56633	15772	25447	45270	25994	12494	27999
00837	45747	11641	47859	53356	35946	47059	94610	87783	43961
63492	82410	76941	68198	98564	22233	80344	84289	27968	00768
63927	54753	53873	11773	46145	14044	52458	18373	69512	06021

Comparison of Graphical Displays

	Skewed Left	Symmetric	Skewed Right
Stem plots	(below)	(below)	(below)

Skewed Left

1	6
2	12
3	2268
4	235556
5	13556679
6	012345556678
7	11223334556666677889
8	2333344555567888
9	4

Symmetric

1	6
2	12
3	22445568
4	2355567778899
5	11223334556666778
6	012334555678
7	112344467
8	2678
9	47

Skewed Right

1	6
2	2223455556677778
3	12233444445567778899
4	23445556789
5	123445579
6	455578
7	2488
8	89
9	4

Histograms

Box and Whisker Plots

Cumulative Frequency Plots

Dotplots

Summary of Inference Methods

Confidence Intervals Using Large Samples

statistic $\pm$ (critical value) $\cdot$ (standard deviation of statistic)

Population Parameter	Sample Estimate	Conditions for Use	Formula
mean μ	$\overline{x}$	Simple Random Sample $n \geq 30$ or population is approximately normal	$\overline{x} \pm z_c \sigma_{\overline{x}}$ where $\sigma_{\overline{x}} = \dfrac{s}{\sqrt{n}}$
proportion p	$\hat{p}$	Simple Random Sample $n\hat{p} \geq 5$, $n\left(1 - \hat{p}\right) \geq 5$ Sample size < 5% of population size	$\hat{p} \pm z_c \sigma_{\hat{p}}$ where $\sigma_{\hat{p}} = \sqrt{\dfrac{\hat{p}\left(1 - \hat{p}\right)}{n}}$
difference of means $\mu_1 - \mu_2$	$\overline{x}_1 - \overline{x}_2$	Independent Simple Random Samples $n_1 \geq 30$ and $n_2 \geq 30$ or population is approximately normal	$\left(\overline{x}_1 - \overline{x}_2\right) \pm z_c \sigma_{\overline{x}_1 - \overline{x}_2}$ where $\sigma_{\overline{x}_1 - \overline{x}_2} = \sqrt{\dfrac{s_1^2}{n_1} + \dfrac{s_2^2}{n_2}}$
difference of proportions $p_1 - p_2$	$\hat{p}_1 - \hat{p}_2$	Independent Simple Random Samples $n_1\hat{p}_1 \geq 5$, $n_1\left(1 - \hat{p}_1\right) \geq 5$ $n_2\hat{p}_2 \geq 5$, $n_2\left(1 - \hat{p}_2\right) \geq 5$	$\left(\hat{p}_1 - \hat{p}_2\right) \pm z_c \sigma_{\hat{p}_1 - \hat{p}_2}$ where $\sigma_{\hat{p}_1 - \hat{p}_2} = \sqrt{\dfrac{\hat{p}_1\left(1 - \hat{p}_1\right)}{n_1} + \dfrac{\hat{p}_2\left(1 - \hat{p}_2\right)}{n_2}}$

Confidence Intervals Using Small Samples

statistic $\pm$ (critical value) $\cdot$ (standard deviation of statistic)

Population Parameter	Sample Estimate	Conditions for Use	Formula
mean μ	$\overline{x}$	Simple Random Sample $n < 30$ Population approximately normal $d.f. = n - 1$	$\overline{x} \pm t_c \sigma_{\overline{x}}$ where $\sigma_{\overline{x}} = \dfrac{s}{\sqrt{n}}$
difference of means $\mu_1 - \mu_2$	$\overline{x}_1 - \overline{x}_2$	Independent Simple Random Samples Variances Not Equal $n_1 < 30$ and/or $n_2 < 30$ $d.f.$ is the smaller of $n_1 - 1$ and $n_2 - 1$	$\left(\overline{x}_1 - \overline{x}_2\right) \pm t_c \sigma_{\overline{x}_1 - \overline{x}_2}$ where $\sigma_{\overline{x}_1 - \overline{x}_2} = \sqrt{\dfrac{s_1^2}{n_1} + \dfrac{s_2^2}{n_2}}$
difference of means $\mu_1 - \mu_2$	$\overline{x}_1 - \overline{x}_2$	Independent Simple Random Samples Variances Equal $n_1 < 30$ and/or $n_2 < 30$ $d.f. = n_1 + n_2 - 2$	$\left(\overline{x}_1 - \overline{x}_2\right) \pm t_c \sigma_{\overline{x}_1 - \overline{x}_2}$ where $\sigma_{\overline{x}_1 - \overline{x}_2} = \sqrt{\dfrac{(n_1 - 1) s_1^2 + (n_2 - 1) s_2^2}{n_1 + n_2 - 2}} \sqrt{\dfrac{1}{n_1} + \dfrac{1}{n_2}}$

Hypothesis Testing Using Large Samples

(statistic − parameter) / standard deviation of statistic

Population Parameter	Sample Estimate	Conditions for Use	Formula
mean μ	$\overline{x}$	Simple Random Sample $n \geq 30$ or population is approximately normal	$z = \dfrac{\overline{x} - \mu}{\sigma_{\overline{x}}}$ where $\sigma_{\overline{x}} = \dfrac{s}{\sqrt{n}}$
proportion p	$\hat{p}$	Simple Random Sample $n\hat{p} \geq 5,\ n\left(1 - \hat{p}\right) \geq 5$	$z = \dfrac{\hat{p} - p}{\sigma_{\hat{p}}}$ where $\sigma_{\hat{p}} = \sqrt{\dfrac{p(1-p)}{n}}$
difference of means $\mu_1 - \mu_2$	$\overline{x}_1 - \overline{x}_2$	Independent Simple Random Samples $n_1 \geq 30$ and $n_2 \geq 30$ or population is approximately normal	$z = \dfrac{\left(\overline{x}_1 - \overline{x}_2\right)\left(\mu_1 - \mu_2\right)}{\sigma_{\overline{x}_1 - \overline{x}_2}}$ where $\sigma_{\overline{x}_1 - \overline{x}_2} = \sqrt{\dfrac{s_1^2}{n_1} + \dfrac{s_2^2}{n_2}}$
difference of proportions $p_1 - p_2$	$\hat{p}_1 - \hat{p}_2$	Independent Simple Random Samples $n_1\hat{p}_1 \geq 5,\ n_1\left(1 - \hat{p}_1\right) \geq 5$ $n_2\hat{p}_2 \geq 5,\ n_2\left(1 - \hat{p}_2\right) \geq 5$	$z = \dfrac{\left(\hat{p}_1 - \hat{p}_2\right) - \left(p_1 - p_2\right)}{\sigma_{\hat{p}_1 - \hat{p}_2}}$ where $\sigma_{\hat{p}_1 - \hat{p}_2} = \sqrt{\hat{p}\left(1 - \hat{p}\right)\left(\dfrac{1}{n_1} + \dfrac{1}{n_2}\right)}$

Hypothesis Testing Using Small Samples

(statistic − parameter) / standard deviation of statistic

Population Parameter	Sample Estimate	Conditions for Use	Formula
mean μ	$\overline{x}$	Simple Random Sample $n < 30$ Population approximately normal $d.f. = n - 1$	$t = \dfrac{\overline{x} - \mu}{\sigma_{\overline{x}}}$ where $\sigma_{\overline{x}} = \dfrac{s}{\sqrt{n}}$
difference of means $\mu_1 - \mu_2$	$\overline{x}_1 - \overline{x}_2$	Independent Simple Random Samples Variances Not Equal $n_1 < 30$ and/or $n_2 < 30$ $d.f.$ is the smaller of $n_1 - 1$ and $n_2 - 1$	$t = \dfrac{\left(\overline{x}_1 - \overline{x}_2\right) - \left(\mu_1 - \mu_2\right)}{\sigma_{\overline{x}_1 - \overline{x}_2}}$ where $\sigma_{\overline{x}_1 - \overline{x}_2} = \sqrt{\dfrac{s_1^2}{n_1} + \dfrac{s_2^2}{n_2}}$
difference of means $\mu_1 - \mu_2$	$\overline{x}_1 - \overline{x}_2$	Independent Simple Random Samples Variances Equal $n_1 < 30$ and/or $n_2 < 30$ $d.f. = n_1 + n_2 - 2$	$t = \dfrac{\left(\overline{x}_1 - \overline{x}_2\right) - \left(\mu_1 - \mu_2\right)}{\sigma_{\overline{x}_1 - \overline{x}_2}}$ where $\sigma_{\overline{x}_1 - \overline{x}_2} = \sqrt{\dfrac{(n_1 - 1)\,s_1^2 + (n_2 - 1)\,s_2^2}{n_1 + n_2 - 2}}\sqrt{\dfrac{1}{n_1} + \dfrac{1}{n_2}}$